SHOW TUNES

SHOW TUNES

1905-1985

The Songs, Shows and Careers of
Broadway's Major Composers

Steven Suskin

DODD, MEAD & COMPANY
NEW YORK

Designed by Erich Hobbing

First Edition

Library of Congress Cataloging in Publication Data
Suskin, Steven.
  Show tunes.

  Bibliography: p.
  Includes indexes.
  1. Composers—United States. 2. Musical, revue,
comedy, etc.—United States. I. Title.
ML390.S983 1985   782.81′092′2 [B]   85-12930
ISBN 0-396-08674-8

Contents

PART 3

PART 4

APPENDIX 1

APPENDIX 2

APPENDIX 3

Preface

It's probably true that a few people are *not* interested in show tunes. This book isn't for them. It *is* for everyone else.

A veritable mountain of material has been written about Broadway musicals. Some volumes focus on individual creators or performers; others discuss shows in general or certain selected shows. Distinct musical theatre forms have been examined, as has the total work of an era. There are biographies—some excellent, some not—of specific composers, or groups of composers, or composers and their lyricists. All concentrate on the hit shows, with summaries of plots, excerpts from reviews, etc.

But the Broadway musical is built on show tunes.

Song soothes the soul. Personal favorites express our feelings better than we can in our own words. Truths captured in music and lyric by the Messrs. Rodgers and Hart, or Gershwin and Gershwin, or Arlen (and on) remain constant. Their songs are on our lips, or in our ears, or at the touch of our fingers whenever we want them, whenever we need them. "Dancing In The Dark" at twilight, "Time On My Hands" at dawn. The plaintive "Someone To Watch Over Me," the importunate "I Can't Get Started." "All The Things You Are" in times rhapsodic, "Spring Is Here" in times unrequited, and "I've Got The World On A String" any old time at all.

This book grew from the assumption that for every well-known Kern or Duke or Youmans treasure, there were two or three unknown gems hidden from view. (An assumption that proved, for the most part, to be correct!) It was quickly discovered that there was no accurate list of *what* to look for. The works of Gershwin and Porter have been fairly well catalogued; information on other composers is inconsistent, haphazard, or simply nonexistent. Shows which closed out of town and "plays with music," particularly, have heretofore been ignored.

The search grew into a quest. Pursuit of accuracy eventually led to a piece-by-piece search through the copyright deposits at the Library of Congress. The Library's vast collection of uncatalogued material inconveniently mixes together all theatre, vaudeville, and motion picture music from America, England, France, Austria, Germany, Italy, Mexico, etc. registered since the turn of the century. In the interests of providing a fairly complete guide to important musical theatre, the number of examined composers trebled.

A list of song titles, though, is ultimately of limited interest, no matter how extensive. Personal involvement in and enthusiasm for the musical theatre led to an investigation of *why* these composers wrote what they did. *How* did they come to work with their various collaborators? Did the songs work in the theatre? What were the effects of success and failure on future work (and the work of others)? The Broadway musical has been examined from the perspective of scholars and musicologists, but rarely from a *theatrical* viewpoint; this book does so.

Show Tunes is my personal paean to (and investigation of) the music that makes me, figuratively, dance on the ceiling. I was born in a trunk full of original cast albums, and I have spent many a night and day—vocationally and avocationally—in the Broadway theatre. I played and examined 6,000 songs, listening with a highly analytical musical ear. Shows by the hundreds (750 or so) were researched in my guise as musical-comedy detective, discovering coincidences, contradictions, surprises and curiosities. Finally, I liberally laced my accounts of songs, shows, and careers with random observations accumulated during my long years as a Broadway production manager. (Editor's note: the author appears to have been born sometime between **Wish You Were Here** and **Wonderful Town**).

The reader will find favorite and (nonfavorite) composers within, perhaps even a few unknowns. For one discriminating individual to enjoy all their songs is virtually impossible. Tastes, even among drama critics, vary. Whether you agree with my comments or not, I trust you will find them provocative and informative.

My reward has been the discovery of hundreds of good songs. The reader's rewards will be a better acquaintance with the show tunes he or she already enjoys, and a guide to new favorites.

Steven Suskin
New York
June 1985

How to Use This Book

Thirty major composers have been selected for discussion. They are divided into three generational groups, with each career discussed separately. An additional group of notable scores by other composers follows.

THE COMPOSERS

This study of the musical theatre starts at the very beginning, with Jerome Kern. Kern entered a theatre dominated by operetta and made radical changes. Other successful American composers chose to remain in operetta: Victor Herbert, Rudolf Friml, and Sigmund Romberg all retain a measure of popularity today. But they wrote operetta and light opera, not show tunes, and therefore are not included. The one early composer who *did* try to create a primitive American musical comedy was George M. Cohan. But his work was extremely primitive.

Hundreds of American composers have been represented on Broadway since Kern discovered musical comedy in 1915. Selecting thirty out of the pack has not been all that difficult, though; most of the choices are obvious. The major criteria are importance of work, in terms of quality or popular success, and a sustained concentration on the musical stage. The lack of a theatre career does not signify the inability to write important musical theatre work, of course. A section of "Notable Scores" has been added to represent such composers and their shows. Again, note that only *American* composers (born or naturalized) are discussed in this book.

For purposes of chronology, composers are arranged by date of their first *important* work. Cole Porter was born just two years after Irving Berlin, and his initial Broadway hearing came in 1915; but the younger George Gershwin, Vincent Youmans, and Richard Rodgers were all firmly established before Porter achieved recognition in 1928.

The individual work of each composer is examined show by show, from the earliest interpolation by Kern through September 1985. Each production is discussed in three parts: Show Data, Song Information, and (usually) Commentary.

SHOW DATA

The Shows

All stage productions from which songs were published or recorded are listed. This includes shows that closed during pre-Broadway tryouts, and others written specifically for production in London. Also included are shows that weren't intended for Broadway presentation. The majority are musicals and revues, but *any* organized stage production for which the composer wrote specific material is included. In addition, many productions for which *no* songs were published are included. Movie and television work is not discussed, except for material written for adaptations of theatrical productions. Revivals are mentioned when the show included previously unheard material. Amateur shows, unproduced musicals, and workshops are included when songs were published; much of the better material, of course, was reused in other productions and published at that time. Following show titles in some cases are subtitles or colorful, descriptive slogans ("A Bubbling Satirical Musical Revue of Plays, Problems and Persons") taken from original advertising material.

Date

The date of the official Broadway (or London) opening is used. For shows which closed during tryout or were not intended to play Broadway or London, date of the first public performance is given in [brackets]. Where exact date is unknown, month and year are given in [brackets].

Theatre and City

The theatre where the show officially opened is listed. All shows were produced in New York City unless indicated. Shows produced in London or other cities are so noted. Complete information is sometimes unknown, particularly for shows that did not play Broadway. This applies to credits and other data as well. In such cases, the listings herein are necessarily incomplete.

Performances

The "official" number of performances is given. Published figures are, unfortunately, often contradictory. The most accurate-sounding

number has been listed, usually from the earliest reliable reference
source.

Credits

Composers

The composer under discussion wrote all music unless specifically
noted. In the Gershwin chapter, for example: "Music also by Sigmund Romberg" means that Gershwin and Romberg each wrote
substantial parts of the score. "Music mostly by Sigmund Romberg"
means that Gershwin supplied interpolated song(s) to a Romberg score.
"Music mostly by Gershwin" means that other composers provided
interpolations. Where numerous composers were involved, the word
"others" is usually used.

Lyricists

The overall lyricist for the production is named in the credit section;
exceptions for specific songs are noted in the song listing. In cases of
partial scores, the principal composer and lyricist are named; but only
songs written by the composer under discussion are listed. Some of
the composers wrote their own lyrics; this is mentioned at the beginning of their chapters, with specific exceptions noted. Songs for which
the composer wrote lyrics *only* are included, but collaboration with
another composer in this book is discussed under the career of the
composer (and cross-referenced).

Others

Librettists, directors, and producers are listed where information is
available. Choreographers are listed for productions in which dance
was an important creative element. Certain cast members are listed:
stars, supporting performers, and others of interest. Future stars in
the chorus are specifically *not* included. Standardized terms are used:
"directed" rather than "staged," "choreographed" rather than "dances
by," "with" rather than "starring."

"Pre-Broadway Title"

When a show underwent a name change during tryouts, songs were
sometimes issued using both titles. In such cases, the original title is
mentioned. Songs cut from these shows might, in fact, have been issued using the earlier title only.

SONG LISTINGS

Song listings include all material from each production which was published or recorded. Information is given on lyricists, other uses of the same material, and related details. The purpose of the section is to provide a complete guide to all songs that *exist*, and which the reader can *find*. (Not all are found easily; suggestions for locating particularly rare material are given with the Bibliography.)

Other reference books are available with titles of published *and* unpublished songs, usually without any differentiation. Unfortunately, most unpublished manuscripts have long since disappeared and cannot be checked. These "unpublished" titles are sometimes songs that actually *were* published—with a different lyric, or merely a different title. Theatre programs can provide unreliable information, as shows-in-crisis make changes faster than a good press agent can keep track of (or wants to). Sometimes proposed titles for never-written songs find their way onto these lists. Accurate information and authorship of unpublished material is simply not verifiable. We have chosen to concentrate only on what is *real*. (Any unpublished manuscripts unearthed in research have been examined, and relevant findings are noted.)

Many of the composers discussed also wrote songs for motion pictures. A few wrote as carefully for film assignments as for theatre. It is regretted that these songs cannot be discussed in this book; but including the important songs would necessitate including them all, and there are hundreds.

CLASSIFICATION OF PUBLICATIONS

Many songs were printed in more than one method: an individually published song was also included in the score (if any), etc. These listings are cumulative, the key phrase being "additional songs." Only songs written by the composer under discussion are included; contributions by other composers in the book are cross-referenced.

Nonsong material is listed where it is a separate composition: "Overture To Candide" as opposed to song-medley overtures, "Slaughter On Tenth Avenue" as opposed to dance music arrangements.

Certain songs were published with subtitles: "The Impossible Dream (The Quest)." In other cases, familiar subtitles follow official title for identification purposes: "He Dances On My Ceiling (Dancing On The Ceiling)." Vocal scores sometimes neglected to print song titles in favor of "Opening Act Two," "Scene And Song," or "Entrance Of Cowgirls." Where necessary, a suitable title or subtitle has been taken from the lyric. Where composer wrote different songs with the same title, they are referred to as [1st] and [2nd]; this does not apply to similarly titled songs by different composers.

Published Songs

Sheet music of individual songs, for sale in stores and theatre lobbies.

Additional Songs Published in Vocal Score

Collections of all musical material needed for performance: songs, dances, underscoring, etc.

Additional Songs Published in Vocal Selection

Collections of selected songs, sometimes including titles not published individually. In some cases revised editions have been issued with different contents.

Additional Songs Published (No Lyric) in Piano Selection

Medleys of songs issued without lyrics, sometimes piano reductions of the overtures. Dozens of believed-to-be-vanished songs by Gershwin, Rodgers, Kern, etc. were published in this manner (and are here catalogued for the first time). In some cases American and British editions have different contents.

Additional Songs Published

Otherwise unpublished material contained in songbooks, collections, scripts, or other publications. So-called "fakebooks" containing lyrics and melody lines (only) are not included.

Additional Songs Recorded

Otherwise unpublished songs that were made available on recordings.

A WORD ABOUT THE INCLUSION OF RECORDED MATERIAL

In olden days, before the Depression, the publisher usually issued the "best" (i.e., most likely to sell) songs even before the tryout began. More numbers were added as demand was shown—if the show ran long enough. Leftover songs appeared only in the vocal score, if any; otherwise they were forgotten or eventually reused in another show. Since the advent of the original cast album, many such songs have been recorded. Others can be heard on "songwriter tributes."

While this book is not about recorded theatre music, songs preserved only in this method are certainly to the point. Therefore, at the end of the song listings are unpublished-but-recorded songs, which appear on original (or studio) cast albums, "songwriter tributes," and other special collections. Recently issued "pirated" albums—live performances taped and pressed without permission of authors or performers—have not been considered; the poor quality makes most of them virtually inaudible, anyway. Live tapes and noncommercial demonstration records are sometimes obtainable: imaginative readers interested in this material can easily track down sources.

Due to space and the desire to concentrate on musical theatre matters, label and number information on unpublished-but-recorded songs is not given; the majority can be found on cast albums. For further information, David Hummel's *Collector's Guide to the American Musical Theatre* is especially recommended.

SONG EXPLANATIONS

Cut Songs

Material cut from shows before or after the opening. As these cases were not accurately chronicled in programs or anywhere else, such listings cannot be complete. By definition, cut material includes songs dropped during rehearsals—and therefore never actually performed.

Reused Songs

Material used in different productions, usually songs cut from their initial show. In some cases an absolutely identical song reappeared with a different title.

New (or Revised) Lyrics

Identical music reused with different lyrics.

Revised Music

At the least, basically similar music reworked. The same song in a different tempo with a new bridge, for example. At the most, virtually new music containing a recognizable theme from the composer's earlier work. (And why not? A good musical idea is well worth rescuing from ignominious obscurity.)

Advertised But Not Published

These might better be labeled *"believed to exist* but not published." Many were advertised by the publishers; other titles first appeared in reference books or song indexes. Nonexistence has been verified by all possible means; the names are included in hopes of ending confusion. Not listed are certain "advertised" titles which have indeed been found—and discovered to be interpolations by other composers.

Issued as Professional Copy (Only)

These were copies distributed for noncommercial use; usually printed without covers, sometimes on poor-quality paper. They were given to singers and recording companies in hopes of arranging performances outside the theatre. For any number of reasons—premature closing of the show, song cut on the road, etc.—some songs were never actually issued for sale, and exist only as professional copies. Irving Berlin, it seems, regularly issued professional copies, more as a form of added copyright protection than as a preliminary to commercial release.

"Initial Publication"

Certain songs were not published until long after the production had closed, usually in connection with a successful movie version or revival. These are listed as such. Because the individually published sheet is our primary source, "initial publication" supersedes an earlier printing in a vocal score or selection. It is regretted that current availability is impossible to indicate; please note that certain long-out-of-print individual sheets are now available in selections and collections.

"Additional Songs"

Songs by the composer *not* from the original production are sometimes interpolated into revivals or movie versions. These are listed only when specifically written by the composer for that purpose, or where use resulted in initial publication or recording of previously unpublished material.

COMMENTARY

Pertinent—and sometimes impertinent—comments are given on the shows, songs, and careers. Other publications can be consulted for plot summaries and the like; my concern is with the *composers. What* they wrote and *whom* they wrote with; *why* and *how* they came to be involved with their chosen projects. All were influenced and/or affected by their counterparts/competitors. They shared the same collaborators and producers, wrote for the same performers. And, the shows were performed in the same theatres for the same audience (and the same reviewers).

Critical comments on contemporary shows come from actual viewing. Opinions on older productions have been derived from analysis of existing material, reviews, and first-hand reports. Certain critics, one finds, can be relied upon for generally insightful comments. Statements of commercial success/failure are derived from financial records.

Show Tunes is not meant to be a total history of the American musical theatre, but rather a look at the more important composers and their work, with incidental miscellania of curiosity and interest included.

CROSS-REFERENCING

Reference to any of the productions discussed in this book is printed with the show title in boldface capitals, followed by composer and date:

SHOW BOAT [Kern: December 27, 1927]

This refers to the chapter on Kern, where the listing can be found chronologically. When reference is to a show written by the composer being discussed, his name will not be given:

(in chapter on Jerome Kern)

SHOW BOAT [December 27, 1927]

When reference is to a show included in the "Notable Scores" section, "PART 4" will be used for composer's name:

A CHORUS LINE [PART 4: April 15, 1975]

When more than one composer wrote for the same production, contributions are discussed in each chapter. This is indicated in the "Show Data" section by naming the other composer in boldface; show title and date are not repeated:

(in chapter on Richard Rodgers)

BETSY
December 28, 1926   New Amsterdam Theatre
39 performances
Music mostly by Rodgers (see **Berlin**)
Lyrics mostly by Lorenz Hart

It will not always be necessary to check the reference, of course; often the date alone is the relevant factor. Finding the location of the most-referred-to chapters might take some getting used to. Specific page numbers for cross-referenced productions can be found in the Chronological Listing Of Productions (Appendix 1).

SOURCES AND CONTRADICTIONS

Standard reference sources—often compiled from earlier standard sources—can contain contradictory information. Titles and names with different spelling or punctuation; different dates, varying "official" numbers of performances; different facts, different facts about the same facts, and more.

Wherever possible, information has been taken directly from published music, theatre programs, reviews, and advertising material. Even primary source materials are often in disagreement. One piece of music can have different titles (or authors) listed on the cover and inside.

Obvious misspellings and errors have been corrected; alternate spellings have been standardized. In dealing with contradictions, the most likely information—usually from the earliest source—has been used. It will be noted that certain experts in the field are consistently reliable, while others are consistently not.

To verify song existence and to provide complete-as-practical reuse information, virtually all individual sheets, scores, selections, etc. have been personally examined and in most cases played. Copyright records and registration deposit copies have been checked to insure the greatest possible accuracy. Even so, we are fairly certain that this volume will contain an error or two.

Exact titles and composer/lyricist information are taken from the published song, as given at the top of the page with the copyright notice. Where reason exists to doubt authorship as credited, copyright and performing-rights organization records have been consulted. Such discrepancies have been included in the interests of completeness and accuracy, and only, of course, where documentation exists.

Acknowledgments

There are many existing sources for statistics, facts, and the like. Songs, though, could not be examined until they were found. The following people were of help in locating materials and clarifying information.

As representatives of the composers: Louis Abend of the Welk Music Group (T. B. Harms), Bob Baumgart, Eric Colodne of Notable Music, Michael Feinstein, John Fearnley, Jack Gottlieb of Amberson Productions, Michael Kerker of ASCAP, Paul McKibbins of the Tommy Valando Publishing Group, Dave Olsen of Columbia Pictures Publishing, Lys Simonette and David Farneth of the Kurt Weill Foundation, Allen Whitehead of Music Theatre International, Joseph Weiss of Eastman and Eastman (Edwin H. Morris), and Allen Whitehead of Music Theatre International. Early support came from Theodore S. Chapin of the Rodgers and Hammerstein (and Hart) Organization, and Mrs. Ceciley Youmans Collins.

For various reasons, only a few of the composers discussed were contacted directly. Jule Styne, Harold Rome, Bob Merrill, and Charles Strouse were all gracious and helpful. Stanley Greene, Edward Jablonski, and Alfred Simon—biographers and friends of several of the composers—were generous with their time and knowledge. Information and insight also came from stage managers, company managers, and press agents.

A number of advanced music collectors have shared their knowledge of the field and helped track down obscure material: Don Stubblebine, Vi Foerster, Stan White, Bill Simon, Lawrence Jay Taylor, Joe Friedman, and Irv Gerst. Special thanks go to James J. Fuld, who offered access to his extensive collections and provided helpful suggestions. Mr. Fuld was also responsible for the unexpected discovery of certain important items.

Much of the research was done at the following institutions: the Music Division and the Billy Rose Theatre Collection of The Performing Arts Research Center at Lincoln Center (thanks to Thor E. Wood and Richard Buck), the Music Reference Collection of The New

York Public Library at Lincoln Center, and the Music Division of the Library of Congress in Washington, D.C. Also the now-defunct Songwriters Hall of Fame Museum (where Frankie MacCormack was of great help), and other private collections, which wish to remain private.

For all sorts of assistance, support, and encouragement, the following are gratefully thanked: Mitchell Erickson, Emily Frankel, Arlene Grayson, Leo and Janice Herbert, Robert Kessler, Carol Patella, Skipp Porteous, Stephanie Ross, Kim Sellon, Mark Sendroff, Dr. Barbara Ann Simon, Mary Jo Slater, Eugene V. Wolsk, Max Woodward, and Kee Young. Jerry Gross, my editor, has been unceasing in his efforts to make this book as comprehensive, useful, and usable as possible. I have repaid his diligence and thoroughness by giving him (and copyeditor Mike Cantalupo) plenty to edit.

Finally, William W. Appleton has been an enthusiastic part of this project since its inception. A discerning theatregoer since 1925, he has graciously spent many hours double-checking song listings and consulting on commentary. His efforts are deeply appreciated.

PART I

Introduction

The century began with American musical theatre dominated by European operettas—English, German, and Austrian. This held firm until 1914, when the Great War quickly ended popularity of things foreign. Jerome Kern, a practiced hand at "Americanizing" imports, finally had a chance to explore his own style; the result was the "modern musical comedy" form. (Actually, the first of many "modern musical comedy" forms.) Irving Berlin, already known to Broadway for pop song hits, tried his hand at complete scores; he was less adventurous than Kern, but highly successful. The postwar years brought three young Kern protégés: George Gershwin, Vincent Youmans, and Richard Rodgers. They surpassed the master with a newer "modern musical comedy" built on dance rhythms; Kern, meanwhile, began development of "musical drama." Cole Porter, of the Kern/Berlin generation, was next to make his mark on Broadway after a long, unapplied apprenticeship. Then came Arthur Schwartz, establishing himself in the months just before the stock market crash. Nineteen thirty saw the entrance of three talented protégés of Gershwin: Harold Arlen, Vernon Duke, and Burton Lane. But the worsening Depression brought Broadway musical opportunity to a near halt.

Jerome Kern

BORN: January 27, 1885   New York, New York
DIED: November 11, 1945   New York, New York

Jerome Kern was raised in Newark, New Jersey, where his father was a merchant. By 1901 Kern was writing songs for amateur groups, leaving high school to work as a song plugger for Edward B. Marks' Lyceum Publishing Company. Lyceum issued Kern's first published piece, the 1902 piano solo "At The Casino." Kern was already set on writing for the theatre; realizing the importance of the publisher in those Tin Pan Alley days, he bought into the small T. B. Harms firm late in 1903. Running the house was the remarkable Max Dreyfus: when Kern's fame began attracting novice composers, Dreyfus selected the most promising and convinced producers to hire the untried Gershwin, Youmans, Porter, Rodgers, Schwartz, etc. At the time, Dreyfus printed American editions of many of the imported British operettas. Interpolations were often needed to "Americanize" the material, so Dreyfus went about getting Kern these assignments.

AN ENGLISH DAISY
January 18, 1904   Casino Theatre   41 performances

Music mostly by A. M. Norden
Lyrics to Kern songs by Edgar Smith
Book by Seymour Hicks and Walter Slaughter
Directed by Ben Teal
Produced by Weber and Fields

Published songs:

"The Downcast Eye"—added to post-Broadway tour
"Wine, Wine! (Champagne Song)"

MR. WIX OF WICKHAM
September 19, 1904   Bijou Theatre   41 performances

Music mostly by Herbert Darnley and George Everard
Lyrics by John H. Wagner

Book by Herbert Darnley and John H. Wagner
Directed and produced by Edward E. Rice
With Julian Eltinge

Published songs:

"Angling By The Babbling Brook"
"From Saturday To Monday"
"Susan" (lyric by Kern)
"Waiting For You"

Broadway heard a Kern sampler of four tunes in **MR. WIX OF WICKHAM.** Broadway was not impressed. Far more successful was Julian Eltinge, beginning his highly respectable career as the most popular female impersonator on the American stage (see **COUSIN LUCY [August 27, 1915]**).

THE SILVER SLIPPER
[Circa April 1905]; post-Broadway tour

Music mostly by Leslie Stuart
Lyrics by W. H. Risqué
Book by Clay M. Greene
(Based on the British book by Owen Hall)
Directed by Cyril Scott
Produced by John C. Fisher
With Samuel Collins, Ben Lodge, and George Tennery

Published song:

"My Celia" (by John Golden and Kern)—added during tour

THE CATCH OF THE SEASON
August 28, 1905   Daly's Theatre   104 performances

Music mostly by W. T. Francis and others
Book by Seymour Hicks and Cosmo Hamilton
Directed by Ben Teal
Produced by Charles Frohman
With Edna May

Published songs:

"Frolic Of A Breeze" (lyric by Clifford Harris)—see **THE BEAUTY OF BATH [March 19, 1906]**
"Molly O'Hallerhan (Edna May's Irish Song)" (lyric by Kern)

"Oh, Mr. Chamberlain" (lyric by Charles H. Taylor)—see **THE BEAUTY OF BATH**
"Raining" (lyric by Harris)
"Take Me On The Merry-Go-Round" (lyric by Kern)
"Tulips (Two Lips)" (lyric by Kern)
"Won't You Kiss Me Once Before I Go?" (lyric by Taylor)

Charles Frohman revolutionized the haphazard American theatre business with innovations still in effect today. By 1900 he was equally active in London, mounting his hits on both sides of the Atlantic. Specializing in British plays and operettas, he regularly refused Kern's offered interpolations until he met the composer in England (and assumed he was English). Kern was soon Frohman's favorite interpolator and good friend—but he never gave Kern a chance at a complete score.

THE BABES AND THE BARON
October 14, 1905   ⟨London⟩
Music mostly by H. E. Haines
Lyrics mostly by Charles H. Taylor
Book by A. M. Thompson and Robert Courtneidge
NOTE: **BABES IN THE WOOD,** post-Broadway title

Published song:

"Farewell, Dear Toys (March)" [instrumental] (partial lyric by Kern)

THE EARL AND THE GIRL
November 4, 1905   Casino Theatre   148 performances
Music mostly by Ivan Caryll
Lyrics mostly by Percy Greenbank
Book by Seymour Hicks
Directed by R. H. Burnside
Produced by Sam S. and Lee Shubert, Inc.
With Eddie Foy

Published songs:

"How'd You Like To Spoon With Me?" (lyric by Edward Laska)—also used in **THE RICH MR. HOGGENHEIMER [October 22, 1906]**
"My Southern Belle" (music by Max Eugene, lyric by Kern)

"How'd You Like To Spoon With Me?" was Kern's first hit song. Composer "Max Eugene" was Max Dreyfus, who had started as a songwriter. The Shubert Brothers (Sam S., Lee, and J. J.) came to Broadway in 1901. Sam, the unanimous favorite, died May 12, 1905 in a train crash en route from **THE EARL AND THE GIRL** tryout in Cincinnati. Lee opted to keep Sam billed for the next few years as coproducer, rather than credit J. J.; this greatly annoyed Jake, which was the intention.

THE BEAUTY OF BATH
March 19, 1906   Aldwych Theatre ⟨London⟩
287 performances

Music mostly by H. E. Haines
Book by Seymour Hicks and Cosmo Hamilton
Choreographed by Edward Royce
Produced by Charles Frohman
With Hicks and Ellaline Terriss (Hicks)

Published song:

"Mr. Chamberlain" (lyric by P. G. Wodehouse and Kern)—revised
   lyric for "Oh, Mr. Chamberlain" from **CATCH OF THE
   SEASON [August 28, 1905]**

Additional song published in vocal score:

"The Frolic Of A Breeze" (lyric by P. G. Wodehouse and Charles
   H. Taylor)—revised lyric for song from **CATCH OF THE
   SEASON**

Astute British showman Seymour Hicks brought Kern and Pelham Grenville Wodehouse together for these interpolations. The young humorist was working as a newspaper columnist; his contributions here indicated lyrical skill, but it wasn't till after the war began that the two resumed collaboration—with revolutionary (for the musical theatre) results. **THE BEAUTY OF BATH** was choreographed by Edward Royce, later to direct a number of important Kern (and non-Kern) American musicals.

THE SPRING CHICKEN
[Circa March 1906]   Gaiety Theatre ⟨London⟩
401 performances

Music mostly by Ivan Caryll and Lionel Monckton
Lyrics mostly by Adrian Ross and Percy Greenbank
Book by George Grossmith
(Based on *Coquin de Printemps* [play] by Jaime and Duval)
With Richard Carle

Published song:

"Rosalie" (lyric by Grossmith)—added after London opening; see
  THE LAUGHING HUSBAND [February 2, 1914]

Although **THE SPRING CHICKEN** opened May 30, 1905, Kern's
contribution wasn't written until the following year. For purposes of
song chronology, the show listing uses the date "Rosalie" was interpolated.

THE LITTLE CHERUB
August 6, 1906   Criterion Theatre   155 performances

Music mostly by Ivan Caryll
Lyrics mostly by Adrian Ross
Book by Owen Hall
Directed by Ben Teal
Produced by Charles Frohman
With Hattie Williams

Published songs:

"Meet Me At Twilight" (lyric by F. Clifford Harris)
"A Plain Rustic Ride ('Neath The Silv'ry Moon)" (music by
  Jackson Gouraud and Kern, lyric by Kern)
"Under The Linden Tree" (lyric by M. E. Rourke)

Michael Elder Rourke, an England-born Irishman, began his Broadway career as a press agent before moving on to lyric writing. He was
to be Kern's major collaborator until the Wodehouse partnership resumed in 1916.

MY LADY'S MAID
September 20, 1906   Casino Theatre   44 performances

Music mostly by Paul Rubens
Lyrics by Rubens and Percy Greenbank
Book by Edward Paulton and R. H. Burnside
(Based on the British musical by Rubens and N. Newnham Davis)

Directed by Burnside
Produced by Sam S. and Lee Shubert
With Madge Crichton

Published song:

"All I Want Is You" (lyric by Paul West)

THE RICH MR. HOGGENHEIMER
October 22, 1906   Wallack's Theatre   187 performances

Music mostly by Ludwig Englander
Book and lyrics mostly by Harry B. Smith
(Based on a character from *The Girl from Kay's* [musical] by Owen Hall)
Directed by Ben Teal
Produced by Charles Frohman
With Sam Bernard

Published songs:

"Bagpipe Serenade" (lyric by Kern)
"Blue, Blue" (lyric by Paul West)
"Don't You Want A Paper Dearie?" (lyric by West)
"How'd You Like To Spoon With Me?" (lyric by Edward
    Laska)—originally used in **THE EARL AND THE GIRL**
    [November 4, 1905]
"I've a Little Favor" (lyric by M. E. Rourke)
"My Hungarian Irish Girl" (lyric by West)
"Poker Love (Card Duet)" (lyric by West and Kern)
"A Recipe" (lyric by Kern and West)—added after opening; also
    used in **THE ORCHID [April 8, 1907]**

THE WHITE CHRYSANTHEMUM
[March 25, 1907]   Garrick Theatre ⟨Philadelphia,
Pennsylvania⟩; closed during pre-Broadway tryout

Music mostly by Howard Talbot
Lyrics mostly by Arthur Anderson
Book by Leedham Hantock and Anderson
With Edna Wallace Hopper and Lawrence Grossmith

Published song:

"I Just Couldn't Do Without You" (lyric by Paul West)
"Bill's A Liar" (lyric by M. E. Rourke)

THE ORCHID
April 8, 1907   Herald Square Theatre   178 performances

Music mostly by Ivan Caryll and Lionel Monckton
Lyrics mostly by Adrian Ross and Percy Greenbank
Book by James T. Tanner and Joseph W. Herbert
Directed by Frank Smithson
Produced by Sam S. and Lee Shubert, Inc.
With Eddie Foy

Published songs:

"Come Around On Our Veranda" (lyric by Paul West and Kern)
"I'm Well Known" (lyric by Kern)
"A Recipe" (lyric by Kern and West)—originally used in **THE
    RICH MR. HOGGENHEIMER [October 22, 1906]**

FASCINATING FLORA
May 20, 1907   Casino Theatre   113 performances

Music mostly by Gustave Kerker
Book by R. H. Burnside and Joseph W. Herbert
Staged by Burnside
Produced by Burnside and Comstock, Inc.

Published songs:

"Ballooning" (lyric by Paul West)
"Katy Was A Business Girl" (lyric by West)
"The Little Church Around the Corner" (lyric by M. E. Rourke)
"Right Now" (music by Fred Fisher, lyric by Kern)
"The Subway Express" (lyric by James O'Dea)

Producer Comstock, an early Kern fan, was to devise the "Princess
Theatre Show" series—and give Kern the assignment (see **NO-
BODY HOME [April 20, 1915]**).

THE DAIRYMAIDS
August 26, 1907   Criterion Theatre   86 performances

Music mostly by Paul A. Rubens and Frank A. Tours
Lyrics to Kern songs by M. E. Rourke
Book by A. M. Thompson and Robert Courtneidge
Directed by A. E. Dodson

Produced by Charles Frohman
With Julia Sanderson

Published songs:

"Cheer Up Girls"
"The Hay Ride"
"I'd Like To Meet Your Father"
"I've A Million Reasons Why I Love You"
"Little Eva"
"Mary McGee"
"Never Marry A Girl With Cold Feet"

Julia Sanderson was one of the top American musical comedy heroines of her day. She starred in a number of Kern musicals.

THE GAY WHITE WAY
October 7, 1907   Casino Theatre   105 performances

Music mostly by Ludwig Englander
Book by Sydney Rosenfeld and J. Clarence Harvey
Directed by R. H. Burnside
Produced by Sam S. and Lee Shubert, Inc.
With Melville Ellis

Published song:
"Without The Girl—Inside!" (lyric by M. E. Rourke and Kern)

THE MORALS OF MARCUS
November 18, 1907   Criterion Theatre   44 performances

Play by William J. Locke
Produced by Charles Frohman
With Marie Doro

Published song:
"Eastern Moon" (lyric by M. E. Rourke)

PETER PAN
Or, The Boy Who Wouldn't Grow Up
⟨First Version⟩
[Circa December 1907]; post-Broadway tour

Play by J. M. Barrie
Produced by Charles Frohman
With Maude Adams and Ernest Lawford

Published song:

"Won't You Have A Little Feather?" (lyric by Paul West)—added
   during tour

The eccentrics Frohman, Maude Adams, and J. M. Barrie formed
an unlikely but enduring personal relationship. Written for Adams,
PETER PAN cast something of a spell over each of their lives (see
ROSY RAPTURE [March 22, 1915]). Adams' debut in the role had
been November 6, 1905; she toured in the play for years. Kern later
wrote a song for Broadway's first non-Adams production of the play,
Marilyn Miller's unsuccessful version **[November 6, 1924]**.

A WALTZ DREAM
January 27, 1908   Broadway Theatre   111 performances

Music mostly by Oscar Strauss
Lyrics mostly by Joseph W. Herbert
Book by Felix Doermann and Leopold Jacobson
(Based on the Austrian musical by Hans Mueller)
Directed by Herbert Gresham
Produced by The Inter-State Amusement Co., Inc.

Published songs:

"The Gay Lothario" (lyric by C. H. Bovill)
"I'd Much Rather Stay At Home" (lyric by Bovill)
"Vienna" (lyric by Adrian Ross)

The course of the musical theatre changed abruptly on June 8, 1907
in London (October 21, 1907 in New York) when Franz Lehar's *Merry
Widow* waltzed in. Kern's "Americanized" interpolations were attracting interest, and he was ready for his break; but now audiences
only wanted Viennese operetta. So Kern began a new round of interpolations.

THE GIRLS OF GOTTENBERG
September 2, 1908   Knickerbocker Theatre
103 performances

Music mostly by Ivan Caryll and Lionel Monckton
Lyrics mostly by C. H. Bovill
Book by George Grossmith and L. E. Berman
Directed by J.A.E. Malone
Produced by Charles Frohman
With Gertie Millar

Published songs:

"Freida" (lyric by M. E. Rourke)
"I Can't Say You're The Only One"
"Nothing At All" (lyric by Rourke)

FLUFFY RUFFLES
September 7, 1908   Criterion Theatre   48 performances

Music mostly by W. T. Francis
Lyrics mostly by Wallace Irwin
Lyrics to Kern songs mostly by C. H. Bovill
Book by John J. McNally
Directed by Ben Teal
Produced by Charles Frohman
With Hattie Williams

Published songs:

"Aida McCluskie"
"Dining Out" (lyric by George Grossmith)
"Meet Her With A Taximeter"
"Mrs. Cockatoo"
"Sweetest Girl, Silly Boy, I Love You" (lyric by Irwin)
"Take Care"
"There's Something Rather Odd About Augustus"
"Won't You Let Me Carry Your Parcel?"

KITTIE GREY
January 25, 1909   New Amsterdam Theatre
48 performances

Music mostly by Augustus Barratt, Howard Talbot, and Lionel Monckton
Lyrics to Kern songs by M. E. Rourke
Book by J. Smyth Pigott
(Based on *Les Fetards* [play] by Mars and Hennequin)
Directed by Austin Hurgon

Produced by Charles Frohman
With Julia Sanderson and G. P. Huntley

Published songs:

"Eulalie"
"If The Girl Wants You (Never Mind The Color Of Her Eyes)"
"Just Good Friends"

THE GAY HUSSARS
July 29, 1909   Knickerbocker Theatre   44 performances

Music by Emmerich Kalman
English lyrics by Grant Stewart
Book by Maurice Browne Kirby
(Based on the Austrian musical by Karl Von Bakonyi and Robert
  Bodansky)
Directed by George Marion
Produced by Henry W. Savage

Published song:

"Shine Out All You Little Stars" (lyric by M. E. Rourke)

THE DOLLAR PRINCESS
September 6, 1909   Knickerbocker Theatre
288 performances

Music mostly by Leo Fall
Book by George Grossmith
(Based on the Austrian musical by Willner and Grunbaum)
Directed by A. E. Malone
Produced by Charles Frohman
With Donald Brian and Valli Valli

Published songs:

"Not Here! Not Here!" (lyric by M. E. Rourke)—see **THE GIRL
  FROM UTAH [August 24, 1914]**
"A Boat Sails on Wednesday [Quartet]" (lyric by Adrian Ross and
  Grossmith)—written for London production [September 25,
  1909]
"Red, White And Blue" (lyric by Ross)—written for London
  production

Prima donna Valli Valli was married to Max Dreyfus's brother Louis,
who ran the London branch of the publishing house.

THE GIRL AND THE WIZARD
September 27, 1909   Casino Theatre   96 performances

Music mostly by Julian Edwards (see **Berlin**)
Lyrics mostly by Robert B. Smith and Edward Madden
Lyrics to Kern songs by Percival Knight
Book by J. Hartley Manners
Directed by Ned Wayburn
Produced by the Messrs. Shubert
With Sam Bernard

Published songs:

"By The Blue Lagoon"
"Frantzi"
"Suzette And Her Pet"

THE GOLDEN WIDOW
[October 26, 1909]   Belasco Theatre ⟨Washington, D.C.⟩;
closed during pre-Broadway tryout

Music mostly by Melville Gideon and Louis Hirsch
Lyrics mostly by Edward Madden
Book by Joseph Herbert
Produced by Sam S. and Lee Shubert
With Louise Dresser

Published song:

"Howdy! How D'You Do?" (lyric by M. E. Rourke)

KING OF CADONIA
January 10, 1910   Daly's Theatre   16 performances

Music also by Sidney Jones
Lyrics to Kern songs by M. E. Rourke
Book by Frederick Lonsdale
Directed by Joseph Herbert
Produced by the Messrs. Shubert
With Marguerite Clark

Published songs:

"The Blue Bulgarian Band"
"Catamarang" (lyric by Percival Knight)—see **SALLY [December 21, 1920]**

"Come Along, Pretty Girl"—also used in **THE GIRL AND THE DRUMMER [Circa August 1910]**
"Coo-coo Coo-coo (Marie)" (lyric by Maurice Stonehill)
"Every Girl I Meet" (lyric by Percival Knight)
"Hippopotamus"
"Lena, Lena"
"Mother And Father"

THE ECHO
August 17, 1910   Globe Theatre   53 performances

Music mostly by Deems Taylor
Book by William Le Baron
Directed by Fred G. Latham
Produced by Charles Dillingham
With John E. Hazzard, Bessie McCoy, and George White

Published song:

"Whistle When You're Lonely" (lyric by M. E. Rourke)

Dillingham, former aide to Charles Frohman, began his producing career in 1903 with a series of Victor Herbert musicals (including THE RED MILL [September 24, 1906]). Through the mid-Twenties he was the most respected producer of American musicals, often in competition with sometime partner (and comanager of the New Amsterdam Theatre) Florenz Ziegfeld, Jr.

OUR MISS GIBBS
August 29, 1910   Knickerbocker Theatre   64 performances

Music mostly by Ivan Caryll and Lionel Monckton
Book by James T. Tanner
Directed by Thomas Reynolds
Produced by Charles Frohman
With Pauline Chase

Published songs:

"Come Tiny Goldfish To Me" (music by Harry Marlow, lyric by Kern)
"Eight Little Girls" (lyric by M. E. Rourke)
"I Don't Want You To Be A Sister To Me" (lyric by Frederick Day)

THE GIRL AND THE DRUMMER
[Circa August 1910]; closed during pre-Broadway tryout

Music mostly by Augustus Barratt (see **Berlin**)
Book and lyrics mostly by George Broadhurst
(Based on *What Happened to Jones* [play] by Broadhurst)
Produced by Wm. A. Brady, Ltd.
With Herbert Corthell and Belle Gold

Published song:

"Come Along, Pretty Girl" (lyric by M. E. Rourke)—originally
   used in **KING OF CADONIA [January 10, 1910]**

THE HENPECKS
February 4, 1911   Broadway Theatre   137 performances

"Notes" mostly by A. Baldwin Sloane
"Rhymes" mostly by E. Ray Goetz
"Words" by Glen MacDonough
Directed by Ned Wayburn
Produced by Lew Fields
With Mr. and Mrs. Sam Watson and Gertrude Quinlan

Published song:

"The Manicure Girl" (lyric by Frederick Day)

LA BELLE PAREE
A Jumble of Jollity
March 20, 1911   Winter Garden Theatre
104 performances

Music also by Frank Tours
Lyrics by Edward Madden
Book by Edgar Smith
Produced by the Messrs. Shubert
With Stella Mayhew, Kitty Gordon, Al Jolson, and Mitzi Hajos

Published songs:

"De Goblin's Glide" (lyric by Frederick Day)
"The Edinboro Wriggle" (lyric by M. E. Rourke)
"I'm The Human Brush (That Paints The Crimson On Paree)"
"Look Me Over Dearie"—added after opening
"Paris Is A Paradise For Coons"
"Sing Trovatore"

"That's All Right For McGilligan" (lyric by Rourke)—added after opening

The Shuberts opened their lavish new musical showplace—formerly a stable—with a vaudeville show featuring the two-act revue **LA BELLE PAREE**. The hit of the evening was Shubert discovery Al Jolson (singing, needless to say, "Paris Is A Paradise For Coons"). He was soon elevated to stardom and became a Winter Garden fixture.

LITTLE MISS FIX-IT
April 3, 1911   Globe Theatre   56 performances

Music and lyrics mostly by Jack Norworth
Book by William J. Hurlbut and Harry B. Smith
Directed by Gustav von Seyfferitz
Produced by Louis F. Werba and Mark A. Luescher
With Nora Bayes and Jack Norworth

Published songs:

"There Is A Happy Land (Tale of Woe)" (lyric by Norworth)
"Turkey Trot" [instrumental] (music by Kern and Dave Stamper)

ZIEGFELD FOLLIES OF 1911
June 26, 1911   Jardin de Paris   80 performances

Music mostly by Maurice Levi and Raymond Hubbell (see **Berlin**)
Book and lyrics mostly by George V. Hobart
Staged by Julian Mitchell
Produced by Florenz Ziegfeld, Jr.
With Bessie McCoy

Published song:

"I'm A Crazy Daffydil" (lyric by Bessie McCoy)

This fifth edition of the series marked Kern's first association with Ziegfeld; despite the producer's indifferent musical ear, he was later responsible for mounting Kern's finest work.

THE SIREN
August 28, 1911   Knickerbocker Theatre   136 performances

Music mostly by Leo Fall
Book and lyrics mostly by Harry B. Smith

(Based on the Austrian musical by Leo Stein and A. M. Willner)
Produced by Charles Frohman
With Donald Brian and Julia Sanderson

Published songs:

"Follow Me Round" (music by Fall, lyric by Adrian Ross and
    Kern)
"In The Valley Of Montbijou" (lyric by Rourke)
"I Want To Sing In Opera" (music and lyric by Morton David,
    George Arthurs, and Kern)
"My Heart I Cannot Give To You" (lyric by Matthew Woodward)

Donald Brian—star of the American MERRY WIDOW [October 21,
1907]—and Julia Sanderson played together in several Kern shows;
he was to introduce Kern's biggest early hit, "They Didn't Believe
Me," in **THE GIRL FROM UTAH [August 24, 1914]**.

THE KISS WALTZ
September 18, 1911   Casino Theatre   88 performances
Music mostly by C. M. Ziehrer
Lyrics by Matthew Woodward
Book by Edgar Smith
Directed by J. C. Huffman
Produced by the Messrs. Shubert
With Adele Rowland

Published songs:

"Fan Me With A Movement Slow"
"Love Is Like A Rubber Band (Hoop Song)"
"Love's Charming Art"
"Ta-Ta, Little Girl"
"There's A Resting Place For Every Girl (Sun Chair Song)"

THE OPERA BALL
February 12, 1912   Liberty Theatre   32 performances
Music mostly by Richard Heuberger
Book by Sydney Rosenfeld
(Based on the Austrian musical by Victor Leon and H. von Waldberg)
With Marie Cahill

Published songs:

"Nurses Are We"—advertised but not published except in piano
   selection

"Sergeant Philip Of The Dancers"—advertised but not published
   except in piano selection

Additional song published (no lyric) in piano selection:

"Marie-Louise"

A WINSOME WIDOW
April 11, 1912   Moulin Rouge Theatre   172 performances

Music mostly by Raymond Hubbell
Lyrics mostly by Harry B. and Robert B. Smith
(Based on *A Trip to Chinatown* [musical] by Charles Hoyt)
Directed by Julian Mitchell
Produced by Florenz Ziegfeld, Jr.

Published song:

"Call Me Flo" (words and music by John Golden and Kern)

"Flo" was Ziegfeld's nickname, but the lyric dealt with a Florence;
Kern didn't call Ziegfeld "Flo" until their Twenties hits together.

THE GIRL FROM MONTMARTRE
August 5, 1912   Criterion Theatre   64 performances

Music mostly by Henry Bereny and Jerome Kern
Book and lyrics mostly by Harry B. and Robert B. Smith
(Based on the French musical by Bereny and Rodolph Schanzer from *La
   Dame de Chez Maxim* [farce] by Georges Feydeau)
Directed by Tom Reynolds
Produced by Charles Frohman
With Hattie Williams and Richard Carle

Published songs:

"Bohemia" (lyric by Robert B. Smith)
"Don't Turn My Picture To The Wall" (lyric by Smith)
"Hoop-La-La, Papa!" (lyric by M. E. Rourke)
"I'll Be Waiting 'Neath Your Window" (written and composed by
   James Duffy and Kern)
"I've Taken Such A Fancy To You" (lyric by Clifford Harris)

"Ooo, Ooo, Lena!" (written and composed by John Golden and
   Kern)

A POLISH WEDDING
A Fascinating Farce With Dainty Music
[August 31, 1912]   Empire Theatre ⟨Syracuse, New York⟩;
closed during pre-Broadway tryout

Music mostly by Jean Gilbert
Book and lyrics mostly by George V. Hobart
(Based on *Die Polnische Wirtschaft* [musical] by Kraatz and Okonkowsky)
Produced by George M. Cohan and Sam H. Harris
With Valli Valli, Ann Pennington, and Genevieve Tobin

Published songs:

"Bygone Days" (lyric by Kern)
"He Must Be Nice To Mother"
"Let Us Build A Little Nest" (lyric by Kern and Hobart)—see
   HEAD OVER HEELS [August 29, 1918]
"You're The Only Girl He Loves"—see **OH, LADY! LADY!!**
   [February 1, 1918]

THE "MIND-THE-PAINT" GIRL
September 9, 1912   Lyceum Theatre   136 performances

Play by Sir Arthur Wing Pinero
Directed by Dion G. Boucicault
Produced by Charles Frohman
With Billie Burke

Published songs:

"If You Would Only Love Me" (words and music by John Crook
   and Kern)
"Mind the Paint" (lyric by Pinero)

Billie Burke was a major Frohman star. The producer demanded that
his leading ladies live secluded, scandal-free lives; he never forgave
Burke when she clandestinely married Ziegfeld in 1914.

THE WOMAN HATERS
October 7, 1912   Astor Theatre   32 performances

Music mostly by Edmund Eysler
Book and lyrics by George V. Hobart
(Based on *Die Frauenfresser* [musical] by Leo Stein and Karl Lindau)
Directed by George Marion
Produced by A. H. Woods
With Dolly Castles

Published song:

"Come On Over Here" (music by Walter Kollo, lyric by Kern and
  Hobart)—also used in **THE DOLL GIRL [August 25, 1913]**

THE RED PETTICOAT
November 13, 1912   Daly's Theatre   61 performances

Lyrics by Paul West
Book by Rida Johnson Young
(Based on *Next* [play] by Young)
Directed by Joseph W. Herbert
Produced by Sam S. and Lee Shubert, Inc.
With Helen Lowell
NOTE: **LOOK WHO'S HERE,** pre-Broadway title

Published songs:

"I Wonder"
"Little Golden Maid"
"My Peaches And Cream"
"Oh, You Beautiful Spring" (lyric by M. E. Rourke)
"The Ragtime Restaurant"
"Since The Days Of Grandmama"

After eight years Kern finally got his chance to write a complete score;
not successfully, though. Kern had heretofore cloaked his individual
style with English and Viennese overtones. Now, as the developing
political situation ended the popularity of things Continental and English imports were halted, Kern's originality launched him into
Broadway prominence.

THE SUNSHINE GIRL
February 3, 1913   Knickerbocker Theatre
160 performances

Music mostly by Paul A. Rubens
Lyrics mostly by Arthur Wimperis and Rubens

Book by Rubens and Cecil Raleigh
Directed by J.A.E. Malone
Produced by Charles Frohman
With Julia Sanderson and Joseph Cawthorn

Published song:

"Honeymoon Lane" (lyric by M. E. Rourke)

THE AMAZONS
April 28, 1913   Empire Theatre   48 performances

Play by Sir Arthur Wing Pinero
Directed by William Seymour
Produced by Charles Frohman
With Billie Burke

Published song:

"My Otaheitee Lady" (lyric by Charles Taylor)

THE DOLL GIRL
August 25, 1913   Globe Theatre   88 performances

Music mostly by Leo Fall
Book and lyrics mostly by Harry B. Smith
(Based on the Austrian musical by Leo Stein and A. M. Willner from
   Riquette et sa Mere [play] by Caillavert and deFlers)
Produced by Charles Frohman
With Hattie Williams and Richard Carle

Published songs:

"Come On Over Here" (music by Walter Kollo, lyric by Smith and
   Kern)—revised lyric for song of same title from **THE WOMAN
   HATERS [October 7, 1912]**
"If We Were On Our Honeymoon (Railway Duet)"
"A Little Thing Like A Kiss"
"When Three Is Company (Cupid Song)" (lyric by M. E.
   Rourke)—see **ZIEGFELD FOLLIES OF 1917 [April 13, 1917]**
"Will It All End In Smoke?"

Additional songs published (no lyric) in piano selection:

"I'm Going Away"
"Opening Act Two (Russian Dance)"

Harry Bache Smith was the most prolific writer in American musical history, with lyrics and librettos for over three hundred shows. His early collaboration with Reginald DeKoven (THE BEGUM [November 21, 1887]) is considered by many the first American comic operetta. In the course of his long career he also did important work with Victor Herbert. Smith's close friendship with Kern included a shared passion for collecting antique books. Kern auctioned off most of his collection early in 1929 for an unheard of $1.7 million . . . which he immediately invested in the stock market!

LIEBER AUGUSTIN
September 3, 1913   Casino Theatre   37 performances

Music mostly by Leo Fall
Book by Edgar Smith
(Based on the Austrian musical by Welisch and Bernauer)
Directed by Al Holbrook and Julian Alfred
Produced by Sam S. and Lee Shubert, Inc.
With DeWolf Hopper and George MacFarlane
NOTE: **MISS CAPRICE,** post-opening Broadway title

Published song:

"Look In Her Eyes" (lyric by Herbert Reynolds [M. E. Rourke]—
    also used (as "Look In His Eyes") in **HAVE A HEART
    [January 11, 1917]**

In 1913, Irish Mike Rourke anglicized his name to Herbert Reynolds. The Shuberts anglicized **LIEBER AUGUSTIN**'s name after the opening, but to no avail.

THE MARRIAGE MARKET
September 22, 1913   Knickerbocker Theatre
80 performances

Music mostly by Victor Jacobi
Lyrics to Kern songs by M. E. Rourke
Book by Gladys Unger
(Based on the Austrian musical by M. Brody and F. Martos)
Directed by Edward Royce
Produced by Charles Frohman
With Donald Brian

Published songs:

"By A Country Stile"
"I'm Looking For An Irish Husband"—cut after opening
"I've Got Money In The Bank"
"A Little Bit Of Silk"—cut after opening
"You're Here And I'm Here" (lyric by Harry B. Smith)—added to
    post-Broadway tour; originally used in **THE LAUGHING
    HUSBAND [February 2, 1914]**

OH, I SAY!
A Riotous Musical Comedy
October 30, 1913   Casino Theatre   68 performances

Music mostly by Kern
Lyrics mostly by Harry B. Smith
Book by Sydney Blowe and Douglas Hoare
(Based on a play by Keroul and Barré)
Directed by J. C. Huffman
Produced by the Messrs. Shubert
With Joseph W. Herbert and Cecil Cunningham
NOTE: **THE WEDDING NIGHT,** post-Broadway title

Published songs:

"Alone At Last" [1st]—different than song with same title from
    VERY GOOD EDDIE [December 23, 1915]; also see **BLUE
    EYES [April 27, 1928]**
"Each Pearl A Thought"
"I Can't Forget Your Eyes"—see **SUNNY [September 22, 1925]**
    and **CRISS-CROSS [October 12, 1926]**
"I Know And She Knows"
"Katy-did"
"A Wifie Of Your Own"

Kern's second complete score—again for the Shuberts—was more
successful than **THE RED PETTICOAT [November 13, 1912]**, if
not particularly special.

THE LAUGHING HUSBAND
February 2, 1914   Knickerbocker Theatre   48 performances

Music mostly by Edmund Eysler
Lyrics to Kern songs by Harry B. Smith

Book by Arthur Wimperis
(Based on the Austrian musical by Julius Brammer and Alfred Grunwald)
Directed by Edward Royce
Produced by Charles Frohman
Starring Courtice Pounds

Published songs:

"Bought And Paid For"

"Love Is Like A Violin"

"Take A Step With Me"—new lyric for "Rosalie" from **THE
   SPRING CHICKEN [Circa March 1906]**

"You're Here And I'm Here"—also used in **THE MARRIAGE
   MARKET [September 22, 1913]**

"You're Here And I'm Here" was another Kern hit song. As the
show had a brief life, the song was inserted into the successfully touring
MARRIAGE MARKET to help sell tickets (and music sheets).

WHEN CLAUDIA SMILES
February 2, 1914   Knickerbocker Theatre   56 performances

Play by Anne Caldwell
(Based on a play by Leo Ditrichstein)
Produced by Frederic McKay
With Blanche Ring

Published song:

"Ssh . . . You'll Waken Mister Doyle" (music by John L. Golden,
   lyric by E. W. Rogers, Golden, and Kern)

THE GIRL FROM UTAH
The Acme Of Musical Comedy
August 24, 1914   Knickerbocker Theatre   120 performances

Music mostly by Paul Rubens and Sydney Jones
Lyrics to Kern songs by Harry B. Smith
Book by James T. Tanner
Directed by J.A.E. Malone
Produced by Charles Frohman
With Donald Brian, Julia Sanderson, and Joseph Cawthorn

Published songs:

"Alice In Wonderland"

"The Land Of 'Let's Pretend' "—revised version of "Not Here! Not

Here!" from **THE DOLLAR PRINCESS** [September 6, 1909]
"The Same Sort Of Girl"—see **ROSY RAPTURE** [March 22,
    1915]
"They Didn't Believe Me" (lyric by Herbert Reynolds)—also used
    in **TONIGHT'S THE NIGHT!** [April 28, 1915]
"We'll Take Care Of You All"—cut; also used in **FADS AND
    FANCIES** [March 8, 1915]
"Why Don't They Dance The Polka Anymore?"
"You Never Can Tell"—cut

Kern's best work thus far included the immensely popular "They
Didn't Believe Me." Already well known to theatre audiences, within
the year Kern was established as Broadway's leading "modern" composer.

NINETY IN THE SHADE
January 25, 1915   Knickerbocker Theatre
40 performances
Music and lyrics also by Clare Kummer
Lyrics to Kern songs by Harry B. Smith
Book by Guy Bolton
Directed by Robert Milton
Produced by Daniel V. Arthur
With Marie Cahill and Richard Carle

Published songs:
"Can't You See I Mean You?" (lyric by Herbert Reynolds)—see
    VERY GOOD EDDIE [December 23, 1915] and **THEODORE
    AND CO.** [September 19, 1916]
"It Isn't Your Fault" (lyric by Reynolds)—initial publication upon
    reuse in **LOVE O' MIKE** [January 15, 1917]
"Love Blossoms"—advertised but not published
"A Package Of Seeds"—initial publication upon reuse in **OH,
    BOY!** [February 20, 1917]
"The Triangle" [musical scene] (lyric by Bolton)—initial
    publication upon reuse in **VERY GOOD EDDIE**
"Where's The Girl For Me?"— advertised but not published;
    initial publication upon reuse in **THE LADY IN RED** [May 12,
    1919]
"Whistling Dan"—advertised but not published; see **LEAVE IT
    TO JANE** [August 28, 1917]

The thirty-year-old Kern entered the second phase of his career, divorcing himself from all European influences (except Arthur Sullivan). At the same time, his collaborators—led by librettist Guy Bolton—began using more realistic situations and contemporary American locales and characters. Bolton, born in England of American parents, followed his father into architecture before entering the theatre in 1912. **NINETY IN THE SHADE** was a failure; but Kern and Bolton were already at work on the first "Princess Theatre Show."

A GIRL OF TODAY
[February 8, 1915] ⟨*Washington, D.C.*⟩; *closed during pre-Broadway tryout*

Play by Porter Emerson Browne
Produced by Charles Frohman
With Ann Murdock

Published song:

"You Know And I Know" (lyric by Schuyler Greene)—see **NOBODY HOME [April 20, 1915]**

FADS AND FANCIES
March 8, 1915   Knickerbocker Theatre   48 performances

Music mostly by Raymond Hubbell
Book and lyrics mostly by Glen MacDonough

Published song:

"We'll Take Care Of You All (Refugee Song)" (lyric by Harry B. Smith)—originally used (cut) in **THE GIRL FROM UTAH [August 24, 1914]**

ROSY RAPTURE, THE PRIDE OF THE BEAUTY CHORUS
March 22, 1915   Duke of York's Theatre ⟨*London*⟩

A burlesque by J. M. Barrie
Produced by Charles Frohman
With Gaby Deslys and Jack Norworth

Published song:

"Best Sort Of Mother, Best Sort Of Child" (lyric by F. W. Mark)—new lyric for "The Same Sort Of Girl" from **THE GIRL FROM UTAH [August 24, 1914]**

A legendary (but unconfirmable) story says that Frohman and Kern booked passage to sail together to England. Kern overslept and missed the departure. On May 7, 1915 the *Lusitania* was sunk by a German torpedo; the gentle Frohman paraphrased his friend Barrie's **PETER PAN [Circa 1907]**—"Why fear Death? It is the most beautiful adventure of Life"—as the ship went down.

NOBODY HOME
April 20, 1915   Princess Theatre   135 performances
Lyrics mostly by Schuyler Greene
Book by Guy Bolton
(Based on *Mr. Popple (of Ippleton)* [musical] by Paul Rubens)
Directed by J. H. Benrimo
Produced by F. Ray Comstock
With Adele Rowland

Published songs:
"Another Little Girl" (lyric by Herbert Reynolds)
"Any Old Night (Is A Wonderful Night)" (music by Otto Motzan
    and Kern, lyric by Greene and Harry B. Smith)—also used in
    TONIGHT'S THE NIGHT! [April 28, 1915]
"At That San Francisco Fair" (music by Ford Dabney, James
    Reese Europe, and Kern)
"The Chaplin Walk" (music by Motzan and Kern)
"In Arcady" (lyric by Reynolds)
"The Magic Melody"
"That Peculiar Tune" (music by Kern and Motzan, lyric by Greene
    and Reynolds)—cut; initial publication as 1916 nonshow song
"Wedding Bells Are Calling Me" (lyric by Smith)—added after
    opening; also used in **VERY GOOD EDDIE [December 23,
    1915]**
"You Know And I Know"—originally used in **A GIRL OF
    TODAY [February 8, 1915]**

F. Ray Comstock managed the 299-seat Princess for the Shuberts, who opened the house in 1913. Having been unable to find suitable attractions for the jewel-box theatre, Comstock and play agent Elisabeth Marbury (see **SEE AMERICA FIRST [Porter: March 28, 1916]**) decided to try a moderately sized, sophisticated musical comedy. **NOBODY HOME,** adapted from a 1905 British musical, was not successful; but the concept worked. The series was quickly es-

tablished with the second "Princess Theatre Show," the very good
VERY GOOD EDDIE [December 23, 1915].

TONIGHT'S THE NIGHT!
April 28, 1915   Gaiety Theatre ⟨London⟩
460 performances

Music mostly by Paul A. Rubens
Lyrics mostly by Rubens and Percy Greenbank
Book by Fred Thompson
(Based on *The Pink Dominos* [play] by James Albery)
Produced by George Grossmith and Edward Laurillard
With Grossmith and Madge Saunders

Published songs:

"Any Old Night (Is A Wonderful Night)" (music by Otto Motzan
   and Kern, lyric by Schuyler Greene and Harry B. Smith)—
   originally used in **NOBODY HOME [April 20, 1915]**
"They Didn't Believe Me" (lyric by Herbert Reynolds)—originally
   used in **THE GIRL FROM UTAH [August 24, 1914]**

A MODERN EVE
May 3, 1915   Casino Theatre   56 performances

Music mostly by Jean Gilbert and Victor Hollaender
Lyrics to Kern songs by Harry B. Smith
Book by Will M. Hough and Benjamin Hapgood Burt
(Based on the German musical by Okonkowsky and Schoenfeld)
Directed by Frank Smithson
Produced by Mort H. Singer

Published songs:

"I'd Love To Dance Through Life With You"
"I've Just Been Waiting For You"

COUSIN LUCY
August 27, 1915   George M. Cohan Theatre
43 performances

Play by Charles Klein
Lyrics by Schuyler Greene
Directed by Robert Milton

Produced by A. H. Woods
With Julian Eltinge

Published songs:

"Society"
"Those 'Come Hither' Eyes"—see **THEODORE AND CO.**
    [September 19, 1916]
"Two Heads Are Better Than One" (lyric by Kern and Greene)—
    see **ROCK-A-BYE BABY [May 22, 1918]**

Eltinge was Broadway's finest female impersonator, immensely popular with the family trade. In 1912 he became only the second performer to have a Broadway theatre built in his honor; Maxine Elliott,
a Lee Shubert mistress, was the first. The charming Eltinge, now called
the Empire, has endured fifty years of 42nd Street abuse and still
survives.

MISS INFORMATION
A Little Comedy with a Little Music
October 5, 1915   George M. Cohan Theatre
47 performances

Play by Paul Dickey and Charles W. Goddard
Music mostly by Jerome Kern (see **Porter**)
Lyrics mostly by Elsie Janis
Book by Paul Dickey and Charles W. Goddard
Directed by Robert Milton
Produced by Charles Dillingham
With Elsie Janis and Irene Bordoni

Published songs:

"A Little Love (But Not For Me)"
"On The Sands Of Wa-Ki-Ki" (music by Henry Kailimai and
    Kern)
"Some Sort of Somebody"
NOTE: all reused in **VERY GOOD EDDIE [December 23, 1915]**

Cole Porter—the first of the Gershwin/Youmans/Rodgers group to
reach Broadway—had his second interpolation in this little comedy,
with little success. Eldest of the new generation, Porter was the only
one *not* particularly influenced by Kern. (Nevertheless, Max Dreyfus
was quick to sign him up.)

VERY GOOD EDDIE
December 23, 1915   Princess Theatre   341 performances

Lyrics mostly by Schuyler Greene and Herbert Reynolds (see **Porter [May 18, 1918]**)
Book by Philip Bartholomae and Guy Bolton
(Based on *Over Night* [play] by Bartholomae)
Directed by Frank McCormick
Produced by the Marbury-Comstock Co.
With Ernest Truex, Alice Dovey, and John E. Hazzard

Published songs:

"Babes In The Wood" (lyric by Kern and Greene)
"Babes In The Wood ('Fox-Trot')"—nonshow dance version
"I'd Like To Have A Million In The Bank" (lyric by Reynolds)
"If I Find The Girl" (lyric by John E. Hazzard and Reynolds)
"Isn't It Great To Be Married?" (lyric by Greene)—new lyric for
   "Can't You See I Mean You" from **NINETY IN THE SHADE
   [January 25, 1915]**; also see **THEODORE AND CO.
   [September 19, 1916]**
"I've Got To Dance" (lyric by Greene)—cut
"Nodding Roses" (lyric by Greene and Reynolds)
"Old Bill Baker (The Undertaker)" (lyric by Ring Lardner)—added
   after opening
"Old Boy Neutral" (lyric by Greene)—music revised from "A
   Little Love" from **MISS INFORMATION [October 5, 1915]**
"On The Shore At Le Lei Wi" (music by Henry Kailimai and
   Kern, lyrics by Reynolds)—new lyric for "On The Sands Of Wa-
   Ki-Ki" from **MISS INFORMATION**
"Some Sort Of Somebody (All Of The Time)" (lyric by Elsie
   Janis)—originally used in **MISS INFORMATION**
"Thirteen Collar" (lyric by Greene)
"Wedding Bells Are Calling Me" (lyric by Harry B. Smith)—
   originally used in **NOBODY HOME [April 20, 1915]**

Additional songs published in vocal score:

"Alone At Last" [2nd] (lyric by Reynolds)—different than song
   with same title from **OH, I SAY! [October 30, 1913]**
"Buffo Dance" [instrumental]
"Dance Trio" [instrumental]
"The Triangle" [musical scene] (lyric by Bolton)—originally used
   (unpublished) in **NINETY IN THE SHADE**
"We're On Our Way" (lyric by Greene)

The first "Princess Theatre Show" had been an Americanized import. Beginning with **VERY GOOD EDDIE,** Kern and Bolton (soon joined by Wodehouse) concentrated on making comedy and song spring directly from situation and character. The practice at the time was to find a loose framework and insert whatever jokes and songs turned up. The difference was immediately noted, and Kern and company went on to continue working out the form. "Babes In The Wood" was Kern's second major song hit in his blossoming style.

ZIEGFELD FOLLIES OF 1916
June 12, 1916   New Amsterdam Theatre
112 performances

Music mostly by Louis Hirsch and Dave Stamper (see **Berlin**)
Book and lyrics mostly by George V. Hobart and Gene Buck
Lyrics to Kern songs by Gene Buck
Directed by Ned Wayburn
Produced by Florenz Ziegfeld, Jr.

Published songs:

"Ain't It Funny What A Difference Just A Few Drinks Make?"
"Have A Heart" [1st]—different than song from **HAVE A HEART**
    [January 11, 1917]
"My Lady Of The Nile"
"When The Lights Are Low"

THEODORE AND CO.
September 19, 1916   Gaiety Theatre ⟨London⟩
503 performances

Music mostly by Ivor Novello
Lyrics by Clifford Grey
Book by H.M. Harwood and George Grossmith
Produced by Grossmith and Edward Laurillard

Songs published in vocal score:

"All That I Want Is Somebody To Love Me"—new lyric for
    "Can't You See I Mean You?" from **NINETY IN THE SHADE**
    [January 25, 1915] and "Isn't It Great To Be Married?" from
    VERY GOOD EDDIE [December 23, 1915]
"The Casino Music Hall"
"That 'Come Hither' Look"—new lyric for "Those 'Come Hither'

Eyes" from **COUSIN LUCY [August 27, 1915]**
"365 Days"

MISS SPRINGTIME
September 25, 1916   New Amsterdam Theatre
224 performances

Music mostly by Emmerich Kalman
Lyrics by P. G. Wodehouse
Book by Guy Bolton
Directed by Herbert Gresham
Produced by Klaw and Erlanger
NOTE: **LITTLE MISS SPRINGTIME,** pre-Broadway title

Published songs:

"All Full Of Talk"
"My Castle In The Air"
"Saturday Night"
"Some One" (lyric by Herbert Reynolds)

At the opening night party for **NOBODY HOME [April 20, 1915]**
Kern ran into Wodehouse and introduced him to Bolton. Wodehouse had been writing stories and plays since **THE BEAUTY OF
BATH [March 19, 1906].** Bolton's next musical was this Kalman
operetta; Wodehouse got the lyric assignment and Kern, suddenly
very popular, helped out with a few songs.

GO TO IT
October 24, 1916   Princess Theatre   23 performances

Music, lyrics and book mostly by John L. Golden, John E. Hazzard, and
    Anne Caldwell
(Based on *A Milk White Flag* [play] by Charles Hoyt)
Directed by William H. Post
Produced by the Comstock-Elliott Co.

Published song:

"When You're In Love You'll Know" (music by Golden and Kern,
    lyric by Golden)

The third "Princess Theatre Show." Kern and Bolton disliked the
idea and turned down the offer; the song contributed was presumably adapted from prior work with Golden. **GO TO IT** was a quick

flop; Kern, Bolton and Wodehouse—already working together on a full-scale musical—agreed to ready something for the Princess.

HAVE A HEART
The Up-To-The-Minute Musical Comedy
January 11, 1917   Liberty Theatre   76 performances

Lyrics by P. G. Wodehouse
Book by Guy Bolton and Wodehouse
Directed by Edward Royce
Produced by Henry W. Savage
With Louise Dresser

Published songs:

"And I Am All Alone" (lyric by Kern and Wodehouse)
"Daisy"
"Have A Heart" [2nd]—different than song from **ZIEGFELD
    FOLLIES OF 1916 [June 12, 1916]**
"Honeymoon Inn"
"I'm So Busy" (lyric by Schuyler Greene and Wodehouse)
"Look In His Eyes" (lyric by Herbert Reynolds)—same song as
    "Look In Her Eyes" from **LIEBER AUGUSTIN [September 3,
    1913]**
"Napoleon"
"Polly Believed In Preparedness"—cut
"The Road That Lies Before"
"They All Look Alike"
"You Said Something" (lyric by Kern and Wodehouse)

Additional songs published in vocal score:

"Bright Lights"
"Finale Act One"
"I'm Here, Little Girls, I'm Here"
"It's A Sure Sign" (by R. P. Weston and Kern)
"The Nightingale (Turk's Song)"
"Opening Act Two"
"Reminiscences" [instrumental]
"Shop"

The Kern and Wodehouse collaboration burst on the scene. The lyricist's humor and crisp language perfectly matched the composer's sprightliness, a modern-day equivalent to Gilbert and Sullivan of the

1880s. The run of **HAVE A HEART** was disappointingly short, but other shows were well underway.

LOVE O' MIKE
January 15, 1917   Shubert Theatre   192 performances

Lyrics by Harry B. Smith
Book by Thomas Sydney
Directed by J. H. Benrimo
Produced by Elizabeth Marbury and Lee Shubert
With Peggy Wood, Luella Gear, and Clifton Webb
NOTE: **FOR LOVE OF MIKE** and **GIRLS WILL BE GIRLS,** pre-Broadway titles

Published songs:

"The Baby Vampire"
"Don't Tempt Me"
"Drift With Me"
"I Wonder Why"
"It Can't Be Done"—cut
"It Wasn't My Fault" (lyric by Herbert Reynolds)—same song as
   "It Isn't Your Fault" (unpublished) from **NINETY IN THE
   SHADE** [January 25, 1915]
"Simple Little Tune"
"We'll See"
"Who Cares?"—cut

Additional songs published (no lyric) in piano selection:

"Life's A Dance"
"Look In The Book"

While the Princess formula called for intimacy, **LOVE O' MIKE** was a full-scale piece which had to play large houses (1,500 seats instead of 300). The show was not particularly memorable, but with a great deal of pre-Broadway revision and care it managed to do well enough.

OH, BOY!
February 20, 1917   Princess Theatre   463 performances

Lyrics by P. G. Wodehouse
Book by Guy Bolton and Wodehouse
Directed by Edward Royce and Robert Milton
Produced by Comstock and Elliott Co.
With Anna Wheaton, Edna May Oliver, and Dorothy Dickson

Published songs:

"Ain't It A Grand And Glorious Feeling?"—cut
"Be A Little Sunbeam"
"The First Day Of May"—written for 1919 British production
    (retitled OH, JOY!)
"Nesting Time In Flatbush" [1st]
"Nesting Time In Flatbush" [2nd] (lyric by Wodehouse and
    Kern)—version with extended lyric
"An Old Fashioned Wife"
"A Package Of Seeds" (lyric by Herbert Reynolds and
    Wodehouse)—revised lyric for song with same title (unpublished)
    from **NINETY IN THE SHADE [January 25, 1915]**
"A Pal Like You"—originally issued as "We're Going To Be Pals"
"Rolled Into One"
"Till The Clouds Roll By" (lyric by Kern and Wodehouse)
"Words Are Not Needed"—originally issued as "Every Day"
"You Never Knew About Me"

Additional songs published (no lyric) in piano selection:

"Flubby Dub"
"Opening Act One"

The most successful of the "Princess Theatre Shows." **OH, BOY!**
set the standard for early musical comedy, with the songs reasonably
interpolated into entertainingly humorous (though often slight) stories. "Till The Clouds Roll By" joined "They Didn't Believe Me"
and "Babes In The Woods" as Kern's three biggest pre-Twenties hits.

ZIEGFELD FOLLIES OF 1917
June 12, 1917   New Amsterdam Theatre
111 performances

Music mostly by Raymond Hubbell and Dave Stamper
Lyrics mostly by Gene Buck
Book by Buck and George V. Hobart
Directed by Ned Wayburn
Produced by Florenz Ziegfeld, Jr.

Published song:

"Just Because You're You"—new lyric for "When Three Is
    Company" from **THE DOLL GIRL [August 25, 1913]**

LEAVE IT TO JANE
August 28, 1917   Longacre Theatre   167 performances

Lyrics by P. G. Wodehouse
Book by Guy Bolton and Wodehouse
(Based on *The College Widow* [play] by George Ade)
Directed by Edward Royce
Produced by William Elliott, F. Ray Comstock, and Morris Gest
With Edith Hallor and Oscar Shaw

Published songs:

"Cleopatterer"
"The Crickets Are Calling"
"I'm Going To Find A Girl"
"It's A Great Big Land"
"Just You Watch My Step"
"Leave It To Jane"—revised version of "Whistling Dan"
  (unpublished) from **NINETY IN THE SHADE** [January 25,
  1915]
"A Peach Of A Life"
"Poor Prune"—cut
"Sir Galahad"
"The Siren's Song"
"The Sun Shines Brighter"
"There It Is Again (When Your Favorite Girl's Not There)"
"What I'm Longing To Say"
"Why?"—cut

Additional song published in vocal selection:

"Wait Till Tomorrow"—initial publication upon reuse in 1959
  revival

Additional songs recorded:

"Football Song (Opening Act Two)"
"Good Old Atwater"
"Just You Watch My Step"

With the tremendously successful **OH, BOY!** [February 20, 1917]
still strong at the Princess, this next show in the series was booked
into a standard-sized, 1,000-seat theatre (which accounts for the considerably shorter run). Model for the college-football musicals of the
future—specifically **GOOD NEWS!** [PART 4: September 6, 1927],
TOO MANY GIRLS [Rodgers: October 18, 1939] and **BEST FOOT**

FORWARD [Martin: October 1, 1941], **LEAVE IT TO JANE** was successfully revived off-Broadway [May 25, 1959] for a 928-performance run.

THE RIVIERA GIRL
September 24, 1917   New Amsterdam Theatre
78 performances

Music mostly by Emmerich Kalman
Lyrics by P. G. Wodehouse
Book by Guy Bolton and Wodehouse
Produced by Klaw and Erlanger

Published song:

"Bungalow In Quogue"

MISS 1917
November 5, 1917   Century Theatre   48 performances

Music also by Victor Herbert
Lyrics by P. G. Wodehouse
Book by Guy Bolton and Wodehouse
Directed by Ned Wayburn
Produced by Charles Dillingham and Florenz Ziegfeld, Jr.
With Lew Fields, Vivienne Segal, Bessie McCoy Davis, and Irene Castle

Published songs:

"Go Little Boat"—cut; also used in **OH, MY DEAR!** [November
    27, 1918]
"I'm The Old Man In The Moon"
"The Land Where The Good Songs Go"
"Peaches"
"The Picture I Want To See"—also used in **OH LADY! LADY!!**
    [February 1, 1918]
"Tell Me All Your Troubles, Cutie"
"We're Crooks"

Dillingham and Ziegfeld had successfully taken over the Century Theatre with **THE CENTURY GIRL [Berlin: November 6, 1916].** For their second presentation they kept cocomposer Victor Herbert on and substituted Kern for Berlin. Kern and Herbert fought. Kern and star Vivienne Segal fought (when she sang Herbert's unauthorized interpolation of "Kiss Me Again" from MLLE. MODISTE [December 25, 1905]. This didn't prevent her from getting the lead in Kern's very next show.). **MISS 1917** wasn't very good, and Dillingham and Ziegfeld let go of the Century. Rehearsal pianist was nineteen-year-old George Gershwin; Harry Askins, company manager, was impressed and sent him to Max Dreyfus.

OH LADY! LADY!!
February 1, 1918   Princess Theatre   219 performances

Lyrics by P. G. Wodehouse
Book by Guy Bolton and Wodehouse
Directed by Robert Milton and Edward Royce
Produced by F. Ray Comstock and William Elliott
With Vivienne Segal and Carl Randall

Published songs:

"Before I Met You"
"Bill"—cut; see **ZIP, GOES A MILLION [December 8, 1919]** and **SHOW BOAT [December 27, 1927]**
"Dear Old Prison Days"
"Greenwich Village"
"It's A Hard Hard World"
"Moon Song"
"Not Yet"—revised version of "You're The Only Girl He Loves" from **A POLISH WEDDING [August 31, 1912]**
"Oh Lady! Lady!!"
"Our Little Nest"
"The Picture I Want To See"—originally used in **MISS 1917 [November 5, 1917]**
"The Sun Starts To Shine Again"
"Waiting Around The Corner"—initially issued as "Some Little Girl"
"Wheatless Day"
"When The Ships Come Home"
"You Found Me And I Found You"

Additional songs published in vocal score:

"Do It Now"
"Do Look At Him"
"Finale Act One"
"Opening Chorus Act One (Wedding Day)"

Despite their enormous success, major disagreements—centering on money and credit—developed between Kern and Wodehouse, and the precedent-setting partnership suddenly ended. Both continued to work individually with Bolton (and were to reunite briefly for unimportant work). The Kern, Bolton, and Wodehouse collaboration made its remarkable contributions to the musical theatre in a period of just sixteen months.

TOOT-TOOT!
A Train Of Mirth And Melody
March 11, 1918   George M. Cohan Theatre
40 performances

Lyrics by Berton Braley
Book by Edgar Allan Woolf
(Based on *Excuse Me* [play] by Rupert Hughes)
Directed by Woolf and Edward Rose
Produced by Henry W. Savage
With Louise Groody and William Kent

Published songs:

"Every Girl In All America"
"Girlie"
"Honeymoon Land"—cut; see **THE NIGHT BOAT [February 2, 1920]**
"I Will Knit A Suit O' Dreams"—cut; originally issued as "Teepee"
"If (There's Anything You Want)"—cut
"If You Only Care Enough"—revised lyric for "If (There's Anything You Want)"
"Let's Go"
"When You Wake Up Dancing"

Additional songs published (no lyric) in piano selection:
"It's Greek To Me"
"Yankee Doodle On The Line"

ROCK-A-BYE BABY
May 22, 1918   Astor Theatre   85 performances

Lyrics by Herbert Reynolds
Book by Edgar Allan Woolf and Margaret Mayo
(Based on *Baby Mine* [play] by Mayo)

Directed by Edward Royce
Produced by Selwyn and Co.
With Louise Dresser, Frank Morgan, and Dorothy Dickson

Published songs:

"The Big Spring Drive"
"I Believed All They Said"
"I Never Thought"
"The Kettle Song"
"Little Tune, Go Away"
"Lullaby."
"My Boy"
"Not You"—cut
"Nursery Fanfare"
"One, Two, Three"
"There's No Better Use For Time Than Kissing"—revised version
   of "Two Heads Are Better Than One" from **COUSIN LUCY**
   [August 27, 1915]

Following his first book musical successes in 1915, Kern finally found
himself in great demand. After ten frustrating years of interpolation
chores, he composed an unprecedented seven-and-a-half full scores
for shows opening within eighteen months. Some of his best early
work was done in this period; naturally, a considerable portion was
rather weak.

HEAD OVER HEELS
August 29, 1918   George M. Cohan Theatre
100 performances

Book and lyrics by Edgar Allan Woolf
(Based on *Shadows* [play] by Lee Arthur and [story] by Nalbro Bartley)
Directed by George Marion
Produced by Henry W. Savage
With Mitzi [Hajos], "The Little Human Dynamo"

Published songs:

"All The World Is Swaying"
"The Big Show"
"Funny Little Something"
"Head Over Heels"
"Head Over Heels (Fox Trot)"—nonshow dance version

"I Was Lonely"
"Let's Build A Little Nest" (lyric by Kern and Woolf)—cut;
    revised lyric for song from **A POLISH WEDDING [August 31,
    1912]**
"Mitzi's Lullaby"
"Moment Of The Dance"

Additional song published (no lyric) in piano selection:
"Spring"

THE CANARY
November 4, 1918   Globe Theatre   152 performances

Music mostly by Ivan Caryll (see **Berlin**)
Book and lyrics mostly by Harry B. Smith
(Based on a play by Georges Barr and Louis Vermeuil)
Directed by Fred C. Latham and Edward Royce
Produced by Charles Dillingham
With Julia Sanderson and Joseph Cawthorn

Published songs:

"Oh Promise Me You'll Write To Him Today" (lyric by Harry
    Clarke)—cut; see **SHE'S A GOOD FELLOW [May 5, 1919]**
"Take A Chance (Little Girl And Learn To Dance)"

OH, MY DEAR!
November 27, 1918   Princess Theatre   189 performances

Music mostly by Louis Hirsch
Lyrics by P. G. Wodehouse
Book by Guy Bolton and Wodehouse
Directed by Robert Milton and Edward Royce
Produced by F. Ray Comstock and William Elliott
With Joseph Santley and Ivy Sawyer (Mr. and Mrs.)

Published song:

"Go Little Boat"—originally used (cut) in **MISS 1917 [November
    5, 1917]**

A non-Kern Princess show, reusing a Kern/Wodehouse song.

SHE'S A GOOD FELLOW
May 5, 1919   Globe Theatre   120 performances

Book and lyrics by Anne Caldwell
Directed by Fred G. Latham and Edward Royce
Produced by Charles Dillingham
With Joseph Santley and Ivy Sawyer
NOTE: **A NEW GIRL**, pre-Broadway title

Published songs:

"The Bull Frog Patrol"
"First Rose Of Summer"—see **THE CABARET GIRL**
    [September 19, 1921]
"Ginger Town"—cut
"A Happy Wedding Day"
"Home Sweet Home"
"I Want My Little Gob"
"I've Been Waiting For You All The Time"—new lyric for "Oh
    Promise Me You'll Write To Him Today" from **THE CANARY**
    [November 4, 1918]
"Jubilo"
"Just A Little Line"
"Letter Song"—cut
"Oh! You Beautiful Person"
"Some Party"
"Teacher, Teacher"

Kern began a series of more-lavish-than-the-Princess shows for Charles
Dillingham: six of eight were hits, albeit with undistinguished scores.
Kern's new lyricist/librettist was Anne Caldwell, the first and (to this
day) most successful woman writer in Broadway musical history.

THE LADY IN RED
May 12, 1919   Lyric Theatre   48 performances

Music mostly by Robert Winterberg (see **Gershwin**)
Book and lyrics mostly by Anne Caldwell
Directed by Frank Smithson
Produced by John P. Slocum

Published song:

"Where's The Girl For Me?" (lyric by Harry B. Smith)—originally
    used (unpublished) in **NINETY IN THE SHADE [January 25,
    1915]**

ZIP, GOES A MILLION

[December 8, 1919]   Worcester Theatre ⟨Worcester, Massachusetts⟩; closed during pre-Broadway tryout

Lyrics by Bud (B. G.) DeSylva
Book by Guy Bolton
(Based on *Brewster's Millions* [play] by Winchell Smith and Byron Ongley, from the novel by George Barr McCutcheon)
Directed by Oscar Eagle
Produced by F. Ray Comstock and Morris Gest
With Harry Fox

Published songs:

"Bill"—unpublished; new lyric for song originally used (cut) in **OH LADY! LADY!!** [February 1, 1918]; also see **SHOW BOAT** [December 27, 1927]
"A Business Of Our Own"
"Forget Me Not"
"Give A Little Thought To Me"
"The Language Of Love"
"The Little Back-Yard Band"
"Look For The Silver Lining"—initial publication upon reuse in **SALLY** [December 21, 1920]
"A Man Around The House"
"Telephone Girls"
"Whip-Poor-Will"—cut; also used in **SALLY**
"You Tell 'Em"

The final "Princess Theatre Show" closed before reaching the Princess. The series had included eight shows (with **LEAVE IT TO JANE** [August 28, 1917] and **ZIP, GOES A MILLION,** which did not actually play the Princess) in only four years. But the work accomplished—the introduction of contemporary sounds and themes into the heretofore make-believe terrain of musical comedy—had immediate and far-reaching effects. Composers George Gershwin, Vincent Youmans, and Richard Rodgers (along with lyricists Ira Gershwin and Lorenz Hart) were just beginning their Broadway careers. Each had been excited and highly stimulated by the "Princess Theatre Shows," and their early work was to show an admitted indebtedness to Kern and Wodehouse.

THE NIGHT BOAT
February 2, 1920   Liberty Theatre   313 performances

Book and lyrics by Anne Caldwell
Directed by Fred G. Latham
Produced by Charles Dillingham
With Louise Groody and John E. Hazzard

Published songs:

"Bob White"—cut
"Chick! Chick! Chick!"—cut; also used in **HITCHY-KOO 1920**
  〈**Fourth Edition**〉 **[October 19, 1920]**
"Don't You Want To Take Me?"
"Good-Night Boat" (lyric by Caldwell and Frank Craven)
"A Heart For Sale"
"I'd Like A Lighthouse"—new lyric for "Honeymoon Land" (cut)
  from **TOOT-TOOT! [March 11, 1918]**
"I Love The Lassies (I Love 'Em All)"
"Left All Alone Again Blues"
"The Lorelei"—cut; initial publication upon reuse in **SALLY**
  [December 21, 1920]
"Rip Van Winkle And His Little Men"—cut
"Whose Baby Are You?"

Additional song published [no lyric] in piano selection:
"Some Fine Day"

THE CHARM SCHOOL
August 2, 1920   Bijou Theatre   87 performances

Play by Alice Duer Miller and Robert Milton
"With A Wee Bit Of Music By Jerome Kern"
Produced and directed by Milton
With Sam Hardy and James Gleason

Published song:

"When I Discover My Man" (lyric by Miller)

HITCHY-KOO 1920
Fourth Edition
October 19, 1920   New Amsterdam Theatre
71 performances

Lyrics by Anne Caldwell
Book by Glen MacDonough
Directed by Ned Wayburn
Produced by Raymond Hitchcock
With Hitchcock and Julia Sanderson

Published songs:

"Bring 'Em Back"—see **SHOW BOAT** [December 27, 1927]
"Buggy Riding"
"Chick! Chick! Chick!"—cut; originally used in **THE NIGHT
    BOAT** [February 2, 1920]
"Cupid, The Winner"
"Ding Dong, It's Kissing Time"
"Girls In The Sea"
"Moon Of Love"
"The Old Town"
"The Star Of Hitchy Koo"
"Sweetie"

SALLY
December 21, 1920   New Amsterdam Theatre
570 performances

Lyrics mostly by Clifford Grey
Book by Guy Bolton
Directed by Edward Royce
Produced by Florenz Ziegfeld, Jr.
With Marilynn Miller, Leon Errol, and Walter Catlett

Published songs:

"The Church 'Round The Corner" (lyric by P. G. Wodehouse and
    Grey)
"Look For The Silver Lining" (lyric by B. G. DeSylva)—originally
    used (cut/unpublished) in **ZIP, GOES A MILLION** [December
    8, 1919]
"The Lorelei" (lyric by Anne Caldwell)—originally used
    (cut/unpublished) in **THE NIGHT BOAT** [February 2, 1920]
"On With The Dance"
"Sally"—revised version of "Catamarang" from **KING OF
    CADONIA** [January 10, 1910]
"The Schnitza Komisski"
"Whip-Poor-Will" (lyric by B. G. DeSylva)—originally used (cut)
    in **ZIP, GOES A MILLION**

"Wild Rose"
"You Can't Keep A Good Girl Down (Joan Of Arc)" (lyric by
   Wodehouse and Grey)
Additional songs published in British vocal score:
"The Night Time"
"Opening Act Two (In Society)"

Ziegfeld, king of the revue, wanted to attain a similar position in the
world of musical comedy: he determined to produce the most lavish,
successful musical comedy to date. Taking advantage of his **FOL-
LIES** talent, facilities, and money, he did just that with **SALLY**. At
the same time, he established his favorite mistress as Broadway's favorite musical comedy star. Marilynn Miller (originally Mary Ellen;
soon to be further contracted to Marilyn, creating the now popular
name) had been discovered in a PASSING SHOW by none other than
Mrs. Billie Burke Ziegfeld. Flo stole her from the Shuberts and placed
her in the **FOLLIES OF 1918 [Berlin: June 18, 1918].** Miller turned
on Ziegfeld by marrying costar Frank Carter; Ziegfeld retaliated by
sending husband Carter on the road. When Carter was killed in a car
crash on May 9, 1920, Ziegfeld made up with Miller and built **SALLY**
around her. For Kern, the success of **SALLY** was deceptive: the better
parts of the score were discards from earlier shows (including the hit
"Look For The Silver Lining" and the very good "Whip-Poor-Will").

ZIEGFELD FOLLIES OF 1921
June 21, 1921   Globe Theatre   119 performances
Music mostly by Victor Herbert, Rudolf Friml, and Dave Stamper
Lyrics mostly by Gene Buck
Directed by Edward Royce
Produced by Florenz Ziegfeld, Jr.

Published song:
"You Must Come Over" (lyric by B. G. DeSylva)

THE CABARET GIRL
September 19, 1921   Winter Garden Theatre ⟨London⟩
361 performances
Lyrics mostly by P. G. Wodehouse
Book by George Grossmith and Wodehouse
Directed by Grossmith

Produced by Grossmith and J.A.E. Malone
With Dorothy Dickson, Grossmith, and Heather Thatcher

Published songs:

"Dancing Time" (lyric by Grossmith)
"First Rose Of Summer" (lyric by Wodehouse and Anne
    Caldwell)—new lyric for song of same title from **SHE'S A
    GOOD FELLOW [May 5, 1919]**
"Journey's End"—also used in **THE CITY CHAP [October 26,
    1925]**
"Ka-Lu-A" (lyric by Anne Caldwell)—added after opening;
    originally used in **GOOD MORNING DEARIE [November 1,
    1921]**
"Looking All Over For You"
"Oriental Dreams" (lyric by Grossmith)
"Shimmy With Me"

Additional songs published in vocal score:

"At The Ball" (lyric by Grossmith)—alternate lyric for "Dancing
    Time"
"Chopin Ad Lib (Opening Chorus)"
"Finaletto Act One"
"Finale Act Two (Vicar Song)"
"London, Dear Old London"
"Mr. Gravvins—Mr. Gripps"
"Nerves"
"The Pergola Patrol"
"Those Days Are Gone Forever"
"Whoop-De-Oodle-Do!"
"You Want The Best Seats, We Have 'Em"

Producers Grossmith and Malone decided to follow the 387-perfor-
mance run of their London production [September 10, 1921] of
SALLY [December 21, 1920] with an original Kern musical. Wodehouse proved amenable, so **THE CABARET GIRL** was written for
the local **SALLY** stars—American Dorothy Dickson, who had been
featured in **OH, BOY! [February 20, 1917]** and **ROCK-A-BYE BABY
[May 22, 1918],** and author/director/producer Grossmith. The success of the venture paved the way for future London musicals by Kern
and other Americans.

GOOD MORNING DEARIE
November 1, 1921   Globe Theatre   347 performances

Book and lyrics by Anne Caldwell
Directed by Edward Royce
Produced by Charles Dillingham
With Louise Groody and Oscar Shaw

Published songs:

"Blue Danube Blues"
"Didn't You Believe?"
"Easy Pickin's"
"Good Morning Dearie"
"Ka-Lu-A"—also used in **THE CABARET GIRL [September 19, 1921]**
"My Lady's Dress"—cut
"Niagara Falls"
"Rose Marie"
"Sing-Song Girl"
"Toddle"
"Way Down Town"

Another Kern/Caldwell hit for Dillingham. Though Kern was writing successful shows, the music was generally stale and uninteresting. At the same time, younger Harms composers George Gershwin and Vincent Youmans were attracting notice with their first Broadway hits; Richard Rodgers was soon to join them. Kern didn't recover from his fallow period until **SHOW BOAT [December 27, 1927]**—when he once again led his contemporaries onto new musical theatre ground. "Ka-Lu-A"—Kern's most popular song between "Look For The Silver Lining" **[ZIP, GOES A MILLION: December 8, 1919]** and "Who?" **[SUNNY: September 22, 1925]**—caused the composer to be sued on plagiarism charges. Publisher/songwriter (and one-time Kern collaborator) Fred Fisher claimed infringement on his 1919 hit "Dardanella." The songs were determined similar enough for Kern to be ruled technically (though unconsciously) guilty, and he was fined a token amount.

THE BUNCH AND JUDY
November 28, 1922   Globe Theatre   65 performances

Book and lyrics by Anne Caldwell
Staged by Fred G. Latham and Edward Royce

Produced by Charles Dillingham
With Fred and Adele Astaire

Published songs:

"Every Day In Every Way"
" 'Have You Forgotten Me?' Blues"
"Hot Dog!"—cut
"How Do You Do, Katinka?"
"Morning Glory"
"The Pale Venetian Moon"
"Peach Girl"

Dillingham had found Fred and Adele Astaire in vaudeville and nurtured them towards stardom, hoping to create a successor to his team of David Montgomery and Fred Stone. But **THE BUNCH AND JUDY** didn't work, and the aging Dillingham let the Astaires get away—to immediate success with George Gershwin and Alex Aarons (see **FOR GOODNESS SAKE [Gershwin: February 20, 1922]**).

ROSE BRIAR
December 25, 1922   Empire Theatre   89 performances

Play by Booth Tarkington
Produced by Florenz Ziegfeld, Jr.
With Billie Burke

Published song:

"Love And The Moon" (lyric by Tarkington)

THE BEAUTY PRIZE
September 5, 1923   Winter Garden Theatre ⟨London⟩
213 performances

Book and lyrics by George Grossmith and P. G. Wodehouse
Directed by Grossmith
Produced by Grossmith and J.A.E. Malone
With Dorothy Dickson, Leslie Henson, and Grossmith

Published songs:

"Honeymoon Isle"
"I'm A Prize"
"It's A Long, Long Day"

"Meet Me Down On Main Street"
"Moon Love"
"Non-Stop Dancing" (lyric by Wodehouse)
"When You Take The Road With Me" (lyric by Wodehouse)
"You Can't Make Love By Wireless"—see **BLUE EYES [April 27, 1928]**

Additional songs published in vocal score:

"A Cottage In Kent"
"For The Man I Love"
"Joy Bells" (lyric by Wodehouse)
"We Will Take The Road Together (Finale)"
"You'll Find Me Playing Mah-Jongg" (lyric by Wodehouse)

Another London success for the **CABARET GIRL [September 19, 1922]** group. Grossmith, as can be seen above, was a versatile man of the theatre. He had been associated with Kern on numerous London shows since 1906.

THE STEPPING STONES
November 6, 1923   Globe Theatre   241 performances

Lyrics by Anne Caldwell
Book by Caldwell and R. H. Burnside
Directed by Burnside
Produced by Charles Dillingham
With Fred Stone (and introducing Dorothy Stone)

Published songs:

"Everybody Calls Me Little Red Riding Hood"
"I Saw The Roses And Remembered You" (lyric by Herbert Reynolds)
"In Love With Love"—see **LADY MARY [February 23, 1928]**
"Once In A Blue Moon"
"Our Lovely Rose"
"Pie"
"Raggedy Ann"
"Stepping Stones"
"Wonderful Dad"

Additional songs included in published vocal score:

"Babbling Babette"
"Because You Love The Singer"

"Cane Dance"
"Dear Little Peter Pan"
"Little Angel Cake"
"Nursery Clock"
"Palace Dance"
"Prelude"

The title was a pun, as the show was built around the talents of dancing Fred Stone, with daughter Dorothy and wife Aileen Crater. Stone and his partner Dave Montgomery (who died in 1917) had been major family-trade stars for Dillingham since Victor Herbert's THE RED MILL [September 24, 1906]. Ivan Caryll was Caldwell's collaborator on the later Stone shows; when he died in 1921, Kern was the logical replacement.

SITTING PRETTY
April 8, 1924   Fulton Theatre   95 performances

Lyrics by P. G. Wodehouse
Book by Guy Bolton and Wodehouse
Directed by Fred G. Latham and Julian Alfred
Produced by F. Ray Comstock and Morris Gest
With Queenie Smith and Gertrude Bryan

Published songs:

"All You Need Is A Girl"
"Bongo On The Congo"
"The Enchanted Train"
"Mr. And Mrs. Rover"
"On A Desert Island With You"
"Shadow Of The Moon"
"Shufflin' Sam"
"Sitting Pretty" (lyric by Kern and Wodehouse)
"Tulip Time In Sing-Sing"
"Worries"
"A Year From Today"

What was to have been a happy return to the "Princess Theatre Show" fell short of expectations. This reunion of Kern, Wodehouse, and Bolton (with producer Comstock) was poorly received, despite a clever and amusing score. The highly polished set of lyrics was Wode-

house's final work with Kern; he soon gave up songwriting altogether.

DEAR SIR
September 23, 1924   Times Square Theatre
15 performances

Lyrics by Howard Dietz
Book by Edgar Selwyn
Directed by David Burton
Produced by Philip Goodman
With Genevieve Tobin, Walter Catlett, and Oscar Shaw

Published songs:

"All Lanes Must Reach A Turning"—see **BLUE EYES [April 27, 1928]**
"Gypsy Caravan"
"If You Think It's Love You're Right"
"I Want To Be There"
"Weeping Willow Tree"—see **BLUE EYES**

This poorly produced show was Kern's worst Broadway experience.
Max Dreyfus discovery Howard Dietz, writing his first show, turned
in a more than respectable set of lyrics; he was to face several bleak
years until **THE LITTLE SHOW [Schwartz: April 30, 1929]** came
along.

PETER PAN
⟨*Second Version*⟩
November 6, 1924   Knickerbocker Theatre
120 performances

Revival of play by J. M. Barrie
Directed by Basil Dean
Produced by Charles Dillingham
With Marilyn Miller

Published song:

"The Sweetest Thing In Life" (lyric by B. G. DeSylva)—new lyric
for "When Three Is Company" from **THE DOLL GIRL
[August 25, 1913]** and "Just Because You're You" from
ZIEGFELD FOLLIES OF 1917 [June 12, 1917]

One of their many spats resulted in Marilyn Miller's temporarily deserting Ziegfeld and signing with the competition. Dillingham worked with Kern to devise another **SALLY [December 21, 1920]**, meanwhile placing his new star in this revival. Kern had written a **PETER PAN** song for the ⟨**First Version**⟩ **[Circa December 1907]**; he got DeSylva to reset an old tune for this one. Miller was somewhat out of place in Maude Adams' old role of the boy who wouldn't grow up, but the Kern musical in preparation made up for that.

SUNNY
September 22, 1925   New Amsterdam Theatre
517 performances

Book and lyrics by Otto Harbach and Oscar Hammerstein 2nd
Directed by Hassard Short
Produced by Charles Dillingham
With Marilyn Miller and Jack Donahue

Published songs:

"D'ye Love Me?"
"Dream A Dream"—cut
"I Might Grow Fond Of You" (lyric by Desmond Carter)—written
    for London production [October 7, 1926]
"I Was Alone"—written for 1930 movie version
"I've Looked For Trouble" (lyric by Carter)—written for London
    production; revised version of "Bought And Paid For" from
    THE LAUGHING HUSBAND [February 2, 1914]; also see
    CRISS-CROSS [October 12, 1926]
"Let's Say Good-night"—written for London production
"Sunny"
"Sunshine"—new lyric for "I Can't Forget Your Eyes" from **OH, I
    SAY!** [October 30, 1913]; also see **CRISS-CROSS**
"Two Little Bluebirds"
"When We Get Our Divorce"—initial publication upon use in
    London production
"Who?"

Additional songs published in British vocal score:

"The Chase"
"Divorcee"
"The Fox Has Left His Lair"

"Here We Are Together Again (Opening Act One)"
"The Hunt Ball"
"It Won't Mean A Thing"
"So's Your Old Man"
"We're Gymnastic"
"Wedding Knell"
"Wedding Scene (Finale Act One)"

Dillingham succeeded in out-Ziegfelding Ziegfeld with this extravaganza. Hiring the Harbach and Hammerstein team on the heels of two long-running hits—**WILDFLOWER [Youmans: February 7, 1923]** and the Friml/Stothart ROSE MARIE [September 2, 1924]—Dillingham joined Kern with his two most important future collaborators. Everything about **SUNNY** was spectacular except the score: nothing but the immense hit "Who?".

THE CITY CHAP
October 26, 1925   Liberty Theatre   72 performances
Lyrics by Anne Caldwell
Book by James Montgomery
(Based on *The Fortune Hunter* [play] by Winchell Smith)
Directed by R. H. Burnside
Produced by Charles Dillingham
With Richard "Skeet" Gallagher, Irene Dunne, and George Raft

Published songs:
"He Is The Type"
"Journey's End" (lyric by P. G. Wodehouse)—originally used in
   THE CABARET GIRL [September 19, 1922]
"No One Knows (How Much I'm In Love)"
"Sympathetic Someone"
"Walking Home With Josie"
"When I Fell In Love With You"—cut after opening

CRISS-CROSS
October 12, 1926   Globe Theatre   206 performances
Book and lyrics by Otto Harbach and Anne Caldwell
Directed by R. H. Burnside
Produced by Charles Dillingham
With Fred and Dorothy Stone

Published songs:

"Bread And Butter"—cut

"Cinderella Girl"

"In Araby With You"—new lyric for "Sunshine" from **SUNNY**
 [September 22, 1925], a revised version of "I Can't Forget Your
 Eyes" from **OH, I SAY!** [October 30, 1913]

"Kiss A Four Leaf Clover"—cut

"Suzie" (lyric by Caldwell)

"That Little Something" (lyric by Bert Kalmar and Harry Ruby)—
 added to post-Broadway tour; originally used in **LUCKY** [March
 22, 1927]

"You Will—Won't You?"—new lyric for "I've Looked For
 Trouble" from London production of **SUNNY**, a revised version
 of "Bought And Paid For" from **THE LAUGHING
 HUSBAND** [February 2, 1914]

LUCKY
March 22, 1927   New Amsterdam Theatre
71 performances

Music mostly by Bert Kalmar and Harry Ruby
Lyrics by Kalmar and Ruby
Book by Otto Harbach, Kalmar and Ruby
Directed by Hassard Short
Produced by Charles Dillingham
With Mary Eaton, Walter Catlett, Ruby Keeler, and Paul Whiteman

Published songs:

"That Little Something"—see **CRISS-CROSS** [October 12, 1926]
"When The Bo-Tree Blossoms Again"

Additional songs published (no lyric) in piano selection
(probably by Kern):

"Ballet"
"Cingalese Village"

SHOW BOAT
December 27, 1927   Ziegfeld Theatre   575 performances

Music mostly by Kern
Book and lyrics by Oscar Hammerstein 2nd
(Based on the novel by Edna Ferber)

Directed by Zeke Colvan
Produced by Florenz Ziegfeld, Jr.
With Charles Winninger, Helen Morgan, Norma Terris, Howard Marsh, Edna May Oliver, and Jules Bledsoe

Published songs:

"Bill" (lyric by P. G. Wodehouse and Hammerstein)—revised version of "Bill" (cut) from **OH LADY! LADY!! [February 1, 1918]** (lyric by Wodehouse) also used (unpublished, lyric by B. G. DeSylva) in **ZIP, GOES A MILLION [December 8, 1919]**
"Can't Help Lovin' Dat Man"
"Dance Away The Night"—written for London production [May 3, 1928]
"I Have The Room Above"—written for 1936 movie version
"I Might Fall Back On You"—initial publication upon use in movie version
"I Still Suits Me"—written for 1936 movie version
"Life Upon The Wicked Stage"—initial publication upon use in movie version
"Make Believe"
"Nobody Else But Me"—written for revival [January 5, 1946]; revised version of "Dream Of A Ladies Cloak Room Attendant" [instrumental] (unpublished) from unproduced 1935 movie *The Flame Within*
"Ol' Man River"
"Why Do I Love You?"
"You Are Love"

Additional songs included in various published vocal scores:
"Captain Andy's Entrance And Ballyhoo"
"Cotton Blossom"
"Dahomey"—revised version of "Bring 'Em Back" from **HITCHY-KOO 1920 ⟨Fourth Edition⟩ [October 19, 1920]**
"Dandies On Parade (The Sports Of Gay Chicago)"
"Finale Act I (Wedding)"
"Hey, Fellah!"
"Mis'ry's Comin Aroun' (Act One, Scene IV)"
"Queenie's Ballyhoo (C'mon Folks, We'se Rarin' To Go)"
" 'Til Good Luck Comes My Way"
"When We Tell Them About It All (Opening Act II)"
"Where's The Mate For Me?"

Kern and Hammerstein knew they were onto something monumental with **SHOW BOAT.** In the musical theatre of the day, other hands—or Kern and Hammerstein two years earlier—might have woven Ferber's setting and romances into a moldy operetta, excising the miscegenation, prejudice, unhappy marriages, etc. (As it was, the authors opted for a weak happy ending.) But Kern and Hammerstein stayed close to the novel, and created a new musical dramatic form. In a period when shows were quickly written and put together, Kern dedicated a full year to **SHOW BOAT;** Hammerstein also lavished an uncommon amount of care on the project, for the first time in his heretofore successful (but hacklike) career displaying his unique theatrical talents. The score was incredibly rich, with Kern developing his highly melodic operetta style in "Make Believe" and "You Are Love." "Can't Help Lovin' Dat Man" and "Life Upon The Wicked Stage" were perfect in their genre, while "Bill" finally found a home (on the third try). With "Ol' Man River," Hammerstein wasn't trying to make a far-reaching social statement: his primary concern was to bring the action downstage while the massive "Cotton Blossom" set was being struck. (Kern wasn't interested in the spot at all—he suggested merely taking the already written "Cotton Blossom" theme and inverting it.) Ziegfeld's lavishness was evident in the physical production, but director-in-fact Hammerstein kept the show boat from overwhelming the powerful material.

LADY MARY
February 23, 1928   Daly's Theatre ⟨London⟩
181 performances

Music mostly by Albert Sirmay and Philip Charig
Lyrics by Harry Graham
Book by Frederick Lonsdale and John Hastings Turner

Published song:

"If You're A Friend Of Mine"—new lyric for "In Love With Love" from **STEPPING STONES [November 6, 1923]**

BLUE EYES
April 27, 1928   Piccadilly Theatre ⟨London⟩
276 performances

Lyrics by Graham John
Book by Guy Bolton and John

Directed by John Harwood
Produced by Lee Ephraim
With Evelyn Laye

Published songs:

"Back To The Heather"
"Blue Eyes"—revised version of "All Lanes Must Reach A Turning"
   from **DEAR SIR [September 23, 1924]**
"Bow Belles"—revised version of "You Can't Make Love by
   Wireless" from **THE BEAUTY PRIZE [September 5, 1923]**
"Do I Do Wrong"—see **ROBERTA [November 18, 1933]**
"Henry"
"In Love"—revised version of "Alone At Last" from **OH, I SAY!**
   [October 30, 1913]
"No One Else But You"

Additional songs published in vocal score:

"Charlie (Opening Act One)"
"The Curtsey"—revised version of "Weeping Willow Tree" from
   DEAR SIR
"A Fair Lady (Opening Act Two)"
"Finale Act One"
"His Majesty's Dragoons"
"Long Live Nancy"
"Praise The Day"
"Romeo And Juliet"
"Someone"
"Trouble About The Drama"

A British historical romance, which was moderately successful but
nonexportable to Broadway.

SWEET ADELINE
A Musical Romance Of the Gay Nineties
September 3, 1929   Hammerstein's Theatre
234 performances

Book and lyrics by Oscar Hammerstein 2nd
Directed by Reginald Hammerstein
Produced by Arthur Hammerstein
With Helen Morgan and Charles Butterworth

Published songs:

"Don't Ever Leave Me"

"Here Am I"

"Lonely Feet"—added to 1935 movie version; originally used in
   THREE SISTERS [April 19, 1934]

"Out Of The Blue"

"The Sun About To Rise"

" 'Twas Not So Long Ago"

"We Were So Young"—written for 1935 movie version

"Why Was I Born?"

Additional song published (no lyric) in piano selection:

"Some Girl Is On Your Mind"

Kern and Hammerstein followed their precedent-breaking **SHOW BOAT [December 27, 1927]** with this nostalgic look at the Nineties. Written to star the torch-singing Helen Morgan (of **SHOW BOAT**), the lovely score was particularly plaintive; but the favorably received **SWEET ADELINE** ran headlong into the stock market crash and could not survive. Producer Arthur Hammerstein, responsible for some of Broadway's most successful operettas (see **WILDFLOWER [February 7, 1923]**), was bankrupt within a year. He lost his theatre and the rights to all his shows (won by the Shuberts at a mysterious auction that nobody else attended).

RIPPLES
The New Musical Extravaganza
February 11, 1930   New Amsterdam Theatre
55 performances

Music mostly by Oscar Levant and Albert Sirmay
Lyrics by Irving Caesar and Graham John
Book and direction by William Anthony McGuire
Produced by Charles Dillingham
With Fred, Dorothy, and (introducing) Paula Stone

Published song:

"Anything May Happen Any Day" (lyric by John)

A circus acrobat in his youth, Fred Stone's appearances always featured a daredevil stunt—like his entrance in THE RED MILL [October 24, 1906], falling backwards down an eighteen-foot ladder. In his midfifties, Stone and neighbor/friend Will Rogers took up the daredevil hobby of flying. A crash landing crushed Stone's legs, forcing him to miss the next scheduled show, Hubbell and Henderson's THREE CHEERS [October 15, 1928]. Daughter Dorothy proved star material on her own, and Rogers—who was to be killed in a 1935 plane crash—stepped into Fred's role. Stone returned to the stage with **RIPPLES,** bringing along Dorothy and his other dancing daughter, Paula. But the accident had aged the ageless Stone, and the times had made the innocent Stone shows obsolete. There was to be one last unsuccessful attempt, Revel and Gordon's SMILING FACES [August 30, 1932].

THE CAT AND THE FIDDLE
A Musical Love Story
October 15, 1931   Globe Theatre   395 performances

Book and lyrics by Otto Harbach
Directed by José Ruben
Produced by Max Gordon
With Bettina Hall, Georges Metaxa, and José Ruben

Published songs:

"Don't Ask Me Not To Sing"—cut
"I Watch The Love Parade"
"Misunderstood"—advertised but not published (apparently a misprint)
"A New Love Is Old"
"The Night Was Made For Love"
"One Moment Alone"
"Poor Pierrot"
"She Didn't Say 'Yes' "
"Try To Forget"

Additional songs published in vocal score:

"Hh! Cha Cha!"
"Opening Act One (Street Vendors)"

Kern was joined by Otto Harbach in this successful integrated-score experiment, song arising naturally from the action. (The leading characters, conveniently, were composers, singers, and street musicians.) A new producer was found for **CAT AND THE FIDDLE:**

Max Gordon, who had overwhelmed the depressed Broadway scene with the Schwartz and Dietz **THREE'S A CROWD** [Schwartz: October 15, 1930] and **THE BAND WAGON** [Schwartz: June 3, 1931]. An unhappy footnote: the financially bereft Charles Dillingham, crushed by the Depression, retained only his beloved (mortgaged) Globe Theatre. In May of 1932 he unaccountably absconded with the box office receipts and fled; his well-deserved reputation was such that Broadway pitied rather than censured him. He existed on charity from still-solvent former associates (including Kern) until his death on August 30, 1934.

MUSIC IN THE AIR
November 8, 1932   Alvin Theatre   342 performances

Book and lyrics by Oscar Hammerstein 2nd
Directed by Kern and Hammerstein
Produced by Peggy Fears
With Natalie Hall, Walter Slezak, Katherine Carrington, and Al Shean

Published songs:

"And Love Was Born"
"I Am So Eager"
"I'm Alone"
"In Egern On The Tegern Sea"
"I've Told Ev'ry Little Star"
"One More Dance"
"The Song Is You"
"There's A Hill Beyond A Hill"
"We Belong Together"
"When The Spring Is In The Air"

Additional songs published in vocal score:

"Hold Your Head Up High" [hymn]
"Melodies Of May" (music by Beethoven, arranged by Kern)
"Prayer"

Working again with Hammerstein, Kern turned out one of his richest scores for this charming Bavarian tale. As in **CAT AND THE FIDDLE** [October 15, 1931], the European setting and musical subject matter enabled close integration of score and book. The authors felt they needed Ziegfeld for the show, but he was in hopeless financial/physical shape and died July 22, 1932. Dillingham and Arthur

Hammerstein were bankrupt; even the Shuberts were bankrupt; and Kern had fought with Max Gordon on **CAT AND THE FIDDLE.** Along came former Follies girl Peggy Fears with rich husband A. C. Blumenthal, who had kept Ziegfeld afloat during his final production (the May 19, 1932 revival of **SHOW BOAT [December 27, 1927]**). Fears—with Blumenthal's money—presented **MUSIC IN THE AIR,** with Hammerstein and Kern doing the actual producing. Hammerstein followed this hit with a ten-year string of flops, until Richard Rodgers called looking to replace Lorenz Hart for **OKLAHOMA! [Rodgers: March 31, 1943].**

ROBERTA
November 18, 1933   New Amsterdam Theatre
295 performances

Book and lyrics by Otto Harbach
(Based on *Gowns by Roberta* [novel] by Alice Duer Miller)
Produced by Max Gordon
With Lyda Roberti, Fay Templeton, Tamara, Sydney Greenstreet, and
  Bob Hope
NOTE: **GOWNS BY ROBERTA,** pre-Broadway title

Published songs:

"Armful Of Trouble"—cut
"I Won't Dance" (lyric by Oscar Hammerstein 2nd, Harbach,
  Dorothy Fields, and Jimmy McHugh)—added to 1935 movie
  version; new lyric for song from **THREE SISTERS [April 19,
  1934]**
"I'll Be Hard To Handle" (lyric by Bernard Dougall)
"Let's Begin"
"Lovely To Look At" (lyric by Fields and McHugh)—written for
  1935 movie version
"Smoke Gets In Your Eyes"
"Something Had To Happen"
"The Touch Of Your Hand"
"Yesterdays"
"You're Devastating"—new lyric for "Do I Do Wrong" from
  BLUE EYES [April 27, 1927]

Additional songs published in vocal score:

"Don't Ask Me Not To Sing"
"Hot Spot"
"Madrigal"

A dreary fashion show with many problems and few attributes. Gordon temporarily patched his shaky relationship with Kern by allowing the composer to direct the show; then he fired Kern out of town and brought in Hassard Short. (No one ultimately received billing.) With less than minimal competition, drastically cut-rate tickets, and the song hit "Smoke Gets In Your Eyes," **ROBERTA** managed a fair run.

THREE SISTERS
April 19, 1934   Theatre Royal, Drury Lane ⟨London⟩
72 performances

Book and lyrics by Oscar Hammerstein 2nd
Directed and produced by Kern and Hammerstein
With Charlotte Greenwood, Adele Dixon, and Stanley Holloway

Published songs:

"Hand In Hand"
"I Won't Dance"—see **ROBERTA [November 18, 1933]**
"Funny Old House"
"Keep Smiling"
"Lonely Feet"—also used in 1935 motion picture version of
   SWEET ADELINE [September 3, 1929]
"Roll On, Rolling Road"
"What Good Are Words?"
"You Are Doing Very Well"

Additional songs published (no lyric) in piano selection:

"Circus Queen"
"Here It Comes"
"Now That I Have Springtime"
"Somebody Wants To Go To Sleep"

An original musical written for the Drury Lane, London home of Hammerstein's hit Twenties operettas. The score contained some particularly lovely work, including "Lonely Feet" and "Hand In Hand"; but the disappointing failure of **THREE SISTERS** sent Kern to Hollywood permanently.

GENTLEMEN UNAFRAID
[June 3, 1938]   Municipal Opera ⟨St. Louis, Missouri⟩
6 performances; summer stock tryout

Book and lyrics by Oscar Hammerstein 2nd and Otto Harbach
(Based on a story by Edward Boykin)
Directed by Zeke Colvan
Produced by St. Louis Municipal Opera
With Ronald Graham, Vicki Cummings, Hope Manning, Avon Long, and
  Richard (Red) Skelton

Published songs:

"Abe Lincoln Had Just One Country"—added to 1942 stock and
  amateur version, retitled **HAYFOOT, STRAWFOOT**; original
  publication as 1941 nonshow song for War Bond drive
"When A New Star" (lyric by Harbach)—initial publication upon
  release of **HAYFOOT, STRAWFOOT**
"Your Dream (Is The Same As My Dream)"—only publication
  upon reuse in 1940 movie *One Night in the Tropics*

This Civil War operetta never got further than its one-week tryout:
no one was interested in taking it to Broadway. **GENTLEMEN
UNAFRAID** was yet another theatrical disappointment for Kern.
HAYFOOT, STRAWFOOT, a revised 1942 version released for stock
and amateur groups, didn't create much more interest.

MAMBA'S DAUGHTERS
January 3, 1939   Empire Theatre   162 performances

Play by Dorothy and DuBose Heyward
(Based on the novel by DuBose Heyward)
Produced and directed by Guthrie McClintic
With Ethel Waters

Published song:

"Lonesome Walls" (lyric by DuBose Heyward)

Kern and Hammerstein had expressed interest in musicalizing Heyward's earlier novel *Porgy* (as an Al Jolson vehicle). By the time of
MAMBA'S DAUGHTERS, Gershwin was no longer alive. Kern was
asked to write the one original song for the play and came up with
the highly effective "Lonesome Walls," a companion to Ethel Waters'
"Supper Time" from **AS THOUSANDS CHEER [Berlin: September 30, 1933].**

VERY WARM FOR MAY
May 17, 1939   Alvin Theatre   59 performances

Book and lyrics by Oscar Hammerstein 2nd
Production staged by Vincente Minnelli
Book staged by Hammerstein
Produced by Max Gordon
With Grace McDonald, Jack Whiting, Eve Arden, Hiram Sherman, Avon
    Long, and Donald Brian

Published songs:

"All In Fun"
"All The Things You Are"
"Heaven In My Arms (Music In My Heart)"
"In Other Words, Seventeen"
"In The Heart Of The Dark"
"That Lucky Fellow"

With no Broadway opportunity since **ROBERTA [November 18, 1933]**, Kern was not in a position to hold out when he was called again by Max Gordon. Things went even worse than on the previous show. Gordon was in Hollywood during the production period; he arrived at the tryout and panicked, demanding radical changes and once again calling Hassard Short for help. **VERY WARM FOR MAY** arrived on Broadway in dismal shape and quickly closed. Gordon still had major hits ahead of him, including the comedies MY SISTER EILEEN [December 26, 1940] and BORN YESTERDAY [February 4, 1946], but his future musicals were all disastrous. Kern's final theatre score contained some fine work, although only "All The Things You Are"—one of the very best musical theatre songs—managed to escape the wreckage. In the mostly youthful cast, incidentally, was early Kern star Donald Brian—who had introduced "They Didn't Believe Me" in **THE GIRL FROM UTAH [August 24, 1914]**. Kern returned to Hollywood where he wrote a number of successful motion picture scores, collaborating with Hammerstein, Ira Gershwin, Dorothy Fields, Johnny Mercer and others. His two Oscars came with Fields for "The Way You Look Tonight" (1936) and Hammerstein for "The Last Time I Saw Paris" (1941). By 1945 Hammerstein and Richard Rodgers had branched into producing. They commissioned Kern and Dorothy Fields to write a musical comedy biography of sharpshooter Annie Oakley for Ethel Merman (see **ANNIE GET YOUR GUN [Berlin: May 16, 1946]**). Simultaneously, Kern and Hammerstein planned to revive **SHOW BOAT [December 27, 1927]** and wrote a new song to be added, "Nobody Else But Me." Arriving in New York for **SHOW BOAT** auditions, Kern suffered a cerebral hemorrhage and collapsed in the street; with no identification, he was taken to the derelict's ward on Welfare Island. Jerome Kern died on November 11, 1945.

Kern entered a musical theatre dominated by foreign operettas. During his thirty-five-year career, the American musical theatre first stood on its own during World War One with the Kern, Bolton, and Wodehouse "Princess Theatre Shows." The early Twenties saw the arrival of the more sophisticated, jazz-influenced Gershwin and Youmans. Then, Kern (with Hammerstein) discovered the dramatic potential of musical theatre with **SHOW BOAT [December 27, 1927]** and succeeding scores. If Kern's early work—with a very few exceptions—is hopelessly dated, it is a case of the experimental being outmoded by the perfected. After more than fifty years, the best of Kern's songs remain high among the very best songs of the American musical theatre.

Irving Berlin

BORN: May 11, 1888   Temun, Russia

Irving Berlin's family fled from religious persecution and came to New York in 1892. The son of a part-time cantor, Berlin took to the streets as a singing panhandler and went on to become a singing waiter at a Chinatown saloon. Here he wrote his first published song, "Marie From Sunny Italy" (music by Nick Nicholson), issued in 1907 by Joseph W. Stern and Company. In 1908 came his first composer/lyricist effort, "Best Of Friends Must Part." Berlin went to work as a staff lyricist (and occasional composer) for publisher/songwriter Ted Snyder and was soon a partner in the firm. As it was then common practice to interpolate songs in Broadway shows, Berlin found a natural showcase for a portion of his increasingly enormous output.

[all music and lyrics by Irving Berlin unless indicated]

THE BOYS AND BETTY
November 2, 1908   Wallack's Theatre   112 performances

Music mostly by Silvio Hein
Book and lyrics mostly by George V. Hobart
Directed by George Marion
Produced by Daniel V. Arthur
With Marie Cahill

Published song:

"She Was A Dear Little Girl" (music by Ted Snyder, lyric by Berlin)

THE GIRL AND THE WIZARD
September 27, 1909   Casino Theatre   96 performances

Music mostly by Julian Edwards (see **Kern**)
Lyrics mostly by Robert B. Smith and Edward Madden

Book by J. Hartley Manners
Directed by Ned Wayburn
Produced by the Messrs. Shubert
With Sam Bernard

Published song:

"Oh, How That German Could Love" (music by Ted Snyder, lyric
  by Berlin)

THE JOLLY BACHELORS
January 6, 1910   Broadway Theatre   84 performances

Music mostly by Raymond Hubbell
Music to Berlin lyrics by Ted Snyder
Book and lyrics mostly by Glen MacDonough
Directed by Ned Wayburn
Produced by Lew Fields
With Stella Mayhew, Nora Bayes (Norworth), Jack Norworth, and Emma
  Carus

Published songs:

"If The Managers Only Thought The Same As Mother"
"Stop That Rag (Keep On Playing, Honey)"
"Sweet Marie, Make-A Rag-A-Time Dance Wid Me"
"That Beautiful Rag"—also used in **UP AND DOWN
  BROADWAY [July 18, 1910]**

ARE YOU A MASON?
[Circa April 1910]; closed during pre-Broadway tour

Play by Leo Ditrichstein
Produced by Rich and Harris
With Ditrichstein and Beth Tate

Published song:

"I'm Going Away On A Long Vacation" (music by Ted Snyder)

ZIEGFELD FOLLIES OF 1910
June 20, 1910   Jardin de Paris Theatre   88 performances

Music mostly by others
Book and lyrics mostly by Harry B. Smith and Gus Edwards
Directed by Julian Mitchell

Produced by Florenz Ziegfeld, Jr.
With Bert Williams, Lillian Lorraine, and Fanny Brice

Published songs:

"The Dance Of The Grizzly Bear" (music by George Botsford)
"Good-Bye Becky Cohen"—advertised but not published

Florenz Ziegfeld, Jr. began his Broadway career in 1896 by importing, featuring, and marrying Parisian star Anna Held in a series of musicals. He came up with his successful revue format with FOLLIES OF 1907 [July 8, 1907]. The editions became more lavish as competition developed in the mid-Teens. The scores were generally contributed by a throng of songwriters, the only exception being Berlin's **ZIEGFELD FOLLIES OF 1927 [August 16, 1927].**

UP AND DOWN BROADWAY
July 18, 1910   Casino Theatre   72 performances

Music mostly by Jean Schwartz
Lyrics mostly by William Jerome
Music to Berlin lyrics by Ted Snyder
Book by Edgar Smith
Directed by William J. Wilson
Produced by Messrs. Shubert
With Eddie Foy, Snyder, and Berlin

Published songs:

"Sweet Italian Love"
"That Beautiful Rag"—originally used in **THE JOLLY
    BACHELORS** [January 6, 1910]

The popularity of the early Snyder and Berlin songs was such that the writers were hired to perform some of their work in this Shubert revue.

THE GIRL AND THE DRUMMER
[Circa August 1910]; closed during pre-Broadway tryout

Music mostly by Augustus Barrett (see **Kern**)
Music to Berlin lyrics by Ted Snyder
Book and lyrics mostly by George Broadhurst
(Based on *What Happened to Jones* [play] by Broadhurst)

Produced by William A. Brady, Ltd.
With Herbert Corthell and Belle Gold

Published songs:

"Herman, Let's Dance That Beautiful Waltz"—also used in **TWO
 MEN AND A GIRL [Circa December 1910]**
"Wishing"

HE CAME FROM MILWAUKEE
September 21, 1910   Casino Theatre   117 performances

Music mostly by Ben M. Jerome and Louis A. Hirsch
Lyrics mostly by Edward Madden
Book by Mark Swan
Directed by Sidney Ellison
Produced by the Messrs. Shubert
With Sam Bernard

Published song:

"Bring Back My Lena To Me" (music and lyric by Berlin and Ted
 Snyder)

GETTING A POLISH
November 7, 1910   Wallack's Theatre   48 performances

Play by Booth Tarkington and Harry Leon Wilson
Music by Ted Snyder
Lyrics by Irving Berlin
Directed by Hugh Ford
Produced by Liebler and Company
With May Irwin
NOTE: **MRS. JIM,** pre-Broadway title

Published songs:

"He Sympathized With Me"
"My Wife Bridget" (music and lyric by Berlin)
"That Opera Rag"

TWO MEN AND A GIRL
[Circa December 1910]; closed during pre-Broadway tryout

Music mostly by Julian Edwards
Book and lyrics mostly by Charles Campbell and Ralph Skinner
With Fred Bailey, Ralph Austin, and Belle Gold

Published song:

"Herman, Let's Dance That Beautiful Waltz" (music by Ted
    Snyder, lyric by Berlin)—originally used in **THE GIRL AND
    THE DRUMMER** [Circa August 1910]

JUMPING JUPITER
March 6, 1911   New York Theatre   24 performances

Music mostly by Karl Hoschna
Lyrics mostly by Richard Carle
Music to Berlin lyrics by Ted Snyder
Book by Carle and Sydney Rosenfeld
Directed by Carle
Produced by H. H. Frazee and George W. Lederer
With Carle and Edna Wallace Hopper

Published songs:

"Angelo"
"It Can't Be Did"
"Thank You Kind Sir! Said She"

GABY
Folies Bergère Revue
April 27, 1911   Folies Bergère Theatre   92 performances

Music and lyrics by Vincent Bryan, Irving Berlin, and Ted Snyder; also
    by others
Book by Harry B. and Robert B. Smith
Directed by George Marion
Produced by Henry B. Harris and Jesse L. Lasky
With Ethel Levey and Otis Harlan

Published songs:

"Answer Me"—advertised but not published
"Down To The Folies Bergère"
"I Beg Your Pardon, Dear Old Broadway" (music and lyric by
    Berlin)
"Keep A Taxi Waiting Dear"
"Spanish Love"

The Folies Bergère opened as a dinner theatre featuring a vaudeville
show. Within five months the house was closed and transformed into

a legitimate theatre, the Fulton (later renamed the Helen Hayes; demolished in 1981). Ethel Levey was the former Mrs. George M. Cohan.

FRIARS' FROLIC OF 1911
Benefit Show
May 28, 1911   New Amsterdam Theatre   1 performance
Music and lyrics mostly by others
Directed by George M. Cohan
Produced by A. L. Erlanger
With Cohan, Berlin, Julian Eltinge, and William Collier
Published song:

"Alexander's Ragtime Band"—published as 1911 nonshow song;
  see **HOKEY-POKEY [February 8, 1912]**

Berlin himself sang his one-month-old hit, which ushered a new sound into popular music. (Not ragtime, though, as it's *not* a rag.) Throughout his career, Berlin had the uncanny ability to express in song what the public was about to feel—just ahead of the competition.

ZIEGFELD FOLLIES OF 1911
June 26, 1911   Jardin de Paris Theatre   80 performances
Music mostly by Maurice Levi and Raymond Hubbell (see **Kern**)
Book and lyrics mostly by George V. Hobart
Directed by Julian Mitchell
Produced by Florenz Ziegfeld, Jr.
With Bessie McCoy, Bert Williams, and Fanny Brice
Published songs:

"Dog Gone That Chilly Man"
"Ephraham Played Upon The Piano" (by Berlin and Vincent
  Bryan)
"Woodman, Woodman, Spare That Tree!" (by Berlin and Bryan)
"You've Built A Fire Down In My Heart"—also used in **THE
  FASCINATING WIDOW [September 11, 1911]**

THE FASCINATING WIDOW
September 11, 1911   Liberty Theatre   56 performances

Music mostly by others
Book and lyrics mostly by Otto Hauerbach (Harbach)
Directed by George Marion
Produced by A. H. Woods
With Julian Eltinge

Published songs:

"Don't Take Your Beau To The Seashore" (by E. Ray Goetz and
    Berlin)
"You've Built A Fire Down In My Heart"—originally used in
    ZIEGFELD FOLLIES OF 1911 [June 26, 1911]

Songwriter/producer E. Ray Goetz was an early collaborator with
Berlin, Gershwin and Porter. Goetz's sister Dorothy became Berlin's
bride in 1912. Tragically, she contracted typhoid fever on the honeymoon and died.

THE LITTLE MILLIONAIRE
September 25, 1911   George M. Cohan Theatre
192 performances

Book, music and lyrics mostly by George M. Cohan
Directed by Cohan
Produced by Cohan and Sam H. Harris
With Cohan, Jerry Cohan and Donald Crisp

Published song:

"Down In My Heart"

Cohan, recognizing Berlin as his natural successor in the popular music
field, befriended and encouraged him. Sam H. Harris, who began his
career producing melodramas, joined Cohan on the hit LITTLE
JOHNNY JONES [November 7, 1904]. They became a major producing firm, presenting not only Cohan's plays and musicals, but others
as well. After breaking up in 1919, Harris formed similar partner-
ships with Berlin and, later, George S. Kaufman.

THE NEVER HOMES
October 5, 1911   Broadway Theatre   92 performances
Music mostly by A. Baldwin Sloane
"Rhymes" mostly by E. Ray Goetz

"Words" by Glen MacDonough
Directed by Ned Wayburn
Produced by Lew Fields

Published song:

"There's A Girl In Havana" (by Goetz, Berlin, and Ted Snyder)

A REAL GIRL
[Circa October 1911]; closed during pre-Broadway tryout

Music and lyrics also by others
Produced by Bonita Amusement Co.
With Bonita and Lew Hearn

Published songs:

"Cuddle Up"
"One O'Clock In The Morning"
"That Mysterious Rag" (by Berlin and Snyder)
"When You're In Town

WINTER GARDEN VAUDEVILLE
[Circa November 1911]   Winter Garden Theatre

Music and lyrics mostly by others
Produced by the Messrs. Shubert
With Dolly Jardon

Published song:

"Sombrero Land" (by E. Ray Goetz, Berlin and Ted Snyder)

SHE KNOWS BETTER NOW
[January 15, 1912]   Plymouth Theatre ⟨Chicago, Illinois⟩; closed during pre-Broadway tryout

Play by Agnes L. Crimmins
Music also by others
Directed by William Collier
Produced by Eisfeldt and Anhalt
With May Irwin and Arthur Byron

Published songs:

"I'm Going Back To Dixie" (music and lyrics by Berlin and Ted
    Snyder)
"The Ragtime Mocking Bird"

HOKEY-POKEY;
And BUNTY, BULLS AND STRINGS
A Potpourri In Two Acts
February 8, 1912   Broadway Theatre   108 performances

Music mostly by John Stromberg and A. Baldwin Sloane
Lyrics mostly by E. Ray Goetz
Sketches by Edgar Smith
Directed by Gus Sohlke
Produced by Weber and Fields
With Joe Weber, Lew Fields, William Collier, Lillian Russell, and Fay
   Templeton

Published song:

"Alexander's Bag-Pipe Band" (by Goetz, Berlin, and Sloane)—
   revised version (take-off) of "Alexander's Ragtime Band" from
   FRIARS' FROLIC [May 28, 1911]

The famous comic acting/producing team of Weber and Fields had
broken up in 1904 after twenty-four years of partnership. Both continued successfully on their own, and with **HOKEY-POKEY** began
occasional "all-star" reunions of their famous music-hall company.
Fields remained a major musical theatre force into the Twenties, when
he discovered and nurtured his son Herbert's colleagues Richard
Rodgers and Lorenz Hart (see **A LONELY ROMEO [Rodgers: June
10, 1919]**).

THE WHIRL OF SOCIETY
March 5, 1912   Winter Garden Theatre   136 performances

Music mostly by Louis A. Hirsch
Lyrics mostly by Harold Atteridge
Book by Harrison Rhodes
Directed by J. C. Huffman
Produced by Winter Garden Co. (Messrs. Shubert)
With Stella Mayhew and Al Jolson

Published songs:

"I Want To Be In Dixie" (by Berlin and Ted Snyder)—also used in
   HULLO, RAGTIME [December 23, 1912]
"Opera Burlesque (On The Sextette From Lucia de
   Lammermoor)"—initial publication upon reuse in **HANKY
   PANKY [August 5, 1912]**
"That Society Bear"

COHAN AND HARRIS MINSTRELS
[Circa April 1912]; post-Broadway tour

Music and lyrics mostly by others
Produced by George M. Cohan and Sam H. Harris
With Happy Lambert

Published song:

"Lead Me To That Beautiful Band" (lyric by E. Ray Goetz)

THE PASSING SHOW OF 1912
July 22, 1912   Winter Garden Theatre   136 performances

Produced by the Messrs. Shubert
With Eugene and Willie Howard, Charlotte Greenwood, and Trixie
  Fraganza

Published song:

"The Ragtime Jockey Man"

HANKY PANKY
A Jumble Of Jollification
August 5, 1912   Broadway Theatre   104 performances

Music mostly by A. Baldwin Sloane
Lyrics mostly by E. Ray Goetz
Book by Edgar Smith
Directed by Gus Sohlke
Produced by Lew Fields
With Carter De Haven, Myrtle Gilbert, and Bobby North

Published songs:

"The Million Dollar Ball" (by Goetz and Berlin)
"Opera Burlesque (On The Sextette From Lucia de
  Lammermoor)"—originally used (unpublished) in **THE WHIRL
  OF SOCIETY [March 8, 1912]**

MY BEST GIRL
September 12, 1912   Park Theatre   68 performances

Music mostly by Clifton Crawford and Augustus Barratt
Book and lyrics mostly by Channing Pollock and Rennold Wolf
Directed by Sidney Ellison
Produced by Henry B. Harris
With Crawford

Published song:
"Follow Me Around"

ZIEGFELD FOLLIES OF 1912
October 21, 1912   Moulin Rouge Theatre   88 performances

Music mostly by Raymond Hubbell
Lyrics mostly by Harry B. Smith
Directed by Julian Mitchell
Produced by Florenz Ziegfeld, Jr.

Published song:
"A Little Bit Of Everything"

THE SUN DODGERS
Fanfare Of Frivolity
November 30, 1912   Broadway Theatre   29 performances

Music mostly by A. Baldwin Sloane
Lyrics mostly by E. Ray Goetz
Book by Edgar Smith and Mark Swan
Directed by Ned Wayburn
Produced by Lew Fields
With Eva Tanguay and George Monroe

Published songs:
"At The Picture Show" (by Goetz and Berlin; issued as by Goetz
   and Sloane)
"Hiram's Band" (music by Goetz and Sloane, lyric by Berlin;
   issued as by Goetz and Sloane)

Exact authorship of a number of 1912 Berlin songs is uncertain, as
Berlin did not take public credit. These songs prove to be by Berlin.

HULLO, RAGTIME!
December 23, 1912   Hippodrome ⟨London⟩
451 performances

Music mostly by Louis Hirsch
Sketches by Max Pemberton and Albert P. De Courville
Directed by Austen Hirgon

Produced by De Courville
With Ethel Levey, Bonita and Lew Hearn

Published songs:

"I Want To Be In Dixie" (by Berlin and Ted Snyder)—originally
   used in **THE WHIRL OF SOCIETY [March 5, 1912]**
"The Ragtime Soldier Man"—initial publication as 1912 nonshow
   song

ALL ABOARD!
June 5, 1913   44th Street Roof Garden Theatre
108 performances

Music mostly by E. Ray Goetz and Malvin Franklin
Lyrics mostly by Goetz
Book by Mark Swan
Directed by Wm. J. Wilson and W. H. Post
Produced by Lew Fields
With Fields, Carter De Haven, and Claire Rochester

Published songs:

"The Monkey Doodle Doo" [1st]—different than song from **THE
   COCOANUTS [December 8, 1925]**
"Somebody's Coming To My House"
"Take Me Back"

THE TRAINED NURSES
Vaudeville Act
Jesse L. Lasky's Most Pretentious Production
[Circa September 1913]

Produced by Lasky
With Gladys Clark and Henry Bergman

Published song:

"If You Don't Want Me (Why Do You Hang Around?)"

THE QUEEN OF THE MOVIES
January 12, 1914   Globe Theatre   104 performances

Music mostly by Jean Gilbert
Book and lyrics mostly by Glen MacDonough

(Based on the German musical by Freund and Okonowski)
Directed by Herbert Gresham
Produced by Thomas W. Ryley

Published song:

"Follow The Crowd"

ALONG CAME RUTH
February 23, 1914   Gaiety Theatre   56 performances

Play by Holman Day
(Based on the French of Fonson and Wicheler)
Directed by George Marion
Produced by Henry W. Savage
With Irene Fenwick

Published song:

"Along Came Ruth"

THE SOCIETY BUDS
Vaudeville Act
[Circa October 1914]

Produced by Jesse L. Lasky
With Gladys Clark and Henry Bergman

Published songs:

"Furnishing A House For Two"
"That's My Idea Of Paradise"

WATCH YOUR STEP
December 8, 1914   Globe Theatre   175 performances

Book by Harry B. Smith
Directed by R. H. Burnside
Produced by Charles Dillingham
With Irene and Vernon Castle, and Frank Tinney

Published songs:

"Come To The Land Of The Argentine"

"Homeward Bound"

"I Hate You"

"I Love To Have The Boys Around Me"

"I'm A Dancing Teacher Now"—advertised but not published

"I've Got A Go Back To Texas"

"Lead Me To Love" (music by Ted Snyder)

"Let's Go 'Round The Town"

"Lock Me In Your Harem And Throw Away The Key"

"The Minstrel Parade"

"Move Over"

"Ragtime Opera Medley"—published in separate edition

"Settle Down In A One-Horse Town"

"Show Us How To Do The Fox Trot"

"Simple Melody"

"The Syncopated Walk"

"They Always Follow Me Around"

"Watch Your Step"—published in separate edition

"What Is Love?"

"When I Discovered You"

"When It's Night Down In Dixie Land"

Additional songs published in vocal score:

"Metropolitan Nights"

"Opening Chorus (Office Hours)"

"Polka (Mr. and Mrs. Castle's Specialty)" [instrumental]

Berlin wrote his first full score for this "syncopated musical," which successfully brought new pop rhythms into the theatre. Producer Charles Dillingham began his career a decade earlier with hit Victor Herbert operettas; he was to play an important part in the Broadway musical field until the stock market crash. Berlin took the opportunity to start his own highly profitable publishing house.

WINTER GARDEN VAUDEVILLE
Did You Ever?
[Circa April 1915]   Winter Garden Theatre

Music and lyrics mostly by others
Produced by the Messrs. Shubert
With Blossom Seeley

Published song:

"My Bird Of Paradise (My Honolulu Girl)"

STOP! LOOK! LISTEN!
December 25, 1915   Globe Theatre   105 performances

Book by Harry B. Smith
Directed by R. H. Burnside
Produced by Charles Dillingham
With Gaby Deslys, Harry Fox, and Justine Johnstone

Published songs:

"And Father Wanted Me To Learn A Trade"
"Blow Your Horn"
"England Every Time For Me"—written for **FOLLOW THE CROWD,** 1916 London version
"Everything In America Is Ragtime"
"The Girl On The Magazine"
"I Love A Piano"
"I Love To Dance"—advertised but not published
"The Law Must Be Obeyed"
"A Pair Of Ordinary Coons"—published in separate edition
"Sailor Song"
"Skating Song"—advertised but not published
"Stop! Look! Listen!"
"Take Off A Little Bit"
"Teach Me How To Love"
"That Hula Hula"
"Until I Fell In Love With You"
"When I Get Back To The U.S.A."
"When I'm Out With You"
"Why Don't They Give Us A Chance?"—advertised but not published

Additional song published (no lyric) in piano selection:

"I Love To Dance"—initial publication in FOLLOW THE CROWD selection

A follow-up to **WATCH YOUR STEP [December 8, 1914],** not quite as successful but with a more satisfying score (including the favorite "I Love A Piano").

FRIARS' FROLIC OF 1916
Benefit Show
May 28, 1916   New Amsterdam Theatre   1 performance

Music and lyrics mostly by others
Directed by George M. Cohan
Produced by Sam H. Harris and A. L. Erlanger
With Cohan, Berlin, William Collier, Frank Tinney, and Harrison Fisher

Published song:

"Friars' Parade"

STEP THIS WAY
May 29, 1916   Shubert Theatre   88 performances

Music mostly by E. Ray Goetz and Bert Grant
Lyrics mostly by Goetz
Book by Edgar Smith
(Based on *The Girl Behind the Counter* [musical] by Smith)
Directed by Frank McCormack
Produced by Lew Fields
With Fields, Gladys Clark, and Henry Bergman

Published song:

"I've Got A Sweet Tooth Bothering Me"
"In Florida Among The Palms"—also used in **ZIEGFELD
    FOLLIES OF 1916 [June 12, 1916]**
"Step This Way"

ZIEGFELD FOLLIES OF 1916
June 12, 1916   New Amsterdam Theatre
112 performances

Music mostly by Louis Hirsch and Dave Stamper (see **Kern**)
Book and lyrics mostly by George V. Hobart and Gene Buck
Directed by Ned Wayburn
Produced by Florenz Ziegfeld, Jr.

Published song:

"In Florida Among The Palms"—originally used in **STEP THIS
    WAY [May 29, 1916]**

THE CENTURY GIRL
November 6, 1916   Century Theatre   200 performances

Music also by Victor Herbert
Lyrics also by Henry Blossom
Produced by Charles Dillingham and Florenz Ziegfeld, Jr.
With Elsie Janis, Hazel Dawn, Frank Tinney, and Sam Bernard

Published songs:

"Alice In Wonderland" [1st]—different than song from **MUSIC
  BOX REVUE** ⟨Fourth⟩ **[December 1, 1924]**
"The Chicken Walk"
"It Takes An Irishman To Make Love" (lyric by Janis and Berlin)

Dillingham and Ziegfeld took the lease on the New Theatre, a white
elephant built to house the short-lived dramatic equivalent to the
Metropolitan Opera. Renamed the Century, it opened with this successful wartime extravaganza. But with the failure of **MISS 1917
[Kern: November 5, 1917]** they gave up on the theatre. The Shuberts eventually bought and demolished the house, replacing it with
their Century Apartments at 25 Central Park West. During the
Depression, employees were "encouraged" to lease apartments.

DANCE AND GROW THIN
Nightclub Show
*[Circa April 1917]   Cocoanut Grove (Atop Century
Theatre)*

Music and lyrics mostly by others
Directed by Ned Wayburn
Produced by Charles Dillingham and Florenz Ziegfeld, Jr.

Published songs:

"Dance And Grow Thin" (music by George W. Meyer)
"There's Something Nice About The South"

RAMBLER ROSE
September 10, 1917   Empire Theatre   72 performances

Music mostly by Victor Jacobi
Book and lyrics mostly by Harry B. Smith
Produced by Charles Frohman, Inc.
With Julia Sanderson and Joseph Cawthorn

Published song:

"Poor Little Rich Girl's Dog"

JACK O'LANTERN
October 16, 1917   Globe Theatre   265 performances

Music mostly by Ivan Caryll
Lyrics mostly by Anne Caldwell
Book by Caldwell and R. H. Burnside
Directed by Burnside
Produced by Charles Dillingham
With Fred Stone

Published song:

"I'll Take You Back To Italy"

GOING UP
December 25, 1917   Liberty Theatre   351 performances

Music mostly by Louis A. Hirsch
Book and lyrics mostly by Otto Harbach
(Based on *The Aviator* [play] by James Montgomery)
Directed by Edward Royce and Montgomery
Produced by George M. Cohan and Sam H. Harris
With Frank Craven and Edith Day

Published songs:

"Come Along To Toy Town"—also used in **EVERYTHING**
    [August 22, 1918]
"When The Curtain Falls"

THE COHAN REVUE OF 1918
A Hit And Run Play
December 31, 1917   New Amsterdam Theatre
96 performances

"Some of the Songs by Irving Berlin, Others by George M. Cohan"
Book "Batted Out by George M. Cohan"
Directed by Cohan
Produced by Cohan and Sam H. Harris
With Nora Bayes and Charles Winninger

Published songs:

"Down Where The Jack O'Lanterns Grow"
"Polly Pretty Polly (Polly With A Past)" (lyric by Cohan)
"Wedding Of Words And Music"—advertised but not published

ZIEGFELD FOLLIES OF 1918
June 18, 1918   New Amsterdam Theatre
151 performances

Music mostly by Louis A. Hirsch
"Lines and lyrics" mostly by Rennold Wolf and Gene Buck
Directed by Ned Wayburn
Produced by Florenz Ziegfeld, Jr.
With Eddie Cantor, Frank Carter, Marilynn Miller, and W. C. Fields

Published songs:

"The Blue Devils Of France" (by Private Irving Berlin)
"I'm Gonna Pin A Medal On The Girl I Left Behind"

YIP-YIP-YAPHANK
*A Military Musical "Mess" Cooked Up By The Boys Of
Camp Upton*
August 19, 1918   Century Theatre   32 performances

Words and music by Sergeant Irving Berlin
Directed by Private William Smith
Produced by Uncle Sam
With Danny Healy, Sammy Lee and Berlin

Published songs:

"Bevo"—also used in **ZIEGFELD FOLLIES OF 1919 [June 23,
   1919]**
"Ding Dong"—also used in **THE CANARY [November 4, 1918]**
"Dream On Little Soldier Boy" (lyric by Jean Havez)
"Ever Since I Put On A Uniform"—advertised but not published
"I Can Always Find A Little Sunshine In The Y.M.C.A."
"Kitchen Police (Poor Little Me)"
"Mandy"—also used in **ZIEGFELD FOLLIES OF 1919**; originally
   issued as "Sterling Silver Moon"
"Oh, How I Hate To Get Up In The Morning"
"Ragtime Razor Brigade"
"Send A Lot Of Jazz Bands Over There"
"We're On Our Way To France"

Berlin's contribution to the war effort was this successful service show (which ended its run with the cast marching out of the theatre to be transported overseas). Berlin appeared, introducing "Oh, How I Hate To Get Up In The Morning"—which he was to revive in his World War Two **THIS IS THE ARMY [July 4, 1942]**.

EVERYTHING
August 22, 1918   Hippodrome Theatre   461 performances

Music mostly by John Philip Sousa and others
Lyrics mostly by John Golden and others
Book and direction by R. H. Burnside
Produced by Charles Dillingham
With De Wolf Hopper

Published songs:

"The Circus Is Coming To Town"
"Come Along To Toy Town"—originally used in **GOING UP**
   [December 25, 1917]

THE CANARY
November 4, 1918   Globe Theatre   152 performances

Music mostly by Ivan Caryll (see **Kern**)
Book and lyrics mostly by Harry B. Smith
(Based on the French play by George Barr and Louis Vermeuil)
Directed by Fred C. Latham and Edward Royce
Produced by Charles Dillingham
With Julia Sanderson and Joseph Cawthorn

Published songs:

"Ding Dong"—cut; originally used in **YIP-YIP-YAPHANK**
   [August 19, 1918]
"I Have Just One Heart For Just One Boy"
"I Wouldn't Give That For The Man Who Couldn't Dance"
"It's The Little Bit Of Irish"—cut
"You're So Beautiful"

THE ROYAL VAGABOND
Opera Comique
February 17, 1919   Cohan and Harris Theatre
208 performances

Music mostly by Anselm Goetzl and George M. Cohan

Lyrics mostly by William Cary Duncan and Cohan
Book by Stephen Ivor Szinnyey and Duncan
Directed by Cohan
Produced by Cohan and Sam H. Harris

Published song:

"That Revolutionary Rag"

Berlin's musical secretary for a very brief time was George Gershwin, who wrote the arrangement for "That Revolutionary Rag." Berlin suggested Gershwin might be better off composing on his own (but did not offer to publish him).

ZIEGFELD FOLLIES OF 1919
June 23, 1919   New Amsterdam Theatre
171 performances

Music and lyrics also by others
Sketches by Rennold Wolf, Gene Buck, and others
Directed by Ned Wayburn
Produced by Florenz Ziegfeld, Jr.
With Bert Williams, Eddie Cantor, Marilynn Miller, and Eddie Dowling

Published songs:

"Bevo"—originally used in **YIP-YIP-YAPHANK [August 19, 1918]**

"Harem Life (Outside Of That Every Little Thing's All Right)"

"I'd Rather See A Minstrel Show"

"I'm The Guy That Guards The Harem (And My Heart's In My Work)"

"Look Out For The Bolsheviki Man"—published in separate edition

"Mandy"—originally used in **YIP-YIP-YAPHANK**

"My Tambourine Girl"

"A Pretty Girl Is Like A Melody"

"A Syncopated Cocktail"

"You Cannot Make Your Shimmy Shake On Tea" (lyric by Wolf and Berlin)

"You'd Be Surprised"—added after opening; published in separate edition

Considered the best edition of the series, Berlin contributed a significant amount of the score—including the most famous **FOLLIES** song, "A Pretty Girl Is Like A Melody."

ZIEGFELD MIDNIGHT FROLIC
October 2, 1919   New Amsterdam Roof   171 performances
Music mostly by Dave Stamper
Book and lyrics mostly by Gene Buck
Directed by Ned Wayburn
Produced by Florenz Ziegfeld, Jr.
With Fanny Brice, Ted Lewis, and W. C. Fields

Published song:

"I'll See You In C-U-B-A"

ZIEGFELD GIRLS OF 1920
A 9 O'Clock Revue
March 8, 1920   New Amsterdam Roof   78 performances
Music mostly by Dave Stamper
Book and lyrics mostly by Gene Buck
Directed by Ned Wayburn
Produced by Florenz Ziegfeld, Jr.
With Fanny Brice, Lillian Lorraine, and W. C. Fields

Published song:

"Metropolitan Ladies"—advertised but not published

ZIEGFELD FOLLIES OF 1920
June 22, 1920   New Amsterdam Theatre
123 performances
Music and lyrics also by others
Sketches by George V. Hobart, James Montgomery, and W. C. Fields
Directed by Edward Royce
Produced by Florenz Ziegfeld, Jr.
With Fanny Brice, W. C. Fields, Mary Eaton, and Charles Winninger

Published songs:

"Bells"
"Chinese Firecrackers"
"Come Along Sextette"
"The Girls Of My Dreams"
"The Leg Of Nations"
"The Syncopated Vamp"
"Tell Me Little Gypsy"

BROADWAY BREVITIES OF 1920
September 29, 1920   Winter Garden Theatre
105 performances

Music mostly by Archie Gottler (see **Gershwin**)
Lyrics mostly by Blair Treynor
Book by George LeMaire
Produced by Rufus LeMaire
With George LeMaire, Eddie Cantor, Edith Hallor, and Bert Williams

Published song:

"Beautiful Faces"

MUSIC BOX REVUE
First Edition
September 22, 1921   Music Box Theatre
440 performances

Sketches by William Collier, George V. Hobart, and others
Directed by Hassard Short
Produced by Sam H. Harris
With Collier, Sam Bernard, and Berlin

Published songs:

"At The Court Around The Corner"
"Behind The Fan"
"Everybody Step"
"I'm A Dumb-Bell"—advertised but not published
"In A Cozy Kitchenette Apartment"
"Legend Of The Pearls"
"My Little Book Of Poetry"
"Say It With Music"
"The Schoolhouse Blues"
"Tell Me With A Melody"—written for 1923 London version
"They Call It Dancing"

Harris (see **THE LITTLE MILLIONAIRE [September 25, 1911]**) and Berlin began their partnership by building the intimate Music Box Theatre and starting their own revue series. Both ventures proved successful. The **MUSIC BOX REVUES** headed away from the overblown, lavish productions of Ziegfeld, White, and Carroll, opting for style and sophistication (and leading to the Thirties revue form of

Arthur Schwartz and others). Guiding the **MUSIC BOX REVUES**, **THE BAND WAGON** [Schwartz: June 3, 1931], and **AS THOUSANDS CHEER** [September 30, 1933] was innovative director/ designer Hassard Short, whose taste and talent were first demonstrated here.

MUSIC BOX REVUE
Second Edition
October 23, 1922   Music Box Theatre   330 performances
Sketches by George V. Hobart, Walter Catlett, and others
Directed by Hassard Short
Produced by Sam H. Harris
With William Gaxton, Charlotte Greenwood, and Bobby Clark and Paul McCullough

Published songs:
"Bring On The Pepper"
"Crinoline Days"
"Dancing Honeymoon"
"Diamond Horseshoe"
"I'm Looking For A Daddy Long Legs"
"Lady Of The Evening"
"The Little Red Lacquer Cage"
"Mont Martre"
"Pack Up Your Sins And Go To The Devil"
"Porcelain Maid"
"Take A Little Wife"
"Three Cheers For The Red, White, And Blue"—advertised but not published
"Will She Come From The East? (East-North-West or South)"

Vaudevillians Gaxton, Clark, and McCullough were to become major musical comedy stars by the end of the decade.

MUSIC BOX REVUE
Third Edition
September 22, 1923   Music Box Theatre
273 performances
Sketches by George S. Kaufman, Robert Benchley, and others
Directed by Hassard Short

Produced by Sam H. Harris
With Frank Tinney, Grace Moore, and Benchley

Published songs:

"Climbing Up The Scale"
"Learn To Do The Strut"
"Little Butterfly"
"Maid Of Mesh"
"One Girl"
"An Orange Grove In California"
"Tell Me A Bedtime Story"
"A Waltz Of Long Ago"
"What'll I Do?"—added after opening; initial publication as 1924
   nonshow song

As the series continued, a marked improvement was noticeable in the
quality of the sketches. George S. Kaufman had already collaborated
with Marc Connelly on two successful comedies; his first musical, with
Connelly, Kalmar, and Ruby, had been the unsuccessful HELEN OF
TROY, N.Y. [June 19, 1923]. To the **MUSIC BOX REVUE** he
contributed the legendary sketch "If Men Played Cards As Women
Do." Soprano Grace Moore went on to stardom; popular Irish song-
and-dance man Tinney went on to obscurity, his career destroyed in
Broadway's equivalent to the Fatty Arbuckle sex scandal. Charles
Chaplin used Tinney as inspiration for his classic film *Limelight*.

THE PUNCH BOWL
May 21, 1924   Duke Of York's Theatre ⟨London⟩
565 performances

Music and lyrics mostly by others
Produced by Archibald De Bears
With Norah Blaney

Published song:

"All Alone"—added after opening; initial publication as 1924 nonshow song; also used in **MUSIC BOX REVUE ⟨Fourth Edition⟩**
   [December 1, 1924]

The romance of immigrant Berlin and socialite heiress Ellin Mackay
created international headlines until their elopement in 1926. "Always," "What'll I Do," and "All Alone" were courtship songs—and

popular hits. Berlin interpolated the last two in his then-running revues.

MUSIC BOX REVUE
Fourth Edition
December 1, 1924   Music Box Theatre   184 performances

Sketches by Bert Kalmar, Harry Ruby, and others
Directed by John Murray Anderson
Produced by Sam H. Harris
With Fanny Brice, Bobby Clark and Paul McCullough, Grace Moore, and
   Oscar Shaw

Published songs:

"Alice In Wonderland" [2nd]—different than song from **THE
   CENTURY GIRL [November 6, 1916]**
"All Alone"—see **THE PUNCH BOWL [May 21, 1924]**
"The Call Of The South"
"Don't Send Me Back (To Petrograd)"
"Don't Wait Too Long"
"I Want To Be A Ballet Dancer"—advertised but not published
"In The Shade Of A Sheltering Tree"
"Listening"
"Rockabye Baby"
"Tell Her In The Springtime"
"Tokio Blues"
"Unlucky In Love"
"Where Is My Little Old New York?"
"Who"

The **MUSIC BOX REVUES** had been expensively and tastefully
produced, but the length of runs had decreased each year, and Harris and Berlin decided to end the series. This jewel box of a theatre
is unable to support large, costly musicals. Except for a brief period
in the Depression (including the most famous Music Box tenant, Harris
and Kaufman's **OF THEE I SING [Gershwin: December 26, 1931]**),
it has usually been booked with straight plays. The theatre is still
tastefully maintained by Berlin, copartnered with the Shuberts.

THE COCOANUTS
December 8, 1925   Lyric Theatre   377 performances

Book by George S. Kaufman
Directed by Oscar Eagle
Produced by Sam H. Harris
With The Marx Brothers and Margaret Dumont

Published songs:

"Everyone In The World Is Doing The Charleston"—added to
   New Summer Edition; issued as professional copy only
"Five O'Clock Tea"
"Florida By The Sea"
"Gentlemen Prefer Blondes"—added to *New Summer Edition;*
   issued as professional copy only
"A Hit With The Ladies"—advertised but not published
"A Little Bungalow"
"Lucky Boy"
"Minstrel Days"—advertised but not published
"The Monkey Doodle-Doo" [2nd]—different than song from **ALL
   ABOARD [June 5, 1913]**
"Tango Melody"
"Ting-A-Ling, The Bells'll Ring"—added to *New Summer Edition*
"Too Many Sweethearts"—issued as professional copy only
"We Should Care" [1st]—cut
"We Should Care" [2nd]—different song than cut version
"When My Dreams Come True"—written for 1929 movie version
"When We're Running A Little Hotel Of Our Own"—advertised
   but not published
"Why Do You Want To Know Why?"—added to *New Summer
   Edition*
"With A Family Reputation"—issued as professional copy only

An unlikely project for Berlin, a Marx Brothers fan who brought them together with Harris and Kaufman. Berlin's score was among his least interesting, except for the raggy "Monkey Doodle-Doo."

BETSY
December 28, 1926   New Amsterdam Theatre
39 performances

Music mostly by Richard **Rodgers**
Lyrics mostly by Lorenz Hart
Book by Irving Caesar and David Freedman

Directed by Wm. Anthony McGuire
Produced by Florenz Ziegfeld, Jr.
With Belle Baker and Al Shean

Published song:

"Blue Skies"

"Blue Skies" was one of Berlin's biggest hits. He wanted belter Belle Baker to sing it. She was in rehearsal for **BETSY,** so Berlin gave the song to Ziegfeld for interpolation (to Rodgers and Hart's displeasure).

ZIEGFELD FOLLIES OF 1927
August 16, 1927   New Amsterdam Theatre
167 performances

Sketches by Harold Atteridge and Eddie Cantor
Directed by Zeke Colvan
Produced by Florenz Ziegfeld, Jr.
With Cantor, Ruth Etting, and Dan Healy

Published songs:

"It"—advertised but not published (probably a misprint)
"It All Belongs To Me"
"It's Up To The Band"
"Jimmy"
"Jungle Jingle"—advertised but not published
"Learn To Sing A Love Song"
"My New York"
"Ooh, Maybe It's You"
"Rainbow Of Girls"
"Ribbons And Bows"—advertised but not published
"Shaking The Blues Away"
"What Makes Me Love You?"—advertised but not published

For the first time in the history of the series, Ziegfeld assigned the entire score to only one songwriter. The strategy backfired, as Berlin's work was mediocre. Cantor was featured as the sole star, also a departure from **FOLLIES** tradition. The show was very expensive and far from the best of the series; Ziegfeld was only able to mount one more edition [July 1, 1931].

SHOOT THE WORKS
July 21, 1931   George M. Cohan Theatre
87 performances

Music and lyrics mostly by others (see **Duke**)
Sketches by Nunnally Johnson, Heywood Broun and others
Directed by Ted Hammerstein
Produced by Broun, with Milton Raison
With Broun, George Murphy, and Imogene Coca

Published song:

"Begging For Love"—published in separate edition

Suffering from major financial losses from the Depression and in the latter part of a creative drought, Berlin interpolated this minor number to this minor production—and turned his attention back to Broadway.

FACE THE MUSIC
February 17, 1932   New Amsterdam Theatre
165 performances

Book by Moss Hart
Book directed by George S. Kaufman
Production staged by Hassard Short
Produced by Sam H. Harris
With Mary Boland, J. Harold Murray, and Katherine Carrington

Published songs:

"I Say It's Spinach"
"Let's Have Another Cup Of Coffee"
"Manhattan Madness"
"My Rhinestone Girl"—advertised but not published
"On A Roof In Manhattan"
"Soft Lights And Sweet Music"

Berlin's career picked up with this mildly satirical success, produced concurrently with Kaufman and Harris's highly satirical smash **OF THEE I SING [Gershwin: December 26, 1931]**. Moss Hart, collaborator with Kaufman on the 1930 comedy ONCE IN A LIFETIME, provided the book; like Kaufman, he went on to important musical theatre work as librettist and director. Berlin regained his ability to sense the public's mood with "Let's Have Another Cup Of Coffee."

AS THOUSANDS CHEER
September 30, 1933   Music Box Theatre
400 performances

Sketches by Moss Hart
Choreographed by Charles Weidman
Directed by Hassard Short
Produced by Sam H. Harris
With Marilyn Miller, Clifton Webb, Helen Broderick, and Ethel Waters

Published songs:

"Easter Parade"—revised version of 1917 nonshow song "Smile
    And Show Your Dimple"
"The Funnies"
"Harlem On My Mind"
"Heat Wave"
"How's Chances"
"Lonely Heart"
"Not For All The Rice In China"
"Supper Time"

Additional song published (no lyric) in piano selection:

"Revolt In Cuba" [instrumental]—initial publication upon reuse in
    London revue STOP PRESS [February 21, 1935]

A high point in Berlin's theatrical career, **AS THOUSANDS CHEER** was a socially conscious revue which succeeded on many levels. Along with his usual gifts, Berlin displayed a poignant, tragic voice in "Supper Time"; he never was to explore this vein further, though. Ethel Waters triumphed in her first white Broadway show, singing that song and the tropical "Heat Wave." For thirty-five-year-old Marilyn Miller it was the end: convinced she was washed up, she retired, married a chorus boy, and died under mysterious circumstances on April 7, 1936. MORE CHEERS, a sequel to **AS THOUSANDS CHEER,** was announced for early 1935 but never produced; Berlin issued a professional copy of the song "Moon Over Napoli." STOP PRESS was a Hassard Short/Moss Hart British revue, using the **AS THOUSANDS CHEER** format and several of the songs. Berlin spent the rest of the Thirties writing movie scores.

LOUISIANA PURCHASE
May 28, 1940   Imperial Theatre   444 performances

Book by Morrie Ryskind
(Based on a story by B. G. DeSylva)
Choreographed by George Balanchine and Carl Randall
Directed by Edgar MacGregor
Produced by DeSylva
With William Gaxton, Vera Zorina, Victor Moore, and Irene Bordoni

Published songs:

"Dance With Me (Tonight At The Mardi Gras)"—originally issued
    as "Tonight At The Mardi Gras"
"Fools Fall In Love"
"I'd Love To Be Shot Out Of A Cannon With You"—cut; issued
    as professional copy only
"It'll Come To You"
"It's A Lovely Day Tomorrow"
"Latins Know How"
"The Lord Done Fixed Up My Soul"
"Louisiana Purchase"
"Outside Of That I Love You"
"What Chance Have I With Love?"
"Wild About You"
"You Can't Brush Me Off"
"You're Lonely And I'm Lonely"

Additional songs published in "special edition" vocal selection:
"Opening Chorus"
"Opening Letter"
"Sex Marches On"

An entertaining hit loosely satirizing Louisiana governor Huey Long.
Gaxton and Moore appeared in their final hit as a team, ably supported by Zorina and Bordoni (the former Mrs. E. Ray Goetz, Berlin's one-time sister-in-law).

THIS IS THE ARMY
July 4, 1942   Broadway Theatre   113 performances

Directed by Ezra Stone
Produced by Uncle Sam
With Stone, Julie Oshins, Anthony Ross, and Berlin

Published songs:

"American Eagles"
"The Army's Made A Man Out Of Me"
"How About A Cheer For The Navy"
"I Left My Heart At The Stage Door Canteen"
"I'm Getting Tired So I Can Sleep"
"My Sergeant And I Are Buddies"
"That Russian Winter"
"That's What The Well-Dressed Man In Harlem Will Wear"
"This Is The Army, Mr. Jones"
"What Does He Look Like"—written for 1943 movie version
"With My Head In The Clouds"

Additional songs published in "special edition" vocal selection:

"Closing"
"Jap-German Sextet"
"Ladies Of The Chorus"
"Opening (The Army And The Shuberts Depend On You)"
"Opening Chorus (Some Dough For The Army Relief)"
"Opening Of Second Act (Jane Cowl Number)"
"This Time"—initial publication as 1942 nonshow song
"Yip Yip Yaphanker's Introduction"

Additional published songs added to Overseas Touring Productions:

"The Fifth Army's Where My Heart Is" (1944)—issued as
   professional copy only
"The Kick In The Pants" (1943)—issued as professional copy only
"I Get Along With The Aussies" (1945)—issued as professional
   copy only
"My British Buddy" (1943)
"There Are No Wings On A Foxhole" (1944)
"Ve Don't Like It" (1943)—issued as professional copy only
"What Are We Going To Do With All The Jeeps?" (1944)

The ultimate wartime service show, successor to **YIP-YIP-YAP-HANK [August 19, 1918]**. Berlin came up with an endless supply of good material; the show provided rousing entertainment and millions of dollars for the Army Emergency Relief.

ANNIE GET YOUR GUN
May 16, 1946   Imperial Theatre   1,147 performances

Book by Herbert and Dorothy Fields
Choreographed by Helen Tamiris
Directed by Joshua Logan
Produced by Rodgers and Hammerstein
With Ethel Merman and Ray Middleton

Published songs:

"Anything You Can Do"
"Colonel Buffalo Bill"
"Doin' What Comes Natur'lly"
"The Girl That I Marry"
"I Got Lost In His Arms"
"I Got The Sun In The Morning"
"I'll Share It All With You"
"I'm A Bad, Bad Man"
"I'm An Indian Too"
"Let's Go West Again"—written for 1950 movie version (cut);
   issued as professional copy only
"Moonshine Lullaby"
"My Defenses Are Down"
"An Old Fashioned Wedding"—written for 1966 revival
"Take It In Your Stride"—cut; advertised but not published
"There's No Business Like Show Business"
"They Say It's Wonderful"
"Who Do You Love, I Hope"
"You Can't Get A Man With A Gun"

Berlin's supreme achievement, one of the most hit-filled scores in
Broadway history. Rodgers and Hammerstein had begun their producing career in 1944 (see **HAPPY BIRTHDAY [Rodgers: October
31, 1946]**). For their first musical they hired Jerome Kern and Dorothy Fields (see **VERY WARM FOR MAY [Kern: November 17,
1939]**). Following Kern's death, Berlin was asked to take on the score.
Fields agreed to withdraw from the lyric assignment and provided
the book with brother Herbert, Rodgers' original librettist. Rodgers
brought along Joshua Logan, frequent associate since **I MARRIED
AN ANGEL [Rodgers: May 11, 1938]**, to direct. To all these
professionals at the top of their creative peak was added Merman,
giving one of the best performances of her career.

MISS LIBERTY
July 15, 1949   Imperial Theatre   308 performances

Book by Robert E. Sherwood
Choreographed by Jerome Robbins
Directed by Moss Hart
Produced by Berlin, Sherwood and Hart
With Allyn McLerie, Eddie Albert, and Mary McCarty

Published songs:

"Business For A Good Girl Is Bad"—cut; issued as professional
  copy only
"Extra! Extra!"
"Falling Out Of Love Can Be Fun"
"Give Me Your Tired, Your Poor " (poem by Emma Lazarus)
"Homework"
"The Hon'rable Profession Of The Fourth Estate"—cut
"I'd Like My Picture Took"
"Just One Way To Say I Love You"
"Let's Take An Old-Fashioned Walk"
"Little Fish In A Big Pond"
"Me An' My Bundle"
"Miss Liberty"
"Mr. Monotony"—cut; initially issued as "Mrs. Monotony"
"The Most Expensive Statue In The World"
"Only For Americans"
"Paris Wakes Up And Smiles"
"The Policeman's Ball"
"The Pulitzer Prize"—cut; advertised but not published
"What Do I Have To Do To Get My Picture In The Paper?"—cut
"You Can Have Him"

A patriotic musical comedy about the Statue of Liberty by Berlin,
Hart, and Pulitzer Prize–winning dramatist/Roosevelt speechwriter
Robert E. Sherwood. The idea sounded a whole lot better than **MISS
LIBERTY** was.

CALL ME MADAM
October 12, 1950   Imperial Theatre   644 performances

Book by Howard Lindsay and Russel Crouse
Choreographed by Jerome Robbins

Directed by George Abbott
Produced by Leland Hayward
With Ethel Merman, Paul Lukas, and Russell Nype

Published songs:

"Anthem For Presentation"—cut; advertised but not published
"The Best Thing For You"
"Can You Use Any Money Today?"—initial publication upon use
    in 1953 movie version
"Free"—cut; revised for 1954 movie *White Christmas* with new lyric
    as "Snow"
"The Hostess With The Mostes' On The Ball"
"It's A Lovely Day Today"
"Lichtenburg"—advertised but not published (except in vocal
    score)
"Marrying For Love"
"Mrs. Sally Adams"—advertised but not published (except in vocal
    score)
"(Dance To The Music Of) The Ocarina"
"Once Upon A Time Today"
"Our Day Of Independence"—cut; advertised but not published
"Something To Dance About"
"They Like Ike"
"Washington Square Dance"
"You're Just In Love (I Wonder Why?)"

This slick entertainment was Berlin's final Broadway hit, carried by
Merman's performance and the eleven-o'clock duet "You're Just In
Love." After some final motion picture work, Berlin went into virtual retirement—which for him meant writing pop songs and contin-
uing his publishing activities.

MR. PRESIDENT
October 20, 1962   St. James Theatre   265 performances

Book by Howard Lindsay and Russel Crouse
Choreographed by Peter Gennaro
Directed by Joshua Logan
Produced by Leland Hayward
With Robert Ryan, Nanette Fabray, and Anita Gillette

Published songs:

"Don't Be Afraid Of Romance"
"Empty Pockets Filled With Love"

"The First Lady"
"Glad To Be Home"
"I'm Gonna Get Him"
"I've Got To Be Around"
"In Our Hide-Away"
"Is He The Only Man In The World?"
"It Gets Lonely In The White House"
"Laugh It Up"
"Let's Go Back To The Waltz"
"Meat And Potatoes"
"Once Every Four Years"—cut
"Pigtails And Freckles"
"Poor Joe"—cut
"The Secret Service"
"Song For Belly Dancer (The Only Dance I Know)"
"They Love Me"
"This Is A Great Country"
"The Washington Twist"

Additional song recorded:

"You Need A Hobby"

Berlin returned to Broadway with yet another politically oriented musical. With a weak score and no support from any of his colleagues, **MR. PRESIDENT** stayed around just long enough to run through a substantial advance sale. The only bright spot: Nanette Fabray as "The First Lady."

Since **MR. PRESIDENT,** Irving Berlin has kept a low profile; his last important song was "An Old Fashioned Wedding," written for the 1966 revival of **ANNIE GET YOUR GUN [May 16, 1946]**. Berlin is unquestionably America's most popular composer, with numerous hits and handfuls of all-time favorites to his credit. His contributions to Broadway were often entertaining and usually profitable—not an altogether bad combination. But Berlin rarely attempted well-rounded musical theatre scores; he always seemed more interested in parades of songs hits, which kept his publisher (i.e., himself) happy. An exception was **ANNIE GET YOUR GUN,** where he was no doubt motivated by the presence of producers Rodgers and Hammerstein. In 1914 Kern and Berlin had led Broadway into a new era. While Kern made musico-dramatic innovation his lifelong quest, Berlin seemed content just writing song hit after song hit.

George Gershwin

BORN: September 26, 1898   Brooklyn, New York
DIED: July 11, 1937   Beverly Hills, California

George Gershwin grew up in Manhattan, where his Russian immigrant father attempted a succession of unsuccessful businesses. At the age of eleven, Gershwin suddenly displayed an unexpected musical aptitude; at fifteen he quit school to work as song plugger for Tin Pan Alley publisher Jerome H. Remick. Supplementing his income by making player-piano rolls, he began writing songs of his own: "When You Want 'Em, You Can't Get 'Em (When You've Got 'Em, You Don't Want 'Em)" (lyric by Murray Roth) was published in 1916. Gershwin felt ready for Broadway, and made his debut at the age of seventeen.

PASSING SHOW OF 1916
The Annual Summer Review
June 22, 1916   Winter Garden Theatre   140 performances
Music mostly by Sigmund Romberg and Otto Motzan
Book and lyrics mostly by Harold Atteridge
Directed by J. C. Huffman
Produced by The Winter Garden Company (Messrs. Shubert)

Published song:

"The Making Of A Girl" (music by Romberg and Gershwin)

Shubert staff composer Sigmund Romberg offered to listen to some of Gershwin's material. He liked one tune enough to use it and had Atteridge write a lyric—taking cocomposer credit for himself. Gershwin remained friendly with Romberg despite their divergent musical styles. Leaving song plugging, Gershwin was hired as rehearsal pianist for **MISS 1917 [Kern: November 5, 1917]**. Gershwin had been deeply influenced by Kern's "Princess Theatre" shows. Kern, on his part, was impressed with the youngster. Gershwin was sent to Max Dreyfus, who signed the eighteen-year-old and began placing his work.

HITCHY-KOO OF 1918
Second Edition
June 6, 1918   Globe Theatre   68 performances

Music mostly by Raymond Hubbell
Book and lyrics mostly by Glen MacDonough
Directed by Leon Errol
Produced by Raymond Hitchcock
With Hitchcock, Errol, and Irene Bordoni

Published song:

"You–oo Just You" (lyric by Irving Caesar)—initial publication as
   1918 nonshow song

Gershwin had accompanied **MISS 1917 [Kern: November 5, 1917]** star Vivienne Segal at concerts. She introduced "You–oo Just You," which soon found its way into **HITCHY-KOO OF 1918**. Gershwin and childhood friend Irving Caesar collaborated on several early songs, including their first major hit "Swanee" **[CAPITOL REVUE: October 24, 1919]**.

LADIES FIRST
October 24, 1918   Broadhurst Theatre   164 performances

Music mostly by A. Baldwin Sloane
Book and lyrics mostly by Harry B. Smith
(Based on *A Contented Woman* [play] by Charles Hoyt)
Directed by Frank Smithson
Produced by H. H. Frazee
With Nora Bayes
NOTE: **LOOK WHO'S HERE,** pre-Broadway title

Published songs:

"The Real American Folk Song (Is A Rag)" (lyric by Arthur
   Francis [Ira Gershwin])—initial publication as 1959 nonshow
   song
"Some Wonderful Sort Of Someone" (lyric by Schuyler Greene)—
   see **THE LADY IN RED [May 12, 1919]**

Gershwin began an occasional collaboration with his older brother Ira. Not wishing to infringe on his brother's reputation—although George was by no means established yet—Ira chose to combine the names of his younger brother and sister for a pseudonym. After dropping out of college, Ira drifted through a series of odd jobs in the same unsuccessful manner as his father had until his first break, **TWO LITTLE GIRLS IN BLUE [Youmans: May 3, 1921]**.

HALF PAST EIGHT
[December 9, 1918]   Empire Theatre ⟨Syracuse, New York⟩; closed during pre-Broadway tryout

Music mostly by Gershwin
Lyrics by Fred Caryll [Edward B. Perkins]
Produced by Perkins
With Joe Cook, Sybil Vane, and the Famous Original Clef Club Band

Published songs:

None

Gershwin wrote his first full score for this ill-assembled revue. Things went so badly that at one of the six performances Gershwin himself was sent on stage to play a medley of his "hits." Producer Perkins borrowed the title from a Paul Rubens revue [August 19, 1916], claiming his show was direct from a nine-month London run; he even billed the lyricist (himself) as "Fred Caryll" (brother of popular British composer Ivan Caryll, perhaps?). Some of the songs resurfaced in **LA, LA LUCILLE [May 26, 1919]** but remained unpublished.

GOOD MORNING JUDGE
February 6, 1919   Shubert Theatre   140 performances

Music mostly by Lionel Monckton and Howard Talbot
Book by Fred Thompson
(Based on *The Magistrate* [play] by Sir Arthur Wing Pinero)
Directed by Wybert Stamford
Produced by the Messrs. Shubert
With Mollie King and Charles King

Published songs:

"I Was So Young (You Were So Beautiful)" (lyric by Irving Caesar and Alfred Bryan)

"There's More To The Kiss Than The X-X-X" (lyric by Caesar)—
see **LA, LA LUCILLE** [May 26, 1919]

THE LADY IN RED
May 12, 1919   Lyric Theatre   48 performances

Music mostly by Robert Winterberg (see **Kern**)
Book and lyrics mostly by Anne Caldwell
Directed by Frank Smithson
Produced by John P. Slocum
With Adele Rowland

Published songs:

"Something About Love" (lyric by Lou Paley)—also used in
London production [April 14, 1926] of **LADY, BE GOOD!**
[December 1, 1924]
"Some Wonderful Sort Of Someone" (lyric by Schuyler Greene)—
revised version of song from **LADIES FIRST** [October 24,
1918]

LA, LA LUCILLE
A New, Up-To-The-Minute Musical Comedy Of Class And Distinction
May 26, 1919   Henry Miller's Theatre   104 performances

Lyrics by Arthur J. Jackson and B. G. DeSylva
Book by Fred Jackson
Directed by Herbert Gresham and Julian Alfred
Produced by Alfred E. Aarons
With Janet Velie and John E. Hazzard

Published songs:

"The Best Of Everything"—see **FOR GOODNESS SAKE**
[February 20, 1922]
"From Now On"
"The Love Of A Wife"—cut
"Nobody But You"—added after opening
"Somehow It Seldom Comes True"
"Tee-Oodle-Um-Bum-Bo"
"There's More To The Kiss Than The Sound" (lyric by Irving
Caesar)—issued in separate edition; revised lyric for "There's
More To The Kiss Than The X-X-X" from **GOOD MORNING
JUDGE** [February 6, 1919]

Gershwin's first complete Broadway score was for this moderately successful "modern" musical. Twenty-four-year-old B. G. DeSylva had already written several Al Jolson hits; he was Gershwin's primary lyricist for the next few years. Turn-of-the-century composer Alfred E. Aarons had become general manager to (and sometime producer for) theatre owner A. L. Erlanger. Aarons' twenty-nine-year-old son Alex was one of the first to praise Gershwin's work: he convinced his father to choose Gershwin over Victor Herbert. Alex produced the post-Broadway tour of **LA, LA LUCILLE** and, beginning in 1924, joined with Vinton Freedley to produce a successful string of hit Gershwin musicals.

CAPITOL REVUE—"Demi-Tasse"
Vaudeville Revue
October 24, 1919   Capitol Theatre

Directed and produced by Ned Wayburn
With Paul Frawley and Muriel DeForrest

Published songs:

"Come To The Moon" (lyric by Ned Wayburn and Lou Paley)—
    see **THE RAINBOW [April 3, 1923]**
"Swanee" (lyric by Irving Caesar)—also used in **SINBAD [Circa December 1919]**

The opening bill for this movie palace included this quickly forgotten stage show; but Al Jolson heard "Swanee" and wanted to sing it. . . . His recording was spectacularly successful and Gershwin had his first hit.

MORRIS GEST'S MIDNIGHT WHIRL
December 27, 1919   Century Grove Theatre
110 performances

Book and lyrics by Bud (B. G.) DeSylva and John Henry Mears
Directed by Julian Mitchell and Dave Bennett
Produced by Morris Gest
With Bessie McCoy Davis and Bernard Granville

Published songs:

"Limehouse Nights"
"Poppyland"

SINBAD
The Winter Garden's Latest Extravaganza
[Circa December 1919]; post-Broadway tour

Music mostly by Sigmund Romberg
Book and lyrics mostly by Harold Atteridge
Directed by J. C. Huffman
Produced by Messrs. Shubert
With Al Jolson

Published songs:

"Swanee" (lyric by Irving Caesar)—originally used in **CAPITOL REVUE [October 24, 1919]**
"Swanee Rose" (lyric by Caesar and B. G. DeSylva)—originally published as "Dixie Rose"

With "Swanee" a hit Jolson record, the singer inserted it into his current show (to help sell more records).

DERE MABLE
[February 2, 1920]   Academy Of Music ⟨Baltimore, Maryland⟩; closed during pre-Broadway tryout

Music mostly by Rosamond Hodges
Lyrics mostly by John Hodges
Book by Edward Streeter and John Hodges
(Based on the books by Streeter)
Directed by George Marion
Produced by Marc Klaw
With Louis Bennison

Published song:

"We're Pals" (lyric by Irving Caesar)

THE ED WYNN CARNIVAL
April 5, 1920   New Amsterdam Theatre   150 performances

Book and songs mostly by Ed Wynn
Directed by Ned Wayburn
Produced by B. C. Whitney
With Ed Wynn

Published song:

"Oo, How I Love To Be Loved By You" (lyric by Lou Paley)

GEORGE WHITE'S SCANDALS
Second Annual Event
June 7, 1920   Globe Theatre   134 performances

Lyrics by Arthur Jackson
Book by Andy Rice and George White
Directed by White and Willie Collier
Produced by White
With Ann Pennington, Lou Holtz, and White

Published songs:

"Idle Dreams"
"My Lady"
"My Old Love Is My New Love"—advertised but not published
"On My Mind The Whole Night Long"
"Queen Isabella"—advertised but not published
"Scandal Walk"
"The Songs Of Long Ago"
"Tum On And Tiss Me"

George White, a featured dancer in THE ZIEGFELD FOLLIES, went into competition with his former boss: stealing Ziegfeld star Ann Pennington he produced the first SCANDALS [June 2, 1919], with a Richard Whiting/Arthur Jackson score. The SCANDALS ran neck and neck with the FOLLIES until the Depression effectively ended both series. While Ziegfeld was lavish, star-laden and traditional, White could be counted on for better music and exciting, modern-dance innovations.

THE SWEETHEART SHOP
The Fascinating Musical Play
August 31, 1920   Knickerbocker Theatre   55 performances

Music mostly by Hugo Felix
Book and lyrics mostly by Anne Caldwell
Directed by Herbert Gresham
Produced by Edgar J. MacGregor and William Moore Patch
Starring Helen Ford

Published song:

"Waiting For The Sun To Come Out" (lyric by Arthur Francis [Ira Gershwin])

This moderately successful interpolation was Ira Gershwin's first published song.

PICCADILLY TO BROADWAY
All Anglo-American Musical Review
[September 27, 1920]   Globe Theatre ⟨Atlantic City, New Jersey⟩; closed during pre-Broadway tryout

Music also by William Daly, Vincent **Youmans,** and others
Sketches and lyrics mostly by Glen MacDonough and E. Ray Goetz
Directed by George Marion and Julian Alfred
Produced by Goetz
With Johnny Dooley, Anna Wheaton, Clifton Webb, and Helen Broderick

Published songs:

None

Gershwin collaborated with Goetz on two songs: "On The Brim Of Her Old-Fashioned Bonnet" and "Baby Blues" (both unpublished, also used in **SNAPSHOTS OF 1921 [June 2, 1921]**). Among the other songwriters on **PICCADILLY TO BROADWAY** were William Daly, an important future Gershwin associate; and the new team of Vincent Youmans and Arthur Francis [Ira Gershwin].

BROADWAY BREVITIES OF 1920
September 29, 1920   Winter Garden Theatre
105 performances

Music mostly by Archie Gottler (see **Berlin**)
Lyrics mostly by Blair Treynor
Book by George LeMaire
Produced by Rufus LeMaire
With George LeMaire, Eddie Cantor, Edith Hallor, and Bert Williams

Published songs:

"Lu Lu" (lyric by Arthur Jackson)
"Snow Flakes" (lyric by Jackson)
"Spanish Love" (lyric by Irving Caesar)

A DANGEROUS MAID
A New TNT Laugh Fest
[March 21, 1921]   Nixon's Apollo Theatre ⟨Atlantic City, New Jersey⟩; closed during pre-Broadway tryout

Lyrics by Arthur Francis [Ira Gershwin]
Book by Charles W. Bell
(Based on *A Dislocated Honeymoon* [play] by Bell)
Produced by Edgar MacGregor
With Vivienne Segal, Amelia Bingham, and Vinton Freedley

Published songs:

"Boy Wanted"—see **PRIMROSE** [September 11, 1924]
"Dancing Shoes"
"Just To Know You Are Mine"
"The Simple Life"
"Some Rain Must Fall"

The first complete score written by the brothers Gershwin was for this quick failure. Ira soon had a Broadway hit, though, **TWO LIT-TLE GIRLS IN BLUE** [Youmans: May 3, 1921].

SNAPSHOTS OF 1921
June 2, 1921   Selwyn Theatre   44 performances

Music mostly by others
Gershwin lyrics by E. Ray Goetz
Directed by Leon Errol
Produced by The Selwyns and Lew Fields
With Nora Bayes, Fields, and DeWolf Hopper

Published songs:

None

Goetz interpolated the leftovers from **PICCADILLY TO BROAD-WAY** [September 27, 1920], which remained unexceptional and un-published. For the post-Broadway tour, Lew Fields assigned the job of conductor to his nineteen-year-old discovery Richard Rodgers.

GEORGE WHITE'S SCANDALS
Third Annual Edition
July 11, 1921   Liberty Theatre   97 performances

Lyrics by Arthur Jackson
Book by Arthur "Bugs" Baer and White
Directed by White and John Meehan
Produced by White
With Ann Pennington, Lester Allen, and White

Published songs:

"Drifting Along With The Tide"
"I Love You"
"She's Just A Baby"
"South Sea Isles"
"Where East Meets West"

Additional song published (no lyric) in piano selection:

"Russian Dance" [instrumental]

THE PERFECT FOOL
November 7, 1921   George M. Cohan Theatre
256 performances

Book, music, and lyrics mostly by Ed Wynn
Directed by Julian Alfred
Produced by B. C. Whitney
Presented by A. L. Erlanger
With Ed Wynn and Janet Velie

Published songs:

"My Log-Cabin Home" (lyric by Irving Caesar and B. G. DeSylva)
"No One Else But That Girl Of Mine" (lyric by Caesar)—see **THE
   DANCING GIRL [January 24, 1923]**

FOR GOODNESS SAKE
February 20, 1922   Lyric Theatre   103 performances

Music mostly by William Daly and Paul Lannin
Lyrics mostly by Arthur Jackson
Lyrics to Gershwin songs by Arthur Francis [Ira Gershwin]
Book by Fred Jackson
Directed by Priestly Morrison
Produced by Alex A. Aarons
With Helen Ford, Vinton Freedley, and Fred and Adele Astaire
NOTE: **STOP FLIRTING!**, London title

Published songs:

"The Best Of Everything" (lyric by Arthur J. Jackson and B. G. DeSylva)—added to London production; revised lyric for song originally used in **LA, LA LUCILLE [May 26, 1919]**

"I'll Build A Stairway To Paradise" (lyric by DeSylva and Arthur Francis [Ira Gershwin])—added to London production; originally used in **GEORGE WHITE'S SCANDALS ⟨Fourth⟩ [August 28, 1922]**

"Someone"

"Tra-La-La"

Additional songs published (no lyrics) in piano selection:

"All By Myself"—written for London production

"Opening Chorus Act One"—written for London production

Aarons' second musical featured the Astaires, on loan from Charles Dillingham (see **THE BUNCH AND JUDY [Kern: November 28, 1922]**). Unsuccessful on Broadway, the show was revamped for London with more Gershwin material for the Astaires. Retitled STOP FLIRTING! [May 30, 1923], it ran an impressive 418 performances. The Nebraskan-born dance team suddenly found themselves major British stage stars, and spent the rest of their theatrical career shuttling across the Atlantic.

THE FRENCH DOLL
February 20, 1922   Lyceum Theatre   120 performances

Play by A. E. Thomas
(Based on a play by Armont and Germedon)
Produced by E. Ray Goetz
With Irene Bordoni (Goetz)

Published song:

"Do It Again" (lyric by B. G. DeSylva)

SPICE OF 1922
July 6, 1922   Winter Garden Theatre   73 performances

"Lyrics and Music by Everybody"
Book by Jack Lait
Directed by Allan K. Foster

Produced by Arman Kaliz
With Georgie Price

Published song:

"The Yankee Doodle Blues" (lyric by Irving Caesar and B. G.
  DeSylva)

GEORGE WHITE'S SCANDALS
Fourth Annual Production
August 28, 1922   Globe Theatre   88 performances

Lyrics by B. G. DeSylva and E. Ray Goetz
Book by Andy Rice and White
Directed and produced by White
With W. C. Fields, Jack MacGowan, White, and Paul Whiteman and His
  Orchestra

Published songs:

"Across The Sea"
"Argentina" (lyric by DeSylva)
"Cinderelatives" (lyric by DeSylva)
"I Found A Four Leaf Clover" (lyric by DeSylva)
"I'll Build A Stairway To Paradise" (lyric by DeSylva and Arthur
  Francis [Ira Gershwin])—see **FOR GOODNESS SAKE
  [February 20, 1922]**
"She Hangs Out In Our Alley"—initially published as "Oh, What
  She Hangs Out"
"Where Is The Man Of My Dreams?"

Additional songs recorded:

"Blue Monday Blues"
"Has Anyone Seen My Joe"—revised version of 1919 string quartet
  "Lullaby" (published 1968)
"I'm Gonna See My Mother"

"I'll Build A Stairway To Paradise" was Gershwin's second hit song.
The one-act opera *Blue Monday* was withdrawn after the opening night
performance. A primitive forerunner of **PORGY AND BESS [October 10, 1935]**, the work marked Gershwin's first attempt at the extended musical form (and included the lovely "Blue Monday Blues").
In 1925 the work was unsuccessfully revised for the concert hall as
135th Street. Fragments of the score are published in Isaac Goldberg's biography of Gershwin.

OUR NELL
A Musical Mellow Drayma
December 4, 1922   Nora Bayes Theatre   40 performances

Music also by William Daly
Lyrics by Brian Hooker
Book by A. E. Thomas and Hooker
Directed by W. H. Gilmore
Produced by Hayseed Productions (Ed Davidow and Rufus LeMaire)
NOTE: **HAYSEED,** pre-Broadway title

Published songs:

"By And By"
"Innocent Ingenue Baby" (music by Gershwin and Daly)—see
    THE RAINBOW [April 3, 1923]
"Walking Home With Angeline"

Daly, principal composer of **FOR GOODNESS SAKE [February 20, 1922]**, became Gershwin's close friend and musical colleague. He was to conduct most of Gershwin's future work. They collaborated here on the playfully chromatic "Innocent Ingenue Baby."

THE DANCING GIRL
January 24, 1923   Winter Garden Theatre
126 performances

Music mostly by Sigmund Romberg and Alfred Goodman
Book and lyrics mostly by Harold Atteridge
Directed by J. C. Huffman
Produced by Messrs. Shubert
With Trini, Marie Dressler, and Jack Pearl

Published song:

"That American Boy Of Mine" (lyric by Irving Caesar)—revised
    lyric for "No One Else But That Girl Of Mine" from **THE
    PERFECT FOOL [November 7, 1921]**

THE RAINBOW
April 3, 1923   Empire Theatre ⟨London⟩
113 performances

Lyrics mostly by Clifford Grey
Book by Albert De Courville, Edgar Wallace, and Noel Scott

Directed by Allan K. Foster
Produced by De Courville
With Grace Hayes

Published songs:

"All Over Town" (lyric by Lou Paley and Grey)—cut; new lyric for
   "Come To The Moon" from **CAPITOL REVUE [October 24,
   1919]**
"Any Little Tune"—advertised but not published
"Beneath The Eastern Moon"
"Give Me My Mammy"—advertised but not published
"Good-Night, My Dear"
"In The Rain"
"Innocent Lonesome Blue Baby" (music by Gershwin and William
   Daly; lyric by Brian Hooker and Grey)—revised lyric for
   "Innocent Ingenue Baby" from **OUR NELL [December 4,
   1922]**
"Moonlight In Versailles"
"Oh! Nina"
"Strut Lady With Me"
"Sunday In London Town"—cut
"Sweetheart, I'm So Glad That I Met You"—see **TELL ME
   MORE! [April 13, 1925]**

Gershwin wrote one of his blandest scores for this uninspired, unsuccessful revue.

GEORGE WHITE'S SCANDALS
Fifth Annual Production
June 18, 1923   Globe Theatre   168 performances
Music mostly by Gershwin
Lyrics mostly by B. G. DeSylva
Book by George White and William K. Wells
Directed and produced by White
With Winnie Lightner and Lester Allen

Published songs:

"Let's Be Lonesome Together" (lyric by DeSylva and E. Ray
   Goetz)
"The Life Of A Rose"
"Lo-La-Lo"
"(On The Beach At) How You've Been"

"There Is Nothing Too Good For You" (lyric by DeSylva and
   Goetz)
"Throw 'Er In High!" (lyric by DeSylva and Goetz)
"Where Is She?"
"You And I (In Old Versailles)" (music by Gershwin and Jack
   Green)

Jack Green, brother of serious composer Louis Gruenberg, was rehearsal pianist; he presumably fashioned a Gershwin dance routine
into "You And I," meriting shared credit. In early 1924 he worked
as a music copyist on the rush preparation of "Rhapsody In Blue"—
and tried to sue Gershwin, claiming coauthorship.

LITTLE MISS BLUEBEARD
August 28, 1923   Lyceum Theatre   175 performances
Play by Avery Hopwood
Produced by Charles Frohman [Inc.] in association with E. Ray Goetz
With Irene Bordoni (Goetz)

Published song:

"I Won't Say I Will (But I Won't Say I Won't)" (lyric by B. G.
   DeSylva and Arthur Francis [Ira Gershwin])

NIFTIES OF 1923
September 25, 1923   Fulton Theatre   47 performances
Music mostly by others
Produced by Charles Dillingham
With Sam Bernard and William Collier

Published songs:

"At Half Past Seven" (lyric by B. G. DeSylva)—see **PRIMROSE
   [September 11, 1924]**
"Nashville Nightingale" (lyric by Irving Caesar)

SWEET LITTLE DEVIL
The Gayest Of Musical Comedies
January 21, 1924   Astor Theatre   120 performances
Lyrics by B. G. DeSylva
Book by Frank Mandel and Laurence Schwab

Directed by Edgar MacGregor
Produced by Schwab
With Constance Binney
NOTE: **A PERFECT LADY,** pre-Broadway title

Published songs:

"Hey! Hey! Let 'Er Go!"
"The Jijibo"
"Mah-Jongg"—cut; also used in **GEORGE WHITE'S
    SCANDALS** ⟨6th⟩ [**June 30, 1924**]
"Pepita"—cut; new lyric and verse for 1921 nonshow song
    "Tomale" (lyric by DeSylva)
"Someone Believes In You"
"Under A One-Man Top"
"Virginia (Don't Go Too Far)"

Gershwin's music had only hinted at the modern rhythms and color-
ings which soon distinguished him (and Vincent Youmans) from his
contemporaries. Then came the "Rhapsody In Blue," introduced
February 12, 1924. The personal renown and radical reputation which
followed this "assault by jazz on the concert hall" helped ease Gershwin away from his often hacklike early work.

GEORGE WHITE'S SCANDALS
Sixth Annual Edition
June 30, 1924   Apollo Theatre   192 performances
Lyrics mostly by B. G. DeSylva
Book by White and William K. Wells
Directed and produced by White
With Winnie Lightner and Lester Allen

Published songs:

"I Need A Garden"
"Kongo Kate"
"Mah-Jongg"—originally used (cut) in **SWEET LITTLE DEVIL**
    [**January 21, 1924**]
"Night Time In Araby"
"Rose Of Madrid"
"Somebody Loves Me" (lyric by DeSylva and Ballard MacDonald)
"Tune In To Station J.O.Y."
"Year After Year"

With increasing fame and more lucrative offers, Gershwin made this edition of the **SCANDALS** his final revue; his work for the series had never been more than adequate, with "Somebody Loves Me" only his second song hit in five scores. Gershwin began to concentrate on contemporary musical comedy—although some of the properties chosen were to be exceedingly thin.

PRIMROSE
*September 11, 1924   Winter Garden Theatre ⟨London⟩
225 performances*

Lyrics mostly by Desmond Carter
Book by George Grossmith and Guy Bolton
Directed by Charles A. Maynard
Produced by Grossmith and J.A.E. Malone
With Heather Thatcher and Leslie Henson

Published songs:

"Boy Wanted" (lyric by Ira Gershwin and Carter)—revised lyric for song of same name from **A DANGEROUS MAID [March 21, 1921]**
"The Country Side (This Is The Life For A Man)"
"Isn't It Wonderful" (lyric by Ira Gershwin and Carter)
"Naughty Baby" (lyric by Ira Gershwin and Carter)
"Some Far-Away Someone" (lyric by Ira Gershwin and B. G. DeSylva)—new Gershwin lyric for "At Half Past Seven" from **NIFTIES OF 1923 [September 25, 1923]**
"That New-Fangled Mother Of Mine"
"Wait A Bit, Susie" (lyric by Ira Gershwin and Carter)—see **ROSALIE [January 10, 1928]**

Additional songs published in vocal score:

"Beau Brummel"
"Berkeley Square And Kew"
"Can We Do Anything?" (lyric by Ira Gershwin and Carter)
"Four Sirens" (lyric by Ira Gershwin)
"I Make Hay While The Moon Shines"
"It Is The Fourteenth Of July"
"Leaving Town While We May"
"The Mophams"
"Roses of France"
"Till I Meet Someone Like You"
"When Toby Is Out Of Town"

Additional song recorded:

"Isn't It Terrible What They Did To Mary Queen Of Scots?"

Gershwin was already extremely popular in England. **PRIMROSE** was the first of a string of Gershwin musicals (the others being remountings of New York work) to achieve great success in London. Ira began writing under his own name. For the sake of clarity, "lyric by Ira" will be used in some cases hereafter.

LADY, BE GOOD!
December 1, 1924   Liberty Theatre   330 performances

Lyrics by Ira Gershwin
Book by Guy Bolton and Fred Thompson
Directed by Felix Edwardes
Produced by Alex A. Aarons and Vinton Freedley
With Fred and Adele Astaire, Walter Catlett, and Cliff Edwards

Published songs:

"Fascinating Rhythm"
"The Half Of It, Dearie, Blues"
"Hang On To Me"
"I'd Rather Charleston" (lyric by Desmond Carter)—written for
   London production [April 14, 1926; 326 performances]
"Little Jazz Bird"
"The Man I Love"—cut; also used in **STRIKE UP THE BAND**
   ⟨First⟩ [August 29, 1927]
"Oh, Lady Be Good"
"So Am I"
"Something About Love" (lyric by Lou Paley)—added to London
   production; originally used in **THE LADY IN RED** [May 12,
   1919]
"Swiss Miss (The Cab-Horse Trot)" (lyric by Ira and Arthur
   Jackson)—only publication (no lyric) upon use in London
   production

Aarons was joined by Vinton Freedley—who had danced in **A DAN-GEROUS MAID** [March 21, 1921] and **FOR GOODNESS SAKE** [February 20, 1922]—in a producing partnership. They commissioned this musical for the Astaires, who were returning as stars from the London production of the latter show. **LADY, BE GOOD!** was Gershwin's biggest success to date, with his fascinating rhythms, jazzy harmonies, and lively melodies (with a touch of humor) consistent throughout the score.

TELL ME MORE!
April 13, 1925   Gaiety Theatre   100 performances

Lyrics by B. G. DeSylva and Ira Gershwin
Book by Fred Thompson and William K. Wells
Directed by John Harwood
Produced by Alfred E. Aarons
With Phyllis Cleveland, Alexander Gray, and Lou Holtz
NOTE: **MY FAIR LADY**, pre-Broadway title

Published songs:

"Baby!" [1st]—new lyric for "Sweetheart, I'm So Glad That I Met You" from **THE RAINBOW [April 3, 1923]**
"Baby!" [2nd]—written for London production; revised music for lyric of "Baby!" [1st]
"Kickin' The Clouds Away"
"Murderous Monty (And Light-Fingered Jane)" (lyric by Desmond Carter)—written for London production
"My Fair Lady"
"Tell Me More"
"Three Times A Day"
"Why Do I Love You?"

Additional songs published (no lyric) in piano selections:

"Love I Never Knew"—written for London production
"Opening Chorus Act One"
"Where The Delicatessen Flows (In Sardinia)"

Alex Aarons' father Alfred (see **LA, LA LUCILLE [May 26, 1919]**) produced this tame musical, which couldn't compare with **LADY, BE GOOD! [December 1, 1924]**. But London had not yet seen the Astaire show; the British Gershwin craze made **TELL ME MORE!** a London [May 6, 1925] hit, running 263 performances. The original title was changed on the road not because they felt **MY FAIR LADY** wouldn't sell, but because audiences turned down the anticipated hit title song in favor of "Tell Me More." (Shows are occasionally renamed for songs that work well during tryouts, **OKLAHOMA! [Rodgers: March 31, 1943]** being a famous example.) There has been confusion as to the proper credits of father and son Aarons, not helped by some programs reading "Al. Aarons presents." For the record:

Alfred was responsible for giving Gershwin and Youmans their first Broadway opportunities (upon advice from his son). Alex took over **LA, LA LUCILLE** for its tour and produced **FOR GOODNESS SAKE [February 20, 1922]**, with Gershwin interpolations. Then he joined dancer Vinton Freedley to produce five George and Ira hits beginning with **LADY, BE GOOD!**

TIP-TOES
December 28, 1925   Liberty Theatre   194 performances

Lyrics by Ira Gershwin
Book by Guy Bolton and Fred Thompson
Directed by John Harwood
Produced by Alex A. Aarons and Vinton Freedley
With Queenie Smith and Allen Kearns

Published songs:

"It's A Great Little World"—cut
"Harlem River Chanty"—initial publication in 1968 nonshow
   choral arrangement
"Looking For A Boy"
"Nice Baby"
"Nightie-Night"
"Sweet And Low-Down"
"That Certain Feeling"
"These Charming People"
"When Do We Dance?"

Additional song published (no lyric) in piano selection:
"Opening Act One"

Another hit for the Gershwins, Aarons, and Freedley. Like **LADY, BE GOOD! [December 1, 1924]** and **OH, KAY! [November 8, 1926]**, **TIP-TOES** had a mindless but fast-paced book coauthored by Guy Bolton—as well as "Sweet And Low-Down" and "That Certain Feeling." During the tryout, Gershwin's "Concerto In F" premiered at Carnegie Hall on December 3, 1925.

SONG OF THE FLAME
December 30, 1925   44th Street Theatre   219 performances

Music by George Gershwin and Herbert Stothart
Book and lyrics by Otto Harbach and Oscar Hammerstein 2nd

Directed by Frank Reicher
Produced by Arthur Hammerstein
With Tessa Kosta and Guy Robertson

Published songs:

"Cossack Love Song"
"Midnight Bells" (music by Gershwin only)
"The Signal" (music by Gershwin only)
"Song Of The Flame"
"Vodka"
"You Are You"—cut

Additional song published (no lyric) in piano selection:

"Tartar"

Arthur Hammerstein had met continued success teaming major composers with his house staff of Stothart, Harbach, and nephew Hammerstein for operettas (including **WILDFLOWER [Youmans: February 7, 1923]** and ROSE-MARIE [Friml: September 2, 1924]). Gershwin was chosen for this Russian operetta, which opened just two days after **TIP-TOES [December 28, 1925]**. The result was successful but pedestrian.

AMERICANA
First Edition
July 26, 1926   Belmont Theatre   224 performances

Music mostly by Con Conrad and Henry Souvaine
Book by J. P. McEvoy
Directed by Allan Dinehart
Produced by Richard Herndon
With Lew Brice and Roy Atwell

Published song:

"That Lost Barber Shop Chord" (lyric by Ira Gershwin)

OH, KAY!
November 8, 1926   Imperial Theatre   256 performances

Lyrics by Ira Gershwin
Book by Guy Bolton and P. G. Wodehouse
Directed by John Harwood

Produced by Alex A. Aarons and Vinton Freedley
With Gertrude Lawrence, Oscar Shaw, and Victor Moore

Published songs:

"Clap Yo' Hands"
"Dear Little Girl"—initial publication upon reuse in 1968 movie
 Star
"Do-Do-Do"
"Fidgety Feet"
"Heaven On Earth" (lyric by Ira and Howard Dietz)—see
 ROSALIE [January 10, 1928]
"Maybe"
"Oh, Kay" (lyric by Ira and Dietz)
"Show Me The Town"—cut; also used in **ROSALIE**
"Someone To Watch Over Me"

Additional songs published in vocal selection:

"Bride And Groom"
"Don't Ask"
"A Woman's Touch"

Gertrude Lawrence had conquered New York with Beatrice Lillie and
Jack Buchanan in CHARLOT'S REVUE [January 9, 1924]; with **OH,
KAY!** she became a star on her own, introducing "Do-Do-Do,"
"Maybe," and the unforgettable "Someone To Watch Over Me."
Comedian Victor Moore—whose last important Broadway role had
been in George M. Cohan's THE TALK OF NEW YORK [December
3, 1907]—began a profitable association with the Gershwins and
Vinton Freedley.

STRIKE UP THE BAND
The Gershwin-Kaufman Musical Play
(First Version—also see January 14, 1930)
*[August 29, 1927] Broadway Theatre ⟨Long Branch,
New Jersey⟩; closed during pre-Broadway tryout*

Lyrics by Ira Gershwin
Book by George S. Kaufman
Directed by R. H. Burnside
Produced by Edgar Selwyn
With Jimmy Savo, Morton Downey, and Edna May Oliver

Published songs:

"The Man I Love"—originally used (cut) in **LADY, BE GOOD!**
   [December 1, 1924]
"Military Dancing Drill"—also used in ⟨**Second Version**⟩
"Seventeen And Twenty-One"
"Strike Up The Band"—also used in ⟨**Second Version**⟩
"Yankee Doodle Rhythm"—also used in **ROSALIE [January 10,
   1928]**

This bitter antiwar satire met a stony reception and quickly closed
"for repairs." "The Man I Love" never made it back to Broadway,
although Marilyn Miller briefly gave it a try in **ROSALIE [January
10, 1928]**. Fortunately it found a well-deserved life of its own outside
the theatre.

FUNNY FACE
November 22, 1927   Alvin Theatre   244 performances

Lyrics by Ira Gershwin
Book by Fred Thompson and Paul Gerard Smith
Directed by Edgar MacGregor
Produced by Alex A. Aarons and Vinton Freedley
With Fred and Adele Astaire, William Kent, Victor Moore, and Allen
   Kearns
NOTE: **SMARTY**, pre-Broadway title

Published songs:

"The Babbitt And The Bromide"
"Dance Alone With You"—cut; see **ROSALIE [January 10, 1928]**
"Funny Face"
"He Loves And She Loves"
"High Hat"
"How Long Has This Been Going On?"—cut; also used in
   ROSALIE
"Let's Kiss And Make Up"
"My One And Only"—originally published as "What Am I Gonna
   Do?"
" 'S Wonderful"
"Tell The Doc"—issued in vocal arrangement; initial publication
   upon use in London production
"The World Is Mine"—cut; see **NINE-FIFTEEN REVUE
   [February 11, 1930]**

Additional song published in vocal selection:
"In The Swim"—initial publication upon reuse in 1983 production
  MY ONE AND ONLY

"Al" Aarons and "Vin" Freedley built the Alvin Theatre with profits
from their three Gershwin musicals, and determined to open it grandly
with another Astaire hit. But **SMARTY** started its pre-Broadway
tryout—immediately after the **STRIKE UP THE BAND** ⟨**First
Version**⟩ **[August 29, 1927]** debacle—with grave problems. Drastic
measures were taken as half the score was discarded, colibrettist Robert
Benchley was replaced, and Victor Moore (from the cast of **OH, KAY!**
[November 8, 1926]) was hurriedly added. The miracle was achieved,
and **FUNNY FACE** came in for a long run, followed by an even
longer run in London [November 8, 1928; 263 performances].

ROSALIE
January 10, 1928   New Amsterdam Theatre
335 performances
Music also by Sigmund Romberg
Lyrics by P. G. Wodehouse and Ira Gershwin
Lyrics to Gershwin songs by Ira Gershwin
Book by Wm. Anthony McGuire and Guy Bolton
Directed by McGuire
Produced by Florenz Ziegfeld, Jr.
With Marilyn Miller, Jack Donahue, and Frank Morgan

Published songs:
"Beautiful Gypsy"—cut; new lyric for "Wait A Bit, Susie" from
  PRIMROSE [September 11, 1924]
"Ev'rybody Knows I Love Somebody"—added after opening; new
  lyric for "Dance Alone With You" from **FUNNY FACE**
  [November 22, 1927]
"How Long Has This Been Going On?"—originally cut from
  FUNNY FACE
"Oh Gee! Oh Joy!" (lyric by Ira and Wodehouse)
"Rosalie"—cut
"Say So!" (lyric by Ira and Wodehouse)
"Show Me The Town"—originally cut from **OH, KAY!**
  [November 8, 1926]
"Yankee Doodle Rhythm"—cut; originally used in **STRIKE UP
  THE BAND** ⟨**First Version**⟩ **[August 29, 1927]**

Additional song published (no lyric) in piano selection:
"Follow The Drum"—added after opening; revised version of
  "Heaven On Earth" from **OH, KAY!**

With Marilyn Miller returning to his management after three Dillingham years (see **PETER PAN ⟨Second Version⟩ [Kern: November 6, 1924]**), Ziegfeld combined Romberg (who had three other shows that fall) and Gershwin (with two) for this modern-day fairy-tale romance. The result was nonmemorable, but successful. Miller was second only to Al Jolson in Twenties musical comedy stardom.

TREASURE GIRL
November 8, 1928   Alvin Theatre   68 performances

Lyrics by Ira Gershwin
Book by Fred Thompson and Vincent Lawrence
Directed by Bertram Harrison
Produced by Alex A. Aarons and Vinton Freedley
With Gertrude Lawrence, Paul Frawley, and Walter Catlett

Published songs:
"Feeling I'm Falling"
"Got A Rainbow"
"I Don't Think I'll Fall In Love Today"
"I've Got A Crush On You"—initial publication upon reuse in
  STRIKE UP THE BAND ⟨Second Version⟩ [January 14, 1930]
"K-ra-zy For You"
"Oh, So Nice"
"What Are We Here For?"
"Where's The Boy? Here's The Girl"

Closely copying the **OH, KAY! [November 8, 1926]** formula, this "sure thing" was a resounding failure in spite of a nice score. Gershwin's third major symphonic work, the tone poem "An American in Paris," premiered on December 13, 1928.

SHOW GIRL
July 2, 1929   Ziegfeld Theatre   111 performances
Music mostly by Gershwin (see **Youmans**)
Lyrics mostly by Gus Kahn and Ira Gershwin
Book and direction by Wm. Anthony McGuire

(Based on the novel by J. P. McEvoy)
Produced by Florenz Ziegfeld, Jr.
With Ruby Keeler Jolson and Clayton, Jackson, and Durante

Published songs:

"Do What You Do!"
"Feeling Sentimental"—cut
"Harlem Serenade"
"I Must Be Home By Twelve O'Clock"
"Liza (All The Clouds'll Roll Away)"
"So Are You! (The Rose Is Red—Violets Are Blue)"

Virtually all the great stage performers of the Twenties—Miller, Cantor, Williams, Fields, Rogers, Brice—starred for Ziegfeld. The sole exception was Jolson, who had been discovered by the Shuberts and stayed with them (as long as they paid him regally). So Ziegfeld decided to make a star out of Jolson's new wife, nineteen-year-old Ruby Keeler. He didn't succeed; **SHOW GIRL** was poor, and if there had been a "Ziegfeld touch" it was by now lost. But he did manage to finally get hold of Jolson, who dropped in (gratis) to serenade his bride as she descended the full-stage staircase to Gershwin's "Liza." She was, it seems, afraid of heights.

STRIKE UP THE BAND
⟨*Second Version—also see August 29, 1927*⟩
January 14, 1930   Times Square Theatre
191 performances

Lyrics by Ira Gershwin
Book by Morrie Ryskind
(Based on a libretto by George S. Kaufman)
Directed by Alexander Leftwich
Produced by Edgar Selwyn
With Bobby Clark and Paul McCullough

Published songs:

"Hangin' Around With You"
"I Mean To Say"
"I Want To Be A War Bride"
"I've Got A Crush On You"—originally used (unpublished) in
    TREASURE GIRL [November 8, 1928]
"Mademoiselle In New Rochelle"

"Soon"

"Strike Up The Band"—originally used in ⟨**First Version**⟩

Additional songs published in vocal score:

"Ding Dong"

"Fletcher's American Chocolate Choral Society (Opening Act One)"

"He Knows Milk"

"How About A Boy Like Me?"

"If I Became The President"

"In The Rattle Of The Battle"

"A Man Of High Degree"

"Military Dancing Drill (Opening Act Two)"—originally used
   (with different verse) in ⟨**First Version**⟩

"Official Resume (First There Was Fletcher)"

"Soldiers' March"

"This Could Go On For Years"

"Three Cheers For The Union!"

"A Typical Self-Made American"

"The Unofficial Spokesman"

Kaufman was unable to solve the problems discovered during the 1927 tryout; he agreed to let Ryskind (with whom he'd scripted the Marx Brothers' ANIMAL CRACKERS [October 23, 1928]) come in to write a new book. Ryskind toned down the bitterness of the satire, changing the source of the plot's international dispute from bad cheese to grade-B chocolate, and post–stock market crash audiences seemed more receptive. With a new cast and heavily revised score, **STRIKE UP THE BAND** was the first hit of the Thirties. More importantly, the Gershwins, Kaufman, and Ryskind were pointed in a new musical theatre direction.

NINE-FIFTEEN REVUE
February 11, 1930   George M. Cohan Theatre
7 performances

Music mostly by others (see **Arlen**)
Lyric to Gershwin song by Ira Gershwin
Directed by Alexander Leftwich
Produced by Ruth Selwyn
With Ruth Etting

Published song:

"Toddlin' Along"—published (cut) only as from **FUNNY FACE**
  [**November 22, 1927**] with original title "The World Is Mine"

GIRL CRAZY
October 14, 1930   Alvin Theatre   272 performances

Lyrics by Ira Gershwin
Book by Guy Bolton and John McGowan
Directed by Alexander Leftwich
Produced by Alex A. Aarons and Vinton Freedley
With Ginger Rogers, Allen Kearns, Willie Howard, Ethel Merman, and
  William Kent

Published songs:

"Bidin' My Time"
"Boy! What Love Has Done To Me!"
"But Not For Me"
"Could You Use Me?"
"Embraceable You"
"I Got Rhythm"
"Sam And Delilah"
"Treat Me Rough!"—initial publication upon reuse in 1943 movie
  version
"You've Got What Gets Me"—written for 1932 movie version

Additional songs published in vocal score:

"Barbary Coast"
"Broncho Busters"
"Goldfarb, That's I'm"
"Land Of The Gay Caballero"
"The Lonesome Cowboy"
"When It's Cactus Time In Arizona"

The last of the great Gershwin/Aarons and Freedley hits, enhanced
by the strong score and stronger singing voice of Ethel Merman (on
"I Got Rhythm" and "Sam And Delilah"). Ginger Rogers, in her
second and final Broadway musical, introduced "But Not For Me"
and "Embraceable You." When help was needed to stage the dance
for the latter song, Gershwin/Aarons and Freedley alumnus Fred Astaire stopped by to show Ginger what to do.

OF THEE I SING
December 26, 1931   Music Box Theatre   441 performances

Lyrics by Ira Gershwin
Book by George S. Kaufman and Morrie Ryskind
Directed by Kaufman
Produced by Sam H. Harris
With William Gaxton, Lois Moran, and Victor Moore

Published songs:

"Because, Because"
"The Illegitimate Daughter"
"Love Is Sweeping The Country"
"Of Thee I Sing"
"Who Cares?"
"Wintergreen For President"—initial publication upon revival
  [May 5, 1952; 72 performances]

Additional songs published in vocal score:

"The Dimple On My Knee"
"Garçon, S'il Vous Plait"
"Hello, Good Morning"
"I Was The Most Beautiful Blossom"
"Jilted, Jilted!"
"A Kiss For Cinderella"
"Never Was There A Girl So Fair"
"On That Matter No One Budges"
"Prosperity Is Just Around The Corner"
"The Senatorial Roll Call"
"Some Girls Can Bake A Pie (Corn Muffins)"
"Trumpeter, Blow Your Golden Horn!"
"Who Is The Lucky Girl To Be?"

Having forged new ground in musical satire with **STRIKE UP THE BAND** ⟨Second Version⟩ **[January 14, 1930]**, Kaufman and Ryskind joined the Gershwins on this epochal piece of musical theatre. Being the first election year of the Depression, the choice target for satire was the Presidency. The score was remarkably cohesive, with the brothers working in extended musical scenes of rhymed dialogue as opposed to songs. Ira—at his very best—paid tribute to his idol, supreme social satirist W. S. Gilbert. All elements combined to make **OF THEE I SING** the most important musical of its time and the first to win the Pulitzer Prize (which went to the librettists and Ira—but not George). Kaufman made his musical directing debut. Several months after the opening he sent his famous telegram to star William Gaxton: "Watching show from back of house stop wish you were here."

PARDON MY ENGLISH
January 20, 1933   Majestic Theatre   46 performances

Lyrics by Ira Gershwin
Book by Herbert Fields
Directed by Vinton Freedley
Produced by Alex A. Aarons and Freedley
With Jack Pearl, Lyda Roberti, and George Givot

Published songs:

"Isn't It A Pity?"
"I've Got To Be There"
"The Lorelei"
"The Luckiest Man In The World"
"My Cousin In Milwaukee"
"So What?"
"Tonight"—initial publication as 1971 nonshow instrumental,
   retitled "Two Waltzes In C"
"Where You Go, I Go"

A disaster produced by the financially desperate Aarons and Freedley, who had already lost their Alvin Theatre. **PARDON MY ENGLISH**'s tryout troubles saw the departure of star Jack Buchanan and colibrettist Morrie Ryskind. Gershwin, busy with concert works, provided "My Cousin In Milwaukee" and the lovely "Isn't It A Pity." As for the producers, Aarons never recovered from his bankruptcy; Freedley, though, rebounded with some of the biggest hits of the next ten years—starting with **ANYTHING GOES [Porter: November 21, 1934]**.

LET 'EM EAT CAKE
October 21, 1933   Imperial Theatre   90 performances

Lyrics by Ira Gershwin
Book by George S. Kaufman and Morrie Ryskind
Directed by Kaufman

Produced by Sam H. Harris
With William Gaxton, Lois Moran, and Victor Moore

Published songs:

"Blue, Blue, Blue"
"Let 'Em Eat Cake"
"Mine"
"On And On And On"
"Union Square"

Additional song recorded:

"Comes The Revolution"

This eagerly awaited sequel to **OF THEE I SING [December 26, 1931]** proved a great disappointment. More bitter than comic, the satire was forced; by the time the authors realized the fundamental creative problems, it was too late to cancel the production. Ironically, the **LET 'EM EAT CAKE** score contains some of the best and most intricate work of the Gershwins. The beautifully chromatic "Comes The Revolution" and "Blue, Blue, Blue," along with the rest, have regrettably all but disappeared.

PORGY AND BESS
October 10, 1935   Alvin Theatre   124 performances

Lyrics by DuBose Heyward and Ira Gershwin
Libretto by DuBose Heyward
(Based on *Porgy* [novel] by DuBose Heyward and [play] by DuBose and
    Dorothy Heyward)
Directed by Rouben Mamoulian
Produced by The Theatre Guild
With Todd Duncan, Anne Brown, John W. Bubbles, and Warren
    Coleman

Published songs:

"Bess, You Is My Woman Now"
"I Got Plenty O' Nuttin' "
"I Loves You Porgy"—initial publication upon use in 1959 movie
    version
"It Ain't Necessarily So" (lyric by Ira)
"My Man's Gone Now" (lyric by Heyward)
"Oh Bess, Oh Where's My Bess?" (lyric by Ira)
"Summertime" (lyric by Heyward)

"There's A Boat Dat's Leavin' Soon For New York" (lyric by Ira)
"A Woman Is A Sometime Thing" (lyric by Heyward)

Additional songs published in vocal score:

"Buzzard Song" (lyric by Heyward)—cut
"Clara, Clara" (lyric by Heyward)
"Crap Game" (lyric by Heyward)
"Gone, Gone, Gone" (lyric by Heyward)
"I Ain't Got No Shame" (lyric by Ira)
"It Takes A Long Pull To Get There" (lyric by Heyward)
"Lawyer Frazier Scene" (lyric by Heyward)
"Leavin' Fo' De Promise' Lan' " (lyric by Heyward)
"Oh De Lawd Shake De Heavens" (lyric by Heyward)
"Oh, Doctor Jesus" (lyric by Heyward)
"Oh, I Can't Sit Down" (lyric by Ira)
"Oh Lawd, I'm On My Way" (lyric by Heyward)
"Overflow" (lyric by Heyward)
"A Red Headed Woman" (lyric by Ira)
"Storm Prayers" (lyric by Heyward)
"Street Cries" (lyric by Heyward)
"They Pass By Singin' " (lyric by Heyward)
"What You Want Wid Bess?" (lyric by Heyward)

Gershwin was interested in *Porgy* upon its publication in 1926, but the Theatre Guild play version was already underway. Over the years, Gershwin had experimented on near-operatic theatre pieces, including "Blue Monday" (see **GEORGE WHITE'S SCANDALS ⟨Fourth⟩ [August 28, 1922]**) and a proposed version of *The Dybbuk* for the Metropolitan Opera. When *Porgy* finally became available, Gershwin was ready. Mamoulian, director of the play version, made a remarkable musical debut. Demanding an exacting control over all production elements, his strong theatricality and sense of movement took Broadway in new directions—as did his next musical, **OKLAHOMA! [Rodgers: March 31, 1943]**. The initial commercial failure of **PORGY AND BESS** was due partially to the overuse of operatic conventions. The piece has been continually successful since Cheryl Crawford's revival [January 22, 1942; 286 performances], which cut the recitatives and presented the piece as more of a book musical.

THE SHOW IS ON
December 25, 1936   Winter Garden Theatre
237 performances

Music mostly by Vernon **Duke** (also see **Arlen, Rodgers,** and **Schwartz**)
Lyric to Gershwin song by Ira Gershwin
Sketches mostly by David Freedman and Moss Hart
Directed by Vincente Minnelli
Produced by Lee Shubert
With Beatrice Lillie and Bert Lahr

Published song:

"By Strauss"

Gershwin contributed his final theatre song to this revue devised by
his close friend Vernon Duke. Following **PORGY AND BESS [Oc-
tober 10, 1935],** Gershwin moved to Hollywood. After writing two
complete film scores for Fred Astaire, Gershwin suddenly fell ill. A
brain tumor was finally diagnosed, but it was too late. George Gershwin died on July 11, 1937 in Beverly Hills. He was thirty-eight years
old.

LET ME HEAR THE MELODY
*[March 9, 1951]   Playhouse Theatre ⟨Wilmington,
Delaware⟩; closed during pre-Broadway tryout*

Play by S. N. Behrman
Incidental music by George Gershwin
Lyric by Ira Gershwin
Directed by Burgess Meredith
Produced by Harold Clurman and Walter Fried
With Melvyn Douglas, Anthony Quinn, Mike Kellin, and Morris
  Carnovsky

Published song:

"Hi-Ho!"—initial publication as 1967 nonshow song

LET ME HEAR THE MELODY, about a songwriter in Hollywood, made use of a considerable amount of Gershwin material. The
jaunty "Hi-Ho!" was the only never-before-heard song; it had been
written for (but unused in) the 1937 Fred Astaire movie *Shall We
Dance.*

George Gershwin brought jazz-influenced rhythms and colors into the
musical theatre, a significant and far-reaching contribution. However, his total output (over a far too brief career) must be judged ad-

mirable but disappointing. Many of the songs remain very good; but practically all of Gershwin's scores were little more than nondramatic song collections. He did attempt two important experiments, resulting in a pair of landmark musicals. For **OF THEE I SING [December 26, 1931],** Gershwin provided an effective setting for Broadway's best political satire; but the dazzling work came from Ira and the librettists. **PORGY AND BESS [October 10, 1935]** stands far above all of Gershwin's other work. He was for once free of his characteristic dependence on strong rhythms and harmonies, seemingly influenced by the soaring melodies and improvisatory style of his protégé Harold Arlen. "Summertime" is unquestionably Gershwin; but the pure, melodic freeness just doesn't exist in his other work. George Gershwin has inspired and attracted more composers, musicians, enthusiasts, etc. than any composer of our time. But with familiarity and increased exposure to Arlen, Youmans, Duke, and Weill, Gershwin love diminishes to Gershwin respect. But Gershwin respect never diminishes.

Vincent Youmans

BORN: September 27, 1898   New York, New York
DIED: April 5, 1946   Denver, Colorado

Vincent Youmans was born the day after George Gershwin. Both played an important part in developing the new 1920s musical comedy, both tried to move into more serious theatre work, and both were struck by fatal illness in their mid-thirties. Unlike Gershwin, Youmans was born on the right side of the New York City tracks. His father, a prosperous hat manufacturer, moved the family to upper-class Larchmont, New York. After wartime Navy service, Youmans became a song plugger at Remick's—where civilian Gershwin had started three years earlier—and wrote his first published song, the 1920 "Country Cousin" (lyric by Alfred Bryan). Youmans moved on to play rehearsal piano for Victor Herbert's 1920 out-of-town failure OUI MADAME, produced by Alfred E. Aarons. Aarons had intended Herbert for his previous musical, but son-and-associate Alex convinced him to gamble on novice Gershwin (see **LA, LA LU-CILLE [Gershwin: May 26, 1919]**). Youmans was to be next. Meanwhile, the ever-alert-for-talent Max Dreyfus signed Youmans at the same time Richard Rodgers was told "come back in a few years." Unlike Gershwin, Rodgers, and Kern, Youmans was established with a Broadway success within the year.

PICCADILLY TO BROADWAY
All Anglo-American Musical Review
[September 27, 1920]   Globe Theatre ⟨Atlantic City, New Jeresy⟩; closed during pre-Broadway tour

Music also by William Daly, George **Gershwin,** and others
Sketches and lyrics mostly by Glen MacDonough and E. Ray Goetz
Lyrics to Youmans songs by Arthur Francis [Ira Gershwin]
Directed by George Marion and Julian Alfred

Produced by Goetz
With Johnny Dooley, Anna Wheaton, Clifton Webb, and Helen Broderick

Published song:

"Who's Who With You?"—initial publication upon reuse in **TWO LITTLE GIRLS IN BLUE [May 3, 1921]**

Max Dreyfus placed interpolations by his two young composers into this thrown-together revue. Youmans was paired with Gershwin's lyric-writing older brother Ira, already briefly heard on Broadway (using the pseudonym Arthur Francis). After the **PICCADILLY TO BROADWAY** failure, Dreyfus held the two Youmans/Francis songs—the playfully catchy "Who's Who With You?" and "Now That We're Mr. And Mrs." (unpublished)—as bait while scouting another opportunity.

TWO LITTLE GIRLS IN BLUE
May 3, 1921   George M. Cohan Theatre
135 performances

Music also by Paul Lannin
Lyrics mostly by Arthur Francis [Ira Gershwin]
Book by Fred Jackson
Directed by Ned Wayburn
Produced by A. L. Erlanger
With The Fairbanks Twins (Madeline and Marion) and Oscar Shaw

Published songs:

"Dolly" (lyric by Francis and Schuyler Greene)
"Oh Me! Oh My!"
"Orienta" (lyric by Irving Caesar and Greene)
"Rice and Shoes" (lyric by Francis and Greene)
"Who's Who With You?"—originally used (unpublished) in **PICCADILLY TO BROADWAY [September 27, 1920]**
"You Started Something"—see **NO, NO, NANETTE [September 16, 1925]**

Producer Alfred Aarons, having done fairly well with **LA, LA LU-CILLE [Gershwin: May 26, 1919]**, offered the composer his next show. Gershwin, already contracted for two complete scores, turned it down but recommended his brother and Youmans for the job. Max Dreyfus sold the team on the strength of the **PICCADILLY TO**

BROADWAY [September 27, 1920] songs. Prior to the tryout, tyrannical theatre-czar A. L. Erlanger took over the production. Aarons was Erlanger's general manager, and it's probable that Aarons' shows were actually owned by A. L. (for Abraham Lincoln, of course). Youmans and Ira contributed the better portion of the score and came up with a moderate success—far more popular than **LA, LA LUCILLE**—and two hit songs, the adequate if undistinguished "Oh Me! Oh My!" and "Dolly."

WILDFLOWER
February 7, 1923   Casino Theatre   477 performances

Music also by Herbert Stothart
Book and lyrics by Otto Harbach and Oscar Hammerstein 2nd
Directed by Oscar Eagle
Produced by Arthur Hammerstein
With Edith Day and Guy Robertson
NOTE: All songs issued as by Youmans and Stothart although written separately. The above were Youmans' actual contributions.

Published songs:

"Bambalina"
"I Can Always Find Another Partner"
"If I Told You"—cut
"I Love You I Love You I Love You"
"Wildflower"
"You Never Can Blame A Girl For Dreaming"—added after
  opening

Additional songs published in vocal score:

"The Chase (Opening Act II)" (probably by Youmans)
"Come Let's Dance Through The Night" (probably by Stothart)
" 'Course I Will" (probably by Youmans)

The competent but unoriginal Stothart had collaborated with Harbach, Hammerstein, and Hammerstein on four competent but unoriginal musicals since 1920. The producer decided to bring in a more inventive cocomposer, resulting in the first of several immensely successful operettas. Broadway discovered Youmans' unconventional rhythmic style in "Bambalina," a top song hit of the early Twenties; the less dynamic "Wildflower" was also enormously popular. For several seasons Gershwin had been intriguing Broadway audiences, but the long-running **WILDFLOWER** established Youmans as the leader of the new breed of composers. Otto Harbach had collaborated with Rudolf Friml on several hit operettas, including Arthur Hammerstein's first production THE FIREFLY [December 2, 1912]. Oscar Greeley Clendenning Hammerstein 2nd—for that was his name—began with his uncle as a stage manager in 1917; Arthur produced Oscar's first play in 1919 (it closed out of town). Then the veteran and the novice lyricist/librettist joined together and began to explore a new musical theatre form.

HAMMERSTEIN'S NINE O'CLOCK REVUE
October 4, 1923   Century Roof Theatre   12 performances
Music and lyrics mostly by Harold Simpson and Morris Harvey
Produced by Arthur Hammerstein

Published song:

"Flannel Petticoat Girl" (lyric by Oscar Hammerstein 2nd and Wm. Cary Duncan)—initial publication upon reuse in **MARY JANE McKANE [December 25, 1923]**

MARY JANE McKANE
December 25, 1923   Imperial Theatre   151 performances
Music also by Herbert Stothart
Book and lyrics by Oscar Hammerstein 2nd and Wm. Cary Duncan
Directed by Alonzo Price
Produced by Arthur Hammerstein
With Mary Hay and Hal Skelly

Published songs:

"Come On And Pet Me"—see **A NIGHT OUT [September 7, 1925]**

"Flannel Petticoat Girl"—originally used (unpublished) in **HAMMERSTEIN'S NINE O'CLOCK REVUE [October 4, 1923]**

"My Boy And I"—see **NO, NO, NANETTE [September 16, 1925]**

"Toodle-Oo"

This moderate success opened the new Imperial Theatre. Youmans began to constantly revise songs and reuse them in future shows. While a standard practice of the day, Youmans came up with a noticeably high proportion of hits in this manner.

LOLLIPOP
January 21, 1924   Knickerbocker Theatre
152 performances

Book and lyrics by Zelda Sears
Directed by Ira Hards
Produced by Henry W. Savage
With Ada May (Weeks), Harry Puck, and Sears
NOTE: **THE LEFT OVER,** pre-Broadway title

Published songs:

"Deep In My Heart"
"Going Rowing"
"Honey-Bun"
"It Must Be Love"—cut; see **A NIGHT OUT [September 7, 1925]**
"Take A Little One-Step"
"Tie A String Around Your Finger"

Additional songs published (no lyric) in piano selection:
"Orphan Girl"
"Spanish"

An old-fashioned, mediocre musical, **LOLLIPOP** drew on family trade for a moderately successful run.

CHARLOT'S REVUE
September 23, 1924   Prince Of Wales's Theatre ⟨London⟩
518 performances

Music mostly by others
Book by Ronald Jeans
Produced by André Charlot

Published song:
"That Forgotten Melody" (lyric by Douglas Furber)

A NIGHT OUT
[September 7, 1925]   Garrick Theatre ⟨Philadelphia, Pennsylvania⟩; closed during pre-Broadway tryout

Lyrics mostly by Clifford Grey and Irving Caesar
Book by George Grossmith and Arthur Miller

(Based on the British musical by Willie Redstone, Grossmith, and Miller
  [see **Porter: September 18, 1920**])
Directed by Thomas Reynolds
Produced by Alfred E. Aarons in association with Edward Laurillard

Published songs:

"I Want A Yes Man" (lyric by Grey, Caesar, and Ira Gershwin)
"Kissing"—revised version of "It Must Be Love" from
  LOLLIPOP [January 21, 1924]
"Like A Bird On The Wing"
"Sometimes I'm Happy" (lyric by Caesar)—revised version of
  "Come On And Pet Me" from **MARY JANE McKANE
  [December 25, 1923]**; also used in **HIT THE DECK [April 25,
  1927]**

In 1924 Youmans had his greatest success, with two of Broadway's
biggest song hits ever; but a prolonged tryout kept **NO, NO, NA-
NETTE [September 16, 1925]** from New York for a while. **A
NIGHT OUT** added an American score to a British book and died
aborning. It was produced by Alfred Aarons, who had discovered both
Gershwin and Youmans. Son Alex had his first major Broadway hit
in **LADY, BE GOOD! [Gershwin: December 1, 1924]**; Alfred produced 1925 flops by both composers. Ira, now collaborating full-time
with brother George, received colyricist credit for "I Want A Yes
Man." This was a leftover reworked from the unused Youmans-Ar-
thur Francis "Robbing Your Father" (probably intended for **TWO
LITTLE GIRLS IN BLUE [May 3, 1921]**). Neither Ira nor Arthur
was consulted or even aware of the new use until after **A NIGHT
OUT** closed. The genial Ira Gershwin was a hard man to alienate,
but Youmans managed to do it.

NO, NO, NANETTE
September 16, 1925   Globe Theatre   321 performances

Lyrics mostly by Irving Caesar
Book by Otto Harbach and Frank Mandel
(Based on *My Lady Friends* [play] by Emil Nyitray and Mandel)
Produced and directed by H. H. Frazee
With Louise Groody, Charles Winninger, and Georgia O'Ramey

Published songs:

"The Boy Next Door" (lyric by Schuyler Greene and Harbach)—
  cut

"I Don't Want A Girlie" (lyric by B. G. DeSylva)—cut
"I Want To Be Happy"
"I've Confessed To The Breeze" (lyric by Harbach)—cut
"No, No, Nanette!" (lyric by Harbach)—revised version of "My
   Boy And I" from **MARY JANE McKANE [December 25, 1923]**
"Santa Claus" (lyric by Harbach)—cut
"Tea For Two"
"Too Many Rings Around Rosie"
" 'Where Has My Hubby Gone?' Blues"
"You Can Dance With Any Girl At All"

Additional songs published in British vocal score:

"Call Of The Sea"
"Fight Over Me"
"Flappers Are We (Opening Act I)"
"Peach On The Beach" (lyric by Harbach)
"Telephone Girlie" (lyric by Harbach)
"Waiting For You"—new lyric for "You Started Something" from
   TWO LITTLE GIRLS IN BLUE [May 3, 1921]
"We're All Of Us Excited (Finale Act II)"
"When You're Sad"

NO, NO, NANETTE played a short tryout in Detroit [beginning
April 23, 1924] before moving on to phenomenal success in Chicago.
Nevertheless, the show underwent major changes: Irving Caesar was
brought in to replace half of Harbach's lyrics, and producer Harry
Frazee—best known as the man who sold Babe Ruth (he owned the
Boston Red Sox)—fired director Edward Royce after all the work was
done and took credit himself. By the time **NANETTE** reached
Broadway there were two road companies, plus a London production
[March 11, 1925], which ran an unprecedented 665 performances. As
in **WILDFLOWER [February 7, 1923],** Youmans provided two smash
hit songs, "Tea For Two" and "I Want To Be Happy." A stylish
Broadway revival (May 16, 1973) played 861 performances.

OH, PLEASE!
December 17, 1926   Fulton Theatre   75 performances

Lyrics by Anne Caldwell
Book by Otto Harbach and Caldwell
(Based on a play by Maurice Hennequin and Pierre Veber)

Directed by Hassard Short
Produced by Charles Dillingham
With Beatrice Lillie, Charles Winninger, and Charles Purcell

Published songs:

"I Know That You Know"
"I'm Waiting For A Wonderful Girl"
"Like He Loves Me"
"Nicodemus"

Having taken New York by storm in CHARLOT'S REVUE [January 29, 1924], Beatrice Lillie and Gertrude Lawrence signed with New York managements Dillingham and Aarons & Freedley, respectively. While Lawrence met immediate success (see **OH, KAY! [Gershwin: November 8, 1926]**), the Canadian-born Lillie suffered from inappropriate vehicles until the Thirties revue format came into place. Youmans had a difficult time dealing with Lillie, as did Richard Rodgers on **SHE'S MY BABY [Rodgers: January 3, 1928]**. Both of Youmans' future wives, incidentally, were in the **OH, PLEASE!** chorus.

HIT THE DECK
A Nautical Musical Comedy
April 25, 1927   Belasco Theatre   352 performances

Lyrics by Leo Robin and Clifford Grey
Book by Herbert Fields
(Based on *Shore Leave* [play] by Hubert Osborne)
Directed by Alexander Leftwich
Produced by Vincent Youmans
With Louise Groody, Charles King, and Stella Mayhew

Published songs:

"Armful Of You"—cut
"Hallelujah!"—revised version of a 1918 march (unpublished)
    written for John Philip Sousa's U.S. Navy Band
"Harbor Of My Heart"
"Join The Navy!"
"Keepin' Myself For You" (lyric by Sidney Clare)—written for
    1929 movie version
"Loo-Loo"
"Lucky Bird"

"Nothing Could Be Sweeter"—cut; see "Why, Oh Why?"
"Sometimes I'm Happy" (lyric by Irving Caesar)—see **A NIGHT
   OUT [September 7, 1925]**
"Why, Oh Why?"—new lyric for "Nothing Could Be Sweeter"

Having suffered from several indifferently mounted productions—and
having seen the financial returns generated by his mother's substantial investment in **NO, NO, NANETTE [September 16, 1925]**—
Youmans resolved to present his own shows. For experienced advice,
librettist Herb Fields' father Lew was invited to coproduce **HIT THE
DECK;** Youmans bought him out immediately after the opening. This
enormously successful producing debut proved to be the disastrous
turning point in Youmans' career: still to write his greatest songs,
HIT THE DECK was his last successful production. Always with
an eye on Gershwin, Youmans—with new hits "Sometimes I'm
Happy" and "Hallelujah!"—was still ahead. But "Rhapsody In Blue"
had startled the musical world in 1924, and Gershwin was composing
a string of popular hits; Richard Rodgers burst on the scene in 1925;
and Kern and Berlin were still very much in evidence. Youmans felt
self-conscious as the only "real" American among this talented group
of Jewish immigrants (and sons of immigrants). Competition prodded him to move away from his reliance on catchy, rhythmic phrases
and develop his new style of soaring melodies and complexly colored
harmonies, initially heard in "Nothing Could Be Sweeter" and
"Keepin' Myself For You."

RAINBOW
November 21, 1928   Gallo Theatre   29 performances

Lyrics and direction by Oscar Hammerstein 2nd
Book by Laurence Stallings and Hammerstein
Produced by Philip Goodman
With Libby Holman, Brian Donlevy, and Charles Ruggles

Published songs:

"The Bride Was Dressed In White"—initial publication upon use
   in 1929 movie version (*Song of the West*)
"Faded Rose"—advertised but not published
"Hay, Straw"
"I Like You As You Are"
"I Look For Love"—advertised but not published

"I Want A Man"

"Let Me Give All My Love To Thee"—initial publication upon use in movie version

"My Mother Told Me Not To Trust A Soldier"—initial publication upon use in movie version

"The One Girl"

"West Wind" (lyric by J. Russell Robinson)—written for movie version

"Who Am I (That You Should Care For Me?)" (lyric by Gus Kahn)—cut

Following the enormous breakthroughs of **SHOW BOAT** [**Kern: February 27, 1927**], Hammerstein rejoined with Youmans for the ambitious **RAINBOW.** Disastrously underrehearsed, the entire premiere was a shambles (highlighted by the legendary opening-night contribution of Fanny the donkey!). Surprisingly patient critics saw the piece as a successor to **SHOW BOAT,** and hoped **RAINBOW** could run long enough to be put into shape. It didn't. The failure of **RAINBOW** sent Hammerstein—ideal collaborator for perfectionist Youmans—back to other composers and (after one last hit) thirteen years of unrelieved failure. This was a crucial loss for Youmans. Unable to sustain relationships with Ira Gershwin, Hammerstein, or Harbach, the rest of his career was spent with uninspired pop-song lyricists. The haphazard production of **RAINBOW** unquestionably killed a potentially important piece, and Youmans became even more determined to produce his own work. Unhappy and insecure with Max Dreyfus (in the company of Kern, Gershwin, Rodgers, et al.) at Harms, he also set up his own publishing company. Distrustful of everyone, Youmans took personal control of everything—and everything began to self-destruct.

SHOW GIRL
July 2, 1929   Ziegfeld Theatre   111 performances

Music mostly by George **Gershwin**

Lyrics mostly by Gus Kahn and Ira Gershwin

Book and direction by Wm. Anthony McGuire

(Based on the novel by J. P. McEvoy)

Produced by Florenz Ziegfeld, Jr.

With Ruby Keeler Jolson and Clayton, Jackson, and Durante

Published song:

"Mississippi Dry" (lyric by J. Russell Robinson)—added after
  opening

Faced with major troubles during the tryout of **GREAT DAY! [Oc-
tober 17, 1929],** Youmans arranged a badly needed cash advance from
Ziegfeld against the promise of a future musical. More as a slap in
the face to Gershwin than an improvement to the mediocre **SHOW
GIRL,** Ziegfeld requested an interpolation from Youmans—who was
to receive his own Ziegfeldian slaps in the face when **SMILES [No-
vember 18, 1930]** came along.

GREAT DAY!
A Musical Play of The Southland
October 17, 1929   Cosmopolitan Theatre   36 performances

Lyrics by William Rose and Edward Eliscu
Book by John Wells and Wm. Cary Duncan
Directed by R. H. Burnside and Frank M. Gillespie
Conceived and produced by Vincent Youmans
With Mayo Methot, Allen Prior, Lois Deppe, and Miller and Lyles

Published songs:

"Great Day!"
"Happy Because I'm In Love"
"More Than You Know"
"One Love"—cut; advertised but not published
"Open Up Your Heart"
"Without A Song"

Over a half dozen librettists and directors came and went, along with
scores of actors (Harold Arlen among the departees) as Youmans prepared his **GREAT DAY!** But the show, anonymously redubbed
"Great Delay!" retained its problems and quickly closed. Three songs
escaped the shambles and became all-time standards: the rhythmic,
spiritualistic "Great Day!"; the moving "Without A Song"; and the
first of four great Youmans ballads, "More Than You Know" (sung
by Mayo Methot, the penultimate Mrs. Humphrey Bogart). Lyricists
were Edward Eliscu, who had helped on **RAINBOW [November 21,
1928],** and Billy Rose. Publisher Youmans thought the pop songwri-

ter's name undignified for serious theatre music, hence "William"
Rose.

SMILES
November 18, 1930   Ziegfeld Theatre   63 performances

Lyrics mostly by Harold Adamson
Book and direction by Wm. Anthony McGuire
(Based on a story by Noël Coward)
Produced by Florenz Ziegfeld, Jr.
With Marilyn Miller and Fred and Adele Astaire

Published songs:

"Be Good To Me" (lyric by Ring Lardner)
"Blue Bowery"—initial publication upon reuse in **TAKE A
  CHANCE [November 26, 1932]** with new lyric "My Lover"
"Carry On, Keep Smiling"
"He Came Along"—cut; initial publication as 1965 nonshow song
"If I Were You, Love (I'd Jump Right In The Lake)" (lyric by
  Lardner)
"I'm Glad I Waited" (lyric by Adamson and Clifford Grey)
"More Than Ever"—cut; advertised but not published
"Time On My Hands" (lyric by Adamson and Mack Gordon)

Additional songs recorded:

"More Than Ever"—cut
"Say, Young Man Of Manhattan"

With three enormous stars and a typically lavish Ziegfeld production, **SMILES** was sure-fire; Ziegfeld, devastated by the stock market crash, certainly hoped so. But the material wasn't there. And
Ziegfeld, Youmans, and McGuire—leading names in Twenties musical comedy—were each on their last professional legs. Occasional-
lyricist Lardner, a close Youmans friend on a similar self-destructive
course, stepped in to help with some of his unique songwords. Youmans' consistent failures since **HIT THE DECK [April 25, 1927]**
combined with financial pressures and emotional problems to trans-
form the difficult perfectionist into an impossible-to-deal-with alco-
holic. Remarkably, his music was not affected by this. The forget-
table **SMILES** contained the unforgettable "Time On My Hands"
(which Marilyn Miller refused to sing) and the rhythmically experi-

mental but fascinating "Be Good To Me" and "Carry On, Keep Smiling."

THROUGH THE YEARS
January 28, 1932   Manhattan Theatre   20 performances

Lyrics by Edward Heyman
Book by Brian Hooker
(Based on *Smilin' Through* [play] by Allan Langdon Martin)
Directed by Edgar MacGregor
Produced by Vincent Youmans
With Natalie Hall and Charles Winninger
NOTE: **SMILING THROUGH,** pre-Broadway title

Published songs:

"Drums In My Heart"
"It's Every Girl's Ambition"
"Kathleen Mine"
"Kinda Like You"
"Through The Years"
"You're Everywhere"

Youmans once more displayed his inability to assemble the elements needed to produce a successful show: **THROUGH THE YEARS** was a much-doctored shambles. Again Youmans managed two hits— "Drums In My Heart" and one of his very best, "Through The Years." The failure took Youmans out of the producing business, and his difficult reputation made him virtually unemployable.

TAKE A CHANCE
November 26, 1932   Apollo Theatre   243 performances

Music mostly by Richard A. Whiting and "Herb Brown Nacio"
Lyrics by B. G. DeSylva
Book by DeSylva and Lawrence Schwab
Directed by Edgar MacGregor
Produced by Schwab and DeSylva
With Ethel Merman, Jack Haley, and Jack Whiting

Published songs:

"I Want To Be With You"—cut
"My Lover"—cut; new lyric for "Blue Bowery" (unpublished)
    from **SMILES [November 18, 1930]**

"Oh, How I Long To Belong To You"
"Rise 'N Shine"
"Should I Be Sweet?"
"So Do I"

When HUMPTY DUMPTY [September 12, 1932] met with disastrous pre-Broadway notices, Schwab and DeSylva decided to take a chance and totally overhaul the piece. Merman remained, while Lou Holtz and Eddie Foy, Jr. were replaced; and DeSylva took an even bigger chance by bringing Youmans in to supplement the score. **TAKE A CHANCE** turned into a hit, though Youmans' contributions (except the spiritualistic "Rise 'N Shine") were overshadowed by HUMPTY DUMPTY leftover "Eadie Was A Lady." Youmans' last great ballad, "I Want To Be With You," was cut and remains neglected to this day. Youmans left Broadway for Hollywood, where he wrote the 1933 *Flying Down to Rio* (which introduced the Astaire/Rogers team). Despite three hit songs, the composer quickly alienated himself from future movie work. Years of heavy drinking and living had resulted in a weakened physical state. Youmans contracted tuberculosis and was forced into a long, discouraging retirement at the age of thirty-four.

VINCENT YOUMANS' BALLET REVUE
[January 27, 1944]   Lyric Theatre ⟨Baltimore, Maryland⟩; closed during pre-Broadway tour

Music by Rimsky-Korsakov, Maurice Ravel, and Ernesto Lecuona
Lyrics by Maria Shelton and Gladys Shelly
Choreographed by Leonide Massine and Eugene von Groza
Directed by Eric Hatch
Produced by Vincent Youmans
With Glenn Anders, Deems Taylor, Mason Adams, and Herbert Ross

Published songs:
None

Youmans had spent the stronger periods of his illness studying composition and experimenting. During a period of remission, Youmans briefly came back into view with this curious dance program featuring music by Mexican Lecuona and others (but no Youmans!). The amateurishly assembled fiasco lasted three weeks and Youmans went

back to his sickbed. After another two years of illness, Vincent Youmans succumbed and died on April 5, 1946 in Denver, Colorado.

Vincent Youmans arrived on Broadway in the early Twenties, experimenting with the same "hot" music as the up-and-coming George
Gershwin. Early success came via **WILDFLOWER [February 7,
1923],** a mild operetta with a difference: one highly syncopated song
hit. Within two years, jazz-based dance rhythms were dominating
entire scores, with **NO, NO, NANETTE [September 16, 1925]** in
the vanguard. Then Youmans' myriad self-inflicted problems—physical, emotional, financial—began to overtake his career. His remaining projects were all hopelessly troubled and ended in failure. In the
midst of this, Youmans developed an incredibly rich melodic style
and wrote some of the most beautiful songs of the musical theatre.
And then his career was over, after just a dozen years.

Richard Rodgers

BORN: June 28, 1902   New York, New York
DIED: December 30, 1979   New York, New York

Richard Rodgers' early years were filled with show tunes: his parents were operetta enthusiasts. From the age of seven his ambition was clearly set on musical theatre. In 1916 Rodgers discovered Kern—a subway-circuit production of **VERY GOOD EDDIE [Kern: December 23, 1915]**—and began writing songs. In May of 1917, Rodgers' older brother took him to the annual Columbia Varsity Show; young Rodgers was impressed by the lyrics, so Mortimer introduced him to fraternity brother Oscar Hammerstein 2nd. The fifteen-year-old decided he was going to go to Columbia and write varsity shows (which he did). In preparation, Rodgers himself published his first song in June 1917: "Auto Show Girl" (lyric by David Dyrenforth).

ONE MINUTE PLEASE
Benefit Revue
December 29, 1917   Plaza Hotel Grand Ballroom
1 performance

Lyrics mostly by Richard C. Rodgers and Ralph G. Engelsman
Book by Engelsman
Directed by Milton Bender
Produced by Bender for The Akron Club

Published songs:

"Auto Show Girl" (lyric by David Dyrenforth)
"Whispers" (lyric by Engelsman and Rodgers)

Mortimer Rodgers was a member of the Akron Club, just then preparing a benefit for funds to send tobacco overseas. As there was no member-composer, Mortimer volunteered his brother; Richard

Rodgers was to continue writing musicals for sixty-two years. "Auto Show Girl," which had not yet created a stir, was used, as was "Whispers." Milton "Doc" Bender, a Broadway dentist, directed and produced. Bender enjoyed one of Broadway's least savory reputations. He was to become Lorenz Hart's agent, "man Friday," and all-around bad influence. Surprisingly, it was through Rodgers—who loathed Bender even more than everyone else did—that Hart first came together with his Svengali.

UP STAGE AND DOWN
Benefit Revue
March 8, 1919   Waldorf Astoria Grand Ballroom
1 performance

Lyrics mostly by Richard C. Rodgers
Book by Myron D. Rosenthal
Directed by Dr. Harry A. Goldberg
Produced by Infants Relief Society
With Phillip Leavitt, Ralph Engelsman, and Rosenthal

Published songs:

"Asiatic Angles"
"Butterfly Love"
"Love Is Not In Vain"
"Love Me By Parcel Post" (lyric by Mortimer W. Rodgers)
"Room For One More" (lyric by Oscar Hammerstein 2nd)—initial
     publication upon reuse in **FLY WITH ME [March 24, 1920]**
"Twinkling Eyes"

The Infants needed Relief, so Rodgers obliged with his second score. He also wrote most of the lyrics, with assists from his brother and Oscar Hammerstein, whose first Broadway show was about to go into rehearsal. Uncle Arthur Hammerstein presented the drama *The Light* [May 21, 1919], which went out after only four New Haven performances. **UP STAGE AND DOWN** at least made it to Broadway with a second benefit performance. Retitled TWINKLING EYES [May 18, 1919], Rodgers—and, for that matter, Hammerstein—played one performance at the 44th Street Theatre. Yet another collaborator lined up by Mortimer was theatrical lawyer Benjamin M. Kaye; the Rodgers-Kaye effort was "Prisms, Plums And Prunes" (unpublished).

A LONELY ROMEO
June 10, 1919   Shubert Theatre   87 performances

Music mostly by Malvin M. Franklin and Robert Hood Bowers
Lyrics mostly by Robert B. Smith
Book by Harry B. Smith and Lew Fields
Directed and produced by Fields
With Lew Fields

Published song:

"Any Old Place With You" (lyric by Lorenz Hart)—added after opening

Following **UP STAGE AND DOWN [March 8, 1919]**, Rodgers began looking for a full-time lyricist. Phillip Leavitt, classmate and friend of Mortimer (and actor in **UP STAGE AND DOWN**), introduced high school student Rodgers to yet another Columbia man who was looking for a composer. Would-be lyricist Lorenz Hart had made little professional headway since graduation. Hart's first contributions to the world of song were three translations for the German-language DIE TOLLE DOLLY [October 23, 1916]—including "Meyer, Your Tights Are Tight" (music by Walter Kollo). The strangely matched pair shared an admiration for the "Princess Theatre Shows" of Kern, Bolton, and Wodehouse and decided to get together for a few songs. Leavitt took songs and songwriters to his neighbor, Broadway star-producer-director Lew Fields (see **HOKEY-POKEY [Berlin: February 8, 1912]**). Fields liked "Any Old Place With You" and added it to **A LONELY ROMEO** (which had moved to the Casino Theatre) on August 26, 1919. It was Rodgers' first professionally published song.

YOU'D BE SURPRISED
An Atrocious Musical Comedy
March 6, 1920   Plaza Hotel Grand Ballroom
1 performance

Lyrics mostly by Lorenz Hart and Milton G. Bender
Book and direction by Bender
Produced by The Akron Club
With Dorothy Fields, Ralph Engelsman, and Phillip Leavitt

Published songs:

"A Breath of Springtime" (lyric by Hart)

"Mary, Queen Of Scots" (lyric by Herbert Fields)—initial
    publication upon reuse in **POOR LITTLE RITZ GIRL [July
    28, 1920]**

"Princess Of The Willow Tree" (lyric by Bender)—see **POOR
    LITTLE RITZ GIRL**

"When We Are Married" (lyric by Bender)

Broadway composer Rodgers entered Columbia in the fall of 1919 even
though he hadn't finished high school. **YOU'D BE SURPRISED** was
a second amateur show for the Akron Club. Rodgers wrote not only
with Hart (and Milton Bender) but with Lew Fields' son Herbert,
who had played a small role in **A LONELY ROMEO [June 10, 1919]**.
Herbert Fields was to become librettist to the successful Rodgers and
Hart team; during the five years of struggle before Broadway success, Herbert filled in as occasional lyricist, choreographer, whatever. **YOU'D BE SURPRISED** also made use of Lew Fields' fifteen-year-old daughter Dorothy, whom producer Rodgers eventually
hired as lyricist (see **ANNIE GET YOUR GUN [Berlin: May 16,
1946]**).

FLY WITH ME
A Futurist Musical Comedy
March 24, 1920   Hotel Astor Grand Ballroom
4 performances

Lyrics mostly by Lorenz Hart
Book by Milton Kroopf and Phillip Leavitt
Choreographed by Herbert Fields
Directed by Ralph Bunker
Produced by The Columbia University Players

Songs published in vocal score:

"Another Melody In F"

"A College On Broadway"

"Don't Love Me Like Othello"—see **POOR LITTLE RITZ GIRL
    [July 28, 1920]**

"Dreaming True"—see **POOR LITTLE RITZ GIRL**

"Gone Are The Days"

"Gunga Din"

"If You Were You"—different than "If I Were You" from **BETSY**
   [December 28, 1926]
"Inspiration"
"Peek In Pekin"—see **POOR LITTLE RITZ GIRL**
"A Penny For Your Thoughts"
"Room For One More" (lyric by Oscar Hammerstein 2nd)—initial
   publication of song originally used in **UP STAGE AND DOWN**
   [March 8, 1919]
"Working For The Government"

Additional songs recorded:

"Kid, I Love You"
"Moonlight And You"
"The Third Degree Of Love"

Freshman Rodgers was selected to write the Columbia Varsity Show
in his first year of eligibility. One of the three-judge panel which accepted **FLY WITH ME** was alumnus Hammerstein, whose first
Broadway show (ALWAYS YOU [January 5, 1920]; music by Herbert Stothart) had just closed after 66 performances. Lew Fields, father
of choreographer Herbert, attended—and hired Rodgers and Hart to
write his next show.

POOR LITTLE RITZ GIRL
July 28, 1920   Central Theatre   119 performances

Music also by Sigmund Romberg
Lyrics to Rodgers songs by Lorenz Hart
Book by George Campbell and Lew Fields
Directed by Ned Wayburn
Produced by Fields
With Charles Purcell and Lulu McConnell

Published songs:

"Boomerang"—cut; advertised but not published
"Lady Raffles Behave"—cut
"Let Me Drink In Your Eyes"—cut; advertised but not published;
   see **YOU'LL NEVER KNOW [April 20, 1921]**
"Love Will Call"
"Love's Intense In Tents"—new lyric for "Peek In Pekin" from
   FLY WITH ME [March 24, 1920]
"Mary, Queen Of Scots" (lyric by Herbert Fields)—originally used

(unpublished) in **YOU'D BE SURPRISED** [March 6, 1920]

"Will You Forgive Me?"—cut; advertised but not published; new lyric for "Princess Of The Willow Tree" from **YOU'D BE SURPRISED**; also see **YOU'LL NEVER KNOW**

"You Can't Fool Your Dreams"—new lyric for "Don't Love Me Like Othello" from **FLY WITH ME** [March 24, 1920]

POOR LITTLE RITZ GIRL tried out in Boston, where it was the opening attraction at the Wilbur Theatre. Rodgers spent the tryout period as a counselor at summer camp. Back in Boston, Fields threw out half the score and brought in Sigmund Romberg. Rodgers didn't discover this until he arrived for the Broadway opening; thereafter he paid more attention to the proper use of his work. It was to be five years before Rodgers and Hart had another Broadway musical opportunity. It might be added that Rodgers' very early work was not overwhelming. Of course, he was still only eighteen.

YOU'LL NEVER KNOW
Columbia 15th Anniversary Varsity Show
April 20, 1921   Hotel Astor Grand Ballroom
4 performances

Lyrics by Lorenz Hart
Choreographed by Herbert Fields
Directed by Oscar Hammerstein 2nd and others
Produced by Players' Club of Columbia University

Songs published in vocal score:

"Chorus Girl Blues"

"I'm Broke"

"Jumping Jack"

"Just A Little Lie"

"Let Me Drink In Your Eyes"—originally used (cut, unpublished) in **POOR LITTLE RITZ GIRL** [July 28, 1920]

"Virtue Wins The Day"

"Watch Yourself"

"When I Go On The Stage" [1st]—different than song from **SHE'S MY BABY** [January 3, 1928]

"Will You Forgive Me?"—originally used (cut, unpublished) in **POOR LITTLE RITZ GIRL**

"You'll Never Know"

"Your Lullaby"

Rodgers wrote his second consecutive Columbia Varsity Show and then left college, entering the Institute of Musical Art (Juilliard). The benefit-show career continued (with no further efforts published) while Rodgers, Hart, and Fields wrote musicals for—and were ignored by—Broadway. Meanwhile, Rodgers went on the road with Papa Fields to conduct the post-Broadway tour of **SNAPSHOTS OF 1921** **[Gershwin: June 2, 1921].**

THE MELODY MAN
May 13, 1924   Central Theatre   56 performances

Play with songs by "Herbert Richard Lorenz"
Directed by Lawrence Marston and Alexander Leftwich
Produced by Lew Fields
With Fields, Frederic Bickel (March), Eva Puck, and Sammy White
NOTE: **THE JAZZ KING,** pre-Broadway title

Published songs:

"I'd Like To Poison Ivy (Because She Clings To Me)"
"Moonlight Mama"

Unable to raise enthusiasm with any of their musicals, Herbert, Richard, and Lorenz combined to create this hackneyed comedy; not unwisely, they kept their names off it. Another year of nonproductive collaboration followed **THE MELODY MAN.** Things for the pair were bad: Hart managed a few assignments with other composers, and the discouraged Rodgers was on the verge of going into babies' underwear.

GARRICK GAIETIES
First Edition
A Bubbling Satirical Musical Revue Of Plays, Problems
and Persons
May 17, 1925   Garrick Theatre   161 performances

Music mostly by Rodgers
Lyrics mostly by Lorenz Hart
Sketches by Benjamin M. Kaye, Morrie Ryskind, and others
Choreographed by Herbert Fields
Directed by Philip Loeb
Produced by The Theatre Guild
With Sterling Holloway, Edith Meiser, Romney Brent, and June Cochrane

Published songs:

"April Fool"
"Do You Love Me? (I Wonder)"
"Manhattan"
"Old Fashioned Girl" (lyric by Edith Meiser)
"On With The Dance"
"Sentimental Me (And Romantic You)"
"The Three Musketeers"—advertised but not published

Additional song published in "Rodgers and Hart Song Book":

"Opening (Gilding The Guild)"

Benjamin Kaye, lyricist of "Prisms, Plums And Prunes" (in **UP STAGE AND DOWN [March 8, 1919]**), asked Rodgers to write another benefit, this time to raise money for drapes in the new Guild Theatre; Kaye was lawyer for the Theatre Guild. Rodgers and Hart put together a bright and inventive score, including "Manhattan" from the unproduced 1923 WINKLE TOWN. The two-performance run was such a success that the **GARRICK GAIETIES** quickly reopened. With "Manhattan" an enormous hit, Rodgers and Hart were no longer in the amateur show market.

JUNE DAYS
August 6, 1925   Astor Theatre   84 performances

Music mostly by J. Fred Coots
Lyrics mostly by Clifford Grey
Book by Cyrus Wood
(Based on *The Charm School* [**Kern: August 2, 1920**])
Directed by J. J. Shubert
Produced by Lee and J. J. Shubert

Published songs:

None

Rodgers and Hart contributed one song, "Anytime, Anywhere, Anyhow."

DEAREST ENEMY
September 18, 1925   Knickerbocker Theatre
286 performances

Lyrics by Lorenz Hart
Book by Herbert Fields

Directed by John Murray Anderson
Produced by George Ford
With Helen Ford and Charles Purcell

Published songs:

"Bye And Bye"
"Cheerio!"
"Here In My Arms"—also used in **LIDO LADY [December 1, 1926]**
"Here's A Kiss"
"Sweet Peter"

Additional songs recorded:

"The Hermits"
"I'd Like To Hide It"
"Where The Hudson River Flows"

With an established hit playing, Rodgers, Hart, and Fields were finally able to get on one of their already written musicals. Musical-comedy star Helen Ford had long been interested in **DEAREST ENEMY**; with Rodgers and Hart now bankable, Ford's husband was able to raise the money. Revue director John Murray Anderson joined in, and the result was a fresh, unpretentious hit. "Here In My Arms" joined "Manhattan" as a popular 1925 song success.

FIFTH AVENUE FOLLIES
A Revue Superb
[Circa January 1926]   Fifth Avenue Nightclub

Lyrics by Lorenz Hart
Directed by Seymour Felix
Produced by Billy Rose
With Cecil Cunningham and Bert Hanlon

Published songs:

"Maybe It's Me"—see **COCHRAN'S 1926 REVUE [April 29, 1926]** and **PEGGY-ANN [December 27, 1926]**
"Where's That Little Girl (In The Little Green Hat)"—see **LIDO LADY [December 1, 1926]**

Rose's first nightclub venture was unsuccessful and short-lived. During his early pop-lyricist days, Rose occasionally used the slightly older (and taller) Hart as ghostwriter. Was it Hart—lyricist of "I'd Love

To Poison Ivy (Because She Clings To Me)" (1923)—who first asked
"Does The Spearmint Lose Its Flavor On The Bedpost Overnight?"
(1924)? The "Green Hat" song, incidentally, was suggested by Michael Arlen's best seller, just then a hit Katharine Cornell vehicle.

THE GIRL FRIEND
March 17, 1926   Vanderbilt Theatre   409 performances

Lyrics by Lorenz Hart
Book by Herbert Fields
Directed by John Harwood
Produced by Lew Fields
With Eva Puck, Sammy White, and June Cochrane

Published songs:

"The Blue Room"
"The Girl Friend"
"Good Fellow Mine"
"Sleepyhead"—cut; also used in **GARRICK GAIETIES** ⟨**Second
   Edition**⟩ **[May 10, 1926]**
"Why Do I?"

Additional songs published (no lyric) in piano selection:

"Look For The Damsel"
"What Is It?"

1926 was a time when Broadway gladly accepted musicals about six-
day bicycle races and such. This second hit firmly established the
Rodgers, Hart, and Fields team, with Lew Fields once again producing. **THE GIRL FRIEND** was written for husband-and-wife dance
team Puck and White, who had been featured in **THE MELODY
MAN [May 13, 1924]**. Their biggest success came as "Frank and
Ellie," the husband-and-wife dance team in **SHOW BOAT [Kern:
December 27, 1927]**. "The Blue Room" was yet another big song
hit; the superb "Sleepyhead" wasn't.

COCHRAN'S 1926 REVUE
April 29, 1926   London Pavilion ⟨London⟩
149 performances

Music mostly by others
Book by Ronald Jeans
Produced by Charles B. Cochran

Published song:

"I'm Crazy 'bout The Charleston" (lyric by Donovan Parsons)—
new lyric for "Maybe It's Me" from **FIFTH AVENUE
FOLLIES [Circa January 1926]** and **PEGGY-ANN [December
27, 1926]**

In an era where song revisions and reuses were not exactly uncommon practice, "Maybe It's Me" stands out. It was initially performed and published in January 1926. When reused in London with a non-Hart lyric, the published sheet also included a second Hart version of the first lyric. In December a *third* Hart version of "Maybe It's Me" appeared. All four were similarly unsuccessful.

GARRICK GAIETIES
Second Edition
May 10, 1926   Garrick Theatre   174 performances

Music mostly by Rodgers
Lyrics mostly by Lorenz Hart
Sketches by Herbert Fields, Benjamin M. Kaye, and others
Choreographed by Fields
Directed by Philip Loeb
Produced by The Theatre Guild
With Sterling Holloway, Romney Brent, Edith Meiser, and Betty
  Starbuck

Published songs:

"Keys To Heaven"
"A Little Souvenir"
"Mountain Greenery"
"Queen Elizabeth"
"Sleepyhead"—originally used (cut) in **THE GIRL FRIEND
  [March 17, 1926]**
"What's The Use Of Talking"

*Additional songs published in USO/Camp Shows "AT EASE"
  (Volume 4):*

The Rose of Arizona, including:
"Back To Nature"
"Davey Crockett"
"It May Rain"
"Say It With Flowers"

A second successful edition of this revue, with "Mountain Greenery" a hit on the level of "Manhattan." Rodgers, Hart, and Fields also contributed the classic one-act operetta spoof, *The Rose of Arizona.*

LIDO LADY
December 1, 1926   Gaiety Theatre ⟨London⟩
529 performances

Lyrics by Lorenz Hart
Book by Guy Bolton, Kalmar and Ruby, and Ronald Jeans
Directed by Herbert M. Darsey
Produced by Jack Hulbert and Paul Murray
With Hulbert, Cicely Courtneidge (Hulbert), and Phyllis Dare

Published songs:

"Atlantic Blues"—see **PRESENT ARMS [April 26, 1928]**
"Here In My Arms"—originally used in **DEAREST ENEMY [September 18, 1925]**
"I Want A Man"—also used in **AMERICA'S SWEETHEART [February 10, 1931]**
"Lido Lady"
"Morning Is Midnight"—also used in **SHE'S MY BABY [January 3, 1928]**
"A Tiny Flat Near Soho Square"—see **SHE'S MY BABY**
"Try Again To-morrow"
"What's The Use?"—new lyric for "Where's That Little Girl (In The Little Green Hat)" from **FIFTH AVENUE FOLLIES [Circa January 1926]**
"You're On The Lido Now"

Additional songs published (no lyric) in piano selection:

"I Must Be Going"
"My Heart Is Sheba Bound"

Rodgers and Hart went to London to write this hit. As with Kern and particularly Gershwin, Rodgers became immensely popular with British audiences through the early Thirties.

PEGGY-ANN
The Utterly Different Musical Comedy
December 27, 1926   Vanderbilt Theatre   333 performances

Lyrics by Lorenz Hart
Book by Herbert Fields
(Based on *Tillie's Nightmare* [musical] by Edgar Smith)
Directed by Robert Milton
Produced by Lew Fields and Lyle D. Andrews
With Helen Ford, Lulu McConnell, Edith Meiser, and Betty Starbuck

Published songs:

"The Country Mouse" (lyric by Desmond Carter)—written for
   1927 London production; new lyric for "A Little Birdie Told Me
   So"
"Give That Little Girl A Hand"—initial publication (as professional
   copy) upon use in London production
"Hello"—initial publication upon use in London production
"Howdy To Broadway"—initial publication (as professional copy)
   upon use in London production
"A Little Birdie Told Me So"
"Maybe It's Me"—revised lyric for song originally used in **FIFTH
   AVENUE FOLLIES [Circa January 1926]**; also see
   COCHRAN'S 1926 REVUE [April 29, 1926]
"A Tree In The Park"
"Where's That Rainbow?"

Additional songs published (no lyric) in piano selection:

"Chuck It!"
"Havana"

A somewhat expressionistic musical, with Helen Ford (of **DEAR-
EST ENEMY [September 18, 1925]**) starring in another Rodgers and
Hart hit.

BETSY
December 28, 1926   New Amsterdam Theatre
39 performances

Music mostly by Rodgers (see **Berlin**)
Lyrics mostly by Lorenz Hart
Book by Irving Caesar and David Freedman
Revised and directed by Wm. Anthony McGuire
Produced by Florenz Ziegfeld, Jr.
With Belle Baker, Al Shean, and Dan Healy

Published songs:

"Come And Tell Me"—cut

"If I Were You"—different than "If You Were You" from **FLY WITH ME [March 24, 1920]**; also used in **LADY LUCK [April 27, 1927]** and **SHE'S MY BABY [January 3, 1928]**

"Sing"—also used in **LADY LUCK** and **LADY FINGERS [January 31, 1929]**

"Stonewall Moscowitz March" (by Caesar, Hart, and Rodgers)

"This Funny World"

"You're The Mother Type"

Rodgers and Hart, with six hits in eighteen months, met disaster the night after **PEGGY-ANN [December 27, 1926]** opened with this Ziegfeldian showcase for vaudeville balladeer Baker. Fanny Brice she wasn't. The songwriters were rudely surprised opening night when Ziegfeld slipped in Irving Berlin's new "Blue Skies"; the song didn't help **BETSY** any, but it did all right by Berlin. Rodgers and Hart's contributions included one of their finest forgotten songs, "This Funny World." The drawing on the sheet music cover shows Baker tying strings around three slightly embarrassed gentlemen. The first two look very much like the composer and lyricist.

LADY LUCK
April 27, 1927   Carlton Theatre ⟨London⟩
324 performances

Music mostly by H. B. Hedley
Lyrics mostly by Greatrex Newman
Lyrics to Rodgers songs by Lorenz Hart
Book by Firth Shepherd
With Laddie Cliff and Leslie Henson

Published songs:

"If I Were You"—originally used in **BETSY [December 28, 1926]**; also used in **SHE'S MY BABY [January 3, 1928]**

"Sing"—originally used in **BETSY**; also used in **LADY FINGERS [January 31, 1929]**

LONDON PAVILION REVUE
"One Dam Thing After Another"
May 20, 1927   London Pavilion ⟨London⟩
237 performances

Lyrics by Lorenz Hart
Book by Ronald Jeans
Directed by Frank Collins
Produced by Charles B. Cochran
With Jessie Matthews, Sonnie Hale, and Melville Cooper

Published songs:

"I Need Some Cooling Off"—also used (unpublished) in **SHE'S
    MY BABY** [January 3, 1928]
"My Heart Stood Still"—also used in **A CONNECTICUT
    YANKEE** [November 3, 1927]
"My Lucky Star"—also used (unpublished) in **SHE'S MY BABY**

Additional songs published (no lyric) in piano selection:

"Danse Grotesque A La Nègre"
"Idles Of The King"
"Make Hey! Make Hey! While The Sun Shines"
"Minuet (Untitled)"
"One Dam Thing After Another"
"Sandwich Girls"
"Shuffle"

Another British hit, memorable for establishing Jessie Matthews as a
star. Matthews introduced the soon-to-be-imported "My Heart Stood
Still," inspired by the near-collision of a Paris taxicab containing
Rodgers and Hart.

A CONNECTICUT YANKEE
⟨*First Version—also see November 17, 1943*⟩
November 3, 1927   Vanderbilt Theatre   418 performances

Lyrics by Lorenz Hart
Book by Herbert Fields
(Based on *A Connecticut Yankee in King Arthur's Court* [novel] by Mark
    Twain)
Directed by Alexander Leftwich
Produced by Lew Fields and Lyle D. Andrews
With William Gaxton, Constance Carpenter, and June Cochrane

Published songs:

"I Blush"—cut
"I Feel At Home With You"
"My Heart Stood Still"—originally used in **LONDON PAVILION
    REVUE** [May 20, 1927]

"On A Desert Island With Thee!"
"Someone Should Tell Them"—cut; see **AMERICA'S
    SWEETHEART [February 10, 1931]**
"Thou Swell"

Additional songs published (no lyric) in piano selection:
"Here's A Toast"
"Nothing's Wrong"

Another smash for Rodgers, Hart, and Fields. Song hits were the
transatlantic "My Heart Stood Still" and the vernacularal "Thou
Swell." Hart, who had displayed skill since **THE GARRICK GAIE-
TIES [May 17, 1925]**, began to exercise his talent for sustained comedy lyrics with "I Feel At Home With You" and "On A Desert Island With Thee!" Rodgers, meanwhile, wrote the first of his
breathtaking waltzes: "Nothing's Wrong," which has all but disappeared. The modern rhythms of Gershwin, Youmans, and Rodgers,
combined with the decline of operetta, ended the popularity of the
waltz. Rodgers, however, developed a distinctive, nonhackneyed waltz
style, resulting in a dozen classics: "Lover," "The Most Beautiful
Girl In The World," "Hello, Young Lovers," and more. Surprisingly, no other theatre composer has made use of the waltz as effectively. **A CONNECTICUT YANKEE** was Rodgers and Hart's eighth
hit in three years; unforeseeably, they were to be without further
Broadway success until 1936.

SHE'S MY BABY
January 3, 1928   Globe Theatre   71 performances
Lyrics by Lorenz Hart
Book by Guy Bolton, Bert Kalmar, and Harry Ruby
Directed by Edward Royce
Produced by Charles Dillingham
With Beatrice Lillie, Clifton Webb, Jack Whiting, and Irene Dunne

Published songs:
"A Baby's Best Friend"
"How Was I To Know?"—cut; see **HEADS UP! [November 11,
    1929]**
"I Need Some Cooling Off"—originally used in (and only
    published as from) **LONDON PAVILION REVUE [May 29,
    1927]**

"If I Were You"—cut; originally used in **BETSY** [December 28, 1926] and **LADY LUCK** [April 27, 1927]

"A Little House In Soho"—revised lyric for "A Tiny Flat Near Soho Square" from **LIDO LADY** [December 1, 1926]

"Morning Is Midnight"—cut; originally used in **LIDO LADY**

"My Lucky Star"—originally used in (and only published as from) **LONDON PAVILION REVUE**

"When I Go On The Stage" [2nd]—different than song from **YOU'LL NEVER KNOW** [April 20, 1921]

"Whoopsie!"

"You're What I Need"

Rodgers and Hart were no more successful with Lillie than Vincent Youmans had been on **OH, PLEASE!** [Youmans: December 17, 1926]); both composers found her difficult to please and were unable to suit her special performing style. Rodgers and Hart eventually did come up with a Lillie gem: "Rhythm" (in the British revue **PLEASE!** [November 16, 1933]), which seems to have been revised from unused **SHE'S MY BABY** material.

PRESENT ARMS!
April 26, 1928   Mansfield Theatre   155 performances

Lyrics by Lorenz Hart
Book by Herbert Fields
Directed by Alexander Leftwich
Produced by Lew Fields
With Charles King, Flora LeBreton, Busby Berkeley, and Joyce Barbour

Published songs:

"Blue Ocean Blues"—new lyric for "Atlantic Blues" from **LIDO LADY** [December 1, 1926]

"Crazy Elbows"

"Do I Hear You Saying (I Love You?)"

"Down By The Sea"

"I'm A Fool, Little One"

"A Kiss For Cinderella"

"You Took Advantage Of Me"

Additional song published (no lyric) in piano selection:

"Tell It To The Marines"

Herb Fields' first non–Rodgers and Hart show had been the monumental hit **HIT THE DECK [Youmans: April 25, 1927].** That musical had a Navy motif; **PRESENT ARMS!** tried the Marines. Nothing from the score attracted attention except "You Took Advantage Of Me," a distant relative of "You're The Mother Type" from **BETSY [December 28, 1926].**

CHEE-CHEE
September 25, 1928   Mansfield Theatre   31 performances

Lyrics by Lorenz Hart
Book by Herbert Fields
(Based on *The Son of the Grand Eunuch* [novel] by Charles Petit)
Directed by Alexander Leftwich
Produced by Lew Fields
With Helen Ford, Betty Starbuck, Philip Loeb, and William Williams

Published songs:

"Better Be Good To Me"
"Dear, Oh Dear!"
"I Must Love You"—see **SIMPLE SIMON [February 18, 1930]**
"Moon Of My Delight"
"Singing A Love Song"—see **SIMPLE SIMON**
"The Tartar Song"

Rodgers, Hart, and Fields decided to try something new, and **CHEE-CHEE** certainly was: Broadway's first Chinese castration musical. After a stony reaction it was withdrawn, and the two Fieldses parted company with Rodgers and Hart. Herbert soon joined Cole Porter for **FIFTY MILLION FRENCHMEN [Porter: November 27, 1929],** the first of seven-out-of-seven hits. Lew's final book musical was the aptly titled **HELLO, DADDY! [December 26, 1928]**—written by Herbert and Dorothy (with Jimmy McHugh).

LADY FINGERS
January 31, 1929   Vanderbilt Theatre   132 performances

Music mostly by Joseph Meyers
Lyrics mostly by Edward Eliscu
Lyrics to Rodgers songs by Lorenz Hart
Book by Eddie Buzzell
(Based on *Easy Come, Easy Go* [play] by Owen Davis)

Directed by Lew Levenson
Produced by Lyle D. Andrews
With Buzzell and John Price Jones

Published songs:

"I Love You More Than Yesterday"
"Sing"—originally used in **BETSY [December 28, 1926]**; also used
  in **LADY LUCK [April 27, 1927]**

SPRING IS HERE
March 11, 1929   Alvin Theatre   104 performances

Lyrics by Lorenz Hart
Book by Owen Davis
(Based on *Shotgun Wedding* [play] by Davis)
Directed by Alexander Leftwich
Produced by Alex A. Aarons and Vinton Freedley
With Glenn Hunter, Lillian Taiz, and Charles Ruggles

Published songs:

"Baby's Awake Now"
"Rich Man, Poor Man"
"Why Can't I?"
"With A Song In My Heart"
"You Never Say Yes"
"Yours Sincerely"

Rodgers and Hart moved from Lew Fields to the Gershwins' Aarons
and Freedley; the association was mutually unprofitable. **SPRING IS
HERE** had two lovely songs—"Baby's Awake Now" and "Why Can't
I?"—and one popular hit, "With A Song In My Heart." The title
song (unpublished) was *not* the superb "Spring Is Here"; that came
later, in **I MARRIED AN ANGEL [May 11, 1938]**.

HEADS UP!
November 11, 1929   Alvin Theatre   144 performances

Lyrics by Lorenz Hart
Book by John McGowan and Paul Gerard Smith
Produced by Alex A. Aarons and Vinton Freedley
With Jack Whiting, Barbara Newberry, Victor Moore, Betty Starbuck,
  and Ray Bolger
NOTE: **ME FOR YOU**, pre-Broadway title

Published songs:

"I Can Do Wonders With You"—cut; also used in **SIMPLE SIMON** [**February 18, 1930**]

"It Must Be Heaven"

"Me For You!"

"My Man Is On The Make"

"A Ship Without A Sail"

"Sky City"—cut

"Why Do You Suppose?"—new lyric for "How Was I To Know" (cut) from **SHE'S MY BABY** [**January 3, 1928**]

Additional songs published (no lyric) in piano selection:

"Daughter Grows Older"

"Knees"

As with Aarons and Freedley's **SMARTY** [**Gershwin: November 22, 1927**], **ME FOR YOU**—with an Owen Davis book—had grave tryout problems. Drastic surgery was performed; but **HEADS UP!,** unlike **FUNNY FACE,** did not respond . . . even with Aarons and Freedley standby Victor Moore in attendance.

SIMPLE SIMON
February 18, 1930   Ziegfeld Theatre   135 performances

Lyrics by Lorenz Hart
Book by Ed Wynn and Guy Bolton
Directed by Zeke Colvan
Produced by Florenz Ziegfeld, Jr.
With Wynn, Ruth Etting, Bobbe Arnst, and Harriet Hoctor

Published songs:

"Don't Tell Your Folks"

"He Dances On My Ceiling (Dancing On The Ceiling)"—cut; also used in **EVER GREEN** [**December 3, 1930**]

"He Was Too Good To Me"—cut

"I Can Do Wonders With You"—cut; originally used (cut) in **HEADS UP!** [**November 11, 1929**]

"I Still Believe In You"—cut; new lyric for "Singing A Love Song" from **CHEE-CHEE** [**September 25, 1928**]

"Send For Me"—new lyric for "I Must Love You" from **CHEE-CHEE**

"Sweetenheart"
"Ten Cents A Dance"

With the Depression in progress and five consecutive failures, Rodgers and Hart could not afford to turn down Ziegfeld's offer (despite their troubles with **BETSY [December 28, 1926]**) and prepared this Ed Wynn vehicle. Matters turned out little better. The score included three very good songs: "He Dances On My Ceiling," which was cut and found a better life; "He Was Too Good To Me," which was cut and didn't; and "Ten Cents A Dance," a truly superb song which can be examined alongside "Love For Sale" (from **THE NEW YORKERS ⟨Second Version⟩ [Porter: December 8, 1930]**). Porter wails, while Hart philosophizes; Hart's downtrodden girl is so very much more *real*, with touches of irony, humor, and sympathy. (She was originally a manicurist, pawed by her male customers.) Porter's music, too, is synthetically dramatic, resting firmly on his oriental scale. Rodgers is weary-but-honest, the unorthodox song structure (A-B-A/B; C-D-A/B) especially fitting the exceptional lyric. Drama is reserved for the remarkable climax, (D into A/B), resulting in a so much more effective song.

EVER GREEN
December 3, 1930   Adelphi Theatre ⟨London⟩
254 performances

Lyrics by Lorenz Hart
Book by Benn W. Levy
(Based on an idea by Rodgers and Hart)
Directed by Frank Collins
Produced by Charles B. Cochran
With Jessie Matthews, Sonny Hale, and Joyce Barbour

Published songs:

"The Colour of Her Eyes"—issued as professional copy
"Dear! Dear!"
"Harlemania"—issued as professional copy
"He Dances On My Ceiling (Dancing On The Ceiling)"—originally used (cut) in **SIMPLE SIMON [February 18, 1930]**
"If I Give In To You"
"In The Cool Of The Evening"
"No Place But Home"

Additional song published (no lyric) in piano selection:
"When The Old World Was New"

This British hit was Rodgers and Hart's only theatrical oasis over a long dry spell. Of particular interest are "No Place But Home" and, to zealous Hart enthusiasts, "The Colour Of Her Eyes," an early attempt at what he perfected in "To Keep My Love Alive" (and other songs). Rodgers and Hart spent much of the early Thirties in Hollywood, their output including the 1932 *Love Me Tonight* (where Rodgers first worked with Rouben Mamoulian) and the 1933 *Hallelujah, I'm a Bum*. Both films are notable for Rodgers' first experiments in the close integration of music and dialogue (and songs like "Mimi," "Lover," and "You Are Too Beautiful").

AMERICA'S SWEETHEART
February 10, 1931   Broadhurst Theatre   135 performances
Lyrics by Lorenz Hart
Book by Herbert Fields
Directed by Monty Woolley
Produced by Lawrence Schwab and Frank Mandel
With Harriette Lake (Ann Sothern), Jack Whiting, and Jean Aubert

Published songs:
"How About It?"
"I've Got Five Dollars"
"I Want A Man"—originally used in **LIDO LADY [December 1, 1926]**
"A Lady Must Live"
"There's So Much More"—revised lyric for "Someone Should Tell Them" from **A CONNECTICUT YANKEE ⟨First Version⟩ [November 3, 1927]**
"We'll Be The Same"

Rodgers, Hart, and Fields met up in Hollywood and returned to Broadway with this satire on Hollywood, and quickly returned to Hollywood. The trip was worth the visit, though, with the carefree, Depression-less "I've Got Five Dollars" and "A Lady Must Live."

CRAZY QUILT
May 19, 1931   44th Street Theatre   79 performances

Music mostly by Harry Warren
Lyrics mostly by Mort Dixon, Billy Rose, and others
Sketches by David Freedman
Produced and directed by Billy Rose
With Fanny Brice (Rose), Phil Baker, and Ted Healy

Published songs:

None

For "Second-Hand" Fanny Brice Rose "of Washington Square,"
Rodgers and Hart supplied "Rest-Room Rose." (Cole Porter tried
"Hot-House Rose," but Brice didn't like it.)

PLEASE!
November 16, 1933   Savoy Theatre ⟨London⟩
108 performances

Music mostly by Vivian Ellis and Austin Croom-Johnson
Lyrics mostly by Dion Titheradge
Lyric to Rodgers song by Lorenz Hart
Book by Titheradge and Robert Macgunigle
Directed by Titheradge
Produced by André Charlot
With Beatrice Lillie and Lupino Lane

Recorded song:

"Rhythm"—also used in **THE SHOW IS ON [December 25, 1936]**

Rodgers and Hart supplied this very special material for the special
Lillie, a minimedley of rhythm songs (see **SHE'S MY BABY [January 3, 1928]**).

SOMETHING GAY
April 29, 1935   Morosco Theatre   72 performances

Play by Adelaide Heilbron
Lyric by Lorenz Hart
Directed by Thomas Mitchell
Produced by the Messrs. Shubert
With Tallulah Bankhead and Walter Pidgeon

Published song:

"You Are So Lovely And I'm So Lonely"

JUMBO
November 16, 1935   Hippodrome Theatre
233 performances

Lyrics by Lorenz Hart
Book by Ben Hecht and Charles MacArthur
Book directed by George Abbott
Directed by John Murray Anderson
Produced by Billy Rose
With Jimmy Durante, Gloria Grafton, Donald Novis, and Paul Whiteman

Published songs:

"The Circus On Parade"
"Diavolo"
"Little Girl Blue"
"The Most Beautiful Girl In The World"
"My Romance"
"Over And Over Again"—song version of "Party Waltz"
    [instrumental] (cut, unpublished) from 1934 movie *Hollywood
    Party*

Additional song recorded:

"Women"

Rodgers and Hart returned to New York with a ballet-vs-jazz dance
show, a proposed movie project Fred Astaire had turned down. In
the meantime, Billy Rose approached the pair to write songs for his
jumbo circus extravaganza. John Murray Anderson, director of
DEAREST ENEMY [September 18, 1925], was the musical comedy veteran on hand. Hecht and MacArthur were writing their first
(and only) musical, and farce playwright/director George Abbott was
hired to stage the book (*his* first musical assignment). Everything about
JUMBO was gargantuan, including Durante's costar "Big Rosie" (in
the title role) and the costs that ultimately overtook the show and
closed it. Rodgers provided a very beautiful waltz, "The Most Beautiful Girl In The World" and a very beautiful nonwaltz, "Little Girl
Blue"—which, come to think of it, includes a waltz interlude (during
which the girls on the flying trapezes flew in).

ON YOUR TOES
April 11, 1936   Imperial Theatre   315 performances

Lyrics by Lorenz Hart
Book by Rodgers and Hart and George Abbott
Choreography by George Balanchine
Directed by Worthington Minor
Produced by Dwight Deere Wiman
With Ray Bolger, Tamara Geva (Balanchine), Monty Woolley, and Doris
    Carson

Published songs:

"Glad To Be Unhappy"
"The Heart Is Quicker Than The Eye"
"It's Got To Be Love"
"On Your Toes"
"Quiet Night"
"Slaughter On Tenth Avenue" [ballet]—issued in separate edition
"There's A Small Hotel"
"Too Good For The Average Man"

Additional songs published in vocal score:

"Princess Zenobia Ballet"
"The Three 'B's"
"Two-A-Day For Keith"

The non–Fred Astaire project turned into one of the finer Rodgers
and Hart shows, with Ray Bolger memorable in the lead. (Marilyn
Miller was announced to costar, but withdrew—no doubt affecting
the development of the project.) With the success of **ON YOUR
TOES,** Rodgers and Hart began a series of musicals with a new creative team. Producer Wiman (see **THE LITTLE SHOW [Schwartz:
April 30, 1929]**) presented five Rodgers and Hart "spring" musicals
over the next seven years; colibrettist Abbott wrote, directed, and
produced four hits; and Wiman's set designer Jo Mielziner became
one of Rodgers' most frequent creative associates. Diaghilev-trained
George Balanchine made his musical comedy debut with two inte-
grally plotted ballets, including the legendary "Slaughter On Tenth
Avenue"; he choreographed four Rodgers and Hart hits. (Hart took
Balanchine, Geva, Zorina, et al. to agent "Doc" Bender.) Besides
"Slaughter," Rodgers contributed "Glad To Be Unhappy" and
"There's A Small Hotel"; while Hart sparkled in "The Heart Is
Quicker Than The Eye" and "It's Got To Be Love." **ON YOUR
TOES** was to have two Broadway revivals, in 1954 and 1982. Abbott
directed both, the second at the age of ninety-two.

THE SHOW IS ON
December 25, 1936   Winter Garden Theatre
237 performances

Music mostly by Vernon **Duke** (see **Arlen, Gershwin,** and **Schwartz**)
Lyric to Rodgers song by Lorenz Hart
Sketches mostly by David Freedman and Moss Hart
Directed by Vincente Minnelli
Produced by Lee Shubert
With Beatrice Lillie and Bert Lahr

Recorded song:

"Rhythm"—originally used in **PLEASE! [November 16, 1933]**

BABES IN ARMS
April 14, 1937   Shubert Theatre   289 performances

Lyrics by Lorenz Hart
Book by Rodgers and Hart
Choreography by George Balanchine
Directed by Robert Sinclair
Produced by Dwight Deere Wiman
With Mitzi Green, Ray Heatherton, Wynn Murray, Alfred Drake, and
  The Nicholas Brothers

Published songs:

"All At Once"
"All Dark People"
"Babes In Arms"
"I Wish I Were In Love Again"
"Johnny One Note"
"The Lady Is A Tramp"
"My Funny Valentine"
"Way Out West"
"Where Or When?"

Additional song published in vocal score:

"Imagine"

Coming off the very good **ON YOUR TOES,** Rodgers and Hart wrote their most hit-laden score. Rodgers was to have other charmed periods in his career, but the late Thirties showed Hart at the very top of his form with "Where Or When?" and "My Funny Valentine"

(Ray Heatherton—father of Joey—played Val), "I Wish I Were In Love Again," and the twin knockouts "Johnny One Note" and "The Lady Is A Tramp." That score is good even by *today's* standards. Rodgers and Hart also provided their first libretto, the one about the group of kids getting together to put on a show; somebody's father had a barn.

I'D RATHER BE RIGHT
November 2, 1937   Alvin Theatre   290 performances

Lyrics by Lorenz Hart
Book by George S. Kaufman and Moss Hart
Directed by Kaufman
Produced by Sam H. Harris
With George M. Cohan, Joy Hodges and Austin Marshall

Published songs:

"Ev'rybody Loves You"—issued as professional copy
"Have You Met Miss Jones?"
"I'd Rather Be Right (Don't Have To Know Much)" [1st]—cut;
    see **TWO WEEKS WITH PAY [June 24, 1940]**
"I'd Rather Be Right (Than Influential)" [2nd]
"Sweet Sixty-Five"
"Take And Take And Take"

Additional song published in "Rodgers And Hart: A Musical Anthology":

"Ev'rybody Loves You"

Additional song recorded:

"Off The Record"

Kaufman and producer Sam Harris decided to attempt another political satire along the lines of **OF THEE I SING [Gershwin: December 26, 1931]** and the unsuccessful **BRING ON THE GIRLS [Schwartz: October 22, 1934].** Kaufman worked extremely well with Gershwin, Berlin, Schwartz, and Loesser; but not Rodgers. The casting of George M. Cohan as Franklin D. Roosevelt made **I'D RATHER BE RIGHT** a highly awaited event: the "Yankee Doodle Boy" had been absent from the musical stage for a decade, and was performing his first non-Cohan score. However, Cohan *hated* Rodgers and Hart; "Gilbert and Sullivan" he called them; what he called Roosevelt in

private is unknown, but the outspoken Cohan interpolated pro–Al
Smith lyrics while G. & S. weren't listening. (Cohan was high on
Broadway's best-hated list. When donations were sought for his Times
Square statue, few professionals contributed—except, curiously, Os-
car Hammerstein 2nd.) **I'D RATHER BE RIGHT** was weak in book,
music, and satire, but the package sold enough tickets for success.
Three fine songs were included: the moderate hit "Have You Met
Miss Jones?" and two cuts, neither of which ever recovered. "I'd Rather
Be Right" [1st] is melodic and lovely; and "Ev'rybody Loves You"
is the team's second tender lullaby, in a class with the equally obscure "Sleepyhead."

I MARRIED AN ANGEL
May 11, 1938   Shubert Theatre   338 performances

Lyrics by Lorenz Hart
Book by Rodgers and Hart
(Based on a play by John Vaszary)
Choreography by George Balanchine
Directed by Joshua Logan
Produced by Dwight Deere Wiman
With Dennis King, Vera Zorina (Balanchine), Vivienne Segal, and Walter
    Slezak

Published songs:

"At The Roxy Music Hall"—issued in professional copy
"Did You Ever Get Stung?"
"How To Win Friends And Influence People"
"I Married An Angel"
"I'll Tell The Man In The Street"
"Spring Is Here"—different than song (unpublished) from
    SPRING IS HERE [March 11, 1929]
"A Twinkle In Your Eye"

*Additional song published in "Rodgers And Hart: A Musical
    Anthology":*

"At The Roxy Music Hall"

Additional song recorded:

"Angel Without Wings"

The angelic Zorina charmed Broadway in this happy, comic-fantasy
hit. Zorina had played the lead in the London production [February

5, 1937] of **ON YOUR TOES** [**April 11, 1936**] and won Tamara
Geva's part in the 1939 film version (and husband Balanchine, too).
I MARRIED AN ANGEL originated as a 1933 Rodgers, Hart, and
Hart (Moss) movie project for Jeanette MacDonald. Rodgers and Hart
(Larry) wrote the stage book themselves, with the score including the
lovely, lonely "Spring Is Here." Operetta stars Dennis King and Vivienne Segal of Friml's THE THREE MUSKETEERS [March 13,
1928] were reunited; the surprise was Segal, now a first-rate musical
comedienne. Rodgers and Hart took note. The Wiman production
team included not only Balanchine and Jo Mielziner, but also directing discovery Joshua Logan. P.S.: Jeanette MacDonald starred in the
1942 movie version.

THE BOYS FROM SYRACUSE
November 23, 1938   Alvin Theatre   235 performances

Lyrics by Lorenz Hart
Book by George Abbott
(Based on *The Comedy of Errors* [play] by William Shakespeare)
Choreography by George Balanchine
Directed and produced by Abbott
With Eddie Albert, Ronald Graham, Teddy Hart, Jimmy Savo, Wynn
  Murray, and Marcy Westcott

Published songs:

"Falling In Love With Love"
"Oh, Diogenes!"
"The Shortest Day Of The Year"
"Sing For Your Supper"
"This Can't Be Love"
"Who Are You?"—written for 1940 movie version
"You Have Cast Your Shadow On The Sea"

Additional songs published in vocal score:

"Big Brother"
"Come With Me"
"Dear Old Syracuse"
"He And She"
"I Had Twins"
"Ladies' Choice" [ballet]
"Ladies Of The Evening"
"Twins' Dance" [ballet]
"What Can You Do With A Man?"

One of the finest of pure-comedy musical comedies. Hart's brother Teddy bore a striking resemblance to burlesque comic Jimmy Savo; when the collaborators began looking at Shakespeare for source material, this potentially perfect casting made *The Comedy of Errors* (about two sets of twins) the obvious choice. Rodgers and Hart continued their association with George Abbott, Broadway's top farce man: the result was a perfect **BOYS FROM SYRACUSE**. Abbott's less-than-satisfying experiences with dilettante producers had led to his presenting his own work. He now entered the musical field (and was soon joined by Rodgers). The excellent score included "This Can't Be Love," "Sing For Your Supper," "Falling In Love With Love," and "Dear Old Syracuse."

TOO MANY GIRLS
October 18, 1939   Imperial Theatre   249 performances

Lyrics by Lorenz Hart
Book by George Marion, Jr.
Choreographed by Robert Alton
Directed and produced by George Abbott
With Marcy Westcott, Richard Kollmar, Desi Arnaz, Eddie Bracken, and
   Mary Jane Walsh

Published songs:

"All Dressed Up (Spic And Spanish)"
"Give It Back To The Indians"
"I Didn't Know What Time It Was"
"I Like To Recognize The Tune"
"Love Never Went To College"
"She Could Shake The Maracas"
"You're Nearer"—written for 1940 movie version

*Additional song published in "Rodgers And Hart: A Musical
   Anthology":*

" 'Cause We Got Cake"

Additional songs recorded:

"Heroes In The Fall"
"Look Out"
"My Prince"
"Pottawatomie"
"Sweethearts Of The Team"
"Tempt Me Not"
"Too Many Girls"

Abbott earned a reputation for fast-paced, youthful entertainments like this college football musical. **TOO MANY GIRLS** was not up to the high Rodgers and Hart caliber, but enjoyable enough to achieve hit status. Hart's years of drinking and dissipation had begun to catch up with him, and he was growing increasingly unreliable; Rodgers occasionally had to fill in during the lyricist's absences. But Hart could still write intricately, as in "Give It Back To The Indians" and "I Like To Recognize The Tune." The score also contained the gentler "I Didn't Know What Time It Was," "My Prince," and "Love Never Went To College." For the movie version, the pair added the tender "You're Nearer." Abbott took most of his youthful cast (including Desi Arnaz) to Hollywood, but lead Marcy Westcott—who introduced the three ballads as well as the earlier "This Can't Be Love"—was replaced by nonsinging starlet Lucille Ball.

HIGHER AND HIGHER
April 4, 1940   Shubert Theatre   108 performances

Lyrics by Lorenz Hart
Book by Gladys Hurlbut and Joshua Logan
(Based on an idea by Irvin Pincus)
Directed by Logan
Produced by Dwight Deere Wiman
With Jack Haley, Shirley Ross, Marta Eggert, Leif Erickson, and Lee
    Dixon

Published songs:

"Ev'ry Sunday Afternoon"
"From Another World"
"It Never Entered My Mind"
"Nothing But You"

*Additional songs published in "Rodgers And Hart: A Musical
    Anthology":*

"Disgustingly Rich"
"It's A Lovely Day For A Murder"—different than "What A
    Lovely Day For A Wedding" from **ALLEGRO [October 10,
    1947]**

Additional songs recorded:

"How's Your Health?"
"Morning's At Seven"

HIGHER AND HIGHER was written for "Angel" Vera Zorina; she wisely opted for **LOUISIANA PURCHASE [Berlin: May 28, 1940]**, and played opposite Gaxton and Moore instead of Sharkey, the scene-stealing seal. One of the very loveliest Rodgers and Hart songs was included, "It Never Entered My Mind," but very little else. The song title "Morning's At Seven" was suggested by Wiman's simultaneous production of Paul Osborn's identically named play.

TWO WEEKS WITH PAY
[June 24, 1940]   Ridgeway Theatre ⟨White Plains, New York⟩; summer stock tryout

Music and lyrics mostly by others
Lyrics to Rodgers song by Lorenz Hart
Sketches by Charles Sherman and others
Created and conceived by Ted Fetter and Richard Lewine
Choreography by Gene Kelly
Directed by Felix Jacoves
Produced by Dorothy and Julien Olney
With Bill Johnson, Marie Nash, Hiram Sherman, and Pat Harrington

Recorded Song:

"Now That I Know You"—new lyric for "I'd Rather Be Right (Don't Have To Know Much)" [1st] (cut) from **I'D RATHER BE RIGHT [November 2, 1937]**

This revue featured interpolations by several composers, compiled by cousins of Porter (Fetter) and Rodgers (Lewine), including the unpublished "Will You Love Me Monday Morning?" (from **LIFE BEGINS AT 8:40 [Arlen: August 27, 1934]**) and "Just Another Page From Your Diary" (cut) from **LEAVE IT TO ME [Porter: November 9, 1938]**). The weak **TWO WEEKS WITH PAY** played two weeks in stock and folded. Gene Kelly, from the chorus of **LEAVE IT TO ME,** had already been chosen for the lead in the next Rodgers and Hart musical; in the meantime, he tried his hand at choreography in White Plains.

PAL JOEY
A Gaily Sophisticated Musical Comedy
December 25, 1940   Ethel Barrymore Theatre
374 performances

Lyrics by Lorenz Hart
Book by John O'Hara

Choreography by Robert Alton
Directed and produced by George Abbott
With Vivienne Segal, Gene Kelly, June Havoc, and Jack Durant

Published songs:

"Bewitched"
"Do It The Hard Way"
"Happy Hunting Horn"—initial publication upon use in 1952
  revival
"I Could Write A Book"
"Plant You Now, Dig You Later"
"Take Him"—initial publication upon use in revival
"What Is A Man?"—initial publication upon use in revival
"You Mustn't Kick It Around"
"Zip"—initial publication upon use in 1962 movie version

Additional song published in "Intimate Songs":

"Den Of Iniquity"

Additional songs published in vocal score:

"Chicago"
"The Flower Garden Of My Heart"
"Pal Joey (What Do I Care For A Dame?)"
"Pal Joey Ballet"
"That Terrific Rainbow"

Additional song recorded:

"I'm Talking To My Pal"—cut

Rodgers, Hart, O'Hara, and producer/director (unbilled coauthor)
Abbott brought a new level of realism to the musical theatre with
PAL JOEY. (Abbott was no doubt influenced by his classic melodrama BROADWAY [September 16, 1926], which had a similar set-
ting and a similar effect.) Reaction was cautious, with a considerable
segment of the audience alienated by the heel of a hero. Gene Kelly
had been acclaimed for his nonmusical performance in Saroyan's THE
TIME OF YOUR LIFE [October 25, 1939]; the cynical antiheroine
Vera was written for operetta star-turned-comedienne Vivienne Segal. Both roles were well cast, written, and performed. Rodgers and
Hart provided a properly cynical score, the one gentler spot being "I
Could Write A Book." Segal was particularly well served with "Bewitched," "Take Him," and "Den Of Iniquity." **PAL JOEY** met with
far greater success (and 542 performances) when revived by Jule Styne

[January 3, 1952], with Segal making her final Broadway appearance. Kelly, meanwhile, choreographed Abbott and Rodgers' **BEST FOOT FORWARD [Martin: October 1, 1941]** before leaving for Hollywood. He returned only once, to direct Rodgers' **FLOWER DRUM SONG [December 1, 1958]**.

BY JUPITER
June 2, 1942   Shubert Theatre   427 performances

Lyrics by Lorenz Hart
Book by Rodgers and Hart
(Based on *The Warrior's Husband* [play] by Julian F. Thompson)
Directed by Joshua Logan
Produced by Dwight Deere Wiman and Rodgers in association with
  Richard Kollmar
With Ray Bolger, Constance Moore, Ronald Graham, and Benay Venuta
NOTE: **ALL'S FAIR,** pre-Broadway title

Published songs:

"Careless Rhapsody"
"Ev'rything I've Got"
"Here's A Hand"
"Jupiter Forbid"
"Nobody's Heart (Ride Amazon Ride!)"
"Wait Till You See Her"

Additional songs recorded:

"Bottoms Up"
"The Boy I Left Behind Me"
"Finale Act One (No, Mother, No)"
"Fool Meets Fool"—cut
"For Jupiter And Greece"
"In The Gateway Of The Temple Of Minerva"
"Life Was Monotonous"—cut
"Life With Father"
"Nothing To Do But Relax"—cut
"Now That I've Got My Strength"

Ray Bolger returned from Hollywood (where he did *not* make the **ON YOUR TOES [April 11, 1936]** movie—Eddie Albert, of **THE BOYS FROM SYRACUSE [November 23, 1938]**, did) to star in this wartime hit. Bolger's performance was enough to insure success, with Rodgers and Hart providing two very good comedy duets—"Ev'rything I've Got" and "Life With Father"—and the rhapsodic "Careless Rhapsody." Rodgers here officially began his producing career, although he was already the silent partner of George Abbott on **BEST FOOT FORWARD [Martin: October 1, 1941]** and the forthcoming BEAT THE BAND [October 14, 1942]. In keeping with Abbott's practice of encouraging young talent, these scores were written by Hugh Martin (vocal arranger of **THE BOYS FROM SYRACUSE** and **TOO MANY GIRLS [October 18, 1939]**) and Johnny Green (conductor of **BY JUPITER**).

OKLAHOMA!
March 31, 1943   St. James Theatre   2,248 performances

Book and lyrics by Oscar Hammerstein 2nd.
(Based on *Green Grow the Lilacs* [play] by Lynn Riggs)
Choreography by Agnes de Mille
Directed by Rouben Mamoulian
Produced by The Theatre Guild
With Alfred Drake, Joan Roberts, Celeste Holm, Howard da Silva and
    Lee Dixon
NOTE: **AWAY WE GO!**, pre-Broadway title

Published songs:

"All 'Er Nothin' "—initial publication upon use in 1955 movie
    version
"Boys And Girls Like You And Me"—cut
"The Farmer And The Cowman"—initial publication upon use in
    movie version
"I Cain't Say No"
"Kansas City"—initial publication upon use in movie version
"Many A New Day"
"Oh, What A Beautiful Mornin' "
"Oklahoma!"
"Out Of My Dreams"
"People Will Say We're In Love"
"Pore Jud"—initial publication upon use in movie version
"The Surrey With The Fringe On Top"

Additional songs published in vocal score:

"It's A Scandal! It's An Outrage!"
"Laurey Makes Up Her Mind" [ballet]
"Lonely Room"

The twenty-four-year-old Theatre Guild was foundering, without a hit since the Lunts' THERE SHALL BE NO NIGHT [April 29, 1940]. Having been surprisingly successful with their first musical (**THE GARRICK GAIETIES [May 17, 1925]**), the Guild asked Rodgers and Hart to adapt a 1931 folk play. The unstable Hart was not interested, so Rodgers convinced the producers to let him collaborate with one of his pre-Hart lyricists: Oscar Hammerstein, author of the landmark **SHOW BOAT [December 27, 1927]** and nothing but flops since 1932. Rouben Mamoulian directed; he had pioneered the integration of music and dialogue in the 1932 Rodgers and Hart movie *Love Me Tonight* and the Guild's folk opera **PORGY AND BESS [Gershwin: October 10, 1935]**. Choreographer Agnes de Mille had been fired from her first two Broadway jobs; but her successful Ballet Russe *Rodeo* [October 16, 1942] indicated her suitability for the assignment. With Mamoulian, Rodgers, Hammerstein, and de Mille approaching their creative peaks, the separate elements of **OKLAHOMA!** were highly superior and excellently integrated. **OKLAHOMA!** set new long-run records not only on Broadway but everywhere.

A CONNECTICUT YANKEE

⟨*Second Version—also see November 3, 1927*⟩
November 17, 1943   Martin Beck Theatre
135 performances

Lyrics by Lorenz Hart
Book by Herbert Fields
(Based on *A Connecticut Yankee in King Arthur's Court* [novel] by Mark Twain)
Directed by John C. Wilson
Produced by Rodgers
With Vivienne Segal, Dick Foran, Julie Warren, Vera-Ellen, and Chester Stratton

New published songs:

"Can't You Do A Friend A Favor?"
"Lunchtime Follies"—advertised but not published
"Something"—advertised but not published (apparently a misprint)
"This Is My Night To Howl"—advertised but not published
"To Keep My Love Alive"
"You Always Love The Same Girl"

Additional song recorded:
"This Is My Night To Howl"

In hope of getting Hart back into working shape, Rodgers produced a new version of the final Rodgers, Hart, and Fields hit. The updated book was not very good, although it did provide a Vivienne Segal starring role. The new songs included one of Hart's best comedy lyrics, "To Keep My Love Alive." But the lyricist was beyond saving; after a two-week binge, he disappeared during the opening night performance. A couple of days later he turned up—with pneumonia. Lorenz Hart died November 22, 1943.

CAROUSEL
April 19, 1945   Majestic Theatre   890 performances
Book and lyrics by Oscar Hammerstein 2nd
(Based on *Liliom* [play] by Ferenc Molnar, as adapted by Benjamin F. Glaser)
Choreography by Agnes de Mille
Directed by Rouben Mamoulian
Produced by The Theatre Guild
With John Raitt, Jan Clayton, Murvyn Vye, and Bambi Linn

Published songs:

"Carousel Waltz" [instrumental]—issued in separate edition
"If I Loved You"
"June Is Bustin' Out All Over"
"Mister Snow"
"A Real Nice Clambake"
"Soliloquy"
"What's The Use Of Wond'rin' "
"When The Children Are Asleep"
"You'll Never Walk Alone"

Additional songs published in vocal score:

"Ballet" [instrumental]
"Blow High, Blow Low"
"Geraniums In The Winder"
"The Highest Judge Of All"
"Stonecutters Cut It On The Stone"
"You're A Queer One, Julie Jordan"

As with **PORGY AND BESS** [Gershwin: October 10, 1935] and **OKLAHOMA!** [March 31, 1943], the Theatre Guild had one of their plays musicalized under the supervision of Mamoulian: in this case the 1921 *Liliom* (which was reputedly ghost-translated by Larry Hart). The creators of **OKLAHOMA!** combined for **CAROUSEL,** one of the very finest American musicals. Rodgers, Hammerstein, and Mamoulian opened with an unconventional, fully staged instrumental prelude (a waltz, naturally); following was a lengthy dramatic scene almost entirely set to music, important segments of which were "You're A Queer One, Julie Jordan," "Mister Snow," and the multi-part "If I Loved You." Innovations abounded with an extended, dramatic "Soliloquy" and a highly effective de Mille ballet. **CAROUSEL** was a substantial hit, although the run was far shorter than four other Rodgers and Hammerstein shows. Nevertheless, many agree with Rodgers' personal selection of **CAROUSEL** as his favorite work.

ANNIE GET YOUR GUN
see Berlin [May 16, 1946]

HAPPY BIRTHDAY
October 31, 1946   Broadhurst Theatre   564 performances

Play by Anita Loos
Lyric by Oscar Hammerstein 2nd
Directed by Joshua Logan
Produced by Rodgers and Hammerstein
With Helen Hayes

Published song:
"I Haven't Got A Worry In The World"

Rodgers and Hammerstein began their producing partnership with the comedy I REMEMBER MAMA [October 19, 1944] (see **I RE-MEMBER MAMA** [May 31, 1979]). This was followed by **ANNIE GET YOUR GUN** [Berlin: May 16, 1946] and others. After six straight hits came two 1950 failures; thereafter the team only produced their own work.

ALLEGRO
October 10, 1947   Majestic Theatre   315 performances

Book and lyrics by Oscar Hammerstein 2nd
Directed and choreographed by Agnes de Mille
Produced by The Theatre Guild
With John Battles, Roberta Jonay, Annamary Dickey, and Lisa Kirk

Published songs:

"Come Home"
"A Fellow Needs A Girl"
"The Gentleman Is A Dope"
"Money Isn't Everything"
"My Wife"—cut; for initial publication see **SOUTH PACIFIC**
    [April 7, 1949]
"So Far"
"You Are Never Away"

Additional songs published in vocal score:

"Allegro"
"A Darn Nice Campus"
"Finale Act 1 (Wedding Introduction)"
"I Know It Can Happen Again"
"It May Be A Good Idea"
"Joseph Taylor, Jr."
"One Foot, Other Foot"
"Poor Joe"
"To Have And To Hold"
"What A Lovely Day For A Wedding"—different than "It's A
    Lovely Day For A Murder" from **HIGHER AND HIGHER**
    [April 4, 1940]
"Wildcats"
"Wish Them Well"
"Ya-Ta-Ta"

This original folk/morality musical approached pretentiousness, and
proved that even Rodgers and Hammerstein could fail. **ALLEGRO**
was inventive, and contained some good material; it just didn't work.
De Mille (with five hit musicals since **OKLAHOMA!** [March 31,
1943]) was given her first of three directing opportunities, each a poorly
staged failure.

SOUTH PACIFIC
April 7, 1949   Majestic Theatre   1,925 performances

Lyrics by Oscar Hammerstein 2nd
Book by Hammerstein and Joshua Logan
(Based on *Tales of the South Pacific* [stories] by James Michener)
Directed by Logan
Produced by Rodgers and Hammerstein in association with Leland
   Hayward and Logan
With Mary Martin, Ezio Pinza, William Tabbert, Myron McCormick, and
   Juanita Hall

Published songs:

"Bali Ha'i"
"A Cockeyed Optimist"
"Dites-Moi"
"Happy Talk"
"Honey Bun"
"I'm Gonna Wash That Man Right Outa My Hair"
"Loneliness Of Evening"—cut, published in separate edition;
   revised version of "Bright Canary Yellow" (cut, unpublished)
"My Girl Back Home"—cut; initial publication upon reuse in 1958
   movie version
"Some Enchanted Evening"
"Suddenly Lucky"—cut; for initial publication see **THE KING
   AND I [March 29, 1951]**
"There Is Nothin' Like A Dame"
"This Nearly Was Mine"
"Will You Marry Me?"—cut; initial publication upon reuse in
   PIPE DREAM [November 30, 1955]
"A Wonderful Guy"
"You've Got To Be Carefully Taught"—initial publication upon use
   in movie version
"Younger Than Springtime"—new lyric for "My Wife" (cut,
   unpublished) from **ALLEGRO [October 10, 1947]**

Additional songs published in vocal score:

"Bloody Mary"
"Now Is The Time"—cut; included (no lyric) as "The Take-Off"
   [instrumental]
"Twin Soliloquies"

Rodgers and Hammerstein (and Logan) won the 1950 Pulitzer for
Drama with this adaptation of James Michener's 1948 Pulitzer winner for Fiction. Logan had directed two Rodgers and Hart hits, as
well as **ANNIE GET YOUR GUN [Berlin: May 16, 1946]**. The

otherwise satisfying **SOUTH PACIFIC** association was marred by the colibrettist/coproducer's public complaints of being cheated out of credit and (especially) money by his collaborators/partners. Mary Martin, who had turned down the lead in **OKLAHOMA! [March 31, 1943]**, was well known to the trio for her performance in the national company [March 10, 1947] of **ANNIE GET YOUR GUN.** She was joined by opera star Pinza, who reluctantly agreed to the necessary eight-performance schedule—but insisted on singing no more than the equivalent of two operatic appearances a week. Therefore, his **SOUTH PACIFIC** singing part consisted of two booming solos and very little else. The score is on a level with **CAROUSEL [April 19, 1945]**, which is to say near perfection. Hammerstein's uncompromising statement against racial intolerance—"You've Got To Be Carefully Taught"—made many 1949 audience members uncomfortable. The song wasn't separately published until a decade later.

THE KING AND I
March 29, 1951   St. James Theatre   1,246 performances

Book and lyrics by Oscar Hammerstein 2nd
(Based on *Anna and the King of Siam* [novel] by Margaret Landon)
Choreography by Jerome Robbins
Directed by John van Druten
Produced by Rodgers and Hammerstein
With Gertrude Lawrence, Yul Brynner, Doretta Morrow, and Dorothy
  Sarnoff

Published songs:

"Getting To Know You"—new lyric for "Suddenly Lucky" (cut,
  unpublished) from **SOUTH PACIFIC [April 7, 1949]**
"Hello, Young Lovers"
"I Have Dreamed"
"I Whistle A Happy Tune"
"March Of The Siamese Children" [instrumental]
"My Lord And Master"
"Shall We Dance?"
"Something Wonderful"
"We Kiss In A Shadow"

Additional songs published in vocal score:

"A Puzzlement"
"The Royal Bangkok Academy"
"Shall I Tell You What I Think Of You?"

"The Small House Of Uncle Thomas" [ballet]
"Western People Funny"

The last of the four great Rodgers and Hammerstein musicals. The team had continually tried to explore musical theatre in their methods and choice of material; hereafter they were to be less ambitious (and less successful). Outstanding from the fine score were "Something Wonderful," the waltz "Hello, Young Lovers," and two instrumental pieces used particularly well by choreographer Jerome Robbins: "The March Of The Siamese Children" and the ballet "The Small House Of Uncle Thomas." Gertrude Lawrence brought the material to Rodgers and Hammerstein, seeing a good role for herself. There was also a good role for Alfred Drake, of **OKLAHOMA! [March 31, 1943]** and **KISS ME, KATE [Porter: December 30, 1948]**. But that was not to be, and the unknown Yul Brynner—whose only credit was opposite Mary Martin in the brief LUTE SONG [February 6, 1946]—became the King and has remained so. During the second year of the run, Gertrude Lawrence died of cancer on September 6, 1952.

ME AND JULIET
May 28, 1953   Majestic Theatre   358 performances

Book and lyrics by Oscar Hammerstein 2nd
Choreographed by Robert Alton
Directed by George Abbott
Produced by Rodgers and Hammerstein
With Isabel Bigley, Joan McCracken, Bill Hayes, and Ray Walston

Published songs:

"The Big Black Giant"
"I'm Your Girl"
"It Feels Good"
"It's Me"
"Keep It Gay"
"Marriage Type Love"
"No Other Love"—revised version of "Beneath The Southern
    Cross" [instrumental] from 1952 TV documentary "Victory at
    Sea"
"That's The Way It Happens"
"A Very Special Day"

Additional songs published in vocal score:

"Intermission Talk (The Theatre Is Dying)"

"Me, Who Am I?"—cut; included (no lyric) in "Opening Of 'Me And Juliet' "

"Opening Of 'Me And Juliet' "

George Abbott's only new work with Rodgers after **PAL JOEY [December 25, 1940]** was this weak backstage play-within-a-weak-play. Now Rodgers was the producer, and things did not work so well. Rodgers and Hammerstein's two original-book musicals were both problematical, but the popularity of the team helped **ME AND JULIET** achieve a slightly profitable run. The tango "No Other Love" and "Intermission Talk" stood out from the score.

PIPE DREAM
November 30, 1955   Shubert Theatre   245 performances

Book and lyrics by Oscar Hammerstein 2nd
(Based on *Sweet Thursday* [novel] by John Steinbeck)
Directed by Harold Clurman
Produced by Rodgers and Hammerstein
With Helen Traubel, Bill Johnson, Judy Tyler, and Mike Kellin

Published songs:

"All At Once You Love Her"
"Everybody's Got A Home But Me"
"The Man I Used To Be"
"The Next Time It Happens"
"Suzy Is A Good Thing"
"Sweet Thursday"

Additional songs published in vocal score:

"All Kinds Of People"
"Bum's Opera (You Can't Get Away From A Dumb Tomato)"
"Dance Fugue" [instrumental]
"Fauna's Song" [1st]—used (no lyric) as "Change Of Scene—#15" [instrumental]
"Fauna's Song [2nd] (Beguine)"
"The Happiest House On The Block"
"How Long?"
"On A Lopsided Bus"
"The Party That We're Gonna Have To-Morrow Night"

"Thinkin' "
"The Tide Pool"
"We Are A Gang Of Witches"
"Will You Marry Me?"—originally used (cut) in **SOUTH
   PACIFIC [April 7, 1949]**

Additional song recorded:

"Fauna's Song" [1st]

What might have made an interesting musical did not work, suffering from strangely varying points of view. Rodgers provided his most
ambitious later score: tuneful, atmospheric, and full of interesting
things. Hammerstein's close friend Steinbeck had previously written
Burning Bright [October 19, 1950], Rodgers and Hammerstein's final
play production. The protagonist of *Sweet Thursday* was fashioned after
the novelist's friend Henry Fonda; but Fonda's singing audition was
weak. Bill Johnson, who starred opposite Dolores Gray in the London production [June 7, 1947] of **ANNIE GET YOUR GUN [Ber-
lin: May 16, 1946],** got the part. Starring as the proprietress of the
"Happiest House On The Block" was miscast opera star Helen
Traubel, as in "second-act Traubel."

FLOWER DRUM SONG
December 1, 1958   St. James Theatre   602 performances

Lyrics by Oscar Hammerstein 2nd
Book by Hammerstein and Joseph Fields
(Based on the novel by C. Y. Lee)
Choreographed by Carol Haney
Directed by Gene Kelly
Produced by Rodgers and Hammerstein in association with Fields
With Miyoshi Umeki, Larry Blyden, Pat Suzuki, and Juanita Hall

Published songs:

"Don't Marry Me"
"Grant Avenue"
"A Hundred Million Miracles"
"I Enjoy Being A Girl"
"Love, Look Away"
"My Best Love"—cut
"Sunday"
"You Are Beautiful"—initially published as "She Is Beautiful"

Additional songs published in vocal score:
"Chop Suey"
"Fan Tan Fannie"
"Gliding Through My Memoree"
"I Am Going To Like It Here"
"Like A God"
"The Other Generation"

Rodgers and Hammerstein returned to an Oriental theme, this time the assimilation of Chinese immigrants in San Francisco. Unlike **SOUTH PACIFIC [April 7, 1949]** and **THE KING AND I [March 29, 1951],** the conflicts were used for comedic purposes only. The resulting musical was unimportant, if moderately successful. Librettist Joseph Fields was number-one son to Lew and brother to Herb, partners-in-crime with Rodgers and Hart on the early Oriental **CHEE-CHEE [September 25, 1928].** Gene Kelly (of **PAL JOEY [December 25, 1940]**) returned from Hollywood to direct. Carol Haney, former Kelly assistant who had been "discovered" in Bob Fosse's **THE PAJAMA GAME [Adler: May 13, 1954],** choreographed. Her not-so-Chinese-American husband, Larry Blyden, took over the leading role during the tryout.

THE SOUND OF MUSIC
November 16, 1959   Lunt-Fontanne Theatre
1,433 performances

Lyrics by Oscar Hammerstein 2nd
Book by Howard Lindsay and Russel Crouse
(Based on *The Trapp Family Singers* [biography] by Maria Augusta Trapp)
Choreographed by Joe Layton
Directed by Vincent J. Donehue
Produced by Leland Hayward, Richard Halliday, Rodgers and
    Hammerstein
With Mary Martin (Halliday), Theodore Bikel, and Patricia Neway

Published songs:

"Climb Ev'ry Mountain"
"Do-Re-Mi"
"Edelweiss"
"I Have Confidence" (lyric by Rodgers)—written for 1965 movie
    version

"The Lonely Goatherd"
"Maria"
"My Favorite Things"
"An Ordinary Couple"
"Sixteen Going On Seventeen"
"So Long, Farewell"—initial publication upon use in movie version
"Something Good" (lyric by Rodgers)—written for movie version
"The Sound Of Music"

Additional songs published in vocal score:

"Alleluia"
"How Can Love Survive"
"No Way To Stop It"
"Preludium"

A huge hit and one of Hollywood's all-time greatest successes, despite an initial critical trouncing. Serious subjects which Rodgers and Hammerstein had sensitively handled in the past came out treacly in Lindsay and Crouse's book; Hammerstein, suffering from cancer, was unable to contribute more than lyrics. Oscar Hammerstein 2nd died on August 23, 1960. The high spot of the final Rodgers and Hammerstein score: "My Favorite Things."

NO STRINGS
March 15, 1962   54th Street Theatre   580 performances

Lyrics by Rodgers
Book by Samuel Taylor
Directed and choreographed by Joe Layton
Produced by Rodgers
With Diahann Carroll, Richard Kiley, Bernice Massi, and Polly Rowles

Published songs:

"Be My Host"
"Eager Beaver"
"La-La-La"
"Loads of Love"
"Look No Further"
"Love Makes The World Go"
"Maine"
"The Man Who Has Everything"
"No Strings"

"Nobody Told Me"
"The Sweetest Sounds"
"You Don't Tell Me"

Additional songs published in vocal score:
"How Sad"
"An Orthodox Fool"

Working as his own lyricist, Rodgers again tried something innovative: using on-stage instrumentalists to counterpoint the moods and emotions of the characters. Unfortunately, there was very little plot; just one situation and the dazzling Diahann Carroll. The experiment was successful enough, and **NO STRINGS** was carried by Carroll to a profitable run.

DO I HEAR A WALTZ?
March 18, 1965   46th Street Theatre   220 performances
Lyrics by Stephen Sondheim
Book by Arthur Laurents
(Based on *The Time of the Cuckoo* [play] by Laurents)
Directed by John Dexter
Produced by Rodgers
With Elizabeth Allen, Sergio Franchi, Carol Bruce, and Madeleine
   Sherwood

Published songs:

"Do I Hear A Waltz?"
"Here We Are Again"
"Moon In My Window"
"Perhaps"—cut
"Someone Like You"
"Stay"
"Take The Moment"
"Thank You So Much"
"Two By Two (By Two)" [1st]—cut; different than song from
   TWO BY TWO [November 10, 1970]

Additional songs published in vocal score:

"Bargaining"
"No Understand"
"Perfectly Lovely Couple"
"Someone Woke Up"
"Thinking"

"This Week Americans"
"We're Gonna Be All Right"
"What Do We Do? We Fly!"

Rodgers and his collaborators—Hammerstein-protégé Sondheim and highly capable librettist Arthur Laurents—got along poisonously; the result was misconceived, miscast, and mistaken. Despite all this, much of the Rodgers and Sondheim work—disowned by both sides—is really quite charming. "Moon In My Window," "Here We Are Again," "Take The Moment," and "Someone Woke Up" all accomplish what they set out to with charm and grace; and in the title song Rodgers came up with his final sweeping waltz.

TWO BY TWO
November 10, 1970   Imperial Theatre   343 performances

Lyrics by Martin Charnin
Book by Peter Stone
(Based on *The Flowering Peach* [play] by Clifford Odets)
Directed and choreographed by Joe Layton
Produced with Rodgers
With Danny Kaye, Harry Goz, and Joan Copeland

Published songs:

"I Do Not Know A Day I Did Not Love You"
"An Old Man"
"Something Doesn't Happen"
"Something, Somewhere"
"Two By Two" [2nd]—different than song (cut) from **DO I HEAR A WALTZ [March 18, 1965]**

Additional songs published in vocal score:

"As Far As I'm Concerned"
"The Covenant"
"The Gitka's Song" [instrumental]
"The Golden Ram"
"Hey, Girlie"
"Ninety Again"
"Poppa Knows Best"
"Put Him Away"
"When It Dries"
"Why Me?"

"You"
"You Have Got To Have A Rudder On The Ark"

In 1970, the sixty-eight-year-old Rodgers suffered a heart attack. He went on to write three more musicals, each without merit. **TWO BY TWO** was an unhappy show and an unhappy experience. There was virtually nothing of interest, including Danny Kaye. The star did what he could to force a run, resulting in a slight profit for producer Rodgers. The best that can be said was that there was one pretty song, "I Do Not Know A Day I Did Not Love You."

REX
April 25, 1976   Lunt-Fontanne Theatre   48 performances
Lyrics by Sheldon Harnick
Book by Sherman Yellen
Directed by Edwin Sherin
Produced by Richard Adler in association with Roger Berlind and Edward
   R. Downe
With Nicol Williamson, Penny Fuller, and Tom Aldredge

Published songs:

"As Once I Loved You"
"Away From You"

Additional songs recorded:

"At The Field Of Cloth Of Gold"
"The Chase"
"Christmas At Hampton Court"
"Elizabeth"
"From Afar"
"In Time"
"No Song More Pleasing"
"So Much You Loved Me"
"Te Deum"
"The Wee Golden Warrior"
"Where Is My Son?"
"Why?"

REX was poorly conceived and badly produced. Michael Bennett was passed over early in the game; he went off to develop **A CHORUS LINE [April 15, 1975]** instead. The directorial reins were entrusted to Edwin Sherin, whose musical experience consisted of being fired from **SEESAW [Coleman: March 18, 1973]** in Detroit (and being replaced by Michael Bennett). On **REX** it was Harold Prince (who had produced Adler's two hits as composer) who was brought to Boston. But it was much too late.

I REMEMBER MAMA
May 31, 1979   Majestic Theatre   108 performances
Lyrics mostly by Martin Charnin
Book by Thomas Meehan
(Based on the play by John van Druten and the stories by Kathryn Forbes)
Directed by Cy Feuer
Produced by Alexander H. Cohen and Hildy Parks
With Liv Ullmann, George Hearn, and George S. Irving

Published songs:

"Ev'ry Day (Comes Something Beautiful)"
"It Is Not The End Of The World"
"Time"
"You Could Not Please Me More"

Alexander H. Cohen assembled a typical Alexander H. Cohen package: star composer, star actress, and the lyricist, librettist, director, designer, etc. from Broadway's most recent smash hit. But Rodgers was seventy-six and in ill health; Liv Ullmann was a musical novice who barely spoke (let alone sang) the language; and the musical-comedy track records of the Messrs. Charnin and Cohen were less than inspiring. Van Druten's **I REMEMBER MAMA** had been a wartime hit (produced by Rodgers and Hammerstein) and a popular Fifties television series. Cohen fired Charnin during the tryout and brought in producer Cy Feuer to direct, along with lyricist Raymond Jessel (of Cohen's **BAKER STREET [Bock: February 16, 1965]**). Cohen was not nominated for the Best Producer Tony, but his musical was nevertheless prominently featured on the Awards telecast (produced by Cohen). **I REMEMBER MAMA** was Richard Rodgers' final work. He died as the decade ended, on December 30, 1979 in New York.

It is impossible to go through the complete work of Richard Rodgers without being overwhelmed by the man's talent. So many wonderful songs! For twenty-five years Rodgers was among the leaders of the field; no one (other than Jerome Kern) was as responsible for the development of the American musical theatre. During a span of less than a decade, Rodgers wrote five innovative, high-quality musicals. **ON YOUR TOES [April 11, 1936]** introduced real ballet to musical comedy—and used it as a plot element. **THE BOYS FROM SYRACUSE [November 23, 1938]** was farce musical comedy par excellence, still unmatched. **PAL JOEY [December 25, 1940]** first brought realistic (if disreputable) characters and subjects onto the musical stage. **OKLAHOMA! [March 31, 1943]** combined all theatrical elements into a cohesive whole. And all culminated in the stunning **CAROUSEL [April 19, 1945]**, serious, dramatic musical theatre. Consider that all five scores are highly effective almost a half century later; during these nine years Rodgers also wrote *five additional* musical successes, including the hit-filled **BABES IN ARMS [April 14, 1937]**; and Rodgers wrote many of his best songs in the years *before* and *after* this golden period (including the **SOUTH PACIFIC [April 7, 1949]** score). A close look at the theatre music of Richard Rodgers shows how very important and enduring his accomplishments, innovations and songs were.

Cole Porter

BORN: June 9, 1891   Peru, Indiana
DIED: October 15, 1964   Santa Monica, California

Cole Porter's father, a druggist, played a very small part in his life; his maternal grandfather, however, was industrial magnate J. O. Cole. While Cole wanted the boy raised to take over his business, Porter's mother cultivated his love of music; she even had an early composition, "Bobolink Waltz," published in 1902. By his fourteenth birthday Porter was away at Eastern schools, and in 1913 he graduated from Yale (where he'd majored in writing football songs—"Bulldog" is still sung—and varsity shows). His first Tin Pan Alley song was the 1910 "Bridget." Porter forsook Indiana for high society. A New York patroness was theatrical agent Elisabeth Marbury, creator of the innovative "Princess Theatre Show" series (see **NOBODY HOME [Kern: April 20, 1915]**). Latching on to the entertaining sophisticate, she went about getting him a Broadway hearing.

[all music and lyrics by Cole Porter unless indicated]

HANDS UP
Musico-Comico-Filmo-Melo-Drama
July 22, 1915   44th Street Theatre   52 performances

Music mostly by E. Ray Goetz and Sigmund Romberg
Book and lyrics mostly by Goetz
Directed by J. H. Benrimo
Produced by the Messrs. Shubert

Published song:

"Esmeralda"

MISS INFORMATION
A Little Play With A Little Music
October 5, 1915   George M. Cohan Theatre
47 performances

Music mostly by Jerome **Kern**
Lyrics mostly by Elsie Janis
Book by Paul Dickey and Charles W. Goddard
Directed by Robert Milton
Produced by Charles Dillingham
With Elsie Janis and Irene Bordoni

Published song:

"Two Big Eyes" (lyric by John Golden)

Irene Bordoni was to star in Porter's first Broadway hit, **PARIS [October 8, 1928]**—thirteen years later!

SEE AMERICA FIRST
A Patriotic Comic Opera
March 28, 1916   Maxine Elliott Theatre   15 performances

Book, music and lyrics by T. Lawrason Riggs and Cole Porter
Directed by J. H. Benrimo
Produced by The Marbury-Comstock Company
With Dorothie Bigelow, John H. Goldsworthy, Leonard Joy, and Clifton
  Webb

Published songs:

"Buy Her A Box At The Opera"
"Ever And Ever Yours"
"I've A Shooting Box In Scotland"
"I've Got An Awful Lot To Learn"
"The Language Of Flowers"
"Lima"
"Oh, Bright Fair Dream"—cut
"Pity Me Please"—cut
"Prithee, Come Crusading"
"See America First"
"Slow Sinks The Sun"—cut
"Something's Got To Be Done"
"When I Used To Lead The Ballet"

Porter's first complete Broadway score was for this vanity production produced by Marbury and her "Princess Theatre Show" partner. Following a highly successful society preview, **SEE AMERICA FIRST**—made up mostly of material written for fraternity musicals—was viewed as a mediocre college show (with surprisingly adept lyrics) and quickly closed. Of interest in the cast was dancer Clifton Webb, who was to be a feature of Broadway's sophisticated Thirties revues before leaving for Hollywood. For the record, Yale man Riggs was Porter's roommate during the latter's brief visit to Harvard Law School (by order of grandfather Cole, who controlled the millions). Following **SEE AMERICA FIRST**, Riggs became a priest.

VERY GOOD EDDIE
May 18, 1918   Palace Theatre ⟨London⟩   46 performances

Music mostly by Jerome **Kern** (see [**December 23, 1915**])
Lyrics mostly by Schuyler Greene and Herbert Reynolds
Book by Philip Bartholomae and Guy Bolton
(Based on *Over Night* [play] by Bartholomae)
Directed by Guy Bragdon
Produced by Alfred Butt and André Charlot
With Nelson Keys

Published song:

"Alone With You" (by Porter and Melville Gideon)

Porter escaped the World War I draft by going to his beloved France, where he was involved with a society-sponsored food distribution program. He spent the war attending and throwing parties, not in the French Foreign Legion (as reported in later years). Songwriting continued as a hobby, with trips across the Channel to interpolate in London musicals. With the exception of a few attempts at revues, Porter spent the next ten years as a very talented dilettante.

TELLING THE TALE
[Circa October 1918]   Ambassador's Theatre ⟨London⟩

Book by Sydney Blow and Douglas Hoare
Produced by Gerald Kirby and John Wyndham
With Birdie Courtenay and Kirby

Published song:

"Altogether Too Fond Of You" (by Melville Gideon, James Heard, and Porter)—also used (cut) in **BUDDIES** [October 27, 1919]

HITCHY-KOO 1919
Third Edition
October 6, 1919   Liberty Theatre   56 performances

Book by George V. Hobart
Directed by Julian Alfred
Produced by Raymond Hitchcock
With Hitchcock and Joe Cook

Published songs:

"Another Sentimental Song"—cut
"Bring Me Back My Butterfly"
"I Introduced"
"In Hitchy's Garden"
"I've Got Somebody Waiting"
"My Cozy Little Corner In The Ritz"
"Old Fashioned Garden"
"Peter Piper/The Sea Is Calling"
"That Black And White Baby Of Mine"—cut
"When I Had A Uniform On"

The war over, Porter returned to America. His already growing reputation as a clever sophisticate resulted in this commission. Hitchcock, a fairly successful comic, began his annual revue series in 1917. Although parts of **HITCHY-KOO**'s score displayed Porter's sophisticated lyricism, it was the simple, sentimental "Old Fashioned Garden" that became his first song hit.

BUDDIES
Comedy Of Quaint Brittany
October 27, 1919   Selwyn Theatre   259 performances

Music and lyrics mostly by B. C. Hilliam
Book by George V. Hobart
Produced by Selwyn and Co.
With Donald Brian, Peggy Wood, and Roland Young

Published songs:

"Altogether Too Fond Of You" (by Melville Gideon, James Heard
    and Porter)—cut before opening; originally used in **TELLING
    THE TALE [Circa October 1918]**

"I Never Realized" (music by Gideon, lyric by Porter; issued as by
    Gideon)—cut before opening; also used in **THE ECLIPSE
    [November 12, 1919]**

"Washington Square" (music by Gideon, lyric by Porter; issued as
    by Gideon)—cut before opening; also see **AS YOU WERE
    [January 27, 1920]** and **THE ECLIPSE**

THE ECLIPSE
November 12, 1919   Garrick Theatre ⟨London⟩
117 performances

Music by Herman Darewski and Melville Gideon
Lyrics mostly by Adrian Ross
Book by Fred Thompson and E. Phillips Oppenheim
Produced by Charles B. Cochran
With Nancy Gibbs and F. Pope Stamper

Published songs:

"I Never Realized" (music by Gideon, lyric by Porter; issued as
    lyric by Adrian Ross)—originally used (cut) in **BUDDIES
    [October 27, 1919]**

"In Chelsea Somewhere" (music by Gideon, lyric by "Col. E.
    Porter" and James Heard)—revised lyric for "Washington Square"
    (cut) from **BUDDIES**

AS YOU WERE
A Fantastic Revue
January 27, 1920   Central Theatre   143 performances

Music mostly by Herman Darewski
Lyrics mostly by Arthur Wimperis and E. Ray Goetz
Book by Glen MacDonough
(Based on *Plus Ça Change* [revue] by Rip)
Produced by Goetz
With Sam Bernard and Irene Bordoni (Goetz)

Published song:

"Washington Square" (music by Melville Gideon, lyric by Porter
    and Goetz)—revised lyric for song originally used (cut) in

BUDDIES [October 27, 1919]; also see THE ECLIPSE [November 12, 1919]

A NIGHT OUT
September 18, 1920   Winter Garden Theatre ⟨London⟩
311 performances

Music mostly by Willie Redstone (see **Youmans [September 7, 1925]**)
Porter lyrics by Clifford Grey
Book by George Grossmith and Arthur Miller
(Based on a farce by Georges Feydeau and Maurice Desvallières)
Directed by Tom Reynolds
Produced by Grossmith and Edward Laurillard
With Leslie Henson and Lily St. John

Published songs:

"Look Around"
"Our Hotel"
"Why Didn't We Meet Before?"

Additional song published in vocal score:

"Finale (It's A Sad Day At This Hotel)"

MAYFAIR AND MONTMARTRE
March 9, 1922   New Oxford Theatre ⟨London⟩
77 performances

Music mostly by others
Book by John Hastings Turner
Directed and produced by Charles B. Cochran
With Alice Delysia, Evelyn Laye, and Joyce Barbour

Published songs:

"The Blue Boy Blues"
"Cocktail Time"
"Olga (Come Back To The Volga)"

PHI-PHI
August 16, 1922   Pavilion Theatre ⟨London⟩
132 performances

Music mostly by Christiné
Lyrics mostly by Clifford Grey

Book by Fred Thompson and Grey
(From the French by Willemetz and Sollar)
Produced by Charles B. Cochran
With Clifton Webb

Published songs:

"The Ragtime Pipes of Pan"

HITCHY-KOO OF 1922
Fifth Edition
[October 10, 1922]   Shubert Theatre ⟨Philadelphia,
Pennsylvania⟩; closed during pre-Broadway tryout

Book by Harold Atteridge
Directed by J. C. Huffman
Produced by Messrs. J. J. and Lee Shubert
With Raymond Hitchcock

Published songs:

"The American Punch"
"The Bandit Band"
"The Harbor Deep Down In My Heart"
"Love Letter Words"
"When My Caravan Comes Home"

Porter wrote his third complete score for this out-of-town failure. On October 25, 1923, Porter's ballet "Within The Quota"—his only attempt at serious music—premiered in Paris.

GREENWICH VILLAGE FOLLIES
Sixth Annual Production
September 16, 1924   Shubert Theatre   127 performances

Book by Lew Fields, Irving Caesar, and others
Directed by John Murray Anderson
Produced by The Bohemians, Inc.
With the Dolly Sisters

Published songs:

"Brittany"
"I'm In Love Again"—added after opening; also used in **UP
   WITH THE LARK [August 25, 1927]**

"Make Every Day A Holiday"
"My Long Ago Girl"
"Two Little Babes In The Wood"—initial publication upon reuse
  in **PARIS [October 8, 1928]**
"Wait For The Moon"

This series had begun life as an intimate, bohemian, off-Broadway revue in 1919; the Shuberts bought the title in 1921 and undressed it. "I'm In Love Again" and "Two Little Babes In The Wood" both became hits—but not until Porter's first wave of popularity in 1928.

UP WITH THE LARK
August 25, 1927   Adelphi Theatre ⟨London⟩

Music mostly by Philip Braham
Lyrics mostly by Douglas Furber
Book by Furber and Hartley Carrick
(Based on *Le Zebre* [play] by Armont and Nancy)
Directed by George Grossmith
Produced by Westland Productions (in association with Martin Henry)
With Allen Kearns, Leslie Sarony, and Charles King

Published song:

"I'm In Love Again"—originally used in **GREENWICH VILLAGE FOLLIES** ⟨Sixth Edition⟩ [September 16, 1924]

LA REVUE DES AMBASSADEURS
Nightclub Revue
May 10, 1928   Les Ambassadeurs ⟨Paris⟩

Music and lyrics mostly by Porter
Directed by Bobby Connolly
Produced by Edmond Sayag
With Morton Downey, Evelyn Hoey, Fred Waring, and Frances Gershwin

Published songs:

"Almiro"
"Hans"
"Military Maids"
"Looking at You"—cut; initial publication upon reuse in **WAKE UP AND DREAM** [March 27, 1929]

"An Old Fashioned Girl"
"You And Me"

Additional songs published in vocal selection:

"Alpine Rose"
"Baby, Let's Dance"
"Blue Hours"
"Fish"
"Fountain Of Youth"
"In A Moorish Garden"
"The Lost Liberty Blues"
"Pilot Me"

This nightclub show was presented for expatriate Americans in Paris. Included in the cast was the Gershwins' talented sister, who sang a medley of Gershwin tunes.

PARIS
October 8, 1928   Music Box Theatre   195 performances

Book by Martin Brown
Directed by W. H. Gilmore
Produced by Gilbert Miller in association with E. Ray Goetz
With Irene Bordoni (Goetz), Louise Closser Hale, and Arthur Margetson

Published songs:

"Don't Look At Me That Way"
"The Heaven Hop"
"Let's Do It"—also used in **WAKE UP AND DREAM** ⟨London⟩
   [March 27, 1929]
"Let's Misbehave"—cut
"Quelque Chose"—cut
"Two Little Babes In The Wood"—originally used in
   GREENWICH VILLAGE FOLLIES ⟨Sixth Edition⟩
   [September 19, 1924]
"Vivienne"
"Which"—cut; also used in **WAKE UP AND DREAM**

Porter's first hit, featuring the saucy Bordoni. The risqué "Let's Do It" was a quick hit, placing Porter in league with Lorenz Hart as Broadway's cleverest and most sophisticated lyricists.

WAKE UP AND DREAM
March 27, 1929   Pavilion Theatre ⟨London⟩
263 performances
December 30, 1929   Selwyn Theatre ⟨New York⟩
136 performances

Music and lyrics mostly by Porter (see **Schwartz [December 30, 1929]**)
Book by John Hastings Turner
Choreography (London) by George Balanchine
Directed by Frank Collins
LONDON: Produced by Charles B. Cochran
With Jessie Matthews and Sonny Hale
NEW YORK: Produced by Arch Selwyn in association with Cochran
With Jessie Matthews and Jack Buchanan

Published songs:

"Agua Sincopada (Tango)"
"The Banjo (That Man Joe Plays)"
"I Dream Of A Girl In A Shawl"—advertised but not published;
   included (no lyric) in piano selection
"I Loved Him But He Didn't Love Me"
"I Want To Be Raided By You"—advertised but not published
"Gigolo"
"Let's Do It"—originally used in **PARIS [October 8, 1928]**
"Looking At You"—originally used (cut/unpublished) in **LA
   REVUE DES AMBASSADEURS [May 10, 1928]**
"Wake Up And Dream"
"What Is This Thing Called Love?"
"Which"—originally used (cut) in **PARIS [October 8, 1928]**

Additional song published in "The Unpublished Cole Porter":

"After All, I'm Only A Schoolgirl"

Additional songs published (no lyric) in piano selection:

"I've Got A Crush On You"

Additional songs recorded:

"I Want To Be Raided By You"
"Pills"

[NOTE: not all songs used in New York edition]

Cochran had been successful in hiring the Americans Rodgers and Hart for his 1927 **LONDON PAVILION REVUE (ONE DAM THING AFTER ANOTHER)** [Rodgers: May 20, 1927]; now he tried Porter, with similarly successful results. The New York production of **WAKE UP AND DREAM** did not do quite as well, hampered by the stock market crash and competition from Porter's just-opened hit **FIFTY MILLION FRENCHMEN** [November 27, 1929].

FIFTY MILLION FRENCHMEN
A Musical Comedy Tour Of Paris
November 27, 1929   Lyric Theatre   254 performances

Book by Herbert Fields
Directed by Monty Woolley
Produced by E. Ray Goetz
With William Gaxton, Genevieve Tobin, and Helen Broderick

Published songs:

"Find Me A Primitive Man"
"The Happy Heaven Of Harlem"
"I Worship You"—cut
"I'm In Love"
"I'm Unlucky At Gambling"
"Let's Step Out"—added after opening
"Paree, What Did You Do To Me?"
"Please Don't Make Me Be Good"—cut
"The Queen Of Terre Haute"—cut
"You Do Something To Me"
"You Don't Know Paree"
"You've Got That Thing"

Additional songs published in "The Unpublished Cole Porter":

"The Tale Of The Oyster"—cut
"Why Don't We Try Staying Home"—cut

Additional song recorded:

"Where Would You Get Your Coat?"

Herbert Fields left his long-time collaborators following the **CHEE-CHEE** [Rodgers: September 25, 1928] debacle, joining Porter in the first of their seven consecutive hits. Gaxton, whose first important role had been as Fields' **CONNECTICUT YANKEE** ⟨**First Ver-**

sion⟩ [Rodgers: November 3, 1927] now became a star. Porter wrote two more hits for Gaxton and future partner Victor Moore. Directing was Porter's close friend and classmate (turned Yale drama professor) Woolley, making his professional debut; he eventually turned to acting. Porter added to his hit songs with "You Do Something To Me" and "You've Got That Thing."

THE NEW YORKERS
⟨Second Version⟩
December 8, 1930   Broadway Theatre   168 performances

Music and lyrics mostly by Porter
Book by Herbert Fields
(Based on a story by Peter Arno and E. Ray Goetz)
Directed by Monty Woolley
Produced by Goetz
With Hope Williams, Ann Pennington, Charles King, and Jimmy Durante

Published songs:

"But He Never Said He Loved Me"—cut; initial publication upon
    reuse in **NYMPH ERRANT [October 6, 1933]** retitled "The
    Physician"
"The Great Indoors"
"I Happen To Like New York"—added after opening
"I'm Getting Myself Ready For You"
"Just One Of Those Things" [1st]—cut; different than hit song
    from **JUBILEE [October 12, 1935]**
"Let's Fly Away"
"Love For Sale"
"Take Me Back To Manhattan"
"Where Have You Been?"

Another hit for Porter, though not as successful as **FIFTY MIL-
LION FRENCHMEN [November 27, 1929]**. Porter continued to earn a reputation for sophistication: lyrics like "Love For Sale" outraged some (but pleased many more).

GAY DIVORCE
November 29, 1932   Ethel Barrymore Theatre
248 performances

Book by Dwight Taylor
Adapted by Kenneth Webb and Samuel Hoffenstein
(Based on an unproduced play by J. Hartley Manners)
Directed by Howard Lindsay
Produced by Dwight Deere Wiman and Tom Weatherly
With Fred Astaire, Claire Luce, and Luella Gear

Published songs:

"After You"
"How's Your Romance"
"I've Got You On My Mind"
"Mister and Missus Fitch"—initial publication as 1954 nonshow
    song
"Night And Day"
"You're In Love"

Additional song published (no lyric) in piano selection:

"I Love Only You"—written for London production [November 2,
    1933]

Additional song recorded:

"Why Marry Them?"

Could Fred Astaire make it on his own following Adele's retirement
after **THE BAND WAGON [Schwartz: June 3, 1931]**? He did
moderately well in **GAY DIVORCE,** which was kept alive by the
popularity of "Night And Day." The 1934 movie version *Gay Divorcee*—which threw out Porter's entire score (except "Night And
Day")—teamed Astaire with Ginger Rogers, and that was the end of
Astaire and Broadway. Hollywood also cut the score for the 1931
version of **FIFTY MILLION FRENCHMEN [November 27, 1928]**
and the 1937 **ROSALIE [Gershwin: January 10, 1928]**—for which
Porter wrote the replacement. Librettist Taylor, later to collaborate
with Porter on **OUT OF THIS WORLD [December 21, 1950],** was
Manners' stepson (and son of actress Laurette).

NYMPH ERRANT
October 6, 1933   Adelphi Theatre ⟨London⟩
154 performances

Book and direction by Romney Brent
(Based on the novel by James Laver)

Produced by Charles B. Cochran
With Gertrude Lawrence, Elisabeth Welch, and David Burns

Published songs:

"Experiment"
"How Could We Be Wrong?"
"I Look At You"—cut; initial publication as 1934 nonshow song
   with new lyric, retitled "You're Too Far Away"
"It's Bad For Me"
"Nymph Errant"
"The Physician"—originally used (cut/unpublished) in **THE NEW
   YORKERS [December 8, 1930]**
"Solomon"
"When Love Comes Your Way"—cut; also used in **JUBILEE
   [October 12, 1935]**

Additional songs published (no lyrics) in piano selection:

"Back To Nature"
"The Castle"
"The Cocotte"
"Georgia Sand"
"Neauville-Sur-Mer"

Additional songs recorded:

"Si Vous Aimez Les Poitrines"
"Sweet Nudity"—cut

A suggestive romp about a staid British nymphomaniac, which thrilled
Continental society but left the staid British lukewarm.

HI DIDDLE DIDDLE

October 3, 1934   Comedy Theatre ⟨London⟩
198 performances

Play by William Walker and Robert Nesbitt
Produced by André Charlot
With Douglas Byng

Published song:

"Miss Otis Regrets"

"Miss Otis Regrets" is one of Porter's Twenties party songs, which
was eventually published and achieved considerable popularity.

ANYTHING GOES
November 21, 1934   Alvin Theatre   420 performances

Book by Guy Bolton and P. G. Wodehouse
Revised by Howard Lindsay and Russel Crouse
Directed by Howard Lindsay
Produced by Vinton Freedley
With William Gaxton, Ethel Merman, Victor Moore, and Bettina Hall

Published songs:

"All Through The Night"
"Anything Goes"
"Blow, Gabriel, Blow"
"Buddie, Beware"—cut after opening
"The Gypsy In Me"
"I Get A Kick Out Of You"
"There'll Always Be A Lady Fair"—initial publication upon reuse
   in 1936 movie version
"Waltz Down The Aisle"—cut; see **KISS ME, KATE [December
   30, 1948]**
"You're The Top"

Additional songs published in vocal score:

"Be Like The Bluebird"
"Bon Voyage"
"Public Enemy Number One (Opening Act Two)"
"Where Are The Men?"

Additional song recorded:

"Kate The Great"—cut

Unquestionably Porter's second best show (after **KISS ME, KATE
[December 30, 1948]**). Freedley, heretofore associated with the
Gershwins, was just recovering from his insolvency (see **PARDON
MY ENGLISH [Gershwin: January 20, 1933]**). Gaxton and Moore
had worked together in **OF THEE I SING [Gershwin: December
25, 1931]** and its sequel **LET 'EM EAT CAKE [Gershwin: October
21, 1933]**; now they established themselves as an ongoing partnership. Ethel Merman, discovered in the final Aarons and Freedley hit
GIRL CRAZY [Gershwin: October 14, 1930], took Broadway by
storm with her renditions of several sparkling Porter gems. **ANY-
THING GOES** played the Alvin, the house that Aarons, Freedley,

and the Gershwins' hits built—except Freedley had to rent it, having lost ownership. The Bolton-Wodehouse libretto about the comic aftermath of a shipwreck was hastily discarded when the *Morro Castle* sank off the New Jersey coast (with 134 dead). The authors being unavailable for revisions, it fell to director Lindsay (from **GAY DIVORCE [November 29, 1932]**) to fashion a new book around the existing songs. Theatre Guild press agent Crouse was brought in to help, forming yet another highly successful partnership. Wodehouse, though, retired from the musical theatre.

JUBILEE
October 12, 1935   Imperial Theatre   169 performances

Book by Moss Hart
Book directed by Monty Woolley
Directed by Hassard Short
Produced by Sam H. Harris and Max Gordon
With Mary Boland, Melville Cooper, and June Knight

Published songs:

"Begin The Beguine"
"Just One Of Those Things" [2nd]—the hit; different than song
   from **THE NEW YORKERS [December 8, 1930]**
"The Kling-Kling Bird On The Divi-Divi Tree"
"Me And Marie"
"A Picture Of Me Without You"
"When Love Comes Your Way"—originally used (cut) in **NYMPH
   ERRANT [October 6, 1933]**
"Why Shouldn't I?"

Additional songs recorded:

"Entrance of Eric"
"Ev'rybod-ee Who's Anybod-ee"
"Sunday Morning, Breakfast Time"
"What A Nice Municipal Park"
"When Me, Mowgli, Love"

Porter rarely needed an excuse to travel; in this case he invited Hart and Woolley along on a five-month world cruise, during which they put together this lavish musical. By the time "Begin The Beguine" and "Just One Of Those Things" caught on, **JUBILEE** was gone—lasting no longer than the cruise and costing a whole lot more.

RED, HOT AND BLUE!
October 29, 1936   Alvin Theatre   183 performances

Book by Howard Lindsay and Russel Crouse
Directed by Lindsay
Produced by Vinton Freedley
With Ethel Merman, Jimmy Durante, and Bob Hope

Published songs:

"Down In The Depths (On The Ninetieth Floor)"
"Goodbye, Little Dream, Goodbye"—cut; see **O MISTRESS
  MINE [December 3, 1936]**
"It's De-Lovely"
"A Little Skipper From Heaven Above"
"Ours"
"The Ozarks Are Calling Me Home"
"Red, Hot And Blue"
"Ridin' High"
"You're A Bad Influence On Me"
"You've Got Something"

Additional songs published in "special edition" vocal selection:

"Perennial Debutantes"
"What A Great Pair We'll Be"

Additional song published in "The Unpublished Cole Porter":

"When Your Troubles Have Started"—cut

Additional song recorded:

"Bertie and Gertie"—cut

An uneven successor to **ANYTHING GOES [November 20, 1934]**
which had some success—not surprisingly, considering the star co-
medians. William Gaxton withdrew when he learned Merman had been
promised equal billing. Durante, in the Victor Moore role, presented
billing problems himself; the two finally settled on a diagonal criss-
cross design. (Merman got first billing when she met Durante again
in **STARS IN YOUR EYES [Schwartz: February 9, 1939]**.) Bob
Hope, fresh from Fanny Brice and the **ZIEGFELD FOLLIES OF
1936 [Duke: January 30, 1936]**, didn't bother with billing: he had a
line of his own below the others, undiagonal and considerably more
readable. Hope followed **RED, HOT AND BLUE!** with Hollywood, never to return. Porter's work was far below his **ANYTHING**

GOES output, but he did come up with a worthy successor to "You're the Top" in "It's De-Lovely." On October 24, 1937, just months after Gershwin's death, Porter was critically injured in a horseback riding accident. Amputation was averted but he suffered constant pain for the rest of his life. After twenty years and thirty operations, his right leg was finally amputated.

O MISTRESS MINE
December 3, 1936   St. James Theatre ⟨London⟩

Play by Ben Travers
Directed and produced by William Mollison
With Yvonne Printemps and Pierre Fresnay

Published song:

"Goodbye, Little Dream, Goodbye"—originally cut from **RED, HOT AND BLUE! [October 29, 1936]**

YOU NEVER KNOW
September 21, 1938   Winter Garden Theatre
78 performances

Music and lyrics also by others
Book and direction by Rowland Leigh
(Based on *Candle Light* [play] by Siegfried Geyer)
Produced by John Shubert
With Clifton Webb, Lupe Velez, and Libby Holman

Published songs:

"At Long Last Love"
"For No Rhyme Or Reason"
"From Alpha To Omega"
"Maria"
"What Is That Tune?"
"What Shall I Do?"
"You Never Know"

Additional song published in "The Unpublished Cole Porter":
"I'm Going In For Love"—cut

Writing in his hospital bed (press releases claim a song was written as he lay crushed beneath the horse, waiting for the ambulance), Porter turned out a mediocre score for a poor musical. The Shuberts brought in other songwriters to try to strengthen the show. As the major problem was the book, and the additional songs weren't even as good as Porter's, this didn't help much.

LEAVE IT TO ME!
November 9, 1938   Imperial Theatre   291 performances

Book by Bella and Samuel Spewack
(Based on *Clear All Wires* [play] by the Spewacks)
Directed by Samuel Spewack
Produced by Vinton Freedley
With William Gaxton, Victor Moore, Sophie Tucker, Tamara, and Mary
   Martin

Published songs:

"Far Away"
"From Now On"
"Get Out Of Town"
"I Want To Go Home"
"Most Gentlemen Don't Like Love"
"My Heart Belongs To Daddy"
"Taking The Steps To Russia"
"To-morrow"

Additional song published in vocal selection:

"Vite, Vite, Vite"—initial publication upon reuse in 1982 movie
   Evil Under the Sun

Porter bounced back with a string of hits well into the war years—although the scores were far below the quality of earlier work. The Spewacks had an enormous success with their George Abbott farce BOY MEETS GIRL [November 27, 1935]; **LEAVE IT TO ME!** was in the same vein. Victor Moore for once had a better role than Gaxton (who was getting a little past the age for romantic leads), and gave one of his funniest performances; red-hot Sophie Tucker played in her only musical comedy role; and Mary Martin overshadowed them all in her Broadway debut, with the auspicious "My Heart Belongs To Daddy" striptease.

THE SUN NEVER SETS
June 9, 1939   Drury Lane Theatre ⟨London⟩

Play by Pat Wallace and Guy Bolton
(Based on stories by Edgar Wallace)
Directed by Basil Dean and Richard Llewellyn
With Todd Duncan, Leslie Banks, Adelaide Hall, and Edna Best

Published song:

"River God"

THE MAN WHO CAME TO DINNER
October 16, 1939   Music Box Theatre   739 performances

Play by Moss Hart and George S. Kaufman
Directed by Kaufman
Produced by Sam H. Harris
With Monty Woolley, Edith Atwater, and David Burns

Song published in acting edition of script:

"What Am I To Do?"

Hart and Kaufman's play satirized mutual friend Alexander Wooll-
cott. Among the characters was a Cowardish personality who whisked
over to the piano and dashed off a little song. Porter, who had brought
college professor Woolley to Broadway, supplied "What Am I To
Do?"—credited to "Noel Porter."

DUBARRY WAS A LADY
December 6, 1939   46th Street Theatre   408 performances

Book by Herbert Fields and B. G. DeSylva
Directed by Edgar MacGregor
Produced by DeSylva
With Bert Lahr, Ethel Merman, Betty Grable, and Benny Baker

Published songs:

"But In The Morning, No"
"Come On In"
"Do I Love You?"
"Ev'ry Day A Holiday"
"Friendship"
"Give Him The Oo-La-La"
"It Was Written In The Stars"
"Katie Went To Haiti"
"Well, Did You Evah?"
"When Love Beckoned (In Fifty-Second Street)"

Additional song recorded:
"It Ain't Etiquette"

Following his 1931 breakup with partners Brown and Henderson, B. G. DeSylva began a highly successful movie producing career. In 1939 he returned to Broadway, producing (and coauthoring librettos for) three major hits in less than a year: two Porter shows and **LOUISIANA PURCHASE [Berlin: May 28, 1940]**. DeSylva brought Herb Fields back from Hollywood, and signed Merman (star of his preceding musical, **TAKE A CHANCE [Youmans: November 26, 1932]**) and Bert Lahr (star of two DeSylva, Brown, and Henderson hits). Also on hand was ingenue Betty Grable, who went right to Hollywood. Porter's score included another classic list song, "Friendship."

PANAMA HATTIE
October 30, 1940   46th Street Theatre   501 performances

Book by Herbert Fields and B. G. DeSylva
Directed by Edgar MacGregor
Produced by DeSylva
With Ethel Merman, James Dunn, and Arthur Treacher

Published songs:

"All I've Got To Get Now Is My Man"
"Fresh As A Daisy"
"I've Still Got My Health"
"Let's Be Buddies"
"Make It Another Old Fashioned, Please"
"My Mother Would Love You"
"Visit Panama"
"Who Would Have Dreamed?"

Additional song published in "The Unpublished Cole Porter":
"I'm Throwing A Ball Tonight"

Another hit for the **DUBARRY WAS A LADY [December 6, 1939]** team, although this wartime entertainment was considerably weaker. Following his threefold success, DeSylva was called back to Hollywood to head Paramount Studios.

LET'S FACE IT
October 29, 1941   Imperial Theatre   547 performances

Music and lyrics mostly by Porter
Book by Herbert and Dorothy Fields
(Based on *The Cradle Snatchers* [play] by Norma Mitchell and Russell Medcraft)
Directed by Edgar MacGregor
Produced by Vinton Freedley
With Danny Kaye, Eve Arden, Benny Baker, Edith Meiser, and Mary Jane Walsh

Published songs:

"Ace In The Hole"
"Ev'rything I Love"
"Farming"
"I Hate You Darling"
"Jerry, My Soldier Boy"
"Let's Not Talk About Love"
"A Little Rumba Numba"
"Rub Your Lamp"
"You Irritate Me So"

Additional songs recorded:

"Get Yourself A Girl"
"A Lady Needs A Rest"
"Pets"—cut
"What Are Little Husbands Made Of"—cut

This wartime hit was bolstered by the starring debut of Danny Kaye (fresh from **LADY IN THE DARK [Weill: January 23, 1941]**). Porter and Freedley had not been getting along well since **RED, HOT AND BLUE! [October 29, 1936]; LET'S FACE IT** was their final show together—and Freedley's final hit. Fields picked up a long-dormant collaboration with his sister Dorothy; he did most of his future work teamed with her.

SOMETHING FOR THE BOYS
January 7, 1943   Alvin Theatre   422 performances

Book by Herbert and Dorothy Fields
Directed by Hassard Short and Herbert Fields
Produced by Michael Todd

With Ethel Merman, Bill Johnson, Allen Jenkins, Betty Garrett, and
   Paula Laurence

Published songs:

"By The Mississinewah"
"Could It Be You?"
"He's A Right Guy"
"Hey, Good Lookin' "
"I'm In Love With A Soldier Boy"
"The Leader Of A Big-Time Band"
"See That You're Born In Texas"
"Something For The Boys"
"When My Baby Goes To Town"

With a new producer, Porter (and Fields) continued their string of
hits. The presence of Merman and the wartime atmosphere ensured
popularity, even for such inferior material as **SOMETHING FOR
THE BOYS**—a long-run success without even one hit song. Dorothy Fields did her second Merman show; it occured to her that her
friend might do well as a musical-comedy Annie Oakley (see **VERY
WARM FOR MAY [Kern: November 17, 1939]**).

MEXICAN HAYRIDE
January 28, 1944   Winter Garden Theatre
481 performances

Book by Herbert and Dorothy Fields
Directed by Hassard Short
Produced by Michael Todd
With Bobby Clark, June Havoc, George Givot, and Wilbur Evans

Published songs:

"Abracadabra"
"Carlotta"
"Count Your Blessings"
"Girls"
"The Good-Will Movement"
"I Love You"
"It Must Be Fun To Be You"—cut
"Sing To Me, Guitar"
"There Must Be Someone For Me"

Additional song published in "The Unpublished Cole Porter":
"It's Just Yours"—cut

Additional songs recorded:
"A Humble Hollywood Executive"—cut
"What A Crazy Way To Spend Sunday"

The final success in Porter's string (and the final one with Herb Fields). Bobby Clark carried the show, while Porter came up with the song hit "I Love You."

SEVEN LIVELY ARTS
December 7, 1944   Ziegfeld Theatre   183 performances
Music also by others
Sketches by Moss Hart, George S. Kaufman, Ben Hecht, and others
Directed by Hassard Short
Produced by Billy Rose
With Beatrice Lillie, Bert Lahr, and Benny Goodman

Published songs:
"The Band Started Swinging A Song"
"Ev'ry Time We Say Goodbye"
"Frahngee-Pahnee"
"Hence It Don't Make Sense"
"Is It The Girl (Or Is It The Gown?)"
"Only Another Boy And Girl"
"When I Was A Little Cuckoo"
"Wow-Ooh-Wolf"

Additional songs recorded:
"Dainty, Quainty Me"—cut
"I Wrote A Play"—cut
"Pretty Little Missus Bell"—cut

Billy Rose followed his greatest theatre success—Oscar Hammerstein 2nd's CARMEN JONES [December 2, 1943]—by purchasing the Ziegfeld Theatre. He determined to open it with a spectacularly Rose-ian spectacle, with Lillie and Lahr and Benny Goodman, Salvador Dali scenic conceptions, and a Broadway ballet composed by no less than Igor Stravinsky. All to no avail, and no thanks to Porter's pedestrian score. For the record, Rose's ego was such that his first production (starring then-wife Fanny Brice) was originally called *Corned Beef and Roses;* revamped after road disasters, it reached Broadway as SWEET AND LOW [November 17, 1930].

AROUND THE WORLD
May 31, 1946   Adelphi Theatre   75 performances

Book and direction by Orson Welles
(Based on *Around the World in Eighty Days* [novel] by Jules Verne)
Produced by The Mercury Theatre (Welles)
With Arthur Margetson, Julie Warren, and Welles

Published songs:

"If You Smile At Me"
"Look What I Found"
"Pipe-Dreaming"
"Should I Tell You I Love You"
"There He Goes, Mister Phileas Fogg"
"Wherever They Fly The Flag Of Old England"

Welles, who had earned a reputation for being wildly creative and totally uncontrollable, returned to Broadway (see **THE CRADLE WILL ROCK [Blitzstein: June 16, 1937]**) and ran amuk with this wildly insane extravaganza. **AROUND THE WORLD** was Porter's biggest flop, losing a record $300,000 in a day when a big musical could be produced for $100,000. (**KISS ME, KATE [December 30, 1948]**, two years later, was mounted for $180,000.) In trying to cover ballooning costs, Welles sold the motion picture rights to recent Porter producer Mike Todd; Todd made the highly successful 1958 movie version without Welles (or, for that matter, Porter).

KISS ME, KATE
December 30, 1948   New Century Theatre
1,077 performances

Book by Bella and Samuel Spewack
(Based on *The Taming of the Shrew* [play] by William Shakespeare)
Choreographed by Hanya Holm
Directed by John C. Wilson
Produced by Arnold Saint-Subber and Lemuel Ayers
With Alfred Drake, Patricia Morison, Harold Lang, and Lisa Kirk

Published songs:

"Always True To You In My Fashion"
"Another Op'nin', Another Show"
"Bianca"
"Brush Up Your Shakespeare"
"From This Moment On"—added to 1953 movie version; originally
    used (cut) in **OUT OF THIS WORLD [December 21, 1950]**
"I Am Ashamed That Women Are So Simple" (lyric by
    Shakespeare)
"I Hate Men"
"I Sing Of Love"
"I've Come To Wive It Wealthily In Padua"
"So In Love"
"Tom, Dick Or Harry"
"Too Darn Hot"
"We Open In Venice"
"Were Thine That Special Face"
"Where Is The Life That Late I Led?"
"Why Can't You Behave?"
"Wunderbar"—revised version of "Waltz Down The Aisle" (cut)
    from **ANYTHING GOES [November 21, 1934]**

Additional song published in vocal score:

"Kiss Me, Kate"

Additional song published in "The Unpublished Cole Porter":

"I'm Afraid, Sweetheart, I Love You"—cut

Additional songs recorded:

"If Ever Married I'm"—cut
"What Does Your Servant Dream About?"—cut

While Kern, Hammerstein, Rodgers, and others had been working
towards integrated musical theatre since the mid-Twenties, Porter
never tried for anything more than the best songs he could write at
the time—many of them rather good—in whatever framework his librettists happened upon. Following a long creative slump, Porter and
the Spewacks (of **LEAVE IT TO ME [November 9, 1938]**) suddenly and unexpectedly came up with one of the very finest musical
comedies in Broadway history. The contemporary backstage setting
gave the composer an opportunity to have swinging musical fun, with
"Too Darn Hot" and "Always True To You In My Fashion"; the

Shakespearean farce-musical excerpts gave the adept lyricist a free dramatic reign to rhyme, with "I've Come To Wive It Wealthily In Padua" and "Where Is The Life That Late I Led?"; and the anachronistic combinations of style—"Bianca" and especially "Brush Up Your Shakespeare"—were delightfully perfect. Porter also included one of his highly effective, carefully constructed ballads, "So In Love." **KISS ME, KATE** was the best, most successful and most personally gratifying show of Porter's career.

OUT OF THIS WORLD
December 21, 1950   New Century Theatre
157 performances

Book by Dwight Taylor and Reginald Lawrence
(Based on the *Amphitryon* legend)
Choreographed by Hanya Holm
Directed by Agnes de Mille
Produced by Saint-Subber and Lemuel Ayers
With Charlotte Greenwood, William Eythe, Priscilla Gillette, and David
    Burns

Published songs:

"Cherry Pies Ought To Be You"
"Climb Up The Mountain"
"From This Moment On"—cut; reused in 1953 motion picture
    version of **KISS ME KATE [December 30, 1948]**
"Hark To The Song Of The Night"
"I Am Loved"
"No Lover"
"Nobody's Chasing Me"
"Use Your Imagination"
"Where, Oh Where?"
"You Don't Remind Me"—cut

Additional song published in "The Unpublished Cole Porter":

"Oh It Must Be Fun"—cut

Additional songs recorded:

"Entrance Of Juno (Hail, Hail, Hail)"
"I Got Beauty"
"I Jupiter, I Rex"
"I Sleep Easier Now"
"Prologue"

"They Couldn't Compare To You"
"What Do You Think About Men?"

As was generally the case, a major hit was followed up with a similarly conceived, highly awaited major flop. Porter provided some of his most intricate lyrics; but his skill was overshadowed by a labored book, and **OUT OF THIS WORLD** was roundly attacked for questionable taste (verbal and visual). The uncredited George Abbott took over from de Mille, but the problems needed more than doctoring. Porter provided some uncharacteristically lovely songs—"I Am Loved" and the waltzing "Where, Oh Where"—along with "From This Moment On." **OUT OF THIS WORLD**'s most striking feature was the most colorful, lavish physical production yet seen on Broadway: co-producer Ayers was an inventive, gifted designer (with **OKLAHOMA! [March 31, 1943]** and **KISS ME, KATE [December 30, 1948]** to his credit) who died in 1955 at the age of forty.

CAN-CAN
May 7, 1953   Shubert Theatre   892 performances
Book and direction by Abe Burrows
Choreographed by Michael Kidd
Produced by Cy Feuer and Ernest Martin
With Lilo, Peter Cookson, Erik Rhodes, Hans Conried, and Gwen Verdon

Published songs:

"Allez-Vous En"
"Can-Can"
"C'est Magnifique"
"Come Along With Me"
"I Am In Love"
"I Love Paris"
"If You Loved Me Truly"
"It's All Right With Me"
"Live And Let Live"
"Montmart"
"Never Give Anything Away"

Additional songs published in vocal score:

"Every Man Is A Stupid Man"
"Maidens Typical Of France"
"Never, Never Be An Artist"

Additional songs published in "The Unpublished Cole Porter":

"To Think That This Could Happen To Me"—cut
"When Love Comes To Call"—cut
"Who Said Gay Paree"—cut

Additional song recorded:

"The Garden Of Eden Ballet" [instrumental]
"Her Heart Was In Her Work"—cut

Feuer and Martin followed their first two shows—hit Loesser musicals—with Porter's final two works. Porter had been undergoing a rough period, with increasing deterioration of his legs, a 1951 nervous breakdown, and the death of his mother (to whom he was devoted) in 1952. **CAN-CAN** managed a fair-sized success despite a lukewarm critical reception, and Porter enjoyed his final hit show tune, "I Love Paris." Stealing the show was dancer Gwen Verdon, in her first major role.

SILK STOCKINGS
February 24, 1955   Imperial Theatre   478 performances

Book by George S. Kaufman, Leueen MacGrath, and Abe Burrows
(Based on *Ninotchka* [movie] from a story by Melchior Lengyel)
Directed by Cy Feuer
Produced by Feuer and Ernest Martin
With Don Ameche, Hildegarde Neff, and Gretchen Wyler

Published songs:

"All Of You"
"As On Through The Seasons We Sail"
"Fated To be Mated"—written for 1957 movie version
"It's A Chemical Reaction, That's All"
"Josephine"
"Paris Loves Lovers"
"Ritz Roll And Rock"—written for 1957 movie version
"Satin And Silk"
"Siberia"
"Silk Stockings"
"Stereophonic Sound"
"Without Love"

Additional song published in "The Unpublished Cole Porter":
"Give Me The Land"—unused

Additional songs recorded:
"Hail Bibinski"
"The Red Blues"
"Too Bad"

Porter's final Broadway show was this painfully assembled, unsatisfying effort. Facing severe out-of-town troubles, librettist/director Kaufman and wife MacGrath were replaced by Burrows, who had been on **GUYS AND DOLLS [Loesser: November 24, 1950]** and **CAN-CAN [May 7, 1953]**. Feuer himself took over as director (as he would on the last Richard Rodgers musical, **I REMEMBER MAMA [Rodgers: May 31, 1979]**). Porter did some final work in Hollywood, including "True Love" for the 1956 film *High Society* and the 1958 TV musical *Aladdin*. In April of 1958 he finally lost his long-time medical battle: his leg had to be amputated. Porter withdrew from public view and stopped writing. After several years of ill health and severe depression, Cole Porter died of pneumonia in Santa Monica, California on October 15, 1964.

Following a lackadaisical twelve-year apprenticeship, Cole Porter startled New York and London in 1928 with sharp, dazzling lyrics and tuneful (if less dazzling) music. His work continued fresh and imaginative until 1935, when he seemed to hit a dry spell. Then came his 1937 accident, which seems to have had a permanent effect on his writing—the fun was gone. The next decade contained an impressive number of successful shows—mostly energetic wartime hits—but few of the songs were at all comparable to the earlier work. With the brilliant **KISS ME, KATE [December 30, 1948]**, Porter instantly caught up with his contemporaries and the newcomers who had passed him by. But the creative renaissance proved to be temporary. It is disconcerting (and somewhat surprising) to discover that the majority of Porter's songs are really quite ordinary. But the good music is often very good, and the good lyrics are always superb, more than enough to earn Porter a well-deserved reputation.

Arthur Schwartz

BORN: November 25, 1900   Brooklyn, New York
DIED: September 3, 1984   Kintnersville, Pennsylvania

Despite an early interest in music, Arthur Schwartz entered law (like his father before him). While attending Columbia, he supported himself by teaching high school English. Schwartz continued his hobby of writing songs; his first published work was the 1923 "Baltimore, Md., That's The Only Doctor For Me" (lyric by Eli Dawson). In 1926, lawyer Schwartz got his first big songwriting chance: writing for an intimate, sophisticated revue.

THE GRAND STREET FOLLIES OF 1926
Third Edition
June 15, 1926   Neighborhood Playhouse ⟨off-Broadway⟩   55 performances

Music also by Lily Hyland and Randall Thompson
Book, lyrics, and direction by Agnes Morgan
Produced by The Neighborhood Playhouse
With Albert Carroll and Morgan

Published songs:

"If You Know What I Mean" (lyric by Theodore Goodwin and
    Carroll)
"Little Igloo For Two"
"Polar Bear Strut"

THE GRAND STREET FOLLIES was an intimate revue providing amusing, contemporary competition to the uptown annuals. The Schwartz contributions were entertaining, if not overwhelming.

THE NEW YORKERS
⟨First Version⟩
March 10, 1927   Edyth Totten Theatre   52 performances

Music also by Edgar Fairchild and Charles M. Schwab
Lyrics by Henry Myers
Book by Jo Swerling
Directed by Milton Bender
Produced by Bender and Myers
NOTE: **1928**, pre-Broadway title

Published song:

"Floating Thru The Air"

Lorenz Hart had written summer-camp songs with Schwartz and was
a firm believer in his talent. **THE NEW YORKERS** was assembled
by his close friend, dentist Milton Bender (see **ONE MINUTE
PLEASE [Rodgers: December 29, 1917]**). "Doc" Bender held Ma-
chiavellian power over Hart, soon giving up his dental career to become the lyricist's agent; his power increased as Hart brought in friends
and coworkers like the Russians Geva, Balanchine, Zorina, and Duke.

GOOD BOY
*September 5, 1928   Hammerstein's Theatre
253 performances*

Music mostly by Harry Ruby and Herbert Stothart
Lyrics mostly by Bert Kalmar
Book by Otto Harbach, Oscar Hammerstein 2nd, and Henry Myers
Directed by Reginald Hammerstein
Produced by Arthur Hammerstein
With Eddie Buzzell and Helen Kane

Published song:

"You're The One" (lyric by Harbach)

This musical comedy featured Helen Kane introducing the Kalmar-
Ruby "I Wanna Be Loved By You"; the lyric of that song swept her
to fame as the "Boop-Boop-A-Doop" girl.

THE RED ROBE
December 25, 1928   Shubert Theatre   167 performances

Music mostly by Jean Gilbert
Book and lyrics mostly by Harry B. Smith
(Based on the novel by Stanley Weyman)
Directed by Stanley Logan
Presented by The Messrs. Shubert
With Walter Woolf and José Ruben

Published song:

"Believe In Me"

This dreary operetta was one of seven Broadway shows to open on that Christmas Night of 1928, none of them distinguished. Hart, meanwhile, prodded Schwartz into giving up his law practice to concentrate on songwriting.

NED WAYBURN'S GAMBOLS
January 15, 1929   Knickerbocker Theatre
31 performances

Music mostly by Walter G. Samuels
Lyrics by Morrie Ryskind
Produced and directed by Ned Wayburn

Published song:

"The Sun Will Shine"

Ned Wayburn, formerly staff director for Lew Fields, Ziegfeld, and the Shuberts, worked on an impressively large number of early revues and musicals. The totally unknown and neglected "The Sun Will Shine" was the first of Schwartz's beautiful ballads. The lyric was by Morrie Ryskind, who went on to do much better work as a satirical librettist (see **STRIKE UP THE BAND ⟨Second Version⟩ [Gershwin: January 14, 1930]**).

THE LITTLE SHOW
April 30, 1929   Music Box Theatre   321 performances

Music mostly by Arthur Schwartz
Lyrics mostly by Howard Dietz
Sketches by Dietz, George S. Kaufman, and others
Directed by Dwight Deere Wiman and Alexander Leftwich

Produced by William A. Brady, Jr. and Wiman, in association with Tom
  Weatherly
With Clifton Webb, Fred Allen, and Libby Holman

Published songs:

"I Guess I'll Have To Change My Plan (The Blue Pajama Song)"—
  new lyric for "I Love To Lie Awake In Bed" (lyric by Lorenz
  Hart; unpublished)
"I've Made A Habit Of You"

Additional songs published (no lyric) in piano selection:

"Get Up On A New Routine"
"The Theme Song"

Following the lead of the **MUSIC BOX [Berlin: September 22, 1921]**
and other intimate revues of the Twenties, **THE LITTLE SHOW**
added sophistication and contemporary comedy to the format. This
new-styled revue was to have great success during the Depression,
with Schwartz and Dietz leading the field. For most of his songwriting career, Howard Dietz was head of publicity at MGM (where he
created that most famous animal actor, Leo the Lion). His first hit
was "Alibi Baby" (music by Stephen Jones) from POPPY [Septem-
ber 3, 1923], although the show's contractual lyricist refused him
credit. But publisher Max Dreyfus was impressed, and sent Dietz to
Kern for the unsuccessful **DEAR SIR [Kern: September 23, 1924]**.
Schwartz recognized something in the lyrics akin to Hart, and tried
to collaborate with Dietz (a Columbia classmate of both Hart and
Hammerstein); Dietz preferred not to go from Kern to an unknown
lawyer, and found very little work (except filling in during Ira Gershwin's appendicitis on **OH, KAY! [Gershwin: November 8, 1926]**).
By 1929 he was ready to reconsider Schwartz's offer, and the successful collaboration began with **THE LITTLE SHOW**—although
the hit song, "Moanin' Low," was composed by Ralph Rainger.

THE GRAND STREET FOLLIES OF 1929
Sixth Edition
May 1, 1929   Booth Theatre   93 performances

Music also by Max Ewing and others
Lyrics mostly by Agnes Morgan
Book and direction by Morgan

Produced by The Actor-Managers, Inc. in association with Paul Moss
With Albert Carroll, Paula Trueman, and James Cagney

Published songs:

"I Love You And I Like You" (lyric by Max and Nathaniel
    Lief)—also used in **HERE COMES THE BRIDE [February 20,
    1930]**
"I Need You So" (lyric by David Goldberg and Howard Dietz)
"What Did Della Wear (When Georgie Came Across?)" (lyric by
    Morgan and Carroll)

For the record: "What Did Della Wear" was introduced by Albert
Carroll, impersonating Fanny Brice. That's what it says on the music
of this revolutionary item.

THE HOUSE THAT JACK BUILT
November 8, 1929   Adelphi Theatre ⟨London⟩
270 performances

Music mostly by Ivor Novello
Lyrics mostly by Donovan Parsons
Book by Ronald Jeans and Douglas Furber
Directed and produced by Jack Hulbert
With Cicely Courtneidge (Hulbert) and Hulbert

Published song:

"She's Such A Comfort To Me" (lyric by Furber and Parsons)—
    also used in **WAKE UP AND DREAM [December 30, 1929]**

WAKE UP AND DREAM
December 30, 1929   Selwyn Theatre   136 performances

Music and lyrics mostly by Cole **Porter** [see **March 27, 1929**]
Book by John Hastings Turner
Directed by Frank Collins
Produced by Arch Selwyn in association with Charles B. Cochran
With Jack Buchanan and Jessie Matthews

Published song:

"She's Such A Comfort To Me" (lyric by Douglas Furber, Max
    and Nathaniel Lief, and Donovan Parsons)—revised lyric for
    song originally used in **THE HOUSE THAT JACK BUILT
    [November 8, 1929]**

HERE COMES THE BRIDE
A Musical Farcical Comedy
February 20, 1930   Piccadilly Theatre ⟨London⟩
175 performances

Lyrics mostly by Desmond Carter
Book by R. P. Weston and Bert Lee
(Based on the play by Edgar MacGregor and Otto Harbach)
Produced by Julian Wylie
With Clifford Mollison and Edmund Gwenn

Published songs:

"High And Low" (lyric by Howard Dietz and Carter)—also used in
   THE BAND WAGON [June 3, 1931]
"Hot" (lyric by Carter and Lew Levinson)
"I Love You And I Like You" (lyric by Max and Nathaniel
   Lief)—originally used in **GRAND STREET FOLLIES OF
   1929 [May 1, 1929]**
"I'll Always Remember" (lyric by Max and Nathaniel Lief and
   Carter)
"I'm Like A Sailor (Home From The Sea)" (lyric by Dietz and
   Carter)
"Rose In Your Hair"

Schwartz's first successful book show, and the first of three Thirties
hits in London. The lyric to the pretty "High And Low" is probably
indeed by Dietz and Carter, although the latter is not credited on
copies of the (identical) song issued from **THE BAND WAGON.**

THE CO-OPTIMISTS OF 1930
A Pierrotic Entertainment
April 4, 1930   Hippodrome ⟨London⟩

Book and lyrics mostly by Greatrex Newman
Directed by Leslie Henson
With Stanley Holloway, Cyril Ritchard, and Elsie Randolph

Published songs:

"The Moment I Saw You" (lyric by Howard Dietz and Newman)—
   also used in **THREE'S A CROWD [October 15, 1931]**
"Steeplejack"
"Sunday Afternoon"

"The Moment I Saw You" was also solely credited to Dietz in its American printing.

THE SECOND LITTLE SHOW
September 2, 1930   Royale Theatre   63 performances

Music mostly by Arthur Schwartz
Lyrics mostly by Howard Dietz
Directed by Dwight Deere Wiman and Monty Woolley
Produced by William A. Brady, Jr. and Wiman, in association with Tom
   Weatherly
With J. C. Flippen and Gloria Grafton

Published songs:

"I Like Your Face"—initially issued as "Foolish Face"
"Lucky Seven"
"What A Case I've Got On You!"
"You're The Sunrise"

The producers of **THE LITTLE SHOW [April 30, 1929]** decided to do a follow-up. Attempting to establish themselves independent of stars, they went ahead without Webb, Allen, and Holman of the first edition. **THE SECOND** and (non-Schwartz and Dietz) **THIRD LITTLE SHOW [Lane: June 1, 1931]** did poorly, while Webb, Allen, and Holman went on to immediate success—in a new Schwartz and Dietz revue. Farm-machinery heir Dwight Deere Wiman entered the theatre in 1925, joining veteran producer William A. Brady. Soon going out on his own, Wiman was associated with the late-Thirties successes of Rodgers and Hart (see **ON YOUR TOES [Rodgers: April 11, 1936]**).

PRINCESS CHARMING
October 13, 1930   Imperial Theatre   56 performances

Music by Albert Sirmay and Arthur Schwartz
Lyrics by Arthur Swanstrom
Book by Jack Donahue
(Based on Arthur Wimperis and Lauri Wylie's British adaptation of the
   Austrian book by F. Martos)
Directed by Bobby Connolly
Produced by Connolly and Swanstrom
With Evelyn Herbert, George Grossmith, and Victor Moore

Published songs:

"I Must Be One Of Those Roses"
"I'll Be There"
"I'll Never Leave You"
"Just A Friend Of Mine"
"Never Mind How"
"Trailing A Shooting Star"
"You"

A not-very-good operetta with an undistinguished score. The one hit song was the interpolated "I Love Love" (music by Robert Dolan, lyrics by Walter O'Keefe). Hungarian-born Sirmay went on to become a major behind-the-scenes figure working closely with Cole Porter and others as editor for the music publishing house of Chappell & Co.

THREE'S A CROWD
October 15, 1930   Selwyn Theatre   271 performances

Music mostly by Arthur Schwartz (see **Duke, Lane**)
Lyrics mostly by Howard Dietz
Sketches by Dietz, Groucho Marx, and others
Choreographed by Albertina Rasch
Directed by Hassard Short
Produced by Max Gordon
With Clifton Webb, Fred Allen, Libby Holman, and Tamara Geva

Published songs:

"The Moment I Saw You"—see **THE CO-OPTIMISTS OF 1930 [April 4, 1930]**
"Right At The Start Of It"
"Something To Remember You By"—new lyric for "I Have No Words (To Say How Much I Love You)" from **LITTLE TOMMY TUCKER [November 19, 1930]**

With the authors and cast of **THE LITTLE SHOW [April 30, 1929]** available, the enterprising Max Gordon (heretofore a vaudeville producer) logically concluded that an unofficial sequel with Webb, Allen, and Holman had a better chance than **THE SECOND LITTLE SHOW [September 2, 1930]**. He was right. Gordon became a major force in the musical theatre through the decade. While "Something

To Remember You By" was a hit, it was Holman singing the interpolated "Body And Soul" (music by Johnny Green, lyric by Edward Heyman and Robert Sour), which created a furor.

LITTLE TOMMY TUCKER
November 19, 1930   Daly's Theatre ⟨London⟩

Music mostly by Vivian Ellis
Lyrics by Desmond Carter
Book by Carter, Caswell Garth, Bert Lee, and R. P. Weston
Directed by William Mollison
Produced by Herbert Clayton
With Ivy Tresmand, Rita Pepe, Jane Welsh, and Melville Cooper

Published songs:

"I Have No Words"—see **THREE'S A CROWD [October 15, 1930]**
"Out Of The Blue" (music by Ellis and Schwartz)

Although **LITTLE TOMMY TUCKER** opened after **THREE'S A CROWD,** "I Have No Words" was published two weeks before the Dietz lyric for the same music, "Something To Remember You By."

THE BAND WAGON
June 3, 1931   New Amsterdam Theatre   260 performances

Lyrics by Howard Dietz
Sketches by George S. Kaufman and Dietz
Choreographed by Albertina Rasch
Directed by Hassard Short
Produced by Max Gordon
With Fred and Adele Astaire, Helen Broderick, Frank Morgan, and Tilly Losch

Published songs:

"Confession"
"Dancing In The Dark"
"High And Low (I've Been Waiting For You)"—see **HERE COMES THE BRIDE [February 20, 1930]**
"Hoops"
"I Love Louisa"
"Miserable With You"
"New Sun In The Sky"

"Sweet Music"

"That's Entertainment"—written for 1953 movie version

"Triplets"—added to 1953 movie version; revised version of song (unpublished) from **BETWEEN THE DEVIL [December 22, 1937]**

Additional number published in piano selection:

"Beggar's Waltz" [instrumental]—subsequently published (1932) as nonshow song "Is It A Dream?" (lyric by Dietz)

Additional songs recorded:

"Ballet Music" [instrumental]

"It Better Be Good (Opening)"

"Nanette"

"Where Can He Be?"

"White Heat"

Schwartz and Dietz had realized the advantage of having the fewest possible writers involved in creating a revue; on **THE BAND WA-GON** they worked solely with George S. Kaufman, who had contributed important sketches to **THE LITTLE SHOW [April 30, 1929]**. Like Dietz, the immensely successful Kaufman kept a full-time "real" job—as drama editor of *The New York Times*. Director Hassard Short, prime force in the **MUSIC BOX REVUES [Berlin: September 22, 1921]**, experimented with moving turntables, mirrors, and novel lighting effects. Songs, sketches, and dances were carefully tailored to the exceptional cast. The result: what is considered the finest revue in Broadway history. **THE BAND WAGON** marked the final professional appearance of Adele Astaire; after spending most of her first thirty years on the stage, she retired to marry a British lord. Broadway wondered if her brother—the less charming, weak-voiced, balding straight man of the team—could succeed on his own.

FLYING COLORS
The Howard Dietz Revue
September 15, 1932   Imperial Theatre   188 performances

Lyrics, sketches, and direction by Dietz
Choreographed by Albertina Rasch
Produced by Max Gordon
With Clifton Webb, Charles Butterworth, Tamara Geva, and Patsy Kelly

Published songs:

"Alone Together"
"Fatal Fascination"
"Louisiana Hayride"
"A Rainy Day"
"A Shine On Your Shoes"
"Smokin' Reefers"
"Two-Faced Woman"—added after opening; published in separate
    edition

Additional song published (no lyric) in piano selection:

"Mein Kleine Acrobat"—initial publication upon reuse in
    FOLLOW THE SUN [February 4, 1936]

Additional song recorded:

"Mother Told Me So"

In their fifth revue together, Schwartz and Dietz had a difficult time
coming through with **FLYING COLORS**. Grave conditions were
faced, including the nervous breakdown (and attempted suicide) of
producer Max Gordon and the last-minute replacement of novice
choreographer Agnes de Mille. The show certainly didn't compare
with **THE BAND WAGON [June 3, 1931]**, although the score had
three hits (including the "Dancing In The Dark" successor, "Alone
Together").

NICE GOINGS ON
September 13, 1933   Strand Theatre ⟨London⟩
221 performances

Lyrics mostly by Frank Eyton
Book by Douglas Furber
Directed by Leslie Henson
Produced by Henson and Firth Shepard
With Henson and Zelma O'Neal

Published songs:

"I Know The Kind Of Girl" (lyric by Furber)
"Sweet One"
" 'Twixt The Devil And The Deep Blue Sea"
"What A Young Girl Ought To Know"
"Whatever You Do"
"With You Here And Me Here"

SHE LOVES ME NOT
November 20, 1933   46th Street Theatre   248 performances

Play by Howard Lindsay
(Based on a novel by Edward Hope)
Lyrics by Edward Heyman
Directed by Lindsay
Produced by Dwight Deere Wiman and Tom Weatherly

Published songs:

"After All, You're All I'm After"
"She Loves Me Not"

BRING ON THE GIRLS
[October 22, 1934]   National Theatre ⟨Washington, D.C.⟩;
closed during pre-Broadway tryout

Play by George S. Kaufman and Morrie Ryskind
Directed by Kaufman
Produced by Sam H. Harris
With Jack Benny, Porter Hall, Claire Carleton and Oscar Polk

Published song:

"Down On The Old-Time Farm" (lyric by Ryskind)

This Kaufman/Ryskind New Deal satire just did not work. Audiences expecting another **OF THEE I SING [Gershwin: December 26, 1931]** were greatly disappointed: to begin with, **BRING ON THE GIRLS** wasn't even a musical.

REVENGE WITH MUSIC
November 28, 1934   New Amsterdam Theatre
158 performances

Book and lyrics by Howard Dietz
(Based on *The Three-cornered Hat* [novel] by Pedro de Alarcon)
Directed by Komisarjevsky and others
Produced by Arch Selwyn and Harold B. Franklin
With Charles Winninger, Libby Holman, and Georges Metaxa

Published songs:

"If There Is Someone Lovelier Than You"
"Maria"
"That Fellow Manuelo"

"Wand'ring Heart"
"When You Love Only One"
"You And The Night And The Music"—revised version of "To-
    Night" (lyric by Desmond Carter) from 1934 movie *The Queen*

Additional song recorded:

"In The Noonday Sun"

The abundant publicity surrounding Libby Holman's return to the
stage after her brief marriage to Zachary Smith Reynolds (which ended
with the young tobacco heir's suicide) wasn't enough to salvage this
first Schwartz and Dietz book musical. "To-Night" was a sweeping
waltz version of what, in Latin tempo, became "You And The Night
And The Music."

AT HOME ABROAD
A Musical Holiday
September 19, 1935   Winter Garden Theatre
198 performances

Lyrics by Howard Dietz
Sketches by Dietz and others
Directed by Vincente Minnelli and Thomas Mitchell
Produced by Messrs. Shubert
With Beatrice Lillie, Ethel Waters, Herb Williams, Reginald Gardiner,
    and Eleanor Powell

Published songs:

"Farewell, My Lovely"
"Got A Bran' New Suit"
"The Hottentot Potentate"
"Love Is A Dancing Thing"
"O Leo"
"That's Not Cricket"
"Thief In The Night"
"What A Wonderful World"

Additional songs published in USO/Camp Shows "AT EASE":

"Get Away From It All"—with revised lyric, retitled "Come Along
    To Our Show" (Volume 4)
"The Lady With The Tap-Tap-Tap"—with revised lyric, retitled
    "The Soldier With The Tap-Tap-Tap" (Volume 3)

Additional songs recorded:

"Get Yourself A Geisha"
"Loadin' Time"
"Paree"

Schwartz and Dietz met Lillie in this first of two hit revues they did together. "Get Yourself A Geisha"—with Lillie at the end of a Japanese chorus line—was classic. Also along on this worldwide travelogue were comics Williams and Gardiner, while Ethel Waters sang and Eleanor Powell tapped her way to Hollywood. Despite their continued Broadway success Dietz remained at MGM, leaving Schwartz a full-time composer with a part-time lyricist. Schwartz began to search for a new collaborator.

FOLLOW THE SUN
February 4, 1936   Adelphi Theatre ⟨London⟩
204 performances

Lyrics by Howard Dietz and Desmond Carter
Book by Ronald Jeans and John Hastings Turner
Produced by Charles B. Cochran
With Claire Luce and Nick Long, Jr.

Published songs:

"Dangerous You" (lyric by Carter)
"How High Can A Little Bird Fly?" (lyric by Dietz)—originally
   used in 1934 radio scrial "The Gibson Family"
"Nicotina" (lyric by Carter)
"Sleigh Bells" (lyric by Dietz)—published in separate edition

Additional songs published (no lyric) in piano selection:

"Follow The Sun"
"Mein Kleine Acrobat"—originally used (unpublished) in **FLYING
   COLORS [September 15, 1932]**
"The Steamboat Whistle"

THE SHOW IS ON
December 25, 1936   Winter Garden Theatre
237 performances

Music mostly by Vernon **Duke** (also see **Arlen, Gershwin** and **Rodgers**)
Lyric to Schwartz song by Howard Dietz

Sketches mostly by David Freedman and Moss Hart
Directed by Vincente Minnelli
Produced by Lee Shubert
With Beatrice Lillie and Bert Lahr

Song published in USO/Camp Shows "AT EASE" (Volume 4):
"Shakespearean Opening"—with revised lyric

VIRGINIA
The American Musical Romance
September 2, 1937   Center Theatre   60 performances

Lyrics by Albert Stillman
Book by Laurence Stallings and Owen Davis
Book directed by Edward Clark Lilley
Staged by Leon Leonidoff
Produced by The Center Theatre
With Anne Booth, Gene Lockhart, Ronald Graham, and Nigel Bruce

Published songs:

"Good And Lucky"
"Good-Bye Jonah"
"If You Were Someone Else"
"My Bridal Gown" (lyric by Stillman and Stallings)
"My Heart Is Dancing"
"An Old Flame Never Dies" (lyric by Stillman and Stallings)
"Virginia"
"You And I Know" (lyric by Stillman and Stallings)

The Rockefellers' initial theatrical attraction at their Music Hall twin
had been Max Gordon's spectacular production of Strauss's THE
GREAT WALTZ [September 22, 1934]. The overwhelming scale of
the house made it difficult to come up with suitable future attractions—a fact which was soon to end the theatre's legitimate career.
The Colonial operetta **VIRGINIA** was overblown and represented a
major financial loss; but Schwartz's work was good, particularly "If
You Were Someone Else" and "You And I Know."

BETWEEN THE DEVIL
December 22, 1937   Imperial Theatre   93 performances

Book and lyrics by Howard Dietz
Directed by Hassard Short

Produced by Messrs. Shubert
With Jack Buchanan, Evelyn Laye, and Adele Dixon

Published songs:

"By Myself"
"Don't Go Away, Monsieur"
"Double Trouble"—advertised but not published
"I Believe In You"—issued as professional copy
"I See Your Face Before Me"
"Why Did You Do It?"
"You Have Everything"

Additional song published in USO/Camp Shows "AT EASE"
  (Volume 3):

"The Uniform"—with revised lyric

Additional songs recorded:

"Imaginist Rhythm"
"Triplets"—initial publication in revised form upon reuse in 1953
  movie version of **THE BAND WAGON [June 3, 1931]**

This second Schwartz/Dietz book show attempt was a dated marital
farce; Dietz never found Broadway success outside the revue format.
Following **BETWEEN THE DEVIL,** the team terminated their collaboration after eight full scores in as many years. Dietz continued
his MGM work and entered a wartime collaboration with Vernon
Duke; Schwartz worked with a variety of lyricists and embarked on
a successful Hollywood career as composer and producer.

STARS IN YOUR EYES
February 9, 1939   Majestic Theatre   127 performances

Lyrics by Dorothy Fields
Book by J. P. McEvoy
Directed by Joshua Logan
Produced by Dwight Deere Wiman
With Ethel Merman, Jimmy Durante, Tamara Toumanova, and Richard
  Carlson

Published songs:

"All The Time"
"I'll Pay The Check"
"It's All Yours"

"Just A Little Bit More"
"A Lady Needs A Change"
"Terribly Attractive"
"This Is It"

What began as a politically tinged satire of the movie industry with
Durante as union organizer lost its bite early on. All that remained
was Merman and Durante, which was nothing to be sneezed at. This
time, incidentally, Merman got first billing without a fight (see **RED,
HOT AND BLUE! [Porter: October 29, 1936]**). Schwartz's new
lyricist was Dorothy Fields, daughter/sister of Lew/Herbert (see
BLACKBIRDS OF 1928 [PART 4: May 9, 1928]) and 1936 Oscar
winner for "The Way You Look Tonight" (music by Jerome Kern).

AMERICAN JUBILEE
May 12, 1940   American Jubilee Theatre,
New York World's Fair

Book and lyrics by Oscar Hammerstein 2nd
Directed by Leon Leonidoff
Produced by Albert Johnson
Presented by New York World's Fair Corporation
With Lucy Monroe (and a cast of 350)

Published songs:

"How Can I Ever Be Alone?"
"My Bicycle Girl"
"Tennessee Fish Fry"
"We Like It Over Here"

A patriotic pageant. The only item of interest was Schwartz's catchy
"Tennessee Fish Fry," which composer Leroy Anderson appears to
have caught. He added sleigh bells and called it "Sleigh Ride," now
a Christmas standard. Following **AMERICAN JUBILEE,** Schwartz
went to Hollywood (not MGM) where he produced two successful
movie musicals: the 1944 Kern/Ira Gershwin *Cover Girl* and the 1946
Cole Porter pseudobiography *Night and Day.*

PARK AVENUE
November 4, 1946   Shubert Theatre   72 performances

Lyrics by Ira Gershwin
Book by Nunnally Johnson and George S. Kaufman

Directed by Kaufman
Produced by Max Gordon
With Leonora Corbett and Arthur Margetson

Published songs:

"For The Life Of Me"
"Goodbye To All That"
"There's No Holding Me"

Additional song published in "Intimate Songs":

"Don't Be A Woman If You Can"

A highly disappointing show from a distinguished set of authors. Left behind was the beautiful ballad "Goodbye To All That." For the fifty-year-old Gershwin, two consecutive flops were enough; he went back home to Hollywood. After several more movies Gershwin permanently retired, but not before writing one last classic, "The Man That Got Away" (music by Harold Arlen), for the 1954 remake of *A Star is Born.*

INSIDE U.S.A.
April 30, 1948   New Century Theatre   399 performances

Lyrics by Howard Dietz
Sketches by Arnold Auerbach, Moss Hart, and Arnold Horwitt
(Title suggested by the book by John Gunther)
Directed by Robert H. Gordon
Produced by Schwartz
With Beatrice Lillie, Jack Haley, Herb Shriner, and Valerie Bettis

Published songs:

"Blue Grass"
"First Prize At The Fair"
"Haunted Heart"
"My Gal Is Mine Once More"
"Rhode Island Is Famous For You"

Additional songs recorded:

"At The Mardi Gras"
"Atlanta"
"Come O Come (To Pittsburgh)"
"Inside U.S.A."
"Protect Me"

Schwartz, reunited with Dietz, produced this sequel to **AT HOME ABROAD [September 19, 1935]. INSIDE U.S.A.** was formatted as a stateside travelogue, whereas the earlier show had an international motif. With a fair score, good sketches and the comedy of Lillie and Haley, **INSIDE U.S.A.** was a moderate hit. Surprisingly, it was to be the final success either writer had (although some of Schwartz's finest work was still to come).

A TREE GROWS IN BROOKLYN
April 19, 1951   Alvin Theatre   270 performances

Lyrics by Dorothy Fields
Book by Betty Smith and George Abbott
(Based on the novel by Smith)
Choreographed by Herbert Ross
Directed by George Abbott
Produced by Abbott with Robert Fryer
With Shirley Booth, Johnny Johnston, Marcia Van Dyke, and Nathaniel
   Frey

Published songs:

"Growing Pains"
"If You Haven't Got A Sweetheart"
"I'll Buy You A Star"
"I'm Like A New Broom"
"Look Who's Dancing"
"Love Is The Reason"
"Make The Man Love Me"

Additional songs recorded:

"Don't Be Afraid Of Anything"
"Halloween" [instrumental]
"He Had Refinement"
"Is That My Prince?"
"Mine 'Til Monday"
"Payday"
"That's How It Goes"

One of Schwartz's richest scores and his best book musical. Based on the popular novel, the librettists sought to balance the story's tragic elements by building up the humorous subplot; this proved a fatal mistake, as the casting of Shirley Booth made a star role out of a sub-ordinate character. Booth's fine performance helped the show achieve a respectable, if unprofitable, run. The usually urbane Schwartz revealed a powerful, emotional side in writing for the unsophisticated, uneducated characters. Resulting treasures (adorned by Fields' best work) included "Make The Man Love Me," "I'll Buy You A Star," and "Don't Be Afraid Of Anything."

BY THE BEAUTIFUL SEA
April 8, 1954   Majestic Theatre   270 performances

Lyrics by Dorothy Fields
Book by Herbert and Dorothy Fields
Directed by Marshall Jamison
Produced by Robert Fryer and Lawrence Carr
With Shirley Booth, Wilbur Evans, and Mae Barnes

Published songs:

"Alone Too Long"
"Hang Up!"
"Happy Habit"
"More Love Than Your Love"
"The Sea Song (By The Beautiful Sea)"

Additional songs recorded:

"Coney Island Boat"
"Good Time Charlie"
"Hooray For George The Third"
"I'd Rather Wake Up By Myself"
"Old Enough To Love"
"Please Don't Send Me Down A Baby Brother"
"Throw The Anchor Away"

Trying to come up with a more successful venture than **A TREE GROWS IN BROOKLYN [April 19, 1951],** the two Fieldses wrote a more comic vehicle for Booth. But without powerful basic material or the strong hand of George Abbott, the result was little more than an old-fashioned costume piece. The Schwartz/Fields score was merely adequate, but Booth's performance gave the show a run of identical length. "I'd Rather Wake Up By Myself" was superb comedy writing.

THE GAY LIFE
November 18, 1961   Shubert Theatre   114 performances

Lyrics by Howard Dietz
Book by Fay and Michael Kanin
(Based on *Anatol* [play] by Arthur Schnitzler)
Directed by Gerald Freedman
Produced by Kermit Bloomgarden
With Walter Chiari, Barbara Cook, and Jules Munshin

Published songs:

"Bloom Is Off The Rose"
"Come A-Wandering With Me"
"For The First Time"
"I'm Glad I'm Single"
"Magic Moment"
"Oh Mein Leibchen"
"Something You Never Had Before"—revised version of "Oh, But
    I Do" (lyric by Leo Robin) from 1946 movie *The Time, The
    Place and The Girl*
"Who Can? You Can!"
"Why Go Anywhere At All?"

Additional songs recorded:

"Bring Your Darling Daughter"
"I Never Had A Chance"
"I Wouldn't Marry You"
"The Label On The Bottle"
"Now I'm Ready For A Frau"
"This Kind Of A Girl"
"What A Charming Couple"
"You Will Never Be Lonely"
"You're Not The Type"

Dietz retired his vice-presidency at MGM in 1957 and reunited with
Schwartz for two final book shows. **THE GAY LIFE** was saddled
with a lifeless book and a lifeless star (Chiari), which defeated the
attributes: a fine, sweeping Viennese score by Schwartz, a *sacher-torte*
physical production—with Tony Award–winning costumes by Lu-
cinda Ballard (Dietz)—and a luscious performance by Barbara Cook.
"Magic Moment," "Why Go Anywhere At All," and "Something You
Never Had Before" were all absolutely lovely.

JENNIE
October 17, 1963   Majestic Theatre   82 performances

Lyrics by Howard Dietz
Book by Arnold Schulman
(Based on *Laurette* [biography] by Marguerite Taylor Courtney)
Directed by Vincent J. Donehue
Produced by Cheryl Crawford and Richard Halliday
With Mary Martin, George Wallace, and Ethel Shutta

Published songs:

"Before I Kiss The World Goodbye"
"Born Again"
"High Is Better Than Low"
"I Believe In Takin' A Chance"
"I Still Look At You That Way"
"On The Other Hand"—cut
"Waitin' For The Evening Train"
"When You're Far Away From New York Town"
"Where You Are"

Additional songs recorded:

"For Better Or Worse"
"Lonely Nights"
"The Night May Be Dark"
"Over Here"
"Sauce Diable" [instrumental]
"See Seattle"

Mary Martin decided against Fanny Brice—she wasn't really right for
FUNNY GIRL [Styne: March 26, 1964]—and chose the feisty, al-
coholic, "Peg O' My Heart" Laurette Taylor instead. Martin also
turned down Dolly Levi. Schwartz's final show was an unhappy experience for all. Dietz had engaged in lyric-suitability battles with
Merman on **SADIE THOMPSON [Duke: November 16, 1944]**, resulting in her replacement. The same problems arose with Mary Martin
. . . who was married to the coproducer. Martin and the enormous
advance sale stayed. **JENNIE** was a shambles, and quickly went the
way of all shambles. A 1960 nonmusical dramatization (*Laurette*) of
the biography by Taylor's daughter, starring the more suitable Judy
Holliday, had closed during tryout; hence the name change. The best
element of **JENNIE** was the music, including the final beautiful

Schwartz ballad: "Before I Kiss The World Goodbye." Schwartz and Dietz both went into virtual retirement. Dietz, who suffered from Parkinson's disease, died July 30, 1983; Schwartz, following a stroke, died September 3, 1984 at his home in Kintnersville, Pennsylvania.

Arthur Schwartz wrote some of the finest theatre music of his time—particularly the minor-key ballads of the Thirties ("Dancing In The Dark," "Alone Together") and the later, much warmer ones ("Make The Man Love Me" and "Magic Moment"). His skill also displayed itself in outstanding rhythmic work ("I Guess I'll Have To Change My Plan" and the 1954 movie song "That's Entertainment"). All of which make it difficult to explain Schwartz's record of *no* successful Broadway book musical. Not having Dietz as a full-time collaborator certainly was part of it, although the lyricist's nonrevue work indicates Schwartz would have done better with, say, Dorothy Fields. However . . . a good number of glorious Arthur Schwartz songs remain.

Harold Arlen

BORN: February 15, 1905   Buffalo, New York

Harold Arlen was the son of a cantor, whose melodic and colorful improvisatory style was to be a tremendous influence on Arlen's work. With his interest firmly in pop music, Arlen began his career as a bandleader and soon moved to New York as an arranger/singer. His first published piece was the 1926 instrumental "Minor Gaff (Blues Fantasy)" (by Harold Arluck and Dick George). His first published song came in 1928, "Jungaleena" (lyric by Herb Magidson and James Cavanaugh); he had by now changed his name to Arlen. His first Broadway experience was as vocalist, rehearsal pianist, and sometime musical secretary to Vincent Youmans for the tryout of **GREAT DAY!** [Youmans: October 17, 1929]. When the troubled show went back into rehearsal for a preopening overhaul, Arlen left the cast. Youmans, who had set up his own doomed-to-failure publishing company, bought and issued Arlen's "Rising Moon" (lyric by Jack Ellis) in the summer of 1929.

NINE-FIFTEEN REVUE
February 11, 1930   George M. Cohan Theatre
7 performances

Music and lyrics mostly by others (see **Gershwin**)
Lyrics to Arlen songs by Ted Koehler
Sketches by Eddie Cantor, George S. Kaufman, Ring Lardner, Wm.
  Anthony McGuire, and others
Directed by Alexander Leftwich
Produced by Ruth Selwyn
With Ruth Etting

Published songs:

"Get Happy"
"You Wanted Me, I Wanted You"

While accompanying dance rehearsals of **GREAT DAY!** **[Youmans:
October 17, 1929],** Arlen improvised a catchy break. He played it
for a friend, pop songwriter Harry Warren; Warren suggested Arlen
get together with lyricist Ted Koehler and turn it into a song. "Get
Happy" was the result, and Arlen switched careers to songwriting
(although he has remained a remarkable blues singer, making occasional recordings of his songs). **NINE-FIFTEEN REVUE** featured
work by many top composers, but it was Arlen's "Get Happy" which
stood out—for the week of the run, anyway. Ruth Etting, who attracted notice with "Love Me Or Leave Me" in **WHOOPEE [PART
4: December 4, 1928],** sang Arlen's first hit. With **NINE-FIFTEEN
REVUE** quickly closed, Etting rushed across Times Square to join
SIMPLE SIMON [Rodgers: February 18, 1930], and introduced her
second song classic of the week, "Ten Cents A Dance."

EARL CARROLL VANITIES
Eighth Edition
America's Greatest Revue
July 1, 1930   New Amsterdam Theatre   215 performances

Music also by Jay Gorney
Lyrics to Arlen songs by Ted Koehler
Book by Eddie Welch and Eugene Conrad
Directed by Priestly Morrison
Produced by Earl Carroll
With Jack Benny, Jimmy Savo, and Herb Williams

Published songs:

"Contagious Rhythm"
"Hittin' The Bottle"
"The March Of Time"
"One Love"
"Out Of A Clear Blue Sky"

"Get Happy" attracted attention to Arlen and Koehler. They were
hired to contribute half the score for this edition of the VANITIES,
the weakest of the three major annual revues. The rest of the songs
were written by another young team, Jay Gorney and E. Y. Harburg, who soon took Koehler's place as Arlen's collaborator.

BROWN SUGAR
Sweet But Unrefined
Nightclub Revue
[Circa December 1930]   *Cotton Club* ⟨*Harlem, New York*⟩

Lyrics by Ted Koehler
Directed by Dan Healy
Produced by The Cotton Club
With Duke Ellington and His Orchestra

Published songs:

"Linda"
"Song Of The Gigolo"

Having tried out Arlen and Koehler material at the Silver Slipper nightclub, proprietors Owney Madden and associates—i.e., the Mob—sent the songwriters uptown to replace McHugh and Fields (who had graduated to Broadway with **BLACKBIRDS OF 1928 [PART 4: May 9, 1928]**). Featuring black performers but catering to an exclusively white clientele, the Cotton Club offered elaborate midnight floor shows to accompany the main business in bootleg liquor. The Arlen/Koehler team did their best work together for the Cotton Club, turning out several blues standards.

YOU SAID IT
The Musicollegiate Comedy Hit
January 19, 1931   *46th Street Theatre*   *168 performances*

Lyrics by Jack Yellen
Book by Yellen and Sid Silvers
Directed by John Harwood
Produced by Yellen and Lou Holtz
With Holtz and Lyda Roberti

Published songs:

"If He Really Loves Me"
"It's Different With Me"
"Learn To Croon"
"Sweet And Hot"
"What Do We Care?"
"While You Are Young"

"You Said It"
"You'll Do"

Arlen was signed to write his first book show by Yellen, a successful
Tin Pan Alley lyricist and former member of Arlen's father's congre-
gation in Buffalo. Though the show was moderately successful, Arlen's work was undistinguished (except for the sweet and hot "Sweet
And Hot"). He returned to Koehler and the revue format.

RHYTH-MANIA
Nightclub Revue
[Circa December 1931]   Cotton Club ⟨Harlem, New York⟩

Lyrics by Ted Koehler
Directed by Dan Healy
Produced by The Cotton Club
With Aida Ward and Cab Calloway

Published songs:

"Between The Devil And The Deep Blue Sea"
"Breakfast Dance"
"Get Up, Get Out, Get Under The Sun"
"I Love A Parade"—issued separately from other songs
"Kickin' The Gong Around"
" 'Neath The Pale Cuban Moon"
"Without Rhythm"

Arlen's second Cotton Club show, with another hit song: "Between
The Devil And The Deep Blue Sea."

EARL CARROLL VANITIES
Tenth Edition
America's Greatest Revue
September 27, 1932   Broadway Theatre   87 performances

Music also by others
Lyrics to Arlen songs by Ted Koehler
Sketches by Jack McGowan
Directed by Edgar J. McGregor
Produced by Earl Carroll
With Will Fyffe, Milton Berle, and Helen Broderick

Published songs:
"I Gotta Right To Sing The Blues"
"Rockin' In Rhythm"

Arlen came up with another treasure—"I Gotta Right To Sing The Blues"—this time for Broadway. Influenced by the improvisatory style of the black jazz underground, Arlen's blues replaced the synthetic-but-popular torch songs of the Twenties for immediate public acceptance.

AMERICANA
Third Edition
A Musical Revue
October 5, 1932   Shubert Theatre   77 performances

Music mostly by Jay Gorney
Lyrics mostly by E. Y. Harburg
Book by J. P. McEvoy
Directed by Harold Johnsrud
Produced by J. P. McEvoy
Presented by Lee Shubert

Published song:
"Satan's Li'l Lamb" (lyric by Harburg and John Mercer)

This short-lived revue is best known for the Gorney/Harburg "Brother, Can You Spare a Dime?" This was the first time Arlen worked with two of his important future collaborators. Johnny Mercer was like Arlen, a fine singer. He was then appearing as a Rhythm Boy with Paul Whiteman's Band (Arlen's younger brother Jerry was also in the trio).

COTTON CLUB PARADE
Twenty-First Edition
Nightclub Revue
October 23, 1932   Cotton Club ⟨Harlem, New York⟩

Lyrics by Ted Koehler
Directed by Dan Healy
Produced by The Cotton Club
With Aida Ward and Cab Calloway

Published songs:

"Harlem Holiday"
"I've Got The World On A String"
"In The Silence Of The Night"
"Minnie The Moocher's Wedding Day"
"New Kind Of Rhythm"
"That's What I Hate About Love"
"The Wail Of The Reefer Man"
"You Gave Me Ev'rything But Love"

GEORGE WHITE'S MUSIC HALL VARIETIES
November 22, 1932   Casino Theatre   71 performances

Music mostly by others
Book by George White and William K. Wells
Produced by White
With Harry Richman, Bert Lahr, and Lily Damita

Published song:

"Two Feet In Two-Four Time" (lyric by Irving Caesar)

THE GREAT MAGOO
December 2, 1932   Selwyn Theatre   11 performances

Play by Ben Hecht and Gene Fowler
Directed by George Abbott
Produced by Billy Rose
With Paul Kelly

Published song:

"If You Believed In Me" (lyrics by E. Y. Harburg and Rose)—
    initial publication upon reuse in **CRAZY QUILT OF 1933 [July
    28, 1933]** retitled "It's Only A Paper Moon"

Arlen's auspicious hit was born in this inauspicious flop; it found
widespread popularity via interpolation in the 1933 movie version of
TAKE A CHANCE [Youmans: November 26, 1932]. Rose, producer of the play, claimed colyricist credit.

COTTON CLUB PARADE
Twenty-Second Edition
Nightclub Revue
April 6, 1933   Cotton Club ⟨Harlem, New York⟩

Lyrics by Ted Koehler
Directed by Dan Healy
Produced by The Cotton Club
With Ethel Waters, George Dewey Washington, and Duke Ellington and
   His Orchestra

Published songs:

"Calico Days"
"Get Yourself A New Broom (And Sweep The Blues Away)"
"Happy As The Day Is Long"
"Muggin' Lightly"
"Raisin' The Rent"
"Stormy Weather"

The most successful edition of the series. Ethel Waters had her first
exposure to a predominantly white audience. Her tear-filled rendi-
tion of "Stormy Weather" was effective enough to convince Irving
Berlin to place her as a lead in his new revue, **AS THOUSANDS
CHEER [Berlin: September 30, 1933]**.

CRAZY QUILT OF 1933
July 28, 1933   ⟨Albany, New York⟩; post-Broadway tour

Music mostly by others
Produced by Billy Rose
With Anita Page

Published song:

"It's Only A Paper Moon" (lyric by E. Y. Harburg and Rose)—
   initial publication of "If You Believed In Me" (unpublished)
   from **THE GREAT MAGOO [December 2, 1932]**

COTTON CLUB PARADE
Twenty-Fourth Edition
Nightclub Revue
March 23, 1934   Cotton Club ⟨Harlem, New York⟩

Lyrics by Ted Koehler
Directed by Dan Healy
Produced by The Cotton Club
With Adelaide Hall and Jimmie Lunceford and His Orchestra

Published songs:

"As Long As I Live"
"Breakfast Ball"
"Here Goes"
"Ill Wind"
"Primitive Prima Donna"

Arlen's final Cotton Club show featured sixteen-year-old chorine Lena
Horne, singing and dancing "As Long As I Live" with Avon Long.

LIFE BEGINS AT 8:40
A Musical Revue
August 27, 1934   Winter Garden Theatre
237 performances

Lyrics by Ira Gershwin and E. Y. Harburg
Sketches mostly by David Freeman
Directed and produced by John Murray Anderson
Presented by Messrs. Shubert
With Ray Bolger, Bert Lahr, Luella Gear, and Frances Williams

Published songs:

"Fun To Be Fooled"
"Let's Take A Walk Around the Block"
"Shoein' The Mare"
"What Can You Say In A Love Song?"
"You're A Builder Upper"

Additional songs published in USO/Camp Shows "AT EASE":

"I Couldn't Hold My Man"—with revised lyric, retitled "I Look
    Bad In Uniform" (Volume 3)
"Life Begins Introduction"—with revised lyric (Volume 4)
"Spring Fever"—(Volume 4)

Additional songs recorded:

"C'est La Vie"
"The Elks And The Masons"
"Quartet Erotica"

"Things"
"Will You Love Me Monday Morning?"

Having broken up with Vernon Duke following the **ZIEGFELD FOLLIES OF 1934 [DUKE: January 4, 1934],** Harburg astutely selected Arlen as his next collaborator. Arlen could not turn down this first major opportunity; the success of **LIFE BEGINS AT 8:40** effectively ended the Arlen/Koehler partnership. Veteran Ira Gershwin, influential in placing college classmate Harburg's early work, became colyricist; George was writing **PORGY AND BESS [Gershwin: October 10, 1935]** with DuBose Heyward (although Ira was soon to join them). Arlen wrote his finest work with Harburg, Gershwin, and Johnny Mercer, songs that Koehler—a decent pop lyricist—could not have kept up with.

THE SHOW IS ON
December 25, 1936   Winter Garden Theater
237 performances

Music mostly by Vernon **Duke** (also see **Gershwin, Rodgers,** and
   Schwartz)
Lyrics to Arlen song by E. Y. Harburg
Sketches by David Freedman and Moss Hart
Directed and designed by Vincente Minnelli
Produced by Lee Shubert
With Beatrice Lillie and Bert Lahr

Song recorded:

"Song Of The Woodman"

Arlen and Harburg's adeptness at Lahr-ese was to continue with "If I Were King Of The Forest" and "If I Only Had The Nerve" for the 1939 movie *The Wizard of Oz*. They also wrote a 1939 Groucho classic, "Lydia, The Tattooed Lady."

HOORAY FOR WHAT!
December 1, 1937   Winter Garden Theatre
200 performances

Lyrics by E. Y. Harburg
Book by Howard Lindsay and Russel Crouse
(Conceived by Harburg)

Choreographed by Robert Alton
Directed by Lindsay
Supervised by Vincente Minnelli
Produced by the Messrs. Shubert
With Ed Wynn, Jack Whiting, June Clyde, and Vivian Vance

Published songs:
"Buds Won't Bud"
"Down With Love"
"God's Country"
"I've Gone Romantic On You"
"In The Shade Of The New Apple Tree"
"Life's A Dance"
"Moanin' In The Mornin' "

Additional song published in USO/Camp Shows "AT EASE"
  (Volume 4):
"Hooray For What!"—with revised lyric, retitled "Hooray For Us!"

What started out as a strong antiwar satire lost much of its bite, along with choreographer Agnes de Mille and costars Kay Thompson and Hannah Williams (Mrs. Jack Dempsey), during its pre-Broadway tryout. What remained—Ed Wynn and the fine score—was more than enough to make **HOORAY FOR WHAT!** a moderate hit. The debut of vocal arranger (and backup singer) Hugh Martin made a striking impression on Broadway: Rodgers, Berlin and Porter immediately put him to work (see **BEST FOOT FORWARD [Martin: October 1, 1941]**). Arlen, who had been writing for the movies since 1934, returned to Hollywood for an extended stay.

BLOOMER GIRL
October 5, 1944   Shubert Theatre   654 performances
Lyrics by E. Y. Harburg
Book by Sig. Herzig and Fred Saidy
(Based on a play by Dan and Lilith James)
Choreographed by Agnes de Mille
Book directed by William Schorr
Production staged by Harburg
Produced by John C. Wilson (in association with Nat Goldstone)
With Celeste Holm, David Brooks, Joan McCracken, and Dooley Wilson

Published songs:

"The Eagle And Me"
"Evelina"
"I Got A Song"
"Right As The Rain"
"T'morra', T'morra' "
"When The Boys Come Home"

Additional songs recorded:

"Civil War Ballet"
"The Farmer's Daughter"
"It Was Good Enough For Grandma"
"Liza Crossing The Ice"
"Lullaby (Satin Gown And Silver Shoe)"
"Man For Sale"
"Never Was Born"
"The Rakish Young Man With The Whiskahs"
"Sunday In Cicero Falls"
"Welcome Hinges"

Arlen returned to Broadway with this Civil War–period costume musical. Trying to follow the success of **OKLAHOMA!** [**Rodgers: March 31, 1943**], **BLOOMER GIRL** employed the same choreographer, designers, and two of the leading players. Though certainly not in the same league, **BLOOMER GIRL** was entertaining and nostalgic enough for wartime audiences and flourished. Arlen's score included "The Eagle And Mc" and the gentle "Evelina."

ST. LOUIS WOMAN
March 30, 1946   Martin Beck Theatre   113 performances

Lyrics by Johnny Mercer
Book by Arna Bontemps and Countee Cullen
(Based on *God Sends Sunday* [novel] by Bontemps)
Directed by Rouben Mamoulian
Produced by Edward Gross
With Ruby Hill, Harold Nicholas, June Hawkins, and Pearl Bailey

Published songs:

"Any Place I Hang My Hat Is Home"
"Cakewalk Your Lady"
"Come Rain Or Come Shine"

"I Had Myself A True Love"
"I Wonder What Became of Me"—cut
"Legalize My Name"
"Ridin' On The Moon"

Additional song published in "Intimate Songs":
"A Woman's Prerogative"

Additional songs recorded:
"Leavin' Time"
"L'il Augie Is A Natural Man"
"Lullaby"
"Sleep Peaceful, Mr. Used-To-Be"

Arlen and Mercer had established their unique chemistry with the
1941 movie *Blues in the Night.* (Who else could have written that song?
"Blues In The Night" is incomparable, two of America's most exciting songwriters combined for their colorful best.) **ST. LOUIS
WOMAN** was another ambitious Mamoulian musical, saddled with
an unfocused script by two first-time librettists—one of whom (Cullen) died before rehearsals. Arlen's theatre music had developed from
his early rhythmic tunes and blues—superb and memorable as they
were—to art songs with beauty, grace, and the unique Arlen coloring. The exquisite "I Wonder What Became Of Me" was cut, and
remains relatively unknown (as does "Sleep Peaceful, Mr. Used-To-
Be"); "Come Rain Or Come Shine" and "Any Place I Hang My Hat
Is Home" managed to find their way to the public. As with all of
Arlen's remaining shows, the scores were overcome by the production's fatal flaws. Arlen and Mercer reworked the **ST. LOUIS
WOMAN** material into the 1959 "blues opera" *Free and Easy,* which
was unsuccessfully performed in Europe.

HOUSE OF FLOWERS
December 30, 1954   Alvin Theatre   165 performances
Lyrics by Truman Capote and Harold Arlen
Book by Capote
(Based on the novella by Capote)
Choreographed by Herbert Ross
Directed by Peter Brook
Produced by Saint-Subber

With Pearl Bailey, Diahann Carroll, Juanita Hall, Ray Walston, and
   Geoffrey Holder

Published songs:

"House Of Flowers"
"I Never Has Seen Snow"
"A Sleepin' Bee"
"Smellin' Of Vanilla (Bamboo Cage)"
"Two Ladies In De Shade Of De Banana Tree"

Additional songs published in vocal selections:

"Can I Leave Off Wearin' My Shoes?"
"Don't Like Goodbyes"
"Jump De Broom" (lyric by Capote)—written for off-Broadway
   revival [January 28, 1968]
"Madame Tango's Particular Tango"—written for revival; different
   than "Madame Tango's Tango" (cut, unpublished) from original
   version
"One Man Ain't Quite Enough"
"Somethin' Cold To Drink"—written for revival
"Waitin' "
"What Is A Friend For?"
"Woman Never Understan' "—written for revival

Additional songs recorded:

"Has I Let You Down"
"Mardi Gras"
"Slide, Boy, Slide"
"Turtle Song (One Brave Man Against The Sea)"
"Waltz" [instrumental]—revised version of 1942 piano solo
   "American Minuet"

A legendary failure with a legendary score. A first-time librettist/colyricist and a very talented director making his musical *and* Broadway debut did not help the situation, and the very special material suffered. The tryout was one continuous, many-sided battle with Pearl Bailey—who had stolen the show in **ST. LOUIS WOMAN [March 30, 1946]**—winning most of the backstage bouts. Diahann Carroll memorably introduced some of Arlen's most beautiful songs and herself. The gems in Arlen's finest score included "A Sleepin' Bee," "I Never Has Seen Snow," and the unique "Two Ladies In De Shade Of De Banana Tree."

JAMAICA
October 31, 1957   Imperial Theatre   557 performances

Lyrics by E. Y. Harburg
Book by Harburg and Fred Saidy
Choreographed by Jack Cole
Directed by Robert Lewis
Produced by David Merrick
With Lena Horne, Ricardo Montalban, and Adelaide Hall

Published songs:

"Ain't It De Truth"—originally used (cut) in 1943 movie version of
   CABIN IN THE SKY [Duke: October 25, 1940]
"Cocoanut Sweet"
"I Don't Think I'll End It All Today"
"Incompatibility"
"Little Biscuit"
"Napoleon"
"Pretty To Walk With"
"Push De Button"
"Savannah"
"Take It Slow, Joe"
"What Good Does It Do?"

Additional songs recorded:

"For Every Fish There's A Little Bigger Fish"
"Hooray For The Yankee Dollar"
"Leave The Atom Alone"
"Monkey In The Mango Tree"
"Pity De Sunset"
"Savannah's Wedding Day"
"Sweet Wind Blowin' My Way"—cut

When calypso star Harry Belafonte withdrew from this project he was
replaced by Lena Horne, who started her career in Arlen's final
**COTTON CLUB PARADE ⟨Twenty-fourth Edition⟩ [March 23,
1934]** and rode to stardom singing the title song in the 1943 movie
Stormy Weather. The unorthodox cast change didn't much matter;
JAMAICA in its final state was little more than Horne singing a string
of songs. Ironically, **JAMAICA** was Arlen's only hit show after
BLOOMER GIRL [October 5, 1944], due to the entrepreneurial fi-
nesse of Merrick. Note that the four Arlen/Harburg shows, as well

as their one complete film musical, *The Wizard of Oz*, were all successes.

SARATOGA
December 7, 1959   Winter Garden Theatre
80 performances

Lyrics by Johnny Mercer
Book and direction by Morton DaCosta
(Based on *Saratoga Trunk* [novel] by Edna Ferber)
Produced by Robert Fryer
With Howard Keel, Carol Lawrence, Carol Brice, and Edith King

Published songs:

"A Game Of Poker"
"Goose Never Be A Peacock"
"Love Held Lightly"
"The Man In My Life"
"Saratoga"

Additional songs published in vocal selection:

"Dog Eat Dog"
"The Parks Of Paris"—cut
"Petticoat High"
"You For Me"—cut

Additional songs recorded:

"Countin' Our Chickens"
"The Cure"
"Gettin' A Man" (music by Mercer)
"Have You Heard (Gossip Song)"
"I'll Be Respectable"
"The Men Who Run The Country" (music by Mercer)
"One Step—Two Step"
"Why Fight This?" (music by Mercer)

A misguided, heavy-handed effort burying some lovely Arlen/Mercer work. **SARATOGA** was in the hands of Morton DaCosta, briefly invincible with NO TIME FOR SERGEANTS [October 20, 1955], AUNTIE MAME [October 31, 1956] and **THE MUSIC MAN [Willson: December 19, 1957]**. Writing his own libretto as well as directing, DaCosta was clearly influenced by and aspiring to the ear-

lier Ferber-based musical **SHOW BOAT [Kern: December 27, 1927]**;
things didn't work out. Mercer's musical contributions came about
when illness forced the composer away from part of the tryout. **SAR-
ATOGA** was Arlen's shortest-running—and final—Broadway show.
Following some additional motion picture work, the composer went
into retirement in the mid-Sixties, but has continued to write some
fine (although presently unpublished) songs.

There are those who place Gershwin and Arlen at the top of the list
of American composers, with the slight lead going to Arlen. Gershwin led the way, scattering delightful surprises ("blue notes," catchy
rhythms, musical whimsy) throughout his work. The younger composer used these same elements, but not for effect: to Arlen they were
natural. Gershwin's fascinatin' rhythms were carefully built and mar-
velously effective; Arlen's—"Get Happy," for example—were infectious and light as air. Gershwin's blues relied on that "blue note," as
in the superb "The Man I Love"; Arlen's blues were ruled only by
his limitless imagination. The music of Harold Arlen has remained
ageless; the songs—theatre, screen, and all—are filled with neverend-
ing magic.

Vernon Duke

BORN: October 10, 1903   Parafianovo (Minsk), Russia
DIED: January 17, 1969   Santa Monica, California

Born to a White Russian family, Vernon Duke was the son of a civil engineer. A highly musical child, Duke studied with Glière and enrolled in the Kiev Conservatory in 1913. Uprooted by the October Revolution of 1917, Duke—with mother and younger brother—fled the country, reaching America in 1921. Unable to find a musical career here, he moved to Paris; in 1924 he composed the successful ballet *Zephyr et Flore* for Serge Diaghilev's Ballet Russe.

KATJA THE DANCER
February 21, 1925   Gaiety Theatre ⟨London⟩
505 performances

Music mostly by Jean Gilbert
Book by Frederick Lonsdale and Harry Graham
(Based on the Austrian musical)
Produced by George Edwardes
With Lilian Davies and Maida Vale

Published songs:

"Back To My Heart" (lyric by Percy Greenbank)—added after
   opening
"Try A Little Kiss" (lyric by Greenbank and Wimperis)—added
   after opening

Arriving in London with his Ballet Russe success, Duke was hired to add contemporary songs to this long-running operetta. "Try A Little Kiss" was his first published popular song. Duke's real name—Vladimir Dukelsky—was contractually restricted to his concert works; George Gershwin, friend and fan since 1921, came up with the pseudonym.

YVONNE
May 22, 1926   Daly's Theatre ⟨London⟩
280 performances

Music also by Jean Gilbert
Book and lyrics by Percy Greenbank
(Based on the Austrian musical)
Directed by Herbert Mason
Produced by George Edwardes
With Ivy Tresmand and Hal Sherman

Published songs:

"Day Dreams"
"It's Nicer To Be Naughty"
"Lucky"
"The Magic Of The Moon"
"We Always Disagree"

Additional songs published in vocal score:

"All Men Are The Same"
"Charming Weather (Opening)"
"Don't Forget The Waiter"

Duke added a half-score to this import, which Noël Coward dubbed "Yvonne The Terrible."

TWO LITTLE GIRLS IN BLUE
[Circa April 1927]   ⟨Portsmouth, England⟩; closed during pre-London tryout

Music mostly by Paul Lannin and Vincent **Youmans [May 3, 1921]**
Lyrics mostly by Ira Gershwin
Book by Fred Jackson
Produced by Norman J. Norman and David Marks
With The Barry Twins and Barrie Oliver

Published song:

"Somebody's Sunday" (music and lyric by Duke)

THE BOW-WOWS
A Hare-m Scare-m Musical Show
October 12, 1927   Prince of Wales's Theatre ⟨London⟩
124 performances

Music and lyrics mostly by others
Directed and produced by Laddie Cliff
With Elsie Gregory and Georges Metaxa

Published song:

"For Goodness' Sake" (lyric by James Dyrenforth)

THE YELLOW MASK
A Mystery Thriller Musical
February 8, 1928   Carlton Theatre ⟨London⟩
218 performances

Lyrics mostly by Desmond Carter
Book by Edgar Wallace
Directed by Laddie Cliff
Produced by Julian Wylie and Cliff
With Bobby Howes, Phyllis Dare and Leslie Henson

Published songs:

"The Bacon And The Egg"
"Blowing The Blues Away" (lyric by Eric Little)
"Deep Sea"
"Half A Kiss" (lyric by Little)
"I Love You So"
"I Still Believe In You" (lyric by Duke and Carter)
"I'm Wonderful"
"You Do, I Don't"

Additional songs published (no lyrics) in piano selection:

"Chinese Ballet"
"Chinese March"
"March"
"Opening Chorus Act One"
"Walking On Air"
"Yellow Mask"

Duke, already attracting notice with his distinctive interpolations in Gershwin-crazy London, wrote his first complete score for this hit. "Blowing The Blues Away" was in the Gershwin "Sweet And Low Down"/"Kickin' The Clouds Away" tradition, only with Duke's more complex natural harmonies; "Half A Kiss" was a pleasant enough fox trot.

OPEN YOUR EYES
[Circa August 1929]   Empire Theatre ⟨Edinburgh⟩; closed during pre-London tryout

Lyrics by Collie Knox
Book by Frederick Jackson
Directed by John Harwood
With Ella Logan, Marie Burke, and Geoffrey Gwyther

Published songs:

"Happily Ever After"
"Jack And Jill"
"Open Your Eyes"
"Such A Funny Feeling"
"Too, Too Divine"—see **GARRICK GAIETIES** ⟨**Third**⟩ **[June 4, 1930]**
"You'd Do For Me—I'd Do For You"

Dukelsky's First Symphony was introduced by mentor/publisher Serge Koussevitzky and the Boston Symphony on March 15, 1929. Duke permanently moved to America in June—before the **OPEN YOUR EYES** production—and became a citizen in 1938.

GARRICK GAIETIES
Third Edition
June 4, 1930   Guild Theatre   170 performances

"Music and Lyrics By Everybody" (see **Blitzstein**)
Lyrics to Duke songs by E. Y. Harburg
Directed by Philip Loeb
Produced by The Theatre Guild
With Sterling Holloway, Edith Meiser, and Imogene Coca

Published songs:

"I Am Only Human After All" (lyric by Ira Gershwin and Harburg)
"Too, Too Divine"—cut after opening; new lyric for song from **OPEN YOUR EYES [Circa August 1929]**; also used with third lyric as "Shavian Shivers" (unpublished)

Ira Gershwin teamed former CCNY classmate (turned Depression-bankrupt electrical-appliance salesman) Harburg and George's friend Duke; the three collaborated on Duke's first American song, "I Am

Only Human After All." While looking for Broadway opportunity, Duke found a background music job at the Paramount film studios in Astoria. Duke and Harburg also wrote additional songs (unpublished) for the post-Broadway tour of this final **GARRICK GAIETIES.**

THREE'S A CROWD
October 15, 1930   Selwyn Theatre   271 performances

Music mostly by Arthur **Schwartz** (see **Lane**)
Lyrics mostly by Howard Dietz
Sketches by Dietz and others
Choreographed by Albertina Rasch
Directed by Hassard Short
Produced by Max Gordon
With Clifton Webb, Fred Allen, Libby Holman, and Tamara Geva

Published songs:

None

Duke contributed Tamara Geva's memorable "Tantalizing Toes" (unpublished). Geva, wife of Balanchine, was the first of Duke's Ballets Russe group to achieve Broadway success.

SHOOT THE WORKS
July 21, 1931   George M. Cohan Theatre
87 performances

Music and lyrics mostly by others (see **Berlin**)
Sketches by Nunnally Johnson, Heywood Broun, and others
Directed by Ted Hammerstein
Produced by Broun, with Milton Raison
With Broun, George Murphy, and Imogene Coca

Published songs:

"Mu-Cha-Cha" (music by Duke and Jay Gorney, lyric by E. Y. Harburg)

WALK A LITTLE FASTER
December 7, 1932   St. James Theatre   119 performances

Lyrics by E. Y. Harburg
Sketches by S. J. Perelman

Directed by Monty Woolley
Produced by Courtney Burr
With Beatrice Lillie, Bobby Clark and Paul McCullough, and Evelyn
  Hoey

Published songs:

"April In Paris"
"Off Again, On Again"
"A Penny For Your Thoughts"
"So Nonchalant" (lyric by Harburg and Charles Tobias)
"Speaking of Love"
"That's Life"
"Where Have We Met Before?"

Duke wrote his most famous song—"April In Paris"—for his first
complete Broadway score. Trained in concert music and jazz ballet,
he quickly attracted notice with his advanced-form theatre songs. Duke
rarely attracted great popularity, but he found (and maintains) an ar-
dent "highbrow" following.

ZIEGFELD FOLLIES OF 1934
January 4, 1934   Winter Garden Theatre
182 performances

Music mostly by Duke
Lyrics mostly by E. Y. Harburg
Directed by Bobby Connolly and John Murray Anderson
Produced by "Mrs. Florenz Ziegfeld" [Messrs. Shubert]
With Fanny Brice, Willie and Eugene Howard, and Jane Froman

Published songs:

"I Like The Likes of You"
"Suddenly" (lyric by Billy Rose and Harburg)
"This Is Not A Song" (lyric by Harburg and E. Hartman)
"What Is There To Say?"

Additional song recorded:

"Water Under The Bridge"

Following Ziegfeld's death in 1932, the Shuberts—longtime second-
rate competition to the **FOLLIES**—bought the rights to the title from
debt-ridden Billie Burke Ziegfeld. Unbilled but acknowledged, they

produced two successful editions with Duke scores (see **ZIEGFELD FOLLIES OF 1936 [January 30, 1936]**).

THUMBS UP
December 27, 1934   St. James Theatre   156 performances

Music and lyrics mostly by others
Directed by John Murray Anderson and Edward Clarke Lilley
Produced by Eddie Dowling
With Bobby Clark and Paul McCullough, Hal LeRoy, and J. Harold
  Murray

Published song:

"Autumn In New York" (lyric by Duke)

Duke's one contribution was his followup to "April In Paris" from **WALK A LITTLE FASTER [December 7, 1932]**. Both shows starred the comedy team of Clark and McCullough (who, of course, did not sing either song).

ZIEGFELD FOLLIES OF 1936
January 30, 1936   Winter Garden Theatre
115 performances

Lyrics by Ira Gershwin
Sketches by David Freedman
Choreographed by George Balanchine
Directed by John Murray Anderson
Produced by "Mrs. Florenz Ziegfeld" [Messrs. Shubert]
With Fanny Brice, Bob Hope, Eve Arden and Josephine Baker

Published songs:

"The Gazooka"
"I Can't Get Started"
"Island In The West Indies"
"My Red Letter Day"
"That Moment Of Moments"
"Words Without Music"

Additional songs published in USO/Camp Shows "AT EASE"
  (Volume 4):

"Economic Situation"—with revised lyric, retitled "New War
  Situation"

"Fancy, Fancy"
"She Hasn't A Thing Except Me"
"Time Marches On"
"We Hope You'll Soon Be Dancing To Our Score"—with revised
    lyric, retitled "We Somehow Feel That You Enjoyed Our Show"

Duke and Harburg—both volatile and opinionated—broke up over
disagreements on the previous **FOLLIES**. Ira Gershwin was free, as
George was busy finishing and orchestrating **PORGY AND BESS**
[October 10, 1935]. Memorable moments: Freedman's creation of the
"Baby Snooks" character for Brice, and Hope introducing the im-
mortal "I Can't Get Started." Also introduced to America was Duke's
Ballets Russe pal, George Balanchine.

THE SHOW IS ON
December 25, 1936   Winter Garden Theatre
237 performances

Music mostly by Duke (see **Arlen, Gershwin, Lane** and **Rodgers**)
Lyrics mostly by Ted Fetter
Sketches mostly by David Freedman and Moss Hart
Directed by Vincente Minnelli
Produced by Lee Shubert
With Beatrice Lillie and Bert Lahr

Published song:

"Now"

Additional song published in USO/Camp Shows "AT EASE"
    (Volume 4):

"The Finale Marches On" (lyric by E. Y. Harburg and Fetter)

Duke wrote songs and ballet music as well as compiling the interpolations from a number of major composers. Following the shock
of Gershwin's death (July 11, 1937), Duke went to Hollywood to
complete his friend's final score for the 1938 movie *The Goldwyn Follies*.

A VAGABOND HERO
A Dashing Musical Romance
*[December 26, 1939]   National Theatre ⟨Washington
D.C.⟩; closed during pre-Broadway tryout*

Music also by Samuel D. Pokrass
Book and lyrics mostly by Charles O. Locke
(Based on *Cyrano de Bergerac* [play] by Edmond Rostand)
Directed by George Houston
Produced by Messrs. Shubert
With Houston, Ruby Mercer, Hope Emerson, and Bill Johnson
NOTE: **THE WHITE PLUME**, original tryout title

Songs issued as professional copies:

"Bonjour, Goodbye"
"I Cling To You (Roxane's Song)" (lyric by Locke and Ted Fetter)
"Shadow Of Love" (lyric by Locke and Fetter)

Cyrano de Bergerac had toured unsuccessfully in 1932. With the
Depression over, the Shuberts decided to remount it (they already
had the costumes) and hired Duke to supplement the score. A week
in Washington as **THE WHITE PLUME,** a week in Pittsburgh as
A VAGABOND HERO—and that was it. "I Cling To You" is particularly lovely.

KEEP OFF THE GRASS
May 23, 1940   Broadhurst Theatre   44 performances
Music mostly by Jimmy McHugh
Lyrics by Al Dubin and Howard Dietz
Sketches by Parke Levy, Norman Panama and Melvin Frank, and others
Choreographed by George Balanchine
Directed by Fred de Cordova and Edward Duryea Dowling
Produced by the Messrs. Shubert
With Ray Bolger, Jimmy Durante, José Limon, Larry Adler, and Jane
    Froman

Published song:

None

Duke provided "Raffles" (unpublished), a ballet for Bolger.

IT HAPPENS ON ICE
An Ice Extravaganza
October 10, 1940   Center Theatre   180 performances
Music also by others
Lyrics by Al Stillman
Staged and devised by Leon Leonidoff

Produced by Sonja Henie and Arthur Wirtz
With Joe Cook

Published songs:

"Don't Blow That Horn, Gabriel" (lyric by Stillman and Will
    Hudson)
"Long Ago"

CABIN IN THE SKY
October 25, 1940   Martin Beck Theatre   156 performances

Lyrics by John Latouche
Book by Lynn Root
Dialogue staged by Albert Lewis
Directed and choreographed by George Balanchine
Produced by Lewis in association with Vinton Freedley
With Ethel Waters, Todd Duncan, Rex Ingram, Dooley Wilson, and
    Katherine Dunham

Published songs:

"Cabin In The Sky"
"Do What You Wanna Do"
"Honey In The Honeycomb"
"In My Old Virginia Home (On The River Nile)"—cut
"Livin' It Up" (lyric by Duke)—written for 1964 revival
"Love Me Tomorrow"
"Love Turned The Light Out"
"Savannah"
"Taking A Chance On Love" (lyric by Latouche and Ted Fetter)

Additional songs recorded:

"Great Day"
"Make Way"
"The Man Upstairs"
"Not So Bad To Be Good"
"Wade In The Water"
"We'll Live All Over Again"—cut

Duke wrote his best and most successful score for this fantasy musical, with friend and compatriot Balanchine not only choreograph-
ing but directing as well. Ethel Waters introduced "Taking A Chance
On Love" in her greatest musical role. Also standing out: "Cabin In
The Sky," "Love Me Tomorrow," and "In My Old Virginia Home."

For the 1944 movie version—made while Duke was serving in the Coast Guard—Harold Arlen and E. Y. Harburg wrote three additional songs, including "Happiness Is Just A Thing Called Joe."

BANJO EYES
December 25, 1941   Hollywood Theatre   126 performances

Music mostly by Duke
Lyrics mostly by John Latouche
Book by Joe Quillan and Izzy Elinson
(Based on *Three Men on a Horse* [play] by John Cecil Holm and George Abbott)
Directed by Hassard Short
Produced by Albert Lewis
With Eddie Cantor, Audrey Christie, June Clyde, and Lionel Stander

Published songs:

"Banjo Eyes"
"Don't Let It Happen Again"—cut; issued as professional copy
"I Always Think of Sally"—issued as professional copy
"I'll Take The City"—issued as professional copy
"Make With The Feet" (lyric by Harold Adamson)
"My Song Without Words"
"A Nickel To My Name"
"Not A Care In The World"
"We're Having A Baby (My Baby and Me)" (lyric by Adamson)
"Who Made The Rumba?"—advertised but not published

Eddie Cantor's only Broadway appearance after **WHOOPEE [PART 4: December 4, 1928]** was in this undistinguished wartime hit, the run cut short by the star's illness. The title character, incidentally, was not Cantor but a rumba-ing racehorse (of the two-person variety). A second musical version of the play was the unsuccessful Livingston and Evans' LET IT RIDE [October 12, 1961]. George Abbott, no fool, knew enough to stay away from both attempts at altering his classic farce.

THE LADY COMES ACROSS
January 9, 1942   44th Street Theatre   3 performances

Lyrics by John Latouche
Book by Fred Thompson and Dawn Powell

Choreography by George Balanchine
Book directed by Romney Brent
Under the supervision of Morrie Ryskind
Produced by George Hale
With Evelyn Wyckoff, Joe E. Lewis, Ronald Graham, Gower Champion,
    and Jeanne Tyler

Songs issued in professional copies:

"I'd Like To Talk About The Weather"
"Lady"
"Summer Is A-Comin' In"—also used in **THE LITTLEST
    REVUE [May 25, 1956]**
"This Is Where I Came In"
"You Took Me By Surprise"

This ill-fated musical started life as the Sammy Fain/Al Dubin *She
Had To Say Yes*, produced and coauthored by (and starring) Dennis
King. Duke and Latouche were called in to doctor; when King closed
the show on the road, George Hale bought the sets and costumes and
assembled **THE LADY COMES ACROSS.** Then the trouble really
started. British musical comedy great Jessie Matthews (see **EVER
GREEN [Rodgers: December 3, 1930]**) came across to star; she
played Boston and disappeared, a victim of shell shock. Evelyn
Wyckoff bravely took over for the Broadway opening; the show got
bombed. Duke entered the Coast Guard.

DANCING IN THE STREETS

*[March 22, 1943]   Shubert Theatre ⟨Boston, Massachusetts⟩;
closed during pre-Broadway tryout*

Lyrics by Howard Dietz
Book by John Cecil Holm and Matt Taylor
Directed by Edgar MacGregor
Produced by Vinton Freedley
With Mary Martin, Dudley Digges, and Ernest Cossart

Published songs:

"Dancing In The Streets"
"Got A Bran' New Daddy"
"Indefinable Charm"
"Irresistible You"

A wartime musical comedy which Duke wrote while serving in
Brooklyn. He had collaborated with Dietz before, on "Tantalizing

Toes" from **THREE'S A CROWD [October 15, 1930]**. Mary Martin had been discovered in **LEAVE IT TO ME [Porter: November 9, 1938]** and signed to a Hollywood contract. She returned East to star in the Ralph Rainger/Leo Robin NICE GOIN' [October 1939], which closed on the road. She turned down the lead in **OKLA-HOMA! [Rodgers: March 31, 1943]** to do **DANCING IN THE STREETS**. It wasn't till her next try that she came up with a hit, **ONE TOUCH OF VENUS [Weill: October 7, 1943]**.

JACKPOT
January 13, 1944   Alvin Theatre   69 performances

Lyrics by Howard Dietz
Book by Guy Bolton, Sidney Sheldon, and Ben Roberts
Directed by Roy Hargrave
Produced by Vinton Freedley
With Nanette Fabray, Betty Garrett, Allan Jones, and Benny Baker

Published songs:

"I've Got A One Track Mind"
"Sugarfoot"
"There Are Yanks (From The Banks Of The Wabash)"
"What Happened?"

Another undistinguished wartime musical comedy. Freedley had lost his touch; he had nothing but flops following **LET'S FACE IT! [Porter: October 29, 1941]**. Retiring in 1950, he spent the rest of his life serving as an officer and ultimately president of the Actors' Fund.

TARS AND SPARS
A Tabloid Recruiting Revue
[Circa April 1944]   United States Coast Guard Show

Music by Lt. Vernon Duke USCGR(T)
Book and lyrics by Howard Dietz
Choreography by Ted Gary and Gower Champion Seaman 1c
Directed and produced by Max Liebman
With Victor Mature CBM, Sidney Caesar Seaman 1c, and Champion

Published songs:

"Arm In Arm"
"Civilian"
"Farewell For A While"

Additional songs published in vocal selection:
"Apprentice Seaman"
"Palm Beach"
"Silver Shield"

The Army had Irving Berlin (**THIS IS THE ARMY [July 4, 1942]**), Frank Loesser, and Harold Rome; the Coast Guard had Duke, and assigned him to put together a recruiting show. Assembling the cast from enlisted men, Sid Caesar was found playing saxophone in the base's band and given comedy routines. **TARS AND SPARS** toured the country, keeping Duke, Caesar, and Champion stateside. SPARS, incidentally, were the Coast Guard's equivalent to WACS.

SADIE THOMPSON
November 16, 1944   Alvin Theatre   60 performances

Lyrics by Howard Dietz
Book by Dietz and Rouben Mamoulian
(Based on *Rain* [play] by W. Somerset Maugham and John Colton)
Directed by Rouben Mamoulian
Produced by A. P. Waxman
With June Havoc, Lansing Hatfield, and Ralph Dumke

Published songs:
"Any Woman Who Is Willing Will Do"—advertised but not
   published
"If You Can't Get The Love You Want"
"Life's A Funny Present From Someone"
"The Love I Long For"
"Poor As A Churchmouse"
"Sailing At Midnight"
"When You Live On An Island"
"You—U.S.A."—advertised but not published

An ambitious failure. **SADIE THOMPSON**'s fate was sealed during the first week of rehearsals, when star Ethel Merman found Dietz's lyrics lacking and quit. Her replacement: "Baby June" Havoc. Duke's fine score disappeared, including the lovely "Sailing At Midnight."

SWEET BYE AND BYE
[October 10, 1946]   Shubert Theatre ⟨New Haven, Connecticut⟩; closed during pre-Broadway tryout

Lyrics by Ogden Nash
Book by S. J. Perelman and Al Hirschfeld
Directed by Curt Conway
Produced by Nat Karson
With Dolores Gray, Erik Rhodes, and Percy Helton

Published songs:

"Just Like A Man"—also used in **TWO'S COMPANY** [December 15, 1952]
"Low and Lazy"
"An Old Fashioned Tune"
"Round About"—also used in **TWO'S COMPANY**
"Sweet Bye And Bye"

Another out-of-town disaster. Beginning with Eddie Cantor's illness which cut short the run of **BANJO EYES** [December 26, 1941], Duke wrote ten consecutive flops (four closing on the road). Not surprisingly, it became increasingly difficult for Duke to get productions, despite the continued quality and inventiveness of his work.

TWO'S COMPANY
December 15, 1952   Alvin Theatre   90 performances

Music mostly by Duke
Lyrics mostly by Ogden Nash
Sketches by Charles Sherman
Choreographed by Jerome Robbins
Directed by Jules Dassin
Produced by James Russo and Michael Ellis
With Bette Davis, Hiram Sherman, and Nora Kaye

Published songs:

"Good Little Girls" (lyric by Sammy Cahn)—cut; also used in
   THE LITTLEST REVUE [May 22, 1956]
"It Just Occurred To Me"
"Just Like A Man"—originally used in **SWEET BYE AND BYE**
   [October 10, 1946]
"Out Of The Clear Blue Sky"
"Round About"—originally used in **SWEET BYE AND BYE**

Additional songs recorded:

"Esther" (lyric by Cahn)
"Haunted Hot Spot"
"Purple Rose"
"Roll Along Sadie"
"The Theatre Is A Lady"
"Turn Me Loose On Broadway"

A turmoil-wracked Broadway failure, with Bette Davis in her musi-cal debut; the not-very-good show had to close when she developed "a sudden illness." Her second musical, the Broadway-bound MISS MOFFAT [October 7, 1974], had to close when she developed "a sudden illness."

THE LITTLEST REVUE
May 22, 1956   Phoenix Theatre   32 performances

Music mostly by Duke (see **Strouse**)
Lyrics mostly by Ogden Nash
Sketches by Nat Hiken, Michael Stewart, and others
Directed by Paul Lammers
Produced by T. Edward Hambleton and Norris Houghton by arrangement
   with Ben Bagley
With Charlotte Rae, Tammy Grimes, and Joel Grey

Published songs:

"Born Too Late"
"Good Little Girls"—originally used in **TWO'S COMPANY**
   [December 15, 1952]
"Madly In Love"
"Summer Is A-Comin' In" (lyric by John Latouche)—originally
   used in **THE LADY COMES ACROSS** [January 9, 1942]
"You're Far From Wonderful"

Additional songs recorded:

"I'm Glad I'm Not A Man"
"Love Is Still In Town"

The Phoenix Theatre had ended its first season with the award-winning Jerome Moross/John Latouche **GOLDEN APPLE [PART 4: March 11, 1954]**. Looking for another musical success, it com-missioned Duke for this intimate revue. Success, however, was not duplicated. Duke's score included the moving and incredible "Born Too Late."

TIME REMEMBERED
November 2, 1957   Morosco Theatre   248 performances

Play by Jean Anouilh
English version by Patricia Moyes
Incidental music and lyrics by Duke
Directed by Albert Marre (see **APRIL SONG [Leigh: July 9, 1980]**)
Produced by The Playwrights' Company in association with Milton
   Sperling
With Helen Hayes, Richard Burton, and Susan Strasberg

Published songs:

"Ages Ago"
"Time Remembered"

This hit drama was, ultimately, Duke's final Broadway effort.

THE PINK JUNGLE
[October 14, 1959]   Alcazar Theatre ⟨San Francisco, California⟩; closed during pre-Broadway tryout

Music and lyrics by Duke
Book by Leslie Stevens
Choreographed by Matt Maddox
Directed by Joseph Anthony
Produced by Paul Gregory
With Ginger Rogers, Leif Erickson, and Agnes Moorehead

Published songs:

None

Ginger Rogers' first Broadway musical since **GIRL CRAZY [Gershwin: October 14, 1930]** was not to be; it closed under a pink cloud of unpaid bills. **THE PINK JUNGLE,** for the record, was the cosmetics game.

ZENDA
A Romantic Musical
[August 5, 1963]   Curran Theatre ⟨San Francisco, California⟩; closed during pre-Broadway tryout

Lyrics mostly by Martin Charnin
Book by Everett Freeman
(Based on *The Prisoner of Zenda* [novel] by Anthony Hope)
Directed by George Schaefer
Produced by Edwin Lester (Civic Light Opera)
With Alfred Drake, Anne Rogers, and Chita Rivera

Published songs:

"Let Her Not Be Beautiful (You Are All That's Beautiful)"
"The Night Is Filled With Wonderful Sounds"

Duke's final show was another road disaster, a costume operetta with
many problems and three different lyricists. Inactive through the rest
of the Sixties, Vernon Duke died of lung cancer on January 17, 1969
in Santa Monica, California.

Vernon Duke began his Broadway career at the worst possible time—
right after the Depression hit the theatre. Harold Arlen and Burton
Lane were also 1930 newcomers; they countered by going to Hollywood, not a viable alternative for the musically intricate Dukelsky.
Duke's Broadway (and Broadway-bound) record is staggering: fourteen complete scores with only three successes. It had to make for a
discouraging career, particularly to a composer who knew that his work
was better than most of his contemporaries. And it was. Duke's advanced harmonies and complex forms were—and are—fascinating.
George Gershwin discovered Duke in the mid-Twenties and was certainly fascinated: Vernon Duke wrote easily in the style Gershwin as-
pired to. Gershwin became Duke's biggest fan, started him writing
for the theatre and encouraged him to come to America. Duke rarely
appealed to the public at large, and his hit songs were few ("April In
Paris," "I Can't Get Started," and "Taking A Chance On Love").
But over the years, Duke's brilliance has attracted—and continues to
attract—many devotees.

Burton Lane

BORN: February 2, 1912   New York, New York

Burton Lane began his musical career at the age of fifteen, when he left school to work as a pianist at Remick's, where Gershwin and Youmans had started a decade earlier. Lane's expert playing attracted attention—Gershwin was a particular fan—and a Shubert offer to write the 1928 edition of the GREENWICH VILLAGE FOLLIES, which was never produced. The sixteen-year-old had to wait another two years before being heard on Broadway.

ARTISTS AND MODELS
Paris-Riviera Edition
June 10, 1930   Majestic Theatre   65 performances

Music mostly by others
Lane lyrics by Samuel Lerner
(Based on *Dear Love* [British musical])
Directed by Frank Smithson
Produced by Messrs. Shubert
With Aileen Stanley and Phil Baker

Published songs:

"My Real Ideal"
"Two Perfect Lovers"

Book troubles were dealt with by throwing out the book and tacking on the name of one of the Shuberts' perennial revues. "Paris-Riviera Edition" explained the sets and costumes. Lane's early songs were bright and tuneful.

THREE'S A CROWD
October 15, 1930   Selwyn Theatre   271 performances

Music mostly by Arthur **Schwartz**
Lyrics mostly by Howard Dietz

Sketches by Dietz, Groucho Marx, and others
Directed by Hassard Short
Produced by Max Gordon
With Clifton Webb, Fred Allen, Libby Holman, and Tamara Geva

Published songs:

"Forget All Your Books" (lyric by Dietz and Samuel Lerner)
"Out In The Open Air" (lyric by Dietz and Ted Pola)

Howard Dietz was impressed with Lane; he fixed up the lyrics of two songs and inserted them into this first Schwartz and Dietz/Max Gordon revue.

THE THIRD LITTLE SHOW
June 1, 1931   Music Box Theatre   136 performances

Music mostly by others
Sketches by Noël Coward, S. J. Perelman, Marc Connelly, and others
Directed by Alexander Leftwich
Produced by Dwight Deere Wiman in association with Tom Weatherly
With Beatrice Lillie, Ernest Truex, and Constance Carpenter

Published song:

"Say The Word" (lyric by Harold Adamson)

THE SECOND LITTLE SHOW [Schwartz: September 2, 1930]— without Webb, Holman and Allen—had done poorly; this final edition, without even Schwartz and Dietz, fared little better.

EARL CARROLL'S VANITIES
Ninth Edition
August 27, 1931   Earl Carroll Theatre   278 performances

Music also by others
Lyrics to Lane songs by Harold Adamson
Sketches by Ralph Spence and Eddie Welch
Directed by Edgar MacGregor
Produced by Earl Carroll
With Will Mahoney, Lillian Roth, and William Demarest

Published songs:

"Goin' To Town"
"Have A Heart"
"Love Come Into My Heart"

The early years of the Depression were not a good time for teenage songwriters on Broadway. Lane and collaborator Harold Adamson went to Hollywood, quickly coming up with the hit "Everything I Have Is Yours." Lane worked successfully through the decade with several lyricists, including Frank Loesser.

HOLD ON TO YOUR HATS
September 11, 1940   Shubert Theatre   158 performances

Lyrics by E. Y. Harburg
Book by Guy Bolton, Matt Brooks, and Eddie Davis
Directed by Edgar MacGregor
Produced by Al Jolson and George Hale
With Jolson, Martha Raye, Jack Whiting, and Bert Gordon

Published songs:

"Don't Let It Get You Down (Love Is A Lovely Thing)"
"Swing Your Calico"—cut; issued as professional copy
"There's A Great Day Coming Mañana"
"The World Is In My Arms"
"Would You Be So Kindly"

Additional songs recorded:

"Down On The Dude Ranch"
"Hold On To Your Hats"
"Life Was Pie For The Pioneer"
"Old Timer"
"She Came, She Saw, She Can-Canned"
"Then You Were Never In Love"
"Walking Along Minding My Business"
"Way Out West"

Al Jolson returned to Broadway after a decade, bringing along Harburg (who with Harold Arlen had written some fine Jolson songs for the 1936 movie *The Singing Kid*). The star/producer also brought along wife Ruby Keeler, who disappeared from show and marriage during the tryout. The Lane/Harburg score was bright and tuneful—although, curiously, without any Jolson hits. After running a few months, the star decided to close the show and left Broadway for good.

LAFFING ROOM ONLY
December 23, 1944   Winter Garden Theatre
233 performances

Lyrics mostly by Lane
Sketches by Ole Olsen and Chic Johnson and others
Directed by John Murray Anderson
Produced by the Messrs. Shubert and Olsen and Johnson
With Olsen and Johnson and Betty Garrett

Published songs:

"Feudin' And Fightin' " (lyric by Lane and Al Dubin)—initial
   publication upon reuse as nonshow song
"Got That Good Time"
"Stop That Dancing"

HELLZAPOPPIN'! [September 22, 1938], the Olsen and Johnson
vaudeville revue, had run a staggering 1,404 performances; the
Shuberts followed it with a string of duplicates including **LAFFING
ROOM ONLY**. "Feudin' And Fightin' " resurfaced several years later
via radio to become a surprise hit.

FINIAN'S RAINBOW
A Completely Captivating Musical
January 10, 1947   46th Street Theatre   725 performances

Lyrics by E. Y. Harburg
Book by Harburg and Fred Saidy
Choreographed by Michael Kidd
Directed by Bretaigne Windust
Produced by Lee Sabinson and William R. Katzell
With Ella Logan, David Wayne, Albert Sharpe, Donald Richards, and
   Anita Alvarez

Published songs:

"The Begat"
"How Are Things In Glocca Morra?"
"If This Isn't Love"
"Look To The Rainbow"
"Necessity"
"Old Devil Moon"
"Something Sort Of Grandish"
"That Great Come And Get It Day"
"When I'm Not Near The Girl I Love"
"When The Idle Poor Become The Idle Rich"

Additional songs published in vocal score:
"Dance Of The Golden Crock" [instrumental]
"This Time Of The Year"

A perfectly fanciful musical comedy, one of the very few to explore the field mined by **OF THEE I SING [Gershwin: December 26, 1931]**. Mixing a little social significance with some fantasy and lots of entertainment, **FINIAN'S RAINBOW** got its message across. Lane wrote a superb, highly melodic score (with bits of Irish charm). Harburg did the best work of his career, probably because he was a leprechaun by nature. The songs are gems, with the shifting harmonies of "Old Devil Moon" and the grand, sweeping-but-hesitating waltz "When I'm Not Near The Girl I Love" the enchanting standouts.

ON A CLEAR DAY YOU CAN SEE FOREVER
October 17, 1965   Mark Hellinger Theatre
280 performances

Book and lyrics by Alan Jay Lerner
Choreographed by Herbert Ross
Directed by Robert Lewis
Produced by Lerner in association with Rogo Productions
With Barbara Harris, John Cullum, Titos Vandis, and William Daniels

Published songs:

"Come Back To Me"
"Go To Sleep"—written for 1970 movie version
"Hurry! It's Lovely Up Here!"
"Love With All The Trimmings"—written for movie version
"Melinda"
"On A Clear Day (You Can See Forever)"
"On The S.S. Bernard Cohn"
"She Wasn't You"
"Wait Till We're Sixty-Five"
"What Did I Have That I Don't Have?"
"When I'm Being Born Again"

Additional songs published in vocal score:

"Solicitor's Song"
"When I Come Around Again"—new lyric for "When I'm Being Born Again"

Additional songs recorded:

"Don't Tamper With My Sister"
"Tosy And Cosh"

Following the 1960 retirement of Frederick Loewe, Alan Jay Lerner
had been unsuccessfully searching for a collaborator. He finally began his ESP project with Richard Rodgers; but Rodgers, used to the
more disciplined Oscar Hammerstein and Lorenz Hart, found Lerner impossible to work with. Lerner turned to Lane, with whom he'd
written the 1951 movie *Royal Wedding* (including the Oscar nominee
"Too Late Now"). The pair wrote an exceedingly fine score, with
the popular "On A Clear Day" and "Come Back To Me," two perfect character songs ("What Did I Have That I Don't Have" and
"Hurry! It's Lovely Up Here!") and the ballads "She Wasn't You"
and "Melinda." All these—plus the performances of Barbara Harris
and John Cullum (who replaced Louis Jourdan during the tryout)—
weren't enough to carry **ON A CLEAR DAY** past a contrived book.

CARMELINA
April 8, 1979   St. James Theatre   17 performances

Lyrics by Alan Jay Lerner
Book by Lerner and Joseph Stein
(Based on *Buona Sera, Mrs. Campbell* [movie])
Choreographed by Peter Gennaro
Directed by José Ferrer
Produced by Roger L. Stevens, J. W. Fisher, Joan Cullman, and
    Jujamcyn Productions
With Georgia Brown, Cesare Siepi, John Michael King, Virginia Martin,
    and Jossie de Guzman

Published songs:

"It's Time For A Love Song"
"One More Walk Around The Garden"

Additional songs recorded:

"All That He Wants Me To Be"
"Carmelina"
"I Must Have Her"
"I'm A Woman"
"The Image Of Me"
"Love Before Breakfast"

"Prayer"
"Signora Campbell"
"Someone In April"
"Why Him?"
"Yankee Doodles Are Coming To Town"

Lane returned to Broadway again with Lerner. The property was poorly selected and poorly executed, with a book far below Lerner's capabilities. Lane's work was the best of the evening, particularly "I'm A Woman" and "Someone In April." The latter song featured especially fine work by Lerner.

In a career that spans fifty years, Burton Lane has chosen to limit his Broadway output to only four musical comedies. Only one of these shows was successful; another is at least somewhat familiar, due more to its Hollywood incarnation than the superior score. Yet Lane's work is so very good that he maintains a position of respect in the musical theatre; and, based on his **CARMELINA** work, he can still write. There is every reason to look forward to Lane's fifth musical—if he chooses to try again.

PART 2

Introduction

Most of the top theatre composers of the Twenties spent the bleak Depression in Hollywood. Broadway's only important new voices of the decade were first heard, fittingly, in politically slanted musicals. The already distinguished Kurt Weill arrived from Germany, where his work had been radical both musically and politically. Marc Blitzstein was deeply influenced by Weill, and even more outspoken. Harold Rome, on the other hand, used comedy and charm to make similar points; not surprisingly, he met with far greater popular success. The Depression ended as the nation geared up for war, and Broadway did its share by providing lively, energetic entertainments. Hugh Martin brought in the pop music sound, both as composer and arranger. Leonard Bernstein made the first of his theatre visits with an extra-lively musical comedy (albeit with a large chunk of modern ballet). After the War it was possible to turn to gentle, more thoughtful musicals. A touch of the European returned with Vienna-born Frederick Loewe. The Forties ended with the entrance of two Hollywood songwriters—Jule Styne and Frank Loesser—whose work quickly established them as important composers of "modern musical comedy." Within a few years Loesser was grooming protégés of his own: pop composers Richard Adler and Meredith Willson, who both enjoyed brief Broadway success.

Kurt Weill

BORN: March 2, 1900   Dessau, Germany
DIED: April 3, 1950   New York, New York

The son of a cantor, Kurt Weill was interested in music at an early age. By 1920 he was studying in Berlin with avant-garde composer Ferruccio Busoni; he soon moved from concert to contemporary work and started writing for the theatre. Caught up in Germany's inflammatory political situation, Weill earned a radical reputation. In 1927 he began collaboration with outspoken playwright/lyricist Bertolt Brecht: the pair received international attention with the success of their controversial DIE DREIGROSCHENOPER [August 28, 1928]. Weill's critical views (and Jewish heritage) made it impossible for him to stay in Germany, and he was forced to flee in 1933.

[Note: Weill's German work is not included except for subsequently presented English-language productions]

THE THREEPENNY OPERA
⟨First Version; see March 10, 1954⟩
April 13, 1933   Empire Theatre   12 performances

Original book and lyrics by Bertolt Brecht
English adaptation by Gifford Cochran and Jerrold Krimsky
(Based on *The Beggar's Opera* by John Gay)
Directed by Francesco von Mendelssohn
Produced by John Krimsky and Cochran
With Robert Chisholm, Steffi Duna, Rex Weber, and Burgess Meredith

Published songs:
None

[Complete vocal score of German version is published]

This heavily Germanic translation of DIE DREIGROSCHENOPER was out of place on Broadway in the midst of the Depression; besides, *The Beggar's Opera* had recently been revived in New York. Neither of the authors was involved in this unsuccessful production. Weill's personal reviews, however, were quite positive.

MARIE GALANTE
December 22, 1934   Théatre de Paris ⟨Paris⟩

Book and lyrics by Jacques Deval
(Based on his novel)
Directed by Andre Lefour
Produced by Leon Volterra
With Florelle, Inkijinoff, Alcover, Serge Nadoud, and Joe Alex

Published songs:

"Les Filles De Bordeaux"
"Le Grand Lustucru"
"J'Attends Un Navire"
"Marche De L'Armée Paneméenne" [instrumental]
"Le Roi D'Aquitaine"—see **A KINGDOM FOR A COW [June 28, 1935]**
"Scène Au Dancing" [instrumental]
"Tango"—advertised but not published; initial publication as 1946 nonshow song "Youkali" (lyric by Roger Fernay)
"Le Train Du Ciel"

Weill spent his first two years of exile in Paris, where he continued his concert compositions, composed the ballet *The Seven Deadly Sins*, and wrote this unsuccessful book musical. "J'Attends Un Navire" is particularly moving.

A KINGDOM FOR A COW
June 28, 1935   Savoy Theatre ⟨London⟩

Lyrics by Desmond Carter
Book by Reginald Arkell and Carter
(Based on *Der Kuhhandel* [musical] by Robert Vambery)
Directed by Ernest Matrai and Felix Weissberger

Published songs:

"As Long As I Love"

"Two Hearts"—new lyric for "Le Roi D'Aquitaine" from **MARIE GALANTE [December 22, 1934]**

Weill moved on briefly to England, where this satire was poorly received and quickly closed. Trying America next, the composer arrived September 10, 1935; he immediately adopted this country and became a citizen in 1943.

JOHNNY JOHNSON
November 19, 1936   44th Street Theatre   68 performances

Book and lyrics by Paul Green
Directed by Lee Strasberg
Produced by The Group Theatre
With Russell Collins, Phoebe Brand, Paula Miller, Lee J. Cobb, Robert Lewis, Luther Adler, and Elia Kazan

Published songs:

"Mon Ami, My Friend"

"Oh, Heart Of Love"

"Oh The Rio Grande"

"To Love You And To Lose You" (lyric by Edward Heyman)— nonshow lyric for "Listen To My Song (Johnny's Song)"

Additional songs published in vocal score:

"Aggie's Song"

"The Allied High Command"

"Asylum Chorus"

"The Ballad Of San Juan Hill"

"The Battle" [instrumental]

"Captain Valentine's Song"

"Democracy's Call"

"A Hymn To Peace" [hymn]

"In No Man's Land" [instrumental]

"In Times Of War and Tumults"

"Interlude After Scene III" [instrumental]

"Introduction" [instrumental]

"Johnny's Dream" [instrumental]

"Laughing Generals" [instrumental]

"Listen To My Song (Johnny's Song)"
"Music Of The Stricken Redeemer" [instrumental]
"Over In Europe"
"The Psychiatry Song"
"The Sea Song"
"Song Of The Goddess"
"Song Of The Guns"
"Song Of The Wounded Frenchmen"

The socially conscious Group Theatre (Harold Clurman, Strasberg and
Cheryl Crawford) commissioned Weill for this antiwar musical. Paul
Green wrote a controversial but muddled book, and the production
suffered from unfocused direction. Although **JOHNNY JOHNSON**
was a failure, Weill's work was well received and he attracted Broadway notice.

THE ETERNAL ROAD
January 7, 1937   Manhattan Opera House
153 performances

Play and lyrics by Franz Werfel
Adapted by William A. Drake
(From a translation by Ludwig Lewisohn)
Directed by Max Reinhardt
Produced by Meyer W. Weisgal and Crosby Gaige
With Thomas Chalmers, Sam Jaffe, Dickie Van Patten, Katherine
   Carrington, and Lotte Lenya (Weill)

Songs published in vocal selection:

"Dance Of The Golden Calf"
"David's Psalm"
"The March To Zion"
"Promise"
"Song Of Miriam"
"Song Of Ruth"

Philanthropist Weisgal had brought Weill to America to work with
emigrés Reinhardt and Werfel on this eternally-in-preparation Bibli-
cal spectacle that illustrated the history of Jewish persecution. Reinhardt had enormous Broadway success in 1924 with his Passion Play
The Miracle; both productions featured spectacular and massive sets

by Norman Bel Geddes. In the cast were Katherine Carrington (Mrs. Arthur Schwartz) and Lotte Lenya, whose career had virtually ended when she joined her husband in exile. Twenty years later, American audiences finally "discovered" her in **THE THREEPENNY OPERA ⟨Second Version⟩ [March 10, 1954].**

KNICKERBOCKER HOLIDAY
October 19, 1938   Ethel Barrymore Theatre
168 performances

Book and lyrics by Maxwell Anderson
(Based on *Knickerbocker History of New York* [stories] by Washington
   Irving)
Directed by Joshua Logan
Produced by The Playwrights' Company
With Walter Huston, Jean Madden, Richard Kollmar, and Ray Middleton

Published songs:

"It Never Was You"
"September Song"
"There's Nowhere To Go But Up"
"Will You Remember Me?"

Additional songs published in vocal selections:

"Ballad Of The Robbers"
"Dirge For A Soldier"
"How Can You Tell An American?"
"May And January"
"The One Indispensable Man"
"Our Ancient Liberties"
"The Scars"
"To War!"
"Washington Irving's Song"
"We Are Cut In Twain"
"Young People Think About Love"

Additional songs published in vocal score:

"The Algonquins From Harlem" [instrumental]
"Clickety-Clack"
"Entrance Of The Council"
"Hush, Hush"
"No Ve Vouldn't Gonto Do It"

"One Touch Of Alchemy (All Hail The Political Honeymoon)"
"Opening (Introduction To Washington Irving's Song)"
"Sitting In Jail"

Pulitzer Prize–winning playwright Anderson saw the tyrannical Peter Stuyvesant (and his councillors) as perfect counterparts to Franklin Roosevelt (and his cabinet). Choosing Weill on the strength of
JOHNNY JOHNSON [November 19, 1936], the two men became
close, lifelong friends and neighbors. The Playwrights' Company was
an organization formed by five distinguished dramatists (Anderson,
S. N. Behrman, Sidney Howard, Elmer Rice, and Robert E. Sherwood) who, dissatisfied with the treatment they were receiving from
producers, decided to present their own works by committee. Weill
became deeply involved in the The Playwrights' Company, eventually becoming a full member. **KNICKERBOCKER HOLIDAY,** their
first production, just missed being a hit; Anderson's criticism was too
bitter. Walter Huston—in his only musical—introduced one of Weill's
few popular hits, "September Song."

RAILROADS ON PARADE
April 30, 1939   New York World's Fair

Pageant by Edward Hungerford
Incidental music by Kurt Weill
Directed by Charles Alan
Produced by Eastern Presidents' Conference

Published song:

"Mile After Mile" (lyric by Charles Alan and Buddy Bernier)

A spectacle presented by the railroad industry.

LADY IN THE DARK
January 23, 1941   Alvin Theatre   467 performances

Lyrics by Ira Gershwin
Book by Moss Hart
Choreographed by Albertina Rasch
Directed by Hassard Short
Produced by Sam H. Harris
With Gertrude Lawrence, Victor Mature, Macdonald Carey, and Danny
    Kaye

Published songs:

"Girl Of The Moment"
"Jenny"
"My Ship"
"One Life To Live"
"The Princess Of Pure Delight"
"This Is New"
"Tschaikowsky"

Additional songs published in vocal score:

"The Best Years Of His Life"
"Dance Of The Tumblers" [instrumental]
"The Greatest Show On Earth"
"Huxley"
"It Looks Like Liza"
"Mapleton High Chorale"
"Oh Fabulous One"

Additional song recorded:

"You Are Unforgettable"—cut

Moss Hart's experience with psychoanalysis provided the inspiration
for this musical play. The score was made up of three extended dream
sequences, with the heroine's dilemma solved in the final song ("My
Ship"). Ira Gershwin, in a dazed retirement since George's death, came
back with absolutely dazzling lyrics. Sam Harris provided Broadway's most technically complicated production to date, as Hassard
Short made novel use of *two* turntables simultaneously. It was the
end of Harris' long career; he died on July 3, 1941. The show's very
greatest asset was its **LADY**; Gertrude Lawrence sat on an acrobat's
swing and bumped-and-ground "The Saga Of Jenny," topping all else
(including young Danny Kaye's startling verbal acrobatics).

ONE TOUCH OF VENUS
October 7, 1943   Imperial Theatre   567 performances

Lyrics by Ogden Nash
Book by S. J. Perelman and Nash
(Based on *The Tinted Venus* [story] by F. Anstey)
Choreography by Agnes de Mille
Directed by Elia Kazan
Produced by Cheryl Crawford

With Mary Martin, Kenny Baker, John Boles, Paula Laurence, Teddy
  Hart, and Sono Osato

Published songs:

"Foolish Heart"—reused in 1948 movie version "(Don't Look
  Now, But) My Heart Is Showing" (lyric by Ann Ronell)
"Speak Low"
"That's Him"
"The Trouble With Women"
"West Wind"—reused in movie version as "My Week" (lyric by
  Ronell)

Additional songs published in vocal selections:

"How Much I Love You"
"I'm A Stranger Here Myself"
"One Touch Of Venus"
"Wooden Wedding"

Additional songs recorded:

"Dr. Crippen"
"Forty Minutes For Lunch" [ballet]
"Love In The Mist"—cut
"Venus In Ozone Heights" [ballet]
"Very, Very, Very"
"Vive La Difference"—cut
"Way Out West In Jersey"—also known as "Plunk, Plunk, Plunk"

Weill's two wartime musical comedies were his only commercial hits.
Mary Martin finally achieved stardom (see **DANCING IN THE
STREETS [Duke: March 22, 1943]**) in a role intended for Marlene
Dietrich. Nash and Perelman's work was witty and funny, as might
be expected. The unlikely team of de Mille and Weill successfully
collaborated on modernist ballets (featuring Sono Osato); and Weill
provided the exceptional "Speak Low." Former Group Theatre producer Cheryl Crawford brought in Elia Kazan (who had appeared in
JOHNNY JOHNSON [November 19, 1936]) to direct his first of
two Weill/Crawford musicals. Weill's other wartime activities included service as production manager for the American Theatre
Wing's morale project, **LUNCHTIME FOLLIES [Rome: June 22,
1942]**.

THE FIREBRAND OF FLORENCE
March 22, 1945 Alvin Theatre 43 performances

Lyrics by Ira Gershwin
Book by Edwin Justus Mayer
(Based on *The Firebrand* [play] by Mayer)
Directed by John Murray Anderson
Produced by Max Gordon
With Earl Wrightson, Beverly Tyler, Melville Cooper, and Lotte
  Lenya (Weill)
NOTE: **MUCH ADO ABOUT LOVE,** pre-Broadway title

Published songs:

"A Rhyme For Angela"
"Sing Me Not A Ballad"
"There'll Be Life, Love And Laughter"
"You're Far Too Near Me"

Additional songs recorded:

"Act One, Scene One"
"Alessandro The Wise"
"Come to Florence"
"Cozy Nook Trio"
"Dizzily, Busily"
"Hangman's Song (Under The Gallows Tree)"
"Just In Case"
"The Little Naked Boy"
"Love Is My Enemy"
"The Nighttime Is No Time For Thinking"
"When The Duchess Is Away"
"You Have To Do What You Do Do"

This lavish costume operetta resoundingly flopped, burying an interesting score and some fine lyrics. Ira Gershwin, in his "Arthur Francis" days, had contributed "The Voice Of Love" (music by Russell Bennett and Maurice Nitke) to the original 1924 production of Mayer's play. Lenya made her only Broadway appearance in a Weill musical; she was woefully miscast and scathingly reviewed.

A FLAG IS BORN
September 5, 1946 Alvin Theatre 120 performances

Play by Ben Hecht
Incidental music by Kurt Weill
Directed by Luther Adler
Produced by The American League For A Free Palestine
With Paul Muni, Marlon Brando, Quentin Reynolds, and Sidney Lumet

Published songs:

None

A fund-raising propaganda play in support of the establishment of Israel.

STREET SCENE
January 9, 1947   Adelphi Theatre   148 performances

Lyrics by Langston Hughes and Elmer Rice
Book by Rice
(Based on the play by Rice)
Choreographed by Anna Sokolow
Directed by Charles Friedman
Produced by Dwight Deere Wiman in association with The Playwrights'
     Company
With Polyna Stoska, Anne Jeffreys, and Norman Cordon

Published songs:

"A Boy Like You" (lyric by Hughes)
"Lonely House" (lyric by Hughes)
"Moon-Faced, Starry-Eyed" (lyric by Hughes)
"We'll Go Away Together" (lyric by Hughes)
"What Good Would The Moon Be?" (lyric by Hughes)

Additional songs published in vocal score:

"Ain't It Awful, The Heat?"
"Blues (Marble and a Star)"
"Catch Me If You Can"
"Don't Forget The Lilac Bush"
"Get A Load Of That"
"I Loved Her Too"
"Ice Cream Sextet"
"Let Things Be Like They Was"
"Lullaby" (lyric by Rice)
"Remember That I Care" (lyric by Hughes)
"Somehow I Never Could Believe" (lyric by Hughes)

"There'll Be Trouble"
"When A Woman Has A Baby"
"The Woman Who Lived Up There"
"Wouldn't You Like To Be On Broadway?"
"Wrapped In A Ribbon And Tied With A Bow"

Additional song recorded:

"Italy In Technicolor"—cut

Since coming to America, Weill had been hoping to create a new musical theatre form combining opera and drama. He did not quite succeed with **STREET SCENE,** a quasi-opera which eventually found success in the opera house. Weill wrote a fine, rich score, and novice lyricists Elmer Rice (the playwright) and Langston Hughes (the poet) did fairly well. Particularly effective were "Somehow I Never Could Believe," "Blues," "What Good Would The Moon Be?" and "Lullaby." But **STREET SCENE** was overlong and overly melodramatic. Weill was by now a full member (with Rice) of the Playwrights' Company, which coproduced the show.

LOVE LIFE
A Vaudeville
October 7, 1948   46th Street Theatre   252 performances

Book and lyrics by Alan Jay Lerner
Directed by Elia Kazan
Produced by Cheryl Crawford
With Nanette Fabray and Ray Middleton

Published songs:

"Economics"
"Green-Up Time"
"Here I'll Stay"
"Is It Him Or Is It Me?"
"Love Song"
"Mr. Right"
"Susan's Dream"—cut
"This Is The Life"

Additional songs recorded:

"I Remember It Well"—different than song from **GIGI [Loewe: November 13, 1973]**

"Locker Room"
"My Kind Of Night"
"What More Do I Want?"—cut
"You Understand Me So"

Crawford's previous musical had been the hit **BRIGADOON [Loewe: March 13, 1947]**. Loewe wasn't interested in this new work, so Crawford teamed Lerner with Weill. They attempted an examination of marriage in vaudeville style, illustrated by one family moving through different eras of American history—not unlike the director's 1942 *Skin of Our Teeth*. But the novel set-up didn't work; Lerner went back to Loewe, Weill to Anderson.

LOST IN THE STARS
October 30, 1949   Music Box Theatre   281 performances

Book and lyrics by Maxwell Anderson
(Based on *Cry the Beloved Country* [novel] by Alan Paton)
Directed by Rouben Mamoulian
Produced by The Playwrights' Company
With Todd Duncan, Inez Matthews, Leslie Banks, and Julian Mayfield

Published songs:

"Big Mole"
"A Bird Of Passage"—issued in choral edition
"The Little Gray House"
"Lost In The Stars"—initial publication as 1946 nonshow song
    (from unproduced musical *Ulysses Africanus*)
"Stay Well"
"Thousands Of Miles"
"Trouble Man"

Additional songs included in published vocal score:

"Cry The Beloved Country"
"Fear!"
"Four O'Clock"
"The Hills Of Ixopo"
"Murder In Parkwold"
"O Tixo, Tixo, Help Me"
"The Search"
"Train To Johannesburg"
"The Wild Justice"
"Who'll Buy"

Weill's final work was this serious piece dealing with racial prejudice in South Africa. While Anderson had great success as a dramatic playwright, he displayed a heavy hand with his two musical librettos; this heaviness worked against **LOST IN THE STARS'** chances for popular success (as it had with **KNICKERBOCKER HOLIDAY [October 19, 1938]**. Shortly after his fiftieth birthday, Kurt Weill had a sudden heart attack; he died April 3, 1950 in New York.

HUCKLEBERRY FINN
[Circa April 1950]; unproduced musical

Lyrics by Maxwell Anderson
(Based on the novel by Mark Twain)

Published songs:

"Apple Jack"
"The Catfish Song"
"Come In, Mornin' "
"River Chanty"
"This Time Next Year"

Weill, whose deep interest in American themes had been displayed in several of his musicals (as well as the 1948 one-act folk opera *Down in the Valley*), was collaborating with Anderson and Rouben Mamoulian on this project at the time of his death. The completed songs were published, and an adaptation of the work was seen on German television.

THE THREEPENNY OPERA
⟨Second Version; see April 13, 1933⟩
March 10, 1954   Theatre de Lys ⟨off-Broadway⟩
2,706 performances

Original book and lyrics by Bertolt Brecht
English adaptation by Marc Blitzstein
(Based on *The Beggar's Opera* by John Gay)
Directed by Carmen Capalbo
Produced by Capalbo and Stanley Chase
With Scott Merrill, Jo Sullivan, Lotte Lenya (Weill), Beatrice Arthur, and
   Charlotte Rae

Published song:

"Mack The Knife"

Additional songs published in vocal selection:
"Army Song"
"Ballad Of Dependency"
"Ballad Of The Easy Life"
"Barbara Song"
"Instead-Of Song"
"Love Song"
"Pirate Jenny"
"Solomon Song"
"Tango Ballad"
"Useless"

Additional songs recorded:
"Call From The Grave"
"Death Message"
"Finale (Reprieved)"
"How To Survive"
"Melodrama"
"Jealousy Duet"
"Morning Anthem"
"The Mounted Messenger"
"Overture"
"Polly's Song"
"Wedding Song"
"The World Is Mean"

Weill's DIE DREIGROSCHENOPER, perhaps his greatest work, remained virtually unknown outside a very small circle. Marc Blitzstein, studying composition in Berlin in 1928, had been deeply influenced by the original production and was a great fan of the piece. In 1950, Blitzstein translated "Pirate Jenny" for a course he was teaching. He called the composer for an opinion, singing over the telephone. Weill enthusiastically suggested they do the entire work; but within the month he was dead. Blitzstein went about the adaptation as a labor of love, without changing a single note of Weill's work. A production scheduled for the spring of 1952 at City Center (where **NO FOR AN ANSWER [Blitzstein: January 5, 1941]** had led its troubled life) was suddenly cancelled, and one more obstacle was placed in the way. Blitzstein's protégé Leonard Bernstein was arranging an arts festival at Brandeis College (Waltham, Massachusetts); he arranged for the piece to debut there (see **TROUBLE IN TAHITI**

[**Bernstein: April 19, 1955**]). With Lenya and David Brooks singing, and Bernstein conducting, the adaptation was performed June 14, 1952. Almost two years later **THE THREEPENNY OPERA** finally opened off-Broadway—for a limited ten-week engagement. Popular demand caused it to reopen, and it became a six-year phenomenon. Lotte Lenya, in her original role of Jenny, began her American career as interpreter of Weill. And "Mack The Knife"—Blitzstein's version of the "Moritat"—became Kurt Weill's biggest hit, some thirty years after it was written.

BRECHT ON BRECHT
January 3, 1962   Theatre de Lys ⟨off-Broadway⟩
440 performances

Staged reading from the works of Bertolt Brecht
Arranged and translated by George Tabori
Music mostly by others
Directed by Gene Frankel
Produced by ANTA and Cheryl Crawford
With Lotte Lenya (Weill), Dane Clark, Anne Jackson, Viveca Lindfors, and George Voskovec

Song recorded:

"Ballad Of The Nazi Soldier's Wife" (translation by Michael Feingold)

THE RISE AND FALL OF THE CITY OF MAHAGONNY
April 28, 1970   Phyllis Anderson Theatre ⟨off-Broadway⟩   8 performances

Original book and lyrics by Bertolt Brecht
English adaptation by Arnold Weinstein
Conceived and directed by Carmen Capalbo
Produced by Capalbo and Abe Margolies
With Barbara Harris, Estelle Parsons, and Frank Poretta

Recorded songs:

"Alabama Song"
"As You Make Your Bed"
"Deep In Alaska"
"Oh, Heavenly Salvation"

A misguided adaptation of the 1929 Berlin piece. Capalbo had produced and directed **THE THREEPENNY OPERA** ⟨Second Version⟩ **[March 10, 1954]**. But in that case Marc Blitzstein was on hand as Weill's surrogate. This **MAHAGONNY** closed "for revision" during previews, at which point Poretta replaced Mort Shuman as the male lead.

HAPPY END
May 7, 1977   Martin Beck Theatre   75 performances

Original book and lyrics by Bertolt Brecht
(Based on a play by Elisabeth Hauptmann)
English adaptation by Michael Feingold
Directed by Michael Kalfin and Patricia Birch
Produced by Michael Harvey and the Chelsea Theatre Center
With Meryl Streep, Christopher Lloyd, and Tony Azito

Recorded songs:

"Bilbao Song"
"Childhood's Bright Endeavor"
"Don't Be Afraid"
"God Bless Rockefeller"
"Mandalay Song"
"March Ahead To The Fight"
"Sailor Tango"

Another unsuccessful attempt to retain the magic of the Weill-Brecht agit-prop style in an American translation. This production was a second Broadway transfer from Chelsea's home at the Brooklyn Academy of Music; the first had been the artistically successful **CANDIDE** ⟨Second Version⟩ **[Bernstein: March 10, 1974]**. But **CANDIDE** had Hal Prince and Stephen Sondheim. **HAPPY END** did not.

Kurt Weill was in America less than fifteen years, little more than half of his creative life. During that time he wrote eight complete musicals, only two of which were financially profitable. Similarly, only two songs—"September Song" and "Speak Low"—became best-selling hits. In the thirty-five years since Weill's death, his work has gradually achieved recognition, chiefly through productions of material written during his early career in Germany. DIE DREIGROS-

CHENOPER [August 28, 1928] brought Weill instant international acclaim; America didn't take to it until the posthumous **Second Version** made **THE THREEPENNY OPERA [March 10, 1954]** Weill's biggest success (and "Mack The Knife" his most popular song). The American shows don't lend as easily to revival, saddled with libretto and production problems; but there is fine musical theatre work throughout.

Marc Blitzstein

BORN: March 2, 1905 Philadelphia, Pennsylvania
DIED: January 22, 1964 Martinique, West Indies

Son of a banker, Marc Blitzstein prepared for a career in serious music. He performed as a piano soloist with the Philadelphia Symphony as early as 1920, and entered the Curtis Institute of Music. In the mid-Twenties he went to Europe to study composition with Nadia Boulanger and Arnold Schoenberg—and was fascinated by the exciting theatre work of Weill and Brecht in Berlin (see **THE THREE-PENNY OPERA** ⟨Second Version⟩ **[Weill: March 10, 1954]**). Blitzstein came to New York before the crash, as a performer and lecturer.

[all music and lyrics by Marc Blitzstein]

GARRICK GAIETIES
Third Edition
June 4, 1930 Guild Theatre 170 performances
"Music and Lyrics by Everybody" (see **Duke**)
Directed by Philip Loeb
Produced by The Theatre Guild
With Sterling Holloway, Edith Meiser, and Imogene Coca

Published songs:
None

The Rose of Arizona, a one-act operetta spoof, had been a popular feature of the **GARRICK GAIETIES** ⟨Second Edition⟩ **[Rodgers: May 19, 1926]**. For this last of the series, another one-act opera was called for: Blitzstein contributed his "progressive opera" *Triple Sec* (text by Ronald Jeans, unpublished), written during his 1928 Berlin days. *Triple Sec*, originally titled *Theatre For Cabaret*, was favorably received despite its avant-garde nature.

PARADE
⟨*First Version*⟩
A Social Revue
May 20, 1935   Guild Theatre   40 performances

Music mostly by Jerome Moross
Lyrics mostly by others
Directed by Philip Loeb
Produced by The Theatre Guild
With Jimmy Savo and Eve Arden

Published songs:

None

Studying and teaching during the early Depression years, Blitzstein developed strong left-wing tendencies. **PARADE** was produced by a young branch of The Theatre Guild, much as the initial **GARRICK GAIETIES [Rodgers: May 17, 1925]** had been. But **PARADE** was extremely political—much to the embarrassment of the Guild—and received a stormy reception. Blitzstein was developing a strong interest in the potential of music as social message, and contributed "Send For The Militia." Principal composer was twenty-one-year-old Jerome Moross, whose one full theatre piece was to be the superlative **GOLDEN APPLE [PART 4: March 11, 1954].**

THE CRADLE WILL ROCK
A Play In Music
June 16, 1937   Venice (Jolson) Theatre   14 performances
December 5, 1937   Mercury Theatre   5 performances
January 3, 1938   Windsor Theatre   104 performances

Book by Blitzstein
Directed by Orson Welles
Produced by Welles and John Houseman
With Will Geer, Howard Da Silva, Olive Stanton, and Blitzstein

Published songs:

"The Cradle Will Rock"
"Croon-Spoon"
"Doctor And Ella"
"Drugstore Scene"

"The Freedom Of The Press"
"Gus And Sadie Love Song"—also included in "Drugstore Scene"
"Honolulu"
"Joe Worker"
"Leaflets!" (and "Art For Art's Sake")
"Nickel Under The Foot"
"The Rich"

Additional songs recorded:

"Let's Do Something Special"
"Moll Song"
"Mrs. Mister And Reverend Salvation"
"Oh, What A Filthy Night Court"

Kurt Weill and Bertolt Brecht, strong influences on Blitzstein, were both now in America. Brecht heard the prostitute's song ("Nickel Under The Foot") and suggested Blitzstein write a full-length music/theatre piece in song, showing all members of establishment as prostitutes. This Blitzstein did, choosing as his hero a union organizer in Steeltown, USA (1936 saw armed riots at Flint, Michigan automobile factories). **THE CRADLE WILL ROCK** was produced by the Federal Theatre Project of the Works Progress Administration, under the supervision of Houseman and twenty-two-year-old director Orson Welles. The government agency—which had approved and funded the project—became nervous after the first preview, and suddenly suspended *all* new WPA activities "to facilitate budget cuts." That night the doors of the sold-out Maxine Elliott Theatre were padlocked; Welles had actor Will Geer perform on the sidewalk to hold the audience while Houseman looked for an empty theatre. Eight hundred people paraded twenty blocks uptown to the Venice, where the performance finally began two hours late. Actors' Equity had forbidden its members to appear; half the cast showed up anyway, delivering their lines from seats in the house while Blitzstein and Welles played and narrated from the stage. **THE CRADLE WILL ROCK** continued at the Venice for two weeks, retaining the exciting performance style born of necessity. Welles and Houseman left the WPA to begin their Mercury Theatre Company (with Blitzstein as resident composer) and revived the piece for Sunday night performances; in January, **THE CRADLE WILL ROCK** was finally opened for a commercial run.

JULIUS CAESAR
November 11, 1937   Mercury Theatre   157 performances

Play by William Shakespeare
Incidental music by Blitzstein
Directed by Orson Welles
Produced by The Mercury Theatre (Welles and John Houseman)
With Welles, George Coulouris, Joseph Cotten, Hiram Sherman, and
    Martin Gabel

Published song:

"Orpheus (Lucius' Song)" (lyric by Shakespeare)

Welles continued to assault the theatre world with a modern-dress version of **JULIUS CAESAR** (in which he played Brutus). The Mercury Theatre Group was to have a brief but notable life, dying with a spectacularly Wellesian failure (the 1939 Shakespearean omnibus *Five Kings*). Orson went to Hollywood and made *Citizen Kane* (1941).

DANTON'S DEATH
"A Drama In Individual Scenes Vignetted By Spotlight"
November 2, 1938   Mercury Theatre   21 performances

Play by Georg Buchner
(Translated by Geoffrey Dunlop)
Songs by Blitzstein
Directed by Orson Welles
Produced by The Mercury Theatre (Welles and John Houseman)
With Welles, Joseph Cotten, Martin Gabel, Arlene Francis, and Ruth
    Ford

Published songs:

None

NO FOR AN ANSWER
January 5, 1941   Mecca Theatre (City Center)
3 performances

Book by Blitzstein
Directed by Walter E. Watts

Produced by "A Committee including Bennett Cerf, Lillian Hellman,
    Arthur Kober and Herman Shumlin"
With Martin Wolfson, Curt Conway, and Carol Channing

Recorded songs:

"Dimples"
"Francie"
"Fraught"
"Gina"
"Make The Heart Be Stone"
"Mike"
"Nick"
"No For An Answer"
"Penny Candy"
"The Purest Kind Of Guy"
"Secret Singing"
"Song Of The Bat"
"Take The Book"

Unable to arrange a full production of **NO FOR AN ANSWER,** a
distinguished group of theatre people sponsored three Sunday-night
staged readings. Public reaction was even more stormy than for **THE
CRADLE WILL ROCK [June 16, 1937],** and the city threatened to
close the theatre for "licensing violations." In the earlier work Blitzstein used stereotyped characters to make his point; here he tried to
create a contemporary, realistic play with a musical base. The subject
matter was again left-wing, dealing with a strike of hotel restaurant
workers. Despite the exciting nature of the work—and the over-
whelmingly positive critical reaction—it was impossible to find back-
ing for a commercial production. Among the cast was nineteen-year-
old Carol Channing, fresh from Bennington. Blitzstein next went to
war, serving with the 8th Air Force in London; his assignments included Director of Music for the American Broadcasting Station in
Europe, supervision of the 1943 American Negro Troops Choral
Concert at Royal Albert Hall, and composition of the 1944 *Airborne
Symphony.*

ANOTHER PART OF THE FOREST
November 20, 1946   Fulton Theatre   182 performances

Play by Lillian Hellman
Incidental music by Blitzstein

(Based on characters from *The Little Foxes* [play] by Hellman)
Directed by Hellman
Produced by Kermit Bloomgarden
With Patricia Neal and Mildred Dunnock

Published songs:

None

Blitzstein continued his association with Lillian Hellman, who had cosponsored **NO FOR AN ANSWER [January 5, 1941]. AN-OTHER PART OF THE FOREST** was actually a prequel to *The Little Foxes*. Blitzstein became engrossed in the Hubbards; with the help of a grant from the American Academy of Arts and Letters, he began his major music theatre work, **REGINA [October 31, 1949].**

ANDROCLES AND THE LION
December 19, 1946   International Theatre
40 performances

Play by George Bernard Shaw
Incidental music by Blitzstein
Directed by Margaret Webster
Produced by American Repertory Theatre (Eva Le Gallienne, Cheryl
  Crawford and Webster)
With Ernest Truex, Richard Waring, and Eli Wallach

Published songs:

None

REGINA
October 31, 1949   46th Street Theatre   56 performances

Book by Blitzstein
(Based on **THE LITTLE FOXES** [play] by Lillian Hellman)
Directed by Robert Lewis
Produced by Cheryl Crawford in association with Clinton Wilder
With Jane Pickens, Priscilla Gillette, Brenda Lewis, and Russell Nype

Published songs:

"The Best Thing Of All"
"Blues"
"Chinkypin"
"Greedy Girl"
"The Rain"—published in choral edition

"Summer Day"—nonshow version of "Two Old Drybones"
"What Will It Be?"

Additional songs published in vocal score:

"Away!"
"Big Rich"
"Deedle-Doodle"
"Finale (Certainly, Lord)"
"Gallop"
"Greetings"
"Horace's Entrance"
"I Don't Know"
"I'm Sick Of You (Horace's Last)"
"Lionnet (Birdie's Aria)"
"Make A Quiet Day (Rain Quartet)"
"Music, Music"
"Regina's Aria"
"Sing Hubbard"
"Small Talk (Marshall)"
"Things (Regina's Waltz)"
"Transition (Bonds)"
"Two Old Drybones"
"The Veranda" [instrumental]
"Want To Join The Angels"

Blitzstein shared Kurt Weill's vision of an opera-inspired American "music drama" form. (Blitzstein was to be responsible for the rediscovery and accessibility of Weill's greatest and most successful work, **THE THREEPENNY OPERA** ⟨Second Version⟩ [Weill: March 10, 1954].) Following the War, Blitzstein had removed himself from the Brecht-influenced political drama, and with **REGINA** created a supreme musical theatre achievement. The advantage of being his own lyricist/librettist enabled a free combination of song and speech, the music written in expanded form or fragmented as it followed the thoughts of the characters. Hellman provided the strong and well-written *The Little Foxes*; Blitzstein used the orchestra to elaborate on the already highly pitched emotions of the little Hubbards. His two earlier scores had been performed with piano accompaniments, due to economic reasons. In **REGINA** the beauties and colors of Blitzstein's music (orchestrated by the composer) were first heard: Alexandra's touching "What Will It Be?," Addie's sympathetic "Blues,"

Regina's dangerous "Things," the "Rain Quartet," and especially Birdie's defeated "Lionnet."

THE THREEPENNY OPERA
see Weill [March 10, 1954]

REUBEN REUBEN
[October 10, 1955]   Shubert Theatre ⟨Boston, Massachusetts⟩; closed during pre-Broadway tryout

Book by Blitzstein
Choreographed by Hanya Holm
Directed by Robert Lewis
Produced by Cheryl Crawford
With Eddie Albert, Kaye Ballard, Evelyn Lear, and George Gaynes

Published songs:

"Be With Me"
"The Hills Of Amalfi"
"Miracle Song"
"Monday Morning Blues"
"Never Get Lost"

This highly ambitious work suffered from an overall lack of focus and direction. **REGINA [October 31, 1949]** had been built upon Lillian Hellman's strong *The Little Foxes;* **REUBEN REUBEN** was original material by Blitzstein (with no relation to the popular novel by Peter de Vries). The far-from-ready show that appeared out of town perplexed audiences, critics, and cast, and was quickly withdrawn. What survives of the score is original, highly imaginative, and often incredibly lovely. "Never Get Lost" and "The Hills Of Amalfi" are tender and fascinating. (Close colleague and friend Leonard Bernstein called Blitzstein's work-failures "falling angels," and named his daughter Nina for the **REUBEN REUBEN** heroine.) Cheryl Crawford, who entered the musical theatre with **JOHNNY JOHNSON [Weill: November 19, 1936]**, produced **REGINA** and **REUBEN REUBEN**. The failures of these last two (along with **FLAHOOLEY [PART 4: May 14, 1951]** and **PAINT YOUR WAGON [Loewe: November 12, 1951]**) caused Crawford to temporarily give up her quest for groundbreaking musical theatre—and drop **WEST SIDE STORY [Bernstein: September 26, 1957]**.

JUNO
March 9, 1959   Winter Garden Theatre   16 performances

Book by Joseph Stein
(Based on *Juno and the Paycock* [play] by Sean O'Casey)
Choreographed by Agnes de Mille
Directed by José Ferrer
Produced by The Playwrights' Company, Oliver Smith, and Oliver Rea
With Shirley Booth, Melvyn Douglas, Jack MacGowran, Jean Stapleton,
    and Sada Thompson

Published songs:

"I Wish It So"
"The Liffey Waltz"
"My True Heart"
"One Kind Word"

Additional songs recorded:

"Bird Upon The Tree"
"Daarlin' Man"
"Farewell, Me Buddy"—cut
"For Love"
"From This Out"—cut
"Hymn"
"Ireland's Eye"—cut
"It's Not Irish"
"Johnny"
"Music In The House"
"Old Sayin's"
"On A Day Like This"
"Quarrel Song"—cut
"Song Of The Ma"
"We Can Be Proud"
"We're Alive"
"What Is The Stars?"
"Where"
"You Poor Thing"
"You're The Girl"—cut

Blitzstein was the perfect choice for this adaptation of O'Casey's strong
drama of the Irish Revolution. However, the commercial management tried to give the show popular appeal, using box-office stars

Shirley Booth (who had appeared on Blitzstein's 1937 radio play *I've Got the Tune*) and Melvyn Douglas. Both were miscast, and the libretto was placed not in the hands of Blitzstein but Joe Stein. The tryout was filled with trouble, with first-time musical director Vincent J. Donehue being replaced by José Ferrer. The dramatic and volatile score worked well, particularly effective in expressing tragedy through de Mille dance. But the book's attempts at lightness and charm matched neither Blitzstein nor O'Casey, and **JUNO** suffered a quick death.

TOYS IN THE ATTIC
February 25, 1960   Hudson Theatre   556 performances

Play by Lillian Hellman
Incidental music by Blitzstein
Directed by Arthur Penn
Produced by Kermit Bloomgarden
With Maureen Stapleton, Jason Robards, Jr., and Irene Worth

Published songs:

None

Blitzstein's final theatre work came on this fourth association with Lillian Hellman. His next project was a music theatre piece based on the Sacco and Vanzetti case. While working on the score, Marc Blitzstein was attacked and killed on the island of Martinique on January 22, 1964.

Marc Blitzstein's strong commitment and uncompromising artistic viewpoint worked against popular success; surprisingly, his scores usually received the highly enthusiastic reviews they deserved. His one commercial project was the labor-of-love adaptation of the work of another composer (**THE THREEPENNY OPERA ⟨Second Version⟩ [Weill: March 10, 1954]**); his own work and name are virtually unknown. But Blitzstein's contributions to the serious musical theatre are of great importance, and point in a direction which has not yet been fully realized.

Harold Rome

BORN: May 27, 1908   Hartford, Connecticut

Harold Rome's musical career began as a college sideline, playing in dance bands to help finance his studies. Upon graduation with an architecture degree in 1934, Rome came to New York during the depths of the Depression. With high qualifications and seven years at Yale, the only architectural work he found was a twenty-four-dollar-a-week WPA job measuring roads and mapping the course of the Hudson River. Spare-time money could be earned playing piano, so Rome took advantage of his musical abilities. In the summer of 1935, Rome got a musical summer job at the Green Mansions resort hotel. Assembling amateur shows for the campers to perform, architect Rome began writing songs. He spent three summers at Green Mansions, writing comic character material for nonperformers.

[all music and lyrics by Harold Rome unless indicated]

PINS AND NEEDLES
November 27, 1937   Labor Stage   1,108 performances
Music and lyrics mostly by Rome
Sketches by Charles Friedman and others
Directed by Friedman
Produced by ILGWU
With The ILGWU Players

Published songs:

"Back To Work"
"Chain Store Daisy (Vassar Girl Finds Job)"
"Doing The Reactionary"
"Four Little Angels Of Peace"
"The General Unveiled (A Satirical Ballet)"
"I've Got The Nerve To Be In Love"

"It's Better With A Union Man (Or Bertha, The Sewing Machine Girl)"

"Mene, Mene, Tekel"—issued in separate edition

"Nobody Makes A Pass At Me"

"Not Cricket To Picket"

"One Big Union For Two"

"Papa Don't Love Mama Any More"

"Sing Me A Song With Social Significance"

"Stay Out, Sammy!"

"Sunday In The Park"

"We Sing America"—issued in separate edition

"What Good Is Love"

"When I Grow Up (G-Man Song)"—issued in separate edition

Additional songs published in vocal score:

"Cream Of Mush Song"

"I'm Just Nuts About You"

"Room For One"

Additional song recorded:

"Status Quo"

NOTE: Due to the topical nature of the piece, various songs cut or added after opening

Louis Schaefer, entertainment director of the International Ladies Garment Workers Union, was looking for an extracurricular morale-building activity. Schaefer heard Rome's work at Green Mansions and commissioned **PINS AND NEEDLES.** The cast was drafted from garment workers; rehearsals were held over a year and a half of evenings and weekends; and the ILGWU renamed the former Princess Theatre "Labor Stage." The nonprofessional show finally opened and attracted Broadway audiences, eventually moving to the larger Windsor Theatre and setting a new record for long-running musicals (the highest mark for the decade had been **OF THEE I SING [Gershwin: December 26, 1931]** with 441 performances). The show spoke for the former middle class, optimistically coping until better times came along. Rome became the first new voice to have an impact on Broadway since Arlen and Duke in 1930. His breezy, lightly rhythmic musical style and pointed but gentle comic lyrics proved an attractive alternative to other attempts at "Social Significance." **PINS AND NEEDLES** flourished, and the WPA lost an architect.

SING OUT THE NEWS
September 24, 1938   Music Box Theatre
105 performances

Sketches by George S. Kaufman and Moss Hart (unbilled)
Directed by Charles Friedman
Produced by Max Gordon in association with Kaufman and Hart
With Philip Loeb, Mary Jane Walsh, Hiram Sherman, Will Geer, and Rex
  Ingram

Published songs:

"F.D.R. Jones"
"How Long Can Love Keep Laughing?"
"My Heart Is Unemployed"
"One Of These Fine Days"
"Ordinary Guy"
"Plaza 6-9423"—issued as professional copy only
"Yip-Ahoy"—issued as professional copy only

PINS AND NEEDLES [November 27, 1937] immediately brought
Rome to the attention of Broadway. Max Gordon and his usually silent partners Kaufman and Hart were excited by Rome's new voice
and sponsored this full-scale revue. Without the ingratiating, nonprofessional charm of the still-running earlier show, **SING OUT THE
NEWS** was unable to compete; but Rome came up with one of his
best songs, the joyful "F.D.R. Jones" (later to be heard sung by vic-
torious Allied troops marching into Germany).

SING FOR YOUR SUPPER
April 24, 1939   Adelphi Theatre   60 performances

Music mostly by others
Lyrics mostly by Robert Sour
Directed by Robert H. Gordon
Produced by WPA Federal Theatre Project
With Paula Laurence and Sonny Tufts

Published song:

"Papa's Got A Job" (music by Ned Lehak, lyric by Hector Troy
  [Harold Rome])

Rome was asked to come up with a lyric in the "F.D.R. Jones" vein;
he wrote "Papa's Got A Job." Not interested in being approached

with lyric-only offers, he came up with the Hector Troy (Rome's nickname is "Heckie") pseudonym.

STREETS OF PARIS
June 19, 1939   Broadhurst Theatre   274 performances

Music mostly by Jimmy McHugh
Lyrics mostly by Al Dubin
Directed by Edward Duryea Dowling and Dennis Murray
Produced by the Shuberts in association with Olsen and Johnson
With Bobby Clark, Abbott and Costello, Luella Gear, and Carmen
  Miranda

Published song:

"History Is Made At Night"

The highlight of this revue was Carmen Miranda, who came out of nowhere with the McHugh/Dubin "South American Way."

THE LITTLE DOG LAUGHED
A Modern Music Comedy
*[July 13, 1940]   Garden Pier ⟨Atlantic City, New Jersey⟩;
closed during pre-Broadway tryout*

Book by Joseph Schrank
Produced and directed by Eddie Dowling
With Mili Monti, Philip Loeb, and Augustin Duncan

Published songs:

"Easy Does It"
"I Have A Song"
"I Want Romance"
"Of The People Stomp"
"You're Your Highness To Me"

An extravagant, idealistic fantasy. The show was backed by a wealthy society matron to showcase her singing "discovery" Mili Monti (who did not overwhelm them in Atlantic City). Rome provided another of his infectiously energetic songs, "Of The People Stomp."

LUNCHTIME FOLLIES
June 22, 1942   Todd Shipyards ⟨Brooklyn, New York⟩

Music and lyrics also by others
Sketches by George S. Kaufman and Moss Hart, Maxwell Anderson, and
     others
Production supervised by Kurt Weill
Produced by The American Theatre Wing

Published songs:

"The Ballad Of Sloppy Joe"
"Dear Joe"
"The Lady's On The Job"
"Men Behind The Man Behind The Gun"—issued in professional
     copy
"On That Old Production Line"
"On Time"
"That's My Pop"
"Victory Symphony, Eight To The Bar"

The **LUNCHTIME FOLLIES** was a series of informal forty-five-
minute presentations mounted as morale builders at war-materiel
production plants. Kurt Weill was production manager for the project, which began with a mostly Rome, Kaufman, and Hart show; other
material was later contributed by a wide range of authors (only Rome's
songs were published).

STAR AND GARTER
June 24, 1942   Music Box Theatre   605 performances
Music and lyrics mostly by others
Directed by Hassard Short
Produced by Michael Todd
With Bobby Clark and Gypsy Rose Lee

Published song:

"Bunny, Bunny, Bunny"

Rome had supplied material for Gypsy Rose Lee in his WPA archi-
tect/Green Mansions days. Mike Todd's burlesque revue was a popular wartime hit.

LET FREEDOM SING
October 5, 1942   Longacre Theatre   8 performances

Music also by others
Sketches by Sam Locke
Directed by Joseph C. Pevney and Robert H. Gordon
Produced by The Youth Theatre
With Mitzi Green, Betty Garrett, and Lee Sullivan

Published songs:

None

An amateurish, poorly done revue with a youthful cast. The only bright
spot was the unknown Betty Garrett, unanimously singled out by the
critics. Rome moved from Broadway to Fort Hamilton, Brooklyn.

STARS AND GRIPES
Fort Hamilton All-Soldier Show
July 13, 1943   War Department Theatre, Ft. Hamilton
⟨*Brooklyn, New York*⟩

Music and lyrics by PFC Harold Rome
Sketches mostly by T4G Ace Goodrich
Directed by PFC Glenn Jordan and PFC Martin Gabel

Published songs:

"The Army Service Forces"
"Hup! Tup! Thrup! Four! (Jack the Sleepy Jeep)"
"Jumping To The Jukebox"—also used in **SKIRTS [January 25,
    1944]**
"The Little Brown Suit My Uncle Bought Me"—also used in
    SKIRTS
"Love Sometimes Has To Wait"
"My Pin-Up Girl"—also used in **SKIRTS**

A morale-builder for the Army.

SKIRTS
An All-American Musical Adventure
January 25, 1944   Cambridge Theatre ⟨*London*⟩

Music and lyrics mostly by PFC Harold Rome and PFC Frank **Loesser**
Choreography by Wendy Toye
Directed by Lt. Arthur G. Brest
Produced by U.S. 8th Air Force, Special Service Section

Published songs:

"The Little Brown Suit My Uncle Bought Me"
"Jumping To The Juke Box"
"My Pin-Up Girl"

NOTE: songs originally used in **STARS AND GRIPES** [July 13, 1943]

The Air Force borrowed these songs from the Army for this commercially presented revue.

CALL ME MISTER
April 18, 1946   National Theatre   734 performances

Sketches by Arnold Auerbach with Arnold Horwitt
Directed by Robert H. Gordon
Produced by Melvyn Douglas and Herman Levin
With Betty Garrett, Jules Munshin, and Lawrence Winters

Published songs:

"Along With Me"
"Call Me Mister"
"The Drugstore Song"
"The Face On The Dime"
"Going Home Train"
"His Old Man"
"Little Surplus Me"
"Love Remains"
"Military Life (The Jerk Song)"
"The Red Ball Express"
"South America, Take It Away"
"Till We Meet Again"

Additional song recorded:

"Yuletide, Park Avenue"

Rome's joy on returning to civilian life was expressed in his infectious "Call Me Mister"—as opposed to "Private"—and provided the basis for this hit revue. Staffed and cast mostly by ex-servicemen and USO women, **CALL ME MISTER** was a happy and energetic entertainment. Betty Garrett established herself as a first-rate comedienne, and Rome's attorney/agent Herman Levin went into the producing business. The score showed Rome moving away from his socially relevant **PINS AND NEEDLES [November 27, 1937]** days: while he could still create hapless characters in comedy lyrics ("Poor Little Surplus Me"), he chose broader subjects for lampooning ("South America, Take It Away"). His music had generally served as support for the lyric; with songs like the Roosevelt eulogy "Face On The Dime," Rome began to develop his gift for dramatic melody.

THAT'S THE TICKET!
[September 24, 1948]   Shubert Theatre ⟨Philadelphia, Pennsylvania⟩; closed during pre-Broadway tryout

Book by Julius J. and Philip G. Epstein
Choreographed by Paul Godkin
Directed by Jerome Robbins
Produced by Joseph Kipness, John Pranksy, and Al Beckman
With Leif Erickson, Loring Smith, and Kaye Ballard

Published songs:

"I Shouldn't Love You"
"The Money Song"
"Take Off The Coat"—also used in **BLESS YOU ALL [December 14, 1950]**
"You Never Know What Hit You (When It's Love)"—also used in **PRETTY PENNY [June 20, 1940]** and **BLESS YOU ALL**

This misguided effort was written by the Hollywood Epstein brothers, authors of the 1941 *Casablanca*. Jerome Robbins made his non–George Abbott directing debut. After a week, everybody went home. "The Money Song" managed to achieve some radio popularity.

PRETTY PENNY
[June 20, 1949]   Bucks County Playhouse ⟨New Hope, Pennsylvania⟩; summer stock tryout

Sketches by Jerome Chodorov
Choreographed by Michael Kidd
Directed by George S. Kaufman
Produced by Leonard Field
With David Burns, Lenore Lonergan, Carl Reiner, Onna White, Peter Gennaro, and Kidd

Published songs:

"Pocketful Of Dreams"—initial publication upon reuse in
  MICHAEL TODD'S PEEP SHOW [June 28, 1950]
"You Never Know What Hit You (When It's Love)"—originally
  used in **THAT'S THE TICKET [September 24, 1948]**

Additional songs recorded:

"Cry, Baby, Cry"—also used in **ALIVE AND KICKING [January
  7, 1950]**
"French With Tears"—also used in **ALIVE AND KICKING**

A recent hit revue with a "looking for investors" motif had been
ANGEL IN THE WINGS [December 11, 1947] with Paul and Grace
Hartman. The similarly formatted **PRETTY PENNY** played the stock
circuit, while actually looking for Broadway investors. David Burns,
a thorough professional with an otherwise unblemished reputation,
uncharacteristically castigated and assaulted Kaufman. The actor received a reprimand from Actors' Equity, tendered his resignation, and
the show did not go on.

ALIVE AND KICKING
January 17, 1950   Winter Garden Theatre
46 performances

Music and lyrics mostly by others
Sketches by Joseph Stein and Will Glickman, I.A.L Diamond, and others
Choreographed by Jack Cole
Directed by Robert H. Gordon
Produced by William R. Katzell and Ray Golden
With Cole, David Burns, Jack Gilford, Carl Reiner, Gwen Verdon, and
  Jack Cassidy

Published song:

"Love, It Hurts So Good"

Additional songs recorded:

"Cry, Baby, Cry"—originally used in **PRETTY PENNY [June 20,
  1949]**
"French With Tears"—originally used in **PRETTY PENNY**

MICHAEL TODD'S PEEP SHOW
June 28, 1950   Winter Garden Theatre   278 performances

Music and lyrics mostly by others (see **Styne**)
Sketches by Bobby Clark, William K. Wells, and others
Scenes directed by "Mr. R. Edwin Clark, Esq."
Directed by Hassard Short
Produced by Michael Todd
With Lina Romay, Clifford Guest, and Lilly Christine

Published songs:

"Gimme The Shimmy"
"Pocketful Of Dreams"—originally used (unpublished) in
    PRETTY PENNY [June 20, 1949]

BLESS YOU ALL
December 14, 1950   Mark Hellinger Theatre
84 performances

Sketches by Arnold Auerbach
Choreographed by Helen Tamiris
Directed by John C. Wilson
Produced by Herman Levin and Oliver Smith
With Mary McCarty, Jules Munshin, Pearl Bailey, Valerie Bettis, and
    Donald Saddler

Published songs:

"I Can Hear It Now"
"Little Things (Meant So Much To Me)"
"Love Letter To Manhattan"
"A Rose Is A Rose"
"Summer Dresses"
"Take Off The Coat"—originally used in **THAT'S THE
    TICKET! [September 24, 1948]**
"You Never Know What Hit You (When It's Love)"—originally
    used in **THAT'S THE TICKET!**

Additional song recorded:

"Don't Wanna Write About The South"

The eagerly awaited follow-up to **CALL ME MISTER [April 18,
1946]** was a distinct disappointment and struggled through a brief run.
The earlier revue had played the considerably smaller National (Billy
Rose/Trafalgar/Nederlander); **BLESS YOU ALL** was not helped by
the extra 400 seats.

WISH YOU WERE HERE
June 24, 1952   Imperial Theatre   598 performances

Book by Arthur Kober and Joshua Logan
(Based on *Having Wonderful Time* [play] by Kober)
Directed by Logan
Produced by Leland Hayward and Logan
With Jack Cassidy, Patricia Marand, Sheila Bond, and Paul Valentine

Published songs:

"Could Be"
"Don José Of Far Rockaway"
"Everybody Loves Everybody"
"Flattery"
"Glimpse Of Love"—cut
"Relax"
"Shopping Around"
"Summer Afternoon"
"They Won't Know Me"
"There's Nothing Nicer Than People"—added after opening
"Tripping The Light Fantastic"
"Where Did The Night Go?"
"Wish You Were Here"

Additional songs published in vocal score:

"Ballad Of A Social Director"
"Camp Kare-free (Opening Act One)"
"Certain Individuals"
"Mix And Mingle"
"Waiter's Song (Bright College Days)"

Additional song recorded:

"Good-bye Love"—cut after opening

The enormous popularity of the title song—and the novelty of a featured swimming pool—carried **WISH YOU WERE HERE** past poor reviews to a long, successful run. The 1937 comedy by Kober (onetime husband to Lillian Hellman) took place at an adult summer camp very much like Green Mansions, where Rome began his career. Logan, who had been disappointed with his treatment as director/coauthor/coproducer of **SOUTH PACIFIC [Rodgers: April 7, 1949],** left his highly successful six-out-of-seven hit association with Rodgers to direct/coauthor/coproduce **WISH YOU WERE HERE.**

For the record, this was not Broadway's first swimming pool: the Majestic had one for the five-performance run of Broadway's first Mexican musical comedy, VIVA O'BRIEN [October 9, 1941], which made a very little splash indeed.

FANNY
November 4, 1954   Majestic Theatre   888 performances

Book by S. N. Behrman and Joshua Logan
(Based on the trilogy by Marcel Pagnol)
Choreographed by Helen Tamiris
Directed by Logan
Produced by David Merrick and Logan
With Ezio Pinza, Walter Slezak, and Florence Henderson

Published songs:

"Be Kind To Your Parents"
"Fanny"
"I Have To Tell You"
"I Like You"
"Love Is A Very Light Thing"
"Never Too Late For Love"
"Octopus"
"Restless Heart"
"To My Wife"
"Welcome Home"
"Why Be Afraid To Dance"

Additional songs published in vocal score:

"Cold Cream Jar Song"
"Hakim's Cellar"
"Happy Birthday (Nursery Round)"
"Oysters, Cockles And Mussels"
"Panisse And Son"
"The Thought Of You"

Attorney/manager/associate producer David Merrick had spent a decade learning the theatre business. Determining to make his musical debut with Pagnol's trilogy, he underwent enormous obstacles before acquiring the rights and hiring Rome. Rome brought in his **WISH YOU WERE HERE [June 25, 1952]** collaborator Logan as director; Logan took Merrick to Rodgers and Hammerstein, a more obvious choice to write the score. Coming off the unsuccessful **ME AND JU-LIET [Rodgers: May 28, 1953],** the pair wanted to do **FANNY**— but only if they could produce it themselves. Merrick had no intention of withdrawing, and went back to Rome. [On their next project, Rodgers and Hammerstein *were* able to buy out original producers Feuer and Martin (**PIPE DREAM [Rodgers: November 30, 1955]**).] The slightly uneven **FANNY** benefited from Merrick's producing and promotional talents to become a long-running hit. Rome departed from his usual musical style to write a moving, highly emotional score. Emphasizing melody, he came up with the soaring title song and "Restless Heart," as well as the tenderly touching "To My Wife."

ROMANOFF AND JULIET
October 10, 1957   Plymouth Theatre   389 performances

Play by Peter Ustinov
Incidental music by Harold Rome
Directed by George S. Kaufman
Produced by David Merrick
With Ustinov, Jack Gilford, Henry Lascoe, and Elizabeth Allen

Published songs:

None

Rome provided a guitar solo for George S. Kaufman's final show.

DESTRY RIDES AGAIN
April 23, 1959   Imperial Theatre   472 performances

Book by Leonard Gershe
(Based on the story by Max Brand)
Directed and choreographed by Michael Kidd
Produced by David Merrick in association with Max Brown
With Andy Griffith, Dolores Gray, and Scott Brady

Published songs:

"Anyone Would Love You"
"Are You Ready, Gyp Watson?"
"Every Once In A While"
"Fair Warning"
"Hoop De Dingle"
"I Know Your Kind"

"I Say Hello"
"Once Knew A Fella"
"Ring On The Finger"
"Rose Lovejoy Of Paradise Alley"

Additional songs published in vocal score:

"Ballad Of A Gun"
"Don't Take Me Back To Bottleneck (Opening)"
"I Hate Him"
"Ladies"
"Not Guilty"
"Only Time Will Tell"
"Respectability"
"Tomorrow Morning"

Merrick and Rome followed **FANNY [November 4, 1954]** with a musical version of the 1939 movie classic. The lavish production and Michael Kidd's exciting staging helped, but the musical **DESTRY** couldn't compete with the memory of James Stewart and Marlene Dietrich.

I CAN GET IT FOR YOU WHOLESALE
March 22, 1962   Shubert Theatre   300 performances

Book by Jerome Weidman
(Based on the novel by Weidman)
Choreographed by Herbert Ross
Directed by Arthur Laurents
Produced by David Merrick
With Elliot Gould, Lillian Roth, Marilyn Cooper, Harold Lang, Bambi
   Linn, and Barbra Streisand

Published songs:

"A Gift Today (The Bar Mitzvah Song)"
"Have I Told You Lately"
"Miss Marmelstein"
"Momma, Momma"
"On My Way To Love"
"The Sound Of Money"
"Too Soon"
"What's In It For Me?"
"Who Knows?"

Additional songs published in vocal score:
"Ballad Of The Garment Trade"
"Eat A Little Something"
"The Family Way"
"I'm Not A Well Man"
"The Way Things Are"
"What Are They Doing To Us Now?"
"When Gemini Meets Capricorn"

Rome was put together with Jerome (**FIORELLO! [Bock: November 23, 1959]**) Weidman for his third consecutive Merrick musical, an adaptation of the 1944 movie *National Velvet*. Weidman's successful 1937 novel seemed a far better idea, and Merrick agreed to go along. Rome returned to his **PINS AND NEEDLES [November 27, 1937]** terrain, the New York City garment district during the Depression; but the music was far richer now, reflecting his melodic experiences with **FANNY [November 4, 1954]**. The combination of an unsympathetic antihero and downbeat subject matter worked against **WHOLESALE.** Bright spots included a young singer from Brooklyn named Streisand who breezed into auditions and was immediately cast in a very minor role. Rome went off and fashioned "Miss Marmelstein" (in his **PINS AND NEEDLES** vein) and "What Are They Doing To Us Now?" to her talents.

THE ZULU AND THE ZAYDA
November 10, 1965   Cort Theatre   179 performances
Play by Howard Da Silva and Felix Leon
Directed by Dore Schary
Produced by Theodore Mann and Schary
With Menasha Skulnik, Ossie Davis, and Louis Gossett

Published songs:
"How Cold, Cold, Cold An Empty Room"
"It's Good To Be Alive"
"Like The Breeze Blows"—see **GONE WITH THE WIND [May 3, 1972]**
"May Your Heart Stay Young (L'Chayim)"
"Out Of This World (Oisgetzaichnet)"
"Rivers Of Tears"
"Some Things"
"Tkambuza (Zulu Hunting Song)"

"The Water Wears Down The Stone"
"Zulu Love Song (Wait For Me)"
Additional songs published in vocal selection:
"Crocodile Wife"

This play with songs attempted to deal with prejudice, telling of an unlikely South African friendship between a Yiddish grandfather and a young Zulu. It didn't work; but Rome, a collector and student of African art, provided a fascinating score in the styles of the two cultures. For a good example of creative song reuse, compare "Like The Wind Blows" with "Bonnie Gone." The worthy original—with its highly idiomatic content—had no life outside **THE ZULU AND THE ZAYDA.** Several years later, Rome effectively used the music as background dirge for the rousing wake in **GONE WITH THE WIND [May 3, 1972]**.

LA GROSSE VALISE
December 14, 1965   54th Street Theatre   7 performances

Music by Gerard Calvi
Lyrics by Harold Rome
Book and direction by Robert Dhery
Produced by Joe Kipness and Arthur Lesser
With Ronald Fraser, Victor Spinetti, and Joyce Jillson

Published songs:

"Delilah Done Me Wrong"
"For You"
"Slippy Sloppy Shoes"
"Xanadu"

David Merrick and Kipness had imported Dhery's previous revue, LA PLUME DE MA TANTE [November 11, 1958], which ran a staggering 835 performances. Merrick passed on the sequel, which was a quick failure. Rome contributed English versions of the lyrics.

GONE WITH THE WIND
The Epic Musical
May 3, 1972   Drury Lane Theatre ⟨London⟩
397 performances

Book by Horton Foote
(Based on the novel by Margaret Mitchell)
Directed and choreographed by Joe Layton
Produced by Harold Fielding
With Harve Presnell and June Ritchie

Published songs:

"Gone With The Wind"—written for American production
"How Often"
"Lonely Stranger"
"Strange And Wonderful"
"We Belong To You"

Additional songs published in vocal selection:

"Blueberry Eyes"
"Little Wonders"
"Scarlett"
"A Time For Love"
"Where Is My Soldier Boy?"

Additional songs recorded:

"Because There's You"—cut
"Blissful Christmas"
"Bonnie Blue Flag"—cut
"Bonnie Gone"—revised version of "Like The Breeze Blows" from
   THE ZULU AND THE ZAYDA [November 10, 1965]
"Gambling Man"
"Goodbye, My Honey"—cut
"Home Again"
"It Doesn't Matter Now"
"Johnny Is My Darling"—cut
"Marrying For Fun"
"My Soldier"
"Newlywed's Song"
"O'Hara"
"A Southern Lady"
"Tara"
"Today's The Day (He Loves Me)"
"Tomorrow Is Another Day"
"Two Of A Kind"
"What Is Love"
"Which Way Is Home?"
"Why Did They Die?"—cut

Rome's final musical began very far out of town when the composer and Joe Layton were invited to Tokyo to create SCARLETT [January 1, 1970], successfully produced by the Japanese in Japanese with a Japanese cast. **GONE WITH THE WIND** jumped across the globe to England, and the burning of Atlanta took London by storm. Troubles were foreseen in America, though, due to the overwhelming familiarity of the 1939 movie version. A less-than-spectacular third production started August 28, 1973 on the nearer side of the Pacific but never made it East—not even to Atlanta. Lesley Ann Warren and Pernell Roberts were the final Scarlett and Rhett.

Harold Rome began his career during the musical theatre drought of the mid-Thirties. He first achieved success with **PINS AND NEEDLES [November 27, 1937]**, using light but pointed political satire. Rome quickly found a place in the revitalized topical revue. His specialty: sparkling comedy lyrics for everyday characters, set to bright and fresh music. But **CALL ME MISTER [April 18, 1946]** was Broadway's last great revue, television variety shows proving fatal to the form. After a period of adjustment, Rome responded with surprisingly rich, emotional scores for **FANNY [November 4, 1954]** and **I CAN GET IT FOR YOU WHOLESALE [March 22, 1962]**. Then came the musical theatre drought of the mid-Sixties, which forced Rome (along with Schwartz, Arlen, and others) into virtual retirement.

Hugh Martin

BORN: August 11, 1914   Birmingham, Alabama

Trained as a pianist, Martin began his Broadway career as a member of Kay Thompson's backup quartet in **HOORAY FOR WHAT!** **[Arlen: December 1, 1937]**. By the end of the tryout Thompson had been replaced; Martin remained and attracted immediate notice with his contemporary, jazz-oriented vocal arrangements. He was quickly hired to bring modernized, swinging choral parts to **THE BOYS FROM SYRACUSE [Rodgers: November 23, 1938], DUBARRY WAS A LADY [Porter: December 6, 1939]** and **CABIN IN THE SKY [Duke: October 25, 1940]**. Martin formed a quartet (The Martins) which sang his arrangements in **LOUISIANA PURCHASE [Berlin: May 28, 1940]**. Also a member of The Martins was fellow songwriter Ralph Blane (born July 26, 1914 in Broken Arrow, Oklahoma).

BEST FOOT FORWARD
A Modern Musical Comedy
October 1, 1941   Ethel Barrymore Theatre
326 performances

Music and lyrics by Hugh Martin and Ralph Blane
Book by John Cecil Holm
Choreographed by Gene Kelly
Produced and directed by George Abbott
With Rosemary Lane, Nancy Walker, Gil Stratton, Jr., and June Allyson

Published songs:

"Buckle Down, Winsocki"
"Ev'ry Time"
"I Know You By Heart"
"Just A Little Joint With A Juke Box"
"A Raving Beauty"—added to 1963 revival; originally used in
   MEET ME IN ST. LOUIS [June 9, 1960]

"Shady Lady Bird"
"That's How I Love The Blues"
"The Three B's"
"What Do You Think I Am?"
"Wish I May"—written for 1943 movie version
"You Are For Loving"—added to revival; originally used in
    MEET ME IN ST. LOUIS
"You're Lucky"—written for movie version

Additional songs recorded:

"Alive And Kicking"—written for movie version
"Don't Sell The Night Short"
"The Guy Who Brought Me"
"Hollywood Story"
"Three Men On A Date"

Abbott was always looking for new talent: Martin worked for him on
BOYS FROM SYRACUSE [Rodgers: November 23, 1938] and
TOO MANY GIRLS [Rodgers: October 18, 1939]. For his next
youth musical, Abbott gave the assignment to the musically up-to-
the-minute Martin and collaborator Blane. Richard Rodgers, relatively inactive due to Larry Hart's deteriorating condition, decided
to get involved and silently coproduced. **BEST FOOD FORWARD**
was a happy success, with the hit football song "Buckle Down, Winsocki" and the poignant "Ev'ry Time." Abbott discovery Nancy
Walker stole the show and went on to a series of Forties Abbott musicals; June Allyson went right to Hollywood—as did Martin and
Blane. Work there included three superlative songs ("The Boy Next
Door," "Have Yourself A Merry Little Christmas," and "The Trolley Song") for the 1944 Judy Garland movie *Meet Me in St. Louis*
(see **June 9, 1960**). Garland's daughter Liza Minnelli was to make
her New York debut in the off-Broadway revival [April 2, 1963] of
BEST FOOT FORWARD.

LOOK, MA, I'M DANCIN'!
January 29, 1948   Adelphi Theatre   188 performances

Music and lyrics by Hugh Martin
Book by Jerome Lawrence and Robert E. Lee
Conceived and choreographed by Jerome Robbins
Directed by George Abbott and Robbins
Produced by Abbott
With Nancy Walker, Harold Lang, and Sandra Deel

Published songs:

"If You'll Be Mine"
"I'm Not So Bright"
"I'm Tired Of Texas"
"The Little Boy Blues"
"Shauny O'Shay"
"Tiny Room"
"The Way It Might Have Been"

Additional songs recorded:

"Gotta Dance"
"I'm The First Girl In The Second Row"
"Mlle. Scandale Ballet" [instrumental]

Abbott, Robbins, and Nancy Walker of **ON THE TOWN [December 28, 1944]** reunited for this comic dance musical. Robbins had his first directing experience here, and Martin worked without a collaborator. The result was entertaining but not quite a hit. Martin provided the delightful "Little Boy Blues" and the lyrically spectacular "I'm The First Girl In The Second Row (Of The Third Scene In The Fourth Number In Fifth Position At Ten O'Clock On The Nose)."

MAKE A WISH!
April 18, 1951   Winter Garden Theatre   102 performances

Music and lyrics by Hugh Martin
Book by Preston Sturges
(Based on *The Good Fairy* [play] by Ferenc Molnar)
Choreographed by Gower Champion
Directed by John C. Wilson
Produced by Harry Rigby and Jule Styne with Alexander H. Cohen
With Nanette Fabray, Melville Cooper, Stephen Douglass, Helen
    Gallagher, and Harold Lang

Published songs:

"Over And Over"
"Paris, France"
"Suits Me Fine"
"That Face"—advertised but not published
"What I Was Warned About"
"When Does This Feeling Go Away?"

Additional songs recorded:

"Hello, Hello, Hello"
"I Wanna Be Good 'N' Bad"
"I'll Never Make A Frenchman Out Of You"
"Make A Wish"
"The Sale" [instrumental]
"Take Me Back To Texas With You"
"That Face"
"Tonight You Are In Paree"
"The Tour Must Go On"
"Who Gives A Sou?"

Composer Jule Styne, with two straight musical hits, was ready to enter the producing field. Martin had done vocal arrangements for both **HIGH BUTTON SHOES [Styne: October 9, 1947]** and **GENTLEMEN PREFER BLONDES [Styne: December 8, 1949];** he auditioned his **MAKE A WISH** score (without a libretto) and Styne agreed to mount it. Alexander Cohen also entered the book musical field, with his first of eight (out of eight) disasters.

LOVE FROM JUDY
September 25, 1952   Saville Theatre ⟨London⟩
594 performances

Lyrics by Hugh Martin and Jack (Timothy) Gray
Book by Eric Maschwitz and Jean Webster
(Based on *Daddy Longlegs* [novel] by Webster)
Choreographed by Pauline Grant
Directed by Charles Hickman
Produced by Emile Littler
With Jeannie Carson, Bill O'Connor, and Adelaide Hall

Published songs:

"Daddy Longlegs"
"Go And Get Your Old Banjo"
"Love From Judy"
"My True Love"

Additional songs published in vocal score:

"Ain't Gonna Marry"
"Ballet" [instrumental]
"Dum Dum Dum"

"Goin' Back To School"
"Here We Are"
"I Never Dream When I Sleep"
"It's Better Rich"
"It's Great To Be An Orphan"
"Kind To Animals"
"Mardi Gras"
"A Touch Of Voodoo"
"What Do I See In You?"

The failure of **MAKE A WISH [April 18, 1951]** virtually ended Martin's Broadway career. He went to London and wrote this highly successful hit with his new collaborator, singer Jack Gray. Strangely enough, both shows were about innocent waiflike orphan girls who find happiness in the world outside the orphanage.

MEET ME IN ST. LOUIS
[June 9, 1960]   Municipal Opera ⟨St. Louis, Missouri⟩
Music and lyrics by Hugh Martin and Ralph Blane
Book by Sally Benson
(Based on stories by Benson and the 1944 movie)

Published songs:

"Almost"
"The Boy Next Door"—originally used in 1944 movie version
"Diamonds In The Starlight"
"Have Yourself A Merry Little Christmas"—originally used in
  movie version
"How Do I Look?"
"If I Had An Igloo"
"A Raving Beauty"—also used in 1963 revival of **BEST FOOT
  FORWARD [October 1, 1941]**
"Skip To My Lou" (adapted from traditional)—originally used in
  movie version
"The Trolley Song"—originally used in movie version
"What's-His-Name"
"You Are For Loving"—also used in revival of **BEST FOOT
  FORWARD**

Martin and Blane were reunited in Hollywood in the late Fifties. **MEET ME IN ST. LOUIS** was a stage version of their popular film, aimed at the stock-and-amateur trade. The summer of 1960 saw several summer stock productions. (Robert Goulet starred in one just prior to making his Broadway debut in **CAMELOT [Loewe: December 3, 1960]**.) The adaptation never reached Broadway, but the new songs included the touching and beautiful "You Are For Loving."

HIGH SPIRITS
An Improbable Musical Comedy
April 7, 1964   Alvin Theatre   375 performances

Book, music and lyrics by Hugh Martin and Timothy Gray
(Based on *Blithe Spirit* [play] by Noël Coward)
Choreographed by Danny Daniels
Directed by Coward
Produced by Lester Osterman, Robert Fletcher, and Richard Horner
With Beatrice Lillie, Tammy Grimes, and Edward Woodward

Published songs:

"The Bicycle Song"—advertised but not published
"Forever And A Day"
"I Know Your Heart"
"If I Gave You"
"Something Tells Me"
"Was She Prettier Than I?"
"You'd Better Love Me"

Additional song published in "professional vocal selection":

"Faster Than Sound"

Additional songs recorded:

"The Bicycle Song"
"Go Into Your Trance"
"Home Sweet Heaven"
"Something Is Coming To Tea"
"Talking To You"
"What In The World Did You Want?"
"Where Is The Man I Married?"

Martin returned to Broadway with this final Bea Lillie vehicle. Coward's five-character farce was out of place in musical comedy, with the addition of an extraneous chorus particularly jarring. This was unfortunate, as an enjoyable score was wasted on the poorly chosen source material.

With the exception of a few vocal arrangement chores—and an un-produced Horatio Alger musical, TATTERED TOM—Hugh Martin has remained inactive in the theatre since 1964. His writing career has been incredibly spotty; but at his best, Martin's distinctive melodic freedom and colorful harmonies made him stand out as a possible successor to Gershwin and Arlen.

Leonard Bernstein

BORN: August 25, 1918   Lawrence, Massachusetts

Leonard Bernstein's first theatre experience came when the twenty-one-year-old Harvard music major mounted the 1939 Boston premiere of **THE CRADLE WILL ROCK [Blitzstein: June 16, 1937].** Bernstein played the onstage accompaniment; the composer attended, was impressed, and the two began a close friendship. Following graduation, Bernstein entered the Curtis Institute of Music in Philadelphia—where Blitzstein had studied—to train for a career in symphonic music. Three years assisting Serge Koussevitzky and Arthur Rodzinski led to the young conductor's break on November 14, 1943: a last-minute illness (and no suitable replacement) resulted in Bernstein conducting a concert by the New York Philharmonic. Being young and *American* brought the event enormous publicity, and Bernstein was suddenly in the serious music spotlight. His first composition was Ballet Theatre's *Fancy Free* [April 18, 1944], choreographed by (and featuring) Jerome Robbins in *his* debut. Robbins had been on Broadway dancing in unsuccessful musicals **GREAT LADY [Loewe: December 1, 1938]** and **KEEP OFF THE GRASS [Duke: May 23, 1940].** *Fancy Free* took the ballet and music world by storm, as the two twenty-five-year-olds brought contemporary dance and jazz into the Metropolitan Opera House. It seemed obvious to take the piece and turn it into a hit musical comedy; *Fancy Free*'s twenty-five-year-old scenic designer Oliver Smith went along as producer.

ON THE TOWN
December 28, 1944   Adelphi Theatre   463 performances

Book and lyrics by Betty Comden and Adolph Green
(Based on *Fancy Free* [ballet] by Bernstein and Robbins)
Choreographed by Jerome Robbins
Directed by George Abbott
Produced by Oliver Smith and Paul Feigay
With Nancy Walker, Sono Osato, Comden, and Green

Published songs:

"I Can Cook Too" (lyric by Bernstein; additional lyric by Comden
    and Green)
"Lonely Town"
"Lucky To Be Me"
"New York, New York"
"Some Other Time"
"Ya Got Me"

Additional songs published in "Bernstein On Broadway":

"Carried Away"
"I Feel Like I'm Not Out Of Bed Yet"
"New York, New York" (complete version)

Additional songs recorded:

"Come Up To My Place"
"Do-Do-Re-Do"
"I'm Blue"
"Imaginary Coney Island Ballet" [instrumental]
"Lonely Town Ballet" [instrumental]
"Miss Turnstile Variations" [instrumental]
"Real Coney Island Ballet" [instrumental]
"She's A Home Loving Girl"
"So Long, Baby"
"Times Square Ballet" [instrumental]

The producers—designer Oliver Smith and twenty-four-year-old
manager Paul Feigay—added on nightclub performers Betty Comden
and Adolph Green, who'd never written book or lyrics or appeared
in a Broadway show, to write the book and lyrics and play featured
roles. They were also in their twenties; Green was a former roommate of Bernstein's. *Then,* somebody brought in George Abbott to
direct. **ON THE TOWN,** of course, was a big hit. Bernstein's score
mixed a handful of ballets (no *Fancy Free* music was used) with his
first songs, including "New York, New York," "Lonely Town," and
some good comedy numbers. Robbins brought along Sono Osato, with
whom he'd danced at Ballet Theatre. She had one Broadway credit,
as Agnes de Mille's lead dancer in **ONE TOUCH OF VENUS [Weill:
October 7, 1943].** Abbott, for his part, brought along Nancy Walker
from **BEST FOOT FORWARD [October 1, 1941].** The veteran's
fast-paced direction was just right for this new-style musical comedy.

Robbins's work was good, Walker and Osato were good, *everything* was good. Comden and Green made a sparklingly impressive debut as lyricist/librettists and began a long and healthy Broadway career. But Bernstein, having conquered Broadway, returned to the world of symphonic music.

PETER PAN
⟨Third Version⟩
April 24, 1950   Imperial Theatre   321 performances

Play by James M. Barrie
Incidental music by Alec Wilder
Songs (music and lyrics) by Leonard Bernstein
Directed by John Burrell
Produced by Peter Lawrence and Roger L. Stevens
With Jean Arthur and Boris Karloff

Published songs:

"My House"
"Never-land"
"Peter, Peter"
"Pirate Song"—issued in choral arrangement only
"Plank Round"—issued in choral arrangement only
"Who Am I?"

Additional song recorded:

"Dream With Me"—cut

Bernstein ended the Forties with an assortment of serious compositions, including the *Jeremiah Symphony*. The Fifties began with this half-dozen-song assignment for the Jean Arthur production of the whimsical Barrie play.

WONDERFUL TOWN
February 25, 1953   Winter Garden Theatre
559 performances

Lyrics by Betty Comden and Adolph Green
Book by Joseph Fields and Jerome Chodorov
(Based on *My Sister Eileen* [play] by Fields and Chodorov from stories by
   Ruth McKenney)
Choreographed by Donald Saddler
Directed by George Abbott

Produced by Robert Fryer
With Rosalind Russell, Edith Adams, George Gaynes, and Henry Lascoe

Published songs:

"It's Love"
"A Little Bit In Love"
"My Darlin' Eileen" (based on an Irish Reel)
"Ohio"
"A Quiet Girl"
"Swing!"
"The Wrong Note Rag"

Additional songs published in "Bernstein On Broadway":

"One Hundred Easy Ways"
"Pass The Football"

Additional songs recorded:

"Ballet At The Village Vortex" [instrumental]
"Christopher Street (opening)"
"Conga!"
"Conquering The City"—cut
"Conversation Piece"
"Lonely Me"—cut
"The Story Of My Life"—cut
"What A Waste"

Comden and Green had cast about for a new composer since **ON THE TOWN [December 28, 1944],** trying out Morton Gould (on the Abbott/Robbins BILLION DOLLAR BABY [December 21, 1945]), Saul Chaplin (on the Broadway-bound BONANZA BOUND [December 26, 1947]), and Jule Styne (**TWO ON THE AISLE [Styne: July 19, 1951]**). The Styne collaboration seemed particularly promising. Meanwhile, Comden and Green went to Hollywood and had just finished the screenplay for the 1952 *Singin' In The Rain* when Abbott called for help. **WONDERFUL TOWN** was just a month away from rehearsals when "artistic differences" among the authors resulted in the withdrawal of songwriters Leroy Anderson and Arnold Horwitt. Bernstein joined Comden and Green to write his second musical score. **ON THE TOWN** had been an experiment in musical/ballet comedy; **WONDERFUL TOWN** was more in the standard musical comedy form, but a well-executed, highly successful example. The score was delightfully evocative of the Thirties period, and in places playfully creative (including "Ohio," "Swing!" and the skillful "Wrong Note

Rag"). Abbott kept things moving at his usual fast pace, and Rosalind Russell made the whole package immensely enjoyable.

ALL IN ONE
[Including TROUBLE IN TAHITI]
April 19, 1955   Playhouse Theatre   49 performances

Opera music and libretto by Bernstein
Directed by David Brooks
Produced by Charles Bowden and Richard Barr
With Alice Ghostley and John Tyers

Opera vocal score published:

"Trouble In Tahiti"
NOTE: Also see **A QUIET PLACE** ⟨Second Version⟩ **[July 22, 1984]**

The one-act opera **TROUBLE IN TAHITI** was first performed in June 1952 at a Brandeis College [Waltham, Massachusetts] arts festival put together by Bernstein. Also introduced was the Marc Blitzstein translation of **THE THREEPENNY OPERA** ⟨Second Version⟩ **[Weill: March 10, 1954]**. (Bernstein dedicated **TROUBLE IN TAHITI** to Blitzstein, and named him godfather of his first child.) Bernstein's opera found its way to a limited Broadway run. The composer found his way to Milan in 1953, when he was the first American to ever conduct opera at La Scala.

THE LARK
November 17, 1955   Longacre Theatre   229 performances

Play by Jean Anouilh
Adaptation by Lillian Hellman
Incidental music and lyrics by Bernstein
Directed by Joseph Anthony
Produced by Kermit Bloomgarden
With Julie Harris, Boris Karloff, and Christopher Plummer

Published songs:

"Soldier's Song"
"Spring Song"

Additional songs published in "Choruses From The Lark":

"Benedictus"
"Court Song"

"Gloria"
"Prelude"
"Requiem"
"Sanctus" [1st]—different than song from **MASS [September 8, 1971]**

A QUIET PLACE
⟨First Version⟩
[November 23, 1955]   Shubert Theatre ⟨New Haven, Connecticut⟩; closed during pre-Broadway tryout

Play by Julian Claman
Title song by Leonard Bernstein
Directed by Delbert Mann
Produced by The Playwrights Company
With Tyrone Power and Leora Dana

Published songs:

None

"A Quiet Place" was an aria from **TROUBLE IN TAHITI [April 19, 1955]**. It was reused as a song in this quick failure. Thirty years later, Bernstein wrote a sequel to **TROUBLE IN TAHITI**—also named **A QUIET PLACE** ⟨Second Version⟩ **[July 22, 1984]**.

CANDIDE
A Comic Operetta
⟨First Version—also see March 10, 1974⟩
December 1, 1956   Martin Beck Theatre   73 performances

Lyrics mostly by Richard Wilbur
Book by Lillian Hellman
(Based on the satire by Voltaire)
Directed by Tyrone Guthrie
Produced by Ethel Linder Reiner in association with Lester Osterman, Jr.
With Max Adrian, Barbara Cook, Robert Rounseville, and Irra Petina

Published songs:

"The Best Of All Possible Worlds"—issued in choral edition
"Buenos Aires Tango (I Am Easily Assimilated)" (lyric by
   Bernstein)

"Glitter And Be Gay"—issued in separate edition
"It Must Be Me"
"Make Our Garden Grow"—issued in choral edition
"What's The Use?"

Additional songs published in vocal score:

"Ballad Of Eldorado" (lyric by Hellman)
"Bon Voyage"
"Dear Boy"—cut
"Lisbon Sequence" (lyric by Bernstein)
"My Love" (lyric by John Latouche and Wilbur)
"Oh, Happy We"
"Overture" [instrumental]
"Pilgrims Procession"
"Quartet Finale"
"Quiet"
"Venice Gambling Scene (Money, Money)" (lyric by Dorothy
   Parker)
"Wedding Chorale"
"You Were Dead, You Know" (lyric by Latouche and Wilbur)

Additional songs recorded:

"Ringaroundarosie"—cut; see ⟨**Second Version**⟩
"We Are Women"—cut; written for 1959 London production

Bernstein wrote one of Broadway's most glorious scores for this glorious failure. Misconceived and misguided, Voltaire's satire was played
as light operetta—not what the author had in mind. Not what the
composer and his lyricists seemed to have in mind, either. John Latouche, best known for **CABIN IN THE SKY [Duke: October 25,
1941],** was fresh from his artistic triumph with **THE GOLDEN AP-
PLE [PART 4: March 11, 1954];** he suffered a heart attack and died
August 7, 1956, at the age of only thirty-eight. Dorothy Parker, librettist Hellman, and even Bernstein contributed lyrics before poet
Richard Wilbur came in.

WEST SIDE STORY
September 26, 1957   Winter Garden Theatre
734 performances

Lyrics by Stephen Sondheim
Book by Arthur Laurents

(Suggested by *Romeo and Juliet* [play] by William Shakespeare)
Choreographed by Jerome Robbins and Peter Gennaro
Conceived and directed by Robbins
Produced by Robert E. Griffith and Harold S. Prince by arrangement with
  Roger L. Stevens
With Larry Kert, Carol Lawrence, Chita Rivera, and Lee Becker

NOTE: Lyrics initially credited to Sondheim and Bernstein

Published songs:

"America"
"Cool"
"Gee, Officer Krupke"—initial publication upon use in 1961 movie
  version
"I Feel Pretty"
"Maria"
"One Hand, One Heart"
"Something's Coming (Could Be)"
"Somewhere"
"Tonight"

Additional songs published in vocal score:

"A Boy Like That" (and "I Have A Love")
"The Dance At The Gym" [instrumental]
"Jet Song"
"Prologue" [instrumental]
"The Rumble" [instrumental]
"Somewhere Ballet" [instrumental]
"Taunting Scene" [instrumental]
"Tonight (Quintet)"

Arthur Laurents entered the theatre with the fine postwar drama
HOME OF THE BRAVE [December 27, 1945]. Discussions in 1945
with Jerome Robbins brought about the idea for an EAST SIDE
STORY—Romeo and Juliet using an interfaith romance. Bernstein
became involved, but the project fell through. When big-city racial
gang wars became news in the mid-Fifties, the idea was reborn.
Bernstein started the lyrics himself; when help was needed, Laurents
brought in Sondheim as colyricist. (Sondheim's contributions to the
score were such that Bernstein relinquished his lyric credit after the
opening.) Producer Cheryl Crawford, whose three Fifties musicals had
been progressive, unconventional flops (**FLAHOOLEY [PART 4:
May 14, 1951], PAINT YOUR WAGON [Loewe: November 12,**

1951] and **REUBEN REUBEN [Blitzstein: October 10, 1955]**), was unable to come up with the financing and abandoned the production. Sondheim called friend Harold Prince, coproducer with Robert Griffith of three big George Abbott/Bob Fosse musicals (see **NEW GIRL IN TOWN [Merrill: May 14, 1957]**), and **WEST SIDE STORY** finally got underway. As with **ON THE TOWN [December 28, 1944]**, **WEST SIDE STORY** was centered on ballet; but not for musical comedy purposes. The modern use of dance for dramatic/plot purposes first worked with de Mille's symbolic "Laurie Makes Up Her Mind" in **OKLAHOMA! [Rodgers: March 31, 1943]**; but here, dance was used as part of the everyday language/movement of the characters. As was to be expected, the exceptional **WEST SIDE STORY** was not a major hit: **THE MUSIC MAN [Willson: December 19, 1957]** took all the awards except Best Choreographer. The legendary status did not develop until the release of the 1961 movie version. After **WEST SIDE STORY** opened, Bernstein once again left the theatre to become music director of the New York Philharmonic.

THE FIRSTBORN
April 29, 1958   Coronet Theatre   38 performances
Play by Christopher Fry
Songs by Leonard Bernstein
Directed by Anthony Quayle
Produced by Katharine Cornell and Roger L. Stevens
With Cornell, Quayle, and Mildred Natwick

Published songs:
None

Katharine Cornell made one of her final stage appearances in this limited engagement.

MASS
A Theatre Piece for Singers, Players and Dancers
[September 8, 1971]   Kennedy Center Opera House
⟨Washington, D.C.⟩; limited engagement
Text from the Liturgy of the Roman Mass
Additional text by Stephen Schwartz and Leonard Bernstein
Choreographed by Alvin Ailey

Directed by Gordon Davidson
Produced by Roger L. Stevens
With Alan Titus

Published songs:

"Almighty Father"
"Gloria Tibi"
"Sanctus" [2nd]—different than song from **THE LARK**
   [November 17, 1955]
"A Simple Song"
"The Word Of The Lord"

Additional songs published in vocal score:

"Agnus Dei"
"Alleluia" [1st]
"Confiteor Alleluia" [2nd]
"Credo In Unum Deum"
"De Profundis"
"Dominus Vobiscum"
"Easy"
"Epiphany"
"Gloria In Excelsis"
"God Said (And It Was Good)"
"Half Of The People" (partial lyric by Paul Simon)
"Hurry"
"I Believe In God"
"I Don't Know"
"I Go On"
"In Nomine Patris"
"Kyrie Eleison"
"Meditation No. 1" [instrumental]
"Meditation No. 2" (on a sequence by Beethoven) [instrumental]
"Non Credo (Possibly Yes, Probably No)"
"Our Father"
"Pax: Communion (Secret Songs)"
"Prefatory Prayers (Street Chorus)"—see **1600 PENNSYLVANIA
   AVENUE [May 4, 1976]**
"Thank You"
"Things Get Broken"
"World Without End"

Bernstein returned to the stage with this spectacular "theatre piece" commissioned for the opening of the John F. Kennedy Center for the Performing Arts. The nature of the work gave the composer freedom to write in all styles, ranging from modal to atonal. Controversy arose over the inclusion of rock music in the religious **MASS**. Others protested objectionable messages political and philosophical; the piece, after all, was paid for by the government. Bernstein's score was incredibly rich, well worth the wait since **WEST SIDE STORY [September 26, 1957]**. The size and scope of **MASS**—soloists, chorus, dance company, boys' choir, full orchestra, etc.—precluded much of an afterlife. A second production [June 28, 1972] played a month at the Metropolitan Opera House, and Kennedy Center mounted a tenth-anniversary revival. **MASS,** most fortunately, remains in full glory on the original cast album.

CANDIDE
⟨Second Version—also see December 1, 1956⟩
March 10, 1974   Broadway Theatre   740 performances

Lyrics mostly by Richard Wilbur
New lyrics by Stephen Sondheim
Book by Hugh Wheeler
(Based on the satire by Voltaire)
Choreographed by Patricia Birch
Directed by Harold Prince
Produced by Chelsea Theatre Center of Brooklyn in conjunction with
    Prince and Ruth Mitchell
With Mark Baker, Lewis J. Stadlen, and Maureen Brennan

Additional songs published in choral arrangements:

"Life Is Happiness Indeed" (lyric by Sondheim)—new lyric for
    "Venice Gambling Scene"
"This World (Candide's Lament)" (lyric by Sondheim)—new lyric
    for "Quartet Finale"

Additional songs published in new vocal score:

"Alleluia" [2nd]
"Auto Da Fe (What A Day)" (lyric by Latouche and Sondheim)—
    revised version of "Ringaroundarosie" (cut) from ⟨**First Version**⟩
"Barcarolle" [instrumental]
"The Best Of All Possible Worlds"—new lyric by Sondheim for
    song of same name
"Sheep's Song" (lyric by Sondheim)

CANDIDE had been unsuccessful in its original production, and a full-scale revival had also failed. The remarkable score had always cried out for a correct mounting; so when Harold Prince was asked to direct the piece off-off-Broadway, he brought in Sondheim and Wheeler from **A LITTLE NIGHT MUSIC [Sondheim: February 25, 1973]**. They removed the costume operetta trappings which had smothered the original, and went back to Voltaire. Success in Brooklyn brought the new **CANDIDE** triumphantly to Broadway—where the cost was too high, the capacity too low, and the union musicians too many. Another failure, but a smashing artistic success . . . and, with the revised version accessible, **CANDIDE** now has a much-deserved life. But the original score is far more glorious.

BY BERNSTEIN
November 23, 1975   Chelsea Westside Theatre ⟨off-Broadway⟩   17 performances

New lyrics mostly by Bernstein
Conceived and written by Betty Comden and Adolph Green
Directed by Michael Bawtree
Produced by Chelsea Theatre Center of Brooklyn
With Patricia Elliott, Kurt Peterson, and Janie Sell

Recorded songs:

"Ain't Got No Tears Left"—based on theme from 1949 symphony
   Age of Anxiety
"Another Love" (lyric by Comden and Green)
"It's Got To Be Good To Be Bad"
"Rio Bamba"—originally written (unpublished) as 1943 nonshow
   song

A revue compiled mostly of cuts and never-performed Bernstein material.

1600 PENNSYLVANIA AVENUE
May 4, 1976   Mark Hellinger Theatre   7 performances

Book and lyrics by Alan Jay Lerner
Choreographed by George Faison
Directed by Gilbert Moses
Produced by Roger L. Stevens and Robert Whitehead
With Ken Howard, Patricia Routledge, Emily Yancy, Gilbert Price, and
   Reid Shelton

Published songs:

"Bright And Black"

"The President Jefferson Sunday Luncheon Party March"—revised
   version of "Prefatory Prayers (Street Chorus)" from **MASS**
   [September 8, 1971]

"Take Care Of This House"

Additional songs published in vocal selection:

"Pity The Poor"

"The Red White And Blues"

"Seena"

"We Must Have A Ball"

Bernstein's first Broadway musical since **WEST SIDE STORY**
[September 26, 1957] was this ill-conceived mistake. The combination of Bernstein, Lerner, and the Bicentennial was enough to get
the Coca-Cola Company to finance the nondevelopable idea. **ON THE
TOWN [December 28, 1944]** and **WEST SIDE** had been close mu-
sic/dance collaborations, with Jerome Robbins and well-constructed
books; **1600 PENNSYLVANIA AVENUE** had an unworkable book
and a small army of directors and choreographers. The impossible
leading role was impossible to cast; the actor finally settled upon was
far from ideal. All the show had going for it was the score (half of
which was very good) and Patricia Routledge (all of whom was very
good). The Bernstein-Lerner team proved itself highly capable, as well
it should have been; but there were long stretches which a strong director or producer or librettist might well have edited, cut, or replaced. Lost but hopefully to reappear in the future were Routledge's perfectly crafted "Duet For One" and the sonata-form
"Overture"—also used for an 1812 minioperetta as the British occu-
pied Washington and set fire to the White House. It was that kind
of evening.

MADWOMAN OF CENTRAL PARK WEST
June 13, 1979   22 Steps Theatre ⟨off-Broadway⟩
86 performances

Music mostly by others
Book by Phyllis Newman and Arthur Laurents
Directed by Laurents

Produced by Gladys Rackmil, Fritz Holt, and Barry M. Brown
With Phyllis Newman

Song published in "Bernstein On Broadway":
"My New Friends" (lyric by Bernstein)

Bernstein contributed this song to Phyllis (Mrs. Adolph Green) Newman's one-woman show.

A QUIET PLACE
⟨Second Version; see November 23, 1955⟩
[July 22, 1984]   Kennedy Center Opera House
⟨Washington, D.C.⟩; limited engagement

Opera by Leonard Bernstein
Libretto and direction by Stephen Wadsworth
(Based on characters from **TROUBLE IN TAHITI [April 19, 1955]**
   [opera] by Bernstein)
Produced by Houston Grand Opera, Kennedy Center and Teatro alla
   Scala
With Robert Galbraith, Beverly Morgan, and Peter Kazaras

A QUIET PLACE was a companion piece to Bernstein's earlier **TROUBLE IN TAHITI.** Following negative reactions to the initial production in Houston, the two one-acts (about succeeding generations of the same family) were combined for engagements at La Scala and Washington. The new version was also unsuccessful at solving the many problems in the material.

Leonard Bernstein has taken time from his serious music career to write just six musicals during forty busy years. Only **WEST SIDE STORY** enjoys legendary status and continues to be performed. From these few theatrical excursions Bernstein has earned his reputation as one of Broadway's leading composers. A man of great overall talents, his theatre work has expanded the horizons of the musical stage. There is more work to be done.

Frederick Loewe

BORN: June 10, 1904   Vienna, Austria

Frederick Loewe was the son of famous tenor Edmund Loewe, who created the role of Prince Danilo in the 1905 world premiere of Lehar's *Die Lustige Witwe (The Merry Widow)*. At the age of fifteen, Frederick wrote the European pop-hit "Katrina," which sold over a million copies; but he wanted a career in serious music, and studied piano and composition with Ferruccio Busoni (Kurt Weill's teacher). Arriving in America in 1924, Loewe was unable to succeed in music and went through a string of unlikely occupations, including prospecting, cowpoking, and professional boxing. In the Thirties he turned again to songwriting.

PETTICOAT FEVER
March 4, 1935   Ritz Theatre   137 performances

Play by Mark Reed
Directed by Alfred DeLiagre, Jr.
Produced by Richard Aldrich and DeLiagre
With Dennis King, Ona Munson, and Leo G. Carroll

Published song:

"Love Tiptoed Through My Heart" (lyric by Irene Alexander)

Twenties operetta star Dennis King was a Lambs' Club friend of Loewe's. He liked this song and sang it in his next show, giving Loewe his Broadway debut.

THE ILLUSTRATORS' SHOW
January 22, 1936   48th Street Theatre   5 performances

Music and lyrics mostly by others (see **Loesser**)
Sketches by Max Liebman, Otto Soglow, and others

Directed by Allen Delano
Produced by Tom Weatherly and The Society of Illustrators

Published song:

"A Waltz Was Born in Vienna" (lyric by Earle Crooker)—also used
  in **SALUTE TO SPRING** [**June 12, 1937**]

This short-lived production also included Frank Loesser's first
Broadway songs. Loesser got a long-term Hollywood contract for his
efforts; Loewe and Crooker didn't.

SALUTE TO SPRING
[June 12, 1937]   Municipal Opera ⟨St. Louis, Missouri⟩;
summer stock tryout

Book and lyrics by Earle Crooker
Directed by Richard H. Berger
Produced by St. Louis Municipal Opera
With Guy Robertson, Berenice Claire, and Olive Olsen

Published songs:

"April Day"
"One Robin"—also used in **LIFE OF THE PARTY** [**October 8,**
  1942]
"Salute To Spring"
"Somehow"—also used in **LIFE OF THE PARTY**
"A Waltz Was Born In Vienna"—originally used in **THE**
  ILLUSTRATORS' SHOW [**January 22, 1936**]

Loewe's first full musical score made for a fairly successful summer
pageant.

GREAT LADY
December 1, 1938   Majestic Theatre   20 performances

Lyrics by Earl Crooker
Book by Crooker and Lowell Brentano
Directed by Bretaigne Windust
Produced by Dwight Deere Wiman and J. H. Del Bondio by arrangement
  with Frank Crumit
With Norma Terris, Irene Bordoni, Helen Ford, and Tullio Carminati

Published songs:

"I Have Room In My Heart"
"May I Suggest Romance?"
"There Had To Be The Waltz"
"Why Can't This Night Last Forever?"

Wiman, in the midst of his successful series of Rodgers and Hart musicals (see **ON YOUR TOES [Rodgers: April 11, 1936]**), produced this operetta failure. Heading the cast were leading ladies of **SHOW BOAT [Kern: December 27, 1927]**, **PARIS [Porter: October 8, 1928]**, and **PEGGY-ANN [Rogers: December 27, 1926]** with very little to sing about.

LIFE OF THE PARTY
*[October 8, 1942]   Wilson Theatre ⟨Detroit, Michigan⟩;
closed during pre-Broadway tryout*

Lyrics by Earle Crooker
Book by Alan Jay Lerner
(Based on *The Patsy* [play] by Barry Connors)
Directed by Russell Filmore
Produced by Henry Duffy
With Dorothy Stone, Charles Collins, Charles Ruggles, and Margaret
  Dumont

Published songs:

"One Robin Doesn't Make A Spring"—originally used in
  SALUTE TO SPRING [June 12, 1937]
"Somehow"—originally used in **SALUTE TO SPRING**

Henry Duffy successfully operated a number of stock companies on the West Coast beginning in the mid-Twenties. Duffy had first presented Fred Stone's dancing daughter Dorothy (with husband Charles Collins) in *Patricia*, a non-Loewe musicalization of *The Patsy*. Loewe's work on **SALUTE TO SPRING [June 12, 1937]** got him the assignment for the new version. Radio scriptwriter Lerner was an aspiring lyricist/librettist recently out of Harvard. Loewe and Lerner knew each other's work from Lambs' Club amateur shows. **LIFE OF THE PARTY** was a rush job, so Loewe invited Lerner along to patch together a book.

WHAT'S UP
A Merry Musical
November 11, 1943   National Theatre   63 performances

Lyrics by Alan Jay Lerner
Book by Arthur Pierson and Lerner
Staged and choreographed by George Balanchine
Book directed by Robert H. Gordon
Produced by Mark Warnow
With Jimmy Savo, Johnny Morgan, and Gloria Warren

Published songs:

"Joshua"
"My Last Love"
"You Wash And I'll Dry"
"You've Got A Hold On Me"
Lerner and Loewe's first Broadway effort was this poor wartime
musical, surprising among their otherwise tasteful, high-quality
body of work.

WHAT'S UP marked Balanchine's second and final directing attempt; the first had been the more successful **CABIN IN THE SKY**
[Duke: October 25, 1940].

THE DAY BEFORE SPRING
November 22, 1945   National Theatre   165 performances

Book and lyrics by Alan Jay Lerner
Book directed by Edward Padula
Staged and produced by John C. Wilson
With Bill Johnson, Irene Manning and Pat Marshall

Published songs:

"The Day Before Spring"
"God's Green World"
"I Love You This Morning"
"A Jug Of Wine"
"My Love Is A Married Man"
"This Is My Holiday"
"You Haven't Changed At All"

This psychoanalytical fantasy received good reviews and attracted fa-
vorable attention to the authors, although the run was disappoint-

ingly short. Director Padula was to resurface as producer of the hit
BYE BYE BIRDIE [Strouse: April 14, 1960].

BRIGADOON
March 13, 1947   Ziegfeld Theatre   581 performances

Book and lyrics by Alan Jay Lerner
Directed by Robert Lewis
Choreography by Agnes de Mille
Produced by Cheryl Crawford
With David Brooks, Marion Bell, Pamela Britton, and James Mitchell

Published songs:

"Almost Like Being In Love"
"Brigadoon"
"Come To Me, Bend To Me"
"Down On MacConnachy Square"
"From This Day On"
"The Heather On The Hill"
"I'll Go Home With Bonnie Jean"
"The Love Of My Life"
"There But For You Go I"
"Waitin' For My Dearie"

Additional songs published in vocal score:

"The Chase"
"Funeral" [instrumental]
"Jeannie's Packin' Up"
"Prologue"
"Sword Dance"
"Vendors' Calls"
"Wedding Dance" [instrumental]

Lerner and Loewe's colorful fantasy of the Scottish Highlands was a
surprise hit, impeccably produced by Cheryl Crawford. The fine work
of de Mille and the colorful trappings helped sustain the magical mood,
but it was the score—not only hits "Almost Like Being In Love"
and "The Heather On The Hill," but also the exquisite "From This
Day On" and "There But For You Go I" which supported the sen-
timent of the evening. It should be pointed out that the hit musicals
of that postwar season were both fantasies, normally an impossible
musical comedy form: the escapist **BRIGADOON,** with its concentrated use of (but not reliance on) dance; and the more successful

(but more quickly dated) **FINIAN'S RAINBOW [Lane: January 10, 1947],** which used elfin charm, a glorious score, and some strong social satire.

PAINT YOUR WAGON
November 12, 1951   Shubert Theatre   289 performances

Book and lyrics by Alan Jay Lerner
Directed by Daniel Mann
Choreography by Agnes de Mille
Produced by Cheryl Crawford
With James Barton, Olga San Juan, Tony Bavaar, and James Mitchell

Published songs:

"Another Autumn"
"Carino Mio"
"I Still See Elisa"
"I Talk To The Trees"
"I'm On My Way"
"Sh!"—cut
"They Call The Wind Maria"
"Wand'rin' Star"

Additional songs published in vocal score:

"All For Him"
"Hand Me Down That Can O' Beans"
"How Can I Wait?"
"In Between"
"Lonely Men" [instrumental]
"Movin' "
"Rope Dance" [instrumental]
"Rumson Town"
"There's A Coach Comin' In"
"Trio (Mormons' Prayer)"
"What's Goin' On Here?"
"Whoop-ti-ay!"

An ambitious but leaden saga of the California Gold Rush. The interwoven use of ballet that worked so well in the Highlands was less scenic on the Prairies, and the subject matter was harsh and cold. In spite of the show's failure, Loewe displayed—as in all his major work—an uncanny ability to write scores indigenous to the time and locale of the characters and plots.

MY FAIR LADY
March 15, 1956   Mark Hellinger Theatre
2,717 performances

Book and lyrics by Alan Jay Lerner
(Based on *Pygmalion* [play] by George Bernard Shaw)
Directed by Moss Hart
Choreographed by Hanya Holm
Produced by Herman Levin
With Rex Harrison, Julie Andrews, Stanley Holloway, and Robert Coote

Published songs:

"Get Me To The Church On Time"
"I Could Have Danced All Night"
"I've Grown Accustomed To Her Face"
"On The Street Where You Live" [2nd]—revised version of [1st]
"The Rain In Spain" [instrumental]
"Say A Prayer For Me Tonight"—cut; initial publication upon
    reuse in 1958 movie *Gigi*
"Show Me"
"With A Little Bit Of Luck"
"Wouldn't It Be Loverly?"

Additional songs published in vocal score:

"Ascot Gavotte"
"The Embassy Waltz" [instrumental]
"A Hymn To Him"
"I'm An Ordinary Man"
"Just You Wait, Henry Higgins"
"The Rain In Spain" [scene version]
"Servants' Chorus"
"Why Can't A Woman Be More Like A Man?"
"Without You"
"You Did It!"

Additional songs recorded:

"Come To The Ball"—cut
"On The Street Where You Live" [1st]—original version

Lerner and Loewe's masterpiece broke the **OKLAHOMA! [Rodgers: March 31, 1943]** long-run record at a time when six-year runs were unheard of. Shaw had ruled all his work off musical limits: he loathed THE CHOCOLATE SOLDIER, the 1909 Oscar Straus operetta of *Arms and the Man*. But Shaw died in 1950, and *Pygmalion* went through several hands before Lerner and Loewe got the chance. For the first time (except for **LIFE OF THE PARTY [October 8, 1942]**) Lerner did an adaptation, reforming the material but wisely retaining Shaw's sparkling language. And *matching* that language in his lyrics. The entire production sparkled, the score contained no less than five ever-popular standards, and everything went exceptionally well. But Shaw would have hated the satisfactorily happy ending.

CAMELOT
December 3, 1960   Majestic Theatre   873 performances

Book and lyrics by Alan Jay Lerner
(Based on *The Once and Future King* [book] by T. H. White)
Directed by Moss Hart
Produced by Lerner, Loewe, and Hart
With Richard Burton, Julie Andrews, Roddy McDowall, Robert Goulet,
    and John Cullum

Published songs:

"Camelot"
"Follow Me"
"How To Handle A Woman"
"I Loved You Once In Silence"
"If Ever I Would Leave You"
"The Lusty Month Of May"
"The Simple Joys Of Maidenhood"
"What Do The Simple Folk Do?"

Additional songs published in vocal score:

"Before I Gaze At You Again"
"C'est Moi"
"The Enchanted Forest"
"Guenevere"
"I Wonder What The King Is Doing Tonight"
"The Invisible Wall" [instrumental]
"The Jousts"
"Madrigal"
"The Persuasion"
"The Seven Deadly Virtues"
"Tent Scene" [instrumental]
"The Tumblers" [instrumental]

Additional songs recorded:

"Fie On Goodness"—cut after opening

"Then You May Take Me To The Fair"—cut after opening;
published in score (no lyric) as "Tent Scene" and "The
Tumblers"

MY FAIR LADY [March 15, 1956] was followed by the Oscar-winning 1958 movie *Gigi*, after which Loewe suffered a massive heart attack. Lerner, Loewe and Hart then began work on the ill-fated **CAMELOT,** during which Hart had a heart attack—causing his death within the year—and Lerner suffered a nervous breakdown. **CAMELOT** was poorly received but did considerably well, thanks to the strong advance sale built on **MY FAIR LADY**'s success and the spirit of the title song. Loewe's nearly fatal illness and the stress caused by extreme personal differences with Lerner were enough to convince him to retire. In 1971 he briefly worked with Lerner on the score for the unsuccessful movie *The Little Prince*.

GIGI
November 13, 1973   Uris Theatre   103 performances

Book and lyrics by Alan Jay Lerner
(Based on the novel by Colette and the 1958 motion picture by Lerner and
   Loewe)
Directed by Joseph Hardy
Produced by Saint-Subber and Edwin Lester (for the Los Angeles and San
   Francisco Light Opera Company)
With Alfred Drake, Agnes Moorehead, Maria Karnilova, and Daniel
   Massey

Published songs originally used in movie version:
"Gigi"
"I Remember It Well"
"I'm Glad I'm Not Young Anymore"
"The Night They Invented Champagne"
"She Is Not Thinking Of Me (Waltz At Maxim's)"
"Thank Heaven For Little Girls"

New songs published in vocal score:
"The Contract"—revised version of "À Toujours" (cut) from
   motion picture version
"The Earth And Other Minor Things"
"I Never Want To Go Home Again"
"In This Wide, Wide World"
"It's A Bore"—originally used (unpublished) in motion picture
   version

"Paris Is Paris Again"
"The Telephone (Opening Act Two)"

Loewe's final score was this partially new stage version of the Oscar-winning 1958 movie. Far inferior to the original, it quickly failed; ironically, inconsistencies in the Tony Award eligibility rules allowed **GIGI** to win that year's award for best score.

Frederick Loewe's musicals were skillfully written and, in places, deeply moving; but he was more craftsman than artist. The enormous success of **MY FAIR LADY [March 15, 1956]** brought the freedom to retire at a relatively early age, which Loewe took advantage of. Displaying little artistic inventiveness, Loewe carefully selected his projects and paid close attention to period. All his mature work, from **BRIGADOON [March 13, 1947]** on, was of significantly high quality and remains effective.

Jule Styne

BORN: December 31, 1905   London, England

Jule Styne was born in the slums of London, son of a butter-and-egg man (and sometime wrestler). The family moved to Chicago in 1912, where Styne had a short career as a piano prodigy: a drill-press accident desensitized a finger, and the preteen switched from the concert hall to the burlesque hall. By the twenties, Styne was leading his own band on the South Side of Chicago, writing a few songs including the 1926 hit "Sunday" (lyric by Ned Miller). In 1934 Styne set up in New York as a vocal coach; four years later he was in Hollywood, working with Shirley Temple and other stars. Opportunity led to assignments writing cowboy songs for B pictures. A short collaboration with lyricist Frank Loesser brought the 1941 hit "I Don't Want To Walk Without You," and Styne began a highly successful Hollywood career.

ICE CAPADES OF 1943
The Magnificent Ice-travaganza
September 4, 1942   Madison Square Garden

Music mostly by others
Directed and choreographed by Chester Hale
Produced by Arena Managers Association (John Harris)
With Vera Hruba

Published song

"The Guy With The Polka-Dot Tie" (lyric by Sol Meyer)

This ice show featured the Czech refugee, who looked a lot prettier than she skated (and she was good on ice). Styne used a jaunty tune he'd composed during high school days, distant cousin to "It's Enough To Make A Lady Fall In Love" from **DARLING OF THE DAY [January 27, 1968]**.

GLAD TO SEE YOU!
[November 13, 1944]   Shubert Theatre ⟨Philadelphia, Pennsylvania⟩; closed during pre-Broadway tryout

Lyrics by Sammy Cahn
Book by Eddie Davis and Fred Thompson
Directed by Busby Berkeley
Produced by David Wolper
With Eddie Foy, Jr., Jane Withers, and June Knight

Published songs:

"Any Fool Can Fall In Love"
"Guess I'll Have To Hang My Tears Out To Dry"
"I Don't Love You No More"

In 1942, Styne began a hit-filled Hollywood collaboration with Sammy Cahn, bolstered by a close association with Frank Sinatra. Styne and Cahn came to Broadway—or, rather, Philadelphia—with the dismal **GLAD TO SEE YOU!** Then it was quickly back to Hollywood, where they wrote "It's Been A Long, Long Time."

HIGH BUTTON SHOES
October 9, 1947   Century Theatre   727 performances

Lyrics by Sammy Cahn
Book by Stephen Longstreet
(Based on *The Sisters Liked Them Handsome* [novel] by Longstreet)
Choreographed by Jerome Robbins
Directed by George Abbott
Produced by Monte Proser and Joseph Kipness
With Phil Silvers, Nanette Fabray, Jack McCauley, Joey Faye, Helen
  Gallagher, and Donald Saddler

Published songs:

"Betwixt And Between"—cut; initial publication upon reuse in
  GYPSY [May 21, 1959] as "Everything's Coming Up Roses"
"Can't You Just See Yourself?"
"Get Away For A Day In The Country"
"I Still Get Jealous"
"On A Sunday By The Sea"
"Papa, Won't You Dance With Me"
"There's Nothing Like A Model 'T' "
"You're My Girl"

Additional songs recorded:

"Bathing Beauty Ballet" [instrumental]
"Nobody Ever Died For Dear Old Rutgers"

Styne and Cahn gave Broadway another try and came up with a long-running hit. The songs were more in the pop than theatre field, led by Nanette Fabray's hits "I Still Get Jealous" and "Papa, Won't You Dance With Me." Styne's outstanding contribution was, surprisingly, his spectacular dance music for Jerome Robbins' legendary "Bathing Beauty Ballet." Choreographer and composer began a profitable association: Robbins was to direct six Broadway musicals, four with Jule Styne scores. George Abbott's fast-paced musical comedy expertise, Phil Silvers' con-man, and the wonderful ballet made **HIGH BUTTON SHOES** very funny (if also very old-fashioned). Styne—already in his midforties—realized that the theatre was where he wanted to be: not just writing songs, but writing for characters in dramatic situations.

GENTLEMEN PREFER BLONDES
⟨*also see LORELEI [January 27, 1974]*⟩
December 8, 1949   Ziegfeld Theatre   740 performances

Lyrics by Leo Robin
Book by Joseph Fields and Anita Loos
(Based on the novel by Loos)
Choreographed by Agnes de Mille
Directed by John C. Wilson
Produced by Herman Levin and Oliver Smith
With Carol Channing, Yvonne Adair, Jack McCauley, and George S.
    Irving

Published songs:

"Bye, Bye, Baby"
"Diamonds Are A Girl's Best Friend"
"It's Delightful Down In Chile"
"Just A Kiss Apart"
"A Little Girl From Little Rock"
"Sunshine"
"You Say You Care"

Additional songs published in vocal selections:

"Homesick Blues"
"I Love What I'm Doing"

"It's High Time"
"Mamie Is Mimi"

Additional songs recorded:

"Gentlemen Prefer Blondes"
"I'm A'Tingle, I'm A'Glow"
"Keeping Cool With Coolidge"
"Scherzo" [instrumental]

The bright and lively **GENTLEMEN PREFER BLONDES** was
dominated by Carol Channing proving "Diamonds Are A Girl's Best
Friend" as she played "A Little Girl From Little Rock." Styne also
provided "Bye, Bye, Baby" and the very good comedy song "It's
Delightful Down In Chile." Styne's new lyricist was Leo Robin, who
had **HIT THE DECK [Youmans: April 25, 1927]** in his pre-Holly-
wood past; Sammy Cahn chose to stay in movies. With **GENTLE-
MEN PREFER BLONDES** a hit, Styne remained in New York and
set out to educate himself in the theatre.

MICHAEL TODD'S PEEP SHOW
June 28, 1950   Winter Garden Theatre   278 performances

Music mostly by others (see **Rome**)
Lyrics to Styne songs by Bob Hilliard
Sketches by Bobby Clark and others
Scenes directed by "Mr. R. Edwin Clark, Esq."
Directed by Hassard Short
Produced by Michael Todd
With Lina Romay, Clifford Guest, and Lilly Christine

Published songs:

"Francie"—issued as professional copy
"Stay With The Happy People"

MAKE A WISH
see Martin [April 18, 1951]

TWO ON THE AISLE
July 19, 1951   Mark Hellinger Theatre   276 performances

Sketches and lyrics by Betty Comden and Adolph Green
Choreographed by Ted Cappy

Directed by Abe Burrows
Produced by Arthur Lesser
With Bert Lahr, Dolores Gray, Elliot Reid, and Colette Marchand

Published songs:

"Everlasting"
"Give A Little, Get A Little"
"Hold Me—Hold Me—Hold Me"
"How Will He Know?"
"So Far—So Good"—cut; issued as professional copy; revised
    version of "Give Me A Song With A Beautiful Melody" from
    1949 movie *It's A Great Feeling*
"There Never Was Another Baby"

Additional songs published in vocal selection:

"Catch Our Act At The Met"—initial publication upon reuse in A
    PARTY WITH COMDEN AND GREEN [December 23, 1958]
"If You Hadn't But You Did"—initial publication upon reuse in A
    PARTY WITH COMDEN AND GREEN

Additional songs recorded:

"The Clown"
"Here She Comes Now"
"Show Train"
"Vaudeville Ain't Dead"

Styne first collaborated with Comden and Green on this summer revue. The comic potential of their partnership was demonstrated by
"If You Hadn't But You Did," "Catch Our Act At The Met," and
the patter for "Show Train." Bert Lahr and some good comedy
sketches helped the flimsily produced **TWO ON THE AISLE** to a
respectable run.

HAZEL FLAGG
February 11, 1953   Mark Hellinger Theatre
190 performances

Lyrics by Bob Hilliard
Book by Ben Hecht
(Based on *Nothing Sacred* [story] by James Street and [movie] by Ben
    Hecht and Charles MacArthur)
Choreographed by Robert Alton

Directed by David Alexander
Produced by Styne in association with Anthony Brady Farrell
With Helen Gallagher, Jack Whiting, Benay Venuta, and Thomas Mitchell

Published songs:

"Champagne And Wedding Cake"—written for *Living It Up*, 1954
    movie version
"Ev'ry Street's A Boulevard (In Old New York)"—initial
    publication upon use in movie version
"How Do You Speak To An Angel?"
"I Feel Like I'm Gonna Live Forever"
"Money Burns A Hole In My Pocket"—written for movie version
"Salomee (With Her Seven Veils)"
"That's What I Like"—written for movie version
"Think How Many People Never Find Love"—cut
"You're Gonna Dance With Me, Willie"

Additional songs recorded:

"Autograph Chant"
"Everybody Loves To Take A Bow"
"Hello, Hazel"
"I'm Glad I'm Leaving"
"Laura De Maupassant"
"A Little More Heart"
"Rutland Bounce" [instrumental]
"Who Is The Bravest?"
"The World Is Beautiful Today"

Styne's Broadway producing career began with a major failure (**MAKE
A WISH! [Martin: April 18, 1951]**), followed by the highly successful revival [January 3, 1952] of **PAL JOEY [Rodgers: December 25,
1940]**. Producer Styne determined to make a star out of Helen Gallagher, who had been prominently featured in **HIGH BUTTON
SHOES [October 9, 1947], MAKE A WISH!** and **PAL JOEY** (with
a Tony Award). The show built around her was not good and failed;
Gallagher's career suffered, with her next big opportunity coming
eighteen years later, when she won another Tony for the revival [Jan-
uary 19, 1971] of **NO, NO, NANETTE [September 16, 1925]**. The
ultimate indignity: for the movie version, Gallagher was passed over,
and her part, originally created on film by Carole Lombard, went to
Jerry Lewis!

PETER PAN
⟨Fourth Version⟩
October 20, 1954   Winter Garden Theatre
149 performances

Music also by Moose Charlap
Lyrics also by Carolyn Leigh
Lyrics to Styne songs by Betty Comden and Adolph Green
(Based on *Peter Pan* [play] by James M. Barrie)
Directed and choreographed by Jerome Robbins
Produced by Richard Halliday and Edwin Lester
With Mary Martin, Cyril Ritchard, Margalo Gilmore, and Sondra Lee

Published songs:

"Captain Hook's Waltz"
"Distant Melody"
"Never Never Land"
"Wendy"

Additional songs recorded:

"Oh My Mysterious Lady"
"Ugg-A-Wugg"

This version of **PETER PAN** began as a Los Angeles Civic Light Opera summer presentation. Mary Martin made her first appearance since **SOUTH PACIFIC [Rodgers: April 7, 1949]**, with Jerome Robbins beginning his career as director/choreographer. The score by Charlap and Leigh was weak, so Robbins called in Styne, Comden, and Green to revamp the show for Broadway. They did, contributing the effective theme song ("Never Never Land") and the felicitous "Wendy." After only five months, the Mary Martin **PETER PAN** was telecast—and the Broadway run was cut short. The piece has remained a favorite with audiences, though, and the revival with Sandy Duncan [September 6, 1979] enjoyed a 578-performance run.

MR. WONDERFUL
see Bock [March 22, 1956]

BELLS ARE RINGING
November 29, 1956   Shubert Theatre   924 performances

Book and lyrics by Betty Comden and Adolph Green
Choreographed by Jerome Robbins and Bob Fosse
Directed by Robbins
Produced by The Theatre Guild
With Judy Holliday, Sydney Chaplin, Jean Stapleton, Eddie Lawrence,
   and Peter Gennaro

Published songs:

"Bells Are Ringing"
"Better Than A Dream"—written for 1960 movie version
"Do It Yourself"—written for movie version
"Drop That Name"
"Hello, Hello There"
"I Met A Girl"
"Independent (On My Own)"
"Just In Time"
"Long Before I Knew You"
"Mu-cha-cha"
"The Party's Over"

Additional songs published in vocal score:

"I'm Going Back"
"Is It A Crime?"
"It's A Perfect Relationship"
"It's A Simple Little System"
"The Midas Touch"
"Salzburg"

Styne's finest musical comedy (not including **GYPSY [May 21, 1959]**).
Comden and Green's sometimes wild comic vision was perfect for this
vehicle, starring their former nightclub-act partner Judy Holliday. The
score was consistently good, with two enormous hits ("Just In Time"
and "The Party's Over"). The whole production worked like a well-
made George Abbott musical, which—with Abbott alumni Robbins,
Fosse, Styne, Comden, and Green on hand—was not exactly surprising. Costarring was Sydney (son of Charles) Chaplin, not much of a
singer but charming and handsome enough to star in two more Styne
musicals. The composer used his vocal coach knowledge to fashion
songs that even Chaplin could sing—like "Just In Time" and "You
Are Woman, I Am Man" (in **FUNNY GIRL [March 26, 1964]**).

SAY, DARLING
A Play About A Musical
April 3, 1958   ANTA Theatre   332 performances

Lyrics by Betty Comden and Adolph Green
Book by Richard and Marian Bissell and Abe Burrows
(Based on the novel by Richard Bissell)
Choreographed by Matt Mattox
Directed by Burrows
Produced by Styne and Lester Osterman
With David Wayne, Vivian Blaine, Johnny Desmond, and Robert Morse

Published songs:

"Dance Only With Me"
"It's The Second Time You Meet That Matters"
"Let The Lower Lights Be Burning"
"My Little Yellow Dress"—cut
"Say, Darling"
"Something's Always Happening On The River"
"Try To Love Me Just As I Am"

Additional songs recorded:

"The Carnival Song"
"Chief Of Love"
"The Husking Bee"
"It's Doom"

Richard Bissell was a Dubuque-born, Harvard-educated former steamboat pilot who came to Broadway to adapt his first novel into **THE PAJAMA GAME [Adler: May 13, 1954]**. Bissell's *Say, Darling* was a very funny "fictionalized" account of Bissell's adventures in musical comedy, complete with caricatures of Abbott, Adler, and producers Griffith and Prince. But the musical-comedy adaptation of the second novel, about the making of the musical-comedy adaptation of the first novel, wasn't as good as any of 'em. Styne, Comden, and Green's score was pastiche musical comedy of little interest. The only true bright spot was the boyish Robert Morse playing the pretentious-but-lovable boyish coproducer.

GYPSY
May 21, 1959   Broadway Theatre   702 performances

Lyrics by Stephen Sondheim
Book by Arthur Laurents
(Based on the memoirs by Gypsy Rose Lee)
Directed and choreographed by Jerome Robbins
Produced by David Merrick and Leland Hayward
With Ethel Merman, Jack Klugman, Sandra Church, and Maria Karnilova

Published songs:

"All I Need Is The Girl"
"Everything's Coming Up Roses"—revised version of "Betwixt
    And Between" (cut, unpublished) from **HIGH BUTTON
    SHOES [October 9, 1947]**
"Let Me Entertain You"
"Little Lamb"
"Mama's Talkin' Soft"—cut
"Mr. Goldstone"
"Small World"
"Some People"
"Together Wherever We Go"
"You'll Never Get Away From Me"—revised version of "I'm In
    Pursuit Of Happiness" from 1956 TV musical *Ruggles of Red
    Gap*

Additional songs published in vocal score:

"Baby June And Her Newsboys"
"Broadway"
"Extra! Extra!"
"Farm Sequence (Caroline)"
"If Momma Was Married"
"Rose's Turn"
"You Gotta Get A Gimmick"

Arthur Laurents, librettist of **WEST SIDE STORY [Bernstein:
September 26, 1957],** came up with the key to musicalizing Gypsy
Rose Lee's autobiography: concentrating on the character of the
mother. David Merrick brought in Laurents' **WEST SIDE STORY**
collaborators Robbins and Sondheim, the latter to make his composing debut. Then Ethel Merman became Rose and she wanted Jule
Styne, who knew how to write for her voice. (Porter and Berlin were
both approached first.) Robbins, of course, had worked very successfully with Styne; and Merrick—before Laurents and Merman—
had initially gone to Styne, Comden, and Green. What Sondheim's

score would have been like is unknown; surely interesting, but one has to be glad things developed as they did. Styne's talent and background were particularly suited to the material, and the combined Styne/Sondheim **GYPSY** ranks high among the theatre's very best, but **THE SOUND OF MUSIC [Rodgers: November 16, 1959]** won the awards and ran twice as long.

DO RE MI
December 26, 1960 St. James Theatre 400 performances

Lyrics by Betty Comden and Adolph Green
Book and direction by Garson Kanin
(Based on the novel by Kanin)
Choreographed by Marc Breaux and Dee Dee Wood
Produced by David Merrick
With Phil Silvers, Nancy Walker, Nancy Dussault, John Reardon, and
  David Burns

Published songs:

"All You Need Is A Quarter"
"Asking For You"
"Cry Like The Wind"
"Fireworks"
"Make Someone Happy"
"What's New At The Zoo?"

Additional songs published in vocal score:

"Adventure"
"All Of My Life"
"Ambition"
"He's A V.I.P."
"I Know About Love"
"It's Legitimate"
"The Late, Late Show"
"Take A Job"
"Waiting"
"Who Is Mr. Big?"

Styne reunited with Comden and Green for this comical musical comedy, which—despite clowns Silvers, Walker, and Dussault, good reviews, and the enormously popular "Make Someone Happy"—had a disappointing run. Expressionistic designer Boris Aronson began his drive to change the way Broadway musicals looked. For this pop music satire, he constructed a spectacular show curtain of stage-to-ceiling jukeboxes, wired for neon and sound.

SUBWAYS ARE FOR SLEEPING
December 27, 1961   St. James Theatre   205 performances

Book and lyrics by Betty Comden and Adolph Green
(Based on stories by Edmund G. Love)
Directed and choreographed by Michael Kidd
Produced by David Merrick
With Sydney Chaplin, Carol Lawrence, Orson Bean, and Phyllis Newman

Published songs:

"Be A Santa"
"Comes Once In A Lifetime"
"How Can You Describe A Face?"
"I'm Just Taking My Time"
"Who Knows What Might Have Been?"

Additional songs recorded:

"Girls Like Me"
"I Just Can't Wait"
"I Said It And I'm Glad"
"I Was A Shoo-In"
"Ride Through The Night"
"Strange Duet"
"Subway Directions"
"Subways Are For Sleeping"
"Swing Your Projects"
"What Is This Feeling In The Air?"

David Merrick pulled the publicity coup of his distinguished publicity career. Using gentlemen with names legitimately identical to the most powerful drama critics of the day, he composed the full-page quote ad of everyone's dreams: "No doubt about it—**SUBWAYS ARE FOR SLEEPING** is the best musical of the century! . . . John Chapman." In order to pull this off, Merrick first had to wait for Brooks Atkinson to retire—there was only one Brooks Atkinson in the phone book. Then he had to wait for a big-budget show with dismal reviews. "One of the few great musicals of the last thirty years" said Merrick's Howard Taubman. Taubman of the *Times* called

SUBWAYS "dull and vapid." Photographs accompanying the seven-out-of-seven raves indicate that in a liberal (for 1961) move, Merrick chose to include a Mr. Richard Watts from Harlem.

ARTURO UI
November 11, 1963   Lunt-Fontanne Theatre
8 performances

Play by Bertolt Brecht
Incidental music by Jule Styne
Directed by Tony Richardson
Produced by David Merrick
With Christopher Plummer, Lionel Stander, Murvyn Vye, and Madeleine
    Sherwood

Published songs:

None

Styne supplied a brilliant barrelhouse jazz accompaniment to this view of Hitler-as-Capone in prohibition Chicago. (In 1927, Capone asked if he could lead Styne's orchestra in "Rhapsody in Blue"; Styne said okay.)

FUNNY GIRL
March 26, 1964   Winter Garden Theatre
1,348 performances

Lyrics by Bob Merrill
Book by Isobel Lennart
(Based on a story by Lennart)
Choreographed by Carol Haney
Directed by Garson Kanin
Production supervised by Jerome Robbins
Produced by Ray Stark
With Barbra Streisand, Sydney Chaplin, Kay Medford, and Jean Stapleton

Published songs:

"Don't Rain On My Parade"
"Funny Girl"—cut; published in standard edition
"His Love Makes Me Beautiful"—initial publication upon use in
    1968 version
"I'm The Greatest Star"—initial publication upon use in movie
    version

"The Music That Makes Me Dance"
"People"
"Who Are You Now?"
"You Are Woman, I Am Man"
"You're A Funny Girl"—written for movie version

Additional songs published in vocal score:

"Cornet Man"
"Downtown Rag" [instrumental]
"Find Yourself A Man"
"Henry Street"
"I Want To Be Seen With You Tonight"
"If A Girl Isn't Pretty"
"Private Schwartz"
"Rat-Tat-Tat-Tat"
"Sadie, Sadie"
"Who Taught Her Everything"

Additional song recorded:

"Roller Skate Rag"

What started as Mary Martin's follow-up to **THE SOUND OF MU-SIC [Rodgers: November 16, 1959]** traveled a particularly tortuous path before finally arriving as a Broadway hit. Fanny Brice's son-in-law Ray Stark initially brought the project to David Merrick, his co-producer on the 1958 *The World of Suzie Wong*. Merrick assembled his **GYPSY [May 21, 1959]** team of Styne, Sondheim, and Robbins. Mary Martin wasn't exactly particularly quite right for Fanny Brice; she moved on to Laurette Taylor (**JENNIE [Schwartz: October 17, 1963]**) instead. By the time Anne Bancroft came in, lyricist Sondheim was **ON THE WAY TO THE FORUM [Sondheim: May 8, 1962].** Bob Merrill (from Merrick's **CARNIVAL! [Merrill: April 13, 1964]**) became Styne's collaborator. Barbra Streisand (from Merrick's **I CAN GET IT FOR YOU WHOLESALE [Rome: March 22, 1962]**) became Fanny Brice, and all was ready. Then Robbins quit. Bob Fosse came in, Bob Fosse went out. Garson Kanin (from Merrick's **DO RE MI [December 26, 1960]**) came in and **FUNNY GIRL** breezed into rehearsal. *Without* David Merrick, who grew tired of it all and let himself be bought out. (Besides, he had **HELLO, DOLLY! [Herman, Strouse, Merrill: January 16, 1964]** to keep him busy.) Tryout troubles unexpectedly arose, and Stark replaced Kanin with: Jerome Robbins. And *then* everything began to work. Styne's score was good, although less adventuresome than usual—influenced, no doubt, by the craftsmanlike Merrill. "Don't Rain On My Parade," "I'm The Greatest Star," and "The Music That Makes Me Dance" were particularly effective, both musically and dramatically. And Streisand sang "People," too.

WONDERWORLD
May 7, 1964   World's Fair Amphitheatre-in-the-Lake
250 performances

Lyrics by Stanley Styne
Choreographed by Michael Kidd
Conceived and directed by Leon Leonidoff
With Chita Rivera and Gretchen Wyler

Published song:

"Wonderworld"

This twenty-eight-show-a-week spectacle—at the old Billy Rose Aquacade arena—closed owing two-and-a-half million dollars. Styne's lyricist was his older son.

FADE OUT—FADE IN
May 26, 1964   Mark Hellinger Theatre   199 *performances*

Book and lyrics by Betty Comden and Adolph Green
Choreographed by Ernest Flatt
Directed by George Abbott
Produced by Lester Osterman and Styne
With Carol Burnett, Jack Cassidy, Lou Jacobi, and Tiger Haynes

Published songs:

"Fade Out—Fade In"
"I'm With You"
"You Mustn't Feel Discouraged"

Additional songs published in vocal selection:

"Call Me Savage"—see **HALLELUJAH, BABY!** [April 26, 1967]
"Go Home Train"
"It's Good To Be Back Home"
"The Usher From The Mezzanine"

Additional songs recorded:

"Close Harmony"
"The Dangerous Age"
"Fear"
"The Fiddler And The Fighter"
"L.Z. In Quest Of His Youth" [ballet]
"Lila Tremaine"
"My Fortune Is My Face"
"My Heart Is Like A Violin"
"Oh Those Thirties"

ABC-Paramount saw fit to invest three million musical-producing dollars with producers Lester Osterman and Jule Styne (with a track record of **MR. WONDERFUL** [Bock: March 22, 1956], SAY, **DARLING [April 3, 1958]** and FIRST IMPRESSIONS [March 19, 1959]). The money went to produce **HIGH SPIRITS [Martin: April 7, 1964], FADE OUT—FADE IN,** and Sammy Fain's SOME-THING MORE [November 5, 1964]—the last directed by Styne himself. After which ABC-Paramount (and Jule Styne) reassessed their Broadway producing careers. **FADE OUT—FADE IN** featured a live seal and did very well until Carol Burnett became indisposed. At its best, Burnett played Shirley Temple—Styne's vexation in Hollywood vocal coaching days—to Tiger Haynes' Bill Robinson in "You Mustn't Feel Discouraged."

HALLELUJAH, BABY!
April 26, 1967   Martin Beck Theatre   293 performances

Lyrics by Betty Comden and Adolph Green
Book by Arthur Laurents
Choreographed by Kevin Carlisle
Directed by Burt Shevelove
Produced by Albert W. Selden and Hal James, Jane C. Nusbaum, and
    Harry Rigby
With Leslie Uggams, Robert Hooks, Allen Case, and Lillian Hayman

Published songs:

"Being Good Isn't Good Enough"
"Hallelujah, Baby!"
"My Own Morning"
"Not Mine"—see **BAR MITZVAH BOY [October 31, 1978]**
"Now's The Time"

"Talking To Yourself"
"When The Weather's Better"—cut

Additional song published in vocal selection:

"I Wanted To Change Him"

Additional songs recorded:

"Another Day"
"Feet Do Yo' Stuff"
"I Don't Know Where She Got It"
"The Slice"
"Smile, Smile"
"Watch My Dust"
"Witches' Brew"—revised version of "Call Me Savage" from
   FADE OUT—FADE IN [May 26, 1964]

Styne, composer of **BELLS ARE RINGING [November 29, 1956]** and **GYPSY [May 21, 1959]**, finally received a Tony Award for this unsuccessful musical—which had long since closed. (**HALLELU-JAH, BABY!** opened after the eligibility cut-off date for 1967; it won the following season.) An unclear (or maybe just poorly executed) concept and a jumbled book made for confusion; racial tensions between cast and staff didn't help, and a better-than-average score wasn't enough. Lost in the shuffle: the rhythmic "When The Weather's Better." Leslie Uggams—in a role intended for Lena Horne—gave a very good performance, and Lillian Hayman was an unforgettable treasure.

DARLING OF THE DAY
January 27, 1968   George Abbott Theatre
32 performances

Lyrics by E. Y. Harburg
Book by Nunnally Johnson (unbilled)
(Based on *The Great Adventure* [play] by Arnold Bennett)
Choreographed by Lee Becker Theodore
Directed by Noel Willman
Produced by The Theatre Guild and Joel Schenker
With Vincent Price, Patricia Routledge, Brenda Forbes, and Teddy Green

Published songs:

"I've Got A Rainbow Working For Me"
"It's Enough To Make A Lady Fall In Love"

"Let's See What Happens"
"Not On Your Nellie"
"Under The Sunset Tree"

Additional songs recorded:

"Butler In The Abbey"
"A Gentleman's Gentleman"
"He's A Genius"
"Money, Money, Money"
"Panache"
"That Something Extra Special"
"To Get Out Of This World Alive"
"What Makes A Marriage Merry?"

It is always a bad sign when a show reaches Broadway with no book writer credited; the disastrously produced **DARLING OF THE DAY** almost opened without a director, either. Styne wrote a particularly good score, with Harburg's lyrics second only to his **FINIAN'S RAINBOW [Lane: March 13, 1947]**. Standing out were "That Something Extra Special," "Let's See What Happens," and the schottische "It's Enough To Make A Lady Fall In Love" (with Harburg's "stork of Damocles"). The lack of interest engendered by Vincent Price (playing the title role) ruined the little chance **DARLING OF THE DAY** might have had under its ill-fated star. Patricia Routledge was superhuman in her efforts, and became the only foreign, unknown-to-Broadway nonstar ever to make her musical debut in a short-run flop and win the Best Actress Tony Award. Arnold Bennett's original novel version of the material was entitled *Buried Alive*.

LOOK TO THE LILIES
March 29, 1970   Lunt-Fontanne Theatre   25 performances

Lyrics by Sammy Cahn
Book by Leonard Spigelgass
(Based on *Lilies of the Field* [novel] by William Barrett)
Directed by Joshua Logan
Produced by Edgar Lansbury, Max Brown, Richard Lewine, and Ralph Nelson
With Shirley Booth, Al Freeman, Jr., Taina Elg, and Carmen Alvarez

Songs published in vocal selection:

"Follow The Lamb!"
"I! Yes, Me! That's Who!"

"I'd Sure Like To Give It A Shot"
"Look To The Lilies"
"One Little Brick At A Time"
"Some Kind Of Man"
"There Comes A Time"

Additional song recorded:

"First Class Number One Bum"

Sammy Cahn—with two non-Styne Broadway flops since **HIGH BUTTON SHOES [October 9, 1947]**—reunited with his former partner for this horror. Even the miscast Shirley Booth (in her final musical) was uninteresting.

PRETTYBELLE
[February 1, 1971]   Shubert Theatre ⟨Boston, Massachusetts⟩; closed during pre-Broadway tryout

Book and lyrics by Bob Merrill
(Based on the novel by Jean Arnold)
Directed and choreographed by Gower Champion
Produced by Alexander H. Cohen
With Angela Lansbury, Charlotte Rae, and Joe Morton

Songs published in vocal selections:

"How Could I Know?"
"I Met A Man"
"I'm In A Tree"
"Individual Thing"
"Prettybelle"
"To A Small Degree"
"When I'm Drunk I'm Beautiful"

Additional songs recorded:

"Back From The Great Beyond"
"God's Garden"
"I Never Did Imagine"
"In The Japanese Gardens"
"Manic Depressives"
"The No-Tell Motel"
"You Ain't Hurtin' Your Ole Lady None"
"You Never Looked Better"

Alexander H. Cohen followed his Broadway failure **DEAR WORLD [Herman: February 6, 1969]** with **PRETTYBELLE,** which fared even worse. A valiant Angela Lansbury suffered through both. Styne's score was only slightly better than **LOOK TO THE LILIES [March 29, 1970].**

SUGAR
April 9, 1972   Majestic Theatre   505 performances

Lyrics by Bob Merrill
Book by Peter Stone
(Based on *Some Like It Hot* [movie] by Billy Wilder and I.A.L. Diamond)
Directed and choreographed by Gower Champion
Produced by David Merrick
With Robert Morse, Tony Roberts, Cyril Ritchard, and Elaine Joyce

Published song:

"(Doing It For) Sugar"

Additional songs recorded:

"Beautiful Through And Through"
"The Beauty That Drives Men Mad"
"Hey, Why Not!"
"It's Always Love"
"November Song (Even Dirty Old Men Need Love)"
"Penniless Bums"
"Sun On My Face"
"We Could Be Close"
"What Do You Give To A Man Who's Had Everything?"
"When You Meet A Man In Chicago"

Somehow or other Merrick managed to get a successful run out of this less-than-satisfying show. Not only was a starring role deleted during the tryout—singer Johnny Desmond as the George Raft gangster—they also threw out Jo Mielziner and his entire set! Styne's Twenties Chicago music was actually pretty good, at least in the first act. The authors were locked out of rehearsals by Champion, and the cutting of the Raft character left the second act void of material. Robert Morse managed to succeed against the memory of the brilliant Jack Lemmon original. Morse's performance of "We Could Be Close" alone was well worth the price of admission (**SUGAR** opened with a record-high $15 top).

LORELEI
Or "Gentlemen Still Prefer Blondes"
⟨also see GENTLEMEN PREFER BLONDES
[December 8, 1949]⟩
January 27, 1974   Palace Theatre   320 performances

New lyrics by Betty Comden and Adolph Green
New book material by Kenny Solms and Gail Parent
(Based on **GENTLEMEN PREFER BLONDES** [musical])
Choreographed by Ernest Flatt
Directed by Robert Moore
Produced by Lee Guber and Shelly Gross
With Carol Channing, Dody Goodman, Tamara Long, and Peter Palmer

New published songs:

"I Won't Let You Get Away"
"Lorelei" [1st]—cut
"Men!"

Additional songs recorded:

"Button Up With Esmond"
"Looking Back"
"Lorelei" [2nd]
"Paris, Paris" (lyric by Comden, Green, and Robin)—cut; revised
   version of "Sunshine" from **GENTLEMEN PREFER
   BLONDES**

With the lack of suitable properties for Carol Channing, an attempt
was made to give Lorelei Lee a facelift. Outfitted with new material
and a streamlined book, the charming original was destroyed. The
same producers did a similar job on **BRING BACK BIRDIE [Strouse:
March 5, 1981]** with similarly dismal results. Prior to Broadway
LORELEI played a year on the road, initially directed and choreographed by Joe Layton.

HELLZAPOPPIN'!
[November 22, 1976]   Mechanic Theatre ⟨Baltimore,
Maryland⟩; closed during pre-Broadway tryout

Music also by Hank Beebe and Cy **Coleman**
Lyrics by Carolyn Leigh and Bill Heyer
Book by Abe Burrows and others

(Based on a format by Olsen and Johnson)
Choreographed by Donald Saddler
Directed by Jerry Adler
Produced by Alexander H. Cohen in association with Maggie and Jerome
  Minskoff
With Jerry Lewis, Lynn Redgrave, Joey Faye, and Brandon Maggart

Published songs:
None

Cohen's second attempt to honor the 1,404-performance Olsen and
Johnson original [September 22, 1938] died aborning. An earlier ver-
sion, which premiered (and died) at Expo '67 in Montreal, starred
Soupy Sales.

BAR MITZVAH BOY
October 31, 1978   Her Majesty's Theatre ⟨London⟩
77 performances

Lyrics by Don Black
Book by Jack Rosenthal
(Based on a TV play by Rosenthal)
Choreographed by Peter Gennaro
Directed by Martin Charnin
Produced by Peter Witt
With Joyce Blair, Harry Towb, Vivienne Martin, and Barry Angel

Songs recorded:
"The Bar Mitzvah Of Eliot Green"
"The Harolds Of This World"—revised version of "Not Mine"
  from **HALLELUJAH, BABY!** [April 26, 1967]
"I've Just Begun"
"If Only A Little Bit Sticks"
"Rita's Request"
"Simchas"
"The Sun Shines Out Of Your Eyes"
"This Time Tomorrow"
"Thou Shalt Not"
"We've Done Alright"
"Where Is The Music Coming From?"
"Why"
"You Wouldn't Be You"

DARLING OF THE DAY [January 27, 1968] and **BAR MITZ-VAH BOY** are Styne's two best scores since **FUNNY GIRL [March 26, 1964]. BAR MITZVAH BOY** was a quick failure, with blame going to everyone involved except the songwriters. The score remains unpublished to date, available only on the presently unavailable original cast album. Styne wrote no less than five tender and lovely songs: "Where Is The Music Coming From," "The Harolds Of This World," "The Sun Shines Out Of Your Eyes," "You Wouldn't Be You," and "We've Done Alright." And then there were good rhythm songs, comedy songs, etc.

ONE NIGHT STAND
[October 20, 1980]   Nederlander Theatre; closed during previews

Book and lyrics by Herb Gardner
Choreographed by Peter Gennaro
Directed by John Dexter
Produced by Joseph Kipness, Lester Osterman, Joan Cullman, James M. Nederlander, and Alfred Taubman
With Jack Weston, Charles Kimbrough, and Catherine Cox

Songs recorded:

"Don't Kick My Dreams Around"
"For You"
"Go Out Big"
"Here Comes Never"
"I'm Writing A Love Song For You"
"Let Me Hear You Love Me"
"A Little Travellin' Music Please"
"Long Way From Home"
"Somebody Stole My Kazoo"
"Someday Soon"
"There Was A Time"
"Too Old To Be So Young"

Another haphazardly assembled enterprise. **ONE NIGHT STAND** was misconceived, and there were no musical theatre professionals involved (except the seventy-five-year-old Styne) capable of even beginning to deal with realities. The composer provided at least one very good song, "Too Old To Be So Young."

Arriving on Broadway in 1947, forty-two-year-old Jule Styne gave up a successful Hollywood career and committed his future to the theatre. (Richard Rodgers, only three years older than Styne, was on Broadway back in 1919.) Styne compensated for his late start by becoming the theatre's most prolific composer of the next twenty-five years. With **BELLS ARE RINGING [November 29, 1956]** he entered the first rank of musical comedy. Then came the classic **GYPSY [May 21, 1959],** which proved him a top musical dramatist as well. The heavy demands of a continuous production schedule—and the occasional selection of less-than-inspired material—resulted in a number of misses. But even the lesser scores have been marked by optimism, warmth, and Styne's exciting musical professionalism.

Frank Loesser

BORN: June 29, 1910   New York, New York
DIED: July 28, 1969   New York, New York

Frank Loesser was the son of a distinguished German-born piano teacher. While his brother Arthur became a renowned concert pianist, Frank was the musical black sheep of the family. Refusing to study the classics, he took up the harmonica and later taught himself piano, playing pop songs on the sly. Dropping out of college early in the Depression, Loesser supported himself with whatever jobs he could get (including a stint as a process server). Always intrigued by wordplay, Loesser's first published lyric was the 1931 pop song "In Love With The Memory Of You" (music by William Schuman, who became a serious composer and president of Juilliard). By the mid-Thirties Loesser was singing and playing in nightclubs, writing lyrics for special material to music by Irving Actman.

[NOTE: All music and lyrics by Frank Loesser unless indicated]

THE ILLUSTRATORS' SHOW
January 22, 1936   48th Street Theatre   5 performances
Music and lyrics mostly by others (see **Loewe**)
Sketches by Max Liebman, Otto Soglow, and others
Directed by Allen Delano
Produced by Tom Weatherly

Published song:

"Bang The Bell Rang" (music by Irving Actman, lyric by Loesser)

This quick flop had very little to distinguish it—except early contributions of Loesser and Loewe. A Hollywood executive liked the few Loesser/Actman songs enough to sign the pair to a contract. Once in Hollywood, Loesser quickly moved on to the top movie composers

of the time, successfully collaborating with Hoagy Carmichael, Jule
Styne, Burton Lane, and Arthur Schwartz. Then Loesser was drafted.
Without a composer on hand, the lyricist started writing his own tunes.
The first was a quick wartime hit, the 1942 "Praise The Lord And
Pass The Ammunition."

SKIRTS
An All American Musical Adventure
January 25, 1944   Cambridge Theatre ⟨London⟩

Music and lyrics mostly by PFC Frank Loesser and PFC Harold **Rome**
Choreography by Wendy Toye
Directed by Lt. Arthur G. Brest
Produced by U.S. 8th Air Force

Published song:

"Skirts"

Loesser (along with other Broadway and Hollywood professionals) had
been assigned to Special Services—the morale-building entertainment branch of the Army—to write material for soldier shows. "Skirts"
was borrowed by the Air Force.

ABOUT FACE!
An Army "Blueprint Special"
May 26, 1944   Camp Shanks, New York

Music and lyrics by PFC Frank Loesser, PFC Jerry Livingston, and
    others
Sketches by PFC Arnold Auerbach and others
Directed by Robert H. Gordon
With Jules Munshin and Vincente Gomez

Published songs:

"First Class Private Mary Brown"—also used in **PFC MARY
    BROWN [Circa November 1944]**
"One Little WAC"
"Why Do They Call A Private A Private? (When His Life's A
    Public Event)" (lyric by T/Sgt. Peter Lind Hayes)

Additional songs published in script:

"Dogface"
"Gee But It's Great To Be In The Army!"

"PX Parade" (probably by Loesser)
"When He Comes Home"—also used in (and separately published
   from) **OK, U.S.A.! [Circa June 1945]**

Special Services decided to put out a series of do-it-yourself soldier
shows, complete with script, songs, designs, publicity material, etc.
Loesser headed the songwriting branch, and wrote a considerable
amount of material over the next two years, his earliest theatre work.
"First Class Private Mary Brown" became another wartime pop hit
for Loesser.

HI, YANK!
An Army "Blueprint Special"
August 7, 1944   Theatre No. 5, Fort Dix ⟨New Jersey⟩

Music and lyrics by PFC Frank Loesser, Lt. Alex North, and others
Skits by PFC Arnold Auerbach and others
Choreographed by PFC José Limon
Directed by Cpl. David E. Fitzgibbon
Produced by Capt. Hy Gardner
With David Brooks and Joshua Shelley

Songs published in script:

"Classification Blues"
"Little Red Rooftops"
"The Most Important Job"
"My Gal And I" (lyric by Lt. Jack Hill)
"Saga Of A Sad Sack" (lyric by PFC Hy Zaret)
"Yank, Yank, Yank"

PFC MARY BROWN
A WAC Musical Revue
[Circa November 1944]

Music and lyrics mostly by PFC Frank Loesser
Sketches by PFC Arnold Auerbach and others

Published songs:

"First Class Private Mary Brown"—originally used in **ABOUT
   FACE! [May 26, 1944]**
"The WAC Hymn"

Additional songs published in script:
"Come On Honey"
"Lonely M.P."
"Lost In A Cloud Of Blue"
"New Style Bonnet"
"Something New"
"Twenty Five Words Or Less"

This WAC show was inspired by Loesser's "Mary Brown" hit. Exact authorship of the songs is unknown, but the score was credited as being "mostly by Loesser."

OK, U.S.A.!
An Army "Blueprint Special"
[Circa June 1945]

Published song:

"When He Comes Home"—originally used in **ABOUT FACE!**
   [May 26, 1944]

Additional songs published in script:

"I Was Down Texas Way"
"My Chicago"
"The Tall Pines"
"Tonight In San Francisco"
"A Trip Round The U.S.A."
"You're OK, U.S.A.!"

Again, exact authorship of the songs in the script is unavailable, but probably by Loesser. After the war, Loesser resumed his movie work, writing his own music. When Hollywood executives Cy Feuer and Ernest Martin decided to become Broadway producers, they invited Loesser along as composer/lyricist. He returned to New York, picking up an Oscar for the 1948 "Baby, It's Cold Outside" from *Neptune's Daughter*.

WHERE'S CHARLEY?
October 11, 1948   St. James Theatre   792 performances
Book and direction by George Abbott
(Based on *Charley's Aunt* [play] by Brandon Thomas)

Choreographed by George Balanchine

Produced by Cy Feuer and Ernest Martin in association with Gwen
   Rickard (Bolger)

With Ray Bolger, Allyn McLerie, and Doretta Morrow

Published songs:

"At The Red Rose Cotillion"—advertised but not published (except
   in vocal score)

"Lovelier Than Ever"

"Make A Miracle"

"My Darling, My Darling"

"The New Ashmolean Marching Society And Students'
   Conservatory Band"

"Once In Love With Amy"

"Pernambuco"

"The Train That Brought You To Town"—cut; advertised but not
   published

"Where's Charley?"

"The Years Before Us"—issued in choral arrangement

Additional songs published in vocal score:

"Better Get Out Of Here"

"The Gossips"

"Serenade With Asides"

"The Woman In His Room"

The novice producers had the foresight to hire veteran Abbott to direct and adapt the 1892 farce. Abbott frequently worked with talented newcomers, shepherding through their first important shows
Hugh Martin, Leonard Bernstein, Jule Styne, Richard Adler, Jerry
Bock, Bob Merrill, Stephen Sondheim, and John Kander. Loesser
and Abbott came up with an energetic showcase for Ray Bolger and
a big success. The score was more than adequate, with two high-
quality, out-of-the-ordinary songs ("Once In Love With Amy" and
"Make A Miracle"). And Broadway novice Loesser was about to unquestionably prove that he was more than just a pop-tune writer from
Hollywood.

GUYS AND DOLLS
A Musical Fable Of Broadway
November 24, 1950   46th Street Theatre
1,200 performances

Book by Jo Swerling and Abe Burrows
(Based on stories and characters by Damon Runyon)
Choreographed by Michael Kidd
Directed by George S. Kaufman
Produced by Feuer and Martin
With Sam Levene, Isabel Bigley, Robert Alda, and Vivian Blaine

Published songs:

"Adelaide"—written for 1955 movie version
"Adelaide's Lament"
"A Bushel And A Peck"
"Follow The Fold"
"Fugue For Tinhorns"
"Guys And Dolls"
"Guys And Dolls Preamble (Roxy)"
"I'll Know"
"I've Never Been In Love Before"
"If I Were A Bell"
"It Feels Like Forever"—cut; advertised but not published
"Luck Be A Lady"
"Marry The Man Today"
"More I Cannot Wish You"
"My Time Of Day"
"The Oldest Established"
"Pet Me, Poppa"—written for movie version
"Shango"—cut; advertised but not published
"Sit Down You're Rockin' The Boat"
"Sue Me"—nonshow version
"Sue Me Argument" [duet]—show version
"Take Back Your Mink"
"Three Cornered Tune"—nonshow version of "Fugue For
   Tinhorns"
"Traveling Light"—cut; advertised but not published
"A Woman In Love"—written for movie version

One of the finest modern-day musical comedies. Loesser displayed
his ability to lovingly (and with dignity) capture his characters and
their vernacular. His "Hot-Box Doll" Adelaide is as sympathetic and
real as Nellie Forbush; her chronic dilemma, while more humorous
than serious to us, is every bit as important to her. Loesser turned
out a hit-filled score (and quickly went into the music publishing
business); the happy fact that these hits were endemic to the char-

acters not only put Loesser in the top rank of theatre composers, but made **GUYS AND DOLLS** the classic it is. An important force on the show was director Kaufman, who had won the first musical Pulitzer for **OF THEE I SING [Gershwin: December 26, 1931]**. Radio writer Abe Burrows was brought in to replace librettist Jo Swerling and provided a fine book in Runyonese; Burrows took Kaufman lessons, and quickly became a musical comedy director himself. It is theorized that the Pulitzer committee was to have selected **GUYS AND DOLLS**; but Burrows was brought before the House Un-American Activities Committee and the politically sensitive prize administrators declined to present any award that year. Loesser and Burrows received a Pulitzer for their next collaboration.

THE MOST HAPPY FELLA
May 3, 1956   Imperial Theatre   676 performances

Book by Frank Loesser
(Based on *They Knew What They Wanted* [play] by Sidney Howard)
Choreographed by Dania Krupska
Directed by Joseph Anthony
Produced by Kermit Bloomgarden and Lynn Loesser
With Robert Weede, Jo Sullivan, Art Lund, and Susan Johnson

Published songs:

"Big D"
"Don't Cry"
"I Like Ev'rybody"
"Joey, Joey, Jocy"
"The Most Happy Fella"
"My Heart Is So Full Of You"
"Somebody, Somewhere"
"Standing On The Corner"
"Warm All Over"

Additional songs published in vocal score:

"Abbondanza"
"Aren't You Glad?"
"Benvenuta"
"Fresno Beauties (Cold And Dead)"
"Goodbye, Darlin' "
"Happy To Make Your Acquaintance"
"Hoedown" [instrumental]

"How Beautiful The Days"
"I Don't Like This Dame"
"I Know How It Is"
"I Love Him"
"I Make A Fist"
"The Letter"
"Love And Kindness"
"Mama, Mama"
"Ooh, My Feet"
"Please Let Me Tell You That I Love You"
"Plenty Bambini"
"Rosabella"
"She's Gonna Come Home With Me"
"Song Of A Summer Night"
"Soon You Gonna Leave Me, Joe"
"Special Delivery! (One Bride)"
"Sposalizio"
"Tony's Thoughts"
"Young People Gotta Dance"

Loesser confounded everyone by following the raucous **GUYS AND DOLLS** with this rich, operatic "musical musical." Writing his own libretto, Loesser came up with this heartwarming piece which, unlike **PORGY AND BESS [Gershwin: October 10, 1935], STREET SCENE [Weill: January 9, 1947]** and **REGINA [Blitzstein: October 31, 1949]**, was a major commercial success. Included were two hit songs, "Standing On The Corner" and "Big D." Loesser also came up with a new wife, divorcing coproducer Lynn and marrying Jo "Rosabella" Sullivan.

GREENWILLOW
March 8, 1960   Alvin Theatre   95 performances

Book by Lesser Samuels and Loesser
(Based on the novel by B. J. Chute)
Choreographed by Joe Layton
Directed by George Roy Hill
Produced by Robert A. Willey in association with Frank (Loesser)
    Productions, Inc.
With Anthony Perkins, Cecil Kellaway, Pert Kelton, and Ellen McCown

Published songs:
"Faraway Boy"
"Gideon Briggs, I Love You"
"Greenwillow Christmas"
"The Music Of Home"
"Never Will I Marry"
"Summertime Love"
"Walking Away Whistling"

Additional song published in vocal selection:
"Clang Dang The Bell"

Additional songs recorded:
"Could've Been A Ring"
"A Day Borrowed From Heaven"
"Dorrie's Wish"
"Greenwillow Walk" [instrumental]
"He Died Good"
"The Sermon"
"What A Blessing (To Know There's A Devil)"

Throughout his career Loesser demonstrated a reluctance to repeat himself, following each project with a radical change of pace. **GREENWILLOW** was a pastoral, folksy, tender musical that played whimsical and dull in performance. Loesser's work, while enchanting, had no life outside the theatre (and very little in it). **GREENWILLOW**'s failure was a major disappointment to Loesser.

HOW TO SUCCEED IN BUSINESS WITHOUT REALLY TRYING
October 14, 1961   46th Street Theatre   1,417 performances
Book by Abe Burrows, Jack Weinstock and Willie Gilbert
(Based on the book by Shepherd Mead)
Choreographed by Hugh Lambert
Musical staging by Bob Fosse
Directed by Burrows
Produced by Feuer and Martin in association with Frank (Loesser)
    Productions, Inc.
With Robert Morse, Rudy Vallee, Bonnie Scott, Virginia Martin, and
    Charles Nelson Reilly

Published songs:

"Brotherhood Of Man"
"Grand Old Ivy"
"Happy To Keep His Dinner Warm"
"How To Succeed"
"I Believe In You"
"Love From A Heart Of Gold"
"Paris Original"

Additional songs published in vocal score:

"Been A Long Day"
"Cinderella, Darling"
"Coffee Break"
"The Company Way"
"Finale—Act One" [trio]
"Rosemary"
"A Secretary Is Not A Toy"
"The Yo-Ho-Ho" [instrumental]

This Pulitzer Prize–winning musical cartoon remains one of the funniest evenings in Broadway history. All elements seemed to merge, although not easily: Burrows again provided a replacement libretto and directed, while Bob Fosse was brought in and came up with some very funny numbers. The performers, led by Morse, were superb; and tongue-in-cheek Loesser gave his hero the hypocritical "Brotherhood Of Man" and the narcissistic "I Believe In You"—both taken out of context to become gigantic popular hits.

PLEASURES AND PALACES
[March 11, 1965]   Fisher Theatre ⟨Detroit, Michigan⟩; closed during pre-Broadway tryout

Book by Sam Spewack and Loesser
(Based on *Once There Was A Russian* [play] by Spewack)
Directed and choreographed by Bob Fosse
Produced by Allen B. Whitehead in association with Frank (Loesser)
    Productions, Inc.
With Phyllis Newman, Jack Cassidy, Hy Hazell, and Sammy Smith

Songs issued in professional copies:

"Barabanchik"
"Far, Far, Far Away"

"In Your Eyes"
"Oh To Be Home Again"
"Pleasures And Palaces"
"Thunder And Lightning"
"Truly Loved"

Spewack had been highly successful with his two previous musicals, **LEAVE IT TO ME** [Porter: November 9, 1938] and **KISS ME, KATE** [Porter: December 30, 1948]; but this comic costume-operetta was a major disaster which quickly closed. The 1961 play version, for that matter, had lasted only one performance on Broadway. It was Loesser's final score. A heavy chain-smoker, Frank Loesser developed lung cancer and died July 28, 1969 in New York.

Lyricist Frank Loesser came from Hollywood with no theatrical experience and only a few years of composing credits. In the next thirteen years he wrote five Broadway scores, two of them good and the other three exceptional. **GUYS AND DOLLS** [November 24, 1950], **THE MOST HAPPY FELLA** [May 3, 1956] and **HOW TO SUCCEED IN BUSINESS WITHOUT REALLY TRYING** [October 14, 1961] all remain among the finest of their genre. Quite significantly, all had first-rate work from librettists, directors, choreographers, designers, and producers: perfectionist Loesser kept a careful eye on all elements of production. His innate cleverness and ease with words, combined with a deep respect for his characters, made him the best comedy lyricist of his time; his music, if not particularly innovative, was tuneful and always highly skillful. Frank Loesser's songs remain bright and golden.

Richard Adler

BORN: August 3, 1921   New York, New York

Like Frank Loesser, Richard Adler was the son of a concert pianist (Clarence Adler); like Loesser, young Adler stayed away from the piano. Following wartime Navy service, Adler went into advertising. In the early Fifties he began writing pop songs with Jerry Ross (born March 9, 1926 in the Bronx), including the 1953 hit "Rags To Riches." Loesser had set up as a music publisher following the success of **GUYS AND DOLLS [Loesser: November 24, 1950],** and he began looking for writers to supplement his own output. Adler and Ross were put under contract.

JOHN MURRAY ANDERSON'S ALMANAC
December 10, 1953   Imperial Theatre   229 performances

Music and lyrics also by others (see **Coleman**)
Adler music and lyrics by Adler and Ross
Sketches by Jean Kerr, William K. Wells, and others
Choreographed by Donald Saddler
Directed by John Murray Anderson and Cyril Ritchard
Produced by Michael Grace, Stanley Gilkey, and Harry Rigby
With Hermione Gingold, Billy DeWolfe, Harry Belafonte, and Orson
  Bean

Published songs:

"Acorn In The Meadow"
"Fini"
"You're So Much A Part Of Me"

Anderson was a veteran revue director with credits including **THE GREENWICH VILLAGE FOLLIES [Porter: September 16, 1924]** and **JUMBO [Rodgers: November 16, 1935].** Known for his taste and lavish use of color, he had gravitated to spectacles and spent much of the Forties doing pageants and the Ringling Brothers Circus. His career virtually at an end, Leonard Sillman had given him one last opportunity with the highly successful NEW FACES OF 1952 [May 16, 1952]. (Sillman had done the same thing with his first NEW FACES [March 15, 1934] when he invited the woebegone Charles Dillingham to supervise the production. Sillman was accused in both cases of merely taking advantage of the formerly illustrious names.) Anderson's NEW FACES prompted the far inferior **JOHN MURRAY ANDERSON'S ALMANAC;** the director died shortly after the opening. But Adler and Ross received their first theatre experience and attracted notice.

THE PAJAMA GAME
May 13, 1954   St. James Theatre   1,063 performances

Music and lyrics by Richard Adler and Jerry Ross
Book by George Abbott and Richard Bissell
(Based on 7½ Cents [novel] by Bissell)
Choreographed by Bob Fosse
Directed by Abbott and Jerome Robbins
Produced by Frederick Brisson, Robert E. Griffith, and Harold S. Prince
With John Raitt, Janis Paige, Eddie Foy, Jr., and Carol Haney

Published songs:

"Hernando's Hideaway"
"Hey There"
"I'm Not At All In Love"
"Small Talk"
"Steam Heat"
"There Once Was A Man"

Additional songs published in vocal score:

"Her Is"
"I'll Never Be Jealous Again"
"A New Town Is A Blue Town"
"Once-A-Year Day"
"The Pajama Game (Opening)"
"Racing With The Clock"
"Seven-And-A-Half Cents"
"Sleep-Tite"
"Think Of The Time I Save"

Griffith was a long-time Abbott stage manager, just then on **WON-DERFUL TOWN [Bernstein: February 25, 1953]** with young Prince as his assistant. The newly formed producing team optioned Bissell's best seller and brought it to their mentor. Unconventional musical comedy material (a labor strike in a Midwest garment factory) made it impossible to find established songwriters. An early choice was Loesser, who sent around his fledgling team; they were finally allowed an audition and got the assignment. Robbins, choreographer of most of Abbott's work since **ON THE TOWN [Bernstein: December 28, 1944],** turned down the dance job but agreed to back up novice Bob Fosse in exchange for codirector billing. Fosse was recommended by wife Joan McCracken, star of Abbott's BILLION DOLLAR BABY [December 21, 1945] and **ME AND JULIET [Rodgers: May 28, 1953].** Thus was this Abbott-trained group of future musical theatre directors brought together. Griffith and Prince called in Brisson, husband of Rosalind Russell (of **WONDERFUL TOWN**) for financing. The gamble on young talents Adler, Ross and Fosse paid off with a staggeringly successful hit with a little help from Loesser (on the one hand) and Robbins (who staged the rousing "Seven-And-A-Half-Cents"). Adler and Ross came up with three immense hits, "Hey There," "Hernando's Hideaway," and "Steam Heat."

DAMN YANKEES
May 5, 1955   46th Street Theatre   1,019 performances

Music and lyrics by Adler and Jerry Ross
Book by George Abbott and Douglas Wallop
(Based on *The Year the Yankees Lost the Pennant* [novel] by Wallop)
Choreographed by Bob Fosse
Directed by Abbott
Produced by Frederick Brisson, Robert E. Griffith, and Harold S. Prince
    in association with Albert Taylor
With Gwen Verdon, Stephen Douglass, and Ray Walston

Published songs:

"Goodbye, Old Girl"
"Heart"
"A Man Doesn't Know"
"Near To You"
"Shoeless Joe From Hannibal, Mo."
"There's Something About An Empty Chair" (music and lyric by
    Adler)—written for 1958 movie version

"Two Lost Souls"
"Whatever Lola Wants (Lola Gets)"
"Who's Got The Pain"

Additional songs published in vocal score:

"The Game"
"A Little Brains—A Little Talent"
"Six Months Out Of Every Year"
"Those Were The Good Old Days"

Follow-up to **THE PAJAMA GAME [May 13, 1954]** was the equally successful—if less well-made—**DAMN YANKEES.** The same team (less Robbins) took another popular off-beat novel and turned it into a fast, funny Fifties musical; even Richard Bissell contributed un-billed book material (jokes). Gwen Verdon, a Jack Cole dancer who stole the show in Michael Kidd's **CAN-CAN [Porter: May 7, 1953]** ballets, became Broadway's new musical comedy dancing star in her first of five Fosse shows. Adler and Ross had another two hit songs, "Heart" and "Whatever Lola Wants." But on November 11, 1955 Ross died of a bronchial ailment.

THE SIN OF PAT MULDOON
March 13, 1957   Cort Theatre   5 performances

Play by John McLian
Directed by Jack Garfein
Produced by Richard Adler and Roger L. Stevens
With James Barton and Elaine Stritch

Published song:

"The Sin Of Pat Muldoon" [music by Adler]—nonshow
  instrumental inspired by play

Adler began his producing career with this quick failure. In the fall of 1957 he wrote and produced two 1957 television musicals, *The Gift of the Magi* (starring Sally Ann Howes) and *Little Women.* Adler mar-ried soprano Howes, Julie Andrews' replacement in **MY FAIR LADY [March 15, 1956],** and began a Broadway project for her.

KWAMINA
October 23, 1961   54th Street Theatre   32 performances

Book by Robert Alan Aurthur
Choreographed by Agnes de Mille

Directed by Robert Lewis
Produced by Alfred de Liagre, Jr.
With Sally Ann Howes, Terry Carter, and Brock Peters

Published songs:

"Another Time, Another Place"
"I'm Seeing Rainbows"—cut
"Nothing More To Look Forward To"
"Ordinary People"
"Something Big"
"What's Wrong With Me?"—also revised and used in 1973 revival
   of **THE PAJAMA GAME [May 13, 1954]** as "Watch Your
   Heart" (unpublished)

Additional songs recorded:

"Cocoa Bean Song"
"Did You Hear That?"
"A Man Can Have No Choice"
"One Wife"
"Seven Sheep, Four Red Shirts, And A Bottle Of Gin"
"The Sun Is Beginning To Crow (You Are Home)"
"Welcome Home"
"What Happened To Me Tonight?"
"You're As English As"

An unsuccessful yet notable attempt. With all good intentions, the
authors created a contemporary "King And I Goes To Africa."
Hammerstein and Rodgers had carefully handled their racial intolerance theme in Siam and Bali H'ai; the **KWAMINA** book was a
poor retread, with bits of Eliza Doolittle thrown in. Adler, though,
came up with a fine, serious score. His work—particularly in the African songs—was far more dramatic than the two pop-song scores with
Jerry Ross. Following the failure of **KWAMINA,** Adler left Broadway. He went back to pop work, wrote the catchy "Let Hertz Put
You In The Driver's Seat" jingle, and produced special events for
the Kennedy and Johnson Administrations.

A MOTHER'S KISSES

*[September 23, 1968]   Shubert Theatre ⟨New Haven,
Connecticut⟩; closed during pre-Broadway tryout*

Music and lyrics by Richard Adler
Book by Bruce Jay Friedman

(Based on the novel by Friedman)
Choreographed by Onna White
Directed by Gene Saks
Produced by Lester Osterman, Richard Horner, and Lawrence Kasha
With Beatrice Arthur (Saks), Bill Callaway, and Carl Ballantine

Published songs:

None

This was the year of the Jewish mother. Hoping to mine theatre party business, two similar items were mounted: the Herbert Martin/Michael Leonard HOW TO BE A JEWISH MOTHER [December 28, 1967], which died after three weeks on Broadway, and **A MOTHER'S KISSES,** which played three deadly weeks on the road. The former was a two-character musical starring the formidable team of Molly Picon and Godfrey Cambridge. Adler next returned to Broadway in 1973 as producer of the unsuccessful interracial revival of **THE PAJAMA GAME [May 13, 1954].**

REX
See Rodgers [April 25, 1976]

MUSIC IS
December 20, 1976   St. James Theatre   8 performances

Music by Richard Adler
Lyrics by Will Holt
Book and direction by George Abbott
(Based on *Twelfth Night* [play] by William Shakespeare)
Choreographed by Patricia Birch
Produced by Adler, Roger Berlind, and Edward R. Downe, Jr.
With Joel Higgins, Catherine Cox, and Christopher Hewett

Published songs:

"Should I Speak"—issued as professional copy

Adler rejoined with Abbott twenty-two years after their initial collaboration. For his (presumably) final book, Abbott attempted to follow his path on **THE BOYS FROM SYRACUSE [November 23, 1938].** But *The Comedy of Errors* lent itself to the farcical treatment that *Twelfth Night* didn't; and, after all, Rodgers and Hart and Balanchine weren't along to contribute. Adler wrote a couple of catchy tunes, but they were of little help; the show was dreary, old-fashioned, and of far less interest than the 1968 off-Broadway rock adaptation YOUR OWN THING.

Richard Adler came to Broadway with two major musical comedy successes. Then collaborator Jerry Ross died, and Adler's career has never recovered. **KWAMINA [October 23, 1961]** showed his potential as a composer of serious theatre work, as well as proving he could write alone; but nothing of worth has been attempted since.

Meredith Willson

BORN: May 8, 1902   Mason City, Iowa
DIED: June 15, 1984   Santa Monica, California

As a small-town child, Meredith Willson did not take up the trumpet and lisp (like Winthrop Paroo in **THE MUSIC MAN [December 19, 1957]**). Rather, he sang barber shop and became proficient on flute and piccolo. His mother gave piano lessons, though. Willson spent the early Twenties in John Philip Sousa's band, then moved over to the New York Philharmonic. After the stock market crash, Willson went to the West Coast and began a profitable career in radio as performer and conductor.

[all music and lyrics by Meredith Willson]

THE LITTLE FOXES
February 15, 1939   National Theatre   410 performances

Play by Lillian Hellman
Incidental music by Meredith Willson
Produced and directed by Herman Shumlin
With Tallulah Bankhead

Published song:

"Never Feel Too Weary To Pray"—initial publication upon use in
  1941 movie version

Willson's career somehow led him to this first of two curious assignments. In 1940, he composed and arranged the score for Charles Chaplin's film *The Great Dictator*. His first song hit was the 1941 pop song "You And I." "May The Good Lord Bless And Keep You," theme song for Tallulah Bankhead's 1950 radio show, was an inspirational hit during the Korean War. In 1948 Willson wrote a slight, nostalgic semiautobiography. Frank Loesser, who had just successfully made the Hollywood-to-Broadway trip with **WHERE'S CHAR-LEY? [October 11, 1948],** suggested that Willson write a musical comedy based on his youth.

THE MUSIC MAN
December 19, 1957   Majestic Theatre   1,375 performances

Book by Meredith Willson with Franklin Lacey
(Based on *And There I Stood with My Piccolo* [memoir] by Willson)
Choreographed by Onna White
Directed by Morton DaCosta
Produced by Kermit Bloomgarden with Herbert Greene in association
   with Frank (Loesser) Productions
With Robert Preston, Barbara Cook, David Burns, and Pert Kelton

Published songs:

"Being In Love"—written for 1962 movie version
"Goodnight, My Someone"
"It's You"
"Lida Rose"
"Seventy-Six Trombones"
"Till There Was You"—revised lyric for 1950 nonshow song "Till
   I Met You"

Additional songs published in vocal score:

"Gary, Indiana"
"Iowa Stubborn"
"Marian The Librarian"
"My White Knight"
"Piano Lesson (If You Don't Mind My Saying So)"
"Pick-A-Little, Talk-A-Little"
"Rock Island (Train Talk)"
"The Sadder-But-Wiser Girl"
"Shipoopi"
"Sincere"
"The Wells Fargo Wagon"
"Will I Ever Tell You?"
"Ya Got Trouble"

After eight years and dozens of different versions, Willson's nostalgic musical finally made it to Broadway. With no theatre training, the composer used inventiveness and humor to come up with a delightful

score full of period musical "examples." **THE MUSIC MAN** became the biggest hit of the post-**MY FAIR LADY [Loewe: March
15, 1956]** Fifties. The heretofore nonsinging Robert Preston was an
inspired casting choice; besides, no one else wanted to do it. Barbara
Cook graduated from **CANDIDE [Bernstein: December 1, 1956]** to
musical comedy heroine. Frank Loesser, instigator of the project,
reaped multiple benefits as associate producer, publisher of the score,
and licensor of rights.

THE UNSINKABLE MOLLY BROWN
November 3, 1960   Winter Garden Theatre
532 performances

Book by Richard Morris
Choreographed by Peter Gennaro
Directed by Dore Schary
Produced by The Theatre Guild and Dore Schary
With Tammy Grimes, Harve Presnell, Cameron Prud'homme, and Edith
  Meiser

Published songs:

"Are You Sure?"
"Bea-u-ti-ful People Of Denver"
"Belly Up To The Bar Boys"
"Bon Jour (The Language Song)"
"Chick-A-Pen"
"Dolce Far Niente"
"He's My Friend"—written for 1964 movie version
"I Ain't Down Yet"
"I'll Never Say No"
"I've A'ready Started In"
"If I Knew"
"Keep-A-Hoppin' "

Additional songs published in vocal score:

"Colorado, My Home"
"Denver Police"
"Happy Birthday, Mrs. J. J. Brown"
"Leadville Johnny Brown (Soliloquy)"
"My Brass Bed"

A second homespun hit with much less appeal than **THE MUSIC
MAN [December 19, 1957]**. What had been spontaneous inventive-

ness in 1957 was too calculated here; but Willson's tunefulness and Tammy Grimes' performance carried the show to moderate success.

HERE'S LOVE
October 3, 1963   Shubert Theatre   334 performances

Book by Willson
(Based on *Miracle on 34th Street* [story] by Valentine Davies)
Choreographed by Michael Kidd
Directed and produced by Stuart Ostrow
With Janis Paige, Craig Stevens, Laurence Naismith, and Fred Gwynne

Published songs:

"Arm In Arm"
"The Big Clown Balloons"
"Dear Mister Santa Claus"—cut
"Expect Things To Happen"
"Here's Love"
"Love, Come Take Me Again"—cut
"My State, My Kansas, My Home"
"My Wish"
"Pine Cones And Holly Berries"—countermelody to 1951 nonshow
    song "It's Beginning To Look Like Christmas"
"That Man Over There"
"You Don't Know"

Additional songs recorded:

"The Bugle"
"Look Little Girl"
"She Hadda Go Back"

A sure-fire family hit based on the Christmas movie classic, **HERE'S LOVE** had no chance: If you can't do something better, don't do it. Director Norman Jewison departed during the tryout; Ostrow, a former Frank Music administrator with no producing *or* directing experience, took over himself. Outside of Michael Kidd's interesting Thanksgiving Day Parade opening, **HERE'S LOVE** had nothing but a decent-sized advance sale.

1491
A Romantic Speculation
[September 2, 1969]   Dorothy Chandler Pavilion ⟨Los Angeles, California⟩; closed during pre-Broadway tryout

Book by Willson and Richard Morris
(Based on an idea by Ed Ainsworth)
Choreographed by Danny Daniels
Directed by Morris
Produced by Edwin Lester (Los Angeles Civic Light Opera)
With John Cullum, Chita Rivera, Jean Fenn and Steve Arlen

Published songs:

None

Willson's final attempt for the theatre was this charmless Christopher Columbus operetta, which suffered a severe critical trouncing and quickly expired. Willson went back into retirement and died June 15, 1984 in Santa Monica, California.

Meredith Willson was not really a theatre composer; rather, he was an inventive novelty writer with one great show in him. **THE MUSIC MAN [December 19, 1957]** will always remain a one-of-a-kind classic. The composer's three other scores, however, are of little interest.

PART 3

Introduction

The late Fifties and early Sixties saw an influx of new theatre composers. Jerry Bock more or less consistently turned out satisfying, well-written scores, the only composer since Jule Styne to do so. Bob Merrill, a nontheatrical pop songwriter, was surprisingly effective. Stephen Sondheim entered the theatre as an exceptional lyricist, but his composing career didn't meet encouragement until the Seventies. Since then he has led the field in progressive *and* worthwhile musical theatre; unfortunately, no one seems capable of following. Charles Strouse and Cy Coleman were seriously trained musicians who reached Broadway with pop-styled musical comedies. Jerry Herman was in the Irving Berlin tradition, concentrating on catchy song hits rather than theatrical technique. The versatile John Kander began his career with a refreshing originality, while Harvey Schmidt has shown an individual, experimental style. Mitch Leigh, from the lower-than-pop field of television jingles, entered the theatre in 1965 with an all-time great musical. In the twenty years since, only one new composer—Stephen Schwartz—has been active enough to warrant inclusion here. Current composers with limited theatre output (Marvin Hamlisch, for example) are represented in Part 4.

Jerry Bock

BORN: November 23, 1928   New Haven, Connecticut

Jerry Bock grew up in Flushing, New York, where his father was a salesman. He began playing the piano at nine, and by high school was writing songs (including an amateur show to help raise money for a Navy hospital ship). In 1945 he went to the University of Wisconsin as a music major.

BIG AS LIFE
University of Wisconsin Golden Jubilee Production
[Circa May 1948]

Music by Jerrold Bock
Lyrics by Jack Royce
Book by Dave Pollard
Produced by The Haresfoot Club

Published songs:

"Everybody Loses"
"Forest In The Sky"—advertised but not published
"Great Wisconsin"
"Starway Lullaby"
"Today"—advertised but not published
"Why Sing A Love Song?"

A struggle between the radio industry and ASCAP over licensing fees caused formation of the competing BMI (Broadcast Music Inc.). For a brief period ASCAP songs were kept from the airwaves, and BMI went searching for substitute material. A scouring of college campuses resulted in the publishing of varsity shows by Bock and Sondheim **[PHINNEY'S RAINBOW: Circa 1948]**, among others. None of this material proved popular, but the college experiment paid off well: while Sondheim quickly moved to ASCAP, Bock remained with BMI and eventually provided them with a strong group of Broadway hits. As for **BIG AS LIFE,** "Why Sing A Love Song?" is interesting, if ultimately unsatisfying. Following graduation in 1949, Bock teamed with lyricist Larry Holofcener. They began writing songs and material for television, including the Sid Caesar "Your Show of Shows" series. They also practiced their craft writing revues at Tamiment, a Pennsylvania adult summer resort similar to Green Mansions (where Harold Rome had begun his career).

CATCH A STAR
September 6, 1955   Plymouth Theatre   23 performances

Music mostly by Sammy Fain and Philip Charig
Lyrics to Bock songs by Larry Holofcener
Sketches by Danny and Neil Simon
Conceived and supervised by Ray Golden
Produced by Sy Kleinman
With Pat Carroll, David Burns, and Marc Breaux

Published songs:

None

The Simon brothers were television writers who had worked with Bock and Holofcener at Tamiment. They gave Broadway a try, bringing along a few Bock-Holofcener songs. The show closed quickly and the Simons went back to television.

MR. WONDERFUL
March 22, 1956   Broadway Theatre   383 performances

Music and lyrics by Bock, Larry Holofcener, and George Weiss
Book by Joseph Stein and Will Glickman
Directed by Jack Donohue
Produced by Jule Styne and George Gilbert in association with Lester Osterman, Jr.
With Sammy Davis, Jr., Jack Carter, Pat Marshall, and Chita Rivera

Published songs:

"Ethel, Baby"
"Jacques D'Iraque"
"Mr. Wonderful"
"There"
"Too Close For Comfort"
"Without You I'm Nothing"

Additional songs recorded:
"Charlie Welch"
"I'm Available"
"I've Been Too Busy"
"Miami"
"1617 Broadway"
"Talk To Him"

Producer Jule Styne decided to bring Sammy Davis, Jr. to Broadway. Unable to assemble a vehicle, they went ahead without one. . . . Styne was too busy with stage, screen, and television projects to write the score himself. He auditioned songwriters and gambled on Bock and Holofcener (later adding pop composer George David Weiss to help). The resulting **MR. WONDERFUL** was a poor show, but the star presence of Davis and two hit songs—the title number and "Too Close For Comfort"—helped keep it alive.

THE ZIEGFELD FOLLIES OF 1956
[April 16, 1956]   Shubert Theatre ⟨Boston, Massachusetts⟩; closed during pre-Broadway tryout

Music mostly by others
Lyrics to Bock songs by Larry Holofcener
Sketches by Arnold B. Horwitt, Ronny Graham and others
Choreographed by Jack Cole
Directed by Christopher Hewett
Produced by Richard Kollmar and James W. Gardiner by arrangement
    with Billie Burke Ziegfeld
With Tallulah Bankhead, David Burns, Mae Barnes, Joan Diener, Carol
    Haney, Lee Becker, and Larry Kert

Published songs:
None

The last successful FOLLIES had been the Shuberts' wartime edition [April 1, 1943]. Since then there have been several unsuccessful attempts, including this disaster which contained the last of the Bock-Holofcener work. At the opening night party for the fabled Harry Warren flop SHANGRI-LA [June 13, 1956], leading man Jack Cassidy introduced Bock to Sheldon Harnick. Harnick had been successfully interpolating music and lyrics for revues, including the classic "Boston Beguine" for Alice Ghostley in NEW FACES OF 1952

[May 16, 1952]. Bock's publisher Tommy Valando went about getting the new team their first assignment.

THE BODY BEAUTIFUL
January 23, 1958   Broadway Theatre   60 performances

Lyrics by Sheldon Harnick
Book by Joseph Stein and Will Glickman
Choreographed by Herbert Ross
Directed by George Schaefer
Produced by Richard Kollmar and Albert W. Selden
With Jack Warden, Mindy Carson, Steve Forrest, and Barbara McNair

Published songs:

"All Of These And More"
"Hidden In My Heart"—cut
"Just My Luck"
"Leave Well Enough Alone"
"Uh-huh, Oh Yeah"

Additional song recorded:

"Summer Is"

Bock and Harnick's debut came with this quick failure. But the score was better than average, and attracted the notice of producers Robert Griffith and Harold Prince.

FIORELLO!
November 23, 1959   Broadhurst Theatre
795 performances

Lyrics by Sheldon Harnick
Book by Jerome Weidman and George Abbott
Choreographed by Peter Gennaro
Directed by Abbott
Produced by Robert E. Griffith and Harold S. Prince
With Tom Bosley, Patricia Wilson, Howard DaSilva, Eileen Rodgers, and
   Pat Stanley

Published songs:

"Gentleman Jimmy"
"I Love A Cop"—advertised but not published (except in vocal
   selection)

"Little Tin Box"
"Politics And Poker"
" 'Til Tomorrow"
"(I'll Marry) The Very Next Man"
"When Did I Fall In Love?"
"Where Do I Go From Here?"—cut

Additional songs recorded:

"The Bum Won"
"Home Again"
"Marie's Law"
"The Name's La Guardia"
"On The Side Of The Angels"
"Unfair"

Arthur Penn, director of the hit drama TWO FOR THE SEESAW [January 16, 1958], came to Griffith and Prince with the idea for his first musical. The producers, whose four hit musicals had been written by veteran Leonard Bernstein and theatrical novices Adler, Ross, Merrill, and Sondheim, selected Bock and Harnick for the score. Novelist Jerome Weidman (**I CAN GET IT FOR YOU WHOLE-SALE [Rome: March 22, 1962]**) was put to work on *his* first theatre project. As the La Guardia biography moved further into the musical comedy vein, Penn departed. Griffith/Prince standby George Abbott took over as director and colibrettist. The resulting **FIORELLO!** was one of Broadway's finest book musicals, joining **OF THEE I SING [Gershwin: December 26, 1931]** and **SOUTH PACIFIC [Rodgers: April 7, 1949]** as a Pulitzer Prize winner. The careful integration of the piece avoided inclusion of potential hit songs; but the score displayed Bock and Harnick's great feel for character work, expressing the thoughts and emotions of the more-or-less contemporary common man. This had been glimpsed in parts of **THE BODY BEAU-TIFUL [January 23, 1958]** score, and was to be seen consistently in the best of the team's work.

TENDERLOIN
October 17, 1960   46th Street Theatre   216 performances
Lyrics by Sheldon Harnick
Book by George Abbott and Jerome Weidman
(Based on the novel by Samuel Hopkins Adams)
Choreographed by Joe Layton

Directed by Abbott
Produced by Robert E. Griffith and Harold S. Prince
With Maurice Evans, Ron Husmann, Eileen Rodgers, and Margery Gray

Published songs:

"Artificial Flowers"
"Good Clean Fun"
"I Wonder What It's Like"—cut
"Lovely Laurie"—cut
"My Gentle Young Johnny"
"My Miss Mary"
"Tommy, Tommy"

Additional songs recorded:

"The Army Of The Just"
"Bless This Land"
"Dear Friend" [1st]—different than song from **SHE LOVES ME**
   [April 23, 1963]
"Dr. Brock"
"How The Money Changes Hands"
"Little Old New York"
"The Picture Of Happiness"
"Reform"
"The Trial"
"What's In It For You?"

Once again, the creators of a landmark musical attempted to follow up with a close copy; once again, the attempt failed. **TENDERLOIN** took place in a little older New York than **FIORELLO!** [**November 23, 1959**], and switched from inside politics to inside vice. Harnick, Layton, and company captured the color of the bad guys so well (in numbers like the opening, "Little Old New York," and the sparkling "Picture Of Happiness") that the good guys seemed bland and sappy. This included the star role, played by Shakespearean actor Maurice Evans. Dull leading characters are fatal to musical comedies. Bock, for his part, wrote a fine period score for **TENDERLOIN,** raucously energetic on the one hand and literately sentimental on the other.

NEVER TOO LATE
November 27, 1962   Playhouse Theatre
1,007 performances

Play by Sumner Arthur Long
Incidental music mostly by John **Kander**
Directed by George Abbott
Produced by Elliot Martin and Daniel Hollywood
With Paul Ford, Maureen O'Sullivan, and Orson Bean

Published song:

"Never Too Late" (lyric by Sheldon Harnick)

MAN IN THE MOON
Marionette Show
April 11, 1963   Biltmore Theatre   7 performances

Lyrics by Sheldon Harnick
Book by Arthur Burns
(Based on a story by Bil Baird)
Directed by Gerald Freedman
Produced by Arthur Cantor and Joseph Harris
With Bil and Cora Baird's Marionettes

Published song:

"Worlds Apart"

Additional songs recorded:

"Ain't You Never Been Afraid?"
"Itch To Be Rich"
"Look Where I Am"
"You Treacherous Man"

Bock and Harnick set a new level for marionette-show songs in this fantasy, which followed Broadway with an overseas State Department tour.

SHE LOVES ME
The Happiest Musical
April 23, 1963   Eugene O'Neill Theatre   302 performances

Lyrics by Sheldon Harnick
Book by Joe Masteroff
(Based on *The Shop Around the Corner* [play] by Miklos Laszlo)
Choreographed by Carol Haney
Directed by Harold Prince
Produced by Prince in association with Lawrence J. Kasha and Philip C.
   McKenna
With Barbara Cook, Daniel Massey, Jack Cassidy, and Barbara Baxley

Published songs:

"Days Gone By"
"Dear Friend" [2nd]—different than song from **TENDERLOIN**
  [October 17, 1960]
"Grand Knowing You"
"Ilona"—advertised but not published (except in vocal selection)
"She Loves Me"
"Tonight At Eight"
"Will He Like Me?"

Additional songs recorded:

"Good Morning, Good Day"
"Good Bye, Georg"
"I Don't Know His Name"
"I Resolve"
"Ice Cream"
"No More Candy"
"Perspective"
"A Romantic Atmosphere"
"Sounds While Selling"
"Tango Tragique"
"Thank You, Madam"
"Three Letters"
"A Trip To The Library"
"Try Me"
"Twelve Days To Christmas"
"Where's My Shoe?"

Director Harold Prince, whose Broadway debut had been as replacement on **A FAMILY AFFAIR [Kander: January 27, 1962]**, now prepared his first musical from inception. Bock and Harnick wrote their finest score for this romantic/comic valentine, which was given a cream-puff production and perfectly played. Yet **SHE LOVES ME** failed, due to unforseeable managerial miscalculations in promotion and booking. The score survives, and remains a joy. Barbara Cook had her best role as the heroine, and Jack Cassidy, who had introduced Bock and Harnick, received a Tony Award for his supporting role. Carol Haney, featured dancer in **THE PAJAMA GAME [Adler: May 13, 1954]**, choreographed.

TO BROADWAY WITH LOVE
April 22, 1964   Texas Pavilion Music Hall ⟨New York World's Fair⟩

Title theme and original material by Jerry Bock
Lyrics to Bock songs by Sheldon Harnick
Choreographed by Donald Saddler
Conceived and directed by Morton DaCosta
Produced by George Schaeffer and Angus G. Wynne, Jr.
With Carmen Alvarez, Patti Karr, Rod Perry, and Sheila Smith

Recorded Songs:

"Beautiful Lady"
"Mata Hari Mine"
"Popsicles In Paris"
"Remember Radio"
"To Broadway With Love"

An unsuccessful World's Fair revue made up mostly of old-time Broadway and popular hits.

FIDDLER ON THE ROOF
September 22, 1964   Imperial Theatre   3,242 performances

Lyrics by Sheldon Harnick
Book by Joseph Stein
(Based on stories by Sholom Aleichem)
Directed and choreographed by Jerome Robbins
Produced by Harold Prince
With Zero Mostel, Maria Karnilova, and Beatrice Arthur

Published songs:

"Anatevka"—initial publication upon use in 1971 movie version
"Do You Love Me?"—initial publication upon use in movie version
"Far From The Home I Love"—initial publication upon use in
    movie version
"Fiddler On The Roof (Theme)"—nonshow lyric
"If I Were A Rich Man"
"Matchmaker, Matchmaker"
"Miracle Of Miracles"—initial publication upon use in movie
    version
"Now I Have Everything"
"Sabbath Prayer"—initial publication upon use in movie version

"Sunrise, Sunset"
"To Life"—initial publication upon use in movie version
"Tradition"—initial publication upon use in movie version

Additional songs published in vocal score:

"Chava Sequence (Little Chavaleh)"
"The Dream"
"The Rumor"
"Tevye's Monologue (They Gave Each Other A Pledge)"
"Tevye's Rebuttal"
"Wedding Dance" [instrumental]

Additional songs recorded:

"How Much Richer Could One Man Be?"—cut
"When Messiah Comes"—cut

One of the most successful and important musicals in Broadway history. Bock and Harnick began work with Joseph Stein, librettist of Bock's first two musicals, following the failure of **TENDERLOIN [October 17, 1960].** In late 1963 producer Fred Coe was joined by Harold Prince (Coe was to disappear from the credits during the pre-Broadway tryout). Prince brought along Jerome Robbins, who had just departed the **FUNNY GIRL** project (see **[Styne: March 26, 1964]**). **FIDDLER**'s strong theme—as interpreted by Robbins—brought the piece worldwide acclaim. But compared to the overall excellence of the show, the score must be judged slightly disappointing. Robbins' previous **WEST SIDE STORY [Bernstein: September 26, 1957]** and **GYPSY [Styne: May 21, 1959]** had music which captured the essence of the material throughout. The same cannot be said for **FIDDLER.** Much of the score was perfect, especially "Tradition," "Sabbath Prayer," "If I Were A Rich Man," and the "Chava Sequence." Other songs—"Matchmaker, Matchmaker" and "Sunrise, Sunset"—became popular hits. But while **FIDDLER ON THE ROOF** was certainly Bock and Harnick's best musical, their best score—at least in this man's opinion—was written for **SHE LOVES ME [April 23, 1963].**

BAKER STREET
February 16, 1965   Broadway Theatre   313 performances

Music and lyrics mostly by Marian Grudeff and Raymond Jessel
Lyrics to Bock songs by Sheldon Harnick

Book by Jerome Coopersmith
(Based on stories by Sir Arthur Conan Doyle)
Choreographed by Lee Becker Theodore
Directed by Harold Prince
Produced by Alexander H. Cohen
With Fritz Weaver, Inga Swenson, and Martin Gabel

Published songs:

"Buffalo Belle"—cut
"Cold, Clear World"
"I Shall Miss You, Holmes"
"I'm In London Again"

Alex Cohen equipped **BAKER STREET** with the most spectacular front-of-house marquee in Broadway history and little else. Bock and Harnick answered Prince's calls for help by interpolating four songs (publicly credited to Grudeff and Jessel).

GENERATION
October 6, 1965   Morosco Theatre   300 performances

Play by William Goodhart
Incidental music by Jerry Bock
Directed by Gene Saks
Produced by Frederick Brisson
With Henry Fonda and Holly Turner

Published songs:

None

Bock wrote a title song to a lyric by the playwright.

THE APPLE TREE
October 18, 1966   Shubert Theatre   463 performances

Lyrics by Sheldon Harnick
Book by Bock and Harnick
Additional material by Jerome Coopersmith
(Based on stories by Mark Twain, Frank R. Stockton, and Jules Feiffer)
Choreographed by Lee Becker Theodore and Herbert Ross
Directed by Mike Nichols
Produced by Stuart Ostrow
With Barbara Harris, Larry Blyden, and Alan Alda

Published songs:

"The Apple Tree (Forbidden Fruit)"
"Beautiful, Beautiful World"
"I'm Lost"—cut
"I've Got What You Want"
"What Makes Me Love Him?"

Additional songs published in vocal score:

"Ai, Ai!"
"Eve"
"Feelings"
"Fish"
"Forbidden Love (In Gaul)"
"Friends"
"Gorgeous"
"Here In Eden"
"I Know"
"I'll Tell You A Truth"
"Lullaby (Go To Sleep Whatever You Are)"
"Make Way"
"Oh, To Be A Movie Star"
"Prisoner, Choose!"
"Razor Teeth"
"Real"
"Tiger, Tiger"
"Wealth"
"Which Door?"
"Who Is She?"

An interesting idea—an evening of three one-act musicals—proved difficult to pull off. Jerome Robbins and Coopersmith left the project early on; musical novice Mike Nichols came in (bringing along *Passionella* from **THE WORLD OF JULES FEIFFER [Sondheim: July, 2, 1962]**). The three bites of **THE APPLE TREE** were sentimental, costume operetta-ish, and contemporary farce-fantasy. Not surprisingly, the third bite brought forth the best of Bock and Harnick, but too late to make up for the pastoral first and dreary second acts.

HER FIRST ROMAN
October 20, 1968   Lunt-Fontanne Theatre
17 performances

Book, music and lyrics mostly by Ervin Drake
Lyrics to Bock songs by Sheldon Harnick
(Based on *Caesar and Cleopatra* [play] by George Bernard Shaw)
Choreographed by Dania Krupska
Directed by Derek Goldby
Produced by Joseph Cates and Henry Fownes (in association with Warner
    Brothers-7 Arts)
With Richard Kiley, Leslie Uggams and Claudia McNeil

Published songs:

None

The producers were successful in securing the closely guarded rights,
only the third musical adaptation of Shaw ever authorized. Then the
assignment was given to pop composer Ervin Drake, who had done
the score for Cates' long-running but unsuccessful WHAT MAKES
SAMMY RUN? [February 27, 1964]; Drake's librettist qualifications
were even less impressive. The director and choreographer (and their
replacements) were replaced on the road. Bock and Harnick came in
for last-minute cosmetic surgery and contributed "Caesar Is Wrong,"
"Old Gentleman," and "Ptolemy" (all unpublished, publicly credited
to Drake).

THE ROTHSCHILDS
October 19, 1970   Lunt-Fontanne Theatre
507 performances

Lyrics by Sheldon Harnick
Book by Sherman Yellen
(Based on the biography by Frederic Morton)
Directed and choreographed by Michael Kidd
Produced by Lester Osterman and Hillard Elkins
With Hal Linden, Leila Martin, Paul Hecht, Keene Curtis, and Jill
    Clayburgh

Published songs:

"I'm In Love! I'm In Love!"
"In My Own Lifetime"
"One Room"
"Valse De Rothschild (Never Again)"

Additional songs published in vocal selection:

"Everything"
"Rothschild And Sons"
"Sons"

Additional songs recorded:

"Allons"
"Bonds"
"Give England Strength"
"Have You Ever Seen A Prettier Little Congress?"
"He Tossed A Coin"
"Pleasure And Privilege"
"Stability"
"They Say"
"This Amazing London Town"

A theatre-party special, calculated to please audiences who were still thronging to the six-year-old **FIDDLER ON THE ROOF [September 22, 1964]**. But Meyer Rothschild and five sons hadn't the charm of Tevye and five daughters. The weak book lacked warmth and interest, Bock and Harnick were a century out of their element, and there was no Robbins or Prince in sight. The producers who assembled the package had a string of poor musicals to their credit. Director Derek Goldby, who had evidently impressed Bock and Harnick when they tried to patch **HER FIRST ROMAN [October 20, 1968]** together, had no other musical experience and was soon gone. Michael Kidd, on hand all along as choreographer, was eventually asked to take over, but much too late to deal with the problems.

Following **THE ROTHSCHILDS,** Bock ended his twelve-year partnership with Sheldon Harnick. The composer then wrote a mystery-musical (with his own lyrics) which was never produced, and nothing since. Bock's reasons for self-imposed retirement are unknown, although his two final shows were criticized for not being as good as **FIDDLER ON THE ROOF [September 22, 1964]**. (Of course they were not as good as **FIDDLER ON THE ROOF;** how many shows are?) Jerry Bock is certainly one of today's finest theatre composers. He hasn't been heard from for fifteen years, and that's not good for Broadway.

Bob Merrill

BORN: May 17, 1920   Atlantic City, New Jersey

Following military service, Bob Merrill went to Hollywood as an MGM dialogue director before moving to television writing. An interest in songwriting led to a highly profitable pop song career, highlighted by the 1950 "If I Knew You Were Comin' I'd've Baked A Cake" (with Al Hoffman and Clem Watts) and "How Much Is That Doggie In The Window?" in 1953. His success with novelty songs was such that he had difficulty getting a serious hearing.

[all music and lyrics by Bob Merrill]

NEW GIRL IN TOWN
May 14, 1957   46th Street Theatre   431 performances

Book and direction by George Abbott
(Based on *Anna Christie* [play] by Eugene O'Neill)
Choreographed by Bob Fosse
Produced by Frederick Brisson, Robert E. Griffith, and Harold S. Prince
With Gwen Verdon, Thelma Ritter, George Wallace, and Cameron
  Prud'homme

Published songs:

"At The Check Apron Ball"
"Did You Close Your Eyes?"
"Flings"
"Here We Are Again"—cut
"If That Was Love"
"It's Good To Be Alive"
"Look At 'Er"
"Theme From New Girl In Town" [instrumental]—nonlyric
  version of "Anna Lilla"
"Sunshine Girl"
"You're My Friend, Ain'tcha?"

Additional songs recorded:

"Anna Lilla"
"Chess And Checkers"
"On The Farm"
"Roll Yer Socks Up"
"There Ain't No Flies On Me"
"Ven I Valse"

MGM dropped *A Saint She Ain't,* their Doris Day musical remake of *Anna Christie.* Griffith, Prince, and Abbott heard the score and brought Merrill to Broadway. Extreme tryout problems resulted in a rift between the producers/authors and the **DAMN YANKEES [Adler: May 5, 1955]** team of Verdon and Fosse. The result was a moderate hit, thanks chiefly to Verdon and Thelma Ritter (who shared the Tony Award for Best Actress in a Musical). Griffith, Prince, and Abbott went looking for new songwriters (**FIORELLO! [Bock: November 23, 1959]**); Fosse and Verdon went looking for new producers (**REDHEAD [PART 4: February 5, 1959]**); and Merrill was called by David Merrick.

TAKE ME ALONG
October 22, 1959   Shubert Theatre   448 performances

Book by Joseph Stein and Robert Russell
(Based on *Ah, Wilderness* [play] by Eugene O'Neill)
Choreographed by Onna White
Directed by Peter Glenville
Produced by David Merrick
With Jackie Gleason, Eileen Herlie, Walter Pidgeon, and Robert Morse

Published songs:

"But Yours"
"I Get Embarrassed"
"I Would Die"
"Little Green Snake"
"Nine O'Clock"
"Promise Me A Rose"
"Sid, Ol' Kid"
"Staying Young"
"Take Me Along"

Additional songs recorded:

"Oh, Please"
"The Parade"
"That's How It Starts"
"Volunteer Firemen Picnic (Ladies With A Liberal Point Of View)"
"We're Home"
"Wint's Song"

Merrill tried a second O'Neill adaptation, this time using the play-wright's more suitable turn-of-the-century comedy. But the librettists concentrated on the secondary comic couple, and Merrill gave them show-stopping material. This could have worked if the George M. Cohan part had been diminished; but with a star (Walter Pidgeon) cast in the role, the relatively colorless character was given an equivalently sized part. **TAKE ME ALONG** might have succeeded anyway; it had a charming score, nostalgic physical production, and fine performances from Eileen Herlie and Robert Morse. But off-stage problems developed with TV star Jackie Gleason, who finally withdrew. Merrill's first show had been successful although not very good; **TAKE ME ALONG** was considerably better but barely managed to break even.

CARNIVAL!
April 13, 1961   Imperial Theatre   719 performances

Book by Michael Stewart
(Based on material by Helen Deutsch)
Directed and choreographed by Gower Champion
Produced by David Merrick
With Anna Maria Alberghetti, Jerry Orbach, Kaye Ballard, James
  Mitchell, and Horr'ble Henry

Published songs:

"Beautiful Candy"
"Grand Imperial Cirque De Paris"
"Her Face"
"It Was Always You"
"Mira (Can You Imagine That?)"
"She's My Love"
"Theme From Carnival! (Love Makes The World Go Round)"

"Three Puppet Songs: Golden, Delicious Fish; The Rich; Yum-
   Ticky-Tum-Tum"
"Yes, My Heart"

Additional song published in piano selection:

"Direct From Vienna"

Additional songs recorded:

"Everybody Likes You"
"Humming"
"I Hate Him"
"I've Got To Find A Reason"
"Sword, Rose And Cape"
"A Very Nice Man"

David Merrick had been particularly successful with Gallic shows,
from **FANNY [Rome: November 4, 1954]** to the revue LA PLUME
DE MA TANTE [September 29, 1960]. Securing the rights to the
popular 1953 movie *Lili,* Merrick wisely put it in the hands of Gower
Champion (and librettist Michael Stewart) of the surprise hit **BYE
BYE BIRDIE [Strouse: April 14, 1960]**. Merrill, who did well enough
on his first Merrick assignment, came up with his best score. **CAR-
NIVAL!** was magical: staging, songs and all (including Broadway's
best puppets ever). Merrill even managed to top the movie's hit theme
song ("Hi-Lili, Hi-Lo") with "Love Makes The World Go Round."

HELLO, DOLLY!
January 16, 1964   St. James Theatre   2,844 performances

Music and lyrics mostly by Jerry **Herman** (also see **Strouse**)
Books by Michael Stewart
(Based on *The Matchmaker* [play] by Thornton Wilder)
Directed and choreographed by Gower Champion
Produced by David Merrick
With Carol Channing, David Burns, Eileen Brennan, and Charles Nelson
   Reilly

Published song:

"Elegance"

Additional song published in vocal score:

"Motherhood March"

Merrill, busy on Merrick's **FUNNY GIRL [Styne: March 26, 1964]**, was asked for help during **DOLLY**'s Detroit dilemma. He had successfully worked with Champion and Stewart on Merrick's **CARNIVAL! [April 13, 1961]**, as had fellow doctors Lee Adams and Charles Strouse on **BYE BYE BIRDIE [April 14, 1960]**. The two Merrill contributions above were interpolated, although publicly credited to Herman. The artful "Elegance," in fact, seems to have been originally written for **NEW GIRL IN TOWN [May 14, 1957]**.

FUNNY GIRL
see Styne [March 26, 1964]

BREAKFAST AT TIFFANY'S
[December 14, 1966]   Majestic Theatre; closed during Broadway previews

Book by Abe Burrows
Book revised by Edward Albee
(Based on the novella by Truman Capote)
Choreographed by Michael Kidd
Directed by Joseph Anthony
Produced by David Merrick
With Mary Tyler Moore, Richard Chamberlain, Art Lund, and Sally
  Kellerman
NOTE: **HOLLY GOLIGHTLY,** pre-Broadway title

Songs issued in professional copies:

"Breakfast At Tiffany's"
"Ciao, Compare"
"Holly Golightly"
"I've Got A Penny"—cut
"Travellin' "—cut
"You've Never Kissed Her"

Merrill, in his fourth Merrick assignment, came up with one of Broadway's all-time fiascos. A popular novel, a smash movie, and two major TV stars added up to a record advance sale; but Merrick chose to close what he considered a hopelessly poor show. A satisfactory point of view for the treatment of the prostitute heroine was never found, even with a drastic tryout revision (Abe Burrows—who took over from Nunnally Johnson—to Edward Albee?). Merrill's work, though, had charm in places, particularly in the two title songs. Mary Tyler Moore's much-heralded musical comedy debut never happened, and she went back to Hollywood to try her luck in her own television series.

HENRY, SWEET HENRY
October 23, 1967   Palace Theatre   80 performances

Book by Nunnally Johnson
(Based on *The World of Henry Orient* [novel] by Nora Johnson)
Choreographed by Michael Bennett
Directed by George Roy Hill
Produced by Edward Specter Productions and Norman Twain
With Don Ameche, Carol Bruce, Robin Wilson, Louise Lasser, and Alice
    Playten

Published songs:

"Dearest Darling"—cut; issued in professional copy
"Do You Ever Go To Boston?"
"Henry, Sweet Henry"
"Here I Am"
"I Wonder How It Is To Dance With A Boy"
"Love Of My Life"—cut; issued in professional copy
"My Kind Of Person"—cut; issued in professional copy
"Somebody Someplace"—cut; issued in professional copy
"Weary Near To Dyin' "
"You Might Get To Like Me"—cut; issued in professional copy

Additional songs recorded:

"Academic Fugue"
"I'm Blue Too"
"In Some Little World"
"Nobody Steps On Kafritz"
"Pillar To Post"
"People Watchers"
"Poor Little Person"—revised version of "My Kind Of Person"
    (cut)
"To Be Artistic"
"Woman In Love"

Merrill adapted another popular novel/movie, again meeting with failure. *Ah, Wilderness* and *Lili* had been warm, tender stories about

innocents; Holly Golightly and Henry Orient were jaded New Yorkers. The sophisticated adults of **HENRY, SWEET HENRY** were
obnoxious and uninteresting; the teenage girls were amusing and
sympathetic. Merrill's tender material for the latter (including "Here
I Am" and "In Some Little World") was overpowered by the former, and the show—in a season where it should have been a hit—
defeated itself. Hired to choreograph was Michael Bennett, a
Michael Kidd dancer in **SUBWAYS ARE FOR SLEEPING [Styne:
December 27, 1961]** and **HERE'S LOVE [Willson: October 3, 1963]**.
Bennett had made his choreographic debut with the short-lived A
JOYFUL NOISE [December 15, 1966].

PRETTYBELLE
see Styne [February 1, 1971]

SUGAR
see Styne [April 9, 1972]

THE PRINCE OF GRAND STREET
*[March 7, 1978]   Forrest Theatre ⟨Philadelphia,
Pennsylvania⟩; closed during pre-Broadway tryout*

Book by Merrill
Choreographed by Lee Becker Theodore
Directed by Gene Saks
Produced by Robert Whitehead, Roger L. Stevens, and The Shubert
    Organization
With Robert Preston, Sam Levene, Neva Small, Werner Klemperer, and
    Bernice Massi

Published songs:

None

Merrill's Broadway career has been virtually ended by the combination of **BREAKFAST AT TIFFANY'S [December 14, 1966]**,
PRETTYBELLE [February 1, 1971] and **THE PRINCE OF
GRAND STREET**—three star vehicles with great potential and heavy
advance theatre party bookings. Producers and theatre owners hate
to give back ticket money. **THE PRINCE OF GRAND STREET**
was patterned after Jacob Adler, patriarch of the Yiddish Theatre.
Robert Preston is one of Broadway's finest and most charming ac-

tors, equally at home in drama and musical—but *Jacob Adler?* (In the second act, the aging Yiddish Prince portrayed Huckleberry Finn. Seems that Adler was a great chum of Mark Twain.) Preston also closed out of town when Stuart Ostrow cast him as Pancho Villa in WE TAKE THE TOWN [February 19, 1962]. The actors and writers get blamed for these things, and suffer through the painful performances (no matter how few). But what about the producers who choose the material?

Bob Merrill's Broadway career has encompassed only six musicals (plus three sets of lyrics to Jule Styne scores). He has been at his best when adapting his pop music style into family entertainment like **CARNIVAL!** [April 13, 1961]; the more sophisticated attempts have been coarse and less appealing. In a day when an **ANNIE [Strouse: April 21, 1977]** can find an audience, Merrill's talents certainly should not be overlooked.

Stephen Sondheim

BORN: March 22, 1930   New York, New York

At the age of ten, Stephen Sondheim moved from Manhattan to Doylestown, Pennsylvania—Doylestown, home of Oscar Hammerstein 2nd. A friendship with the lyricist's son led to a close teacher/student relationship with the man who had set new musical theatre boundaries in his work with Jerome Kern, and who was just then writing **OKLAHOMA! [Rodgers: March 31, 1943]** and **CAROUSEL [Rodgers: April 19, 1945]**. There was little question of career choice, and Sondheim was already writing amateur shows during the War. As Hammerstein was struggling through **ALLEGRO [Rodgers: October 10, 1947]** and future Broadway lyricists were no doubt delighting over E. Y. Harburg's **FINIAN'S RAINBOW [Lane: January 10, 1947]** conundrums, Sondheim went off to Williams College as a music major.

[all music and lyrics by Stephen Sondheim unless indicated]

PHINNEY'S RAINBOW
Williams College Show
[Circa May 1948]   Adams Memorial Theatre
⟨Williamstown, Massachusetts⟩

Book by Sondheim and Josiah T. S. Horton
Directed by David C. Bryant
Produced by Cap and Bells, Inc.

Published songs:

"How Do I Know?"
"Phinney's Rainbow"
"Still Got My Heart"

Sondheim's first published theatre work came from this college show, courtesy of the BMI talent search (see **BIG AS LIFE [Bock: Circa**

May 1948]). The title was borrowed from a recent Broadway hit; the songs, though, were far removed from Glocca Morra. As composer Sondheim's first Broadway musical wasn't until fourteen years later, it's interesting to see his first works as advanced as they are. The title song has a strong, complex rhythm (which gets *too* complex along the way); the lyric—oddly enough—is upbeat inspirational, closely echoing the less rhythmic "You'll Never Walk Alone." "Still Got My Heart" is particularly interesting for its effective harmonic wanderings and a couple of syncopational tricks.

ALL THAT GLITTERS
Williams College Show
[March 19, 1949]   Adams Memorial Theatre
⟨*Williamstown, Massachusetts*⟩

Book by Sondheim
(Based on *Beggar on Horseback* [play] by George S. Kaufman and Moss Hart)
Directed by David C. Bryant
Produced by Cap and Bells, Inc.
With Ronald Moir, Betty Dissell, Jeanette Forsey, and Donald Rackerby

Songs published in vocal selection:

"I Love You Etcetera"
"I Must Be Dreaming"
"I Need Love"
"Let's Not Fall In Love"
"When I See You"

Sondheim's first Kaufman and Hart adaptation was far more favorably received than his second. "When I See You" stands out, surely his prettiest ballad until **ANYONE CAN WHISTLE [April 4, 1964]**. One is struck by the complexities—nineteen-year-old Sondheim tried things no one else in those days (except Blitzstein or Duke) was doing. One wonders, though, how a 1949 college soprano coped with the key shifts into and throughout the fascinating bridge. "Let's Not Fall In Love" is the best of the others, a light rhythm number. Surprisingly, in these first eight songs Sondheim was least advanced in lyric and melody; rhythmically, he was often *too* intricate.

GIRLS OF SUMMER
November 19, 1956   Longacre Theatre   56 performances

Play by N. Richard Nash
Incidental music by Sondheim
Directed by Jack Garfein
Produced by Cheryl Crawford
With Shelley Winters, Pat Hingle, and George Peppard

Published song:

"Girls Of Summer"

Graduating from Williams, Sondheim studied with avant-garde composer Milton Babbitt on a fellowship. He then worked with George
Oppenheimer scripting the aprés-garde TV series "Topper." Sondheim's first Broadway assignment came in 1954, writing music and
lyrics for the unproduced SATURDAY NIGHT; the show was abandoned when producer/designer Lemuel Ayers (see **OUT OF THIS
WORLD [Porter: December 21, 1950]**) died. By 1956 Sondheim was
collaborating on the lyrics to **WEST SIDE STORY [Bernstein:
September 26, 1957]**. The producer (at the time) was Cheryl Crawford; she gave Sondheim his first Broadway hearing with the incidental music assignment on **GIRLS OF SUMMER**. The title song is
Sondheim at his jazziest.

WEST SIDE STORY
see Bernstein [September 26, 1957]

GYPSY
see Styne [May 21, 1959]

INVITATION TO A MARCH
October 29, 1960   Music Box Theatre   113 performances

Play by Arthur Laurents
Incidental music by Sondheim
Directed by Laurents
Produced by The Theatre Guild
With Celeste Holm, Madeleine Sherwood, Eileen Heckart, Jane Fonda,
   and James MacArthur

Published songs:

None

Arthur Laurents had been responsible for bringing Sondheim in on
WEST SIDE STORY [Bernstein: September 26, 1957]; he had also

done the libretto for Sondheim's **GYPSY** [Styne: May 21, 1959]. The pair were to work together twice more, with less satisfying results.

A FUNNY THING HAPPENED ON THE WAY TO THE FORUM
May 8, 1962   Alvin Theatre   964 performances

Book by Burt Shevelove and Larry Gelbart
(Based on plays by Plautus)
Choreographed by Jack Cole
Directed by George Abbott
Produced by Harold Prince
With Zero Mostel, Jack Gilford, David Burns, and John Carradine

Published songs:

"Comedy Tonight"
"Everybody Ought To Have A Maid"
"I Do Like You"—cut
"Love, I Hear"
"Love Is In The Air"—cut
"Lovely"
"That'll Show Him"
"Your Eyes Are Blue"—cut

Additional songs published in vocal score:

"Bring Me My Bride"
"Free"
"Funeral Sequence"
"The House Of Marcus Lycus" [2nd]—scene version
"I'm Calm"
"Impossible"
"Pretty Little Picture"
"That Dirty Old Man"

Additional songs recorded:

"Echo Song"—cut
"The House Of Marcus Lycus" [1st]—cut; song version
"There's Something About A War"

Composer Sondheim—already highly successful as a lyricist—finally came to Broadway with this very funny vaudeville farce. The material demanded a score far less adventurous than Sondheim's previous work; the result worked well, with the fine comedy lyrics on level with the book. The music was slightly tamer, except for the delectable "Everybody Ought To Have A Maid." It wasn't until **COMPANY [April 26, 1970]**—a long eight years later—that the composer began to receive recognition. Harold Prince produced his first musical on his own: partner Robert Griffith died June 7, 1961. George Abbott had his final musical success (with an assist from Jerome Robbins, who had initially been on the project). Zero Mostel became an unlikely musical comedy hero, and Jack Gilford became an unlikelier musical comedy "heroine."

THE WORLD OF JULES FEIFFER
[July 2, 1962]   Hunterdon Hills Playhouse ⟨Clinton, New Jersey⟩; summer stock tryout

Sketches by Jules Feiffer
Music and lyrics by Stephen Sondheim
Directed by Mike Nichols
Produced by Lewis Allen and Harry Rigby
With Ronny Graham, Dorothy Loudon, and Paul Sand

Published songs:
None

Mike Nichols first tried his hand at legit directing with this comedy revue. Included was a one-act musical version of Feiffer's *Passionella*. What has surfaced of Sondheim's work—"I'd Be Truly Content"—compares favorably with the rather good "Oh, To Be A Movie Star" from **THE APPLE TREE [Bock: October 18, 1966]**. And Dorothy Loudon, who spent the next fifteen years giving life to a string of musical fatalities (until Nichols put her in **ANNIE [Strouse: April 21, 1977]**), surely must have made an interesting "mooo-vie" star.

HOT SPOT
April 19, 1963   Majestic Theatre. 43 performances

Music mostly by Mary Rodgers
Lyrics mostly by Martin Charnin
Book by Jack Weinstock and Willie Gilbert
Choreographed by Onna White
Directed by Morton DaCosta

Produced by Robert Fryer and Lawrence Carr, in association with John
  Herman
With Judy Holliday, Joseph Campanella, Joe Bova, Mary Louise Wilson,
  and George Furth

Published songs:

None

Sondheim, friend of composer Rodgers, came in to help out on the
opening number, "Don't Laugh" (music and lyrics by Rodgers,
Sondheim and Charnin). But **HOT SPOT**—Broadway's Peace Corps
musical comedy—was beyond aid.

ANYONE CAN WHISTLE
A Wild New Musical
April 4, 1964   Majestic Theatre   9 performances

Book and direction by Arthur Laurents
Choreographed by Herbert Ross
Produced by Kermit Bloomgarden and Diana Krasny
With Angela Lansbury, Lee Remick, and Harry Guardino

Published songs:

"Anyone Can Whistle"
"Come Play Wiz Me"
"Everybody Says Don't"
"I've Got You To Lean On"
"A Parade In Town"
"See What It Gets You"
"There Won't Be Trumpets"—cut
"With So Little To Be Sure Of"

Additional songs published in vocal score:

"A-1 March"
"Cora's Chase (Lock 'Em Up)"
"I'm Like The Bluebird"
"Me And My Town"
"Miracle Song"
"Opposites"
"Run For Your Lives"
"Simple (A Is One)"
"Watchcries"

This wild new musical was *too* wild and new (and muddled) to compete with **HELLO, DOLLY!** [Herman: January 16, 1964] and **FUNNY GIRL** [Styne: March 26, 1964]. The score showed composer Sondheim well developed, with exciting extended musical sequences, intricate choral work and many surprises. **ANYONE CAN WHISTLE** was complex enough to scare away composing jobs for the rest of the decade. Angela Lansbury soon became an important musical comedy star—but not via Sondheim.

DO I HEAR A WALTZ?
see Rodgers [March 18, 1965]

THE MAD SHOW
January 9, 1966   New Theatre ⟨off-Broadway⟩
871 performances

Music by Mary Rodgers
Lyrics mostly by Marshall Barer
Book by Larry Siegel and Stan Hart
(Based on *Mad* magazine)
Directed by Steven Vinaver
Produced by Ivor David Balding
With Linda Lavin, Paul Sand, Dick Libertini and Jo Anne Worley

Song published in "Hansen Treasury of Stephen Sondheim Songs":

"The Boy From" (music by Rodgers, lyric by "Esteban Ria Nido")

Sondheim contributed this nonsense lyric in the Ipanema vein to music by Mary Rodgers. Sondheim's only musical activity between **ANYONE CAN WHISTLE [April 4, 1964]** and **COMPANY [April 26, 1970]** was for the one-performance TV mini-musical *Evening Primrose* [November 16, 1966].

COMPANY
April 26, 1970   Alvin Theatre   706 performances

Book by George Furth
Choreographed by Michael Bennett
Directed by Harold Prince
Produced by Prince in association with Ruth Mitchell
With Dean Jones, Elaine Stritch, Barbara Barrie, and Donna McKechnie

Published songs:

"Another Hundred People"
"Being Alive"
"Company"
"The Ladies Who Lunch"
"The Little Things You Do Together"
"Side By Side By Side"
"Someone Is Waiting"
"Sorry-Grateful"
"You Could Drive A Person Crazy"

Additional songs published in vocal score:

"Barcelona"
"Getting Married Today"
"Have I Got A Girl For You"
"Overture (Bobby, Bobby)"
"Poor Baby"
"Tick-Tock" [instrumental]
"What Would We Do Without You?"

Additional songs recorded:

"Happily Ever After"—cut
"Marry Me A Little"—cut

Sondheim returned to Broadway with the most important new musical since **FIDDLER ON THE ROOF [Bock: September 24, 1964].** Director Harold Prince had broken ground with **CABARET [Kander: November 20, 1966],** in which only the physical production and parts of the score kept pace. In Sondheim, Prince found an equally innovative collaborator. They began a highly imaginative, not always artistically successful (but always worthwhile) collaboration. Important co-workers: the Messrs. Bennett, Aronson and Tunick. "Another Hundred People," "Being Alive," "Sorry-Grateful," and "Company" advanced the sound of the Broadway musical at a time when advance was desperately needed. The entire score worked well, although it showed Sondheim at his least adventurous except for **A FUNNY THING HAPPENED ON THE WAY TO THE FORUM [May 8, 1962].** Not surprisingly, **COMPANY** is composer Sondheim's biggest hit to date—except for **A FUNNY THING.**
(NOTE: As Sondheim's popularity increased in the Seventies, many of the songs cut from his shows began to appear on recordings. Titles are listed as above.)

FOLLIES
April 4, 1971   Winter Garden Theatre   522 performances

Book by James Goldman
Choreographed by Michael Bennett
Directed by Harold Prince and Bennett
Produced by Prince in association with Ruth Mitchell
With Alexis Smith, Dorothy Collins, Gene Nelson, and John McMartin

Published songs:

"Broadway Baby"
"Follies (Beautiful Girls)"
"Losing My Mind"
"Too Many Mornings"

Additional songs published in vocal score:

"Ah, Paris!"
"Buddy's Blues (The God-Why-Don't-You-Love-Me Blues)"
"Could I Leave You?"
"Don't Look At Me"
"Fox-Trot" [instrumental]—nonlyric version of "Can That Boy
    Fox-Trot!" (cut; initial publication in *Hansen Treasury Of Stephen
    Sondheim Songs*)
"I'm Still Here"
"In Buddy's Eyes"
"Live, Laugh, Love"
"Love Will See Us Through"
"Loveland"
"Lucy And Jessie"
"One More Kiss"
"Rain On The Roof"
"The Road You Didn't Take"
"Vincent And Vanessa Dance" [instrumental]
"Waiting For The Girls Upstairs"
"Who's That Woman?"
"You're Gonna Love Tomorrow"

Additional songs recorded:

"All Things Bright And Beautiful"—cut
"It Wasn't Meant To Happen"—cut
"Pleasant Little Kingdom"—cut
"Uptown, Downtown"—cut
"Who Could Be Blue?"—cut

One of Sondheim's richest scores was overwhelmed by a bloated concept, aiming for surrealism but settling for pretension. The "layered ghosts" approach used to illustrate the characters' psychoneuroses— Sally flirting with Young Ben fighting with Phyllis commiserating with Young Buddy mooning over Young Sally, while a couple of Heidis sang soprano—came across rather silly. The adventurous work by all (except the librettist) suffered. It wasn't really the librettist's fault: the blame rested on what became of that concept. (The authors had been working on the project for five years; as THE GIRLS UPSTAIRS, it had no ghosts, no flashbacks, and only one set of characters.) The score, staging, and production made **FOLLIES** a staggering experience by the third viewing, when you no longer paid attention to the book, but that wasn't good enough for the bored businessman. For the listener, the rewards were numerous: "Losing My Mind," "I'm Still Here," "Too Many Mornings," "Broadway Baby," "Who's That Woman?," "One More Kiss," and on. For the producer, the reward for an important and worthwhile experiment was financial nightmare. The listener definitely came out best.

A LITTLE NIGHT MUSIC
February 25, 1973   Shubert Theatre   601 performances

Book by Hugh Wheeler
(Based on *Smiles of a Summer Night* [film] by Ingmar Bergman)
Choreographed by Patricia Birch
Directed by Harold Prince
Produced by Prince in association with Ruth Mitchell
With Glynis Johns, Len Cariou, Hermione Gingold, and Victoria Mallory

Published songs:

"A Little Night Music (The Sun Won't Set)" [instrumental
   version]
"The Miller's Son"
"Remember?"
"Send In The Clowns"
"You Must Meet My Wife"

Additional songs published in vocal score:

"Every Day A Little Death"
"The Glamorous Life" [1st]
"In Praise Of Women"

"It Would Have Been Wonderful"
"Later"
"Liaisons"
"Night Waltz II (The Sun Sits Low)"
"Now"
"Perpetual Anticipation"
"Soon"
"The Sun Won't Set" [song version]
"A Weekend In The Country"

Additional songs recorded:

"Bang"—cut
"The Glamorous Life" [2nd] ("The Letter Song")—written for
   1978 movie version
"Love Takes Time"—written for movie version; new lyric for "The
   Sun Won't Set"
"Silly People"—cut
"Two Fairy Tales"—cut

A waltzing operetta hit, with a book only half as tangled as **FOL-
LIES [April 4, 1971]**. No harm, as Sondheim did everything so very
well and inventively: the duet "Every Day A Little Death," the trio
of soliloquies, the ensemble "The Glamorous Life," and the quintet
with their "Sun Won't Set." "A Weekend In The Country" was musical, lyrical and choral perfection—not only delightful, but covering
what would otherwise have been pages and pages and pages of li-
brettical explication. Sondheim also came up with "Send In The
Clowns," his only popular hit (as composer) to date.

CANDIDE
⟨*Second Version*⟩
see Bernstein [March 10, 1974]

THE FROGS
*[May 20, 1974]   Yale University Swimming Pool ⟨New
Haven, Connecticut⟩   8 performances*

Book and direction by Burt Shevelove
(Based on the play by Aristophanes)
Choreographed by Carmen de Lavallade

Produced by the Yale Repertory Theatre
With Larry Blyden, Alvin Epstein, de Lavallade, Anthony Holland,
    Christopher Durang, Meryl Streep, and Sigourney Weaver

Recorded songs:

"Fear No More" (lyric by William Shakespeare)
"Invocation To The Gods And Instructions To The Audience"

This Yale experiment created quite a splash. The built-in obstacles,
though, made it more curious than theatrical. And there were severe
echo problems.

PACIFIC OVERTURES
January 11, 1976   Winter Garden Theatre
193 performances

Book by John Weidman
Additional material by Hugh Wheeler
Choreographed by Patricia Birch
Directed by Harold Prince
Produced by Prince in association with Ruth Mitchell
With Mako, Soon-Teck Oh, Sab Shimono, and Yuki Shimoda

Songs published in vocal score:

"The Advantages Of Floating In The Middle Of The Sea"
"A Bowler Hat"
"Chrysanthemum Tea"
"Four Black Dragons"
"Lion Dance" [instrumental]
"Next"
"Please Hello"
"Poems"
"Pretty Lady"
"Someone In A Tree"
"There Is No Other Way"
"Welcome To Kanagawa"

Sondheim and Prince attempted something different, and they certainly succeeded. Once again, the work was inaccessible due to an
uninvolving book (although that wasn't the only problem). Sondheim's score took repeated hearings to enjoy, with "Pretty Lady" and
"Someone In A Tree" standing out. "A Bowler Hat" was excep-

tional writing: a lucid statement of the show's overall theme, with the character himself ironically illustrating the point. Meanwhile, the high point of the evening was a set change.

SIDE BY SIDE BY SONDHEIM
May 4, 1976   Mermaid Theatre ⟨London⟩
April 18, 1977   Music Box Theatre ⟨New York⟩
390 performances

Directed by Ned Sherrin
Produced ⟨London⟩ by H. M. Tennent, Ltd. and Cameron MacKintosh
Produced ⟨New York⟩ by Harold Prince in association with Ruth Mitchell
and the Incomes Company, Ltd.
With Millicent Martin, Julia McKenzie, David Kernan, and Sherrin

Published song:

"I Never Do Anything Twice"—initial publication in *Hansen
Treasury of Stephen Sondheim Songs;* originally used in 1975 movie
The 7½% Solution

London, which had only seen productions of half of the Sondheim musicals, mounted this successful anthology revue. The Broadway transfer did quite well, too, until the cast was replaced by—of all people—Kukla, Fran, and Ollie.

SWEENEY TODD
The Demon Barber of Fleet Street
March 1, 1979   Uris Theatre   558 performances

Book by Hugh Wheeler
(Based on a play by Christopher Bond)
Choreographed by Larry Fuller
Directed by Harold Prince
Produced by Richard Barr, Charles Woodward, Robert Fryer, Mary Lea
Johnson, and Martin Richards
With Len Cariou, Angela Lansbury, Victor Garber, Ken Jennings, and
Edmund Lyndeck

Published songs:

"Johanna"
"Not While I'm Around"
"Pretty Women"

Additional songs published in vocal score:
"Ah, Miss"
"The Ballad Of Sweeney Todd"
"The Barber And His Wife"
"By The Sea"
"City On Fire!"
"The Contest"
"Epiphany"
"Final Scene"
"God, That's Good!"
"Green Finch And Linnet Bird"
"Kiss Me"
"Johanna (Turpin Version)"—cut
"Ladies In Their Sensitivities"
"The Letter (Quintet)"
"A Little Priest"
"My Friends"
"No Place Like London"
"Parlor Songs"
"Pirelli's Miracle Elixir"
"Poor Thing"
"Wait"
"The Worst Pies In London"

Sondheim's finest work to date. The other Sondheim/Prince shows had less than ideal books; **SWEENEY TODD,** with more plot than its predecessors, was constructed of music—and worked far better. The composer wrote an extensive and varied score, ranging from moments of tender beauty ("Pretty Women" and "Not While I'm Around") to moments of madness ("Johanna—Turpin Version") and suppressed emotion ("The Barber And His Wife"). The "Epiphany" scene is unquestionably one of the most extraordinary segments in musical theatre writing. Len Cariou (of **A LITTLE NIGHT MU-SIC [February 25, 1973]**) and Angela Lansbury (who had followed **ANYONE CAN WHISTLE [April 4, 1964]** with Tony Award-winning performances in two Jerry Herman musicals) were breathtaking.

MARRY ME A LITTLE
March 12, 1981   Actors Playhouse ⟨off-Broadway⟩
96 performances

Conceived and developed by Craig Lucas and Norman René
Directed by René
Produced by Diane de Mailly in association with William B. Young
With Lucas and Suzanne Henry

Recorded songs:

"Little White House"
"A Moment With You"—written for unproduced 1954 musical
    SATURDAY NIGHT
"Pour Le Sport"—written for unproduced 1956 musical THE
    LAST RESORTS
"Saturday Night"—written for SATURDAY NIGHT
"So Many People"—written for SATURDAY NIGHT

This revue featured cut and previously unused Sondheim material.
(Songs from produced musicals are listed with the original scores.)
THE LAST RESORTS was a short-lived Griffith and Prince project,
with a Jean Kerr book (based on Cleveland Amory material). Prince
produced Sondheim's first musicals as lyricist and composer, taking
both properties over from other producers. Prince did originate
COMPANY [April 26, 1970] but not **FOLLIES [April 4, 1971],** which
began in the mid-Sixties with David Merrick. Merrick had been ma-
neuvered off of **A FUNNY THING [May 8, 1962];** he was no doubt
glad *not* to be waiting around for the THE GIRLS UPSTAIRS after
the curtain came down.

MERRILY WE ROLL ALONG
November 16, 1981   Alvin Theatre   16 performances

Book by George Furth
(Based on the play by George S. Kaufman and Moss Hart)
Choreographed by Larry Fuller
Directed by Harold Prince
Produced by Lord Grade, Martin Starger, Robert Fryer, and Prince
With Jim Walton, Ann Morrison, and Lonny Price

Published songs:

"Good Thing Going"
"Not A Day Goes By"

Additional songs published in vocal score:

"Bobby And Jackie And Jack"
"Franklin Shepard, Inc."
"The Hills Of Tomorrow"

"It's A Hit"
"Like It Was"
"Meet The Blob"
"Merrily We Roll Along"
"Now You Know"
"Old Friends"
"Opening Doors"
"Our Time"
"Rich And Happy"

Additional song published in vocal selection:

"Honey"—cut

The Sondheim/Prince collaboration ran aground on this curious project. The unsuccessful 1934 Kaufman and Hart play had unsolvable problems; its only distinction was the revolutionary-for-Broadway device of moving backwards in time. In 1981 the same unsolvable problems existed—and the novelty was no longer novel. The use of youthful actors and a jungle-gym production might have seemed workable at first, but something went wrong. Rather than adjusting, Sondheim, Prince, and company appear to have merrily worked along in their own separate vacuums. The songs came off best, of course, Sondheim providing "Not A Day Goes By," "Old Friends," and "Now You Know." The use of "Merrily We Roll Along" to move back through time worked better than the other conceptual choices of the evening. And mention must be made of the composer's choral work and Jonathan Tunick's orchestrations: dazzlingly brilliant!

SUNDAY IN THE PARK WITH GEORGE
May 2, 1984   Booth Theatre
604 performances

Book and direction by James Lapine
(Suggested by a painting by Georges Seurat)
Produced by The Shubert Organization and Emanuel Azenberg in
    association with Playwrights Horizons
With Mandy Patinkin, Bernadette Peters, Dana Ivey, and Charles
    Kimbrough

Songs published in vocal selection:

"Beautiful"
"Children And Art"

"Finishing The Hat"
"Move On"
"Sunday"

Additional songs recorded:

"Chromolume #7" [instrumental]
"Color And Light"
"The Day Off"
"Everybody Loves Louis"
"Gossip"
"It's Hot Up Here"
"Lesson #8"
"No Life"
"Putting It Together"
"Sunday In The Park With George"
"We Do Not Belong Together"

Working without Harold Prince for the first time since 1970, Sond-heim wrote the very special, Pulitzer Prize-winning **SUNDAY IN THE PARK WITH GEORGE.** The score, here, was the thing; and Broadway musicalizing did *not* work in the piece's favor. Minor weaknesses were only magnified by "theatrical" production values thought necessary for commercial success. Taking his cue from the palette of painter Seurat, Sondheim attempted musical pointillism and produced a first act of color and light: "Sunday," lyric and music, illustrated the *painting* illustrating the *painter*. The people of 1884 on the island in Paris were real and relevant and interesting. Not so the Impressionist's model's grandson, with his laser-beam art and his doddering musical-comedy grandmother. The authors seemed to think they needed 1984 to prove their point, in the same unsuccessful way **PACIFIC OVERTURES [January 11, 1976]** jumped the century. But their 1884 was far more relevant. As for musical *laser*ism, there seems to be no such thing; and practical lasers beamed over the head of the audience bought realism at the expense of imagery. Mean-while, Sondheim was at the top of his form (make that *anyone's* form) in "Finishing The Hat." This was his second perfect hat song, fol-lowing the "Bowler"; one can only hope for more. (Does anyone still *wear* a hat? . . .)

Stephen Sondheim has written thirteen Broadway shows, music and/or lyrics. While only half were successful, all but one have been innovative, experimental, and well worthwhile. Sondheim has *never* settled for the merely adequate; virtually every song is special in its own right. Ironically, composer Sondheim has been given a strong book only once, on his very first show. He might do far better working with a heretofore untried librettist: himself. Certainly he is capable, with a scriptwriting past and years of practical observation. Sondheim has an inveterate passion for puzzles, and what better word puzzle than a musical libretto? (Except maybe a Sondheim lyric.) Stephen Sondheim is not only the most important composer writing for Broadway today; he is the *only* important composer writing for Broadway today.

Charles Strouse

BORN: June 7, 1928   New York, New York

Charles Strouse began his musical career with a training in serious composition. After graduating from the Eastman School of Music, he studied with Nadia Boulanger in Paris and Aaron Copland before changing over to popular music. His first theatre composing came in 1953, writing summer amateur shows at Green Mansions (Harold Rome's training ground); his collaborator was Lee Adams, a magazine editor. For three years Strouse supported himself as a rehearsal pianist and accompanist, returning to Green Mansions for summers of high-pressure songwriting.

SHOESTRING REVUE
February 28, 1955   President Theatre ⟨off-Broadway⟩
100 performances

Music and lyrics mostly by others
Lyrics to Strouse songs by Michael Stewart
Sketches by Stewart, Sheldon Harnick, and others
Directed by Christopher Hewett
Produced by Ben Bagley in association with Mr. and Mrs. Judson S. Todd
With Dorothy Greener, Beatrice Arthur, Dody Goodman, and Chita
   Rivera

Recorded songs:

"The History Of The World"
"Man's Inhumanity To Man"
"Three Loves"

Twenty-two-year-old Ben Bagley came to New York and compiled three memorable (if not overly successful) off-Broadway revues in two seasons; featured were early songs and sketches by novices Strouse, Stewart, Adams, Harnick, and Schmidt & Jones. Bagley then left the theatre, eventually alighting in the record business. Strouse was musical director for the first **SHOESTRING REVUE** and placed interpolations in all three Bagley revues, this first in collaboration with Mike Stewart.

THE LITTLEST REVUE
May 22, 1956   Phoenix Theatre ⟨off-Broadway⟩
32 performances

Music mostly by Vernon **Duke**
Lyrics mostly by Ogden Nash
Sketches by Nat Hiken, Michael Stewart, and others
Directed by Paul Lammers
Produced by T. Edward Hambleton and Norris Houghton, with Ben
    Bagley
With Tammy Grimes, Charlotte Rae, Joel Grey, and Larry Storch

Recorded Songs:

"I Lost The Rhythm" (lyric by Strouse)
"Spring Doth Let Her Colours Fly" (lyric by Lee Adams)

"Spring Doth Let Her Colours Fly" was written for Charlotte Rae as an opera star doing a nightclub act. It was a very funny cartoon in words and (Wagnerian) music, suitable for the first New York work of Adams and Strouse.

SHOESTRING '57
November 5, 1956   Barbizon Plaza Theatre ⟨off-Broadway⟩   110 performances

Music mostly by others (see **Schmidt**)
Lyrics by Sheldon Harnick, Mike Stewart, Tom Jones, Carolyn Leigh,
    and others
Lyrics to Strouse songs by Lee Adams
Choreographed by Danny Daniels
Directed by Paul Lammers
Produced by Ben Bagley in association with E. H. Morris
With Dody Goodman, Dorothy Greener, and Paul Mazursky

Recorded Song:

"The Arts"

E. H. Morris was a music publisher, using a new method for arranging interpolations: coproducing (financing) the show himself. While nothing of interest came from **SHOESTRING '57**, Morris signed three of the important early Sixties composers: Strouse, Carolyn Leigh's new partner Cy Coleman, and Jerry Herman. (Herman remains with the Morris group, now owned by Paul McCartney.)

BYE BYE BIRDIE
April 14, 1960   Martin Beck Theatre   607 performances

Lyrics by Lee Adams
Book by Michael Stewart
Directed and choreographed by Gower Champion
Produced by Edward Padula in association with L. Slade Brown
With Chita Rivera, Dick Van Dyke, Susan Watson, Dick Gautier, and
   Kay Medford

Published Songs:

"Baby, Talk To Me"
"Bye Bye Birdie"—written for 1963 movie version
"How Lovely To Be A Woman"
"Kids!"
"A Lot Of Livin' To Do"
"One Boy"
"One Last Kiss"
"Put On A Happy Face"
"Rosie"

Additional songs published in vocal score:

"An English Teacher"
"A Healthy, Normal American Boy"
"One Hundred Ways Ballet" [instrumental]
"Shriner's Ballet" [instrumental]
"Spanish Rose"
"We Love You Conrad"
"What Did I Ever See In Him?"

To the surprise of everyone (including the authors), this cartoon musical was an enormously popular hit. After going through a number of different librettists including nightclub performer Mike Nichols, Michael Stewart—a TV writer for Sid Caesar and Strouse's lyricist for **SHOESTRING REVUE [February 28, 1955]**—came up with a book that worked. Gower (and Marge) Champion had been approached to star; instead, he directed his first book musical and became a major musical comedy force for a decade. Strouse, doing arrangements for the two-week flop GIRLS AGAINST THE BOYS [November 2, 1959], recommended the show's featured comic; he couldn't dance like Gower, but . . . Dick Van Dyke was joined by **SHOESTRING REVUE** alumna Chita Rivera, just back from the London production of **WEST SIDE STORY [Bernstein: September 26, 1957]**. Seriously inclined composer Strouse attempted simple pop tunes and rock lampoons—and found himself with "Put On A Happy Face," "A Lot Of Livin' To Do," "Rosie," and the pretty "Baby, Talk To Me."

ALL AMERICAN
March 19, 1962   Winter Garden Theatre   80 performances

Lyrics by Lee Adams
Book by Mel Brooks
(Based on *Professor Fodorski* [novel] by Robert Lewis Taylor)
Choreographed by Danny Daniels
Directed by Joshua Logan
Produced by Edward Padula in association with L. Slade Brown
With Ray Bolger, Eileen Herlie, Fritz Weaver, Ron Husmann, and Anita
   Gillette

Published songs:

"The Fight Song"
"If I Were You"
"I'm Fascinating"
"It's Fun To Think"
"I've Just Seen Her (As Nobody Else Has Seen Her)"
"Nightlife"
"Once Upon A Time"
"Our Children"
"We Speak The Same Language"
"What A Country!"

Additional songs recorded:

"Have A Dream"
"I Couldn't Have Done It Alone"
"Melt Us"
"Physical Fitness"

"The Real Me"
"Which Way?"

The **BYE BYE BIRDIE [April 14, 1960]** team was quickly split: David Merrick snapped up Gower Champion and Mike Stewart to do, initially, **CARNIVAL! [Merrill: April 13, 1961]**. Strouse, Adams, and their producers turned to veteran Joshua Logan (directing his first of five musicals since **FANNY [Rome: November 4, 1954]**—all increasingly disastrous failures). The new librettist was another Sid Caesar comedy writer Strouse had met while composing dance music for "Your Show of Shows." Mel Brooks's one book show had been SHINBONE ALLEY [April 13, 1957], the stage version of *archie and mehitabel*. Watching the troubled **ALL AMERICAN** tryout, Brooks began to wonder what'd happen if someone actually *tried* to produce a sure-fire musical bomb. The result: the 1968 Oscar-winning screenplay for *The Producers*. The charm of Ray Bolger and Eileen Herlie wasn't enough to carry this charmless college football musical, which did include the gentle hit "Once Upon A Time" and the feathery soft-shoe "I'm Fascinating."

HELLO, DOLLY!
January 16, 1964   St. James Theatre   2,844 performances

Music and lyrics mostly by Jerry **Herman** (also see **Merrill**)
Book by Michael Stewart
(Based on *The Matchmaker* [play] by Thornton Wilder)
Directed and choreographed by Gower Champion
Produced by David Merrick
With Carol Channing, David Burns, Eileen Brennan, and Charles Nelson
  Reilly

Published song:
"Before The Parade Passes By"

While Merrick called in Bob Merrill (from the Champion/Stewart hit **CARNIVAL! [April 13, 1961]**) to help the troubled-but-fixable **DOLLY,** Champion called in Strouse and Adams (from **BYE BYE BIRDIE [April 14, 1960]**). The original "Before The Parade Passes By"—written in Detroit—was by Strouse and Adams. Herman kept the lyric, reworked the music, and received sole public credit for the entire score.

GOLDEN BOY
October 20, 1964   Majestic Theatre   569 performances

Lyrics by Lee Adams
Book by Clifford Odets and William Gibson
(Based on the play by Odets)
Choreographed by Donald McKayle
Directed by Arthur Penn
Produced by Hillard Elkins
With Sammy Davis, Jr., Billy Daniels, and Paula Wayne

Published songs

"Can't You See It?"
"Gimme Some"
"Golden Boy"
"I Want To Be With You"
"Lorna's Here"
"Night Song"
"Stick Around"
"This Is The Life"
"While The City Sleeps"

Additional songs published in vocal selection:

"Colorful"
"Don't Forget 127th Street"
"Everything's Great"
"No More"

Additional song recorded:

"What Became Of Me?"—written for 1968 London production; see
  DANCE A LITTLE CLOSER [May 11, 1983]
"Workout"

The second Sammy Davis, Jr. Broadway vehicle had as many problems as the first (**MR. WONDERFUL [Bock: March 22, 1956]**); this time, at least, they started with strong basic material. But the 1937 Odets play was already clichéd; and the harried white manager, the young black newcomer who makes it big, etc. were familiar enough from both **MR. WONDERFUL** and the boxing **BODY BEAUTIFUL [Bock: January 23, 1958]**. The intent of the librettists (Odets died during the writing; Gibson came in, precipitating the replacement of Peter Coe by Arthur Penn) was admirable enough, but the results were anything but satisfying. Strouse had his first Broadway opportunity to write an emotional, nonlampoon score; what seemed like a complex departure from his **BYE BYE BIRDIE [April 14, 1960]** success was actually a return to his abstract training. "Night Song," "Lorna's Here," "I Want To Be With You," and "Golden Boy" were all highly moving and fascinating in structure; and the seductive "While The City Sleeps" perfectly expressed what should have been the tone of the entire production. With **GOLDEN BOY**'s failure Strouse went back to writing contemporary, pop musicals; his work hasn't shown such inventiveness and texture since.

"IT'S A BIRD, IT'S A PLANE, IT'S SUPERMAN"
March 29, 1966   Alvin Theatre   129 performances

Lyrics by Lee Adams
Book by David Newman and Robert Benton
(Based on the comic strip)
Choreographed by Ernest Flatt
Directed by Harold Prince
Produced by Prince in association with Ruth Mitchell
With Jack Cassidy, Patricia Marand, Bob Holiday, Michael O'Sullivan,
    and Linda Lavin

Published songs:

"It's Superman"
"Love Theme From Superman" [instrumental]—nonlyric version of
    "What I've Always Wanted"
"Superman Theme"
"What I've Always Wanted"
"You've Got Possibilities"

Additional songs published in vocal selection:

"Doing Good"
"I'm Not Finished Yet"
"It's Super Nice"
"Ooh, Do You Love You!"
"Pow! Bam! Zonk!"
"Revenge"
"So Long, Big Guy"
"The Strongest Man In The World"
"We Don't Matter At All"
"We Need Him"
"The Woman For The Man Who Has Everything"
"You've Got What I Need, Baby"

Strouse turned to comic-strip music for this comic-strip musical, with a particularly fine set of comedy lyrics by the underrated Lee Adams. Librettists Newman and Benton held on to their Superman treatment and successfully duplicated it a decade later in Hollywood—without Strouse, Adams, and Prince. For director/producer Prince it was the end of his standard-musical-comedy days: he determined to move away from the world of Abbott to the progressive world of Prince (via Robbins). First stop: **CABARET [Kander: November 20, 1966].**

APLAUSE

March 30, 1970   Palace Theatre   896 performances

Lyrics by Lee Adams
Book by Betty Comden and Adolph Green
(Based on *All About Eve* [story] by Mary Orr)
Directed and choreographed by Ron Field
Produced by Joseph Kipness, Lawrence Kasha, James M. Nederlander,
    and George Steinbrenner III
With Lauren Bacall, Len Cariou, Penny Fuller, and Bonnie Franklin

Published songs:

"Applause"
"Backstage Babble"
"The Best Night Of My Life"
"But Alive"
"Good Friends"
"Hurry Back"
"It Was Always You"—cut
"Love Comes First"—cut
"One Of A Kind"
"She's No Longer A Gypsy"
"Something Greater"
"Think How It's Gonna Be (When We're Together Again)"
"Welcome To The Theatre"

Additional songs published in vocal score:

"Fasten Your Seat Belts"
"Inner Thoughts"
"One Hallowe'en"
"Who's That Girl?"

Strouse and Adams had their second hit with this Lauren Bacall vehicle. The star ably carried her first musical, with assists from Len

Cariou and the energetic Bonnie Franklin. Ron Field, fresh from two Harold Prince shows, did a fine job; but the score was not very good at all. Comden and Green provided book without lyrics for the first time in their career, as tryout replacements for Sidney Michaels.

SIX
April 12, 1971   Cricket Theatre ⟨off-Broadway⟩
8 performances

Book and lyrics by Strouse
Directed by Peter Coe
Produced by Slade Brown
With Lee Beery, Gilbert Price, Hal Watters, and Alvin Ing

Published songs:

None

Reestablished on Broadway, Strouse expressed his abstract background with the experimental **SIX**. Produced on a small scale, the piece baffled audiences and was quickly withdrawn.

I AND ALBERT
November 6, 1972   Piccadilly Theatre ⟨London⟩
120 performances

Lyrics by Lee Adams
Book by Jay Presson Allen
Directed by John Schlesinger
Produced by Lewis M. Allen and Si Litvinoff
With Polly James and Sven-Bertil Taube

Published songs:

"I And Albert"
"Just You And Me"
"This Gentle Land"
"Victoria"
"Victoria And Albert Waltz" [instrumental]

Additional songs recorded:

"All Bless The Genius Of Man"
"Draw The Blinds"
"Enough!"
"Go It, Old Girl!"

"Hans"
"His Royal Highness"
"I've 'Eard The Bloody 'Indoos 'As It Worse"
"It Has All Begun"
"Leave It Alone"
"No One To Call Me Victoria"
"Vivat! Vivat Regina!"
"When You Speak With A Lady"
"The Widow At Windsor"

Strouse and Adams seemed an unlikely pair to write a Victorian British musical about Queen and Consort. London audiences were not amused.

ANNIE
April 21, 1977   Alvin Theatre   2,377 performances

Lyrics by Martin Charnin
Book by Thomas Meehan
(Based on "Little Orphan Annie" [comic strip])
Choreographed by Peter Gennaro
Directed by Charnin
Produced by Mike Nichols, Irwin Meyer, Stephen Friedman, and Lewis
   Allen
With Reid Shelton, Dorothy Loudon, Andrea McArdle, and Robert Fitch

Published songs:

"Annie"
"Easy Street"
"I Don't Need Anything But You"
"It's The Hard-Knock Life"
"Let's Go To The Movies"—written for 1982 movie version
"Little Girls"
"Maybe"
"N.Y.C."
"Sandy (Dumb Dog)"—written for movie version
"Sign"—written for movie version
"Tomorrow"
"We Got Annie!"—cut; initial publication upon reuse in movie
   version
"You're Never Fully Dressed Without A Smile"

Additional songs published in vocal score:

"I Think I'm Gonna Like It Here"
"A New Deal For Christmas"
"Something Was Missing"
"We'd Like To Thank You, Herbert Hoover"
"You Won't Be An Orphan For Long"

An unlikely, impossible-to-get-produced cartoon musical finally got mounted—and was the runaway smash hit of the decade (second only to **A CHORUS LINE [PART 4: April 15, 1975]**). A 1976 summerstock tryout at the Goodspeed Opera House finally got **ANNIE** on her feet, but just barely. Then Mike Nichols came in to produce, assuring financing and offering helpful suggestions. Like adding a starring role for Dorothy Loudon, his original "Passionella" in **THE WORLD OF JULES FEIFFER [Sondheim: July 2, 1962]**). For Loudon, **ANNIE** was reward for consistently outstanding valor on such battlefields as Sidney Lumet's NOWHERE TO GO BUT UP [November 10, 1962], George Abbott's THE FIG LEAVES ARE FALLING [January 2, 1969], and Alan Jay Lerner's LOLITA, MY LOVE [February 16, 1971]. The score was synthetic and banal; although Strouse's work far outclassed the lyrics. The only originality in the piece was the delightfully sassy "We Got Annie." They cut out the melody, cut out the rhythm, and retained the counter-melody for an insipid title song.

A BROADWAY MUSICAL
December 21, 1978   Lunt-Fontanne Theatre
1 performance

Lyrics by Lee Adams
Book by William F. Brown
Directed and choreographed by Gower Champion
Produced by Norman Kean and Garth H. Drabinsky
With Warren Berlinger, Larry Marshall, Patti Karr, and Tiger Haynes

Published songs:

None

A poorly produced musical about a poorly produced musical, **A BROADWAY MUSICAL** played its out-of-town tryout *up*town. Librettist Brown (of **THE WIZ [PART 4: January 5, 1975]**) and Strouse and Adams (of **GOLDEN BOY [October 20, 1964]**) prepared a good-natured description of their experiences as white writers on black musicals. Things took on the very racial overtones they were trying to avoid when black director/choreographer George Faison (from the hit **WIZ**) was replaced by the white Gower Champion (in a slump since 1966). Opening in time for Broadway's big holiday week, **A BROADWAY MUSICAL** was long gone by Christmas Eve.

FLOWERS FOR ALGERNON
June 14, 1979   Queen's Theatre ⟨London⟩
28 performances
CHARLIE AND ALGERNON
September 14, 1980   Helen Hayes Theatre
⟨New York⟩   17 performances

Book and lyrics by David Rogers
(Based on "Flowers for Algernon" [story] by Daniel Keyes)
Directed [London] by Peter Coe
Directed [New York] by Louis W. Scheeder
Produced [London] by Michael White in association with Isobel Robins
    Konecky
Produced [New York] by Kennedy Center, Konecky, Fisher Theatre
    Foundation, and Folger Theatre Group
With [London] Michael Crawford and Cheryl Rogers
With [New York] P. J. Benjamin and Sandy Faison

Published songs:

"Charlie"
"I Got A Friend"
"Midnight Riding"
"No Surprises"
"Whatever Time There Is"

Additional songs recorded:

"Charlie And Algernon"
"Dream Safe With Me"
"His Name Is Charlie Gordon"
"Hey Look At Me!"
"I Can't Tell You"
"I Really Loved You"
"The Maze"

"Now"
"Our Boy Charlie"
"Reading"
"Some Bright Morning"

Strouse once again departed from the conventional with seemingly impossible-to-handle subject matter. What had been pulled off in the 1968 movie *Charly* was too painful for a live audience. After a tryout in Ontario, the piece was unsuccessfully mounted in London. The production which eventually reached Broadway was of stock-company caliber (except for the sensitive performance by P. J. Benjamin) and an even quicker failure.

BRING BACK BIRDIE
March 5, 1981   Martin Beck Theatre   4 performances

Lyrics by Lee Adams
Book by Michael Stewart
(Based on characters from **BYE BYE BIRDIE** [April 14, 1960])
Directed and choreographed by Joe Layton
Produced by Lee Guber, Shelly Gross, Slade Brown, and Jim Milford
With Donald O'Connor, Chita Rivera, Maria Karnilova, and Maurice
  Hines

Songs recorded:

"Baby, You Can Count On Me"
"Back In Show Business Again"
"Bring Back Birdie"
"Half Of A Couple"
"I Like What I Do"
"I Love 'Em All"
"Inner Peace"
"A Man Worth Fightin' For"
"Middle Age Blues"
"Movin' Out"
"There's A Brand New Beat In Heaven"
"Twenty Happy Years"
"Well, I'm Not"
"When Will Grown-ups Grow Up?"
"You Can Never Go Back"
"Young"

BYE BYE BIRDIE's phenomenal success in the stock and amateur field (i.e., high school and community group production) prompted the authors to write a sequel—for that market. **BRING BACK BIRDIE** was *not* written or suitable for Broadway. Overenthusiastic stock producers got hold of the piece. They'd have been much better off bringing back **BIRDIE.**

UPSTAIRS AT O'NEALS
Cabaret Revue
October 28, 1982   O'Neal's Restaurant ⟨off-Broadway⟩

Music and lyrics mostly by others
Conceived and directed by Martin Charnin
Produced by Charnin and Michael and Patrick O'Neal

Song recorded:

"Boy Do We Need It Now" (music and lyric by Strouse)

Strouse contributed this song to a revue devised by **ANNIE [April 21, 1977]** collaborator Charnin. The year 1982 also saw the premiere of *The Nightingale* (text by Strouse), a children's opera.

DANCE A LITTLE CLOSER
May 11, 1983   Minskoff Theatre   1 performance

Book, lyrics and direction by Alan Jay Lerner
(Based on *Idiot's Delight* [play] by Robert E. Sherwood)
Choreography by Billy Wilson
Produced by Frederick Brisson, Jerome Minskoff, James Nederlander,
    and Kennedy Center
With Len Cariou, Liz Robertson (Lerner), and George Rose

Published songs:

"Another Life"
"Dance A Little Closer"—new lyric for "What Became Of Me?"
    written for 1968 London production of **GOLDEN BOY**
    [October 20, 1964]
"I Never Want To See You Again"
"There's Always One You Can't Forget"

DANCE A LITTLE CLOSER was a total, if momentary, shambles. However, two of the surviving songs—"Another Life" and

"There's Always One You Can't Forget"—are particularly worthwhile. Strouse here displayed more emotion and melodic inventiveness than in anything he's written since **GOLDEN BOY [October 20, 1964]**.

MAYOR
May 13, 1985   Village Gate Upstairs ⟨off-Broadway⟩; [still running as of October 1, 1985]

Music and lyrics by Charles Strouse
Book by Warren Leight
(Based on the autobiography by Edward I. Koch)
Choreographed by Barbara Siman (Strouse)
Directed by Jeffrey B. Moss
Produced by Martin Richards, Jerry Kravat, Mary Lea Johnson with the
  New York Music Company
With Lenny Wolpe

Published songs:

None

As of October 1, 1985, the following songs have been recorded: "Ballad," "Good Times," "Hootspa," "How'm I Doin'?," "I Want To Be The Mayor," "The Last 'I Love New York' Song," "March Of The Yuppies," "Mayor," "My City," "We Are One (I'll Never Leave You)," "What You See Is What You Get," "You Can Be A New Yorker, Too!," "You're Not The Mayor."

Strouse wrote his own lyrics for this harmless, minor cabaret revue.

Charles Strouse's record shows eleven full scale musicals, eight of which were failures. Most disheartening are the years since **ANNIE [April 21, 1977]**: four quick flops, three closing overnight. This is not encouraging. **ANNIE**, of course, was as big a hit as any composer needs; and the indifferent **APPLAUSE [March 30, 1970]** was also successful in lean times. Only two Strouse scores have been particularly exciting, the early **BYE BYE BIRDIE [April 14, 1960]** and **GOLDEN BOY [October 20, 1964]**. However, Strouse is certainly capable of good work; he has the freedom and time to choose more suitable projects; and his most recent songs show cause for optimism.

Cy Coleman

BORN: June 14, 1929   Bronx, New York

A piano prodigy, Cy Coleman began his musical training in serious music before turning to pop in the late Forties. Coleman started writing songs with lyricist Joseph McCarthy, Jr. (whose father wrote **IRENE [PART 4: November 1, 1919]**) while playing in nightclubs.

JOHN MURRAY ANDERSON'S ALMANAC
December 10, 1953   Imperial Theatre   229 performances

Music mostly by Richard **Adler** and Jerry Ross
Sketches by Jean Kerr, William K. Wells, and others
Choreographed by Donald Saddler
Directed by John Murray Anderson and Cyril Ritchard
Produced by Michael Grace, Stanley Gilkey, and Harry Rigby
With Hermione Gingold, Billy DeWolfe, Harry Belafonte, and Orson
  Bean

Published song:

"Tin Pan Alley" (lyric by Joseph McCarthy, Jr.)

Coleman interpolated this song, which held its own against the rest of the **JOHN MURRAY ANDERSON'S ALMANAC** score.

COMPULSION
October 24, 1957   Ambassador Theatre   140 performances

Play by Meyer Levin
Original music by Cy Coleman
Directed by Alex Segal
Produced by Michael Myerberg
With Roddy McDowall and Dean Stockwell

Published song:

"Compulsion" [instrumental]

Coleman first worked in the theatre as musical director of this drama based on the Leopold and Loeb case. At about the same time, he found a new lyricist: Carolyn Leigh, best known for her work on the Mary Martin **PETER PAN** ⟨**Fourth Version**⟩ **[Styne: October 20, 1954]**. Their collaboration immediately turned out pop hits like the 1957 "Witchcraft."

DEMI-DOZEN
Nightclub Revue
October 11, 1958   Upstairs at the Downstairs
⟨*off-Broadway*⟩

Music mostly by Harvey **Schmidt**
Directed by John Heawood
Produced by Julius Monk
With Jane Connell and Gerry Matthews

Published song:

"You Fascinate Me So" (lyric by Carolyn Leigh)

MEDIUM RARE
An Intimate Musical Revue
June 29, 1960   Happy Medium Theatre ⟨*Chicago, Illinois*⟩
1,210 performances

Music mostly by others
Directed by Bill Penn
Produced by Robert Weiner
With Anne Meara, Jerry Stiller, and Bobo Lewis

Published song:

"The Tempo Of The Times" (lyric by Carolyn Leigh)

WILDCAT
December 16, 1960   Alvin Theatre   172 performances

Lyrics by Carolyn Leigh
Book by N. Richard Nash
Directed and choreographed by Michael Kidd
Produced by Kidd and Nash
With Lucille Ball, Keith Andes, Edith King, Paula Stewart, and Swen
  Swenson

Published songs:

"Angelina"—cut
"Give A Little Whistle"
"Hey, Look Me Over!"
"One Day We Dance"
"Tall Hope"
"What Takes My Fancy"
"You're Far Away From Home"—cut
"You've Come Home"

Additional songs published in vocal score:

"Corduroy Road"
"Dancing On My Tippy-Tippy Toes"
"El Sombrero"
"Oil!"
"You're A Liar!"

Additional songs recorded:

"That's What I Want For Janie"

The successful pop songs of Coleman and Leigh resulted in this assignment, Lucille Ball's Broadway musical debut (and farewell). Manufactured solely for the purpose of cashing in on Ball's television popularity, **WILDCAT** had little of interest in it; when Ball "became ill," the show quickly closed. Coleman came up with the hit "Hey, Look Me Over!" and the melodic "You've Come Home."

LITTLE ME
November 17, 1962   Lunt-Fontanne Theatre
257 performances

Lyrics by Carolyn Leigh
Book by Neil Simon
(Based on the novel by Patrick Dennis)
Choreographed by Bob Fosse
Directed by Cy Feuer and Fosse
Produced by Feuer and Ernest Martin
With Sid Caesar, Virginia Martin, Nancy Andrews, and Swen Swenson

Published songs:

"Deep Down Inside"
"Dimples"

"Don't Ask A Lady"—written for 1982 revival
"Here's To Us"
"I Wanna Be Yours"—written for revival
"I've Got Your Number"
"Le Grand Boom-Boom"
"Little Me"
"On The Other Side Of The Tracks"
"Poor Little Hollywood Star"
"Real Live Girl"
"To Be A Performer!"

Additional songs recorded:

"Goodbye (The Prince's Farewell)"
"I Love You"
"The Truth"

Feuer and Martin followed **HOW TO SUCCEED IN BUSINESS WITHOUT REALLY TRYING [Loesser: October 14, 1961]** with another fast-paced, brash musical. Comedienne Virginia Martin was brought along, as well as choreographer Fosse (codirecting with Feuer). Coleman combined his two strongest musical traits—rhythmic jazz and humor—in a gem of a score, to sparkling Leigh lyrics. Neil Simon, whose only musical work had been in television, provided one of the very funniest librettos. And Sid Caesar headed the good cast. Yet, **LITTLE ME** was a disappointing failure—possibly because it had no heart. When the authors tried to "fix" **LITTLE ME** twenty years later, the changes made it pale, weak, and not even funny.

SWEET CHARITY
January 30, 1966   Palace Theatre   608 performances

Lyrics by Dorothy Fields
Book by Neil Simon
(Based on *Nights of Cabiria* [movie] by Federico Fellini, Tullio Pinelli, and Ennio Flaiano)
Conceived, directed and choreographed by Bob Fosse
Produced by Fryer, Carr, and Harris
With Gwen Verdon, John McMartin, Helen Gallagher, and Thelma Oliver

Published songs:

"Baby, Dream Your Dream"
"Big Spender"

"Gimme A Rain Check"—cut

"I Love To Cry At Weddings"

"I'm A Brass Band"

"I'm The Bravest Individual (I Have Ever Met)"

"If My Friends Could See Me Now"

"It's A Nice Face"—written for 1969 movie version

"My Personal Property"—written for movie version

"Poor Everybody Else"—cut; also used in **SEESAW [March 18, 1973]**

"The Rhythm Of Life"

"Sweet Charity" [1st] ("Charity's Theme") [instrumental]

"Sweet Charity" [2nd]—new lyric for "You Wanna Bet" (cut)

"Sweet Charity" [3rd]—written for movie version; new music for lyric of "Sweet Charity" [2nd]

"There's Gotta Be Something Better Than This"

"Too Many Tomorrows"

"Where Am I Going?"

"You Should See Yourself"

"You Wanna Bet"—cut; used with new lyric as "Sweet Charity" [2nd]

Additional songs recorded:

"Charity's Soliloquy"

"Pompeii Club" ("Rich Man's Frug" [2nd]) [instrumental]— written for movie version

"Rebirth (Finale)" [instrumental]—written for movie version

"Rich Man's Frug" [1st] [instrumental]

Since **REDHEAD [PART 4: February 5, 1959]**, Bob Fosse's only success had been as replacement choreographer on **HOW TO SUC-CEED IN BUSINESS WITHOUT REALLY TRYING [Loesser: October 14, 1961]**. With **SWEET CHARITY,** Fosse entered a new stage in his career. Leaving the confines of the Abbott-influenced well-made book musical, the director/choreographer began to imprint his influence on the material more fully than even Robbins did. **CHAR-ITY** boasted the return to the stage of Gwen Verdon, who had followed **REDHEAD** by marrying Fosse. **REDHEAD** lyricist Dorothy Fields was partnered with Coleman from **LITTLE ME [November 17, 1962]**. Facing book problems, Fosse replaced librettist Bert Lewis (i.e., Bob Fosse) with Neil Simon; the result was a cartoon musical valentine. Some of the material was uneven, but Verdon and Fosse kept things moving. In places like the "Big Spender" number, all theatrical elements blended perfectly.

KEEP IT IN THE FAMILY
September 27, 1967   Plymouth Theatre   5 performances

Play by Bill Naughton
Directed by Allan Davis
Produced by David Merrick
With Maureen O'Sullivan, Patrick Magee, and Karen Black

Published song:

"Keep It In The Family" (lyric by Dorothy Fields)

SEESAW
March 18, 1973   Uris Theatre   296 performances

Lyrics by Dorothy Fields
Book and direction by Michael Bennett
(Based on *Two for the Seesaw* [play] by William Gibson)
Choreographed by Bennett and Grover Dale
Produced by Joseph Kipness, Lawrence Kasha, James Nederlander, and
   George Steinbrenner III
With Michele Lee, Ken Howard, and Tommy Tune

Published songs:

"He's Good For Me"
"I'm Way Ahead"
"In Tune"
"It's Not Where You Start"
"My City"
"Nobody Does It Like Me"
"Poor Everybody Else"—originally used in (cut from) **SWEET
   CHARITY [January 20, 1966]**
"Ride Out The Storm"
"Seesaw"
"Spanglish"
"We've Got It"
"Welcome To Holiday Inn"
"You're A Lovable Lunatic"

Additional song recorded:

"Chapter 54, Number 1909"

William Gibson's two-character play was blown up into a massive, trouble-ridden production. Star Lainie Kazan and director Edwin Sherin were both replaced in Detroit. Michael Bennett came in to redirect and replace a good deal of the choreography; he also took credit for the book after Mike Stewart departed. The best moments: the inventively staged and well-written title song and the finale "I'm Way Ahead." **SEESAW** was the final show of Dorothy Fields' long career. She died March 28, 1974.

STRAWS IN THE WIND
February 21, 1975   American Place Theatre ⟨off-Broadway⟩   33 performances

Music mostly by others
Lyrics to Coleman songs by Betty Comden and Adolph Green
Directed by Phyllis Newman
Produced by American Place Theatre
With Tovah Feldshuh, Brandon Maggart, and Josh Mostel

Recorded songs:

"The Lost Word"
"Simplified Language"

HELLZAPOPPIN'!
[November 22, 1976]   Mechanic Theatre ⟨Baltimore, Maryland⟩; closed during pre-Broadway tryout

Music mostly by Hank Beebe and Jule **Styne**
Lyrics by Carolyn Leigh and Bill Heyer
Book by Abe Burrows and others
(Based on a format by Olsen and Johnson)
Choreographed by Donald Saddler
Directed by Jerry Adler
Produced by Alexander H. Cohen in association with Maggie and Jerome
   Minskoff
With Jerry Lewis, Lynn Redgrave, Joey Faye, and Brandon Maggart

Published songs:

None

I LOVE MY WIFE
April 17, 1977   Ethel Barrymore Theatre
857 performances

Book and lyrics by Michael Stewart
(Based on a play by Luis Rego)
Choreographed by Onna White
Directed by Gene Saks
Produced by Terry Allen Kramer and Harry Rigby by arrangement with
   Joseph Kipness
With Lenny Baker, James Naughton, Joanna Gleason, and Ilene Graff

Published songs:
"Hey There, Good Times"
"I Love My Wife"
"Love Revolution"
"Someone Wonderful I Missed"

Additional songs published in vocal selection:
"By Threes"
"Ev'rybody Today Is Turning On"
"Lovers On Christmas Eve"
"Married Couple Seeks Married Couple"
"Monica"
"A Mover's Life"
"Scream"
"Sexually Free"
"We're Still Friends"

Following Dorothy Fields' death, Coleman teamed up with Comden
and Green for **ON THE TWENTIETH CENTURY [February 19,
1978]**. While that show was in preparation, Mike Stewart (who had
worked with Coleman on **SEESAW [March 18, 1973]**) found this
French comedy and proposed an intimate musical. Stewart wrote his
first lyrics since the **SHOESTRING REVUE [Strouse: November
5, 1955]**) and **I LOVE MY WIFE** was a surprise hit—boasting the
charm of Lenny Baker, an on-stage combo wearing Santa Claus suits,
and little else.

ON THE TWENTIETH CENTURY
February 19, 1978   St. James Theatre   449 performances

Book and lyrics by Betty Comden and Adolph Green
(Based on *Twentieth Century* [play] by Ben Hecht and Charles MacArthur)
Choreographed by Larry Fuller
Directed by Harold Prince

Produced by Robert Fryer, Mary Lea Johnson, James Cresson, and
  Martin Richards
With John Cullum, Madeline Kahn, Imogene Coca, and Kevin Kline

Published songs:

"Never"
"On The Twentieth Century"
"Our Private World"

Additional songs published in vocal selection:

"Five Zeros"
"I Rise Again"
"I've Got It All"
"The Legacy"
"Life Is Like A Train"
"Mine"
"Repent"
"She's A Nut"
"Sign, Lily, Sign (Sextet)"
"Stranded Again"
"Together"
"Veronique"

Additional song recorded:

"Babette"
"Lily, Oscar"

Despite Tony Award-winning performances by John Cullum and
Kevin Kline and a lavish art deco production by Robin Wagner, **ON
THE TWENTIETH CENTURY** was top-heavy and ran out of
steam. Coleman deserted his normal style for mock operetta, an experiment which didn't work. But Wagner's train, in life-size and
miniature, did.

HOME AGAIN, HOME AGAIN
*[March 12, 1979]   American Shakespeare Theatre
⟨Stratford, Connecticut⟩; closed during pre-Broadway tryout*

Lyrics by Barbara Fried
Book by Russell Baker
Choreographed by Onna White
Directed by Gene Saks

Produced by Irwin Meyer and Stephen R. Friedman
With Lisa Kirk, Dick Shawn, Anita Morris, and Mike Kellin

Published songs:

None

With a book by *The New York Times* columnist Russell Baker and staging by the **I LOVE MY WIFE [April 17, 1977]** team, **HOME AGAIN, HOME AGAIN** held some promise. But the producers (from the **ANNIE [April 21, 1977]** team) ran into nontheatrical problems and **HOME AGAIN** was stranded on the road.

BARNUM

April 30, 1980   St. James Theatre   854 performances

Lyrics by Michael Stewart
Book by Mark Bramble
Directed and choreographed by Joe Layton
Produced by Coleman, Judy Gordon, and Maurice and Lois F. Rosenfield
With Jim Dale, Glenn Close, and Marianne Tatum

Published songs:

"The Colors Of My Life"
"Come Follow The Band"
"Join The Circus"
"One Brick At A Time"
"There Is A Sucker Born Every Minute"

Additional songs published in vocal selection:

"Bigger Isn't Better"
"Black And White"
"I Like Your Style"
"Love Makes Such Fools Of Us All"
"Museum Song"
"Out There"
"The Prince Of Humbug"
"Thank God I'm Old"

The concept of **BARNUM**—a circus atmosphere overtaking the theatre space and spilling through the audience—combined with Jim Dale's bravura performance to make for a moderate hit. After less than inspiring management on **SEESAW [March 18, 1973]** and

HOME AGAIN, HOME AGAIN [March 12, 1979], Coleman tried his hand at coproducing, with more satisfactory results.

Cy Coleman's early Neil Simon/Bob Fosse collaborations—**LITTLE ME [November 17, 1962]** and **SWEET CHARITY [January 30, 1966]**—had bright, exciting scores. Slightly lacking in heart, perhaps, but well-suited to the material. **CHARITY** was followed by a long inactive period with only one show in eleven years. His five scores since 1966 have been almost devoid of interest. This is disappointing and rather baffling. Coleman is a capable musician with good ideas; one can only look to his future work with hope.

Jerry Herman

BORN: July 10, 1933   New York, New York

Jerry Herman grew up in Jersey City, son of a summer-camp owner. A self-taught musician, Herman started training as an interior decorator at the Parsons School of Design before switching to drama at the University of Miami.

[all music and lyrics by Jerry Herman unless indicated]

I FEEL WONDERFUL
October 18, 1954   Theatre de Lys ⟨off-Broadway⟩
48 performances

Sketches by Barry Alan Grael
Directed by Herman
Produced by Sidney S. Oshrin
With Phyllis Newman and Richard Tone

Published songs:

None

Herman graduated from Miami and brought back this college show, which was promising if slightly amateurish.

NIGHTCAP
Nightclub Revue
May 18, 1958   Showplace ⟨off-Broadway⟩

Choreographed by Phyllis Newman
Directed by Herman
Produced by Jim Paul Eilers
With Kenneth Nelson, Charles Nelson Reilly, Fia Karin, and Estelle
  Parsons

Published songs:

"Show Tune In 2/4"—initial publication upon reuse in **PARADE**
  ⟨**Second Version**⟩ [**January 20, 1960**]; see **MAME** [**May 24,
  1966**]
"Your Good Morning"—initial publication upon reuse in **PARADE**

Additional songs recorded:

"Confession To A Park Avenue Mother"—initial recording upon
  reuse in **PARADE**
"Jolly Theatrical Season"—initial recording upon reuse in
  PARADE

Herman, playing piano at the Showplace, talked the owner into putting on this intimate, late-night revue, which ran almost a year. "Show
Tune In 2/4" was a lively, catchy show tune in 2/4, and "Jolly Theatrical Season" was cleverly amusing.

PARADE
⟨*Second Version*⟩
January 20, 1960   Players Theatre ⟨*off-Broadway*⟩
95 performances

Book and direction by Herman
Choreographed by Richard Tone
Produced by Lawrence N. Kasha
With Dody Goodman, Charles Nelson Reilly, Fia Karin, and Tone

Published songs:

"Next Time I Love"
"Show Tune In 2/4"—originally used in **NIGHTCAP** [**May 18,
  1958**]; see **MAME** [**May 24, 1966**]
"The Wonderful World Of The Two-A-Day"
"Your Good Morning"—originally used in **NIGHTCAP**
"Your Hand In Mine"

Additional songs recorded:

"Another Candle"
"The Antique Man"
"Confession To A Park Avenue Mother"—originally used in
  NIGHTCAP
"Jolly Theatrical Season"—originally used in **NIGHTCAP**

"Just Plain Folks"
"Maria In Spats"
"Overture"—see **MACK AND MABEL** [October 6, 1974]
"Save The Village"

PARADE was Herman's first professional show. Charles Nelson
Reilly—who repeated his songs from **NIGHTCAP** [May 18, 1958]—
left the cast to go to Broadway with **BYE BYE BIRDIE** [Strouse:
April 14, 1960]; he was to give very good Broadway performances
over the next few years in **HOW TO SUCCEED . . .** [Loesser:
October 14, 1961] and Herman's own **HELLO, DOLLY!** [January
16, 1964].

FROM A TO Z
April 20, 1960   Brooks Atkinson Theatre   21 performances
Music mostly by others
Lyrics mostly by Fred Ebb and others
Sketches by Woody Allen and others
Directed by Christopher Hewett
Produced by Carroll and Harris Masterson
With Hermione Gingold, Bob Dishy, and Elliot Reid

Published songs:
None

Herman contributed the opening number, "Best Gold," to this short-
lived revue.

MILK AND HONEY
October 10, 1961   Martin Beck Theatre   543 performances
Book by Don Appell
Choreographed by Donald Saddler
Directed by Albert Marre
Produced by Gerard Ostreicher
With Robert Weede, Mimi Benzell, Molly Picon, and Tommy Rall

Published songs:

"As Simple As That"
"Chin Up, Ladies"
"I Will Follow You"

"Independence Day Hora"
"Let's Not Waste A Moment"
"Milk And Honey"
"Shalom"
"That Was Yesterday"
"There's No Reason In The World"

Additional songs published in vocal score:

"Hymn To Hymie"
"Like A Young Man"
"Sheep Song"
"The Wedding"

An Israel-based musical seemed a safe bet for theatre parties—particularly with Yiddish theatre favorite Molly Picon on hand. The novice producer believed in the novice composer and gave him the assignment; Herman did well enough, attracting attention with the highly melodic, minor-key "Shalom." **MILK AND HONEY** became the first Broadway musical to run over five hundred performances and still lose money (now a commonplace occurrence).

MADAME APHRODITE
December 29, 1961   Orpheum Theatre ⟨off-Broadway⟩
13 performances

Book by Tad Mosel
Directed by Robert Turoff
Produced by Howard Barker, Cynthia Baer, and Robert Chambers
With Nancy Andrews, Cherry Davis, and Jack Drummond

Published songs:

"Beautiful"—see **LA CAGE AUX FOLLES [August 21, 1983]**
"The Girls Who Sit And Wait"
"Only, Only Love"
"Take A Good Look Around"

HELLO, DOLLY!
January 16, 1964   St. James Theatre   2,844 performances

Music and lyrics mostly by Jerry Herman
Book by Michael Stewart
(Based on *The Matchmaker* [play] by Thornton Wilder)

Directed and choreographed by Gower Champion
Produced by David Merrick
With Carol Channing, David Burns, Eileen Brennan, and Charles Nelson
  Reilly

Published songs:

"Before The Parade Passes By"—see Charles **Strouse**
"Dancing"
"Hello, Dolly!"
"It Only Takes A Moment"
"It Takes A Woman"—initial publication upon use in 1965 London
  production
"Just Leave Everything To Me"—written for 1969 movie version
"Love Is Only Love"—written for movie version
"Love, Look In My Window"—added after opening (1970)
"Put On Your Sunday Clothes"
"Ribbons Down My Back"
"So Long, Dearie"
"World, Take Me Back"—added after opening (1970)

Additional songs published in vocal score:

"Elegance"—see Bob **Merrill**
"I Put My Hand In"
"Motherhood March"—see Bob **Merrill**
"Waiter's Gallop" [instrumental]

HELLO, DOLLY! galloped on to Broadway as the biggest hit of the
young decade, and remained so despite competition from the illustrious **FIDDLER ON THE ROOF [Bock: September 22, 1964]** and
MAN OF LA MANCHA [Leigh: November 22, 1965]. Gower
Champion's magic, Carol Channing's charisma (in a part nobody
wanted and everybody eventually played), David Merrick's show-
manship (rejuvenating a fading hit into a sellout simply by adding
Pearl Bailey and Cab Calloway), and Jerry Herman's title song did
it. Herman paid a $275,000 settlement on a plagiarism claim brought
by Mack David, brother of **PROMISES, PROMISES [PART 4:
December 1, 1968]** lyricist Hal David. "Hello, Dolly!" is certainly
more than similar to the 1948 pop hit "Sunflower," but surely an
unconscious borrowing on Herman's part. Other parts of the score
were not borrowed but bought. At any rate, **DOLLY** was immensely
entertaining and, after twenty years, is still "glowin' and crowin' and
goin' strong."

BEN FRANKLIN IN PARIS
October 27, 1964   Lunt-Fontanne Theatre
215 performances

Music mostly by Mark Sandrich, Jr.
Book and lyrics by Sidney Michaels
Directed and choreographed by Michael Kidd
Produced by George W. George and Harvey Granat
With Robert Preston, Ulla Sallert, and Susan Watson

Published song:

"To Be Alone With You"

Additional song published in vocal selection:

"Too Charming"

BEN FRANKLIN IN Boston was having the miseries. Surgeons were
called in; but the troubles were terminal. This time Herman was the
song doctor; the two songs were publicly credited to Sandrich and
Michaels. "To Be Alone With You" is a very pretty ballad, on a level
with the best of Herman's work.

MAME
May 24, 1966   Winter Garden Theatre
1,508 performances

Book by Jerome Lawrence and Robert E. Lee
(Based on *Auntie Mame* [novel] by Patrick Dennis)
Choreographed by Onna White
Directed by Gene Saks
Produced by Fryer, Carr, and Harris
With Angela Lansbury, Beatrice Arthur (Saks), Jane Connell, Charles
   Braswell, and Frankie Michaels

Published songs:

"If He Walked Into My Life"
"It's Today"—revised version of "Show Tune In 2/4" from
   NIGHTCAP [May 18, 1958]
"Loving You"—written for 1974 movie version
"Mame"
"My Best Girl"
"Open A New Window"
"That's How Young I Feel"
"We Need A Little Christmas"

Additional songs published in vocal score:

"Bosom Buddies"
"The Fox Hunt (Fall Off, Auntie Mame)"
"Gooch's Song"
"The Man In The Moon"
"St. Bridget"

Herman's best show. **MAME** had great style in every department, thanks to director Gene Saks, who replaced original director/colibrettist Joshua Logan. Angela Lansbury, Jane Connell, and Beatrice Arthur were three clowns with superb material. Herman, needing no last-minute "help," provided a fine score without a weak link. His ballad, "If He Walked Into My Life," was good, and his comedy numbers "Gooch's Song" and "Bosom Bodies" were perfect. "Mame" joined "Hello, Dolly!" in the popular title-song sweepstakes; and the show had a long and successful run (though not so spectacular as her sister from Yonkers). **MAME,** incidentally, was produced in tandem with yet another lady, **SWEET CHARITY [Coleman: January 30, 1966].**

DEAR WORLD
February 6, 1969   Mark Hellinger Theatre
132 performances

Book by Jerome Lawrence and Robert E. Lee
(Based on *The Madwoman of Chaillot* [play] by Jean Giradoux)
Directed and choreographed by Joe Layton
Produced by Alexander H. Cohen
With Angela Lansbury, Jane Connell, and Milo O'Shea

Published songs:

"And I Was Beautiful"
"Dear World"
"Garbage" [instrumental]
"I Don't Want To Know"
"I've Never Said I Love You"
"Kiss Her Now"
"One Person"

Additional songs published in vocal selection:

"Dickie"
"Each Tomorrow Morning"

"Memories"
"Pearls"
"The Spring Of Next Year"
"Thoughts"
"Voices"

Additional song recorded:

"Garbage" [song version]

Alexander Cohen assembled the authors and stars of **MAME [May 24, 1966]** for this lavishly packaged, sure-fire, misguided failure. Herman's music was actually rather tuneful, but the lyrics were way far below his usual level. The rest of **DEAR WORLD** suffered from lack of direction. The director was Joe Layton replacing Peter Glenville replacing Lucia Victor.

MACK AND MABEL
October 6, 1974   Majestic Theatre   65 performances

Book by Michael Stewart
(Based on an idea by Leonard Spigelgass)
Directed and choreographed by Gower Champion
Produced by David Merrick
With Robert Preston, Bernadette Peters, Lisa Kirk, and James Mitchell

Published songs:

"Hundreds Of Girls"
"I Promise You A Happy Ending"
"I Won't Send Roses"
"Tap Your Troubles Away"
"Time Heals Everything"
"Today I'm Gonna Think About Me"—cut
"When Mabel Comes In The Room"
"Wherever He Ain't"

Additional songs published in vocal selection:

"Big Time"
"I Wanna Make The World Laugh"—new lyric for unspecified song originally used in **PARADE ⟨Second Version⟩ [January 20, 1960]**
"Look What Happened To Mabel"
"Movies Were Movies"

Additional song recorded:
"My Heart Leaps Up"

Another poorly conceived, ill-manufactured musical comedy. Herman displayed his ability to write perfect material for the female lead in "Look What Happened To Mabel" and "Time Heals Everything," but the rest of the score was barren. Gower Champion, meanwhile, had long since lost his touch. His career following **I DO! I DO! [December 5, 1966]** was marked by six of the bigger financial disasters of the era, including **THE HAPPY TIME [Kander: January 18, 1968], PRETTYBELLE [Styne: February 1, 1971],** and the indescribable ROCKABYE HAMLET [February 17, 1976]. Robert Preston gave his usual superb performance, and Bernadette Peters was sympathetic in an unsympathetic role.

THE GRAND TOUR
January 11, 1979   Palace Theatre   61 performances
Book by Michael Stewart and Mark Bramble
(Based on *Jacobowsky and the Colonel* [play] by Franz Werfel)
Choreographed by Donald Saddler
Directed by Gerald Freedman
Produced by James Nederlander, Diana Shumlin, and Jack Schlissel
With Joel Grey, Ron Holgate, and Florence Lacey

Published songs:
"I'll Be Here Tomorrow"
"Marianne"
"You I Like"

Additional songs published in vocal selection:
"For Poland"
"I Belong Here"
"I Think I Think"
"Mazel Tov"
"More And More/Less And Less"
"Mrs. S. L. Jacobowsky"
"One Extraordinary Thing"
"We're Almost There"

A charmless show, not helped by a miscast star and a poorly directed production. Herman provided a very good opening—"I'll Be Here

Tomorrow"—which created sympathy and interest; then things hit bottom and continued to descend. As is the norm in such cases, they fired the choreographer.

A DAY IN HOLLYWOOD/A NIGHT IN THE UKRAINE
May 1, 1980   John Golden Theatre   588 performances

Music mostly by Frank Lazarus
Book and lyrics mostly by Dick Vosburgh
Additional music and lyrics by Herman
Directed and choreographed by Tommy Tune
Produced by Alexander H. Cohen and Hildy Parks
With Priscilla Lopez, David Garrison, and Lazarus

Published song:

"The Best In The World"

Additional songs published in vocal selection:

"Just Go To The Movies"
"Nelson"

This revue needed some beefing up; Herman, at the lowest point in his professional career, contributed three numbers (including the effective "Nelson").

LA CAGE AUX FOLLES
August 21, 1983   Palace Theatre   [still running as of October 1, 1985]

Book by Harvey Fierstein
(Based on the play by Jean Poiret)
Choreographed by Scott Salmon
Directed by Arthur Laurents
Produced by Allan Carr, Kenneth-Mark Productions, Marvin A. Krauss, Stewart F. Lane, James M. Nederlander, Martin Richards, and Fritz Holt and Barry Brown
With George Hearn and Gene Barry

Published songs:

"The Best Of Times"
"La Cage Aux Folles"
"I Am What I Am"

"Look Over There"
"Song On The Sand (La Da Da Da)"
"With You On My Arm"

Additional songs published in vocal selection:

"A Little More Mascara"—revised version of "Beautiful" from
  MADAME APHRODITE [December 29, 1961]
"Masculinity"
"We Are What We Are"—alternate lyric for "I Am What I Am"

Additional song recorded:

"Cocktail Counterpoint"

Herman had been without a hit since **MAME [May 24, 1966]**; it was
assumed that his "popular touch" was outdated, too old-fashioned.
Then came **LA CAGE AUX FOLLES,** Broadway's biggest hit since
ANNIE [Strouse: April 21, 1977]. Curiously enough, considering the
diversity in subject matter, **LA CAGE** and **ANNIE** were pretty much
equally matched in quality of score, book, and direction, which is to
say monotonously mediocre. The **LA CAGE** package was very empty
indeed. Herman wrote his blandest score to date, without a single
interesting moment. And the book played much better in the movie
version, with English subtitles. But Broadway audiences loved it, and
a hit is a hit. Right?

Jerry Herman wrote one of the most successful musicals of the Sixties, as well as what seems likely to be one of the biggest hits of the
Eighties. A third show, **MAME [May 24, 1966],** was also a major
hit. Herman's record compares more than favorably with other important theatre composers', yet his work is continually attacked as
being banal and derivative. There's a good reason for this. However,
it must be remembered that he *has* proven himself highly capable with
the score for **MAME** and a half dozen fine songs scattered through
his other shows.

John Kander

BORN: March 18, 1927   Kansas City, Missouri

John Kander began his musical training at Oberlin College, where he wrote songs with childhood friend James Goldman. Coming to New York to get a Masters Degree from Columbia, Kander began working as an accompanist. His first Broadway assignments came as dance music arranger for **GYPSY [Styne: May 21, 1959]** and Marguerite Monnot's IRMA LA DOUCE [September 29, 1960], two shows with particularly good dance arrangements.

A FAMILY AFFAIR
January 27, 1962   Billy Rose Theatre   65 performances

Book and lyrics by James and William Goldman
Directed by Harold Prince
Produced by Andrew Siff
With Shelley Berman, Eileen Heckart, Morris Carnovsky, Larry Kert, and Rita Gardner

Published songs:

"Beautiful"
"A Family Affair"
"Harmony"
"Mamie In The Afternoon"—cut
"There's A Room In My House"

Additional songs recorded:

"Anything For You"
"Every Girl Wants To Get Married"
"Football Game (Marching Songs)"
"I'm Worse Than Anybody"
"Kalua Bay"
"My Son, The Lawyer"
"Now Morris"

"Revenge"
"Right Girls"
"Summer Is Over"
"What I Say Goes"
"Wonderful Party"

James Goldman's first play, the 1961 THEY MIGHT BE GIANTS, closed during its 1961 pre–West End tryout. The producers: Robert Griffith and Harold Prince. Goldman's second effort was **A FAMILY AFFAIR,** written with brother William (best known in theatre circles for his 1969 Broadway chronicle *The Season*) and Kander. The intimate musical featured three semi-names, none of whom had ever appeared in a musical. The authors had never done a Broadway show, the producer had never done a Broadway show, even the director— Word Baker of **THE FANTASTICKS [Schmidt: May 3, 1960]**— had never done a Broadway show. Out of town, **A FAMILY AFFAIR** had problems. A call went to Harold Prince, who had never directed *anything*. Prince helped somewhat, and gained valuable experience. He also kept Kander—whose work came off best—in mind. James Goldman, too, was to work once more with director Prince (on **FOLLIES [Sondheim: April 4, 1971]**).

NEVER TOO LATE
November 27, 1962   Playhouse Theatre
1,007 performances

Play by Sumner Arthur Long
Incidental music by John Kander
Song by Jerry **Bock** and Sheldon Harnick
Directed by George Abbott
Produced by Elliot Martin and Daniel Hollywood
With Paul Ford, Maureen O'Sullivan, and Orson Bean

Published songs:

None

Kander provided incidental music for this surprise hit, George Abbott's final smash. The one song used, though, was provided by Bock and Harnick.

FLORA, THE RED MENACE
May 11, 1965   Alvin Theatre   87 performances

Lyrics by Fred Ebb
Book by George Abbott and Robert Russell
(Based on *Love Is Just Around the Corner* [novel] by Lester Atwell)
Choreographed by Lee Theodore
Directed by Abbott
Produced by Harold Prince
With Liza Minnelli, Bob Dishy, Mary Louise Wilson, Cathryn Damon, and James Cresson

Published songs:

"All I Need (Is One Good Break)"
"Dear Love"
"Express Yourself"
"I Believe You"—cut
"Knock Knock"
"Not Every Day Of The Week"
"A Quiet Thing"
"Sing Happy"

Additional songs recorded:

"The Flame"
"Hello Waves"
"Palomino Pal"
"Sign Here"
"Unafraid"
"You Are You"

Publisher Tommy Valando, who had nurtured Jerry Bock, brought Kander and lyricist Fred Ebb together. Ebb had been contributing undistinguished songs (with music by Norman Martin) to late-Fifties revues. The new team immediately came up with the 1962 pop hit "My Coloring Book." Harold Prince had been impressed with Kander on **A FAMILY AFFAIR [January 27, 1962]**; he gave the pair their first Broadway assignment. **FLORA, THE RED MENACE** was the last of the Abbott-Prince shows; the old formula was becoming outmoded, and Prince decided to move on without Abbott and direct future shows himself. What was good about **FLORA** was the bright, funny score and Liza Minnelli, who won a Tony Award in her Broadway debut.

CABARET
November 20, 1966   Broadhurst Theatre
1,165 performances

Lyrics by Fred Ebb
Book by Joe Masteroff
(Based on *I Am a Camera* [play] by John van Druten from stories by
  Christopher Isherwood)
Choreographed by Ronald Field
Directed by Harold Prince
Produced by Prince in association with Ruth Mitchell
With Jill Haworth, Jack Gilford, Lotte Lenya, and Joel Grey

Published songs:

"Cabaret"
"I Don't Care Much"—cut
"Married"
"Maybe This Time"—added to 1972 movie version; initial use of
  1963 nonshow song
"Meeskite"
"Mein Herr"—written for movie version
"Money, Money (Makes The World Go Round)"—written for
  movie version
"Tomorrow Belongs To Me"
"Why Should I Wake Up?"
"Wilkommen (Welcome)"

Additional songs published in vocal score:

"Don't Tell Mama"
"If You Could See Her"
"It Couldn't Please Me More (The Pineapple Song)"
"Perfectly Marvelous"
"Sitting Pretty (Money Song)"
"So What"
"Telephone Song"
"Two Ladies"
"What Would You Do?"

Kander and Ebb's first and biggest hit came with this first of the new-
style Harold Prince musicals. Prince had experimented as director on
four musical comedies; he now successfully moved ahead into a more
conceptualized musical theatre (aided by Boris Aronson's striking
physical production which drew the audience into the proceedings).
The score was effective, if uneven: the Kit Kat Club solos ("Wilkommen" and "Cabaret") and the M.C.'s comic specialties on the
one hand, the bland songs accompanying the weak love story on the
other. The music was highly influenced by Kurt Weill, accentuated

by the presence of Lenya; Kander and Ebb wrote one of their best songs for her, "What Would You Do?" Jack Gilford supplied pathos, and the brilliantly conceived role of the M.C. was well performed by the chilling Joel Grey.

THE HAPPY TIME
January 18, 1968   Broadway Theatre   286 performances

Lyrics by Fred Ebb
Book by N. Richard Nash
(Based on the novel by Robert L. Fontaine)
Directed and choreographed by Gower Champion
Produced by David Merrick
With Robert Goulet, David Wayne, Mike Rupert, and George S. Irving

Published songs:

"A Certain Girl"
"The Happy Time"
"I Don't Remember You"
"Seeing Things"
"Tomorrow Morning"
"(Walking) Among My Yesterdays"

Additional songs published in vocal selection:

"The Life Of The Party"
"Please Stay"
"St. Pierre"
"Without Me"

Additional songs recorded:

"Catch My Garter"
"He's Back"

Kander and Ebb came up with a charming score for a charming, intimate musical—which was given an overblown, heavy production. When Champion decided to turn **THE HAPPY TIME** into a multi-media photography show, all was lost. Broadway had its first million-dollar bomb, and Champion received two Tony Awards.

ZORBA
November 17, 1968   Imperial Theatre   305 performances

Lyrics by Fred Ebb
Book by Joseph Stein

(Based on *Zorba the Greek* [novel] by Nikos Kazantzakis)
Choreographed by Ronald Field
Directed by Harold Prince
Produced by Prince in association with Ruth Mitchell
With Herschel Bernardi, Maria Karnilova, John Cunningham, and
   Lorraine Serabian

Published songs:

"The First Time"
"Happy Birthday To Me"
"No Boom Boom"
"Only Love"
"Why Can't I Speak?"
"Woman"—written for 1983 revival
"Zorba Theme (Life Is)" [instrumental]

Additional songs published in vocal selection:

"I Am Free"
"The Top Of The Hill"

Additional songs recorded:

"The Butterfly"
"The Crow"
"Goodbye, Canavaro"
"Grandpapa (Zorba's Dance)"
"Life Is"
"Y'assou"

An attempt to follow a hit—**CABARET [November 20, 1966]**—with
a similarly assembled, advance-sale blockbuster was once again unsuccessful. There were also overtones of Prince's longest-running
FIDDLER ON THE ROOF [Bock: September 22, 1964], represented by stars Bernardi (a long-time Tevye) and Karnilova. While
Kander under the influence of Weill was right for the earlier show,
the manufactured Greek music of **ZORBA** had little of the composer's voice in it. After struggling on a while, the stars got sick—separately—and the show passed away.

70, GIRLS, 70
April 15, 1971   Broadhurst Theatre   35 performances

Lyrics by Fred Ebb
Book by Ebb and Norman L. Martin
(Based on *Breath of Spring* [play] by Peter Coke)

Choreographed by Onna White
Directed by Paul Aaron
Produced by Arthur Whitelaw
With Mildred Natwick, Lillian Roth, Lillian Hayman, and Hans Conried

Published songs:
"The Elephant Song"
"Yes"

Additional songs published in vocal selection:
"Believe"
"Boom Ditty Boom"
"Broadway, My Street"
"Coffee (In A Cardboard Cup)"
"Do We?"
"Go Visit Your Grandmother"
"Home"
"Old Folks"
"70, Girls, 70"

Additional songs recorded:
"The Caper"
"Hit It, Lorraine"
"See The Light"
"You And I, Love"

Kander and Ebb came back with another charming, if imperfect, score. As with **FLORA, THE RED MENACE [May 11, 1965]** and **THE HAPPY TIME [January 18, 1968],** problems in other areas took their toll. **70, GIRLS, 70** also suffered from an unlikely audience identification problem: **FOLLIES [Sondheim: April 4, 1971]** had recently opened to cautious reviews and worse word-of-mouth among the older, traditional musical comedy fans. The Kander-Ebb/Prince connection, the presence of old-time actors, and the Follies Girls titles confused theatregoers and the intimate musical quickly folded. (The extravaganza died more slowly, painfully.) Ebb wrote the book with Norman Martin, his pre-Kander collaborator. A tragedy of the **70, GIRLS, 70** tryout: veteran David Burns suffered a heart attack doing the "Grandmother" number and died March 12, 1971 in Philadelphia.

CHICAGO
A Musical Vaudeville
June 1, 1975   46th Street Theatre   923 performances

Lyrics by Fred Ebb
Book by Ebb and Bob Fosse
(Based on the play by Maurine Dallas Watkins)
Directed and choreographed by Fosse
Produced by Robert Fryer and James Cresson
With Gwen Verdon, Chita Rivera, Jerry Orbach, and Barney Martin

Published songs:

"And All That Jazz"
"Mr. Cellophane"
"Me And My Baby"
"My Own Best Friend"
"Razzle Dazzle"
"Roxie"

Additional songs published in vocal selection:

"All I Care About"
"Class"
"Funny Honey"
"I Can't Do It Alone"
"A Little Bit Of Good"
"Nowadays"
"When You're Good To Mama"

Additional songs recorded:

"Cell Block Tango"
"We Both Reached For The Gun"
"When Velma Takes The Stand"

Fosse had **CHICAGO** built to order around his concept, as he'd done with **PIPPIN [S. Schwartz: October 23, 1972].** While the earlier show had at least some effective musical moments, the **CHICAGO** score merely filled Fosse's needs and sounded "authentic." But Fosse, Gwen Verdon (in her first musical since **SWEET CHARITY [Coleman: January 30, 1966],** and Chita Rivera (in her first since BAJOUR [November 23, 1964]) provided enough reason to give Kander his second-longest run.

THE ACT
October 29, 1977   Majestic Theatre   233 performances

Lyrics by Fred Ebb
Book by George Furth
Choreographed by Ron Lewis
Directed by Martin Scorsese
Produced by The Shubert Organization and Feuer and Martin
With Liza Minnelli and Barry Nelson

Published songs:

"City Lights"
"It's The Strangest Thing"
"My Own Space"
"Shine It On"

Additional songs recorded:

"Arthur In The Afternoon"
"Bobo's"
"Hot Enough For You?"
"Little Do They Know"
"The Money Tree"
"There When I Need Him"
"Turning (Shaker Hymn)"
"Walking Papers"

CHICAGO [June 1, 1975] had Bob Fosse to help triumph over weak components; **THE ACT** had weaker material, no Fosse, and one Liza in place of Verdon and Rivera. But Minnelli's popularity at the time made her a sure-fire ticket seller, enabling **THE ACT** to get away with a lot on very little. First facing Broadway in **FLORA, THE RED MENACE [May 11, 1965]**, Minnelli became a superstar in Fosse's 1972 movie version of **CABARET [November 20, 1966]**. She had subbed for the ailing Verdon in **CHICAGO,** and Kander and Ebb supplied much of her special material for nightclubs and television. So, Minnelli was closely tied to the songwriters; hence, **THE ACT.** Gower Champion replaced Scorsese (without credit); he also made his final stage appearance when he replaced Barry Nelson late in the run.

WOMAN OF THE YEAR
March 29, 1981   Palace Theatre   770 performances

Lyrics by Fred Ebb
Book by Peter Stone

(Based on the screenplay by Ring Lardner, Jr. and Michael Kanin)
Choreographed by Tony Charmoli
Directed by Robert Moore
Produced by Lawrence Kasha, David S. Landay, James M. Nederlander,
    Warner Communications, Carole J. Shorenstein, and Stewart F. Lane
With Lauren Bacall, Harry Guardino, Roderick Cook, and Rex Everhart

Published songs:

"One Of The Girls"
"See You In The Funny Papers"
"Sometimes A Day Goes By"
"We're Gonna Work It Out"

Additional songs published in vocal selection:

"The Grass Is Always Greener"
"I Wrote The Book"
"The Two Of Us"
"Woman Of The Year"

Additional songs recorded:

"Happy In The Morning"
"I Told You So"
"It Isn't Working"
"The Poker Game"
"Shut Up, Gerald"
"So What Else Is New?"
"Table Talk"
"When You're Right, You're Right"

Lauren Bacall managed to carry this show for a decent though unprofitable run. The well-written and literate Oscar-winning screenplay was turned into a one-sided comic strip, leaving nothing much
to amuse audiences but Marilyn Cooper. Tommy Tune helped out
during the tryout and Joe Layton redid the show (with some new
material) for the post-Broadway tour. All told, a star vehicle with one
of the few stars still capable of carrying a capsized ship.

THE RINK

February 9, 1984   Martin Beck Theatre   204 performances

Lyrics by Fred Ebb
Book by Terrence McNally
Choreographed by Graciela Daniele
Directed by A. J. Antoon

Produced by Jules Fisher, Roger Berlind and Joan Cullman, Milbro
    Productions, Kenneth-John Productions in association with Jonathan
    Farkas
With Chita Rivera and Liza Minnelli

Songs published in vocal selection:
"All The Children In A Row"
"Blue Crystal"
"Chief Cook And Bottle Washer"
"Colored Lights"
"Marry Me"
"The Rink"
"Under The Roller-Coaster"
"Wallflower"
"We Can Make It"

Additional songs recorded:
"After All These Years"
"Angel's Rink And Social Center"
"The Apple Doesn't Fall"
"Don't 'Ah, Ma' Me"
"Mrs. A."
"Not Enough Magic"
"What Happened To The Old Days?"

Even Minnelli and the exceptional Rivera weren't enough to attract
any interest to **THE RINK,** a heartless show (like its predecessors)
built around nothing. Attempts to shock the audience were repug-
nant, and the stars were wasted. A good sign, though: both Kander
and Ebb showed more inventiveness and originality than they had in
years, particularly in "Colored Lights" and some of the comedy
numbers.

John Kander's first six Broadway scores (through **70, GIRLS, 70
[April 15, 1971]**) were interesting and worthwhile, although only
CABARET [November 20, 1966] was a hit. The four star vehicles
since have shown none of Kander's former creativity. Again, only one
show was successful. The overall record is less than encouraging, and
it is surprising to find only two song hits ("Cabaret" and "Wilkommen") in the lot. Even so, Kander is one of the more talented composers of his generation. It is to be hoped that recent failures will
influence him to go back to his distinctive personal style.

Harvey Schmidt

BORN: September 12, 1929   Dallas, Texas

The son of a Methodist minister, Schmidt was studying art at the University of Texas when he met fellow Texan Tom Jones. A mutual interest in theatre led the pair to a songwriting collaboration on college shows. After serving in the Army, both men came to New York. Jones began directing nightclub revues while Schmidt worked as a commercial artist.

SHOESTRING '57
November 5, 1956   Barbizon Plaza Theatre
⟨off-Broadway⟩   110 performances

Music mostly by others (see **Strouse**)
Lyrics by Sheldon Harnick, Mike Stewart, Lee Adams, Carolyn Leigh, and others
Choreographed by Danny Daniels
Directed by Paul Lammers
Produced by Ben Bagley in association with E. H. Morris
With Dody Goodman, Dorothy Greener, and Paul Mazursky

Recorded song:
"At Twenty-Two" (lyric by Tom Jones)

This revue was a sequel to Ben Bagley's first **SHOESTRING RE-VUE [Strouse: February 28, 1955]**. Bagley was to leave off-Broadway for a record producing career, specializing in less familiar theatre music; the artist Schmidt was to provide distinctive jacket paintings for the series.

DEMI-DOZEN
Nightclub Revue
October 11, 1958   Upstairs At The Downstairs

Music also by others (see **Coleman**)
Lyrics to Schmidt songs by Tom Jones
Directed by John Heawood
Produced by Jules Monk
With Gerry Matthews and Jane Connell

Recorded songs:

"Grand Opening"
"The Holy Man And The Yankee"
"Mini Off-Broadway"
"One And All" (lyric by Schmidt)
"Race Of The Lexington Avenue Express"
"A Seasonal Sonatina"
"Statehood Hula"

Jones had been involved as a director with the Julius Monk night-club revue series. With **DEMI-DOZEN** Jones and Schmidt received their first New York break (and little notice).

THE FANTASTICKS
May 3, 1960   Sullivan Street Theatre ⟨off-Broadway⟩
[still running as of October 1, 1985]

Book and lyrics by Tom Jones
(Based on *Les Romantiques* [play] by Edmond Rostand)
Directed by Word Baker
Produced by Lore Noto
With Jerry Orbach, Kenneth Nelson, Rita Gardner, and Thomas Bruce
   (Jones)

Published songs:

"Soon It's Gonna Rain"
"They Were You"
"Try To Remember"

Additional songs published in vocal score:

"Happy Ending"
"I Can See It"
"It Depends On What You Pay"
"Metaphor"
"Much More"
"Never Say No"
"Overture" [instrumental]

"Plant A Radish"
"Rape Ballet" [instrumental]
" 'Round And 'Round"
"This Plum Is Too Ripe"

Fellow University of Texas student Word Baker renewed acquaintance with Schmidt and Jones when he served as associate director/producer of **DEMI-DOZEN [October 11, 1958].** With the opportunity to mount an original one-act musical at a Barnard College (New York) summer program, Baker asked Schmidt and Jones if they could finish the piece they had been working on; the one-act **FANTASTICKS** played a week [opening August 3, 1959]. Novice producer Lore Noto optioned it and brought the revised version to Sullivan Street back in 1960. The popularity of "Try To Remember" sustained the show for a dozen years or so, and "Soon It's Gonna Rain" accounted for another decade. The simplicity and theatrical inventiveness (and relatively low operating cost) keep **THE FANTASTICKS** with us.

110 IN THE SHADE
October 24, 1963   Broadhurst Theatre   330 performances

Lyrics by Tom Jones
Book by N. Richard Nash
(Based on *The Rainmaker* [play] by Nash)
Choreographed by Agnes de Mille
Directed by Joseph Anthony
Produced by David Merrick
With Inga Swenson, Robert Horton, Stephen Douglass, and Lesley Ann
    Warren

Published songs:

"Everything Beautiful Happens At Night"
"Is It Really Me?"
"Love, Don't Turn Away"
"A Man And A Woman"
"110 In The Shade"—written for 1967 London production
"Simple Little Things"
"Too Many People Alone"—cut

Additional songs published in vocal score:

"Cinderella"
"Gonna Be Another Hot Day"

"The Hungry Men"
"Little Red Hat"
"Lizzie's Comin' Home"
"Melisande"
"Old Maid"
"Poker Polka"
"The Rain Song"
"Raunchy"
"Wonderful Music"
"You're Not Fooling Me"

David Merrick brought Schmidt and Jones to Broadway and put them together with Nash's 1954 hit *The Rainmaker*. The odd combination came up with a surprisingly effective and well-crafted piece. Particularly impressive: "The Rain Song," "Gonna Be Another Hot Day," and the soliloquy "Old Maid." By season's end, though, the competition of Merrick's own **HELLO, DOLLY!** [**Herman: January 16, 1964**] and **FUNNY GIRL** [**Styne: March 26, 1964**] had overwhelmed the intimate **110 IN THE SHADE.**

I DO! I DO!
December 5, 1966   46th Street Theatre   561 performances

Book and lyrics by Tom Jones
(Based on *The Fourposter* [play] by Jan de Hartog)
Directed and choreographed by Gower Champion
Produced by David Merrick
With Mary Martin and Robert Preston

Published songs:

"The Honeymoon Is Over"
"I Do! I Do!"
"My Cup Runneth Over"
"Thousands Of Flowers"—cut
"Together Forever"
"What Is A Woman?"

Additional songs published in vocal score:

"All The Dearly Beloved"
"The Father Of The Bride"
"Flaming Agnes"
"Goodnight"

"I Love My Wife"
"Love Isn't Everything"
"Nobody's Perfect"
"Roll Up The Ribbons"
"Someone Needs Me"
"Something Has Happened"
"This House"
"A Well Known Fact"
"When The Kids Get Married"
"Where Are The Snows?"

Although inventiveness and sparseness were Schmidt and Jones' stock in trade, **I DO! I DO!** was a curious paradox: a plotless, two-character, sweetly sentimental duet *and* a full-scale, big-budget star vehicle. The results were less than inspired, but Merrick and Champion managed to sell the Martin-Preston package to Broadway for a profitable run (cut short by the 1968 Actors' Equity strike).

CELEBRATION
January 22, 1969   Ambassador Theatre   110 performances

Book, lyrics, and direction by Tom Jones
Choreographed by Vernon Lusby
Produced by Cheryl Crawford and Richard Chandler
With Keith Charles, Susan Watson, Ted Thurston, and Michael Glenn-Smith

Published songs:

"Celebration"
"I'm Glad To See You've Got What You Want"
"Love Song"
"My Garden"
"Under The Tree"

Additional songs published in vocal score:

"Beautician Ballet" [instrumental]
"Bored"
"Fifty Million Years Ago"
"It's You Who Makes Me Young"
"Not My Problem"
"Orphan In The Storm"
"Saturnalia" [instrumental]

"Somebody"
"Survive"
"Where Did It Go?"
"Winter And Summer"

After two successful (yet relatively traditional) Merrick musicals, Schmidt and Jones returned to the experimental field of THE FANTASTICKS [May 3, 1960] under the auspices of Cheryl Crawford. Both shows shared a similar theatrical simplicity; but THE FANTASTICKS was slightly metaphoric while the baffling CELEBRATION was heavily symbolic. After the show's quick failure, Schmidt and Jones retreated to their off-off-Broadway studio to work on future experiments away from commercial theatre pressures.

COLETTE
⟨First Version⟩
May 6, 1970   Ellen Stewart Theatre ⟨off-Broadway⟩
101 performances

Play by Elinor Jones
(Based on *Earthly Paradise* [autobiographical stories] by Colette)
Incidental music by Harvey Schmidt
Lyrics by Tom Jones
Directed by Gerald Freedman
Produced by Cheryl Crawford in association with Mary W. John
With Zoe Caldwell, Mildred Dunnock, Keene Curtis, Barry Bostwick, and
    Schmidt

Published song:
"Earthly Paradise"

Additional songs recorded:
"The Bouilloux Girls"
"Femme Du Monde"

Tom Jones' wife wrote this rather acclaimed piece. Schmidt performed the on-stage piano accompaniment.

PHILEMON
April 8, 1975   Portfolio Theatre ⟨off-off-Broadway⟩
60 performances

Book and lyrics by Tom Jones
Directed by Lester Collins (a.k.a. Harvey Schmidt)
Produced by Jones and Schmidt
With Michael Glenn-Smith, Leila Martin, Dick Latessa, and Kathrin
  King Segal

Published songs:

None

Another experiment in the **CELEBRATION [January 22, 1969]**
mode.

COLETTE
⟨Second Version⟩
*[February 9, 1982]   Fifth Avenue Theatre ⟨Seattle,
Washington⟩; closed during pre-Broadway tryout*

Book and lyrics by Tom Jones
Choreographed by Carl Jablonski
Directed by Dennis Rosa
Produced by Harry Rigby and The John F. Kennedy Center in association
  with the Denver Center and James M. Nederlander
With Diana Rigg, Robert Helpmann, John Reardon, Martin Vidnovic,
  and Marta Eggert

Published songs:

None

Schmidt and Jones returned to the commcrical theatre with a full-
scale, full-sized musical that quickly collapsed. This **COLETTE**, incidentally, was not based on the ⟨**First Version**⟩ **[May 6, 1970]**.

Harvey Schmidt and collaborator Tom Jones displayed creativity and
inventiveness in their work during the Sixties. The pair were never
comfortable working on the large scale necessary for Broadway, and
until recently have been in self-imposed exile. Just now Broadway
needs creativity and inventiveness, and Schmidt and Jones might very
well have something to say. Meanwhile, **THE FANTASTICKS [May
3, 1960]** keeps running.

Mitch Leigh

BORN: January 31, 1928 Brooklyn, New York

Mitch Leigh prepared for his musical career at Yale, studying composition with Paul Hindemith. Upon receiving his Masters, he entered the world of advertising and became an expert at television jingles (his most popular work—after "The Impossible Dream"—remains "Nobody Doesn't Like Sara Lee"). By the mid-Sixties, the highly successful jingle writer was ready to put his musical training to a more creative use.

TOO TRUE TO BE GOOD
March 12, 1963   54th Street Theatre   94 performances

Play by George Bernard Shaw
Incidental music by Mitch Leigh
Directed by Albert Marre
Produced by Paul Vroom, Buff Cobb, and Burry Frederick
With Lillian Gish, Robert Preston, David Wayne, Cedric Hardwicke,
   Eileen Heckart, Cyril Ritchard, Glynis Johns, and Ray Middleton

Published songs:
None

Leigh began a career-long association with director Albert Marre on this all-star revival. Marre's only musical hit was KISMET [December 3, 1953]; more recently, he'd done **MILK AND HONEY [Herman: October 10, 1961]**. Leigh and Marre began discussing a musical adaptation of Dale Wasserman's 1960 teleplay *I, Don Quixote*. The ambitious composer began the adaptation with poet W. H. Auden as lyricist.

NEVER LIVE OVER A PRETZEL FACTORY
March 28, 1964   Eugene O'Neill Theatre   9 performances

Play by Jerry Devine
Incidental music by Mitch Leigh
Directed by Albert Marre
Produced by Paul Vroom, Buff Cobb, and Marre
With Dennis O'Keefe and Martin Sheen

Published songs:

None

Leigh's first Broadway song to be heard—for a week—was "In This Town" (lyric by Jack Wohl).

MAN OF LA MANCHA
November 22, 1965   ANTA Washington Square Theatre
2,328 performances

Lyrics by Joe Darion
Book by Dale Wasserman
(Based on *Don Quixote* [novel] by Miguel de Cervantes)
Choreographed by Jack Cole
Directed by Albert Marre
Produced by Albert W. Selden and Hal James
With Richard Kiley, Joan Diener (Marre), Irving Jacobson, Ray
  Middleton, and Robert Rounseville

Published songs:

"Aldonza"
"Dulcinea"
"I Really Like Him"
"The Impossible Dream (The Quest)"
"Knight Of The Woeful Countenance (The Dubbing)"
"Little Bird, Little Bird"
"A Little Gossip"
"Man Of La Mancha (I, Don Quixote)"
"To Each His Dulcinea (To Every Man His Dream)"

Additional songs published in vocal score:

"Barber's Song"
"The Combat"
"Golden Helmet"
"I'm Only Thinking Of Him"
"It's All The Same"
"Knight Of The Mirrors"

"The Psalm"
"What Do You Want Of Me?"

A summer stock tryout at the Goodspeed Opera House in East Haddam, Connecticut brought forth this monumental worldwide hit (see **CHU-CHEM [November 15, 1966]**). Lyricist Joe Darion, W. H. Auden's replacement, had one Broadway musical (SHINBONE ALLEY [April 13, 1957]) to his credit; composer Leigh and librettist Wasserman had none. While the separate elements were not perfect in themselves, everything joined together magically. Leigh's highly theatrical, strongly rhythmic score played an important part in overriding the sometimes saccharine book, with "The Impossible Dream" affecting the public conscience as "Camelot" had five years earlier. Performances by Richard Kiley, Joan Diener and the others; Marre's inventive staging; Howard Bay's dungeon and windmill set—everything worked.

CHU-CHEM
[November 15, 1966]   New Locust Street Theatre
⟨Philadelphia, Pennsylvania⟩; closed during pre-Broadway
tryout

Lyrics by Jim Haines and Jack Wohl
Book by Ted Allan
Choreographed by Jack Cole
Directed by Albert Marre
Produced by Cheryl Crawford and Mitch Leigh
With Menasha Skulnick and Molly Picon

Published songs:
None

The summer of 1965 saw an ambitious project at the newly restored Goodspeed Opera House in East Haddam, Connecticut: producer Albert Selden and director Albert Marre planned a season of three new musicals with Mitch Leigh scores. Their intention was to move them to Broadway, in turn, for four-week runs. The first opened June 24 at Goodspeed, and took several months to get to New York; but **MAN OF LA MANCHA [November 22, 1965]** lasted longer than four weeks! The second was a short-lived musical adaptation of Sean O'Casey's 1940 *Purple Dust;* Marre had been trying to mount a production of the play since 1952. The third musical, **CHU-CHEM,** holds the distinction of being the only Chinese-Yiddish musical comedy to ever almost reach Broadway.

CRY FOR US ALL
April 8, 1970   Broadhurst Theatre   9 performances

Lyrics by William Alfred and Phyllis Robinson
Book by Alfred and Albert Marre
(Based on *Hogan's Goat* [play] by Alfred)
Directed by Marre
Produced by Mitch Leigh in association with L. Gerald Goldsmith
With Robert Weede, Joan Diener (Marre), Steve Arlen, Helen Gallagher,
   and Tommy Rall

Published songs:

"Cry For Us All"
"That Slavery Is Love"
"The Verandah Waltz"

Additional songs recorded:

"Aggie, Oh Aggie"
"The Cruelty Man"
"The End Of My Race"
"How Are Ya, Since?"
"The Leg Of The Duck"
"The Mayor's Chair"
"Search Your Heart"
"Swing Your Bag"
"This Cornucopian Land"
"The Wages Of Sin"
"Who To Love If Not A Stranger"

Leigh returned to Broadway with his most serious work. **CRY FOR US ALL** was a musical drama verging on the operatic; but a muddy book weighed down the already heavy subject matter, and an even heavier set proved far more depressing than the Inquisition prison of **MAN OF LA MANCHA [November 22, 1965].** Yet the score was finely written, Leigh working with constantly shifting rhythms for highly emotional effects. All through his career Leigh has suffered from the same problem as Vincent Youmans, Vernon Duke, and others: the inability to sustain working relationships with collaborators. **CRY FOR US ALL** had potential as a serious musical theatre piece. The music was of suitable caliber, but the other elements assembled were lacking.

HALLOWEEN
[March 20, 1972]   Bucks County Playhouse ⟨New Hope, Pennsylvania⟩; stock tryout

Book and lyrics by Sidney Michaels
Directed by Albert Marre
Produced by Albert W. Selden and Jerome Minskoff
With David Wayne, Margot Moser, and Dick Shawn

Published songs:
None

Again working with a collaborator undistinguished in the musical theatre, Leigh turned out the strange, experimental **HALLOWEEN**, which quickly disappeared.

HOME SWEET HOMER
January 4, 1976   Palace Theatre   1 performance

Lyrics by Charles Burr and Forman Brown
Book by Roland Kibbee and Albert Marre
(Based on *The Odyssey* by Homer)
Directed by Marre
Produced by The John F. Kennedy Center
With Yul Brynner and Joan Diener (Marre)
NOTE: **ODYSSEY,** pre-Broadway title

Published songs:
None

A fabled Broadway flop, a rare case of the lyricist/librettist—Erich (*Love Story*) Segal—quitting during the tryout tour and pulling his material. Everything worked out splendidly, though: a battery of new writers was brought in, the show was renamed, and **HOME SWEET HOMER** ended its epic odyssey on Broadway.

SARAVA
February 23, 1979   Mark Hellinger Theatre
177 performances

Book and lyrics by N. Richard Nash
(Based on *Dona Flor and Her Two Husbands* [novel] by Jorge Amado)
Directed and choreographed by Rick Atwell
Produced by Eugene V. Wolsk
With Tovah Feldshuh, P. J. Benjamin, and Michael Ingraham

Published song:

"Sarava"

Additional song recorded:

"You Do"

Leigh chose yet another amateur lyricist as collaborator. Playwright N. Richard Nash had provided the rather good book for **110 IN THE SHADE [Schmidt: October 24, 1963]** and the less happy **HAPPY TIME [Kander: January 18, 1968]** and **WILDCAT [Coleman: December 16, 1960]**. **SARAVA** was undistinguished, and even a skillfully designed Mitch Leigh advertising campaign didn't help.

APRIL SONG
[July 9, 1980]   John Drew Theatre ⟨East Hampton, New York⟩; summer stock tryout

Lyrics by Sammy Cahn
Book by Albert Marre
(Based on *Leocadia* [play] by Jean Anouilh)
Directed by Marre
Produced by Marre and Leigh
With Glynis Johns

Published songs:

None

Something impelled Marre to take the Anouilh play—which he had successfully directed in an earlier nonmusical translation (**TIME REMEMBERED [Duke: November 1957]**)—and turn it into a play with songs. Whatever the intentions were, they didn't work.

Mitch Leigh entered the musical theatre with the instant classic **MAN OF LA MANCHA [November 22, 1965].** He has returned with six consecutive failures, best attributed to poor choice of material and collaborators. Leigh is a well-trained, serious composer with avant-garde leanings. He has satisfactorily displayed ability in **LA MANCHA** and **CRY FOR US ALL [April 8, 1970];** what he has *not* displayed, of late, is the dedication to exercise those talents.

Stephen Schwartz

BORN: March 6, 1948   Roslyn Heights, New York

The dearth of musical comedy production since the late Sixties has resulted in the lack of a new generation of theatre writers. Only one composer of the Seventies has shown the ability (and interest) to work principally in the theatre. Stephen Schwartz is a full twenty years younger than the Kander/Bock/Strouse/Schmidt/Coleman group; and no one has come along since Schwartz. After attending Carnegie-Mellon University, the twenty-one-year-old songwriter came to New York to begin his career.

[all music and lyrics by Stephen Schwartz]

BUTTERFLIES ARE FREE
October 21, 1969   Booth Theatre   1,128 performances

Play by Leonard Gershe
Directed by Milton Katselas
Produced by Arthur Whitelaw, Max J. Brown, and Byron Goldman
With Keir Dullea, Eileen Heckart, and Blythe Danner

Published song:

"Butterflies Are Free"

Schwartz got his first New York hearing with this singer-and-guitar title song. The play was a surprise hit; the song pleasant.

GODSPELL
May 17, 1971   Cherry Lane Theatre ⟨off-Broadway⟩
2,124 performances
June 22, 1976   Broadhurst Theatre   527 performances

Book and direction by John-Michael Tebelak
(Based on The Gospel According to St. Matthew)

Produced by Edgar Lansbury, Stuart Duncan, and Joseph Beruh
With Stephen Nathan and David Haskell

Published songs:

"All For The Best"
"All Good Gifts"
"Day By Day"
"Finale (Long Live God)"
"Learn Your Lessons Well"
"Light Of The World"
"O Bless The Lord"
"On The Willows"
"Prepare Ye The Way Of The Lord"
"Save The People"
"Turn Back, O Man"
"We Beseech Thee"

Additional songs published in vocal score:

"Alas For You"
"Bless The Lord"
"Prologue"
"Tower Of Babble"

Schwartz's success began with this pop-Biblical revue, the **FAN-TASTICKS [Schmidt: May 3, 1960]** of the Seventies, although **GODSPELL**'s run was far shorter, only six-plus years. The score was easy and tuneful, with "Day By Day" bringing Schwartz to the attention of Broadway.

MASS
see Bernstein [September 8, 1971]

PIPPIN
October 23, 1972   Imperial Theatre   1,944 performances

Book by Roger O. Hirson
Directed and choreographed by Bob Fosse
Produced by Stuart Ostrow
With John Rubinstein, Ben Vereen, Irene Ryan, and Jill Clayburgh

Published songs:

"Corner Of The Sky"
"Goodtime Ladies Rag"

"I Guess I'll Miss The Man"
"Just Between The Two Of Us"—cut
"Morning Glow"

Additional songs published in vocal selections:

"Extraordinary"
"Kind Of Woman"
"Love Song"
"Magic To Do"
"No Time At All"
"Pippin"
"Simple Joys"
"Spread A Little Sunshine"
"With You"

Additional songs recorded:

"Glory"
"On The Right Track"
"War Is A Science"

With the success of **GODSPELL [May 17, 1971]**, a college project of Schwartz's found its way to Broadway. Inability to raise money resulted in a drastically cut budget; hence, the imaginative, minimal production (and a skeletal replacement for the intended set). What **PIPPIN** did have was Bob Fosse at his inventive best, more than making up for the less-than-staggering score and more-than-lackluster book. Ben Vereen and designers Tony Walton and Patricia Zipprodt made valuable contributions; and a revolutionary (for the theatre) TV advertising campaign kept **PIPPIN** running for almost five years.

THE MAGIC SHOW
May 28, 1974   Cort Theatre   1,920 performances

Book by Bob Randall
(Based on magic by Doug Henning)
Directed and choreographed by Grover Dale
Produced by Edgar Lansbury, Joseph Beruh, and Ivan Reitman
With Henning, Dale Soules, Anita Morris, and David Ogden Stiers

Published song:

"Lion Tamer"

Additional songs published in vocal selection:

"Before Your Very Eyes"
"Charmin's Lament"
"Solid Silver Platform Shoes"
"Style"
"Sweet, Sweet, Sweet"
"Two's Company"
"Up To His Old Tricks"
"West End Avenue"

The great magic feat here was pulling a long-run hit out of a very empty hat. **THE MAGIC SHOW** ran 1,920 performances; **A LIT-TLE NIGHT MUSIC [Sondheim: February 25, 1973],** in comparison, barely broke 600.

THE BAKER'S WIFE
[May 11, 1976]   Dorothy Chandler Pavilion ⟨Los Angeles⟩; closed during pre-Broadway tryout

Book by Joseph Stein
(Based on *La Femme de Boulanger* [movie] by Marcel Pagnol and Jean
   Giono)
Choreographed by Robert Tucker
Directed by John Berry
Produced by David Merrick
With Topol (replaced by Paul Sorvino), Patti LuPone, Keene Curtis,
   Portia Nelson, and David Rounds

Songs recorded:

"Any-Day-Now-Day"
"Chanson"
"Endless Delights"
"Gifts Of Love"
"If I Have To Live Alone"
"Meadowlark"—cut
"Merci, Madame"
"Proud Lady"
"Serenade"
"Where Is The Warmth?"

Stephen Schwartz's track record led to this assignment on the biggest musical of the season. David Merrick brought together Topol, the

Israeli-born star of the London and Hollywood **FIDDLER ON THE ROOF [Bock: September 22, 1964]**, and Joe Stein, that musical's librettist, for a big-budget, sure-fire hit . . . like **BREAKFAST AT TIFFANY'S [Merrill: December 14, 1966]**. Director Joseph Hardy left midway through the tryout; star Topol lasted till the next-to-last stop. Paul Sorvino could not handle the problematic material nearly so well, and **THE BAKER'S WIFE** was quickly no more. Schwartz's score was the most melodic and theatrical of his career to date.

WORKING
May 14, 1978   46th Street Theatre   25 performances

Music and lyrics also by others
Book and direction by Stephen Schwartz
(Based on the book by Studs Terkel)
Choreographed by Onna White
Produced by Stephen R. Friedman and Irwin Meyer (in association with
    Joseph Harris)
With Lenora Nemetz, Rex Everhart, Bobo Lewis, Patti LuPone, and
    Arny Freeman

Songs published in vocal selection:

"All The Livelong Day" (lyric including "I Hear America Singing"
    by Walt Whitman)
"Fathers And Sons"
"It's An Art"
"Neat To Be A Newsboy"

If Broadway can be said to take retribution for undeserved hits, then Broadway took retribution on composer Schwartz with **THE BAKER'S WIFE [May 11, 1976]**. Then they did it again, more publicly. Schwartz conceived, directed, and cowrote **WORKING,** which didn't work at all.

Stephen Schwartz's career has not yet recovered from his two highly visible, expensive failures. But with three highly lucrative, long-running goldmines to his name, he's sure to be produced again. Schwartz has already proven his ability to occasionally write pleasant tunes. There is every reason to expect that he will write more, or maybe even something better.

PART 4

Introduction

The following section contains additional shows which merit discussion. Some were enormous hits and are included for that reason only; others were written by popular or interesting composers who never found Broadway success; and a handful are included because of the high quality of the work. Until the late Sixties, Broadway was virtually dominated by the thirty composers already discussed. It is anticipated and hoped that some of the current writers represented here will soon prove themselves major theatre composers.

Notable Broadway Scores
by Other Composers

IRENE
November 1, 1919   Vanderbilt Theatre   675 performances

Music by Harry Tierney
Lyrics by Joseph McCarthy
Book by James Montgomery
Directed by Edward Royce
Produced by Vanderbilt Producing Corp.
With Edith Day

Published songs:

"Alice Blue Gown"
"Castle Of Dreams"
"The Family Tree" (additional lyric by Charles Gaynor)—initial
   publication upon use in 1973 revival
"Hobbies"
"Irene"
"The Last Part Of Ev'ry Party"
"The 'Paul Jones' "
"Skyrocket"
"Talk Of The Town"
"To Be Worthy (Worthy Of You)"
"We're Getting Away With It"
"You've Got Me Out On A Limb"—written for 1940 movie version

Additional songs published in vocal score:

"To Love You"—countermelody to "To Be Worthy"
"Too Much Bowden (Opening Chorus Act 2, Scene 2)"

Tin Pan Alley composer Harry Tierney (1895–1965) made occasional
Broadway visits. His first and most successful, **IRENE,** set the mold

for the "American Cinderella" musicals. (The Shuberts, ever on the lookout for a catchy title, actually came up with SALLY, IRENE & MARY [September 4, 1922]; **SALLY** being **Kern [December 21, 1920]**, and MARY [October 18, 1920] being Louis Hirsch's "Love Nest" musical.) **IRENE** waltzed to a record-length run in her "Alice Blue Gown," unsurpassed until **PINS AND NEEDLES [Rome: November 27, 1937]** set a new mark of 1,108. Tierney and McCarthy wrote two other successful shows, both for Ziegfeld: Eddie Cantor's KID BOOTS [December 31, 1923] and RIO RITA [February 2, 1927].

SHUFFLE ALONG
A Musical Melange
May 23, 1921   63rd Street Music Hall   484 performances

Music by Eubie Blake
Lyrics by Noble Sissle
Book by Flournoy Miller and Aubrey Lyles
(Conceived by Miller and Lyles)
Directed by Miller
Produced by Nikko Producing Co.
With Blake, Sissle, Miller, Lyles, and Florence Mills

Published songs:

"Aintcha Comin' Back, Mary Ann, To Maryland"
"Baltimore Buzz"
"Bandana Days"
"Daddy Won't You Please Come Home"
"Everything Reminds Me Of You"
"Gypsy Blues"
"Good Night, Angeline"
"I'm Craving For That Kind Of Love (Kiss Me)"
"I'm Just Simply Full Of Jazz"
"I'm Just Wild About Harry"—new melody for lyric revised from
    1916 nonshow song "My Loving Baby"
"If You've Never Been Vamped By A Brown Skin (You've Never
    Been Vamped At All)"
"In Honeysuckle Time (When Emaline Said She'd Be Mine)"
"Kentucky Sue"
"Love Will Find A Way"
"Liza Quit Vamping Me"—advertised but not published

"Low Down Blues"
"Old Black Joe And Uncle Tom"
"Oriental Blues"
"Pickaninny Shoes"
"Shuffle Along"
"Sing Me To Sleep, Dear Mammy (With A Hush-A-Bye
  Pickaninny Tune)"
"Vision Girl"
NOTE: Songs cut or added after the opening not so noted

This shoestring revue set a standard for ragtag black musicals. A surprise hit, **SHUFFLE ALONG** outran most shows of the time and then toured for years. Two revised versions [December 26, 1932] and [May 8, 1952]—both headed by Sissle and Blake—lasted twenty-one performances combined. Eubie Blake (1883–1983) had no success with his other Broadway work; EUBIE! [September 20, 1978], an anthology revue, attempted to cash in on the overflow from the Fats Waller success AIN'T MISBEHAVIN' [May 8, 1978].

GEORGE WHITE'S SCANDALS OF 1926
Eighth Edition
June 14, 1926   Apollo Theatre   432 performances

Music by Ray Henderson
Lyrics by B. G. DeSylva and Lew Brown
Sketches by George White and W. K. Wells
Directed and produced by White
With Ann Pennington, Willie and Eugene Howard, and Harry Richman

Published songs:

"The Birth Of The Blues"
"Black Bottom"
"The Girl Is You And The Boy Is Me"
"Here I Am"—added after opening; published in separate edition
"It All Depends On You"—added after opening; published in
  separate edition
"Lucky Day"
"Sevilla"
"Tweet Tweet"

Ray Henderson (1896–1970) became a force in the pop music field with hits like "That Old Gang Of Mine" and "Bye Bye Blackbird."

When George Gershwin left the *Scandals* to concentrate on book musicals, White turned to Henderson, pop lyricist Lew Brown, and DeSylva (Gershwin's *Scandals* collaborator). Thus was born the most successful songwriting team of the late Twenties. This edition of the SCANDALS alone had four hits, including "Black Bottom"—which launched a dance craze—and the fine "Birth Of The Blues." Gershwin's five editions had brought forth only two worthwhile songs, "I'll Build A Stairway To Paradise" and "Somebody Loves Me"—both with DeSylva as colyricist.

GOOD NEWS!
The Collegiate Musical
September 6, 1927   Chanin's 46th Street Theatre
551 performances

Music by Ray Henderson
Lyrics by B. G. DeSylva and Lew Brown
Book by Laurence Schwab and DeSylva
Choreographed by Bobby Connolly
Directed by Edgar MacGregor
Produced by Schwab and Frank Mandel
With Mary Lawlor, John Price Jones, Zelma O'Neal, and George Olsen
   and his Orchestra

Published songs:

"The Best Things In Life Are Free"
"A Girl Of The Pi Beta Phi"
"Good News"
"Happy Days"
"He's A Ladies' Man"
"Just Imagine"
"Lucky In Love"
"The Varsity Drag"

Additional songs published in vocal score:

"Baby! What?"
"Flaming Youth"
"In The Meantime"
"On The Campus"
"Tait Song"
"Today's The Day"

DeSylva, Brown, and Henderson entered the book musical field with five hits in a row. Following FLYING HIGH [March 3, 1930], the team went to Hollywood—where DeSylva soon moved on to a producing career (see **DUBARRY WAS A LADY [Porter: December 6, 1939]**). Henderson and Brown continued writing (together and individually) but never equalled the success of their five great years. **GOOD NEWS!** was a mindless football musical in the **LEAVE IT TO JANE [Kern: August 28, 1917]** tradition; "The Best Things In Life Are Free" and "The Varsity Drag" were hits in the DeSylva, Brown, and Henderson tradition.

BLACKBIRDS OF 1928
May 9, 1928   Liberty Theatre   519 performances

Music by Jimmy McHugh
Lyrics by Dorothy Fields
Directed and produced by Lew Leslie
With Bill Robinson, Adelaide Hall, and Aida Ward

Published songs:

"Baby!"
"Bandanna Babies"
"Diga-Diga-Doo"
"Dixie"
"Doin' The New Low Down"
"Here Comes My Blackbird"
"I Can't Give You Anything But Love"
"I Must Have That Man!"
"Porgy"
"Magnolia's Wedding Day"
"Shuffle Your Feet And Just Roll Along"

Pop songwriter Jimmy McHugh (1894–1969) began contributing material to Harlem's Cotton Club in 1921. In 1927 he found a new lyricist: Dorothy Fields, of the familiar show business family. Cotton Club work got them the assignment for the highly successful **BLACKBIRDS OF 1928**, which, unlike **SHUFFLE ALONG [PART 4: May 23, 1921]**, was a professional, high-caliber production. The score brought McHugh and Fields immediate acclaim, with "I Can't Give You Anything But Love" and "Diga-Diga-Doo" leading the way. The team moved to Hollywood for successful work (including "I'm In The Mood For Love") until Jerome Kern needed a new lyric for his 1935 movie version of **ROBERTA [November 18, 1933]**. Fields, on staff at RKO, got the chance and wrote "Lovely To Look At." McHugh, per terms of his contract, shared credit for the lyric; but Kern claimed Fields as his new collaborator. McHugh wrote for another twenty-five years—including a handful of Broadway musicals—but never so well as during his Dorothy Fields days.

WHOOPEE
December 4, 1928   New Amsterdam Theatre
255 performances

Music mostly by Walter Donaldson
Lyrics mostly by Gus Kahn
Book and direction by Wm. Anthony McGuire
(Based on *The Nervous Wreck* [play] by Owen Davis)
Produced by Florenz Ziegfeld, Jr.
With Eddie Cantor, Ruth Etting, and George Olsen and his Orchestra

Published songs:

"Come West, Little Girl, Come West"
"A Girl Friend Of A Boy Friend Of Mine"—written for 1930
   movie version
"Gypsy Joe"
"The Gypsy Song (Where Sunset Meets The Sea)"
"Here's To The Girl Of My Heart!"
"I'm Bringing A Red, Red Rose"
"Love Me Or Leave Me"
"Makin' Whoopee!"
"My Baby Just Cares For Me"—written for movie version
"The Song Of The Setting Sun"
"Until You Get Somebody Else"

Walter Donaldson (1893–1947) was a top Tin Pan Alley composer, with hits like "How Ya Gonna Keep 'Em Down On The Farm?," "My Blue Heaven" and Al Jolson's "My Mammy." Although he occasionally contributed interpolations, his only full stage score was this Ziegfeld hit for Eddie Cantor. Donaldson's popular touch was evident in "Makin' Whoopee!" and "Love Me Or Leave Me."

FINE AND DANDY
September 23, 1930   Erlanger Theatre   255 performances

Music by Kay Swift
Lyrics by Paul James
Book by Donald Ogden Stewart
"Many Nonsensical Moments Created by Joe Cook"
Directed by Morris Green
Produced by Green and Lewis Gensler
With Joe Cook, Nell O'Day, Dave Chasen, and Eleanor Powell

Published songs:

"Can This Be Love?"
"Fine And Dandy"
"The Jig Hop"
"Let's Go Eat Worms In The Garden"
"Nobody Breaks My Heart"
"Rich Or Poor"
"Starting At The Bottom"

A handful of female lyricists have been successful in the theatre, starting with Anne Caldwell, Dorothy (THE STUDENT PRINCE [Romberg: December 2, 1924]) Donnelly and Dorothy Fields. But for some unaccountable reason, almost no women composers have had Broadway impact. Kay Swift (born 1907) made a promising start with notable interpolations in **THE LITTLE SHOW [Schwartz: April 30, 1929]** and **NINE-FIFTEEN REVUE [Arlen: February 11, 1930].** Her first and only book musical was **FINE AND DANDY,** with one of the best scores of the season. Swift wrote three extraspecial songs: "Can't We Be Friends?" (from **THE LITTLE SHOW**), "Can This Be Love?" and the dandy "Fine And Dandy." She then left her lyricist-husband Paul James (Warburg) and began a professional/personal relationship with George Gershwin. Her only return to Broadway was with songs for Cornelia Otis Skinner's one-woman PARIS '90 [March 4, 1952]. Irene Dunne played Swift in her 1952 movie semi-biography. Other early women composers included Alma Sanders (who wrote a string of unimportant Twenties musicals with lyricist-husband Monte Carlo) and Ann Ronell, another Gershwin protégé best known for her lyric to the 1939 "Who's Afraid Of The Big Bad Wolf?" In more recent times, Mary Rodgers and Carol Hall were both successful with transfers from off-Broadway's old Yiddish Art (Phoenix/Entermedia) Theatre, ONCE UPON A MATTRESS [May 11, 1959] and **THE BEST LITTLE WHOREHOUSE IN TEXAS [PART 4: April 17, 1978].**

WALK WITH MUSIC
June 4, 1940   Ethel Barrymore Theatre   55 performances

Music mostly by Hoagy Carmichael
Lyrics mostly by Johnny Mercer
Book by Guy Bolton, Parke Levy, and Alan Prescott
(Based on *Three Blind Mice* [play] by Stephen Powys)
Directed by Clarke Lilley
Produced by Ruth Selwyn in association with the Messrs. Shubert
With Simone Simon, Mitzi Green, and Stepin' Fetchit
NOTE: **THREE AFTER THREE,** pre-Broadway title

Published songs:

"Darn Clever, These Chinee"—advertised but not published
"Everything Happens To Me"—advertised but not published
"How Nice For Me"—issued in professional copy only
"I Walk With Music"
"Ooh! What You Said"
"The Rumba Jumps!"
"Way Back In 1939 A.D."
"What'll They Think Of Next"

Additional songs published in USO/Camp Shows "AT EASE"
   (Volume 3):

"Break It Up, Cinderella"—with revised lyric, retitled "Break It
   Now, Buck Private"
"Wait Till You See Me In The Morning"—with revised lyric

Hoagy Carmichael (1899–1981) was best known for "Stardust" and
his performance of "How Little We Know" in the 1945 Humphrey
Bogart movie *To Have and Have Not.* A prewar Hollywood collaboration with Frank Loesser turned out hits like "Two Sleepy People" and "Heart And Soul" (second only to "Chopsticks" in popularity with piano duetists). His periodic collaboration with Johnny
Mercer resulted in "Lazy Bones" and the 1951 Oscar winner "In The
Cool, Cool, Cool Of The Evening." **WALK WITH MUSIC,** Carmichael's only complete score, was a quick failure; his one Broadway
song hit was "Little Old Lady" (lyric by Stanley Adams), interpolated into **THE SHOW IS ON [Arlen, Duke, Gershwin, Rodgers,
Schwartz: December 25, 1936].** For the record, Stephen Powys, author of **WALK WITH MUSIC's** original work, was the pseudonym
of Virginia De Lanty (the fourth Mrs. Guy Bolton).

EARLY TO BED
June 17, 1943   Broadhurst Theatre   380 performances

Music by Thomas (Fats) Waller
Book and lyrics by George Marion, Jr.
Choreographed by Robert Alton
Produced by Richard Kollmar and Alfred Bloomingdale
With Kollmar, Muriel Angelus, and Mary Small

Published songs:

"The Ladies Who Sing With A Band"
"Slightly Less Than Wonderful"
"There's A Man In My Life"
"This Is So Nice"
"When The Nylons Bloom Again"—issued as professional copy
    only

Additional songs recorded:

"Hi-De-Ho-Hi"

Fats Waller (1904–1943) was a jazz pianist/singer with a distinctive style. One of his very few Broadway visits brought "Ain't Misbehavin'," from the revue HOT CHOCOLATES [June 20, 1929]. Waller's second and final complete score was **EARLY TO BED,** which began a decent wartime run shortly before the composer's death. An anthology revue of Waller's work, AIN'T MISBEHAVIN' [May 8, 1978], was a major success. Collaborator Marion's father was a popular early musical comedy director. Producer/star Kollmar, husband to columnist Dorothy Kilgallen, had been the juvenile in **KNICKERBOCKER HOLIDAY [Weill: October 19, 1938]** and **TOO MANY GIRLS [Rodgers: October 18, 1939].**

BEGGAR'S HOLIDAY
December 26, 1946   Broadway Theatre   108 performances

Music by Duke Ellington
Book and lyrics by John Latouche
(Based on *The Beggar's Opera* by John Gay)
Choreographed by Valerie Bettis
Directed by Nicholas Ray
Produced by Perry Watkins and John R. Sheppard, Jr.
With Alfred Drake, Bernice Parks, Marie Bryant, and Zero Mostel

Published songs:

"On The Wrong Side Of The Railroad Tracks"
"Take Love Easy"
"Tomorrow Mountain"
"When I Walk With You"

Additional songs published in vocal selection:

"Brown Penny" [instrumental]
"I've Got Me"
"Maybe I Should Change My Ways"
"Tooth And Claw"
"Wanna Be Bad"

This ambitious musical was the first book show by band-leader/composer Duke Ellington (1899–1974). Based on *The Beggar's Opera*—at a time when the Weill/Brecht adaptation was virtually unknown in this country (see **THE THREEPENNY OPERA ⟨Second Version⟩ [Weill: March 10, 1954]**)—**BEGGAR'S HOLIDAY** ran into tryout trouble when star Libby Holman quit. Audiences looking for a happy, black revusical from the Duke were confronted by Zero Mostel's perplexing Poppa Peachum. Ellington came back once more with POUSSE-CAFE [March 18, 1966], which lasted three performances. The black composer anthology fad of the late Seventies brought forth an Ellington revue, SOPHISTICATED LADIES [March 1, 1981].

FLAHOOLEY
May 14, 1951   Broadhurst Theatre   40 performances

Music mostly by Sammy Fain
Lyrics mostly by E. Y. Harburg
Book and direction by Harburg and Fred Saidy
Choreographed by Helen Tamiris
Produced by Cheryl Crawford in association with Harburg and Saidy
With Ernest Truex, Yma Sumac, Barbara Cook, Edith Atwater, and Irwin
  Corey

Published songs:

"Come Back, Little Genie"—advertised but not published
"Flahooley"
"He's Only Wonderful"
"Here's To Your Illusions"

"How Lucky Can You Get?"—written for 1952 production
  [JOLLYANNA]
"The Springtime Cometh"
"Who Says There Ain't No Santa Claus?"—advertised but not
  published
"The World Is Your Balloon"

Additional songs recorded:

"B. G. Bigelow, Inc."
"Come Back, Little Genie"
"Jump, Little Chillun!"
"Sing The Merry"
"Who Says There Ain't No Santa Claus?"
"You Too Can Be A Puppet"

Sammy Fain was the only successful movie composer who continually returned to Broadway throughout his career—coming up with eight flops. The unconventional **FLAHOOLEY** stands out for its above-average score and very good intentions. In **FINIAN'S RAINBOW [Lane: January 10, 1947]** Harburg slyly cloaked his points with humor; but during the witch-hunt days of **FLAHOOLEY,** Harburg couldn't laugh. (He could, though, provide the lyrically dazzling "You Too Can Be A Puppet.") Cheryl Crawford once again gambled on an important, uncommercial musical and paid the price.

TOP BANANA
November 1, 1951   Winter Garden Theatre
350 performances

Music and lyrics by Johnny Mercer
Book by H. S. Kraft
Choreographed by Ron Fletcher
Directed by Jack Donohue
Produced by Paula Stone and Mike Sloane
With Phil Silvers, Rose Marie, Joey Faye, and Bob Scheerer

Published songs:

"Be My Guest"
"My Home Is In My Shoes"
"O.K. For T.V."
"Only If You're In Love"
"Sans Souci"

"That's For Sure"
"Top Banana"

Additional songs recorded:

"A Dog Is A Man's Best Friend"
"The Elevator Song (Going Up)"
"Havin' A Ball"
"I Fought Every Step Of The Way"
"The Man Of The Year This Week"
"Meet Miss Blendo"
"A Word A Day"
"You're So Beautiful That . . ."

Exceptional pop lyricist Johnny Mercer (1909–1976) occasionally wrote his own music—including movie song hits "I'm An Old Cowhand" and "Something's Gotta Give." **TOP BANANA** was a burlesque musical featuring Phil Silvers, a handful of clowns, and a dog named Ted "Sport" Morgan (who sang an inspired duet with Silvers). The show, which did not quite make it, was coproduced by Paula Stone (of the Stepping Stones—see **RIPPLES [Kern: February 11, 1930]**).

THE GOLDEN APPLE
March 11, 1954   Phoenix Theatre ⟨off-Broadway⟩
46 performances
April 20, 1954   Alvin Theatre   127 performances

Music by Jerome Moross
Book and lyrics by John Latouche
(Based on *The Odyssey* by Homer)
Choreographed by Hanya Holm
Directed by Norman Lloyd
Produced by The Phoenix Theatre (T. Edward Hambleton and Norris
    Houghton)
With Priscilla Gillette, Stephen Douglass, Kaye Ballard, Jack Whiting,
    and Jonathan Lucas

Published songs:

"Goona-Goona"
"It's The Going Home Together"
"Lazy Afternoon"
"Store-Bought Suit"
"Windflowers"—initially issued as "When We Were Young"

Additional songs recorded:

"Calypso"
"Circe, Circe"
"Come Along, Boys (Raise A Ruckus Tonight)"
"Departure For Rhododendron (1st Act Finale)"
"Doomed, Doomed, Doomed"
"Hector's Song (People Like You And Like Me)"
"Helen Is Always Willing"
"The Heroes Come Home"
"It Was A Glad Adventure"
"Judgement Of Paris"
"Mother Hare's Prophecy"
"My Love Is On The Way"
"My Picture In The Papers"
"Overture" [instrumental]
"Scylla And Charybdis"
"Sewing Bee"
"The Tirade (Finale)"
"Ulysses' Soliloquy (Despair Cuts Through Me Like A Knife)"

A brilliant musical theatre experiment. Jerome Moross (1913–1983) had been principal composer of the radical **PARADE ⟨First Version⟩ [Blitzstein: May 20, 1935],** but most of his career was spent scoring motion pictures. John Latouche's best work had been on **CABIN IN THE SKY [Duke: October 25, 1940]. THE GOLDEN APPLE** benefited from a perfect blend of theatrical elements, but it was the more-than-glorious score that carried it all the way to Broadway. The musical received the 1954 New York Drama Critics' Circle Award.

LI'L ABNER
November 15, 1956   St. James Theatre   693 performances

Music by Gene de Paul
Lyrics by Johnny Mercer
Book by Norman Panama and Melvin Frank
(Based on the comic strip by Al Capp)
Directed and choreographed by Michael Kidd
Produced by Panama, Frank, and Kidd
With Edith Adams, Peter Palmer, Stubby Kaye, and Charlotte Rae

Published songs:

"If I Had My Druthers"
"It's A Nuisance Having You Around"—cut

"Jubilation T. Cornpone"
"Love In A Home"
"Namely You"
"Otherwise (I Wish It Could Be)"—advertised but not published
"Unnecessary Town"

Additional songs published in vocal score:

"The Country's In The Very Best Of Hands"
"Dogpatch Dance" [instrumental]
"It's A Typical Day"
"The Matrimonial Stomp"
"Oh, Happy Day"
"Past My Prime"
"Progress Is The Root Of All Evil"
"Put 'Em Back"
"Rag Off'n The Bush"
"Sadie Hawkins Ballet"
"There's Room Enough For Us"
"What's Good For General Bullmoose"

Choreographer Michael Kidd came to Broadway with the magical **FINIAN'S RAINBOW [Lane: January 10, 1947]**, and attained genius status (and three quick Tony Awards) with his work on **GUYS AND DOLLS [Loesser: November 24, 1950]** and **CAN-CAN [Porter: May 7, 1953]**. Kidd was in league with Jerome Robbins, setting a new dance style for Broadway. The pair had, incidentally, danced the 1944 premiere of the latter's *Fancy Free* (see **ON THE TOWN [Bernstein: December 28, 1944]**). Kidd went to MGM for their 1953 version of **THE BAND WAGON [Schwartz: June 3, 1931]**. This was followed by a second movie musical classic, the 1954 *Seven Brides for Seven Brothers* (with a fine score by pop composer Gene de Paul and Johnny Mercer). Screenwriters Panama and Frank combined with Kidd—here making his directing debut—to produce **LI'L ABNER**. Al Capp's cartoon characters had been looking for a stage role for several years, but Broadway writers had given up on them. Kidd and company did just fine, with Johnny Mercer's most sparkling stage lyrics and extra-especially Kidd's "Sadie Hawkins Ballet." The choreographer won his fourth Tony, and was to receive another for his next musical (**DESTRY RIDES AGAIN [Rome: April 23, 1959]**). However, the talented Kidd has had nothing but flops since.

REDHEAD
February 5, 1959   46th Street Theatre   452 performances

Music by Albert Hague
Lyrics by Dorothy Fields
Book by Herbert and Dorothy Fields, Sidney Sheldon, and David Shaw
Directed and choreographed by Bob Fosse
Produced by Robert Fryer and Lawrence Carr
With Gwen Verdon, Richard Kiley, and Leonard Stone

Published songs:

"I Feel Merely Marvelous"
"I'm Back In Circulation"
"It Doesn't Take A Minute"—cut
"Just For Once"
"Look Who's In Love"
"My Girl Is Just Enough Woman For Me"
"The Right Finger Of My Left Hand"
"Two Faces In The Dark"

Additional songs published in vocal score:

"Behave Yourself"
"Chase" [instrumental]
"Dream Dance" [instrumental]
" 'Erbie Fitch's Dilemma"
"I'll Try"
"Pickpocket Tango" [instrumental]
"The Simpson Sisters"
"Uncle Sam Rag"
"We Loves Ya, Jimey"

German-born Albert Hague made his Broadway debut with the moderate hit PLAIN AND FANCY [January 27, 1955]. Next came the
mediocre hit **REDHEAD,** winner of the Best Musical Tony Award—
with Hague, the librettists, choreographer Fosse, and stars Verdon
and Kiley all winning as well. (One can imagine the overall quality
of the season!) This was Fosse's third Tony in five years, Verdon's
fourth in six; they got married. Fosse's next assignment was as choreographer on THE CONQUERING HERO [January 16, 1961], a
project so vanquished that it arrived on Broadway with no director
(Albert Marre) *or* choreographer credited. Fosse didn't return as full
director/choreographer until **SWEET CHARITY [Coleman: Janu-**

ary 30, 1966], seven years after the seven-Tony **REDHEAD**. For Hague, currently a popular TV actor, there have been three disasters since: CAFE CROWN [April 17, 1964], THE FIG LEAVES ARE FALLING [January 2, 1969] and MISS MOFFAT [October 7, 1970].

HAIR
The American Tribal Love-Rock Musical
April 29, 1968   Biltmore Theatre   1,742 performances

Music by Galt MacDermot
Book and lyrics by James Rado and Gerome Ragni
Choreographed by Julie Arenal
Directed by Tom O'Horgan
Produced by Michael Butler
With Rado, Ragni, Lynn Kellogg, Melba Moore, and Diane Keaton

Published songs:

"Aquarius"
"Easy To Be Hard"
"Frank Mills"
"Good Morning Starshine"
"Hair"
"Let The Sunshine In"—initially issued as "The Flesh Failures"
"Where Do I Go?"

Additional songs published in vocal selection(s):

"Abie Baby/Fourscore"
"Ain't Got No"
"Air"
"Black Boys"
"Donna"
"Electric Blues/Old Fashioned Melody"
"Hashish"
"I Got Life"
"I'm Black"
"Initials"
"Manchester England"
"Somebody To Love"—written for 1979 movie version
"Three-Five-Zero-Zero"
"Walking In Space"
"What A Piece Of Work Is Man" (lyric by William Shakespeare)
"White Boys"

Additional songs recorded:

"Be-In"
"The Bed"
"Colored Spade"
"Don't Put It Down"
"My Conviction"
"Sodomy"

NOTE: additional cut and unused material has been recorded

HAIR had a pre-Broadway tryout of sorts, playing three months at the New York Shakespeare Festival [October 29, 1967] before briefly moving to the Cheetah discotheque. A new production team was then assembled, led by director Tom O'Horgan (replacing Gerald Freedman). Invading the sacred precincts of Broadway, **HAIR** shocked, insulted, enraged, etc. But the show quickly won over most of the audience, with its strong overall viewpoint (credit director Tom O'Horgan) and a very good, tuneful score. "Where Do I Go," "Easy To Be Hard," "Aquarius": Broadway audiences were comfortable enough with the songs, and non-Broadway audiences first discovered theatre courtesy of the American Tribal Love-Rock Musical. Canadian-born composer Galt MacDermot's next project was John Guare's successful pop adaptation of TWO GENTLEMEN OF VERONA [December 1, 1971]. Broadway adventures since have all been imaginative failures.

PROMISES, PROMISES
December 1, 1968   Shubert Theatre   1,281 performances

Music by Burt Bacharach
Lyrics by Hal David
Book by Neil Simon
(Based on *The Apartment* [movie] by Billy Wilder and I.A.L. Diamond)
Choreographed by Michael Bennett
Directed by Robert Moore
Produced by David Merrick
With Jerry Orbach, Jill O'Hara, A. Larry Haines, Marian Mercer, and
    Donna McKechnie

Published songs:

"Christmas Day"
"I'll Never Fall In Love Again"

"Knowing When To Leave"
"Promises, Promises"
"Wanting Things"
"Whoever You Are I Love You"

Additional songs published in vocal score:

"A Fact Can Be A Beautiful Thing"
"Grapes Of Roth" [instrumental]
"Half As Big As Life"
"It's Our Little Secret"
"She Likes Basketball"
"Turkey Lurkey Time"
"Upstairs"
"Where Can You Take A Girl?"
"You'll Think Of Someone"
"A Young Pretty Girl Like You"

The mid-Sixties saw pop composer Burt Bacharach rise to celebrity status, with a string of hits ("What The World Needs Now," "Alfie," etc.) and a personable personality. David Merrick brought Bacharach and his less-visible collaborator to Broadway, putting them together with Neil Simon and a classic Billy Wilder screenplay. Simon wrote his best libretto to date, Bacharach and David wrote a lively score (bordering on the over-bouncy), and Merrick supplied a good director, Robert Moore. Also hired were choreographer Michael Bennett (who had performed unbilled salvage work on Merrick's unsalvagable HOW NOW, DOW JONES [December 7, 1967]) and designer Robin Wagner (who made his Broadway musical debut with **HAIR [PART 4: April 29, 1968]**). Bennett and Wagner began experimenting with choreographed set changes, with immediately gratifying results. The assignment of adapting Bacharach's pop recording sound to live theatre went to Jonathan Tunick, who began his reign as the musical theatre's finest modern-day orchestrator.

1776
March 16, 1969   46th Street Theatre   1,217 performances

Music and lyrics by Sherman Edwards
Book by Peter Stone
Choreographed by Onna White
Directed by Peter Hunt

Produced by Stuart Ostrow
With William Daniels, Howard Da Silva, Ken Howard, Virginia Vestoff,
   Paul Hecht, and Ronald Holgate

Published songs:

"He Plays The Violin"
"Is Anybody There?"
"Momma Look Sharp"
"Yours, Yours, Yours!"

Additional songs published in vocal selection:

"But, Mr. Adams"
"Cool, Cool, Considerate Men"
"The Egg"
"The Lees Of Old Virginia"
"Molasses To Rum"
"Piddle, Twiddle And Resolve"
"Sit Down, John"
"Till Then"

Theatrical novice Sherman Edwards (1919–1981) decided to musi-
calize the suspenseful tale of John Adams, Ben Franklin, and Tom
Jefferson writing the Declaration of Independence. Edwards received
encouragement and tutelage from Frank Loesser, as had Meredith
Willson with **THE MUSIC MAN [Willson: December 19, 1957].**
Producer Ostrow, a former Frank (Loesser) Music executive, took
up the unlikely project. The result was not particularly well made,
but a surprise hit.

GREASE
February 14, 1972   Eden Theatre ⟨off-Broadway⟩
128 performances
June 7, 1972   Broadhurst Theatre   3,388 performances

Book, music and lyrics by Jim Jacobs and Warren Casey
Choreographed by Patricia Birch
Directed by Tom Moore
Produced by Kenneth Waissman and Maxine Fox
With Barry Bostwick, Carole Demas, and Adrienne Barbeau

Published songs:

"Freddy, My Love"
"Summer Nights"

"There Are Worse Things I Could Do"
"Those Magic Changes"

Additional songs published in vocal score:

"All Choked Up"
"Alone At A Drive-In Movie"
"Beauty School Dropout"
"Born To Hand Jive"
"Greased Lightnin' "
"It's Raining On Prom Night"
"Look At Me, I'm Sandra Dee"
"Mooning"
"Rock 'n Roll Party Queen"
"Rydell Alma Mater"
"Rydell's Fight Song"
"Shakin' At The High School Hop"
"We Go Together"

Like **HAIR [PART 4: April 29, 1968]**—but without its quality or charm—**GREASE** moved from off-Broadway and attracted many, many theatregoers for many years. Most of them left **GREASE** satisfied; a significant number returned again and again.

THE WIZ
January 5, 1975   Majestic Theatre   1,672 performances

Music and lyrics by Charlie Smalls
Book by William F. Brown
(Based on *The Wizard of Oz* [novel] by L. Frank Baum)
Choreographed by George Faison
Directed by Geoffrey Holder
Produced by Ken Harper
With Stephanie Mills, Tiger Haynes, Hinton Battle, and DeeDee
  Bridgewater

Published songs:

"Be A Lion"
"Don't Cry Girl"
"Ease On Down The Road"
"Everybody Rejoice"
"He's The Wizard"
"Home"

"If You Believe"
"A Rested Body Is A Rested Mind"

Additional songs published in vocal selections:

"Don't Nobody Bring Me No Bad News"
"The Feeling We Once Had"
"I Was Born On The Day Before Yesterday"
"I'm A Mean Ole Lion"
"Slide Some Oil To Me"
"So You Want To See The Wizard"
"Soon As I Get Home"
"Tornado"
"What Would I Do If I Could Feel"
"Who, Who Do You Think You Are?"
"Y'all Got It"
"You Can't Win"—initial publication upon use in 1978 movie
   version

Another negligible but highly successful musical. "Ease On Down
The Road" became the first blockbuster Broadway song hit of the
Seventies and helped pull **THE WIZ** past a dismal initial reception.

SHENANDOAH
January 7, 1975   Alvin Theatre   1,050 performances

Music by Gary Geld
Lyrics by Peter Udell
Book by James Lee Barrett, Philip Rose and Udell
(Based on the screenplay by Barrett)
Choreographed by Robert Tucker
Directed by Rose
Produced by Rose, and Gloria and Louis K. Sher
With John Cullum, Donna Theodore, Joel Higgins, and Penelope Milford

Published songs:

"Freedom"
"Pass The Cross"
"We Make A Beautiful Pair"

Additional songs published in vocal score:

"I've Heard It All Before"
"It's A Boy"
"Meditation (This Land Don't Belong To Virginia)"

"Next To Lovin' (I Like Fightin' Best)"
"The Only Home I Know"
"Over The Hill"
"Papa's Gonna Make It Alright"
"The Pickers Are Comin' "
"Raise The Flag"
"Violets And Silverbells"
"Why Am I Me?"

Pop writers Gary Geld and Peter Udell first came to Broadway with producer/director/librettist Philip Rose and PURLIE [March 15, 1970]. Cleavon Little, Melba Moore, and "I Got Love" helped the show to a long (but financially unsuccessful) run of almost two years. **SHEN-ANDOAH** lasted six months longer and managed to break even. John Cullum carried the show with his strong performance in a heavy singing/acting role, written for Robert Ryan (who died before rehearsals). The property had potential as a serious musical in the **CAROUSEL [Rodgers: April 19, 1945]** vein; but no Hammerstein, Mamoulian, or Rodgers was on hand. Don Walker, skillful orchestrator of **CAROUSEL** and other classics, *was* on hand; you could tell. The final Geld, Udell, and Rose musical was the Thomas Wolfe-based ANGEL [May 10, 1978], which played five performances before giving up the ghost.

A CHORUS LINE
April 15, 1975   Public Theatre ⟨off-Broadway⟩
101 performances
July 25, 1975   Shubert Theatre   [still running as of October 1, 1985]

Music by Marvin Hamlisch
Lyrics by Edward Kleban
Book by James Kirkwood and Nicholas Dante
Choreographed by Michael Bennett and Bob Avian
Directed and conceived by Bennett
Produced by Joseph Papp
With Donna McKechnie, Priscilla Lopez, Carole Bishop, Sammy Williams
   and Pamela Blair

Published songs:

"I Can Do That"
"One"
"What I Did For Love"

Additional songs published in vocal score:

"And . . ."
"At The Ballet"
"Dance Ten, Looks Three"
"Hello Twelve, Hello Thirteen, Hello Love"
"I Hope I Get It"
"The Music And The Mirror"
"Nothing"
"Sing!"

Michael Bennett, codirector of **FOLLIES [Sondheim: April 4, 1971],** had an idea for a musical. Rather than placing it in the hands of writers, he assembled a group of dancers and developed the idea in workshop. Marvin Hamlisch, Bennett's dance arranger on **HENRY, SWEET HENRY [Merrill: October 23, 1967],** came in to compose. Hamlisch was the Burt Bacharach of the Seventies, achieving fame and acclaim with a burst of recording and movie work. Bennett's idea was brilliantly realized, and **A CHORUS LINE** went on to become Broadway's long-run champ. (**OKLAHOMA! [March 31, 1943]** held the record for fifteen years. Nowadays, the title changes frequently.) Nothing on the horizon seems likely to surpass **A CHORUS LINE,** but that's what they said about **FIDDLER ON THE ROOF [September 22, 1964].**

THE ROBBER BRIDEGROOM
October 9, 1976   Biltmore Theatre   145 performances

Music by Robert Waldman
Book and lyrics by Alfred Uhry
(Based on the novella by Eudora Welty)
Choreographed by Donald Saddler
Directed by Gerald Freedman
Produced by John Houseman, Margot Harley, and Michael B. Kapon
With Barry Bostwick, Rhonda Coullet, and Barbara Lang

Published songs:

"Deeper In The Woods"
"Nothin' Up"
"Sleepy Man"

Additional songs published in vocal selection:

"Goodbye Salome"
"Love Stolen"

"Once Upon The Natchez Trace"
"The Pricklepear Bloom"
"Poor Tied Up Darlin' "
"Riches"
"Rosamund's Dream"
"Steal With Style"
"Two Heads"
"Where Oh Where"

An inventive but uncommercial musical. **THE ROBBER BRIDE-GROOM** never reached the proper audience, and died with a struggle. Robert Waldman and Alfred Uhry have had two other short-lived opportunities, the *East of Eden* musical HERE'S WHERE I BELONG [March 3, 1968] and Stuart Ostrow's out-of-town fiasco SWING [February 25, 1980]. **THE ROBBER BRIDEGROOM** was initially presented for a limited engagement at the Harkness Theatre [October 7, 1975] by John Houseman's Acting Company (from Juilliard). Playing the bridegroom and bride: Kevin Kline and Patti LuPone.

THE BEST LITTLE WHOREHOUSE IN TEXAS
April 17, 1978   Entermedia Theatre   85 performances
June 19, 1978   46th Street Theatre   1,584 performances

Music and lyrics by Carol Hall
Book by Larry L. King and Peter Masterson
(Based on an article by King)
Choreographed by Tommy Tune
Directed by Masterson and Tune
Produced by Universal Pictures
With Carlin Glynn, Henderson Forsythe, Pamela Blair, Delores Hall, and
  Jay Garner

Songs published in vocal selection:

"The Aggie Song"
"Bus From Amarillo"
"Doatsy Mae"
"Girl, You're A Woman"
"Good Old Girl"
"Hard Candy Christmas"
"A Li'l Ole Bitty Pissant Country Place"
"No Lies"

"The Sidestep"
"Texas Has A Whorehouse In It"
"Twenty Fans"
"Twenty-Four Hours Of Lovin' "
"Watch Dog Theme"

A potentially good musical settled for being just a crowd-pleasing li'l ole hit. Theatrical novices Carol Hall and Larry King did well enough, although the effectiveness of their material was diminished by pre-opening "improvements" from the experienced hands on hand.

MARCH OF THE FALSETTOS
April 1, 1981   Playwrights Horizons
⟨*off-off-Broadway*⟩   *170 performances*
November 9, 1981   Westside Arts Center
⟨*off-Broadway*⟩   *128 performances*

Book, music and lyrics by William Finn
Directed by James Lapine
Produced by Playwrights Horizons (Andre Bishop)
With Michael Rupert, Alison Fraser, Chip Zien, Stephen Bogardus, and
   James Kushner

Recorded songs:

"The Chess Game"
"Everyone Tells Jason To See A Psychiatrist"
"Father To Son"
"Four Jews In A Room Bitching"
"The Games I Play"
"I Never Wanted To Love You"
"Jason's Therapy"
"Love Is Blind"
"Making A Home"
"March Of The Falsettos"
"A Marriage Proposal"
"Marvin At The Psychiatrist" [A 3-Part Mini-Opera]
"Marvin Hits Trina"
"My Father's A Homo"
"Please Come To My House"
"This Had Better Come To A Stop"
"The Thrill Of First Love"

"A Tight-Knit Family"
"Trina's Song"

A highly original, highly exciting piece which—surprisingly—was
immediately recognized and enthusiastically supported. William Finn
adhered to no structure: music and lyrics just went where they needed
to go, forming a tapestry of strong, emotional musical themes. The
author displayed a keen ability at drawing his characters in "Four
Jews In A Room Bitching," "Trina's Song," and "The Games I Play."
Particularly stunning were the intricately written musical conversa-
tions for combinations of the five characters: "This Had Better Come
To A Stop," "Love Is Blind," "The Chess Game," and "I Never
Wanted To Love You." A very special theatre work! (Also see **IN
TROUSERS [PART 4; March 26, 1985]**).

DREAMGIRLS
December 20, 1981   Imperial Theatre   1,522 performances
Music by Henry Krieger
Book and lyrics by Tom Eyen
Choreographed by Michael Bennett and Michael Peters
Directed by Bennett
Produced by Bennett, Bob Avian, Geffen Records, and the Shubert
    Organization
With Jennifer Holliday, Loretta Devine, Sheryl Lee Ralph, Cleavant
    Derricks, Obba Babatunde, and Ben Harney

Songs published in vocal selection:

"Ain't No Party"
"And I Am Telling You I'm Not Going"
"Cadillac Car"
"Dreamgirls"
"Fake Your Way To The Top"
"Family"
"Hard To Say Goodbye, My Love"
"I Am Changing"
"Move (You're Steppin' On My Heart)"
"One Night Only"
"Steppin' To The Bad Side"
"When I First Saw You"

Additional songs recorded:

"Firing Of Jimmy"
"I Meant You No Harm"

"I Miss You Old Friend"
"Press Conference"
"The Rap"

Michael Bennett and Bob Fosse have perfected the concept musical, built on plenty of concept and (often) little else. Talent frees them from relying on book, music, lyrics: instead of assembling a production around written material, they seem to start with *movement* and add on songs, plot, etc. Jerome Robbins worked in the same way, but he insisted on first-rate material—which explains his absence since **FIDDLER ON THE ROOF [Bock: September 22, 1964]**. Bennett and designer Robin Wagner have been experimenting with "choreographed sets" since **PROMISES, PROMISES [PART 4: December 1, 1968]** and **SEESAW [Coleman: March 18, 1973]**. While Wagner scenery has been known to overpower weak material (i.e., **ON THE TWENTIETH CENTURY [Coleman: February 19, 1978]**), the **DREAMGIRLS** set enhanced and carried the show. Bennett's work as *director* was particularly impressive, with the six principal actors—singer/dancers with little dramatic experience—each giving fine performances. The score of **DREAMGIRLS** was slightly more than adequate, with a slightly puzzling tendency to switch from high-gear Motown to decidedly non-Motown quasi-*recitative*. Composer Henry Krieger's second musical, THE TAP DANCE KID [December 21, 1983], was of little interest.

NINE
May 9, 1982   46th Street Theatre   739 performances

Music and lyrics by Maury Yeston
Book by Arthur Kopit
(Based on Mario Fratti's adaptation of 8½ [movie] by Federico Fellini,
   Tullio Pinelli, and Ennio Flaiano)
Choreographed by Thommie Walsh
Directed by Tommy Tune
Produced by Michel Stuart, Harvey J. Klaris, Roger S. Berlind, James M.
   Nederlander, Francine LeFrak and Kenneth D. Greenblatt
With Raul Julia, Liliane Montevecchi, Karen Akers, Anita Morris, Taina
   Elg, and Shelly Burch

Published songs:

"Be Italian"
"Be On Your Own"

"Only With You"
"Simple"
"Unusual Way"

Additional songs published in vocal selection:

"A Call From The Vatican"
"Folies Bergère"
"Getting Tall"
"Guido's Song"
"My Husband Makes Movies"
"Nine"

Additional songs recorded:

"The Bells Of St. Sebastian"
"The Germans At The Spa"
"Grand Canal Sequence"
"A Man Like You"
"Not Since Chaplin"
"Overture Delle Donne"
"Ti Voglio Bene"

Yale professor Maury Yeston arrived on Broadway with good music and an interesting musical—which only partially survived its libretto and production. A parade of fine supporting performances helped alleviate one-gimmick-concept problems, while the dazzling costumes by William Ivey Long took advantage of the strictures. Yeston's inventive and highly melodic score suffered in spots from lower-grade lyrics; but he certainly can write music. After **NINE** came a score for **LA CAGE AUX FOLLES [Herman: August 21, 1983]**; but Yeston's version was not used. He seems likely to become an important musical theatre contributor.

BABY
December 4, 1983   Ethel Barrymore Theatre
241 performances

Music by David Shire
Lyrics by Richard Maltby, Jr.
Book by Sybille Pearson
(Based on a story by Susan Yankowitz)
Choreographed by Wayne Cilento
Directed by Maltby

Produced by James B. Freydberg and Ivan Bloch, Kenneth-John
    Productions, and Suzanne J. Schwartz
With Liz Callaway, James Congdon, Catherine Cox, Beth Fowler, Todd
    Graff, and Martin Vidnovic

Published song:

"I Want It All"

Additional songs published in vocal selection:

"And What If We Had Loved Like That?"
"At Night She Comes Home To Me"
"Baby, Baby, Baby"
"Easier To Love"
"Fatherhood Blues"
"I Chose Right"
"Patterns"—cut
"The Story Goes On"
"Two People In Love"
"With You"

Additional songs recorded:

"The Birth"
"The Ladies Singing Their Song"
"Opening"
"The Plaza Song"
"Romance"
"We Start Today"
"What Could Be Better Than That?"

A very special musical which Broadway audiences just never discovered. A more creative promotional campaign might have helped; but
it wasn't, and it didn't. **BABY** was warm, pink and tender, with a
better score than Broadway had heard in a long while: "Baby, Baby,
Baby," "And What If We Had Loved Like That," the especially
moving "The Story Goes On," and more. Ingratiating performances
from Catherine Cox, Liz Callaway, Todd Graff, and Martin Vidnovic
added to the charms, as did an inventive and functional John Lee
Beatty set. **BABY** was slightly weakened, though, by the lack of
Broadway experience among director, librettist, and the courageous
producers. David Shire and Richard Maltby had been around since
the off-Broadway SAP OF LIFE [October 2, 1961]. The cabaret revue STARTING HERE, STARTING NOW [March 7, 1977] was

far more successful, but their one previous Broadway attempt (LOVE MATCH [November 3, 1968]) closed during its tryout. Maltby had reached Broadway a few years earlier, as director of the off-Broadway transfer AIN'T MISBEHAVIN' [May 8, 1978]. **BABY** was a very sad failure.

IN TROUSERS
March 26, 1985   Promenade Theatre ⟨off-Broadway⟩
16 performances

Book, music, and lyrics by William Finn
Directed by Matt Casella
Produced by Roger Berlind, Franklin R. Levy and Gregory Harrison
With Catherine Cox, Tony Cummings, Kathy Garrick, and Sherry Hursey

Published songs:

None

Recorded songs:

"Another Sleepless Night"
"Breakfast Over Sugar"
"High School Ladies At Five O'Clock"
"How Marvin Eats His Breakfast"
"How The Body Falls Apart"
"I Am Wearing A Hat (Marvin Takes A Wife)"—cut
"In Trousers (The Dream)"
"Love Me For What I Am"
"Marvin Takes A Victory Shower"—cut
"Marvin's Giddy Seizures"
"My Chance To Survive The Night"—cut
"My High School Sweetheart"
"The Nausea Before The Game"—cut
"The Rape Of Miss Goldberg"
"Set Those Sails"
"Whizzer Going Down"
"Your Lips And Me"—cut

IN TROUSERS began life in 1978 as a developmental workshop at Playwrights Horizons. Then came a sequel: the brilliant **MARCH OF THE FALSETTOS [April 1, 1981],** which transferred to a commercial run. A revised version of the earlier work was successfully mounted in Los Angeles in 1984, resulting in this off-Broadway production. William Finn's score for **IN TROUSERS** was exciting and impressive, the best work heard during the dismal 1984–1985 musical season. The libretto, though, suffered from structural problems and dramatic immaturity. Poor direction and casting did not help. The one exception was Catherine Cox, particularly outstanding in Finn's "Love Me For What I Am" and "I'm Breaking Down." Most of **IN TROUSERS** was written prior to **MARCH OF THE FALSETTOS**. What is desperately needed is work from the William Finn of today. One can confidently look forward to whatever he does next. But soon, please?

BIG RIVER
April 25, 1985   Eugene O'Neill Theatre   [still running as of October 1, 1985]

Music and lyrics by Roger Miller
Book by William Hauptman
(Based on *Huckleberry Finn* [novel] by Mark Twain)
Directed by Des McAnuff
Produced by Rocco Landesman, Heidi Landesman, Rick Steiner,
   M. Anthony Fisher, and Dodger Productions
With Daniel H. Jenkins, Ron Richardson, Bob Gunton, and Rene
   Auberjonois

Published songs:
None

BIG RIVER was the best musical of the worst season for Broadway musicals in seventy years. The score by country songwriter Roger Miller was dramatically ineffective and the book was weak, but Mark Twain and the lack of competition—with an assist from director McAnuff—managed to give **BIG RIVER** some life.

APPENDIX 1

All productions discussed are listed below in chronological order.

Dates represent the official New York or London ⟨L⟩ opening. Brackets represent date of first performance of productions which did not play New York or London. Approximate dates are given as [c. month] (c. standing for "circa").

Where more than one composer contributed to the same production, each is named. Song listings will be found in the respective chapters.

The page number in the final column represents the *primary* discussion(s) of each production; for further mention of the show, see the show index.

Chronological Listing of Productions

1908

January 27	A WALTZ DREAM	Kern	11
September 2	THE GIRLS OF GOTTEN- BERG	Kern	11
September 7	FLUFFY RUFFLES	Kern	12
November 2	THE BOYS AND BETTY	Berlin	68

1909

January 25	KITTIE GREY	Kern	12
July 29	THE GAY HUSSARS	Kern	13
September 6	THE DOLLAR PRINCESS	Kern	13
September 27	THE GIRL AND THE WIZ- ARD	Berlin/ Kern	68 14
[October 26]	THE GOLDEN WIDOW	Kern	14

1910

January 6	THE JOLLY BACHELORS	Berlin	69
January 10	KING OF CADONIA	Kern	14
[c. April]	ARE YOU A MASON?	Berlin	69
June 20	ZIEGFELD FOLLIES OF 1910	Berlin	69
July 18	UP AND DOWN BROAD- WAY	Berlin	70
August 17	THE ECHO	Kern	15
August 29	OUR MISS GIBBS	Kern	15
[c. August]	THE GIRL AND THE DRUMMER	Berlin/ Kern	70 16
September 21	HE CAME FROM MIL- WAUKEE	Berlin	71
November 7	GETTING A POLISH	Berlin	71
[c. December]	TWO MEN AND A GIRL	Berlin	71

1911

February 4	THE HENPECKS	Kern	16
March 6	JUMPING JUPITER	Berlin	72
March 20	LA BELLE PAREE	Kern	16
April 3	LITTLE MISS FIX-IT	Kern	17
April 27	GABY (FOLIES BERGÈRE)	Berlin	72
May 28	FRIARS' FROLIC OF 1911	Berlin	73
June 26	ZIEGFELD FOLLIES OF 1911	Berlin/ Kern	73 17

August 28	THE SIREN	Kern	17
September 11	THE FASCINATING WIDOW	Berlin	73
September 18	THE KISS WALTZ	Kern	18
September 25	THE LITTLE MILLION-AIRE	Berlin	74
October 5	THE NEVER HOMES	Berlin	74
[c. October]	A REAL GIRL	Berlin	75
[c. November]	WINTER GARDEN	Berlin	75

1912

[January 15]	SHE KNOWS BETTER NOW	Berlin	75
February 8	HOKEY-POKEY	Berlin	76
February 12	THE OPERA BALL	Kern	18
March 5	THE WHIRL OF SOCIETY	Berlin	76
April 11	A WINSOME WIDOW	Kern	19
[c. April]	COHAN AND HARRIS MINSTRELS	Berlin	77
July 22	PASSING SHOW OF 1912	Berlin	77
August 5	THE GIRL FROM MONT-MARTRE	Kern	19
August 5	HANKY PANKY	Berlin	77
[August 31]	A POLISH WEDDING	Kern	20
September 9	THE "MIND-THE-PAINT" GIRL	Kern	20
September 12	MY BEST GIRL	Berlin	77
October 7	THE WOMAN HATERS	Kern	20
October 21	ZIEGFELD FOLLIES OF 1912	Berlin	78
November 13	THE RED PETTICOAT	Kern	21
November 30	THE SUN DODGERS	Berlin	78
December 23 ⟨L⟩	HULLO, RAGTIME!	Berlin	78

1913

February 3	THE SUNSHINE GIRL	Kern	21
April 28	THE AMAZONS	Kern	22
June 5	ALL ABOARD!	Berlin	79
August 25	THE DOLL GIRL	Kern	22
September 3	LIEBER AUGUSTIN	Kern	23
September 22	THE MARRIAGE MARKET	Kern	23
[c. September]	TRAINED NURSES	Berlin	79
October 30	OH, I SAY!	Kern	24

1914

January 12	THE QUEEN OF THE MOVIES	Berlin	79
February 2	THE LAUGHING HUS-BAND	Kern	24
February 2	WHEN CLAUDIA SMILES	Kern	25
February 23	ALONG CAME RUTH	Berlin	80
August 24	THE GIRL FROM UTAH	Kern	25
[c. October]	THE SOCIETY BUDS	Berlin	80
December 8	WATCH YOUR STEP	Berlin	80

1915

January 25	NINETY IN THE SHADE	Kern	26
[February 8]	A GIRL OF TODAY	Kern	27
March 8	FADS AND FANCIES	Kern	27
March 22 ⟨L⟩	ROSY RAPTURE	Kern	27
April 20	NOBODY HOME	Kern	28
April 28 ⟨L⟩	TONIGHT'S THE NIGHT!	Kern	29
[c. April]	WINTER GARDEN	Berlin	81
May 3	A MODERN EVE	Kern	29
July 22	HANDS UP	Porter	204
August 27	COUSIN LUCY	Kern	29
October 5	MISS INFORMATION	Kern/	30
		Porter	205
December 23	VERY GOOD EDDIE	Kern	31
December 25	STOP! LOOK! LISTEN!	Berlin	82

1916

March 28	SEE AMERICA FIRST	Porter	205
May 28	FRIARS' FROLIC OF 1916	Berlin	83
May 29	STEP THIS WAY	Berlin	83
June 12	ZIEGFELD FOLLIES OF 1916	Berlin/	83
		Kern	32
June 22	PASSING SHOW OF 1916	Gershwin	104
September 19 ⟨L⟩	THEODORE AND CO.	Kern	32
September 25	MISS SPRINGTIME	Kern	33
October 24	GO TO IT	Kern	33
November 6	THE CENTURY GIRL	Berlin	83

1917

January 11	HAVE A HEART	Kern	34
January 15	LOVE O' MIKE	Kern	35

February 20	OH, BOY!	Kern	35
[c. April]	DANCE AND GROW THIN	Berlin	84
June 12	ZIEGFELD FOLLIES OF 1917	Kern	36
August 28	LEAVE IT TO JANE	Kern	37
September 10	RAMBLER ROSE	Berlin	84
September 24	THE RIVIERA GIRL	Kern	38
October 16	JACK O'LANTERN	Berlin	85
November 5	MISS 1917	Kern	38
December 25	GOING UP	Berlin	85
December 29	ONE MINUTE PLEASE	Rodgers	153
December 31	THE COHAN REVUE OF 1918	Berlin	85

1918

February 1	OH LADY! LADY!!	Kern	39
March 11	TOOT-TOOT!	Kern	40
May 18 ⟨L⟩	VERY GOOD EDDIE	Porter	206
May 22	ROCK-A-BYE BABY	Kern	40
June 6	HITCHY-KOO OF 1918	Gershwin	105
June 18	ZIEGFELD FOLLIES OF 1918	Berlin	86
August 19	YIP-YIP-YAPHANK	Berlin	86
August 22	EVERYTHING	Berlin	87
August 29	HEAD OVER HEELS	Kern	41
October 24	LADIES FIRST	Gershwin	105
[c. October] ⟨L⟩	TELLING THE TALE	Porter	206
November 4	THE CANARY	Berlin/ Kern	87 42
November 27	OH, MY DEAR	Kern	42
[December 9]	HALF-PAST EIGHT	Gershwin	106

1919

February 6	GOOD MORNING JUDGE	Gershwin	106
February 17	THE ROYAL VAGABOND	Berlin	87
March 8	UP STAGE AND DOWN	Rodgers	154
May 5	SHE'S A GOOD FELLOW	Kern	42
May 12	THE LADY IN RED	Gershwin/ Kern	107 43
May 26	LA, LA LUCILLE	Gershwin	107
June 10	A LONELY ROMEO	Rodgers	155
June 23	ZIEGFELD FOLLIES OF 1919	Berlin	88

October 2	ZIEGFELD MIDNIGHT FROLICS	Berlin	89
October 6	HITCHY-KOO 1919	Porter	207
October 24	CAPITOL REVUE	Gershwin	108
October 27	BUDDIES	Porter	207
November 1	IRENE	PART 4	537
November 12 ⟨L⟩	THE ECLIPSE	Porter	208
[December 8]	ZIP, GOES A MILLION	Kern	44
December 27	MORRIS GEST'S MID-NIGHT WHIRL	Gershwin	108
[c. December]	SINBAD	Gershwin	109

1920

January 27	AS YOU WERE	Porter	208
February 2	THE NIGHT BOAT	Kern	45
[February 2]	DERE MABLE	Gershwin	109
March 6	YOU'D BE SURPRISED	Rodgers	155
March 8	ZIEGFELD GIRLS OF 1920	Berlin	89
March 24	FLY WITH ME	Rodgers	156
April 5	THE ED WYNN CARNI-VAL	Gershwin	109
June 7	GEORGE WHITE'S SCAN-DALS 1920	Gershwin	110
June 22	ZIEGFELD FOLLIES OF 1920	Berlin	89
July 28	POOR LITTLE RITZ GIRL	Rodgers	157
August 2	THE CHARM SCHOOL	Kern	45
August 31	THE SWEETHEART SHOP	Gershwin	110
September 18 ⟨L⟩	A NIGHT OUT	Porter	209
[September 27]	PICCADILLY TO BROAD-WAY	Gershwin/ Youmans	111 138
September 29	BROADWAY BREVITIES OF 1920	Berlin/ Gershwin	90 11
October 19	HITCHY-KOO 1920	Kern	45
December 21	SALLY	Kern	46

1921

[March 21]	A DANGEROUS MAID	Gershwin	112
April 20	YOU'LL NEVER KNOW	Rodgers	158
May 3	TWO LITTLE GIRLS IN BLUE	Youmans	139
May 23	SHUFFLE ALONG	PART 4	538

June 2	SNAPSHOTS OF 1921	Gershwin	112
June 21	THE ZIEGFELD FOLLIES OF 1921	Kern	47
July 11	GEORGE WHITE'S SCANDALS 1921	Gershwin	112
September 19 ⟨L⟩	THE CABARET GIRL	Kern	47
September 22	MUSIC BOX REVUE	Berlin	90
November 1	GOOD MORNING DEARIE	Kern	49
November 7	THE PERFECT FOOL	Gershwin	113

1922

February 20	FOR GOODNESS SAKE	Gershwin	113
February 20	THE FRENCH DOLL	Gershwin	114
March 9 ⟨L⟩	MAYFAIR AND MONTMARTRE	Porter	209
July 6	SPICE OF 1922	Gershwin	114
August 16 ⟨L⟩	PHI-PHI	Porter	209
August 28	GEORGE WHITE'S SCANDALS 1922	Gershwin	115
[October 10]	HITCHY-KOO OF 1922	Porter	210
October 23	MUSIC BOX REVUE ⟨second⟩	Berlin	91
November 28	THE BUNCH AND JUDY	Kern	49
December 4	OUR NELL	Gershwin	116
December 25	ROSE BRIAR	Kern	50

1923

January 24	THE DANCING GIRL	Gershwin	116
February 7	WILDFLOWER	Youmans	140
April 3 ⟨L⟩	THE RAINBOW	Gershwin	116
June 18	GEORGE WHITE'S SCANDALS 1923	Gershwin	117
August 28	LITTLE MISS BLUEBEARD	Gershwin	118
September 5 ⟨L⟩	THE BEAUTY PRIZE	Kern	50
September 22	MUSIC BOX REVUE ⟨third⟩	Berlin	91
September 25	NIFTIES OF 1923	Gershwin	118
October 4	HAMMERSTEIN'S NINE O'CLOCK REVUE	Youmans	141
November 6	THE STEPPING STONES	Kern	51
December 25	MARY JANE McKANE	Youmans	141

1924

January 21	LOLLIPOP	Youmans	142
January 21	SWEET LITTLE DEVIL	Gershwin	118
April 8	SITTING PRETTY	Kern	52
May 13	THE MELODY MAN	Rodgers	159
May 21 ⟨L⟩	THE PUNCH BOWL	Berlin	92
June 30	GEORGE WHITE'S SCAN- DALS 1924	Gershwin	119
September 11 ⟨L⟩	PRIMROSE	Gershwin	120
September 16	GREENWICH VILLAGE FOLLIES 1924	Porter	210
September 23 ⟨L⟩	CHARLOT'S REVUE	Youmans	142
September 23	DEAR SIR	Kern	53
November 6	PETER PAN ⟨second⟩	Kern	53
December 1	LADY, BE GOOD!	Gershwin	12
December 1	MUSIC BOX REVUE ⟨fourth⟩	Berlin	93

1925

February 21 ⟨L⟩	KATJA THE DANCER	Duke	273
April 13	TELL ME MORE	Gershwin	122
May 17	GARRICK GAIETIES ⟨first⟩	Rodgers	159
August 6	JUNE DAYS	Rodgers	160
[September 7]	A NIGHT OUT	Youmans	142
September 16	NO, NO, NANETTE	Youmans	143
September 18	DEAREST ENEMY	Rodgers	160
September 22	SUNNY	Kern	54
October 26	THE CITY CHAP	Kern	55
December 8	THE COCOANUTS	Berlin	93
December 28	TIP-TOES	Gershwin	123
December 30	SONG OF THE FLAME	Gershwin	123

1926

[c. January]	FIFTH AVENUE FOLLIES	Rodgers	161
March 17	THE GIRL FRIEND	Rodgers	162
April 29 ⟨L⟩	COCHRAN'S 1926 REVUE	Rodgers	162
May 10	GARRICK GAIETIES ⟨sec- ond⟩	Rodgers	163
May 22 ⟨L⟩	YVONNE	Duke	274
June 14	GEORGE WHITE'S SCAN- DALS ⟨eighth⟩	PART 4	539

1927

1928

September 25	CHEE-CHEE	Rodgers	170
October 8	PARIS	Porter	212
November 8	TREASURE GIRL	Gershwin	128
November 21	RAINBOW	Youmans	146
December 4	WHOOPEE	PART 4	542
December 25	THE RED ROBE	Schwartz	235

1929

January 15	NED WAYBURN'S GAM-BOLS	Schwartz	236
January 31	LADY FINGERS	Rodgers	170
March 11	SPRING IS HERE	Rodgers	171
March 27 ⟨L⟩	WAKE UP AND DREAM	Porter	213
April 30	THE LITTLE SHOW	Schwartz	236
May 1	GRAND STREET FOLLIES OF 1929	Schwartz	237
July 2	SHOW GIRL	Gershwin/	128
		Youmans	147
[c. August] ⟨L⟩	OPEN YOUR EYES	Duke	276
September 3	SWEET ADELINE	Kern	59
October 17	GREAT DAY!	Youmans	148
November 8 ⟨L⟩	HOUSE THAT JACK BUILT	Schwartz	238
November 11	HEADS UP!	Rodgers	171
November 27	FIFTY MILLION FRENCHMEN	Porter	214
December 30	WAKE UP AND DREAM	Schwartz	238

1930

January 14	STRIKE UP THE BAND	Gershwin	129
February 11	NINE-FIFTEEN REVUE	Arlen/	130
		Gershwin	257
February 11	RIPPLES	Kern	60
February 18	SIMPLE SIMON	Rodgers	172
February 20 ⟨L⟩	HERE COMES THE BRIDE	Schwartz	239
April 4 ⟨L⟩	CO-OPTIMISTS OF 1930	Schwartz	239
June 4	GARRICK GAIETIES ⟨third⟩	Blitzstein/	318
		Duke	276
June 10	ARTISTS AND MODELS	Lane	291
July 1	EARL CARROLL VANI-TIES ⟨eighth⟩	Arlen	258
September 2	THE SECOND LITTLE SHOW	Schwartz	240

1931

1932

| December 2 | THE GREAT MAGOO | Arlen | 262 |
| December 7 | WALK A LITTLE FASTER | Duke | 277 |

1933

January 20	PARDON MY ENGLISH	Gershwin	133
April 6	COTTON CLUB PARADE ⟨twenty-second⟩	Arlen	263
April 13	THREEPENNY OPERA ⟨first⟩	Weill	301
[July 28]	CRAZY QUILT OF 1933	Arlen	263
September 13 ⟨L⟩	NICE GOINGS ON	Schwartz	244
September 30	AS THOUSANDS CHEER	Berlin	97
October 6 ⟨L⟩	NYMPH ERRANT	Porter	216
October 21	LET 'EM EAT CAKE	Gershwin	133
November 16 ⟨L⟩	PLEASE!	Rodgers	175
November 18	ROBERTA	Kern	63
November 20	SHE LOVES ME NOT	Schwartz	245

1934

January 4	ZIEGFELD FOLLIES OF 1934	Duke	278
March 23	COTTON CLUB PARADE ⟨twenty-fourth⟩	Arlen	263
April 19 ⟨L⟩	THREE SISTERS	Kern	64
August 27	LIFE BEGINS AT 8:40	Arlen	264
October 3 ⟨L⟩	HI DIDDLE DIDDLE	Porter	217
[October 22]	BRING ON THE GIRLS	Schwartz	245
November 21	ANYTHING GOES	Porter	218
November 28	REVENGE WITH MUSIC	Schwartz	245
[December 22]	MARIE GALANTE	Weill	302
December 27	THUMBS UP!	Duke	279

1935

March 4	PETTICOAT FEVER	Loewe	367
April 29	SOMETHING GAY	Rodgers	175
May 20	PARADE ⟨first⟩	Blitzstein	319
June 28 ⟨L⟩	A KINGDOM FOR A COW	Weill	302
September 19	AT HOME ABROAD	Schwartz	246
October 10	PORGY AND BESS	Gershwin	134
October 12	JUBILEE	Porter	219
November 16	JUMBO	Rodgers	176

1936

January 22	THE ILLUSTRATORS' SHOW	Loesser/ Loewe	401 367
January 30	ZIEGFELD FOLLIES (OF 1936)	Duke	279
February 4 ⟨L⟩	FOLLOW THE SUN	Schwartz	247
April 11	ON YOUR TOES	Rodgers	176
October 29	RED, HOT AND BLUE!	Porter	220
November 19	JOHNNY JOHNSON	Weill	303
December 3 ⟨L⟩	O MISTRESS MINE	Porter	221
December 25	THE SHOW IS ON	Duke/ Arlen/ Gershwin/ Rodgers/ Schwartz	265 247 280 135 178

1937

January 7	THE ETERNAL ROAD	Weill	304
April 14	BABES IN ARMS	Rodgers	178
[June 12]	SALUTE TO SPRING	Loewe	368
June 16	THE CRADLE WILL ROCK	Blitzstein	319
September 2	VIRGINIA	Schwartz	248
November 2	I'D RATHER BE RIGHT	Rodgers	179
November 11	JULIUS CAESAR	Blitzstein	321
November 27	PINS AND NEEDLES	Rome	328
December 1	HOORAY FOR WHAT!	Arlen	265
December 22	BETWEEN THE DEVIL	Schwartz	248

1938

May 11	I MARRIED AN ANGEL	Rodgers	180
[June 3]	GENTLEMEN UNAFRAID	Kern	64
September 21	YOU NEVER KNOW	Porter	221
September 24	SING OUT THE NEWS	Rome	330
October 19	KNICKERBOCKER HOLI-DAY	Weill	305
November 2	DANTON'S DEATH	Blitzstein	321
November 9	LEAVE IT TO ME!	Porter	222
November 23	THE BOYS FROM SYRA-CUSE	Rodgers	181
December 1	GREAT LADY	Loewe	368

1939

January 3	MAMBA'S DAUGHTERS	Kern	65
February 9	STARS IN YOUR EYES	Schwartz	249
February 15	THE LITTLE FOXES	Willson	419
April 24	SING FOR YOUR SUPPER	Rome	330
April 30	RAILROADS ON PARADE	Weill	306
June 9 ⟨L⟩	THE SUN NEVER SETS	Porter	222
June 19	STREETS OF PARIS	Rome	331
October 16	THE MAN WHO CAME TO DINNER	Porter	223
October 18	TOO MANY GIRLS	Rodgers	182
November 17	VERY WARM FOR MAY	Kern	65
December 6	DUBARRY WAS A LADY	Porter	223
[December 26]	VAGABOND HERO	Duke	280

1940

April 4	HIGHER AND HIGHER	Rodgers	183
May 12	AMERICAN JUBILEE	Schwartz	250
May 23	KEEP OFF THE GRASS	Duke	281
May 28	LOUISIANA PURCHASE	Berlin	98
June 4	WALK WITH MUSIC	PART 4	544
[June 24]	TWO WEEKS WITH PAY	Rodgers	184
[July 13]	LITTLE DOG LAUGHED	Rome	331
September 11	HOLD ON TO YOUR HATS	Lane	293
October 10	IT HAPPENS ON ICE	Duke	281
October 25	CABIN IN THE SKY	Duke	282
October 30	PANAMA HATTIE	Porter	224
December 25	PAL JOEY	Rodgers	184

1941

January 5	NO FOR AN ANSWER	Blitzstein	321
January 23	LADY IN THE DARK	Weill	306
October 1	BEST FOOT FORWARD	Martin	346
October 29	LET'S FACE IT	Porter	225
December 25	BANJO EYES	Duke	283

1942

January 9	THE LADY COMES ACROSS	Duke	283
June 2	BY JUPITER	Rodgers	186

June 22	LUNCHTIME FOLLIES	Rome	331
June 24	STAR AND GARTER	Rome	332
July 4	THIS IS THE ARMY	Berlin	98
September 4	ICE CAPADES OF 1942	Styne	377
October 5	LET FREEDOM SING	Rome	332
[October 8]	LIFE OF THE PARTY	Loewe	369

1943

January 7	SOMETHING FOR THE BOYS	Porter	225
[March 22]	DANCING IN THE STREETS	Duke	284
March 31	OKLAHOMA!	Rodgers	187
June 17	EARLY TO BED	PART 4	545
[July 13]	STARS AND GRIPES	Rome	333
October 7	ONE TOUCH OF VENUS	Weill	307
November 11	WHAT'S UP	Loewe	370
November 17	A CONNECTICUT YAN-KEE ⟨second⟩	Rodgers	188

1944

January 13	JACKPOT	Duke	285
January 25	SKIRTS	Loesser/	402
		Rome	333
[January 27]	VINCENT YOUMANS' BALLET REVUE	Youmans	151
January 28	MEXICAN HAYRIDE	Porter	226
[c. April]	TARS AND SPARS	Duke	285
[May 26]	ABOUT FACE!	Loesser	402
[August 7]	HI, YANK!	Loesser	403
October 5	BLOOMER GIRL	Arlen	266
[November 13]	GLAD TO SEE YOU!	Styne	378
November 16	SADIE THOMPSON	Duke	286
[c. November]	PFC MARY BROWN	Loesser	403
December 7	SEVEN LIVELY ARTS	Porter	227
December 23	LAFFING ROOM ONLY	Lane	293
December 28	ON THE TOWN	Bernstein	353

1945

| March 22 | FIREBRAND OF FLOR-ENCE | Weill | 309 |
| April 19 | CAROUSEL | Rodgers | 189 |

[c. June]	OK, U.S.A.!	Loesser	404
November 22	THE DAY BEFORE SPRING	Loewe	370

1946

March 30	ST. LOUIS WOMAN	Arlen	267
April 18	CALL ME MISTER	Rome	334
May 16	ANNIE GET YOUR GUN	Berlin	99
May 31	AROUND THE WORLD	Porter	228
September 5	A FLAG IS BORN	Weill	309
[October 10]	SWEET BYE AND BYE	Duke	287
October 31	HAPPY BIRTHDAY	Rodgers	190
November 20	ANOTHER PART OF THE FOREST	Blitzstein	322
November 4	PARK AVENUE	Schwartz	250
December 19	ANDROCLES AND THE LION	Blitzstein	323
December 26	BEGGAR'S HOLIDAY	PART 4	545

1947

January 9	STREET SCENE	Weill	310
January 10	FINIAN'S RAINBOW	Lane	294
March 13	BRIGADOON	Loewe	371
October 9	HIGH BUTTON SHOES	Styne	378
October 10	ALLEGRO	Rodgers	190

1948

January 29	LOOK, MA, I'M DANCIN'!	Martin	347
April 30	INSIDE U.S.A.	Schwartz	251
[c. May]	BIG AS LIFE	Bock	427
[c. May]	PHINNEY'S RAINBOW	Sondheim	449
[September 24]	THAT'S THE TICKET!	Rome	335
October 7	LOVE LIFE	Weill	311
October 11	WHERE'S CHARLEY?	Loesser	404
December 30	KISS ME, KATE	Porter	228

1949

[March 19]	ALL THAT GLITTERS	Sondheim	450
April 7	SOUTH PACIFIC	Rodgers	191
[June 20]	PRETTY PENNY	Rome	335

July 15	MISS LIBERTY	Berlin	101
October 30	LOST IN THE STARS	Weill	312
October 31	REGINA	Blitzstein	323
December 8	GENTLEMEN PREFER BLONDES	Styne	379

1950

January 17	ALIVE AND KICKING	Rome	336
April 24	PETER PAN ⟨third⟩	Bernstein	355
[c. April]	HUCKLEBERRY FINN	Weill	313
June 28	MICHAEL TODD'S PEEP	Rome/	336
	SHOW	Styne	380
October 12	CALL ME MADAM	Berlin	101
November 24	GUYS AND DOLLS	Loesser	405
December 14	BLESS YOU ALL	Rome	337
December 21	OUT OF THIS WORLD	Porter	230

1951

[March 9]	LET ME HEAR THE MEL-ODY	Gershwin	136
March 29	THE KING AND I	Rodgers	193
April 18	MAKE A WISH!	Martin	348
April 19	A TREE GROWS IN BROOKLYN	Schwartz	252
May 14	FLAHOOLEY	PART 4	546
July 19	TWO ON THE AISLE	Styne	380
November 1	TOP BANANA	PART 4	547
November 12	PAINT YOUR WAGON	Loewe	372

1952

June 25	WISH YOU WERE HERE	Rome	338
September 25 ⟨L⟩	LOVE FROM JUDY	Martin	349
December 15	TWO'S COMPANY	Duke	287

1953

February 11	HAZEL FLAGG	Styne	381
February 25	WONDERFUL TOWN	Bernstein	355
May 7	CAN-CAN	Porter	231
May 28	ME AND JULIET	Rodgers	194
December 10	JOHN MURRAY ANDER-SON'S ALMANAC	Adler/	412
		Coleman	482

1954

March 10	THREEPENNY OPERA ⟨second⟩	Weill	313
March 11	THE GOLDEN APPLE	PART 4	548
April 8	BY THE BEAUTIFUL SEA	Schwartz	253
May 13	PAJAMA GAME	Adler	413
October 18	I FEEL WONDERFUL	Herman	493
October 20	PETER PAN ⟨fourth⟩	Styne	383
November 4	FANNY	Rome	339
December 30	HOUSE OF FLOWERS	Arlen	268

1955

February 24	SILK STOCKINGS	Porter	232
February 28	SHOESTRING REVUE	Strouse	467
April 19	ALL IN ONE	Bernstein	357
May 5	DAMN YANKEES	Adler	414
September 6	CATCH A STAR	Bock	428
[October 10]	REUBEN REUBEN	Blitzstein	325
November 17	THE LARK	Bernstein	357
[November 23]	A QUIET PLACE ⟨first⟩	Bernstein	358
November 30	PIPE DREAM	Rodgers	195

1956

March 15	MY FAIR LADY	Loewe	373
March 22	MR. WONDERFUL	Bock	428
[April 16]	ZIEGFELD FOLLIES OF 1956	Bock	429
May 3	THE MOST HAPPY FELLA	Loesser	407
May 22	THE LITTLEST REVUE	Duke/ Strouse	288 468
November 5	SHOESTRING '57	Schmidt/ Strouse	515 468
November 15	LI'L ABNER	PART 4	549
November 19	GIRLS OF SUMMER	Sondheim	450
November 29	BELLS ARE RINGING	Styne	383
December 1	CANDIDE ⟨first⟩	Bernstein	358

1957

March 13	THE SIN OF PAT MUL-DOON	Adler	415

May 14	NEW GIRL IN TOWN	Merrill	441
September 26	WEST SIDE STORY	Bernstein	359
October 10	ROMANOFF AND JULIET	Rome	340
October 24	COMPULSION	Coleman	482
October 31	JAMAICA	Arlen	270
November 2	TIME REMEMBERED	Duke	289
December 19	THE MUSIC MAN	Willson	420

1958

January 23	THE BODY BEAUTIFUL	Bock	430
April 3	SAY, DARLING	Styne	385
April 29	THE FIRSTBORN	Bernstein	361
May 18	NIGHTCAP	Herman	493
October 11	DEMI-DOZEN	Coleman/	483
		Schmidt	515
December 1	FLOWER DRUM SONG	Rodgers	196

1959

February 5	REDHEAD	PART 4	551
March 9	JUNO	Blitzstein	326
April 23	DESTRY RIDES AGAIN	Rome	340
May 21	GYPSY	Styne	385
[October 14]	THE PINK JUNGLE	Duke	289
October 22	TAKE ME ALONG	Merrill	442
November 16	THE SOUND OF MUSIC	Rodgers	197
November 23	FIORELLO!	Bock	430
December 7	SARATOGA	Arlen	271

1960

January 20	PARADE ⟨second⟩	Herman	494
February 25	TOYS IN THE ATTIC	Blitzstein	327
March 8	GREENWILLOW	Loesser	408
April 14	BYE BYE BIRDIE	Strouse	469
April 20	FROM A TO Z	Herman	495
May 3	THE FANTASTICKS	Schmidt	516
[June 9]	MEET ME IN ST. LOUIS	Martin	350
[June 29]	MEDIUM RARE	Coleman	483
October 17	TENDERLOIN	Bock	431
October 29	INVITATION TO A MARCH	Sondheim	451
November 3	UNSINKABLE MOLLY BROWN	Willson	421

December 3	CAMELOT	Loewe	374
December 16	WILDCAT	Coleman	483
December 26	DO RE MI	Styne	387

1961

April 13	CARNIVAL!	Merrill	443
October 10	MILK AND HONEY	Herman	495
October 14	HOW TO SUCCEED IN BUSINESS . . .	Loesser	400
October 23	KWAMINA	Adler	415
November 18	THE GAY LIFE	Schwartz	254
December 27	SUBWAYS ARE FOR SLEEPING	Styne	388
December 29	MADAME APHRODITE	Herman	496

1962

January 3	BRECHT ON BRECHT	Weill	315
January 27	A FAMILY AFFAIR	Kander	504
March 15	NO STRINGS	Rodgers	198
March 19	ALL AMERICAN	Strouse	470
March 22	I CAN GET IT FOR YOU WHOLESALE	Rome	341
May 8	A FUNNY THING . . .	Sondheim	452
[July 2]	WORLD OF JULES FEIFFER	Sondheim	453
October 20	MR. PRESIDENT	Berlin	102
November 17	LITTLE ME	Coleman	484
November 27	NEVER TOO LATE	Bock/	432
		Kander	505

1963

March 12	TOO TRUE TO BE GOOD	Leigh	522
April 11	MAN IN THE MOON	Bock	433
April 19	HOT SPOT	Sondheim	453
April 23	SHE LOVES ME	Bock	433
[August 5]	ZENDA	Duke	289
October 3	HERE'S LOVE	Willson	422
October 17	JENNIE	Schwartz	255
October 24	110 IN THE SHADE	Schmidt	517
November 11	ARTURO UI	Styne	389

1964

January 16	HELLO, DOLLY!	Herman/	496
		Merrill/	444
		Strouse	471
March 26	FUNNY GIRL	Styne	389
March 28	NEVER LIVE OVER A	Leigh	522
	PRETZEL FACTORY		
April 4	ANYONE CAN WHISTLE	Sondheim	454
April 7	HIGH SPIRITS	Martin	351
April 22	TO BROADWAY WITH	Bock	435
	LOVE		
May 7	WONDERWORLD	Styne	391
May 26	FADE OUT—FADE IN	Styne	391
September 22	FIDDLER ON THE ROOF	Bock	435
October 13	BEN FRANKLIN IN PARIS	Herman	498
October 20	GOLDEN BOY	Strouse	472

1965

February 16	BAKER STREET	Bock	436
[March 11]	PLEASURES AND PAL-	Loesser	410
	ACES		
March 18	DO I HEAR A WALTZ?	Rodgers	199
May 11	FLORA, THE RED MEN-	Kander	505
	ACE		
October 6	GENERATION	Bock	437
October 17	ON A CLEAR DAY . . .	Lane	295
November 10	THE ZULU AND THE	Rome	342
	ZAYDA		
November 22	MAN OF LA MANCHA	Leigh	523
December 14	LA GROSSE VALISE	Rome	343

1966

January 9	THE MAD SHOW	Sondheim	455
January 30	SWEET CHARITY	Coleman	485
March 29	"IT'S . . . SUPERMAN"	Strouse	473
May 24	MAME	Herman	498
October 18	THE APPLE TREE	Bock	437
[November 15]	CHU-CHEM	Leigh	524
November 20	CABARET	Kander	506
December 5	I DO! I DO!	Schmidt	518

[December 14]   BREAKFAST AT TIF-   Merrill   445
                 FANY'S

1967

April 26   HALLELUJAH, BABY!   Styne   392
September 27   KEEP IT IN THE FAMILY   Coleman   487
October 23   HENRY, SWEET HENRY   Merrill   446

1968

January 18   THE HAPPY TIME   Kander   508
January 27   DARLING OF THE DAY   Styne   393
April 29   HAIR   PART 4   552
[September 23]   A MOTHER'S KISSES   Adler   416
October 20   HER FIRST ROMAN   Bock   438
November 17   ZORBA   Kander   508
December 1   PROMISES, PROMISES   PART 4   553

1969

January 22   CELEBRATION   Schmidt   519
February 6   DEAR WORLD   Herman   499
March 16   1776   PART 4   554
[September 2]   1491   Willson   422
October 21   BUTTERFLIES ARE FREE   S. Schwartz   529

1970

March 29   LOOK TO THE LILIES   Styne   394
March 30   APPLAUSE   Strouse   474
April 8   CRY FOR US ALL   Leigh   525
April 26   COMPANY   Sondheim   455
April 28   RISE AND FALL OF MA-   Weill   315
                 HAGONNY
May 6   COLETTE ⟨first⟩   Schmidt   520
October 19   THE ROTHSCHILDS   Bock   439
November 10   TWO BY TWO   Rodgers   200

1971

[February 1]   PRETTYBELLE   Styne   395
April 4   FOLLIES   Sondheim   457
April 12   SIX   Strouse   475

April 15	70, GIRLS, 70	Kander	509
May 17	GODSPELL	S. Schwartz	529
[September 8]	MASS	Bernstein	361

1972

February 14	GREASE	PART 4	555
[March 20]	HALLOWEEN	Leigh	526
April 9	SUGAR	Styne	396
May 3 ⟨L⟩	GONE WITH THE WIND	Rome	434
October 23	PIPPIN	S. Schwartz	530
November 6 ⟨L⟩	I AND ALBERT	Strouse	475

1973

February 25	A LITTLE NIGHT MUSIC	Sondheim	458
March 18	SEESAW	Coleman	487
November 13	GIGI	Loewe	375

1974

January 27	LORELEI	Styne	397
March 10	CANDIDE ⟨second⟩	Bernstein	363
[May 20]	THE FROGS	Sondheim	459
May 28	THE MAGIC SHOW	Schwartz	531
October 6	MACK AND MABEL	Herman	500

1975

January 5	THE WIZ	PART 4	556
January 7	SHENANDOAH	PART 4	557
February 21	STRAWS IN THE WIND	Coleman	488
April 8	PHILOMEN	Schmidt	520
April 15	A CHORUS LINE	PART 4	558
June 1	CHICAGO	Kander	511
November 23	BY BERNSTEIN	Bernstein	364

1976

January 4	HOME SWEET HOMER	Leigh	526
January 11	PACIFIC OVERTURES	Sondheim	460
April 25	REX	Rodgers	201
May 4	1600 PENNSYLVANIA AV- ENUE	Bernstein	364

May 4 ⟨L⟩	SIDE BY SIDE BY SONDHEIM	Sondheim	461
[May 11]	THE BAKER'S WIFE	S. Schwartz	532
October 9	THE ROBBER BRIDE-GROOM	PART 4	559
[November 22]	HELLZAPOPPIN'!	Coleman/	488
		Styne	397
December 20	MUSIC IS	Adler	417

1977

April 17	I LOVE MY WIFE	Coleman	488
April 21	ANNIE	Strouse	476
May 7	HAPPY END	Weill	316
October 29	THE ACT	Kander	512

1978

February 19	ON THE TWENTIETH CENTURY	Coleman	489
[March 7]	PRINCE OF GRAND STREET	Merrill	447
April 17	BEST LITTLE WHORE-HOUSE IN TEXAS	PART 4	560
May 14	WORKING	S. Schwartz	533
October 31 ⟨L⟩	BAR MITZVAH BOY	Styne	398
December 21	A BROADWAY MUSICAL	Strouse	477

1979

January 11	THE GRAND TOUR	Herman	501
February 23	SARAVA	Leigh	527
March 1	SWEENEY TODD	Sondheim	461
[March 12]	HOME AGAIN, HOME AGAIN	Coleman	490
April 8	CARMELINA	Lane	296
May 31	I REMEMBER MAMA	Rodgers	202
June 13	MADWOMAN OF CEN-TRAL PARK WEST	Bernstein	365
June 14 ⟨L⟩	FLOWERS FOR ALGER-NON	Strouse	478

1980

April 30	BARNUM	Coleman	491
May 1	A DAY IN HOLLY-WOOD . . .	Herman	502
[July 9]	APRIL SONG	Leigh	527
[October 20]	ONE NIGHT STAND	Styne	399

1981

March 5	BRING BACK BIRDIE	Strouse	479
March 12	MARRY ME A LITTLE	Sondheim	462
March 29	WOMAN OF THE YEAR	Kander	512
April 1	MARCH OF THE FALSET-TOS	PART 4	561
November 16	MERRILY WE ROLL ALONG	Sondheim	463
December 20	DREAMGIRLS	PART 4	562

1982

[February 9]	COLETTE ⟨second⟩	Schmidt	521
May 9	NINE	PART 4	563
October 28	UPSTAIRS AT O'NEALS	Strouse	480

1983

May 11	DANCE A LITTLE CLOSER	Strouse	480
August 21	LA CAGE AUX FOLLES	Herman	502
December 4	BABY	PART 4	564

1984

February 9	THE RINK	Kander	513
May 2	SUNDAY IN THE PARK WITH GEORGE	Sondheim	464
July 22	A QUIET PLACE ⟨second⟩	Bernstein	366

1985

March 26	IN TROUSERS	PART 4	566
April 25	BIG RIVER	PART 4	567
May 13	MAYOR	Strouse	481

APPENDIX 2

The reader will have noted certain collaborators regularly mentioned throughout this book. There was a core of lyricists, librettists, directors, choreographers and producers who shared responsibility for the better shows and more important innovations.

The lyricists, of course, were especial contributors to the musical theatre. Many of them have been praised far too little (or not at all) in this book; that's not to say they are unappreciated.

As an added reference, forty of these collaborators have been selected for this appendix. Productions they collaborated on are listed, giving a partial view of their careers. (Only shows discussed in this book are listed.) Included are unofficial credits: where they were unbilled "helpers," replaced during the tryout, etc. Acting credits are not included.

The usual function(s) performed are mentioned. The collaborator did not necessarily serve in all capacities on each production.

The format remains as elsewhere, except that the dates given do not reflect shows which closed out of town.

This reference guide can serve as just that: a guide. The work of the collaborators has been discussed only as it affected the composers; most are worthy of separate study.

Collaborator Reference Listing

ALEXANDER A. AARONS
Producer

BORN: [Circa 1891]   Philadelphia, Pennsylvania
DIED: March 14, 1943   Beverly Hills, California

May 26, 1919	Gershwin	LA, LA LUCILLE
May 3, 1921	Youmans	TWO LITTLE GIRLS IN BLUE
February 20, 1922	Gershwin	FOR GOODNESS SAKE
December 1, 1924	Gershwin	LADY, BE GOOD!
December 28, 1925	Gershwin	TIP-TOES
November 8, 1926	Gershwin	OK, KAY!
November 22, 1927	Gershwin	FUNNY FACE
November 8, 1928	Gershwin	TREASURE GIRL
March 11, 1929	Rodgers	SPRING IS HERE
November 11, 1929	Rodgers	HEADS UP!
October 14, 1930	Gershwin	GIRL CRAZY
January 20, 1933	Gershwin	PARDON MY ENGLISH

GEORGE ABBOTT
Librettist, Director, Producer

BORN: June 25, 1887   Forrestville, New York

December 2, 1932	Arlen	THE GREAT MAGOO
November 16, 1935	Rodgers	JUMBO
April 11, 1936	Rodgers	ON YOUR TOES
November 23, 1938	Rodgers	THE BOYS FROM SYRACUSE
October 18, 1939	Rodgers	TOO MANY GIRLS
December 25, 1940	Rodgers	PAL JOEY
October 1, 1941	Martin	BEST FOOT FORWARD
December 28, 1944	Bernstein	ON THE TOWN
October 9, 1947	Styne	HIGH BUTTON SHOES
January 29, 1948	Martin	LOOK, MA, I'M DANCIN'!
October 11, 1948	Loesser	WHERE'S CHARLEY?

October 12, 1950	Berlin	CALL ME MADAM
December 21, 1950	Porter	OUT OF THIS WORLD
April 19, 1951	Schwartz	A TREE GROWS IN BROOKLYN
February 25, 1953	Bernstein	WONDERFUL TOWN
May 28, 1953	Rodgers	ME AND JULIET
May 13, 1954	Adler	THE PAJAMA GAME
May 5, 1955	Adler	DAMN YANKEES
May 14, 1957	Merrill	NEW GIRL IN TOWN
November 23, 1959	Bock	FIORELLO!
October 17, 1960	Bock	TENDERLOIN
May 8, 1962	Sondheim	A FUNNY THING
November 27, 1962	Bock/ Kander	NEVER TOO LATE
May 26, 1964	Styne	FADE OUT—FADE IN
May 11, 1965	Kander	FLORA, THE RED MENACE
December 20, 1976	Adler	MUSIC IS

LEE ADAMS
Lyricist

BORN: August 14, 1924   Mansfield, Ohio

May 22, 1956	Strouse	THE LITTLEST REVUE
November 5, 1956	Strouse	SHOESTRING '57
April 14, 1960	Strouse	BYE BYE BIRDIE
March 19, 1962	Strouse	ALL AMERICAN
January 16, 1964	Strouse	HELLO, DOLLY!
October 20, 1964	Strouse	GOLDEN BOY
March 29, 1966	Strouse	"IT'S . . . SUPERMAN"
March 30, 1970	Strouse	APPLAUSE
November 6, 1972 ⟨L⟩	Strouse	I AND ALBERT
December 21, 1978	Strouse	A BROADWAY MUSICAL
March 5, 1981	Strouse	BRING BACK BIRDIE

GEORGE BALANCHINE
Choreographer, Director

BORN: January 9, 1904   St. Petersburg, Russia
DIED: April 30, 1983   New York, New York

March 27, 1929 ⟨L⟩	Porter	WAKE UP AND DREAM
January 30, 1936	Duke	ZIEGFELD FOLLIES OF 1936
April 11, 1936	Rodgers	ON YOUR TOES
April 14, 1937	Rodgers	BABES IN ARMS

May 11, 1938	Rodgers	I MARRIED AN ANGEL
November 23, 1938	Rodgers	THE BOYS FROM SYRACUSE
May 23, 1940	Duke	KEEP OFF THE GRASS
May 28, 1940	Berlin	LOUISIANA PURCHASE
October 25, 1940	Duke	CABIN IN THE SKY
January 9, 1942	Duke	THE LADY COMES ACROSS
November 11, 1943	Loewe	WHAT'S UP
October 11, 1948	Loesser	WHERE'S CHARLEY?

MICHAEL BENNETT
Director, Choreographer

BORN: April 8, 1943   Buffalo, New York

October 23, 1967	Merrill	HENRY SWEET HENRY
December 1, 1968	[PART 4]	PROMISES, PROMISES
April 26, 1970	Sondheim	COMPANY
April 4, 1971	Sondheim	FOLLIES
March 18, 1973	Coleman	SEESAW
April 15, 1975	[PART 4]	A CHORUS LINE
December 20, 1981	[PART 4]	DREAMGIRLS

GUY BOLTON
Librettist

BORN: November 23, 1884   Broxbourne, England
DIED: September 5, 1979   London, England

January 25, 1915	Kern	NINETY IN THE SHADE
April 20, 1915	Kern	NOBODY HOME
December 23, 1915	Kern	VERY GOOD EDDIE
September 25, 1916	Kern	MISS SPRINGTIME
January 11, 1917	Kern	HAVE A HEART
February 20, 1917	Kern	OH, BOY!
August 28, 1917	Kern	LEAVE IT TO JANE
September 24, 1917	Kern	THE RIVIERA GIRL
November 5, 1917	Kern	MISS 1917
February 1, 1918	Kern	OH LADY! LADY!!
May 18, 1918 ⟨L⟩	Porter	VERY GOOD EDDIE
November 27, 1918	Kern	OH, MY DEAR!
February 21, 1920	Kern	SALLY
April 8, 1924	Kern	SITTING PRETTY
September 11, 1924 ⟨L⟩	Gershwin	PRIMROSE
December 1, 1924	Gershwin	LADY BE GOOD

December 28, 1925	Gershwin	TIP-TOES
November 8, 1926	Gershwin	OH, KAY!
January 3, 1928	Rodgers	SHE'S MY BABY
January 10, 1928	Gershwin	ROSALIE
April 27, 1928 ⟨L⟩	Kern	BLUE EYES
February 18, 1930	Rodgers	SIMPLE SIMON
October 14, 1930	Gershwin	GIRL CRAZY
November 21, 1934	Porter	ANYTHING GOES
June 9, 1939 ⟨L⟩	Porter	THE SUN NEVER SETS
June 4, 1940	[PART 4]	WALK WITH MUSIC
January 13, 1944	Duke	JACKPOT

ANNE CALDWELL
Lyricist, Librettist

BORN: August 30, 1867   Boston, Massachusetts
DIED: October 22, 1936   Beverly Hills, California

February 2, 1914	Kern	WHEN CLAUDIA SMILES
May 5, 1919	Kern	SHE'S A GOOD FELLOW
May 12, 1919	Gershwin/ Kern	THE LADY IN RED
February 2, 1920	Kern	THE NIGHT BOAT
August 31, 1920	Gershwin	THE SWEETHEART SHOP
October 19, 1920	Kern	HITCHY-KOO 1920
November 1, 1921	Kern	GOOD MORNING DEARIE
November 28, 1922	Kern	THE BUNCH AND JUDY
November 6, 1923	Kern	THE STEPPING STONES
October 26, 1925	Kern	THE CITY CHAP
October 12, 1926	Kern	CRISS-CROSS
December 17, 1926	Youmans	OH, PLEASE!

GOWER CHAMPION
Director, Choreographer

BORN: June 22, 1920   Geneva, Illinois
DIED: August 25, 1980   New York, New York

[C. April 1944]	Duke	TARS AND SPARS
April 18, 1951	Martin	MAKE A WISH
April 14, 1960	Strouse	BYE BYE BIRDIE
April 13, 1961	Merrill	CARNIVAL!
January 16, 1964	Herman/ Merrill/ Strouse	HELLO, DOLLY!

December 5, 1966	Schmidt	I DO! I DO!
January 18, 1968	Kander	THE HAPPY TIME
February 1, 1971	Styne	PRETTYBELLE
April 9, 1972	Styne	SUGAR
October 6, 1974	Herman	MACK AND MABEL
October 29, 1979	Kander	THE ACT
December 21, 1978	Strouse	A BROADWAY MUSICAL

BETTY COMDEN
Lyricist, Librettist

BORN: May 3, 1915
Brooklyn, New York

ADOLPH GREEN
Lyricist, Librettist

BORN: December 2, 1915
Bronx, New York

December 28, 1944	Bernstein	ON THE TOWN
July 19, 1951	Styne	TWO ON THE AISLE
February 25, 1953	Bernstein	WONDERFUL TOWN
October 20, 1954	Styne	PETER PAN ⟨fourth⟩
November 29, 1956	Styne	BELLS ARE RINGING
April 3, 1958	Styne	SAY, DARLING
December 26, 1960	Styne	DO RE MI
December 27, 1961	Styne	SUBWAYS ARE FOR SLEEPING
May 26, 1964	Styne	FADE OUT—FADE IN
April 26, 1967	Styne	HALLELUJAH, BABY!
March 30, 1970	Strouse	APPLAUSE
January 27, 1974	Styne	LORELEI
February 21, 1975	Coleman	STRAWS IN THE WIND
November 23, 1975	Bernstein	BY BERNSTEIN
February 19, 1978	Coleman	ON THE TWENTIETH CEN-TURY

CHERYL CRAWFORD
Producer

BORN: September 24, 1902   Akron, Ohio

November 19, 1936	Weill	JOHNNY JOHNSON
October 7, 1943	Weill	ONE TOUCH OF VENUS
December 19, 1946	Blitzstein	ANDROCLES AND THE LION
March 13, 1947	Loewe	BRIGADOON
October 7, 1948	Weill	LOVE LIFE
October 31, 1949	Blitzstein	REGINA
May 14, 1951	[PART 4]	FLAHOOLEY
November 12, 1951	Loewe	PAINT YOUR WAGON
October 10, 1955	Blitzstein	REUBEN REUBEN

November 19, 1956	Sondheim	THE GIRLS OF SUMMER
October 17, 1963	Schwartz	JENNIE
November 15, 1966	Leigh	CHU-CHEM
January 22, 1969	Schmidt	CELEBRATION
May 6, 1970	Schmidt	COLETTE ⟨first⟩

AGNES de MILLE
Choreographer, Director

BORN: [circa 1905]   New York, New York

September 15, 1932	Schwartz	FLYING COLORS
October 6, 1933 ⟨L⟩	Porter	NYMPH ERRANT
December 1, 1937	Arlen	HOORAY FOR WHAT!
March 31, 1943	Rodgers	OKLAHOMA!
October 7, 1943	Weill	ONE TOUCH OF VENUS
October 5, 1944	Arlen	BLOOMER GIRL
April 19, 1945	Rodgers	CAROUSEL
March 13, 1947	Loewe	BRIGADOON
October 10, 1947	Rodgers	ALLEGRO
December 8, 1949	Styne	GENTLEMEN PREFER BLONDES
December 21, 1950	Porter	OUT OF THIS WORLD
November 12, 1951	Loewe	PAINT YOUR WAGON
March 9, 1959	Blitzstein	JUNO
October 23, 1961	Adler	KWAMINA
October 24, 1963	Schmidt	110 IN THE SHADE

B. G. DeSYLVA
Lyricist, Librettist, Producer

BORN: January 27, 1895   New York, New York
DIED: July 11, 1950   Los Angeles, California

May 26, 1919	Gershwin	LA, LA LUCILLE
December 8, 1919	Kern	ZIP, GOES A MILLION
December 27, 1919	Gershwin	MORRIS GEST'S MIDNIGHT WHIRL
[c. December 1919]	Gershwin	SINBAD
December 21, 1920	Kern	SALLY
June 21, 1921	Kern	ZIEGFELD FOLLIES OF 1921
November 7, 1921	Gershwin	THE PERFECT FOOL
February 20, 1922	Gershwin	THE FRENCH DOLL
July 6, 1922	Gershwin	SPICE OF 1922

August 28, 1922	Gershwin	GEO. WHITE'S SCANDALS ⟨fourth⟩
June 18, 1923	Gershwin	GEO. WHITE'S SCANDALS ⟨fifth⟩
August 28, 1923	Gershwin	LITTLE MISS BLUEBEARD
January 21, 1924	Gershwin	SWEET LITTLE DEVIL
June 30, 1924	Gershwin	GEO. WHITE'S SCANDALS ⟨sixth⟩
September 11, 1924 ⟨L⟩	Gershwin	PRIMROSE
November 6, 1924	Kern	PETER PAN ⟨second⟩
April 13, 1925	Gershwin	TELL ME MORE
June 14, 1926	[PART 4]	GEO. WHITE'S SCANDALS ⟨eighth⟩
September 6, 1927	[PART 4]	GOOD NEWS!
November 26, 1932	Youmans	TAKE A CHANCE
December 6, 1939	Porter	DUBARRY WAS A LADY
May 28, 1940	Berlin	LOUISIANA PURCHASE
October 30, 1940	Porter	PANAMA HATTIE

HOWARD DIETZ
Lyricist, Librettist

BORN: September 8, 1896 New York, New York
DIED: July 30, 1983 New York, New York

September 23, 1924	Kern	DEAR SIR
November 8, 1926	Gershwin	OH, KAY!
April 30, 1929	Schwartz	THE LITTLE SHOW
May 1, 1929	Schwartz	GRAND STREET FOLLIES ⟨sixth⟩
February 20, 1930 ⟨L⟩	Schwartz	HERE COMES THE BRIDE
April 4, 1930 ⟨L⟩	Schwartz	CO-OPTIMISTS OF 1930
September 2, 1930	Schwartz	SECOND LITTLE SHOW
October 15, 1930	Schwartz/ Duke/ Lane	THREE'S A CROWD
June 3, 1931	Schwartz	THE BAND WAGON
September 15, 1932	Schwartz	FLYING COLORS
November 28, 1934	Schwartz	REVENGE WITH MUSIC
September 19, 1935	Schwartz	AT HOME ABROAD
February 4, 1936 ⟨L⟩	Schwartz	FOLLOW THE SUN
December 25, 1936	Schwartz	THE SHOW IS ON
December 22, 1937	Schwartz	BETWEEN THE DEVIL
May 23, 1940	Duke	KEEP OFF THE GRASS
March 22, 1943	Duke	DANCING IN THE STREETS
January 13, 1944	Duke	JACKPOT

[c. April 1944]	Duke	TARS AND SPARS
November 16, 1944	Duke	SADIE THOMPSON
April 30, 1948	Schwartz	INSIDE U.S.A.
November 18, 1961	Schwartz	THE GAY LIFE
October 17, 1963	Schwartz	JENNIE

CHARLES B. DILLINGHAM
Producer

BORN: May 30, 1868   Hartford, Connecticut
DIED: August 30, 1934   New York, New York

August 17, 1910	Kern	THE ECHO
December 8, 1914	Berlin	WATCH YOUR STEP
October 5, 1915	Kern/ Porter	MISS INFORMATION
December 25, 1915	Berlin	STOP! LOOK! LISTEN!
November 6, 1916	Berlin	THE CENTURY GIRL
[C. April 1917]	Berlin	DANCE AND GROW THIN
October 16, 1917	Berlin	JACK O'LANTERN
November 5, 1917	Kern	MISS 1917
August 22, 1918	Berlin	EVERYTHING
November 4, 1918	Berlin/ Kern	THE CANARY
May 5, 1919	Kern	SHE'S A GOOD FELLOW
February 2, 1920	Kern	THE NIGHT BOAT
November 1, 1921	Kern	GOOD MORNING DEARIE
November 28, 1922	Kern	THE BUNCH AND JUDY
November 6, 1923	Kern	THE STEPPING STONES
November 6, 1924	Kern	PETER PAN (second)
September 22, 1925	Kern	SUNNY
October 26, 1925	Kern	THE CITY CHAP
October 12, 1926	Kern	CRISS-CROSS
December 17, 1926	Youmans	OH, PLEASE!
March 22, 1927	Kern	LUCKY
January 3, 1928	Rodgers	SHE'S MY BABY
February 11, 1930	Kern	RIPPLES

FRED EBB
Lyricist

BORN: April 8, 1932   New York, New York

April 20, 1960	Herman	FROM A TO Z
May 11, 1965	Kander	FLORA, THE RED MENACE

November 20, 1966	Kander	CABARET
January 18, 1968	Kander	THE HAPPY TIME
November 17, 1968	Kander	ZORBA
April 15, 1971	Kander	70, GIRLS, 70
June 1, 1975	Kander	CHICAGO
October 29, 1977	Kander	THE ACT
March 29, 1981	Kander	WOMAN OF THE YEAR
February 9, 1984	Kander	THE RINK

DOROTHY FIELDS
Lyricist, Librettist

BORN: July 15, 1905   Allenhurst, New Jersey
DIED: March 28, 1974   New York, New York

May 9, 1928	[PART 4]	BLACKBIRDS OF 1928
February 9, 1939	Schwartz	STARS IN YOUR EYES
October 29, 1941	Porter	LET'S FACE IT
January 7, 1943	Porter	SOMETHING FOR THE BOYS
January 28, 1944	Porter	MEXICAN HAYRIDE
May 16, 1946	Berlin	ANNIE GET YOUR GUN
April 19, 1951	Schwartz	A TREE GROWS IN BROOKLYN
April 8, 1954	Schwartz	BY THE BEAUTIFUL SEA
February 5, 1959	[PART 4]	REDHEAD
January 29, 1966	Coleman	SWEET CHARITY
September 27, 1967	Coleman	KEEP IT IN THE FAMILY
March 18, 1973	Coleman	SEESAW

HERBERT FIELDS
Librettist

BORN: July 26, 1897   New York, New York
DIED: March 24, 1958   New York, New York

March 6, 1920	Rodgers	YOU'D BE SURPRISED
March 24, 1920	Rodgers	FLY WITH ME
July 28, 1920	Rodgers	POOR LITTLE RITZ GIRL
April 20, 1921	Rodgers	YOU'LL NEVER KNOW
May 13, 1924	Rodgers	THE MELODY MAN
May 17, 1925	Rodgers	GARRICK GAIETIES ⟨first⟩
September 18, 1925	Rodgers	DEAREST ENEMY
March 17, 1926	Rodgers	THE GIRL FRIEND
May 10, 1926	Rodgers	GARRICK GAIETIES ⟨second⟩
December 27, 1926	Rodgers	PEGGY-ANN
April 25, 1927	Youmans	HIT THE DECK

November 3, 1927	Rodgers	A CONNECTICUT YANKEE ⟨first⟩
April 26, 1928	Rodgers	PRESENT ARMS!
September 25, 1928	Rodgers	CHEE-CHEE
November 27, 1929	Porter	FIFTY MILLION FRENCHMEN
December 8, 1930	Porter	THE NEW YORKERS
February 10, 1931	Rodgers	AMERICA'S SWEETHEART
January 20, 1933	Gershwin	PARDON MY ENGLISH
December 6, 1939	Porter	DUBARRY WAS A LADY
October 30, 1940	Porter	PANAMA HATTIE
October 29, 1941	Porter	LET'S FACE IT!
January 7, 1943	Porter	SOMETHING FOR THE BOYS
November 17, 1943	Rodgers	A CONNECTICUT YANKEE ⟨second⟩
January 28, 1944	Porter	MEXICAN HAYRIDE
May 16, 1946	Berlin	ANNIE GET YOUR GUN
April 8, 1954	Schwartz	BY THE BEAUTIFUL SEA
February 5, 1959	[PART 4]	REDHEAD

BOB FOSSE
Director, Choreographer

BORN: June 23, 1927   Chicago, Illinois

May 13, 1954	Adler	THE PAJAMA GAME
May 5, 1955	Adler	DAMN YANKEES
November 29, 1956	Styne	BELLS ARE RINGING
May 14, 1957	Merrill	NEW GIRL IN TOWN
February 5, 1959	[PART 4]	REDHEAD
October 14, 1961	Loesser	HOW TO SUCCEED . . .
November 17, 1962	Coleman	LITTLE ME
March 11, 1965	Loesser	PLEASURES AND PALACES
January 30, 1966	Coleman	SWEET CHARITY
October 23, 1972	Schwartz	PIPPIN
June 1, 1975	Kander	CHICAGO

VINTON FREEDLEY
Producer

BORN: November 5, 1891   Philadelphia, Pennsylvania
DIED: June 5, 1969   New York, New York

| December 1, 1924 | Gershwin | LADY, BE GOOD! |
| December 28, 1925 | Gershwin | TIP-TOES |

November 8, 1926	Gershwin	OH, KAY!
November 22, 1927	Gershwin	FUNNY FACE
November 8, 1928	Gershwin	TREASURE GIRL
March 11, 1929	Rodgers	SPRING IS HERE
November 11, 1929	Rodgers	HEADS UP!
October 14, 1930	Gershwin	GIRL CRAZY
January 20, 1933	Gershwin	PARDON MY ENGLISH
November 21, 1934	Porter	ANYTHING GOES
October 29, 1936	Porter	RED, HOT AND BLUE!
November 9, 1938	Porter	LEAVE IT TO ME
October 24, 1940	Duke	CABIN IN THE SKY
October 29, 1941	Porter	LET'S FACE IT
March 22, 1943	Duke	DANCING IN THE STREETS
January 13, 1944	Duke	JACKPOT

IRA GERSHWIN
Lyricist

BORN: December 6, 1896   New York, New York
DIED: August 17, 1983   Beverly Hills, California

October 24, 1918	Gershwin	LADIES FIRST
August 31, 1920	Gershwin	THE SWEETHEART SHOP
September 27, 1920	Youmans	PICCADILLY TO BROADWAY
March 21, 1921	Gershwin	A DANGEROUS MAID
May 3, 1921	Youmans	TWO LITTLE GIRLS IN BLUE
February 20, 1922	Gershwin	FOR GOODNESS SAKE
August 28, 1922	Gershwin	GEO. WHITE'S SCANDALS ⟨fourth⟩
August 28, 1923	Gershwin	LITTLE MISS BLUEBEARD

NOTE: above lyrics credited to "Arthur Francis"

September 11, 1924 ⟨L⟩	Gershwin	PRIMROSE
December 1, 1924	Gershwin	LADY, BE GOOD!
April 13, 1925	Gershwin	TELL ME MORE
September 7, 1925	Youmans	A NIGHT OUT
December 28, 1925	Gershwin	TIP-TOES
July 26, 1926	Gershwin	AMERICANA ⟨first⟩
November 8, 1926	Gershwin	OH, KAY!
[c. April 1927] ⟨L⟩	Duke	TWO LITTLE GIRLS IN BLUE
August 29, 1927	Gershwin	STRIKE UP THE BAND ⟨first⟩
November 22, 1927	Gershwin	FUNNY FACE
January 10, 1928	Gershwin	ROSALIE
November 8, 1928	Gershwin	TREASURE GIRL
July 2, 1929	Gershwin	SHOW GIRL

January 14, 1930	Gershwin	STRIKE UP THE BAND ⟨second⟩
February 11, 1930	Gershwin	NINE-FIFTEEN REVUE
June 4, 1930	Duke	GARRICK GAIETIES ⟨third⟩
October 14, 1930	Gershwin	GIRL CRAZY
December 26, 1931	Gershwin	OF THEE I SING
January 20, 1933	Gershwin	PARDON MY ENGLISH
October 21, 1933	Gershwin	LET 'EM EAT CAKE
August 27, 1934	Arlen	LIFE BEGINS AT 8:40
October 10, 1935	Gershwin	PORGY AND BESS
January 30, 1936	Duke	ZIEGFELD FOLLIES ⟨OF 1936⟩
December 25, 1936	Gershwin	THE SHOW IS ON
January 23, 1941	Weill	LADY IN THE DARK
March 22, 1945	Weill	THE FIREBRAND OF FLOR-ENCE
November 4, 1946	Schwartz	PARK AVENUE
March 9, 1951	Gershwin	LET ME HEAR THE MELODY

MAX GORDON
Producer

BORN: June 28, 1892   New York, New York
DIED: November 2, 1978   New York, New York

October 15, 1930	Schwartz	THREE'S A CROWD
June 3, 1931	Schwartz	THE BAND WAGON
October 15, 1931	Kern	THE CAT AND THE FIDDLE
September 15, 1932	Schwartz	FLYING COLORS
November 18, 1933	Kern	ROBERTA
October 12, 1935	Porter	JUBILEE
September 24, 1938	Rome	SING OUT THE NEWS
November 17, 1939	Kern	VERY WARM FOR MAY
March 22, 1945	Weill	FIREBRAND OF FLORENCE
November 4, 1946	Schwartz	PARK AVENUE

OSCAR HAMMERSTEIN 2ND
Lyricist, Librettist, Producer

BORN: July 12, 1895   New York, New York
DIED: August 23, 1960   Doylestown, Pennsylvania

[c. March 1919]	Rodgers	UP STAGE AND DOWN
March 24, 1920	Rodgers	FLY WITH ME
February 7, 1923	Youmans	WILDFLOWER
December 25, 1923	Youmans	MARY JANE McKANE

September 22, 1925	Kern	SUNNY
December 30, 1925	Gershwin	SONG OF THE FLAME
December 27, 1927	Kern	SHOW BOAT
September 5, 1928	Schwartz	GOOD BOY
November 21, 1928	Youmans	RAINBOW
September 2, 1929	Kern	SWEET ADELINE
November 8, 1932	Kern	MUSIC IN THE AIR
April 9, 1934 ⟨L⟩	Kern	THREE SISTERS
June 3, 1938	Kern	GENTLEMEN UNAFRAID
November 17, 1939	Kern	VERY WARM FOR MAY
May 12, 1940	Schwartz	AMERICAN JUBILEE
March 31, 1943	Rodgers	OKLAHOMA!
April 19, 1945	Rodgers	CAROUSEL
May 16, 1946	Berlin	ANNIE GET YOUR GUN
October 31, 1946	Rodgers	HAPPY BIRTHDAY
October 10, 1947	Rodgers	ALLEGRO
April 7, 1949	Rodgers	SOUTH PACIFIC
March 29, 1951	Rodgers	THE KING AND I
May 28, 1953	Rodgers	ME AND JULIET
November 30, 1955	Rodgers	PIPE DREAM
December 1, 1958	Rodgers	FLOWER DRUM SONG
November 16, 1959	Rodgers	THE SOUND OF MUSIC

OTTO HARBACH
Lyricist, Librettist

BORN: August 18, 1873   Salt Lake City, Utah
DIED: January 24, 1963   New York, New York

September 11, 1911	Berlin	THE FASCINATING WIDOW
December 25, 1917	Berlin	GOING UP
February 7, 1923	Youmans	WILDFLOWER
September 16, 1925	Youmans	NO, NO, NANETTE
September 22, 1925	Kern	SUNNY
December 30, 1925	Gershwin	SONG OF THE FLAME
October 12, 1926	Kern	CRISS-CROSS
December 17, 1926	Youmans	OH, PLEASE!
March 22, 1927	Kern	LUCKY
September 5, 1928	Schwartz	GOOD BOY
February 20, 1930	Schwartz	HERE COMES THE BRIDE
October 15, 1931	Kern	THE CAT AND THE FIDDLE
November 18, 1933	Kern	ROBERTA
June 3, 1938	Kern	GENTLEMEN UNAFRAID

E. Y. HARBURG
Lyricist, Librettist

BORN: April 8, 1898   New York, New York
DIED: March 5, 1981   Los Angeles, California

June 4, 1930	Duke	GARRICK GAIETIES ⟨third⟩
July 1, 1930	Arlen	EARL CARROLL VANITIES ⟨eighth⟩
October 5, 1932	Arlen	AMERICANA ⟨third⟩
December 2, 1932	Arlen	THE GREAT MAGOO
December 7, 1932	Duke	WALK A LITTLE FASTER
July 28, 1933	Arlen	CRAZY QUILT OF 1933
January 4, 1934	Duke	ZIEGFELD FOLLIES OF 1934
August 27, 1934	Arlen	LIFE BEGINS AT 8:40
December 25, 1936	Arlen	THE SHOW IS ON
December 1, 1937	Arlen	HOORAY FOR WHAT!
September 11, 1940	Lane	HOLD ON TO YOUR HATS
October 5, 1944	Arlen	BLOOMER GIRL
January 10, 1947	Lane	FINIAN'S RAINBOW
May 14, 1951	[PART 4]	FLAHOOLEY
October 31, 1957	Arlen	JAMAICA
January 27, 1968	Styne	DARLING OF THE DAY

SHELDON HARNICK
Lyricist

BORN: December 27, 1924   Chicago, Illinois

February 28, 1955	Strouse	SHOESTRING REVUE
November 5, 1956	Strouse	SHOESTRING '57
January 23, 1958	Bock	THE BODY BEAUTIFUL
November 23, 1959	Bock	FIORELLO!
October 17, 1960	Bock	TENDERLOIN
November 27, 1962	Bock	NEVER TOO LATE
April 11, 1963	Bock	MAN IN THE MOON
April 23, 1963	Bock	SHE LOVES ME
April 22, 1964	Bock	TO BROADWAY WITH LOVE
September 22, 1964	Bock	FIDDLER ON THE ROOF
February 16, 1965	Bock	BAKER STREET
October 18, 1966	Bock	THE APPLE TREE
October 20, 1968	Bock	HER FIRST ROMAN
October 19, 1970	Bock	THE ROTHSCHILDS
April 25, 1976	Rodgers	REX

SAM H. HARRIS
Producer

BORN: February 3, 1872   New York, New York
DIED: July 3, 1941   New York, New York

September 25, 1911	Berlin	THE LITTLE MILLIONAIRE
[c. April 1912]	Berlin	COHAN AND HARRIS MIN-STRELS
August 31, 1912	Kern	A POLISH WEDDING
May 28, 1916	Berlin	FRIARS' FROLIC OF 1916
December 25, 1917	Berlin	GOING UP
December 31, 1917	Berlin	THE COHAN REVUE OF 1918
February 17, 1919	Berlin	THE ROYAL VAGABOND
September 22, 1921	Berlin	MUSIC BOX REVUE ⟨first⟩
October 23, 1922	Berlin	MUSIC BOX REVUE ⟨second⟩
September 22, 1923	Berlin	MUSIC BOX REVUE ⟨third⟩
December 1, 1924	Berlin	MUSIC BOX REVUE ⟨fourth⟩
December 8, 1925	Berlin	THE COCOANUTS
December 26, 1931	Gershwin	OF THEE I SING
February 17, 1932	Berlin	FACE THE MUSIC
September 30, 1933	Berlin	AS THOUSANDS CHEER
October 21, 1933	Gershwin	LET 'EM EAT CAKE
October 12, 1935	Porter	JUBILEE
November 2, 1937	Rodgers	I'D RATHER BE RIGHT
January 23, 1941	Weill	LADY IN THE DARK

LORENZ HART
Lyricist, Librettist

BORN: May 2, 1895   New York, New York
DIED: November 22, 1943   New York, New York

June 10, 1919	Rodgers	A LONELY ROMEO
March 6, 1920	Rodgers	YOU'D BE SURPRISED
March 24, 1920	Rodgers	FLY WITH ME
July 28, 1920	Rodgers	POOR LITTLE RITZ GIRL
April 20, 1921	Rodgers	YOU'LL NEVER KNOW
May 13, 1924	Rodgers	THE MELODY MAN
May 17, 1925	Rodgers	GARRICK GAIETIES ⟨first⟩
August 6, 1925	Rodgers	JUNE DAYS
September 18, 1925	Rodgers	DEAREST ENEMY
[c. January 1926]	Rodgers	FIFTH AVENUE FOLLIES
March 17, 1926	Rodgers	THE GIRL FRIEND

April 29, 1926 ⟨L⟩	Rodgers	COCHRAN'S 1926 REVUE
May 10, 1926	Rodgers	GARRICK GAIETIES ⟨second⟩
December 1, 1926 ⟨L⟩	Rodgers	LIDO LADY
December 27, 1926	Rodgers	PEGGY-ANN
December 28, 1926	Rodgers	BETSY
April 27, 1927 ⟨L⟩	Rodgers	LADY LUCK
May 20, 1927 ⟨L⟩	Rodgers	LONDON PAVILION REVUE
November 3, 1927	Rodgers	A CONNECTICUT YANKEE ⟨first⟩
January 3, 1928	Rodgers	SHE'S MY BABY
April 26, 1928	Rodgers	PRESENT ARMS!
September 25, 1928	Rodgers	CHEE-CHEE
January 31, 1929	Rodgers	LADY FINGERS
March 11, 1929	Rodgers	SPRING IS HERE
November 11, 1929	Rodgers	HEADS UP!
February 18, 1930	Rodgers	SIMPLE SIMON
December 3, 1930 ⟨L⟩	Rodgers	EVER GREEN
February 10, 1931	Rodgers	AMERICA'S SWEETHEART
May 19, 1931	Rodgers	CRAZY QUILT
November 16, 1933 ⟨L⟩	Rodgers	PLEASE!
April 29, 1935	Rodgers	SOMETHING GAY
November 16, 1935	Rodgers	JUMBO
April 11, 1936	Rodgers	ON YOUR TOES
December 25, 1936	Rodgers	THE SHOW IS ON
April 14, 1937	Rodgers	BABES IN ARMS
November 2, 1937	Rodgers	I'D RATHER BE RIGHT
May 11, 1938	Rodgers	I MARRIED AN ANGEL
November 23, 1938	Rodgers	THE BOYS FROM SYRACUSE
October 18, 1939	Rodgers	TOO MANY GIRLS
April 4, 1940	Rodgers	HIGHER AND HIGHER
June 24, 1940	Rodgers	TWO WEEKS WITH PAY
December 25, 1940	Rodgers	PAL JOEY
June 2, 1942	Rodgers	BY JUPITER
November 17, 1943	Rodgers	A CONNECTICUT YANKEE ⟨second⟩

MOSS HART
Librettist, Director, Producer

BORN: October 24, 1904   New York, New York
DIED: December 20, 1961   Palm Springs, California

February 17, 1932	Berlin	FACE THE MUSIC
September 30, 1933	Berlin	AS THOUSANDS CHEER

October 12, 1935	Porter	JUBILEE
December 25, 1936	Duke	THE SHOW IS ON
November 2, 1937	Rodgers	I'D RATHER BE RIGHT
September 24, 1938	Rome	SING OUT THE NEWS
October 16, 1939	Porter	THE MAN WHO CAME TO DIN-NER
January 23, 1941	Weill	LADY IN THE DARK
June 22, 1942	Rome	LUNCHTIME FOLLIES
December 7, 1944	Porter	SEVEN LIVELY ARTS
April 30, 1948	Schwartz	INSIDE U.S.A.
July 15, 1949	Berlin	MISS LIBERTY
March 15, 1956	Loewe	MY FAIR LADY
December 3, 1960	Loewe	CAMELOT

TOM JONES
Lyricist, Librettist

BORN: February 17, 1928   Littlefield, Texas

November 5, 1956	Schmidt	SHOESTRING '57
October 11, 1958	Schmidt	DEMI-DOZEN
May 3, 1960	Schmidt	THE FANTASTICKS
October 24, 1963	Schmidt	110 IN THE SHADE
December 5, 1966	Schmidt	I DO! I DO!
January 22, 1969	Schmidt	CELEBRATION
May 6, 1970	Schmidt	COLETTE ⟨first⟩
April 8, 1975	Schmidt	PHILEMON
February 9, 1982	Schmidt	COLETTE ⟨second⟩

GEORGE S. KAUFMAN
Lyricist, Librettist, Director, Producer

BORN: November 14, 1889   Pittsburgh, Pennsylvania
DIED: June 2, 1961   New York, New York

September 22, 1923	Berlin	MUSIC BOX REVUE ⟨third⟩
December 8, 1925	Berlin	THE COCOANUTS
August 29, 1927	Gershwin	STRIKE UP THE BAND ⟨first⟩
April 30, 1929	Schwartz	THE LITTLE SHOW
January 14, 1930	Gershwin	STRIKE UP THE BAND ⟨second⟩
February 11, 1930	Arlen	NINE-FIFTEEN REVUE
June 3, 1931	Schwartz	THE BAND WAGON
December 26, 1931	Gershwin	OF THEE I SING
February 17, 1932	Berlin	FACE THE MUSIC

October 21, 1933	Gershwin	LET 'EM EAT CAKE
October 22, 1934	Schwartz	BRING ON THE GIRLS
December 25, 1936	Duke	THE SHOW IS ON
September 24, 1938	Rome	SING OUT THE NEWS
October 16, 1939	Porter	THE MAN WHO CAME TO DIN-NER
June 22, 1942	Rome	LUNCHTIME FOLLIES
December 7, 1944	Porter	SEVEN LIVELY ARTS
November 4, 1946	Schwartz	PARK AVENUE
June 20, 1949	Rome	PRETTY PENNY
November 24, 1950	Loesser	GUYS AND DOLLS
February 24, 1955	Porter	SILK STOCKINGS
October 10, 1957	Rome	ROMANOFF AND JULIET

MICHAEL KIDD
Director, Choreographer

BORN: August 12, 1919   New York, New York

January 10, 1947	Lane	FINIAN'S RAINBOW
June 20, 1949	Rome	PRETTY PENNY
November 24, 1950	Loesser	GUYS AND DOLLS
May 7, 1953	Porter	CAN-CAN
November 15, 1956	[PART 4]	LI'L ABNER
April 23, 1959	Rome	DESTRY RIDES AGAIN
December 16, 1960	Coleman	WILDCAT
December 27, 1961	Styne	SUBWAYS ARE FOR SLEEPING
October 3, 1963	Willson	HERE'S LOVE
May 7, 1964	Styne	WONDERWORLD
October 27, 1964	Herman	BEN FRANKLIN IN PARIS
December 14, 1966	Merrill	BREAKFAST AT TIFFANY'S
October 19, 1970	Bock	THE ROTHSCHILDS

ALAN JAY LERNER
Lyricist, Librettist

BORN: August 31, 1918   New York, New York

October 8, 1942	Loewe	LIFE OF THE PARTY
November 11, 1943	Loewe	WHAT'S UP
November 22, 1945	Loewe	THE DAY BEFORE SPRING
March 13, 1947	Loewe	BRIGADOON
October 7, 1948	Weill	LOVE LIFE

November 12, 1951	Loewe	PAINT YOUR WAGON
March 15, 1956	Loewe	MY FAIR LADY
December 3, 1960	Loewe	CAMELOT
October 17, 1965	Lane	ON A CLEAR DAY YOU CAN SEE FOREVER
May 4, 1976	Bernstein	1600 PENNSYLVANIA AVENUE
April 8, 1979	Lane	CARMELINA
May 11, 1983	Strouse	DANCE A LITTLE CLOSER

JOSHUA LOGAN
Director, Librettist, Producer

BORN: October 5, 1908   Texarkana, Texas

May 11, 1938	Rodgers	I MARRIED AN ANGEL
December 19, 1938	Weill	KNICKERBOCKER HOLIDAY
February 9, 1939	Schwartz	STARS IN YOUR EYES
April 4, 1940	Rodgers	HIGHER AND HIGHER
June 3, 1942	Rodgers	BY JUPITER
July 4, 1942	Berlin	THIS IS THE ARMY
May 16, 1946	Berlin	ANNIE GET YOUR GUN
October 3, 1946	Rodgers	HAPPY BIRTHDAY
April 7, 1949	Rodgers	SOUTH PACIFIC
June 25, 1952	Rome	WISH YOU WERE HERE
November 4, 1954	Rome	FANNY
March 19, 1962	Strouse	ALL AMERICAN
October 20, 1962	Berlin	MR. PRESIDENT
May 24, 1966	Herman	MAME
March 29, 1970	Styne	LOOK TO THE LILIES

ROUBEN MAMOULIAN
Director

BORN: October 8, 1898   Tiflis, Russia

October 10, 1935	Gershwin	PORGY AND BESS
March 31, 1943	Rodgers	OKLAHOMA!
November 16, 1944	Duke	SADIE THOMPSON
April 19, 1945	Rodgers	CAROUSEL
March 30, 1946	Arlen	ST. LOUIS WOMAN
October 30, 1949	Weill	LOST IN THE STARS
[c. April 1950]	Weill	HUCKLEBERRY FINN

DAVID MERRICK
Producer

BORN: November 27, 1911   St. Louis, Missouri

November 4, 1954	Rome	FANNY
October 10, 1957	Rome	ROMANOFF AND JULIET
October 31, 1957	Arlen	JAMAICA
April 23, 1959	Rome	DESTRY RIDES AGAIN
May 21, 1959	Styne	GYPSY
October 22, 1959	Merrill	TAKE ME ALONG
December 26, 1960	Styne	DO RE MI
April 13, 1961	Merrill	CARNIVAL!
December 27, 1961	Styne	SUBWAYS ARE FOR SLEEPING
March 22, 1962	Rome	I CAN GET IT FOR YOU WHOLESALE
October 24, 1963	Schmidt	110 IN THE SHADE
November 11, 1963	Styne	ARTURO UI
January 16, 1964	Herman/ Merrill/ Strouse	HELLO, DOLLY!
December 5, 1966	Schmidt	I DO! I DO!
December 14, 1966	Merrill	BREAKFAST AT TIFFANY'S
September 27, 1967	Coleman	KEEP IT IN THE FAMILY
January 18, 1968	Kander	THE HAPPY TIME
December 1, 1968	[PART 4]	PROMISES, PROMISES
April 9, 1972	Styne	SUGAR
October 6, 1974	Herman	MACK AND MABEL
May 11, 1974	S. Schwartz	THE BAKER'S WIFE

HAROLD PRINCE
Producer, Director

BORN: January 30, 1928   New York, New York

May 13, 1954	Adler	THE PAJAMA GAME
May 5, 1955	Adler	DAMN YANKEES
May 14, 1957	Merrill	NEW GIRL IN TOWN
September 26, 1957	Bernstein	WEST SIDE STORY
November 23, 1959	Bock	FIORELLO!
October 17, 1960	Bock	TENDERLOIN
January 27, 1962	Kander	A FAMILY AFFAIR
May 8, 1962	Sondheim	A FUNNY THING . . .
April 23, 1963	Bock	SHE LOVES ME
September 22, 1964	Bock	FIDDLER ON THE ROOF
February 16, 1965	Bock	BAKER STREET

May 11, 1965	Kander	FLORA, THE RED MENACE
March 29, 1966	Strouse	"ITS . . . SUPERMAN"
November 20, 1966	Kander	CABARET
November 17, 1968	Kander	ZORBA
April 26, 1970	Sondheim	COMPANY
April 4, 1971	Sondheim	FOLLIES
February 25, 1973	Sondheim	A LITTLE NIGHT MUSIC
March 10, 1974	Bernstein	CANDIDE ⟨second⟩
January 11, 1976	Sondheim	PACIFIC OVERTURES
April 25, 1976	Rodgers	REX
February 19, 1978	Coleman	ON THE TWENTIETH CEN-TURY
March 1, 1979	Sondheim	SWEENEY TODD
November 16, 1981	Sondheim	MERRILY WE ROLL ALONG

JEROME ROBBINS
Director, Choreographer

BORN: October 11, 1918   New York, New York

December 28, 1944	Bernstein	ON THE TOWN
October 9, 1947	Styne	HIGH BUTTON SHOES
January 29, 1948	Martin	LOOK, MA, I'M DANCIN'!
September 24, 1948	Rome	THAT'S THE TICKET!
July 15, 1949	Berlin	MISS LIBERTY
October 12, 1950	Berlin	CALL ME MADAM
March 29, 1951	Rodgers	THE KING AND I
December 15, 1952	Duke	TWO'S COMPANY
May 13, 1954	Adler	THE PAJAMA GAME
October 20, 1954	Styne	PETER PAN ⟨fourth⟩
November 29, 1956	Styne	BELLS ARE RINGING
September 26, 1957	Bernstein	WEST SIDE STORY
May 21, 1959	Styne	GYPSY
May 8, 1962	Sondheim	A FUNNY THING . . .
March 26, 1964	Styne	FUNNY GIRL
September 22, 1964	Bock	FIDDLER ON THE ROOF

HASSARD SHORT
Director

BORN: October 15, 1877   Edlington, Lincs, England
DIED: October 9, 1956   Nice, France

| September 22, 1921 | Berlin | MUSIC BOX REVUE ⟨first⟩ |
| October 23, 1922 | Berlin | MUSIC BOX REVUE ⟨second⟩ |

September 22, 1923	Berlin	MUSIC BOX REVUE ⟨third⟩
September 22, 1925	Kern	SUNNY
December 17, 1926	Youmans	OH, PLEASE!
March 22, 1927	Kern	LUCKY
October 15, 1930	Schwartz	THREE'S A CROWD
June 3, 1931	Schwartz	THE BAND WAGON
February 17, 1932	Berlin	FACE THE MUSIC
September 30, 1933	Berlin	AS THOUSANDS CHEER
November 18, 1933	Kern	ROBERTA
October 12, 1935	Porter	JUBILEE
December 22, 1937	Schwartz	BETWEEN THE DEVIL
November 17, 1939	Kern	VERY WARM FOR MAY
January 23, 1941	Weill	LADY IN THE DARK
December 25, 1941	Duke	BANJO EYES
June 24, 1942	Rome	STAR AND GARTER
January 7, 1943	Porter	SOMETHING FOR THE BOYS
January 28, 1944	Porter	MEXICAN HAYRIDE
December 7, 1944	Porter	SEVEN LIVELY ARTS
June 28, 1950	Rome	MICHAEL TODD'S PEEP SHOW

MICHAEL STEWART
Librettist, Lyricist

BORN: August 1, 1929   New York, New York

February 28, 1955	Strouse	SHOESTRING REVUE
May 22, 1956	Strouse	THE LITTLEST REVUE
November 5, 1956	Strouse	SHOESTRING '57
April 14, 1960	Strouse	BYE BYE BIRDIE
April 13, 1961	Merrill	CARNIVAL!
January 16, 1964	Herman/ Merrill/ Strouse	HELLO, DOLLY!
March 18, 1973	Coleman	SEESAW
October 6, 1974	Herman	MACK AND MABEL
April 17, 1977	Coleman	I LOVE MY WIFE
January 11, 1979	Herman	THE GRAND TOUR
April 30, 1980	Coleman	BARNUM
March 5, 1981	Strouse	BRING BACK BIRDIE

DWIGHT DEERE WIMAN
Producer

BORN: August 8, 1895   Moline, Illinois
DIED: January 20, 1951   Hudson, New York

April 30, 1929	Schwartz	THE LITTLE SHOW
September 2, 1930	Schwartz	THE SECOND LITTLE SHOW
June 1, 1931	Lane	THE THIRD LITTLE SHOW
November 29, 1932	Porter	THE GAY DIVORCE
November 20, 1933	Schwartz	SHE LOVES ME NOT
April 11, 1936	Rodgers	ON YOUR TOES
April 14, 1937	Rodgers	BABES IN ARMS
May 11, 1938	Rodgers	I MARRIED AN ANGEL
December 1, 1938	Loewe	GREAT LADY
February 9, 1939	Schwartz	STARS IN YOUR EYES
April 4, 1940	Rodgers	HIGHER AND HIGHER
June 2, 1942	Rodgers	BY JUPITER
January 9, 1947	Weill	STREET SCENE

P. G. WODEHOUSE
Librettist

BORN: October 15, 1881   Guildford, England
DIED: February 14, 1975   Southampton, New York

March 19, 1906 〈L〉	Kern	THE BEAUTY OF BATH
September 25, 1916	Kern	MISS SPRINGTIME
January 11, 1917	Kern	HAVE A HEART
February 20, 1917	Kern	OH, BOY!
August 28, 1917	Kern	LEAVE IT TO JANE
September 24, 1917	Kern	THE RIVIERA GIRL
November 5, 1917	Kern	MISS 1917
February 1, 1918	Kern	OH LADY! LADY!!
November 27, 1918	Kern	OH, MY DEAR!
February 21, 1920	Kern	SALLY
September 19, 1921 〈L〉	Kern	THE CABARET GIRL
September 5, 1923 〈L〉	Kern	THE BEAUTY PRIZE
April 8, 1924	Kern	SITTING PRETTY
November 8, 1926	Gershwin	OH, KAY!
December 27, 1927	Kern	SHOW BOAT
January 10, 1928	Gershwin	ROSALIE
November 21, 1934	Porter	ANYTHING GOES

FLORENZ ZIEGFELD, JR.
Producer

BORN: March 15, 1867   Chicago, Illinois
DIED: July 22, 1932   Los Angeles, California

June 20, 1910	Berlin	ZIEGFELD FOLLIES OF 1910
June 26, 1911	Berlin/ Kern	ZIEGFELD FOLLIES OF 1911
April 11, 1912	Kern	A WINSOME WIDOW
October 21, 1912	Berlin	ZIEGFELD FOLLIES OF 1912
June 12, 1916	Berlin/ Kern	ZIEGFELD FOLLIES OF 1916
November 6, 1916	Berlin	THE CENTURY GIRL
[c. April 1917]	Berlin	DANCE AND GROW THIN
June 12, 1917	Kern	ZIEGFELD FOLLIES OF 1917
November 5, 1917	Kern	MISS 1917
June 18, 1918	Berlin	ZIEGFELD FOLLIES OF 1918
June 23, 1919	Berlin	ZIEGFELD FOLLIES OF 1919
October 2, 1919	Berlin	ZIEGFELD MIDNIGHT FROLIC
March 8, 1920	Berlin	ZIEGFELD GIRLS OF 1920
June 22, 1920	Berlin	ZIEGFELD FOLLIES OF 1920
December 21, 1920	Kern	SALLY
June 21, 1921	Kern	ZIEGFELD FOLLIES OF 1921
December 25, 1922	Kern	ROSE BRIAR
December 28, 1926	Rodgers/ Berlin	BETSY
August 16, 1927	Berlin	ZIEGFELD FOLLIES OF 1927
December 27, 1927	Kern	SHOW BOAT
January 10, 1928	Gershwin	ROSALIE
December 4, 1928	[PART 4]	WHOOPEE
July 2, 1929	Gershwin/ Youmans	SHOW GIRL
February 18, 1930	Rodgers	SIMPLE SIMON
November 18, 1930	Youmans	SMILES

APPENDIX 3
Bibliography and A Word About Finding Music

BIBLIOGRAPHY

This section lists the more helpful sources used in the preparation of this book. The most important material has been the songs, over 6,000 of them: for obvious reasons, printed music, scores, and collections are not included below. Neither are newspaper reviews and articles, theatre programs, souvenir programs, record album notes, etc.

Abbott, George. *Mister Abbott*. New York: Random House, 1963.

ASCAP Index of Performed Compositions (Four Editions). New York: American Society Of Composers, Authors And Publishers, 1952 through 1978.

Astaire, Fred. *Steps In Time*. New York: Harper & Brothers, 1959.

Bernstein, Leonard. *Findings*. New York: Simon And Schuster, 1982.

Blum, Daniel, editor. *Theatre World, Vols. 1–4*. New York: Daniel C. Blum/Theatre World, 1945–1948; *Vols. 5–13*. New York: Greenberg Publisher, 1949–1957; *Vols. 14–20*. Philadelphia: Chilton Books, 1958–1964.

Boardman, Gerald. *American Musical Theatre*. New York: Oxford University Press, 1978.

Boardman, Gerald. *Days To Be Happy, Years To Be Sad*. New York: Oxford University Press, 1982.

Boardman, Gerald. *Jerome Kern*. New York, Oxford University Press, 1980.

Burrows, Abe. *Honest Abe*. Boston: Little, Brown & Co., 1980.

Cantor, Eddie. *My Life Is In Your Hands*. New York: Blue Ribbon Books, 1932.

Chapman, John, editor. *The Best Play Series, Vols. 1947–1948* through *1951–1952*. New York: Dodd, Mead & Company, 1948–1952.

[Chappell Group]. *Comprehensive Catalogue of Vocal Solos*. New York: Chappell Group, [Circa 1953].

Crawford, Cheryl. *One Naked Individual*. Indianapolis: Bobbs-Merrill Co., 1977.

de Mille, Agnes. *Dance To The Piper*. Boston: Little, Brown and Co., 1952.

Dietz, Howard. *Dancing In The Dark*. New York: Quadrangle, 1974.

Duke, Vernon. *Passport To Paris*. Boston: Little, Brown & Co., 1955.

Ewen, David. *New Complete Book Of The American Musical Theatre*. Holt, Rinehart and Winston, 1970.

Ewen, David. *Popular American Composers*. New York: H. W. Wilson Co., 1962. *First Supplement,* 1972.

Fordin, Hugh. *Getting To Know Him*. New York: Random House, 1977.

Freedland, Michael. *Irving Berlin*. New York: Stein & Day, 1974.

Gershwin, Ira. *Lyrics On Several Occasions*. New York: Alfred A. Knopf, 1959.

Goldberg, Isaac, supplemented by Garson, Edith. *George Gershwin: A Study In American Music*. New York: Frederick Ungar Publishing Co., 1958.

Gordon, Max and Funke, Lewis. *Max Gordon Presents*. New York: Bernard Geis, 1963.

Green, Stanley. *Encyclopedia Of The Musical Theatre*. New York: Dodd, Mead & Co., 1976.

Green, Stanley. *Ring Bells! Sing Songs!* New York: Arlington House, 1971.

Green, Stanley, editor. *Rodgers And Hammerstein Fact Book*. New York: Rodgers And Hammerstein, 1955. *Supplement,* 1961.

Green, Stanley. *The World Of Musical Comedy (Revised And Enlarged Fourth Edition)*. San Diego: A. S. Barnes & Co., 1980.

Guernsey, Jr., Otis L., editor. *The Best Plays Series, Vols. 1964–1965* through *1982–1983*. New York: Dodd, Mead & Company, 1965–1983.

Hart, Dorothy. *Thou Swell, Thou Witty*. New York: Harper & Row, 1976.

Hellman, Lillian. *Pentimento: A Book Of Portraits*. Boston: Little, Brown and Company, 1973.

Hewes, Henry, editor. *The Best Plays Series, Vols. 1961–1962* through *1963–1964*. New York: Dodd, Mead & Co., 1962–1964.

Higham, Charles. *Ziegfeld*. Chicago: Henry Regnery, 1972.

Hughes, Elinor. *Passing Through To Broadway*. Boston: Waverly House, 1948.

Hummel, David. *The Collector's Guide To The Musical Theatre*. Metuchen, N.J.: Scarecrow Press, 1984.

Jablonski, Edward and Stewart, Lawrence D. *The Gershwin Years*. Garden City, N.Y.: Doubleday and Company, Inc., 1973.

Jablonski, Edward. *Harold Arlen: Happy With The Blues*. New York: Doubleday & Co., 1961.

Jay, Dave. *The Irving Berlin Songography*. New Rochelle: Arlington House, 1969.

Kimball, Robert, editor. *Cole*. New York: Holt, Rinehart and Winston, 1971.

Kimball, Robert, editor. *The Complete Lyrics Of Cole Porter*. New York: Alfred A. Knopf, 1983.

Kimball, Robert, and Simon, Alfred. *The Gershwins*. New York: Atheneum, 1973.

Kronenberger, Louis, editor. *The Best Plays Series, Vols. 1952–1953* through *1960–1961*. New York: Dodd, Mead & Co., 1953–1961.

Lamb, Andrew. *Jerome Kern In Edwardian London*. East Preston, West Sussex, England: Andrew Lamb, 1981.

Leonard, William Torbert. *Broadway Bound*. Metuchen, N.J.: Scarecrow Press, 1983.

Lerner, Alan Jay. *The Street Where I Live*. New York: W. W. Norton & Co., 1978.

Lewine, Richard, and Simon, Alfred. *Encyclopedia Of Theatre Music*. New York: Random House, 1961.

Lewine, Richard, and Simon, Alfred. *Songs Of The American Theatre*. New York: Dodd, Mead and Company, 1973.

Logan, Joshua. *Josh*. New York: Delacorte Press, 1976.

Mantle, Burns, editor. *The Best Plays Series, Vols. 1919–1920* through *1923–1924*. Boston: Small, Maynard & Co., 1920–1924; *Vols. 1924–1925* through *1946–1947*. New York: Dodd, Mead & Co., 1925–1947.

Mantle, Burns, and Sherwood, Garrison P., editors. *The Best Plays of 1899–1909; The Best Plays of 1909–1919*. New York: Dodd, Mead & Co., 1944; 1933.

Marx, Samuel and Clayton, Jan. *Rodgers & Hart: Bewitched, Bothered And Bedeviled*. New York: G. P. Putnam's Sons, 1976.

McNamara, Daniel, editor. *The ASCAP Biographical Dictionary Of Composers, Authors & Publishers*. New York: Thomas Y. Crowell Co., 1948.

Meredith, Scott. *George S. Kaufman And His Friends*. Garden City: Doubleday & Co., 1974.

Nathan, George Jean. *The Theatre Book Of The Year, Vols. 1941–1942* through *1950–1951*. New York: Alfred A. Knopf, 1943–1951.

New York Theatre Critics Reviews, Vols. 1 through *30*. New York: Critics' Theatre Reviews, Inc., 1940–1970.

The New York Times Directory Of The Film. New York: Arno Press, 1971.

The New York Times Directory Of the Theatre. New York: Arno Press, 1973.

Nolan, Frederick. *The Sound Of Their Music*. New York: Walker & Co., 1978.

Parker, John, editor. *Who's Who In The Theatre, 1st* through *16th Editions*. London: Sir Isaac Pitman & Sons, 1912 through 1977.

Prince, Hal. *Contradictions: Notes On Twenty-Six Years In The Theatre*. New York: Dodd, Mead & Company, 1974.

Rigdon, Walter, editor. *Biographical Encyclopedia And Who's Who Of The American Theatre*. New York: Heineman, 1966.

Rodgers, Richard. *Musical Stages*. New York: Random House, 1975.

Sanders, Ronald. *The Days Grow Short: The Life And Music Of Kurt Weill*. New York: Holt, Rinehart & Winston, 1980.

Schwartz, Charles. *Cole Porter*. New York: Dial Press, 1977.

Schwartz, Charles. *Gershwin: His Life And Music*. New York: Bobbs-Merrill, 1973.

Stagg, Jerry. *The Brothers Shubert*. New York: Random House, 1968.

Stone, Fred. *Rolling Stone*. New York: Whittlesey House, 1945.

Stott, William, with Fehl, Fred and Stott, Jane. *On Broadway*. Austin: University of Texas Press, 1978.

Taylor, Theodore. *Jule: The Story Of Composer Jule Styne*. New York: Random House, 1979.

Teichmann, Howard. *George S. Kaufman: An Intimate Portrait*. New York: Atheneum, 1972.

Toohey, John L. *A History Of The Pulitzer Prize Plays*. New York: Citadel Press, 1967.

[U.S. Army Service Forces]. *About Face!* New York: Special Services Division, [Circa 1944].

[U.S. Army Service Forces]. *Hi, Yank!* New York: Special Services Division, [Circa 1944].

[U.S. Army Service Forces]. *OK, U.S.A.!* New York: Special Services Division, [Circa 1945].

[U.S. Army Service Forces]. *PFC Mary Brown*. New York: Special Services Division, [Circa 1944].

Wharton, John. *Life Among The Playwrights*. New York: Quadrangle, 1974.

Willis, John, editor. *Theatre World, Vols. 21* through *39*. New York: Crown Publishers, 1965–1984.

Wintergreen, John P. *Diary Of An Ex-President*. New York: Minton, Balch and Company, 1932.

[Writers and Material Committee for Soldier Shows]. *At Ease, Vols. III* and *IV*. USO-Camp Shows, Inc., 1943.

Zadan, Craig. *Sondheim And Co*. New York: Macmillan And Co., Inc. 1974.

A WORD ABOUT FINDING MUSIC

Recently issued songs and still-popular standards can best be found in local music stores. Many vocal scores and selections are still in print. Recently, certain publishers have reissued long-out-of-print songs in new vocal selections and composer anthologies; in some cases these include previously unpublished work. Chain stores which sell only top 50 hits won't be of much help; but any place which carries instruction books, classical music, etc. will have (or gladly order) these items. Publishers can be contacted directly for in-print material. Some long-established music stores still have out-of-print material in stock.

An increasing number of stores now carry out-of-print music, especially dealers in used and rare books and antiques. If they don't handle music, they will generally know of others who do. There are dozens of mail-order dealers specializing in music; they advertise in newspapers and journals for antique dealers and collectors, or can be found through the music societies listed below. Flea markets and antique shows can also be good places to find music.

The best place to find specific out-of-print songs is in one of several libraries with specialized collections. Those listed below are particularly recommended. (Other collections also exist; check with your local library or university library.) Individual policies vary, but many of these facilities will allow photocopying of out-of-print material for noncommercial use. The UCLA and Buffalo Libraries have indicated that they try to accommodate mail requests for specific songs.

LIBRARY OF CONGRESS
Music Division—Room 113
Madison Building
1st Avenue and Independence, S.E.
Washington, DC 20540
(202) 287-5504

NEW YORK PUBLIC LIBRARY
Performing Arts Research Center
Music Division—Third Floor
111 Amsterdam Avenue
New York, NY 10023
(212) 870-1650

NEW YORK PUBLIC LIBRARY
General Library of the Performing Arts
Music Circulation—First Floor
111 Amsterdam Avenue
New York, NY 10023
(212) 870-1625

BROWN UNIVERSITY
John Hay Collection
Box A
20 Prospect Street
Providence, RI 02912
(401) 863-2146

BUFFALO AND ERIE COUNTY PUBLIC LIBRARY
Lafayette Square
Buffalo, NY 14203
(716) 856-7525

CHICAGO PUBLIC LIBRARY
Music Section, Fine Arts Division
78 East Washington

Chicago, IL 60602
(312) 269–2886

INDIANA UNIVERSITY
Lilly Library
Bloomington, IN 47405
(812) 335–2452

UCLA MUSIC LIBRARY
Archive of Popular Music
Los Angeles, CA 90024
Attn: Dr. David Morton
(213) 825–1665

Listed below are organizations of sheet music hobbyists. Member-
ship in these groups brings contact with collectors and dealers who
can help locate songs. The New York and Los Angeles groups have
monthly meetings, where members buy, sell, and trade music.

NATIONAL SHEET MUSIC SOCIETY
1597 Fair Park Avenue
Los Angeles, CA 90041

NEW YORK SHEET MUSIC SOCIETY
P. O. Box 1126
East Orange, NJ 07019

REMEMBER THAT SONG
5623 North 64th Avenue
Glendale, AZ 85301

The majority of the recorded songs mentioned are included on original cast albums. The *Schwann Catalog* lists those presently in print,
which any dealer can order. Labels specializing in reissues and rari-
ties are no doubt familiar to collectors of records. These companies
offer catalogues and welcome personal correspondence (current mail-
ing addresses are on the record jackets). Any of several books cata-
loguing record albums can be consulted for further information and
recommended retail stores. Public libraries often have circulating
collections of recorded theatre music.

Song Title Index

Please Hello, 460
Please Let Me Tell You That I Love You, 408
Please Stay, 508
Pleasure And Privilege, 440
Pleasures And Palaces, 411
Plenty Bambini, 408
Plunk, Plunk, Plunk, 308
Pocketful Of Dreams, 336–37
Poems, 460
Poker Game, The, 513
Poker Love (Card Duet), 8
Poker Polka, 518
Polar Bear Strut, 234
Policemen's Ball, The, 101
Politics And Poker, 431
Polka (Castle Specialty), 81
Polly Believed In Preparedness, 34
Polly Pretty Polly, 86
Polly's Song, 314
Pompeii Club, 487
Poor As A Churchmouse, 286
Poor Baby, 456
Poor Everybody Else, 486–87
Poor Joe (Berlin), 103
Poor Joe (Rodgers), 191
Poor Little Hollywood Star, 485
Poor Little Me, 86
Poor Little Person, 446
Poor Little Rich Girl's Dog, 85
Poor Pierrot, 61
Poor Prune, 37
Poor Thing, 462
Poor Tied Up Darlin', 560
Poppa Knows Best, 200
Poppyland, 108
Popsicles In Paris, 435
Porcelain Maid, 91
Pore Jud, 187
Porgy, 541
Pottawatomie, 182
Pour Le Sport, 463
Pow! Bam! Zonk!, 473
Praise The Day, 59
Praise The Lord And Pass The Ammunition, 402
Prayer (Kern), 62
Prayer (Lane), 297

Prefatory Prayers, 362
Prelude (Bernstein), 358
Prelude (Kern), 52
Preludium, 198
Prepare Ye The Way Of The Lord, 530
President Jefferson Sunday Luncheon March, 365
Press Conference, 563
Pretty Girl Is Like A Melody, A, 88
Pretty Lady, 460
Pretty Little Missus Bell, 227
Pretty Little Picture, 452
Pretty To Walk With, 270
Pretty Women, 461–62
Prettybelle, 395
Pricklepear Bloom, The, 560
Primitive Prima Donna, 264
Prince Of Humbug, The, 491
Princess Of Pure Delight, The, 307
Princess Of The Willow Tree, 156, 158
Princess Zenobia Ballet, 177
Prisms, Plums And Prunes, 154, 160
Prisoner, Choose!, 438
Prithee, Come Crusading, 205
Private Schwartz, 390
Progress Is The Root Of All Evil, 550
Prologue (*Brigadoon*), 371
Prologue (*Godspell*), 530
Prologue (*Out Of This World*), 230
Prologue (*West Side Story*), 360
Promise, 304
Promise Me A Rose, 442
Promises, Promises, 554
Prosperity Is Just Around The Corner, 132
Protect Me, 251
Proud Lady, 532
Psalm, The, 524
Psychiatry Song, The, 304
Ptolemy, 439
Public Enemy Number One, 218
Pulitzer Prize, The, 101
Purest Kind Of Guy, The, 322
Purple Rose, 288
Push De Button, 270
Put 'Em Back, 550
Put Him Away, 200
Put On A Happy Face, 469–70

Show Index

The Show Index includes all musicals and plays as well as basic property material, motion pictures, etc. The principal listings for productions written by the major composers (or included as Notable Scores) are denoted by boldface page numbers.

People Index

The People Index contains many, but not all, of the persons mentioned in this book. Those who worked importantly or primarily in musical theatre are included. Demands of space, time, and interest, though, have limited the inclusion of some only tangentially associated with the songs, shows, and careers of the major composers. For ease of usage, page numbers of the primary discussion of each of the major composers are in boldface.